The College of Law
of England and Wales

LIBRARY SERVICES

The College of Law, Braboeuf Manor, St. Catherines, Portsmouth Road, Guildford, GU3 1HA
Telephone: 01483 216788   E-mail: library.gld@lawcol.co.uk

This book MUST be returned on or before the last date stamped below.
Failure to do so will result in a fine.

Birmingham · Chester · Guildford · London · Manchester · York

A GUIDE TO THE
LCIA ARBITRATION RULES

A GUIDE TO THE LCIA ARBITRATION RULES

Peter Turner
Reza Mohtashami

OXFORD

UNIVERSITY PRESS

OXFORD

UNIVERSITY PRESS

Great Clarendon Street, Oxford ox2 6DP

Oxford University Press is a department of the University of Oxford.
It furthers the University's objective of excellence in research, scholarship,
and education by publishing worldwide in

Oxford New York

Auckland Cape Town Dar es Salaam Hong Kong Karachi
Kuala Lumpur Madrid Melbourne Mexico City Nairobi
New Delhi Shanghai Taipei Toronto

With offices in

Argentina Austria Brazil Chile Czech Republic France Greece
Guatemala Hungary Italy Japan Poland Portugal Singapore
South Korea Switzerland Thailand Turkey Ukraine Vietnam

Oxford is a registered trade mark of Oxford University Press
in the UK and in certain other countries

Published in the United States
by Oxford University Press Inc., New York

British Library Cataloguing in Publication Data

Data available

Library of Congress Cataloging in Publication Data

Data available

Typeset by Cepha Imaging Private Ltd., Bangalore, India
Printed in Great Britain
on acid-free paper by
CPI Antony Rowe

ISBN 978–0–19–923443–1

1 3 5 7 9 10 8 6 4 2

FOREWORD

Nearly seventeen years ago, I returned to my law firm in Montreal after four years in New York as Canada's Permanent Representative and Ambassador to the United Nations in New York. I was interested in learning more about international arbitration, and I did not hesitate to make known my interest to all whom I felt could be of assistance. My inquiries soon led me to the London Chambers of the late Michael Kerr. 'Mr International Arbitration', he was called. Perhaps even more intriguing to me was his moniker, 'Mr LCIA'.

I was invited by Michael to a splendid luncheon at Lincoln's Inn where I received a primer on both international arbitration and the LCIA. Further sessions with that brilliant and gracious man followed.

For many years, Michael, with the legendary Bertie Vigrass, had been running the LCIA, in effect, out of his vest pocket. I remember distinctly the passion with which Michael explained to me not only why he believed that international commercial arbitration was a dispute resolution mechanism whose time had come, but why the LCIA in particular was ideally suited to administer the many cases which he was convinced loomed on the horizon.

In both respects, time has proven Michael to have been prescient. This excellent book, which is being published at a time when the LCIA's docket of cases and international reach are expanding impressively, is in many respects a testament to that prescience.

How pleased Michael would be today—how pleased all of our forebears would be—to learn that the 1998 Arbitration Rules of the LCIA are finally the subject of a full and learned commentary. It is, if I may say so, about time.

I commend Peter Turner and Reza Mohtashami for having undertaken this important task. Their scholarship will be of immense assistance to all users of LCIA arbitration—parties, counsel and arbitrators alike—in addition to students of international arbitration generally. The authors' article-by-article commentary provides a comprehensive guide to the LCIA Rules, their origins and their application. It is user friendly and insightful, and I predict that it will rank as an essential work in every practitioner's library.

L Yves Fortier, CC, OQ, QC
Honorary Vice President and former President of the LCIA Arbitration Court
25 September 2008

PREFACE

The impetus behind this book was the realization on the part of both authors that there was nowhere to go to for a full commentary on the LCIA Arbitration Rules. We had both been used to referring to the commentary on the ICC Rules of Arbitration by Yves Derains and Eric Schwartz for ICC cases, and felt that something similar should exist for the LCIA Rules.

We therefore set ourselves the task of writing a practitioner's guide to the LCIA Rules to meet what we perceived as a need and to fill this gap. Feeling as we did that the excellent work by Derains and Schwartz should be emulated for the LCIA Rules, we have attempted to produce a commentary on the LCIA Rules that followed their approach of an article-by-article commentary, with emphasis on the operation of the Rules rather than as a general commentary on international arbitration. We have therefore dealt with general topics of arbitration law only to the extent that we deemed necessary to provide context to the discussion of the Rules themselves.

In approaching our task, we quickly ran into what probably accounts for the fact that there has hitherto been no comprehensive guide to the LCIA Rules, namely that there exists no publicly available body of LCIA arbitral awards, such as exists for ICC arbitration. It is to be hoped that the decision to publish decisions of divisions of the LCIA Arbitration Court on challenges to arbitrators will provide future commentators with more material and it may be that the LCIA will in the future revise its position of not publishing even sanitized versions of awards.

Given the lack of primary material on the operation of the Rules in practice, we were extremely fortunate in obtaining the help of the LCIA itself in conducting research into LCIA cases and in persuading Adrian Winstanley, the LCIA's Director-General, to give freely of his time to answer our questions as to how the Rules operate in practice, where the bare text itself is of little help. We are greatly in his debt.

Our research was actually carried out by two of the LCIA's excellent research assistants, Wing Shek and Hannah Guest, rather than by ourselves, to ensure that the confidentiality of the proceedings was respected. They worked and re-worked the results of their activities as we continually revised the aims of the research and managed to retain their good humour throughout. We hope that the work that they did will be of more general benefit to the LCIA than just for our book. As with Adrian, we express our deep thanks to both Wing and Hannah.

Notwithstanding the great help extended to us by the LCIA in the preparation of the groundwork for the book, it in no way represents an LCIA-sponsored official commentary on its Rules. Nor is it an explanation of the original intentions as to the operation of the Rules by those who drafted them. The views contained herein are the authors' own. Furthermore, it should of course be understood that the practices of the LCIA Court and Registrar described in the book may change over time; just because a certain practice has been adopted in the past does not mean that it always will be in the future.

One of the ways in which the future development of the LCIA could be influenced in ways as yet unforeseen is the recent expansion of the LCIA onto the international stage. The proposed opening of branches in Barbados and India, and especially the existing partnership with the Dubai International Financial Centre, are likely to take the LCIA far from its London roots and could well see it embark on new journeys. Time will tell. It is in any event indicative of the gradual distancing of the LCIA from its status as the 'English' arbitration institution into one that is truly international. In that context it is perhaps fitting that this book should be written by two Paris-based practitioners, albeit both English.

We should like to take this opportunity to thank our respective wives, Sybille and Sophie, who have suffered more than most from the gestation of this project, and without whose support it would not have been possible. We also extend our thanks to Alan Redfern for graciously agreeing to review the draft manuscript and making many valuable suggestions, and also Catherine Redmond and Manju Manglani at OUP, whose forbearance in the matter of serially missed deadlines has been exemplary.

Peter Turner
Reza Mohtashami
Paris, 29 September 2008

CONTENTS—SUMMARY

Table of Authorities   xv

Table of Legislation   xix

Arbitration Rules   xxi

International Instruments   xxiii

List of Abbreviations   xxv

1. Introduction   1

2. The Role of the LCIA's Organs (Articles 3 and 29)   17

3. Starting the Arbitration (Articles 1, 2, and 4)   27

4. The Arbitral Tribunal: Formation and Challenge (Articles 5 to 13)   47

5. Conduct of the Arbitration (Articles 14 to 21)   91

6. The Powers of the Arbitral Tribunal (Articles 22, 23, and 25)   137

7. Awards (Articles 26 and 27)   179

8. Costs (Articles 24 and 28)   199

9. Miscellaneous Provisions (Articles 30, 31, and 32)   219

Appendices   235

Bibliography   375

Index   379

CONTENTS

Table of Authorities   xv
Table of Legislation   xix
Arbitration Rules   xxi
International Instruments   xxiii
List of Abbreviations   xxv

1. Introduction

  A. The London Court of International Arbitration   1.02

  B. The LCIA Arbitration Rules   1.38

  C. The LCIA as Appointing Authority under the UNCITRAL
     Arbitration Rules   1.47

  D. The Softwood Lumber Arbitrations   1.50

  E. Other Forms of Dispute Resolution Administered by the LCIA 1.54

2. The Role of the LCIA's Organs (Articles 3 and 29)

  A. Article 3 – The LCIA Court and Registrar   2.02

  B. Article 29 – Decisions by the LCIA Court   2.21

3. Starting the Arbitration (Articles 1, 2, and 4)

  A. Article 1 – The Request for Arbitration   3.02

  B. Article 2 – The Response   3.24

  C. Article 4 – Notices and Periods of Time   3.39

4. The Arbitral Tribunal: Formation and Challenge (Articles 5 to 13)

  A. Article 5 – Formation of the Arbitral Tribunal   4.06

  B. Article 6 – Nationality of Arbitrators   4.50

  C. Article 7 – Party and Other Nominations   4.69

  D. Article 8 – Three or More Parties   4.75

  E. Article 9 – Expedited Formation   4.86

  F. Article 10 – Revocation of Arbitrator's Appointment   4.109

G. Article 11 – Nomination and Replacement of Arbitrators 4.129

H. Article 12 – Majority Power to Continue Proceedings 4.137

I. Article 13 – Communications between Parties and the
Arbitral Tribunal 4.158

5. **Conduct of the Arbitration (Articles 14 to 21)**

A. Article 14 – Conduct of the Proceedings 5.02

B. Article 15 – Submission of Written Statements and Documents 5.30

C. Article 16 – Seat of Arbitration and Place of Hearings 5.58

D. Article 17 – Language of Arbitration 5.72

E. Article 18 – Party Representation 5.81

F. Article 19 – Hearings 5.86

G. Article 20 – Witnesses 5.99

H. Article 21 – Experts to the Arbitral Tribunal 5.114

6. **The Powers of the Arbitral Tribunal (Articles 22, 23, and 25)**

A. Article 22 – Additional Powers of the Arbitral Tribunal 6.03

B. Article 23 – Jurisdiction of the Arbitral Tribunal 6.82

C. Article 25 – Interim and Conservatory Measures 6.107

7. **Awards (Articles 26 and 27)**

A. Article 26 – The Award 7.02

B. Article 27 – Correction of Award and Additional Awards 7.38

8. **Costs (Articles 24 and 28)**

A. Article 28 – Arbitration and Legal Costs 8.02

B. Article 24 – Deposits 8.35

9. **Miscellaneous Provisions (Articles 30, 31, and 32)**

A. Article 30 – Confidentiality 9.03

B. Article 31 – Exclusion of Liability 9.30

C. Article 32 – General Rules 9.36

Appendix 1. Recommended LCIA Arbitration Clauses 237

Appendix 2. LCIA Arbitration Rules 239

Contents

Appendix 3. Schedule of the LCIA's Arbitration Fees and Costs   255

Appendix 4. Constitution of the LCIA Arbitration Court   259

Appendix 5. Membership of the LCIA Arbitration Court   261

Appendix 6. Directives of the LCIA Arbitration Court under
    Articles 24, 26, and 28   263

Appendix 7. Constitution of the LCIA Users' Councils   267

Appendix 8. The English Arbitration Act 1996   271

Appendix 9. UNCITRAL Model Law on International
    Commercial Arbitration   323

Appendix 10. LCIA Mediation Procedure   355

Appendix 11. DIFC-LCIA Arbitration Rules   359

Bibliography   375
Index   379

TABLE OF AUTHORITIES

ARBITRAL DECISIONS

Antoine Biloune et al v Ghana Investments et al, Award on Damages and
Costs, (1994) 19 YCA 11, 22 . . . . 7.46
CDC Group PLC v Republic of the Seychelles (ICSID Case No ARB/02/14) 6.117
Himpurna California Energy Ltd v Republic of Indonesia (2000)
25 YCA 186 . . . . 4.139–4.140, 4.145, 9.53
ICC Case No 12171 [2005] ASA Bull 2770 . . . . 6.47
Partial Award in ICC Case No 3896, 23 December 1982 . . . . 6.125
Ram International Industries, Inc and Others v The Air Force of the Islamic
Republic of Iran, Iran-US Claims Tribunal, Decision No DEC 118-148-1 . . . . 7.46
Salini Costruttori SpA v Ethiopia (ICC Case No 10623) Award regarding the
Suspension of the Proceedings and Jurisdiction, 7 December 2001 . . . . 5.66
Suez, Sociedad General de Aguas de Barcelona SA and InterAguas Servicios
Integrales de Agua SA v The Argentine Republic (ICSID Case No ARB/03/17) 4.19
Suez, Sociedad General de Aguas de Barcelona SA and InterAguas Servicios Integrales
de Agua SA v The Argentine Republic (ICSID Case No ARB/03/19) 4.19
Tanzania Electric Supply Company Limited v Independent Power Tanzania Limited
(ICSID Case No ARB/98/8). 7.44
Wena Hotels Limited v Arab Republic of Egypt (ICSID Case No ARB/98/4) 7.44

EUROPEAN COURT OF JUSTICE

Eco Swiss China Time Ltd v Benetton International NV (C-126/97) [1999]
2 All ER (Comm) 44; [1999] ECR I-3055; [1999] UKCLR 183; [2000] 5
CMLR 816, ECJ 6.73–6.74

DECISIONS OF NATIONAL COURTS

Argentina

Procuración del Tesoro v International Chamber of Commerce 2.660/2006
(Decision 15-XII-05) 2.28, 9.34

Australia

Esso Australia Resources Ltd & Ors v The Honourable Sidney James Plowman &
Ors (1995) 128 ALR 391 . . . . 9.18
The Commonwealth of Australia v John Fairfax and Sons Ltd (1995) 128 ALR 391 . . . . 9.19

Canada

Dell Computer Corporation v Union des Consommateurs and Olivier Dumoulin,
2007 SCC 34 . . . . 1.34, 6.90

England and Wales

ABB AG v Hochtief Airport GmbH [2006] EWHC 388 (Comm) 7.06

Aegis v European Re [2003] UKPC 11 . . . . .9.11, 9.23
Ali Shipping v Shipyard Trogir [1996] 1 Lloyd's Rep 643, CA, 65 . . . . .9.08, 9.11
Ashville Investments Ltd v Elmer Contractors Ltd; Sub Nom Elmer Contractors
    Ltd v Ashville Investments Ltd [1989] QB 488, CA 6.42
ASM Shipping Ltd v Harris [2007] EWHC 1513 (Comm). 4.18
ASM Shipping Ltd of India v TTMI Ltd of England [2005] EWHC 2238
    (Comm). 4.10, 4.18
Associated Electric & Gas Insurance Services Ltd v European Reinsurance Co of
    Zurich [2003] UKPC 11 . . . . 9.10
AT&T Corp and Anor v Saudi Cable Co [2000] 1 All ER 201 (Comm) CA 4.41
Bay Hotel and Resort Ltd v Cavalier Construction Co Ltd [2001] UKPC 34,
    PC (TCI) 6.45
Compagnie d'Armement Maritime v Compagnie Tunisienne de Navigation;
    Sub Nom Compagnie d'Armement Maritime SA v Compagnie Tunisienne
    de Navigation SA [1971] AC 572 . . . . 6.70
Coppée-Lavalin SA/NV v Ken-Ren Chemicals and Fertilizers Ltd
    (In Liquidation) [1994] 2 All ER 449, HL 6.152–6.153, 6.158
Elektrim SA v Vivendi Universal SA (No 2) [2007] 2 Lloyd's Rep 8, 19 . . . . 5.08, 5.26, 7.27
Emmott v Michael Wilson & Partners Ltd [2008] EWCA Civ 184 . . . . 9.12
Fiona Trust & Holding Corp v Privalov; Sub Nom: Premium Nafta Products
    Ltd v Fili Shipping Co Ltd [2007] UKHL 40, HL; [2007] EWCA Civ 20,
    CA (Civ Div) 6.94, 6.96
Hiscox v Outhwaite (No.1) [1992] 1 AC 562; [1991] 3 WLR 297; [1991] 3
    All ER 641; [1991] 2 Lloyd's Rep 435, HL 5.67, 7.09
Home and Overseas Insurance v Mentor Insurance [1989] 1 Lloyd's Rep 473, CA. 6.78
Laker Airways v FLS Aerospace [1999] 2 Lloyd's Rep 45 . . . . 4.26
Lesotho Highlands Development Authority v Impregilo SpA [2006] 1 AC 221, HL 7.35
Ronly Holdings Ltd v JSC Zestafoni G Nikoladze Ferralloy Plant [2004]
    EWHC 1354 . . . . 6.133
Smith Ltd v H&S International [1991] 2 Lloyd's Rep 127, 130. 5.24
Soleimany v Soleimany [1999] QB 785, CA. 6.72

France

Cass Civ, 7 January 1992, Sociétés BKMI et Siemens c société Dutco, [1992]
    Rev arb 470 . . . . .4.01, 4.03
Cass Civ 1re, 25 May 1992, Fougerolle SA c Procofrance SA 7.47
Cass Civ 1re, 6 July 2000, Gouvernement de l'Etat du Qatar c Creighton Ltd,
    [2001] Rev arb 114. . . . . 7.38
Cass Civ 1re, 20 February 2001, Société Cubic Defense Systems Inc c Chambre de
    Commerce Internationale. 9.33
Cass Civ 1re, 25 October 2005, Société Omenex c M Hugon, [2006] Rev arb 106 . . . . 6.93
Cass Civ 1re, 4 June 2008, Société SNF SAS c Société Cytec Industries BV, Bull
    civ I No 06-15.320 . . . . 6.74
Cour d'Appel de Paris, 18 February 1986, Aita c Ojjeh, [1986] Rev arb 583 . . . . 9.13
Cour d'Appel de Paris, 28 June 1991, KFTCIC c Kori Estero, [1992] Rev arb 568 . . . . 4.26
Cour d'Appel de Paris, 1 July 1999, Société Braspetro Oil Services (Brasoil) c GMRA,
    [1999] Rev arb 834. . . . . 7.29
Cour d'Appel de Paris, 4 March 2004, Société Nihon Plast Co Ltd c Société
    Takata-Petri Aktiengesellschaft, [2004] Rev arb 452 . . . . 9.45
Cour d'Appel de Paris, 18 November 2004, Thalès Air Defence BV c GIE Euromissile,
    EADS France and EADS Deutschland GmbH, [2005] Rev arb 529 . . . . 6.74
Cour d'Appel de Paris, 21 April 2005, Malecki c Long, [2006] Rev arb 673. . . . . 4.153

Switzerland

Swiss Federal Supreme Court, Ivan Milutinovic PIM v Deutsche Babcock AG,
BGE 117 Ia 166 . . . . 4.140
Swiss Federal Supreme Court, 11 March 1992, Société P c Société S Ltd, [1993]
Rev arb 115 . . . . 7.47
Westland Helicopters Ltd v Arab Organization for Industrialization, [1989]
Rev arb 514; BGE 120 II 155; [1996] ASA Bull 496 . . . . 9.34

Sweden

Stockholm City Court, AI Trade Finance Inc v Bulgarian Foreign Trade Bank Ltd
(1999) YCA 321 . . . . 9.14, 9.23
Svea Court of Appeal, 15 June 2003, Czech Republic v CME Czech Republic BV,
Case No T 8735-01 (2003) 42 ILM 915 . . . . 9.35
Supreme Court, 19 November 2007, Lind Case Case No T 2448-06 [2007]
Stockholm Int Arb Rev 167, 174 . . . . 4.24

The Netherlands

District Ct, Republic of Ghana v Telekom Malaysia [2005] ASA Bull 186 . . . . . . 4.14–4.15, 4.35

United States of America

United States v Panhandle Eastern Corp et al 118 FRD 346 (D Del 1988) 9.17

TABLE OF LEGISLATION

STATUTES

Belgium
Judicial Code
    art 1717 . . . . 5.26
    (4) 7.36

China
Contract Law 1999
    art 54 . . . . 6.40

Finland
Contracts Act 1929 (as amended)
    s 36 . . . . 6.40

France
Code de procédure civile
    art 1492 . . . . 5.69
    art 1502 . . . . 5.69
    art 1504 . . . . 5.69, 7.36

Germany
Zivilprozessordnung (code of civil
    procedure)
    s 1041(2) 6.129

Netherlands
Arbitration Act 1986
    Art 1030(1) 4.131
    Art 1068. . . . . 7.47
    Art 1073. . . . . 5.68

Sweden
Arbitration Act 1999
    s 25 . . . . 6.137
    s 51 . . . . 5.26

Switzerland
Civil Code
    art 2 . . . . 6.40

Private International Law Act 1986
    Art 176(1) 5.68
    Art 179. . . . . 4.131
    Art 183. . . . . 6.108
    (2) 6.129
    Art 186(2) 3.34
    Art 192. . . . . 5.26, 7.36

United Arab Emirates
Dubai International Financial Centre Arbit-
    ration Law 2008 . . . . 1.31

United Kingdom
Arbitration Act 1950
    s 19A 7.23
    s 20 . . . . 7.24
Arbitration Act 1996 . . . . 1.11, 1.21,
    1.38, 1.40, 2.24, 3.06, 4.26, 4.44, 5.25,
    5.35, 5.58, 5.68, 5.71, 6.57, 6.148, 7.27,
    7.45, 8.30, App8
    s 3 . . . . 5.58, 5.64, 5.68
    s 4(3) 5.22
    (5) 5.71
    s 5(1) 5.14
    (2) 3.06
    s 6 . . . . 6.49
    s 9 . . . . 6.94
    s 24 . . . . 2.23, 2.26, 4.18
    (1) 4.02
    (a) 4.11
    (2) 2.26
    s 27(1) 4.131
    s 29 . . . . 9.30, 9.33
    s 30 . . . . 6.86
    s 31(4) 6.103
    s 33(1) 1.39, 5.03, 5.08, 5.13,
    5.35, 7.11

Arbitration Act 1996 (*cont.*)

(a)	1.42, 4.117
(b)	1.42
s 34	5.16
(2)	5.37
(f)	6.37
(g)	5.35, 5.96, 6.22
s 35	6.56, 6.59
s 38	6.133
(1)	6.133, 6.138
(3)	6.154
(4)	6.140
s 39	6.131, 6.133, 6.143
(1)	1.39, 6.132–6.133
s 40	7.23
(1)	5.27
s 41	5.27, 5.56
(6)	6.156
s 42	6.129, 6.150
s 46(1)(b)	6.68, 6.78
(2)	6.64
(3)	6.64
s 47(1)	7.25
s 49(3)	7.24
(b)	7.24
(4)	7.24
s 51(2)	7.30
s 52(1)	7.03
(2)	7.03, 7.07
(3)	7.10
s 53	5.67, 7.09
s 57(3)	7.45
(a)	7.45
s 60	8.30
s 61	8.26, 8.27
s 67	7.36
(2)	6.104
s 68	7.06, 7.36
(3)(a)	9.49
s 69	7.35
s 73	9.37, 9.40
(1)(d)	9.43
s 74	2.24, 9.30, 9.33
s 76	9.31
s 100(2)(b)	5.67

Supreme Court Act 1981

s 37	7.27

STATUTORY INSTRUMENTS

Civil Procedure Rules SI 1998/3132	5.33
Pt 36	8.31

ARBITRATION RULES

AAA Arbitration Rules . . . 4.153, 6.65, 6.131

CIETAC Rules

  Art 7. . . . . 6.128

  Art 17. . . . . 6.128

  Art 18. . . . . 6.128

DIFC-LCIA Arbitration Rules . . . . . . App 11

  art 16.1. . . . . 5.60

ICC Arbitration Rules 1.08, 3.08, 3.14,
    3.28, 4.08, 4.12, 4.41, 4.77, 4.132,
    4.147, 4.149, 5.31, 5.64, 6.04, 6.55,
    6.87, 6.131, 6.145, 6.160, 7.11, 7.33,
    8.02, 8.07–8.08, 8.39, 8.41, 9.47, 9.49

  Art 1(3) 2.10

  Art 3. . . . . 3.39

  Art 4(3) 3.18

     (c) 3.10

    (4) 3.18

    (5) 3.19

    (6) 6.55

  Art 5. . . . . 3.24

    (2) 3.28–3.29, 3.49

    (4) 3.19

  Art 6(2) 3.08, 6.87

    (3) 5.56

  Art 7(1) 4.11

    (5) 4.114

  Art 8(4) 3.14

    (5) 6.153

  Art 10. . . . . 4.83

    (2) 4.83

  Art 12(4) 4.130, 4.132

    (5) 4.144, 4.150

  Art 13. . . . . 8.38

  Art 14(1) 5.60

    (2) 5.65–5.66

Art 15. . . . . 5.21

  (1) 5.05

  (2) 4.11, 5.07, 5.12, 5.21, 5.67

Art 16. . . . . 5.72

Art 17(1) 6.65

  (2) 6.62

Art 18(2) 3.49

Art 19. . . . . 5.21, 6.09, 6.11

Art 20. . . . . 5.21

  (1) 5.21, 5.31

  (2) 5.88

  (3) 5.104

  (4) 5.115

  (5) 6.27

Art 21. . . . . 5.21

  (2) 5.56

Art 22. . . . . 5.21

Art 23(1) 6.131

Art 24(1) 7.11

  (2) 3.49

Art 25(3) 7.09

Art 26. . . . . 7.30

Art 27. . . . . 7.20

Art 28(1) 7.22

  (6) 7.35, 7.37

Art 29(2) 7.43

Art 30(2) 8.39

  (3) 8.40, 8.48

  (4) 8.54

Art 31(1) 8.02

  (2) 5.29

Art 33. . . . . 9.38

Art 34. . . . . 9.31, 9.33

Art 35. . . . . 9.49

ICC Rules 1998 . . . . .6.152

ICDR Rules 4.88, 4.94, 5.31

  art 3 . . . . .3.24

  art 13 . . . . .5.60

  art 13.2 . . . . .5.65

  art 14 . . . . .5.72

  art 16 . . . . .5.05

  art 16.1 . . . . .5.07

  art 16.3 . . . . .5.104

  art 17.1 . . . . .5.31

  art 18 . . . . .3.39

  art 22 . . . . .5.115

  art 23 . . . . .5.56

  art 26.2 . . . . .5.29

  art 27.3 . . . . .5.67

  art 34 . . . . .9.04

  art 35 . . . . .9.31

  art 37 . . . . 4.88, 4.91

  art 39.5 . . . . .4.90

ICSID Arbitration Rules 4.08, 4.19

  r 41 . . . . .3.34

LCIA Rules 1985 . . . . .1.06, 1.12, 1.38,
    3.16, 4.79, 5.02, 5.05, 5.21, 5.64, 5.87,
    7.23, 7.34, 7.38, 7.43–7.44

  Art 2.1 . . . . .3.29

  Art 3.4 . . . . .3.16

  Art 3.5 . . . . .4.130

  Art 7.1 . . . . .5.64

  Art 8.1 . . . . 5.73, 5.78

  Art 17. . . . . .5.73

  Art 18.2 . . . . .8.04

NAI Rules 4.08, 4.88, 4.94

  Arts 42a–42o 4.88

SCC Rules 6.15, 6.55, 6.65, 6.127, 9.47

  art 19(1). 5.05

  art 20 . . . . .5.60

  art 31 . . . . .9.38

  art 32(1). 6.131

  art 35(2). 5.29

  art 46 . . . . .9.04

Swiss Rules

  art 4(2). 6.51

  art 16(1). 5.60

  art 43(1). 9.04

UNCITRAL Arbitration Rules 1.09,
    1.47–1.48, 3.14, 3.24, 4.14, 4.57,
    4.132, 4.139, 5.31, 6.51, 6.131, 8.02,
    9.53

  art 1.1 . . . . .5.05

  art 2 . . . . .3.39

  art 7.1 . . . . .3.14

  art 11.3 . . . . .4.114

  art 14 . . . . .4.132

  art 15.1 . . . . 5.07, 5.12

  art 16 . . . . .5.60

  art 16.2 . . . . .5.65

  art 17 . . . . .5.72

  art 18 . . . . 5.31, 6.12

  art 19 . . . . 5.31, 6.12

  art 20 . . . . 6.12, 6.19

  art 22 . . . . .5.31

  art 25.6 . . . . .5.104

  art 26.2 . . . . .5.29

  art 27 . . . . .5.115

  art 28 . . . . .5.56

  art 30 . . . . .9.38

    (1) 7.14

  art 35 . . . . 7.43–7.44

  art 36 . . . . .7.43

  art 37 . . . . .7.43

  art 38 . . . . .8.02

WIPO Arbitration Rules. 4.89, 6.65

  Art 4. . . . . .3.39

  Art 35. . . . . 4.142

  Art 46(b) 1.21

  Art 77. . . . . 9.31

INTERNATIONAL INSTRUMENTS

Treaty establishing the European Community (Rome, 25 February 1957, as amended) [1997] OJ C350/173

Art 17(1) 4.68

Art 81 . . . . 6.73

Art 82 . . . . 6.73

Convention on the Recognition and Enforcement of Foreign Arbitral Awards (New York, 10 June 1958) (1959) 330 UNTS 3 . . . . . . 4.02, 5.58, 5.68, 6.48

Art I(3) 5.58

Art II 6.49

Art V 5.68

(1)(a) 5.68

(b) 3.42, 5.11, 5.26

(d) 5.26, 5.68

(e) 5.69

Convention on the Settlement of Investment Disputes between States and Nationals of other States (Washington, 18 March 1965) (1966) 575 UNTS 159

art 45 . . . . 5.56

art 50 . . . . 7.43–7.44

art 51 . . . . 7.43

Convention on the Law Applicable to Contractual Obligations (Rome, 19 June 1980) [1980] OJ L266/1 . . . . 6.72

Art 3(1) 6.65

(3) 6.72

United Nations Convention on Contracts for the International Sale of Goods (Vienna, 11 April 1980) (1980) 1489 UNTS 53 . . . . 6.69

UNCITRAL Model Law on International Commercial Arbitration 24 ILM 1302 (1985) 5.25, 5.68, 6.110, 6.149, App9

art 1(2) 5.68

(3) 1.11

art 4 . . . . 9.37

art 7(2) 3.06

art 12 . . . . 4.02

art 13(3) 2.26

art 14(2) 4.114

art 15 . . . . 4.131

art 16 . . . . 6.86

(2) 6.99

(3) 6.104

art 17 . . . . 6.126

(2) 6.111

(a) 6.126

(b) 6.126

(3)(b) 6.117

art 17.A 6.112, 6.117, 6.120, 6.123

(1)(a) 6.121

(2) 6.113

art 17.E(1) 6.136

art 18 . . . . 5.03, 5.12

art 19 . . . . 5.07

(1) 5.05

art 25 . . . . 5.56

art 26 . . . . 5.114

art 28 . . . . 6.65

art 31(1) 7.03, 7.07, 7.10

(3) 5.67

art 33 . . . . 7.38

art 36(1)(a)(ii) 3.42

Treaty on European Union (Maastricht, February 1992) [1992] OJ C191/1 . . . . 4.68

North American Free Trade Agreement
(17 December 1992) (1993)
32 ILM 605 (1993) 1.51–1.52

Softwood Lumber Agreement between
the Government of Canada and the

Government of the United States
of America (Ottawa, 12 September
2006, as amended) 1.50, 1.52,
5.115, 9.22

LIST OF ABBREVIATIONS

AAA	American Arbitration Association
Am Rev Int Arb	*American Review of International Arbitration*
Arbitration	*Arbitration: The Journal of the Chartered Institute of Arbitrators*
Arb Int	*Arbitration International*
ASA Bull	*Bulletin of the Swiss Arbitration Association*
Bull civ	*Bulletin des arrêts de la Cour de cassation, chambre civile*
CIETAC	China International Economic and Trade Arbitration Commission
Commentary	'Commentary on a Discussion Draft of the LCIA Rules' (1996) 1(2) LCIA Newsletter 10
Craig, Park, Paulsson	WL Craig, W Park and J Paulsson, *International Chamber of Commerce Arbitration* (3rd edn, Oceana/ICC, 2000)
DAC Report	Departmental advisory committee on arbitration law: Report on the Arbitration Bill, reprinted in (1997) 12 Arb Int 275.
Derains & Schwartz	Y Derains and E Schwartz, *A Guide to the ICC Rules of Arbitration* (2nd edn, Kluwer, 2005)
DIFC	Dubai International Financial Centre
Fouchard, Gaillard, Goldman	E Gaillard and J Savage (eds), *Fouchard, Gaillard, Goldman on International Commercial Arbitration* (Kluwer, 2000)
Hunter & Paulsson	M Hunter and J Paulsson, 'A Commentary on the Rules of the London Court of International Arbitration' (1985) 10 YCA 167
IBA Arb News	*International Bar Association Arbitration Newsletter*
IBA Guidelines	Guidelines on Conflicts of Interest in International Arbitration adopted by the Council of the International Bar Association on 22 May 2004
IBA Rules	Rules on the Taking of Evidence in International Commercial Arbitration adopted by the Council of the International Bar Association on 1 June 1999
ICC	International Chamber of Commerce
ICC Bull	*ICC International Court of Arbitration Bulletin*
ICDR	International Centre for Dispute Resolution
ICSID	International Centre for Settlement of Investment Disputes

IDRC	International Dispute Resolution Centre
ILM	*International Legal Materials*
Int ALR	*International Arbitration Law Review*
Iran-US Cl Trib Rep	*Iran-US Claims Tribunal Reports*
JDI	*Journal du droit international*
J Int Arb	*Journal of International Arbitration*
JT	*Journal des Tribunaux*
Lew, Mistelis, Kröll	J Lew, L Mistelis and S Kröll, *Comparative International Commercial Arbitration* (Kluwer, 2003)
Mealey's Int Arb Rep	*Mealey's International Arbitration Reports*
NAI	Netherlands Arbitration Institute
New York Convention	Convention on the Recognition and Enforcement of Foreign Arbitral Awards (New York, 10 June 1958), (1959) 330 UNTS 3
Nicholas & Partasides	G Nicholas and C Partasides, 'LCIA Court Decisions on Challenges to Arbitrators: A Proposal to Publish' (2007) 23 Arb Int 1
PILA	Swiss Federal Statute on Private International Law
Poudret & Besson	JF Poudret and S Besson, *Comparative Law of International Arbitration* (2nd edn, Sweet & Maxwell, 2007)
RCDIP	*Revue critique du droit international privé*
Redfern & Hunter	A Redfern and M Hunter with N Blackaby and C Partasides, *Law and Practice of International Commercial Arbitration* (4th edn, Sweet & Maxwell, 2004)
Rev arb	*Revue de l'arbitrage*
Russell	D St John Sutton, J Gill and M Gearing, *Russell on Arbitration* (23rd edn, Sweet & Maxwell, 2007)
SCC	Arbitration Institute of the Stockholm Chamber of Commerce
SchiedsVZ	*Zeitschrift für Schiedsverfahren*
Stockholm Int Arb Rev	*Stockholm International Arbitration Review*
Swiss Rules	Swiss Rules of International Arbitration
TDM	Transnational Dispute Management, accessible at <http://www.transnational-dispute-management.com>
UNCITRAL	United Nations Commission on International Trade Law
UNCITRAL Model Law	UNCITRAL Model Law on International Commercial Arbitration, as amended in 2006, contained in UN documents A/40/17 (1985) and A/61/17 (2006)
UNCITRAL Rules	UNCITRAL Arbitration Rules, adopted by General Assembly Resolution 31/98 on 15 December 1976
WIPO	World Intellectual Property Organization
YCA	*Yearbook Commercial Arbitration*
ZPO	*Zivilprozessordung*, German Code of Civil Procedure

1

INTRODUCTION

A. The London Court of International Arbitration	1.02
B. The LCIA Arbitration Rules	1.38
C. The LCIA as Appointing Authority under the UNCITRAL Arbitration Rules	1.47
D. The Softwood Lumber Arbitrations	1.50
E. Other Forms of Dispute Resolution Administered by the LCIA	1.54

1.01 The London Court of International Arbitration is probably the oldest continuously established international arbitration institution in the world.[1] Its longevity is matched by its continuing vitality: in the first six months of 2008 it had registered 137 new cases, an increase of 34 per cent over the same period in 2007.[2]

A. The London Court of International Arbitration

1.02 The LCIA was inaugurated in November 1892 as the 'London Chamber of Arbitration' at the initiative of the Corporation of London, with the hope that

---

[1] The International Court of Arbitration (until 1989 the Court of Arbitration) of the International Chamber of Commerce was founded in 1923.

[2] For a general discussion of the history of the LCIA, see Sir M Kerr, 'The London Court of International Arbitration 1892–1992' (1992) 8 Arb Int 317; JL Delvolvé, 'Le centenaire de la LCIA (London Court of International Arbitration)' [1993] Rev arb 599; Sir M Kerr, 'London Court of International Arbitration' in *ICCA Congress Series No 7* (Kluwer, 1996) 213; VV Veeder, 'London Court of International Arbitration – The New 1998 LCIA Rules' (1998) 23 YCA 366; and A Winstanley, 'The LCIA – history, constitution and rules' in A Berkeley and J Mimms (eds), *International Commercial Arbitration: Practical Perspectives* (Centre of Construction Law & Management, 2001) 21.

it would expedite the resolution of business disputes. Its foundation was reported thus in a now-famous commentary:

> This Chamber is to have all the virtues which the law lacks. It is to be expeditious where the law is slow, cheap where the law is costly, simple where the law is technical, a peacemaker instead of a stirrer-up of strife.[3]

1.03 Whether the LCIA (it became the London Court of Arbitration in 1903 and the adjective 'International' was added in 1981 to emphasize its worldwide vocation and ambition), or indeed international commercial arbitration in any of its manifestations, achieves these ideals is another matter (or even aspires to them, in some cases, since the wish to be a peacemaker may smack more of mediation and its fellow-travellers than arbitration). What is apparent has been the LCIA's durability, due to its popularity with users and its flexibility of approach.

The organization of the LCIA

1.04 The LCIA has a complicated constitution. There are three levels of administration, a company, the Arbitration Court, and the Secretariat.[4]

The company

1.05 The LCIA is incorporated in England and Wales as a not-for-profit company limited by guarantee. It should be noted that the Board of Directors of the LCIA has no responsibility for the administration of the Rules, still less of individual arbitrations, and primarily concerns itself with the development of the LCIA itself, as well, of course, as its operational efficiency and its compliance with English company law.[5]

The Arbitration Court

1.06 The LCIA Court is the primary body, with the Secretariat, that administers arbitrations under the LCIA Rules.[6] Indeed, it is mentioned no less than 91 times in the Rules.[7] It is the final authority for the appointment of tribunals, determining

---

[3] (1893) IX LQR 86.

[4] Although the word 'secretariat' nowhere appears in the Rules, it is used as the term to describe all of the LCIA's casework staff even in the LCIA's own materials and, for example, in Winstanley (n 2 above).

[5] The overwhelmingly London-based composition of the Board does not detract from the LCIA's international nature. It is, rather, efficient for the governing body of the English company to be able to meet without due expense and delay and to be familiar with English company law.

[6] The LCIA Court was set up under the 1985 Rules: see Winstanley (n 2 above) 26.

[7] Of course, some of these references are multiple, contained in the same Article, but the impression of the importance of the role of the Court created by such statistics is absolutely right, despite the fact that the LCIA Court does not have the same role of scrutiny of awards as the ICC Court does.

challenges to arbitrators, and controlling costs. Its role will be described more fully in chapter 2 below.

In stark contrast to the Board, the Court has a truly international membership.[8] **1.07**
Indeed, its Constitution provides that no more than six members (out of a total of 35) may be UK citizens at any given time.[9]

The Court does not have the same functions as the perhaps better-known **1.08**
International Court of Arbitration of the ICC. In particular, the LCIA Arbitration Court does not scrutinize draft awards before they are released to the parties. The scrutiny of draft awards by the ICC's Court, together with the Terms of Reference required by the ICC Rules but not those of the LCIA, is a distinguishing feature of the ICC's procedure and parties will need to consider, when choosing a set of institutional arbitration rules, whether they are necessary or desirable in the context of the potential or actual dispute that they are facing.[10] A discussion of the relative advantages to the parties that these differences may give is contained in chapters 5 and 7 below. In contrast, the LCIA Court has a greater role in the selection of tribunals than does the ICC Court, as discussed in chapter 4 below.

The Secretariat

The Secretariat is responsible for the day-to-day administration of LCIA arbitra- **1.09**
tions (and LCIA-administered arbitrations under the UNCITRAL Arbitration Rules) and mediations (which are not the subject of this book). Again, its role and function (and in particular that of the Registrar) is discussed in chapter 2 below.

The Secretariat currently consists of the Director-General (currently also man- **1.10**
dated to serve as Registrar), the Registrar and Deputy Director-General, and three casework administrators.[11] This lean organization reflects the role of the LCIA as an institution: it facilitates the task of the tribunal but its administrative hand is very light. In this it is to be contrasted with the ICC.

The LCIA today

Although the LCIA has an overwhelmingly international user base, it does not restrict **1.11**
itself to 'international' arbitration as such.[12] It can thus (although in practice it does

---

8 The membership of the Court as at the date of publication is set out in app 5.

9 The Constitution of the LCIA Arbitration Court, as amended in 2002, is at app 4.

10 While there are many commentaries on the ICC Arbitration Rules, the two best-known and most comprehensive are *Derains & Schwartz* and *Craig, Park, Paulsson*.

11 Plus secondees, research assistants, and membership assistants.

12 In any event, there is more than one definition of what constitutes international, as opposed to domestic, arbitration. The appropriate definition would have to depend on both the governing law of the contract and/or the arbitration clause and the arbitration law of the seat of the arbitration. In England and Wales, the definition is contained in the Arbitration Act 1996 (a copy of which

so very rarely) deal with domestic English (or other) arbitration as well as international cases, however defined.

1.12   Although it has a history of over 100 years, the LCIA stayed a very London-centred organization (albeit dealing with many non-English parties and international disputes, as indeed did, and does, the English Commercial Court, both phenomena being due to London's eminence as a commercial and shipping centre) until 1985, when its Arbitration Court was established and new rules, more international in nature, were introduced. One can indeed almost talk of the LCIA's refoundation as a genuinely international body as of that date (which would of course effectively see the title of the world's oldest international arbitration institution slip away, probably to Paris). Indeed, given that the rebirth of the LCIA took place only in the early 1980s, its growth since then has been nothing short of remarkable.

1.13   Since 1985, while the LCIA has largely succeeded in its mission to internationalize its users, it is still widely perceived as a very English institution. The general feeling is that the LCIA Rules are chosen as a complement to a choice of English governing law and thus justifying a choice of London as a seat and the consequent retention of English lawyers, this last choice very often including the full panoply of the English split legal profession, with solicitors instructing barristers to present the oral argument and sometimes even the use of a common law-biased procedure with extensive document disclosure and lengthy hearings, leading to high legal fees by international standards.[13] While, as shown below, this

---

is at app 8), which provides in s 85 that a domestic arbitration agreement is one to which none of the parties is '(a) an individual who is a national of, or habitually resident in, a state other than the United Kingdom, or (b) a body corporate which is incorporated in, or whose central control and management is exercised in, a state other than the United Kingdom, and under which the seat of the arbitration (if the seat has been designated or determined) is in the United Kingdom'. The UNCITRAL Model Law (a copy of which is at app 9), promulgated in 1985 (under the direction of Prof Dr Gerold Hermann, a past President of the LCIA and now an Honorary Vice President) and revised in 2006, defines in art 1(3) an arbitration as international if:

   (a) the parties to an arbitration agreement have, at the time of the conclusion of that agreement, their places of business in different States; or

   (b) one of the following places is situated outside the State in which the parties have their places of business:

      (i) the place of arbitration if determined in, or pursuant to, the arbitration agreement;

      (ii) any place where a substantial part of the obligations of the commercial relationship is to be performed or the place with which the subject-matter of the dispute is most closely connected; or

   (c) the parties have expressly agreed that the subject-matter of the arbitration agreement relates to more than one country.

[13]   Although it should be noted that the procedure in the English Commercial Court has itself recently been considerably streamlined.

perception is not wholly accurate (not only is there an increasingly international look to the LCIA's arbitrators, but the traditional split between solicitors preparing the case and barristers presenting the argument is seen less even where parties opt for English legal representation, and the use of the IBA Rules often greatly limits document disclosure), it is still true that LCIA arbitration is usually very closely related to England, English law, and an English seat.

The perception of the LCIA as London-centric is not helped by the fact that even the 1998 Rules provide that London is the default seat (Article 16.1) and that English is the default language of the arbitration for non-participating parties and the invariable language of communication with the Registrar (Article 17.1). Furthermore, the Rules themselves are authentic only in their English-language version and the translations into the various languages that appear on the LCIA's website are unofficial.[14]

1.14

Moreover, it is interesting to note that the LCIA's own statistics show that, in 2007, no fewer than 77 per cent of party-nominated arbitrators were of UK nationality. This is a rise from the 2006 figure of 70 per cent, again showing that the perceived Englishness of LCIA arbitration is at least in part derived from the parties' own choices and can thus be seen as a positive asset in attracting users. In the same period, the LCIA Court appointed (without party nomination) only 35 UK nationals as arbitrators, out of a total of 70, namely 50 per cent, down from 54 per cent in 2006.[15]

1.15

These statistics, of arbitrators nominated by the parties (or party-nominated arbitrators), on the one hand, and appointed directly by the LCIA Court, on the other, are of particular interest. They show both (a) parties' perceptions of the LCIA as an English organization, for English cases, needing English arbitrators (it is assumed that the overwhelming majority of the UK nationals nominated by the parties were English-qualified, rather than qualified in Scotland or Northern Ireland) and (b) the LCIA's own efforts to reduce that perception by appointing a lower percentage of English arbitrators than the parties themselves (50 per cent may seem a lot, but it is on a downward trend from 54 per cent from the previous year and far below the 74 per cent of English arbitrators nominated by the parties, which is on an upward trend).

1.16

In the course of preparing this book, the authors have been given unprecedented access to the LCIA's records. We have been able to review all 701 fully-administered cases that have been introduced under the 1998 Rules from their

1.17

---

[14] The following translations of the LCIA Rules are available on the LCIA's website: Arabic, Chinese, French, German, Italian, Portuguese, Russian, and Spanish. See <http://www.lcia-arbitration.com>

[15] For the 2006 figures, see the Director General's report for 2006, available on the LCIA's website at <http://www.lcia-arbitration.com>

inception until the end of 2007. In order to preserve the principle of the confidentiality of the proceedings mandated by Article 30 (discussed in chapter 9 below), this research has been carried out at the authors' direction by the LCIA's own research assistants. It has proved a very rich source of information about how tribunals, the LCIA Court, and the Registrar apply the Rules in practice.

1.18 With the benefit of such a source of information, the authors have been able to make reference to specific cases in the discussion of individual provisions of the LCIA Rules that follows. Since the cases are confidential and the awards unpublished, there can be no citations to individual cases. The value of the research material as a guide to LCIA arbitration in practice cannot, however, be underestimated.

1.19 In the course of our research, we have been able to complement the LCIA's own statistics referred to above. In the light of that research, is the perception that LCIA cases are mostly English-law and -language, and have a London seat, justified? It would seem so. From our research, it can be seen that only seven out of 701 (ie, less than 1 per cent) were wholly conducted in a language other than English,[16] some 12 only were conducted in English and another language, and the rest were English-language alone. As to the governing law,[17] no less than 501 (representing 71 per cent) of the cases surveyed were governed by English law; in a further 10 cases, the contracts had governing law clauses specifying English law and another law in one form or another.[18]

1.20 Similarly, some 503 out of 701 cases had their seat in London, with another six elsewhere in England and Wales, while a mere 18 (3 per cent) had their seat elsewhere.[19] Given that 173 cases had unknown or unspecified seats, and given the provision for a default seat in London under Article 16.1, it is to be imagined that nearly all if not all of these 173 had (or would have had, in the case of arbitrations that settled before the seat was designated) their seat in London. One can thus see the overwhelming dominance of England and Wales (and particularly London) as the seat of arbitration for cases under the LCIA Rules.

---

[16] Six cases in Russian and one in Italian.

[17] All of the cases reviewed were contract-based; as far as we are aware, the LCIA has not been used as an institution in investment-treaty arbitrations, although, as discussed further below, it has been chosen by the governments of Canada and the United States to administer the 'softwood lumber' arbitrations.

[18] The rest had no governing law clause.

[19] Three in Geneva, two each in New York, Vancouver and Vienna, and one each in Barcelona, Berlin, Bermuda, Miami, Mumbai, Osaka, Paris, Singapore, and Washington DC.

This explains the great care that has been taken, as is seen time and time again   **1.21**
when considering the 1998 Rules, to ensure that the Rules are always in
conformity with the English Arbitration Act 1996, or make choices about the
powers of the tribunal where the Arbitration Act allows such choices to be made
by the parties. This does not render the Rules any less usable in other seats (indeed,
the Rules have also been markedly influenced by the UNCITRAL Model Law),
but it would clearly have been a derogation of duty by the drafters of the Rules
not to have taken great care to ensure that the Rules did not cause problems for
arbitrations with their seat in England and Wales.[20]

It is also the case that parties overwhelmingly choose English-based counsel to   **1.22**
represent them in LCIA arbitrations. Claimants chose London-based counsel
about two-thirds of the time (on a few, but really not very many (20-odd out of
well over 400) occasions, with lawyers from elsewhere). Some 30-odd other claimants had counsel based elsewhere in England and one in Wales. To show the extent
to which it is perceived necessary to have lawyers based in London, claimants
chose counsel based in Paris (which is both nearby and the base of a very large
number of experienced arbitration practitioners) only 12 times (and one of those
was with London counsel as well).

As to respondents, they chose London counsel (less than 10 per cent of the time   **1.23**
with lawyers from elsewhere) slightly under half the time (in 335 out of 701 cases
reviewed), lawyers from the rest of England in 30-odd cases and Paris (again, the
most popular place in which to seek representation after London) trailing far
behind with only eight mentions.[21]

On the other hand, the epithet 'international' is certainly more than justified   **1.24**
by the origins of the parties to LCIA arbitrations. Although in 135 cases there
was at least one UK-based claimant, and in 120 cases there was at least one
UK-based respondent, this represents under 20 per cent of the total. Since
in some cases, although a small minority for both claimants and respondents,
there was also an overseas-based co-claimant or -respondent, as the case may be,
this means that the number of cases with only UK-based claimants or respondents
is far less than the number of London seats or English governing-law clauses
would suggest.

---

[20] A commentary for the German-speaking market remarks that the LCIA Rules are in fact
very international and that the only specifically English provision is the ability to award security
for costs (in art 25.2, discussed in ch 6 below), which, they note, is also present in art 46(b) WIPO
Rules: V Triebel and R Hunter, 'Kommentar LCIA-Schiedsregeln' in R Schütze (ed), *Institutionelle
Schiedsgerichtsbarkeit* (Carl Heymanns Verlag, 2006) 356.

[21] Astonishingly, 30 claimants were not represented, whether by in-house or outside counsel.
The same is true for 138 respondents, which is less surprising as some claims will be left undefended.
It is still a very high proportion (20 per cent) of the sample.

1.25 It seems as though, while its users come from far and wide, the LCIA is seen by those users as an English institution to decide matters under English law, with English arbitrators and English lawyers, in London, in the English language.

1.26 As to arbitrators, over the whole sample of 701 fully administered cases, tribunals had UK nationals as chairman or sole arbitrator in 352 cases (almost exactly half), and one or more UK co-arbitrators in 185 cases, well under a third of the total. There have been, in all cases started under the 1998 Rules up to the end of 2007, all-UK tribunals in only 91 out of 701 cases. Thus, whatever the perceived advantages to the parties of a London seat and English substantive law, they do not want (or get, as the Court makes many of these appointments) only English-qualified lawyers to decide their cases.

1.27 The perception of the LCIA as an English, specifically London, organization is thus still current despite the LCIA's considerable efforts, with the establishment of Users' Councils all over the world,[22] and its holding of very successful and well-attended conferences every year in several parts of the world, on the popular 'Tylney Hall'[23] model, where there are no set speeches but rather moderated debates. This has meant that the LCIA has prospered with the widespread use of English law for commercial agreements containing arbitration clauses but has also led to its being seen as the junior partner to other institutions, especially the ICC, which are seen as more international in origin. It may be that the relative absence of commentary and academic study of the LCIA Rules has also contributed to the (false) view that the LCIA is only for arbitration in London under English law.

1.28 In any event, whatever the perception of the LCIA as English, it does not seem to have detracted from the international nature of its users. As noted above, the parties to LCIA arbitrations are far from being mainly from the UK. In 2007, only 16 per cent came from the UK (down from 19 per cent in 2006, a further indication of the downward trend in English participation also remarked upon in connection with arbitrators appointed by the LCIA Court). This was still, however, the largest single national contingent. The USA was the next most heavily represented at 10 per cent (down from 12.75 per cent in 2006). The national origins of the remaining users show a fragmented picture. In 2007, therefore, 7.5 per cent each of parties came from Africa, the Middle East

---

[22] The LCIA's Users' Councils are (in alphabetical order) the African Users' Council, the Arab Users' Council, the Asia-Pacific Users' Council (including Australia and New Zealand), the European Users' Council, the Latin-American and Caribbean Users' Council, and the North American Users' Council (including Mexico). Full details of the Users' Councils are set out in app 7.

[23] Named after the hotel in Hampshire, southern England, where the LCIA holds conferences of this type (although it also uses a larger venue due to the great popularity of the format).

(which augurs well for the future success of the DIFC joint venture, discussed below) and 'other Asia-Pacific', after deduction of Singapore (2 per cent by itself). An interesting statistic is that the Caribbean almost matches western Europe in supplying parties to LCIA arbitrations: the British Virgin Islands alone supply some 7 per cent and the rest of the Caribbean another 6.5 per cent for a total of 13.5 per cent of users, while Western Europe (excluding the UK), supplies 14.5 per cent (Switzerland providing the largest contribution, despite its own reputation as a centre for international arbitration, at 5 per cent of parties). This Caribbean influence no doubt hides many interests from elsewhere, often from Russia and other former Soviet states. Russia itself provided only 2 per cent of parties directly (and other CIS countries another 3.5 per cent) but the representation of Russian or CIS interests is surely far greater. On any view, therefore, whether perceived as of use primarily for English-language or English law-related disputes, the LCIA is clearly succeeding in spreading its message far and wide around the globe.

Moreover, despite what some might feel is the handicap of being seen as more **1.29** national than international (or at least as being the standard-bearer of a particularly English way of conducting arbitration), the LCIA is at the very forefront of the development of the institution of arbitration. There is the ground-breaking decision to publish decisions of the Court on challenges to arbitrators, and even more recently the decision to sponsor the Corporate Counsel International Arbitration Group, an independent body that represents the real users of arbitration, namely in-house counsel (for it is they, or rather the companies for whom they work) whom the LCIA and the other arbitration institutions are ultimately there to serve, not the cohorts of arbitration counsel and arbitrators who actually work in the system.

International reach

Even more noteworthy is the LCIA's international expansion. There are two **1.30** distinct models of this expansion. The first is the setting-up of LCIA branch offices. At present, these are planned for India and Barbados. The branch offices will function as a devolved part of the existing LCIA Secretariat, with a local Registrar. Arbitrations could be started in the local branch, or started by sending the Request for Arbitration to the London head office and subsequently administered from the local branch. Either way, the idea would be to have a presence in India and the Caribbean that should encourage locally based parties to consider the LCIA as a local institution, or at least not one that deals only with English-related disputes.

More daringly, however, the LCIA has entered into a partnership with the Dubai **1.31** International Financial Centre (the DIFC), whereby the two organizations have established the DIFC-LCIA Arbitration Centre. This is the first time that the LCIA has entered into a strategic partnership of this kind. This centre has its own rules (the 1998 LCIA Rules suitably changed to make reference to the

DIFC-LCIA Arbitration Centre and to provide a default seat (in the absence of party choice) of the DIFC[24] rather than London)[25] and arbitrations will be administered locally, albeit with the assistance of the LCIA Registrar in London. The LCIA Court will play the same role as in LCIA arbitrations, but the DIFC-LCIA Arbitration Centre will otherwise be a largely autonomous institution.

1.32   Much has been written about the DIFC, its unique 'state-within-a-state' position within the judicial fabric of Dubai and the United Arab Emirates, and its own unique system of dispute resolution for disputes between DIFC members,[26] and this book is not the place to discuss it and its wider policy implications. Given that the DIFC-LCIA Arbitration Centre will be open to all parties, however, not just members of the DIFC, it has the potential to become a beacon of international arbitration in the Middle East, with which the LCIA has done well to be associated.

1.33   All of these developments bode very well for the future of the LCIA. It has done well to date as an institution catering for parties who have chosen English law to govern their relations and who want an English-style dispute resolution mechanism to go with that choice.[27] Its challenge now is to keep that market, while also broadening its appeal. The branch offices seem to play to its existing strengths, the DIFC joint venture to belong more to the search for new horizons, even if one of the DIFC's own selling points is an English-language legal system closely modelled on English law, including a common law procedure in the DIFC courts (which will have supervisory jurisdiction over DIFC-LCIA Arbitration Centre arbitrations with their seat in the DIFC), applied by a roster of judges composed of retired members of the judiciaries of England and other Commonwealth countries.

1.34   While considering the LCIA's international ambitions, one can also mention the *amicus curiae* brief that the institution submitted in the Supreme Court of Canada in the *Dell Computer* case.[28] This case is discussed further in chapter 6 below in the context of the tribunal's jurisdiction and the principle of *compétence-compétence*, but the fact that the LCIA was (at its own cost) prepared to support the principle in the Supreme Court of Canada shows that it sees itself as having a mandate to support and encourage positive developments in arbitration wherever they may be taking place.

---

[24] An autonomous jurisdiction where the civil and commercial laws of the UAE do not apply. The enactment of the DIFC Arbitration Law (DIFC Law No 1 of 2008) on 1 September 2008 opened up the DIFC as a possible seat of arbitration to all parties.

[25] A copy of the DIFC-LCIA Arbitration Centre Arbitration Rules is at app 11.

[26] R Mohtashami, 'Recent Arbitration-related Developments in the UAE' (2008) 25 J Int Arb 631; and P Bourke and D Hennessy, 'Brighter times – developments in arbitration in the United Arab Emirates' (2008) 13(2) IBA Arb News 24.

[27] Quite how similar or dissimilar to an English court action is the typical LCIA arbitration is discussed in ch 5 below.

[28] *Dell Computer Corporation v Union des Consommateurs and Olivier Dumoulin* 2007 SCC 34.

In addition, the LCIA was the pioneer in the setting-up of the now ubiquitous **1.35** 'young arbitrators' groups. The Young International Arbitration Group of the LCIA was founded in 1997 and provides an opportunity for practitioners aged 40 or under to meet and discuss topics without feeling overshadowed by their seniors (in age, if not in wisdom). This very successful format has been followed by several other international arbitration institutions.[29]

Finally, on the topic of the LCIA's vocation to be at the head of best international **1.36** arbitration practice, can be added the setting-up and sponsoring of the International Dispute Resolution Centre or IDRC in London, a dedicated arbitration facility unmatched in any other major arbitration centre. The LCIA was at the forefront of its conception and realization and has its offices in the IDRC's offices on Fleet Street, in what the IDRC itself terms 'the heart of legal London'. While the IDRC is an independent body, and any parties, using whatever rules, can choose to have their hearings there, it is of huge benefit for the LCIA that London (which is the seat of so many LCIA arbitrations, as discussed above) should have such a facility for staging hearings and procedural meetings.[30]

It is developments such as these that set the LCIA apart and will perhaps ensure **1.37** that it stays on course to fulfil at least some of the hopes that were expressed at its inauguration some 107 years ago.

B. The LCIA Arbitration Rules

The 1998 Rules replaced those of 1985,[31] which were the first that marked the **1.38** LCIA's ambition to become a truly international organization.[32] The impetus

---

[29] Such as 'ASA Under 40' in Switzerland, 'ICDR Young and International' from the AAA, 'DIS40' in Germany, the ICC's 'Young Arbitrators' Forum', and many others.

[30] It is interesting that the ICC has now followed suit in setting up a dedicated hearing centre in Paris. This is on a smaller scale than the IDRC (it has only three hearing rooms) and has not followed the IDRC model of independence from its sponsoring institution, although it will be available for non-ICC arbitrations.

[31] For commentaries on the 1985 Rules, see *Hunter & Paulsson*; C Salans, 'The 1985 Rules of the London Court of International Arbitration' (1986) 2 Arb Int 40; and S Lebedev, 'The LCIA Rules for International Commercial Arbitration' (1992) 8 Arb Int 321.

[32] For commentaries on the 1998 Rules, see A Winstanley, 'The New Rules of the London Court of International Arbitration', (1997) 8 Am Rev Int Arb 59; D Rivkin, '1997: A Year of Rule Changes' Int ALR 1998 1(2) 91; A Samuel, 'Jurisdiction, interim relief and awards under the LCIA Rules' in A Berkeley and J Mimms (eds), *International Commercial Arbitration: Practical Perspectives* (Centre of Construction Law & Management, 2001) 35; A Diamond, 'Procedure and Hearings' in A Berkeley and J Mimms (eds), *International Commercial Arbitration: Practical Perspectives* (Centre of Construction Law & Management, 2001) 49; WL Craig, 'The LCIA and the ICC Rules: the 1998 revisions compared' in A Berkeley and J Mimms (eds), *International Commercial Arbitration: Practical Perspectives* (Centre of Construction Law & Management, 2001) 79; Veeder (n 2 above); and Triebel & Hunter (n 20 above).

behind the 1998 Rules was the passing of the English Arbitration Act 1996,[33] and, as previously stated and as will be seen below, the Rules very often follow the Arbitration Act, to which considerable reference is made in the following chapters. While it could be said that this somewhat puts the lie to the LCIA's international pretensions, that would be unfair. The simple fact is that, as noted above, the overwhelming majority of LCIA arbitrations have their seat in England and Wales (usually London) and for the LCIA not to have taken studious care to ensure that their new Rules were in harmony with the new English legislation would have been an act of Quixotic folly.

1.39 One could point to a number of examples where the Rules track the Arbitration Act with the utmost fidelity. One is Article 25.1(c), dealing with the arbitral tribunal's powers to order interim and conservatory measures, which is a near-verbatim reproduction of section 39(1) of the Arbitration Act. Another is Article 14.1, which reproduces the language of section 33(1) of the Arbitration Act in setting out the general duties of the arbitral tribunal.

1.40 It is thus the case that the Rules and the Arbitration Act go hand in glove, and that an LCIA arbitration is perfectly suited to a seat in England. This is not to say that it is not suited to seats in other places, but parties choosing LCIA arbitration with seats elsewhere than England should at least be aware that many features of the Rules reflect mandatory provisions of the English Act. They will therefore want to take into account whether, and if so to what extent, this could prove in conflict with the arbitration law of the seat.

1.41 The Rules do, however, provide for the parties to derogate from them and shape their own procedure to a quite unprecedented degree, thus enabling the parties to adapt them to any exigencies of the seat (or the needs of their particular dispute). This principle of overriding party autonomy is set out in Article 14.1, which is dealt with in more detail in chapter 5 below, and which states that '[t]he parties may agree on the conduct of their arbitral proceedings and they are encouraged to do so . . .'. Of particular note is the recognition by the use of the word 'their' that the arbitration does indeed belong to the parties, and not to the institution, the arbitrators, or counsel. This provision has been described by one prominent commentator as the 'Magna Carta' of the LCIA Rules.[34] The party autonomy thus recognized is almost unlimited, and is to be contrasted with the far more restrictive approach adopted by, for example, the ICC Rules: in an ICC arbitration, the parties cannot derogate from the requirements of terms of reference, a procedural timetable, and the scrutiny of awards by the ICC Court, to name but those.

---

[33] Veeder (n 2 above) 366.
[34] Veeder (n 2 above) 367.

It is nonetheless important to recognize that there are limits on the ability of the **1.42** parties to define their own procedure. The tribunal is enjoined by Article 14.1, sub-paragraphs (i) and (ii), in words almost identical to those in section 33(1)(a) and (b) of the Arbitration Act, to respect the principles of natural justice and procedural fairness, on the one hand, and to ensure the resolution of the dispute 'avoiding unnecessary delay and expense' on the other. The tribunal could, therefore, no doubt stop the parties from agreeing to a grossly unbalanced allocation of time to present their respective cases at the hearing, for example, or to have an unfeasibly large number of rounds of written submissions with very long deadlines for the submission of each one.

A further illustration of the guiding principle of the Rules being to leave the **1.43** parties to conduct 'their' arbitration as they wish is the very limited role of the LCIA Court. The Rules place responsibility for almost all matters in the hands of the tribunal, once formed, rather than the Court. Thus the Court cannot, for example, extend any time limits under the Rules (again, unlike the ICC Court). The Court's concerns are effectively limited to the appointment and removal of arbitrators and ensuring that the LCIA is in funds to pay the arbitrators pursuant to Article 24. For this reason, it has been argued that LCIA arbitration 'occupies a position halfway between full institutional arbitration and ad hoc forms of arbitration'.[35]

On the other hand, the parties, in practice, very rarely specify in advance of an **1.44** arbitration the procedure they intend to follow, restricting themselves to a choice of institutional rules. In that regard, it is noteworthy that the Rules (while not providing a complete procedural code) are considerably more prescriptive in setting out the procedure to be followed than most other sets of arbitration rules. Thus, the Rules provide for a detailed procedure for the written stage of the proceedings in default of party agreement or procedural directions from the tribunal, as well as detailed rules for the language of the arbitration, the conduct of the hearing, the submission of witness evidence, etc.[36] They also set out a lengthy list of 'additional powers' of the tribunal and a very prescriptive description of the interim and conservatory measures that a tribunal may order.[37]

One is therefore faced with the apparent contradiction of an unprecedented **1.45** respect for the principle of party autonomy, and a very limited role for the institution in the conduct of an arbitration under its Rules, on the one hand, and a very detailed template for the procedure that will be followed in the absence of

---

[35] Veeder (n 2 above) 366.
[36] Arts 15, 17, 19, and 20 respectively. These are all discussed in ch 5 below.
[37] Arts 22 and 25 respectively. These are discussed in ch 6 below.

party agreement to the contrary, on the other. The LCIA Rules are, therefore, considerably longer than those of, for example, the ICC, which allow less party autonomy but also prescribe far less by way of the procedure to be followed. This is perhaps best illustrated by the example of language: despite the fact that less than 1 per cent of the 701 arbitrations that were the subject of our research were wholly conducted in a language other than English, Article 17 devotes four detailed sub-articles to describing how language issues are to be treated. By contrast, the ICC Rules (under which arbitrations are conducted in many different languages) deal with language in four lines in Article 16.

1.46 This book will examine the LCIA's 1998 Rules by theme, largely, but not exclusively, in order (for example, Articles 1, 2, and 4, which deal with the starting of an arbitration under the LCIA Rules, will be dealt with only in chapter 3). In the light of the relative paucity of academic commentary and judicial decisions dealing with the LCIA Rules, and, as a result of the prohibition on publication contained in Article 30.3,[38] the total absence of compilations of even sanitized versions of awards and decisions of arbitral tribunals established under the LCIA Rules or of the LCIA Court,[39] we have adopted an approach to our description of the Rules that addresses them, where this is helpful, by reference to other arbitration rules that have been the subject of more detailed study.

C. The LCIA as Appointing Authority under the UNCITRAL Arbitration Rules

1.47 The LCIA will (in contrast to the ICC, for example) not only act as the appointing authority under the UNCITRAL Rules, but will also administer UNCITRAL arbitrations.

1.48 It is of note that, with 18 cases administered under the UNCITRAL Rules in 2006 and 2007, the LCIA has more such cases than any other arbitral institution. Of those cases, four are cases arising under investment treaties. The LCIA acts as appointing authority under the UNCITRAL rules in eight further cases, chosen as such by the parties five times and by the Permanent Court of Arbitration in the remaining three.

---

[38] Discussed in ch 9 below.

[39] Although decisions of the LCIA Court on challenges to arbitrators will now be published following a report to the LCIA Court that has now been published in *Arbitration International*: see *Nicholas & Partasides*. Indeed, a major step towards the realization of this unique initiative, which will be of inestimable benefit to practitioners (arbitrators and counsel alike) was taken with the publication, as an annex to *Nicholas & Partasides*, of their survey of the decisions on challenges to arbitrators that had already been made by the Court.

The LCIA's UNCITRAL cases have given rise to more than their fair share **1.49** of challenges to arbitrators, discussed in chapter 4 below.

D. The Softwood Lumber Arbitrations

The LCIA made arbitration history when, on 12 September 2006, the govern- **1.50** ments of the United States and Canada adopted the Softwood Lumber Agreement (the SLA), submitting disputes under the SLA to LCIA arbitration (with certain modifications of the 1998 Rules).

The SLA seeks to bring to an end years of disputes between the United States and **1.51** Canada over duties and regulations on softwood lumber. Its importance for the purposes of this discussion resides in its choice of LCIA arbitration for the resolution of disputes arising out of the agreement (to the exclusion of alternatives such as the dispute resolution mechanisms of the World Trade Organization and the North American Free Trade Agreement).[40]

The parties to the SLA agreed to a number of modifications to the 1998 Rules **1.52** (which are stated to apply to all disputes even if the Rules are subsequently amended): Article 21 (appointment of experts to the arbitral tribunal) is excluded; the parties agree not to nominate US or Canadian citizens as arbitrators (the LCIA would of course in any event not appoint a chairman of the nationality of one of the parties without express agreement pursuant to Article 6.1, as discussed in chapter 4 below); the LCIA Court agrees (despite its not being a party to the SLA) to use its best endeavours to appoint the tribunal once all its members have been nominated (one by each party and the Chair by the party-nominated arbitrators); the tribunal is to use its best endeavours to render an award within 180 days of its appointment by the LCIA Court; and the parties agree that the tribunal shall not award the costs of the proceedings (following a practice that is becoming more common in investment-treaty arbitration as well). There are also specific provisions in the dispute settlement clause as to the publication of submissions and the like, following established practice in NAFTA arbitrations, thereby effectively derogating from the confidentiality obligation in Article 30 (discussed in chapter 9 below).

---

[40] Two arbitrations under the SLA are currently under way. The arbitral tribunals constituted are, in the so-called 'adjustment factor' arbitration, V V Veeder, QC (nominated by the USA), Prof Bernard Hanotiau (nominated by Canada) with Prof Dr Karl-Heinz Böckstiegel as Chair, while in the 'Ontario/Québec programs' arbitration, the United States nominated David Williams, QC, Canada nominated Prof Albert Jan van den Berg, and Prof Gabrielle Kaufmann-Kohler serves as Chair.

1.53   We will consider the implications of these adaptations at the appropriate places in the detailed discussion of the Rules below, but the mere fact that the LCIA has been chosen for such a task (in the context of an embittered dispute and in an atmosphere of some political distrust of international arbitration in cases involving the public interest on the part of both Canada and the United States as a result of NAFTA cases) is a ringing endorsement of its status as a premier international arbitration institution.

E. Other Forms of Dispute Resolution Administered by the LCIA

1.54   The LCIA has a Mediation Procedure (published in 1999)[41] and will also act as appointing authority for and administer other forms of alternative dispute resolution procedure for which it has not published rules. This could encompass any form of ADR (which is inherently flexible and not susceptible to an exhaustive definition), such as adjudication, early neutral evaluation, and expert determination. The LCIA publishes recommended clauses for the last-cited (in alternative forms in which it is to act as appointing authority only or as both appointing authority and administrator).

1.55   Given the popularity of stepped dispute resolution clauses,[42] involving one or more forms of ADR (for example, adjudication or mediation) before having resort to arbitration, the LCIA could thus see the parties through from the beginning to the end of a dispute that spans several distinct phases.

---

[41]   Reproduced in app 10.
[42]   Recommended LCIA arbitration clauses are reproduced at app 1.

2

THE ROLE OF THE LCIA'S ORGANS (ARTICLES 3 AND 29)

A. Article 3 – The LCIA Court and Registrar	2.02
Article 3.1	2.03
F. – Appointment of Arbitrators and Mediators	2.13
Article 3.2	2.15
Article 3.3	2.17
Article G – Functions of the Registrar and Deputy Registrar	2.20
B. Article 29 – Decisions by the LCIA Court	2.21
Article 29.1	2.22
Article 29.2	2.23

The LCIA Rules follow a slightly disconcerting pattern in that they explain the **2.01** role and function of the Court and Registrar (ie the Secretariat) in several places throughout the body of the Rules, beginning after the process of starting the arbitration itself has begun (in Articles 1 and 2). Given that, in order to understand how the Rules work, the role played by the Court and Registrar respectively must first be understood, we start with the disparate Articles that explain and define those roles. Articles 3 and 29 cover, respectively, the overall roles of the Court and Registrar (Article 3) and decisions of the Court (Article 29). The related topic of the limitation of the LCIA's (and its constituent bodies' and officers') liability for the administration of the arbitration is contained in Article 31, discussed in chapter 9 below.

A. Article 3 – The LCIA Court and Registrar

Article 3 describes the mode of working of the LCIA Court and the Registrar, **2.02** rather than their respective roles in the conduct of an arbitration under the LCIA Rules, which are set out in the relevant articles. It establishes three principles: the Court only acts through sub-divisions, never as a plenary body; the Registrar operates under the supervision of the Court; and the Registrar acts as the go-between for the Court and parties and arbitrators, receiving and transmitting any communications.

Article 3.1

The functions of the LCIA Court under these Rules shall be performed in its name by the President or a Vice President of the LCIA Court or by a division of three or five members of the LCIA Court appointed by the President or a Vice President of the LCIA Court, as determined by the President.

The composition of the LCIA Court

2.03   The LCIA Court is not a 'court' in the sense that it decides the outcome of LCIA arbitrations. It is a purely administrative body charged under the Rules with the carrying-out of a number of functions in connection with the arbitration. Article 3 does not spell out those functions, which are spread around the body of the Rules, but it does set out how those functions are to be performed and in particular that they shall always be performed on a delegated basis rather than by the whole Court of 35 members.[1] Thus, the President alone can perform any of the Court's functions (and usually does so with respect to the appointment of arbitrators) as can any Vice President. The Court can also be sub-divided into divisions of three or five members, appointed by the President or a Vice President.

2.04   The current (as at the date of publication) President of the Court is Jan Paulsson, based in Paris. He was appointed President in 2004 for a renewable three-year term. He succeeded three equally distinguished arbitrators, all of whom remain members of the Court as Honorary Vice Presidents: they are Professor Dr Karl-Heinz Böckstiegel of Germany, L Yves Fortier, the former Canadian Ambassador to the United Nations, and Professor Dr Gerold Hermann, also of Germany, the former Secretary-General of UNCITRAL. This tradition of having as President a respected and prominent arbitrator from outside England (and not of UK nationality) has, it would seem, been consciously adopted as a policy by the LCIA to emphasize its global vocation. It should not be forgotten, however, that it was under the long presidency of the late Sir Michael Kerr (ably assisted by the then-Registrar, Bertie Vigrass) that the LCIA began to re-emerge from a lengthy period in the doldrums, and so one would hope that no irrevocable decision has been taken to exclude London residents or UK citizens from the presidency.

---

[1] The composition of the Court as at the date of publication is set out at app 5. Its Constitution is reproduced at app 4. The Constitution is itself the result of a decision of the LCIA's Board and the LCIA Court. It was last revised in 2008.

The six Vice Presidents come from the United States, Germany, Ireland, **2.05**
Switzerland, and the UK (there are in fact two Americans and two Swiss but only
one Englishman, although the Irishman lives in the UK), once again emphasizing
the international nature of the institution. All are lawyers and all bar one are in
private practice, the exception being Professor William W 'Rusty' Park of the
University of Boston. Among the other members of the Court the same pattern is
perpetuated: all of the 28 Honorary Vice Presidents and ordinary members of the
Court are lawyers or university teachers of law, with one (Andrew Clarke of
ExxonMobil, a founder-member of the Corporate Counsel International
Arbitration Group) working in-house. There is no representative of the formerly
rich stream of non-lawyer arbitrators, coming from the engineering or other professions, who now seem to have almost entirely made way for lawyers, as an effect
(or perhaps in some measure a cause) of the now well-established 'judicialization'
of arbitration.

The members of the Court are appointed by the LCIA's Board, on the recommen- **2.06**
dation of the Court. There is currently some overlap between the memberships of
the two bodies. In appointing members of the Court, apart from the injunction
in Article A.1 of the Court's Constitution not to appoint more than six citizens of
the UK (the actual words used in Article A.1 are 'from the United Kingdom', but
this is taken as a reference to nationality rather than simply residence), there are
no guides as to whom the Court should appoint or what criteria it should apply.
On any view, the membership reflects the international character of the parties to
LCIA arbitrations, which is probably one of the most important criteria for the
appointment of members of the Court. The current members of the Court include
only five British citizens, including one dual national with British and Canadian
nationality resident in Canada, and also including the Chairman of the Board and
the Director-General, who are members of the Court *ex officio*. There is one
further UK-resident member who does not hold British nationality.

The Court should be composed of members who understand and care for the **2.07**
institution of arbitration as a means of resolving disputes as well as representing
the wide geographical coverage of the LCIA Users' Councils. As to the former
criterion, it has already been remarked that there is only one real 'user' of arbitration on the Court at the time of going to press, in the sense of a representative of
parties to an arbitration, namely Andrew Clarke of ExxonMobil, and not one
non-lawyer arbitrator. It could be argued that a little more representation of these
other groups could only give the LCIA Court more insight into the issues facing
international arbitration as it continues its development. As to the second major
criterion, there can be no doubt that the Board has appointed some of the most
prominent members of the arbitration community over the last decades. Further
criteria for appointment will obviously be the wish and ability to devote the time

needed to fulfil the functions of a Court member, including service on divisions of the Court, and a wish to promote the activities of the LCIA as an institution.

The exercise of delegated authority

2.08   As Article 3.1 explains, the Court's functions can be exercised by its President, one of the Vice Presidents, or by a division of three or five members. This increases the speed with which the Court can fulfil its many roles under the Rules and ensures efficient service to users. If, for example, a party applies to the Court for the expedited formation of a tribunal under Article 9,[2] it would utterly defeat the purpose of Article 9 for the Court to wait for a plenary meeting in order to appoint the tribunal.

2.09   The principle established by Article 3.1 is therefore to ensure that the Court as such in fact rarely takes decisions, most of which are taken by the President, Vice Presidents, or a division. As a rule, therefore, the Court itself thus needs to meet only twice a year. (Administrative functions are delegated to the Registrar or a deputy Registrar under Article 3.2, as discussed below.) The Court's Constitution goes further and actually specifies that all arbitral appointments shall be made by the President or, if he or she (always he, to date) is unavailable, one of the Vice Presidents, to the exclusion of a three- or five-member division.[3]

2.10   This exercise of the Court's functions exclusively by delegated bodies is to be contrasted with the regime under the ICC Rules. Article 1(3) of the ICC Rules provides only that the Chairman of the ICC Court or, in his absence, one of the Vice-Chairmen, can take urgent decisions on behalf of the ICC Court. This leaves begging the question of what is urgent: for example, it can certainly be argued with some cogency that any decision regarding the constitution of an arbitral tribunal is urgent to at least some degree. The LCIA's choice of delegating the Court's authority should, at least in theory, dispense with debates about what is or is not urgent.[4]

2.11   Apart from that example, there is nothing in the Court's Constitution that determines when a particular role should be exercised by the President, a Vice President, or a division of the Court, but it is interesting to note that it has been the practice of Presidents to appoint a three-member division to hear challenges to arbitrators under Article 10.[5]

---

[2] Art 9 is discussed in ch 4 below.
[3] Art F.1 of the Court's Constitution.
[4] For a discussion of the powers of the ICC Court, see *Derains & Schwartz*.
[5] Challenges are discussed in ch 4 below. See also *Nicholas & Partasides*.

Court members serving as arbitrator

One of the Court's most important functions is of course the initial appointment **2.12** of a tribunal. As the Court (and *a fortiori* its President and Vice Presidents) is composed for the most part of eminent arbitration practitioners, most or all of whom could expect to be on a short-list for most arbitral appointments, the following provision of the Court's Constitution is particularly important in allaying any fears that the Court may be tempted to do favours for those who are at that time its members:

F. – Appointment of Arbitrators and Mediators

1. All appointments of arbitrators and mediators in the name of the Court pursuant to D.1(a) and D.1(b) shall be made by the President or by a Vice President on the President's behalf pursuant to B.2 above.

2. All members of the Court shall be eligible for appointment as arbitrators. However:

   a. the President shall only be eligible if the parties agree to nominate him as sole arbitrator or as Chairman;[6] and

   b. the Vice Presidents shall only be eligible to serve as arbitrators if nominated by a party or the parties.

   The President or Vice Presidents so nominated shall take no part in the appointment of an arbitral tribunal to which they have been nominated or in any other function of the Court relating to such an arbitration.

This provision is essential to ensure that there is no doubt as to the integrity of the **2.13** process of formation of a tribunal and also to remove any possibility for a serving arbitrator who is also an office-holder of the Court to use improper influence in the conduct and oversight of an arbitration in which he or she is sitting. It would have been a self-defeating measure, indeed it would have looked like the LCIA cutting off its nose to spite its face, for all members of the Court to be disqualified from sitting as arbitrators in LCIA arbitrations, since this would have deprived the parties and the LCIA of the services of prominent members of the arbitration community for no substantive benefit. The compromise embodied by Article F.2 of the Court's Constitution is both necessary, to guard against the appearance of any impropriety, and also sufficient in avoiding any actual conflict of interest for the members of the Court.

---

⁶ This provision raises an interesting philosophical point. Co-arbitrators are required to be as neutral as presiding arbitrators. So why, therefore, is the restriction on the President's acting as a party-nominated arbitrator written into the Court's Constitution? The answer has to be that the notion of the independence of party-nominated arbitrators may not yet be wholly and universally accepted, leading the LCIA to err on the side of caution.

2.14 There is no prohibition on any member of the Court acting as a party's counsel. This does not in practice seem to have posed any problem, although one would imagine that the President, in particular, would need to watch appearances very carefully to avoid negating the positive effect of the Constitution of the Court as regards arbitral appointments.

Article 3.2

The functions of the Registrar under these Rules shall be performed by the Registrar or any deputy Registrar of the LCIA Court under the supervision of the LCIA Court.

The role of the Registrar

2.15 The Registrar is the head of the LCIA's Secretariat and can be assisted in his functions by a number of deputy Registrars. The two posts are expressly recognized by Article 3.2, which provides that they shall exercise their functions under the supervision of the Court. Currently, the Director-General also acts as an additional Registrar, alongside the actual Registrar (who is also deputy Director-General).

2.16 The Registrar is responsible for all administrative functions of the LCIA. The LCIA Secretariat is based at the IDRC in London, where many of its hearings are held. The Registrar's functions under the Rules are purely administrative in nature. He (or perhaps in the future she[7]) is involved at the very beginning of an LCIA arbitration, in that he receives the Request for Arbitration and verifies whether it complies with the requirements set out in the Rules.[8]

Article 3.3

All communications from any party or arbitrator to the LCIA Court shall be addressed to the Registrar.

2.17 The Registrar not only receives copies of correspondence between parties and arbitrators and the Court: he also receives copies of all correspondence between the parties and the arbitral tribunal (and he alone receives it before the formation of the tribunal) and he keeps the records of the case at the LCIA. He also prepares the reports to the LCIA Court that form the basis of the decisions taken by the Court. The parties thus have no direct contact with the Court: all day-to-day communication,

---

[7] Art 5.1 actually confirms that the use of the masculine in the Rules when referring to the Registrar, arbitrators, and officers and members of the LCIA Court is to be taken as including the feminine.

[8] The role of the Registrar in the early stages of an arbitration is discussed in ch 3 below.

and all party contact, is with the Registrar, and such communication is, in the overwhelming number of cases, conducted in English, which is the sole working language of the Secretariat. The LCIA differs sharply from the ICC in this respect. The ICC International Court of Arbitration has 'teams' of counsels dealing with cases arising in different areas of the world and capable of doing business in various languages. Thus, correspondence with the ICC Secretariat will generally be in the language of the arbitration. The international developments referred to in chapter 1 above, namely the LCIA's establishment of local branches and the joint venture with the DIFC, are unlikely to change this to any great degree, at least in the short term.

The Secretariat is also responsible for ensuring that deposits on account of costs are paid, and if not to advise tribunals as to the consequences.[9] The Secretariat will provide financial summaries to the parties, and the members of the Secretariat are generally available to help the parties (and, even more frequently, arbitrators) with questions about the application of the Rules and the progress of the case. This can cover all the stages of an arbitration, from initial advice as to the drafting of the Request through evidential matters and preparations for hearings to the making of awards. It is therefore vital that the members of the casework Secretariat have sufficient expertise to help often inexperienced parties and counsel and even (relatively) inexperienced party-nominated arbitrators. Naturally, the Secretariat has to maintain a strict neutrality in dealing with requests for advice from the parties and their representatives, but within those bounds it is able to provide considerable help and guidance as to the application and interpretation of the Rules. **2.18**

The Registrar also carries out such of the Court's functions as are delegated to him from time to time by the President of the Court. Article G of the Court's Constitution provides that: **2.19**

Article G – Functions of the Registrar and Deputy Registrar

The Registrar and the Deputy Registrar shall:

i. carry out in the name of the Court such day to day operations of the Court and administrative functions under any applicable arbitration, mediation or conciliation rules as may be authorised by the President from time to time; and

ii. . . .

Under this provision of its Constitution, the LCIA Court not only authorizes the Registrar to do that which the Rules require him to do, but can also delegate further of its administrative functions to him, always to be exercised under the Court's supervision. Thus, the Court has issued three directives delegating certain of its **2.20**

---

[9] See ch 8 below for a discussion of all aspects of the costs of LCIA arbitrations.

powers to the Registrar. It has issued a directive under Article 26.5, in respect of the issuance of awards, one under Article 24 concerning the directions for the payment of deposits on account of costs and one clarifying the procedure to be followed by the Registrar and the Court for the purposes of determining the costs of the arbitration pursuant to Article 28. These directives are discussed in chapters 7 and 8 below respectively.[10]

B. Article 29 – Decisions by the LCIA Court

2.21 Article 29's importance stems from the fact that it establishes not only the administrative, rather than judicial, character of the LCIA Court, but also the principle of finality for its decisions. If one of the most oft-cited advantages of arbitration is the final nature of awards and the very limited grounds of recourse against them by way of setting-aside actions, it would be odd indeed if dissatisfied parties were able to get around that principle by starting actions against the LCIA Court. This provision therefore not only reinforces the finality of arbitral awards and the arbitral process in general, it also (as with Article 31, discussed below) reduces the scope for satellite litigation.

Article 29.1

The decisions of the LCIA Court with respect to all matters relating to the arbitration shall be conclusive and binding upon the parties and the Arbitral Tribunal. Such decisions are to be treated as administrative in nature and the LCIA Court shall not be required to give any reasons.

2.22 As an administrative, rather than judicial or quasi-judicial, body, the LCIA Court does not have to give reasons for its decisions, and it is therefore all the more remarkable (and certainly all the more laudable) that it does so with regard to challenges to arbitrators.

Article 29.2

To the extent permitted by the law of the seat of the arbitration, the parties shall be taken to have waived any right of appeal or review in respect of any such decisions of the LCIA Court to any state court or other judicial authority. If such appeals or review remain possible due to mandatory provisions of any applicable law, the LCIA Court shall, subject to the provisions of that applicable law, decide whether the arbitral proceedings are to continue, notwithstanding an appeal or review.

2.23 Article 29.2 deals with the circumstance of a party's feeling dissatisfied with a decision of the Court and seeking to challenge it. It is not intended to stop a genuine

---

[10] Copies of these directives appear at app 6.

challenge to LCIA Court decisions (indeed actions in the English Court with regard to decisions on challenges to arbitrators have been threatened in England under section 24 of the Arbitration Act, discussed below). It is rather intended to stop 'wrecking tactics' by a party with no legitimate grievance. It is a different point to the finality and binding nature of an arbitral award, which is dealt with in the discussion of Article 26.9.[11] It seems rather clear that the decisions of the Court that would be most likely to give rise to dissatisfaction and possible challenge are those dealing with the appointment and, much more so, the removal of arbitrators. The aim of this provision can therefore be seen to restrict the parties' ability to appeal to state courts in respect of decisions of the LCIA Court on challenges to arbitrators for lack of independence and impartiality.[12]

What is interesting is the formulation that the parties waive such a right 'to the extent permitted by the law of the seat of the arbitration'. It is unclear how many arbitration laws deal with recourse against decisions of arbitral institutions (as opposed to the question of recourse or appeals against *awards*, dealt with in chapter 7 below) in a general way. The English Arbitration Act, for example, which has by far the greatest significance in this area as the arbitration law of the seat of almost all LCIA arbitrations, contains the principle of the immunity of arbitral institutions, in section 74, discussed in the context of Article 31 in chapter 9 below. **2.24**

It is also rather unclear why the law of the seat (if not England and Wales) would have any role to play in any proceeding brought against the LCIA as such: the LCIA is an English company and one would have expected it to be sued (if at all) in the English court. Nonetheless, this provision can be seen as a 'belt and braces' attempt to prevent the possibility of actions against the Court and its inclusion may indeed have prevented such actions being brought, although this is of course by definition unknowable. **2.25**

In the context of challenges to arbitrators, however, the position is different. For arbitrations with their seat in England and Wales, section 24 of the Arbitration Act provides the English court with a right to remove arbitrators that the parties to the arbitration cannot opt out of. Section 24(2) makes this clear: in requiring parties to exhaust 'any available recourse to [the] institution' before making an application to the court, the English Act makes it plain that decisions of the LCIA Court in respect of challenges to arbitrators are effectively appealable. The position is the same under Article 13(3) of the UNCITRAL Model Law. In both cases, the tribunal can continue with the arbitration while the challenge is pending, and even make an award. **2.26**

---

[11] See ch 7 below.
[12] Dealt with in ch 4 below.

2.27 Article 29.2 itself reflects this in providing that the LCIA Court retains the discretion to allow the arbitration to continue notwithstanding a challenge to one of its decisions. In practice, the LCIA Court would, it is surmised, leave it to the tribunal hearing the case to decide whether the arbitration should continue while a challenge in the state courts is under way. This would be consistent with the philosophy of the LCIA Rules in letting the tribunal decide all matters concerned with the actual running of the arbitration, rather than pure questions of administration.

2.28 It can thus be seen that, at least so far as decisions on challenges to arbitrators are concerned, the attempt to limit recourse by the parties against such decisions in Article 29.2 is ineffective if (as they nearly all do) the arbitration has its seat in England and Wales. It is still worth having, however, as other jurisdictions (including France) do not allow challenges to institutional decisions to remove or not remove arbitrators. There are no known instances of parties actually bringing challenges to decisions of the LCIA Court in local state courts.[13]

---

[13] In contrast to the fate of its ICC equivalent. *Derains & Schwartz* have a full discussion. More recently, Argentina has started an action against the ICC in the Argentine courts in relation to the refusal of the ICC Court to provide reasons for its rejection of a challenge brought by Argentina to an arbitrator in an investment-treaty claim brought by National Grid plc of the UK: Causa 2.660/2006 *Procuración del Tesoro v International Chamber of Commerce* (Deci 15-XII-05).

3

STARTING THE ARBITRATION
(ARTICLES 1, 2, AND 4)

A.	Article 1 – The Request for Arbitration	3.02
	Article 1.1	3.03
	Article 1.2	3.21
B.	Article 2 – The Response	3.24
	Article 2.1	3.25
	Article 2.2	3.33
	Article 2.3	3.34
C.	Article 4 – Notices and Periods of Time	3.39
	Article 4.1	3.40
	Article 4.2	3.41
	Article 4.3	3.43
	Article 4.4	3.44
	Article 4.5	3.45
	Article 4.6	3.47
	Article 4.7	3.48

This chapter addresses the commencement of arbitration proceedings under the **3.01** Rules and the initial steps taken thereafter, which are covered by Articles 1 and 2 of the Rules, dealing with the Request for Arbitration and the Response, respectively. We also cover Article 4 in this chapter, relating to notices and periods of time.

A. Article 1 – The Request for Arbitration

An arbitration under the Rules is started by filing a Request for Arbitration with **3.02** the Registrar. While the Request is not intended to contain full particulars of the claimant's case, as a statement of case and supporting documents are usually submitted at a later stage,[1] the Request is intended to comprise more than a bare

---

[1] Art 15.2; although the claimant can elect to treat the Request as its statement of case.

notice of arbitration. As discussed in more detail below, the Request should set out brief particulars as to the nature and circumstances of the dispute, including the claims advanced by the claimant. The Request should also deal with matters relating to the conduct of the arbitration, such as the language and the seat of arbitration, and the number of arbitrators, including any agreed or proposed method for their nomination. In short, the Request should set out the claimant's claims and, together with the Response, if submitted,[2] serves the purpose of defining the dispute referred to arbitration. This is particularly relevant in informing the LCIA Court about the nature of the parties' dispute, in connection with the Court's duty to appoint the arbitral tribunal as soon as practicable after the submission of the Request and the Response.[3]

Article 1.1

Any party wishing to commence an arbitration under these Rules ('the Claimant') shall send to the Registrar of the LCIA Court ('the Registrar') a written request for arbitration ('the Request'), containing or accompanied by:

(a) the names, addresses, telephone, facsimile, telex and e-mail numbers (if known) of the parties to the arbitration and of their legal representatives;

(b) a copy of the written arbitration clause or separate written arbitration agreement invoked by the Claimant ('the Arbitration Agreement'), together with a copy of the contractual documentation in which the arbitration clause is contained or in respect of which the arbitration arises;

(c) a brief statement describing the nature and circumstances of the dispute, and specifying the claims advanced by the Claimant against another party to the arbitration ('the Respondent');

(d) a statement of any matters (such as the seat or language(s) of the arbitration, or the number of arbitrators, or their qualifications or identities) on which the parties have already agreed in writing for the arbitration or in respect of which the Claimant wishes to make a proposal;

(e) if the Arbitration Agreement calls for party nomination of arbitrators, the name, address, telephone, facsimile, telex and e-mail numbers (if known) of the Claimant's nominee;

(f) the fee prescribed in the Schedule of Costs (without which the Request shall be treated as not having been received by the Registrar and the arbitration as not having been commenced); and

---

[2] As regards the optional nature of the Response, see the discussion below in the context of arts 2.1 and 2.3.

[3] Art 5.4. In the event of an expedited formation of the tribunal, the Court often appoints the tribunal prior to the submission of the Response (see the discussion in ch 4 below in the context of art 9).

(g) confirmation to the Registrar that copies of the Request (including all accompanying documents) have been or are being served simultaneously on all other parties to the arbitration by one or more means of service to be identified in such confirmation.

Pursuant to Article 1.1, the commencement of an arbitration under the Rules is **3.03**
by means of submission to the Registrar of a Request. The service of the Request should conform to the requirements set forth in Article 4 of the Rules, which are discussed below. As already noted, the Request is intended to be more than a bare notice of arbitration, and should cover the various elements set forth in Article 1.1 of the Rules, which are addressed next. This being said, the Rules allow the claimant significant discretion as to how much detail to provide in the Request concerning the merits of its claims, subject to satisfying the minimum requirements of Article 1.1(c).

Description of the parties

Pursuant to the first sub-paragraph of Article 1.1, the Request should contain **3.04**
the names and pertinent contact details of the parties to the arbitration and of their legal representatives. It falls to the claimant therefore, at the outset of the arbitration, and subject only to the power of the tribunal to order the subsequent joinder of third parties,[4] to determine who shall be the parties to the arbitration. This is an important right with significant consequences for the parties so designated.

The Request should contain the full contact details (including e-mails, if known) **3.05**
of all the parties to the arbitration, including their legal representatives. There is no requirement under the Rules for the claimant to furnish details of a power of attorney authorizing its representation by legal counsel or any other third party, together with the Request.[5] Subsequent to its constitution, the tribunal may require from any party proof of authority granted to its representatives.[6]

The arbitration agreement and other relevant contractual documentation

Together with the Request, the claimant should provide a copy of the written **3.06**
arbitration clause (or the contract in which it appears) or separate arbitration agreement which is invoked by the claimant, as well as the relevant contractual documentation in respect of which the arbitration arises.[7] The Rules therefore

---

[4] Art 22.1(h).
[5] It is nonetheless good practice to furnish such proof of authority at the outset of the proceedings.
[6] Art 18.2.
[7] Art 1.1(b).

appear to rule out the prospect of an oral arbitration agreement, which is otherwise valid under English law (and the laws of several other countries), although not subject to the English Arbitration Act 1996.[8] Although the Rules mandate the submission of a written arbitration agreement, the written require-ment is broadly construed by the LCIA Court – in accordance with modern practice in international arbitration[9] – as part of the LCIA's initial review of the Request (discussed below). To take, perhaps, the most common such example, an unsigned arbitration agreement that is otherwise evidenced in writing, typically by the parties' subsequent correspondence or signed minutes of meetings, clearly satisfies the written requirement under Article 1.1(c) of the Rules. The Court therefore adopts a liberal interpretation of this provision. The Court's decision to set the arbitration in motion is subject, of course, to the tribunal's determination of the existence and validity of the arbitration agreement, in the event of a jurisdictional objection.[10]

3.07   The submission of the relevant arbitration agreement and contractual documen-tation invoked by the claimant is essential to enable the respondent to determine both the jurisdictional basis for the arbitration and the legal grounds for the claims brought against it, and to prepare its Response to the Request.

The LCIA's initial review of the Request

3.08   Upon its receipt, the Registrar reviews the Request (and any accompanying documents) in order to determine that it contains the information required to be included in a Request under the Rules, in particular, to determine the existence of an arbitration agreement providing for the adjudication of the parties' dispute under the Rules. The Registrar's initial review of the Request is comparable to a similar review conducted by the ICC Secretariat in ICC arbitration. There are, however, important differences. In an ICC arbitration, if the respondent raises a plea of lack of jurisdiction or fails to submit an answer, the ICC Secretariat first conducts a prima facie review of the existence of an arbitration agreement between the parties to the arbitration. Only if it is satisfied that an agreement exists will the debate progress to the second stage, which is the determination by the arbitral tribunal of its own jurisdiction.[11] Unlike under the ICC Rules, there is no formal two-stage process for deciding jurisdiction in LCIA arbitration. In practice, though, something rather similar happens, albeit informally. In such circumstances,

---

   [8]   *Russell* para 2-015.
   [9]   eg, art 7(2) UNCITRAL Model Law (although the 2006 revisions to the Model Law also allow oral agreements as an option that a state may adopt) and s 5(2) Arbitration Act 1996.
   [10]   Pursuant to art 23.1.
   [11]   Art 6(2) ICC Rules; and *Derains & Schwartz* 76–110.

where the Rules do not contain explicit provisions, it is necessary for the Registrar to exercise his judgment and (in consultation with the LCIA Court) to act in the 'spirit' of the Rules, as mandated by Article 32.[12]

If, on review of the documents submitted, the Registrar (following consultation **3.09** with the LCIA Court) considers that there is doubt either as to the existence of an arbitration agreement, or as to whether it covers the parties to or the subject-matter of the dispute, the Registrar will invite comments from the respondent and enter into discussions with the claimant to seek to resolve the apparent anomaly. If, following such discussions, there is no glaring or obvious inconsistency, but the LCIA's jurisdiction remains contested by the respondent, the matter will be referred to the arbitral tribunal for decision under Article 23.1. There are occasions, however, where the LCIA is faced with an obvious or glaring inconsistency, and a recalcitrant claimant who nonetheless insists on proceeding under the Rules. Although it is difficult to summarize the practice of the Court on such occasions, as each case is decided on its facts, unless the Court considers the matter to be clear cut, for example, if the arbitration agreement unequivocally provides for arbitration under the ICC Rules, the Court is likely to decide to proceed with the arbitration proceedings. In so doing, the Court may direct the claimant alone to bear the costs of the arbitration under Article 24.1 until the tribunal has determined the issue of its jurisdiction. The LCIA thus takes the view that, under the Rules, the claimant will bear the financial risk of its insistence to proceed with the arbitration.[13] There is much merit in this practice, as it requires the arbitrators to rule on their own jurisdiction rather than the institution, which should be focusing on the administration of the parties' dispute rather than its adjudication. It is only in the most glaring or clear-cut cases, which by their nature are exceptional, that the LCIA Court will refuse to set the arbitration in motion.

Description of the parties' dispute and the claims advanced

Article 1.1 next requires that the claimant sets out in the Request a brief statement **3.10** describing the nature and circumstances of the dispute, and specifies the claims advanced against the respondent. The Rules contemplate the provision of

---

[12] The basis for the Registrar's initial review of the Request and the invoked arbitration agreement may also be found in the preamble to the Rules which addresses the applicability of the Rules as follows:

> Where any agreement, submission or reference provides in writing and in whatsoever manner for arbitration under the rules of the LCIA or by the Court of the LCIA ('the LCIA Court'), the parties shall be taken to have agreed in writing that the arbitration shall be conducted in accordance with the following rules ('the Rules') or such amended rules as the LCIA may have adopted hereafter to take effect before the commencement of the arbitration.

[13] See art 24.1 and the discussion in ch 8 below.

a minimum amount of information concerning the parties' dispute and the claims being advanced, but nonetheless allow the claimant to decide how much detail to provide. As discussed earlier, the Request should contain sufficient detail to enable the respondent party to understand the claims presented against it and to formulate its defences in the Response. The Request should, at a minimum, therefore, set out every cause of action and head of claim pursued by the claimant.[14] The Rules do not require the claimant to provide an indication of the amount in dispute, unlike under the ICC Rules.[15] Indeed, the inclusion of such a requirement was expressly rejected during the drafting process of the Rules.[16] Although an indication of the amounts at stake may be useful to the LCIA Court in its selection and appointment of arbitrators, such information is not strictly necessary since the costs of an LCIA arbitration are not determined on the basis of the amounts at stake, unlike in ICC arbitration.[17]

3.11 Further, it is in the interests of the claimant to provide sufficient detail in the Request to assist the Registrar in his task of preparing a summary of the case which is then submitted to the LCIA Court. The Court, in turn, will rely on the case summary to inform its selection of suitable arbitrator candidates and, in the case of party nomination, to ensure the suitability of the nominated arbitrators prior to their appointment. If the Registrar determines that the Request is insufficiently complete in order to prepare a suitable case summary, he will request the claimant to provide a fuller description of the dispute or, as the case may be, the relief sought in the arbitration. Typically, it is the respondent, rather than the Registrar, who is more likely to raise the issue of an incomplete Request. In such circumstances, the Registrar may seek the provision of further and better particulars from the claimant. In so doing, however, and in any ensuing correspondence that may follow, the Registrar must remain neutral and studiously avoid arguing any party's case.

3.12 In circumstances where there is plainly a dispute between the parties as to the sufficiency of the detail set out in the Request, and the claimant refuses to furnish the additional requested information, the Registrar may seize the LCIA Court. As discussed in the next chapter, the LCIA Court may proceed with the formation of the arbitral tribunal notwithstanding that the Request is incomplete or the Response is missing, late, or incomplete.[18] If the Court decides that it cannot proceed with the formulation of the tribunal on the basis of the Request as submitted,

---

[14] As discussed in ch 6 below, the parties subsequently are able to amend or supplement any claim, counterclaim, defence and reply, in accordance with art 22.1(a).

[15] Art 4(3)(c) ICC Rules.

[16] *Commentary* 10

[17] The basis on which the costs of arbitration are determined by the LCIA Court pursuant to art 28.1 is discussed in ch 8 below.

[18] Art 5.4.

then the arbitration cannot progress further until the missing information is furnished by the claimant. The Court can, and occasionally does, decide to proceed with the arbitration in spite of an incomplete Request, even if this means that the Respondent is, in turn, unable to submit a complete Response. The practice of the LCIA Court is, in this respect, guided by its policy to constitute the arbitral tribunal as soon as practicable and to let the arbitrators adjudicate the parties' dispute. Consistent with this policy is the fact that the respondent is not prejudiced by a failure to submit a Response. Indeed, as discussed below, Article 2.3 of the Rules explicitly affirms the optional nature of the Response. It follows, moreover, that the deadline of 30 days for the submission of a Response, which runs from the respondent's receipt of the Request,[19] is not generally disrupted by the submission of an incomplete Request (see the discussion below).

Other matters relating to the conduct of the arbitration and appointment of the arbitral tribunal

Article 1.1(d) provides the claimant with the opportunity to address other **3.13** matters regarding the conduct of the arbitration, such as the language and seat of the arbitration, or the number (and relevant qualifications) of the arbitrators. To the extent that these matters are addressed in the parties' arbitration agreement, the Request should identify the parties' agreement in respect of these matters. Conversely, if such matters are not dealt with by a written agreement of the parties, the claimant has the opportunity to submit its proposals as to these matters, which are all matters that the LCIA Court may be required to take into consideration in setting the arbitration proceedings in motion,[20] and in appointing the arbitral tribunal.[21]

Claimant's nomination of an arbitrator

As discussed in the next chapter, only the LCIA court is empowered to appoint **3.14** members of the tribunal. Moreover, there is no default provision under the Rules that provides the parties with the opportunity to nominate arbitrators – unlike the ICC or UNCITRAL Rules, where each party enjoys the right to nominate (or appoint under the UNCITRAL Rules) one arbitrator.[22] The default provision under the LCIA Rules provides for appointment of all arbitrators by the LCIA Court. The parties may nonetheless provide in their arbitration agreement that each party shall nominate an arbitrator, subject to the nominee's appointment

---

[19] Art 2.1.
[20] See arts 16 and 17 as regards the seat and language of the arbitration, respectively.
[21] Arts 5.5 and 7.1.
[22] Art 8(4) ICC Rules and art 7.1 UNCITRAL Rules.

by the Court.[23] Alternatively, the parties may seek to agree the process for nomination of arbitrators following the commencement of the arbitration.

3.15 If the arbitration agreement calls for party nomination of arbitrators, then the claimant should designate its nominee in the Request and set out the nominee's relevant contact details. Although the claimant's failure to do so does not irrevocably waive the claimant's right to effect such a nomination at a later time, the LCIA Court may appoint an arbitrator on behalf of the claimant in the absence of such a nomination in the Request and without regard to a later nomination.

3.16 On its face, the power of the LCIA Court to appoint an arbitrator in the absence of a nomination in the Request, or without regard to a late nomination, may appear somewhat draconian.[24] This is particularly so, as in a significant number of cases, claimants fail to nominate an arbitrator in the Request, in accordance with the terms of the parties' arbitration agreement. It is important to note, however, that the LCIA Court has a discretion in the exercise of its power to effect an appointment in place of the claimant. Indeed, Article 5.4 of the Rules represents somewhat of a softening of the previous version of this provision in the 1985 Rules, which was drafted in mandatory form.[25] In practice, and in accordance with its policy to encourage party autonomy and participation in the arbitration process, the LCIA Court does not rush to usurp the claimant's right to nominate an arbitrator and instead encourages the claimant to effect its nomination in a timely fashion. Indeed, our research revealed no instances where the LCIA Court has exercised its discretion to appoint an arbitrator due to a claimant party's default to effect a timely nomination in the Request. This is discussed in more detail in chapter 4 below.

The registration fee

3.17 The Request should be accompanied by the appropriate registration fee prescribed in the Schedule of Arbitration Fees and Costs (the **Schedule of Costs**)

---

[23] It is worth noting that the LCIA's recommended arbitration clauses (at app 1) do not include such language, although the Secretariat can advise interested parties as to suitable language.

[24] Art 7.2. The situation faced by a tardy respondent is more severe still, as the respondent's right to nominate an arbitrator pursuant to the parties' arbitration agreement is irrevocably waived if not exercised in the Response or within 30 days following receipt of the Request, as per art 2.3. In practice, as discussed in ch 4 below, the court does not readily ignore tardy nominations.

[25] Art 3.4 1985 Rules provided that in the event that the arbitration agreement calls for party nominations, and 'if the Request does not contain a nomination by the Claimant, and the Claimant fails to make such a nomination [within 30 days of the Respondent's receipt of the Request], the Court will likewise make that appointment'. See also C Salans, 'The 1985 Rules of the London Court of International Arbitration' (1986) 2 Arb Int 40, 43.

in force at the time. The Rules include the Schedule of Costs in effect at the commencement of the arbitration, as separately amended from time to time by the LCIA Court.[26] According to the current Schedule of Costs, which came into effect in May 2007, the non-refundable registration fee currently stands at £1500. Without the registration fee, the Request is treated as not having been received by the Registrar and the arbitration as not having been commenced.

It is interesting to contrast this provision with practice under the ICC Rules, **3.18** where the required advance payment of the ICC's administrative expenses is not deemed to form part of the Request.[27] Therefore, the commencement of the arbitration proceedings can proceed even in the absence of the requisite registration fee, albeit subject to the ICC Secretariat's mandate to close the file if payment is not forthcoming within the time limit to be specified by the Secretariat. The Registrar enjoys no such power under the LCIA Rules.

Confirmation of service of the Request on all parties

The Request should also contain confirmation to the Registrar by the claimant **3.19** that copies of the Request and all accompanying documents have been or are being served simultaneously on all other parties to the arbitration. The Request should further indicate the means by which such service is effected. This is different to the practice in arbitrations governed by the ICC Rules, where the ICC Secretariat takes responsibility for serving the request for arbitration and the answer thereto upon the respondent or claimant respectively.[28]

The direct service of the Request upon the respondent, and the provision in **3.20** Article 2.1 of the Rules that the deadline for submission of the Response runs from the respondent's receipt of the Request, means that the deadline for the submission of the Response may start to run before the formal commencement of the arbitration if, for example, there is a delay in transmission of the Request to the Registrar. Any such time difference is likely to be minimal, however, particularly as Article 1.1(g) requires the simultaneous service of the Request upon the Registrar and the respondent (see discussion below).

Article 1.2

The date of receipt by the Registrar of the Request shall be treated as the date on which the arbitration has commenced for all purposes. The Request (including all accompanying documents) should be submitted to the Registrar in two copies where a sole arbitrator should be appointed, or, if the parties have agreed or the Claimant considers that three arbitrators should be appointed, in four copies.

---

[26] Preamble to the Rules.
[27] Arts 4(3) and 4(4) ICC Rules; and *Derains & Schwartz* 55.
[28] Arts 4(5) and 5(4) ICC Rules.

3.21   Article 1.2 establishes the principle that the date of receipt by the Registrar of the Request shall be treated as the date on which the arbitration has commenced for all purposes. This provision appears to be at odds with Article 2.1 which states that the deadline for the submission of the Response, including the possible nomination of the respondent's arbitrator, runs as of the date of the respondent's receipt of the Request (which is served directly on the respondent by the claimant) and not from the date of commencement of the arbitration. The Court has clarified any possible mismatch in the Rules by confirming that the deadline for submission of the Response (or nomination of an arbitrator) does not start to run before the formal commencement of the arbitration, which, inter alia, is conditioned on the Registrar's receipt of the registration fee (discussed above).

3.22   The Registrar reviews the Request upon its receipt in order to determine that it contains the information required to be included in a Request under the Rules. Subject to the circumstances described above in the discussion of Article 1.1, the Registrar will acknowledge receipt of the Request by writing to all parties designated in the Request. In so doing, the Registrar will typically cite the relevant arbitration agreement invoked by the claimant and affirm the parties' agreement, or the claimant's proposals, as regards the language and seat of the arbitration and any other matters relating to the conduct of the arbitration, including as to the number and method of nomination of arbitrators. The Registrar will also remind the respondent that it should submit a Response within 30 days of receipt of the Request (or an earlier date in the event of an expedited formation of the tribunal pursuant to Article 9).

3.23   Article 1.2 also specifies the number of copies of the Request (and any accompanying documents) to be submitted in accordance with the number of arbitrators. The Registrar will invite the claimant to provide additional copies of the Request in the event that insufficient copies have been submitted.

B.   Article 2 – The Response

3.24   Article 2 deals with the submission of a Response to the Request by the respondent, which should include a brief statement as to the nature and circumstances of any counterclaims advanced by the respondent. The submission of a Response prior to the constitution of the tribunal is an important feature of proceedings under the Rules, which is also common to arbitrations conducted under the ICC and ICDR Rules,[29] but not to certain other arbitration rules.[30] As discussed below, however, the submission of the Response is not a requirement under the Rules,

---

[29]   Art 5 ICC Rules and art 3 ICDR Rules.
[30]   eg, arbitrations conducted under the UNCITRAL Rules or in ICSID arbitration.

and there are no adverse consequences to the respondent's decision not to submit one. The submission of the Response is nonetheless useful, particularly in informing the LCIA Court in its task of selecting suitable arbitrator candidates, or in the case of party nomination, to ensure the suitability of the nominated arbitrators prior to their appointment.

Article 2.1

Within 30 days of service of the Request on the Respondent, (or such lesser period fixed by the LCIA Court), the Respondent shall send to the Registrar a written response to the Request ('the Response'), containing or accompanied by:

(a) confirmation or denial of all or part of the claims advanced by the Claimant in the Request;

(b) a brief statement describing the nature and circumstances of any counterclaims advanced by the Respondent against the Claimant;

(c) comment in response to any statements contained in the Request, as called for under Article 1.1(d), on matters relating to the conduct of the arbitration;

(d) if the Arbitration Agreement calls for party nomination of arbitrators, the name, address, telephone, facsimile, telex and e-mail numbers (if known) of the Respondent's nominee; and

(e) confirmation to the Registrar that copies of the Response (including all accompanying documents) have been or are being served simultaneously on all other parties to the arbitration by one or more means of service to be identified in such confirmation.

3.25 Article 2.1 establishes the time period for the submission of the Response and sets forth its required contents.

Time period

3.26 Article 2.1 provides that the respondent must file its Response within 30 days of its receipt of the Request, or such lesser period as fixed by the LCIA Court. The service of the Response and the calculation of the time period should conform to the requirements set forth in Article 4 of the Rules, which are discussed below.

3.27 In spite of the discussion earlier in the context of Article 1.1, it bears emphasis that although the period of 30 days under Article 1 runs from the date of receipt of the Request, rather than the commencement of the arbitration pursuant to Article 1.2, as a matter of practice, the 30-day time period under Article 2.1 does not start to run before the formal commencement of the arbitration in the event that the respondent were to receive the Request ahead of the Registrar.

3.28 It is also worth reiterating that, unlike under the ICC Rules, there is no scope under the Rules for the respondent to seek an extension of the time period for the submission of the Response from the LCIA Court or the Registrar.[31] In fact, the LCIA Court has no explicit power under the Rules to extend any of the time periods set forth therein, contrary to the arbitral tribunal.[32] The Court is nonetheless empowered to curtail or abridge the period of 30 days under Article 2.1 in the event of a request for the formation of an expedited tribunal.[33] As we saw above, moreover, the time period under Article 2.1 continues to run even if the submitted Request is considered by the Registrar to be incomplete, but sufficiently detailed to enable the Court to proceed with formation of the tribunal.

3.29 The inflexible nature of the Rules in this regard stems from the optional nature of the Response and the LCIA's concern for combating dilatory tactics by the parties, particularly respondents. As to the optional nature of the Response, and as discussed below, the failure to submit a Response is without great consequence.[34] Thus, the respondent is not precluded from defending any claim or pursuing a counterclaim in the arbitration as a consequence of its failure to submit a late Response or one at all. As regards concerns of dilatory tactics, the intention behind the Rules is to enable the LCIA Court to proceed with the formation of the arbitral tribunal as soon as practicable in the face of parties' efforts to delay the arbitration proceedings under Article 5.4.[35] The flexibility of the time limit for the submission of the Response was, in fact, considered during the revision process of the current version of the Rules.[36] In light of the two considerations mentioned above, however, no revision of this provision was proposed.[37]

3.30 While there is considerable merit to the LCIA's tough stance for combating dilatory tactics by parties, the inflexibility of the time limit under Article 2.1 is likely to penalize parties who might have genuine and reasonable grounds for an extension of time in connection with the submission of the Response, for example, due to the inevitable delay caused by the instruction of external counsel. A degree of flexibility in the LCIA's approach would therefore be welcome. At present, such flexibility is only possible if the parties agree to an extension of time for the submission of the Response.

---

[31] Art 5(2) ICC Rules; and *Derains & Schwartz* 67–8.

[32] See the discussion below in ch 4 in the context of art 4.7.

[33] Art 9.3.

[34] Art 2.3.

[35] *Hunter & Paulsson* 167–9.

[36] It is interesting to note that an interim draft of the Rules did, in fact, empower the LCIA Court to extend the 30-day time limit under Article 2.1 'for cause shown', which is similar to the practice in ICC arbitration under art 5(2) ICC Rules (*Commentary* 13).

[37] *Commentary* 10–11. Further, whereas art 2.1 is now drafted in mandatory terms, the same provision in the 1985 Rules provided that 'the Respondent *may* send to the Registrar a Response' (emphasis added).

Content of the Response

Apart from the nomination of its arbitrator, if so provided in the arbitration **3.31** agreement, the Rules do not impose any rigid requirements as to the form of the Response or the amount of detail that the respondent should provide with respect to the merits of the case, including as regards any counterclaims advanced. Indeed, it is not unusual for respondents simply to foreshadow the prospect of future counterclaims without further elucidation. The respondent will have additional opportunities to introduce or elaborate upon its defences, or counterclaims, during the arbitration, notably, in its Statement of Defence.[38] In practice, how much the respondent chooses to include in the Response will likely depend on the circumstances of the case and the content of the Request.

Even if the respondent is not inclined to submit a Response dealing with the **3.32** substance of the parties' dispute, it should nonetheless endeavour to comment in response to any statements contained in the Request, as called for under Article 1.1(d), relating to the conduct of the arbitration. In particular, if such matters are not covered by the arbitration agreement, it is in the interests of the respondent to respond to any proposals made by the claimant as to the number and possible nomination of arbitrators (as well as the language and seat of the arbitration), or it runs the risk that, when deciding on such matters, the LCIA Court will not have the benefit of the respondent's view of the case.[39]

Article 2.2

The Response (including all accompanying documents) should be submitted to the Registrar in two copies, or if the parties have agreed or the Respondent considers that three arbitrators should be appointed, in four copies.

This Article mirrors the provisions of Article 1.2 as to the numbers of copies of **3.33** the Response to be submitted to the Registrar. A copy of the Response should separately be served on all the parties to the arbitration, as per Article 2.1(e).

Article 2.3

Failure to send a Response shall not preclude the Respondent from denying any claim or from advancing a counterclaim in the arbitration. However, if the Arbitration Agreement calls for party nomination of arbitrators, failure to send a Response or to nominate an arbitrator within time or at all shall constitute an irrevocable waiver of that party's opportunity to nominate an arbitrator.

---

[38] Art 15.3.
[39] Although the Court will specifically canvass the parties' views as regards the language and seat of the arbitration prior to making any determination pursuant to arts 16 and 17.

Optional nature of the Response

3.34   As already mentioned, Article 2.3 affirms the optional nature of the Response by providing that failure to send a Response does not preclude the respondent from defending claims raised against it or from advancing any counterclaims in the arbitration. Subject to the discussion below as to the nomination of arbitrators, there is therefore no sanction under the Rules for a respondent's failure to submit a Response on time, or at all. The respondent has further opportunities, such as the Statement of Defence, to submit its defences to the merits of the claims brought against it, or to advance counterclaims. Nor do the Rules require the respondent to raise any jurisdictional defences in the Response. Any such defence must be raised, however, no later than the Statement of Defence, or they are deemed to be irrevocably waived.[40] It is nonetheless good practice and in the interests of the respondent for it to raise any jurisdictional defences as soon as possible, especially if it wishes the tribunal to determine the issue of its jurisdiction in a preliminary phase of the arbitration and before consideration of the merits of the case.[41]

Waiver of the respondent's right to nominate an arbitrator

3.35   Article 2.3 establishes that, if the parties' arbitration agreement provides for the nomination of arbitrators by the parties (subject to their subsequent appointment by the LCIA Court), the respondent's failure to send a Response or otherwise to nominate an arbitrator within time or at all constitutes an irrevocable waiver of that party's opportunity to nominate an arbitrator. In order to avoid the severe sanction set forth in this provision, the respondent must either submit a Response, which contains the nomination of an arbitrator,[42] or, alternatively, if it chooses not to submit a Response, nominate an arbitrator within 30 days of its receipt of the Request. As discussed earlier in the context of Article 2.1, the purpose of this condition is to combat the delaying tactics often employed by respondent parties. Article 2.3 is therefore designed to dissuade parties from abusing opportunities to nominate arbitrators.[43] The drafters of the Rules fully recognized the potential seriousness of this provision. They rather hoped that the Rules would seldom have to be applied in their full severity, and that their very existence would

---

[40]   Art 23.2.

[41]   Art 186(2) PILA requires any objection to jurisdiction to be raised prior to any defence on the merits. Rule 41 ICSID Arbitration Rules also requires that any jurisdictional objections be raised as early as possible, and no later than the time fixed for submission of the counter-memorial.

[42]   Art 2.1(d).

[43]   *Hunter & Paulsson* 168–9.

'cause parties to behave reasonably, and in the process contribute to the development of a generally acceptable deontology of international arbitration'.[44]

The irrevocable waiver of a party's right to nominate an arbitrator under Article 2.3 should be considered in conjunction with Articles 7.1 and 5.4 which are discussed in the next chapter. It suffices to note here that Article 7.1 provides that, where the parties have agreed that the respondent is to nominate an arbitrator, the LCIA Court may appoint an arbitrator notwithstanding the absence of the nomination and without regard to any late nomination. Article 5.4 mandates the LCIA Court to appoint the tribunal as soon as practicable after receipt by the Registrar of the Request or after expiry of 30 days following service of the Request upon the respondent if no Response is submitted. Furthermore, the LCIA Court may proceed with the formation of the tribunal in spite of a missing, late, or incomplete Response. **3.36**

While both provisions empower the LCIA Court to proceed with the arbitration in the event of a late or absent nomination by the respondent, the Court retains a discretion in proceeding with the formation of the tribunal which provides a welcome degree of flexibility in the Court's practice in the face of the potentially severe consequences of Article 2.3. As a matter of practice, the Court is likely to be sympathetic to a nomination that arrives only a few days late, whereas a nomination that is received by the Registrar a few weeks late is likely to be too late. As we discuss in the next chapter, our research revealed many instances where the LCIA Court has exercised its power under Article 7.2 in the absence of a timely nomination by the respondent. **3.37**

One difficult situation that may arise in this context is when, faced with the nomination of an arbitrator by the claimant in the Request, the respondent disputes the validity of the claimant's nomination on the basis of an alleged ambiguity in the arbitration agreement. In such circumstances, it falls to the Court to construe the arbitration agreement for the purposes of Article 2.3 and to determine the existence of a prior agreement of the parties providing for the nomination of arbitrators.[45] Another potentially difficult situation arises in the event that the respondent contends that the Request is defective because the claims are not sufficiently described and that it should not be required to nominate an arbitrator, until the Request has been rectified. As a general rule, the incomplete nature of the Request does not stop the time period under Article 2.3 for the nomination of an arbitrator from running, except if the LCIA Court were to decide not to proceed **3.38**

---

[44] Ibid.

[45] Notwithstanding the absence of a prior agreement between the parties as to either the number of arbitrators or the method for their nomination, claimants occasionally nominate an arbitrator in their Request while, at the same time, seeking the respondent's consent to such party nomination of arbitrators.

with the formation of the tribunal due to the incomplete nature of the Request, in accordance with Article 5.4.

C. Article 4 – Notices and Periods of Time

3.39 Article 4 sets out in comprehensive detail the procedures to be followed in respect of written communications among the parties, the arbitrators, and the Registrar during the arbitration. This article was introduced for the first time in the current version of the Rules and the text essentially follows Article 4 of the WIPO Arbitration Rules.[46] The intention of the drafters was to avoid sterile argument (and dilatory practice by parties) over the precise date, time, and method of service of documents, as provided for in the Rules, directed by the tribunal, or agreed between the parties, by setting out 'chapter and verse' on means of communication, and on dates of commencement and expiry of time limits.[47] All modern arbitration rules now contain similar provisions, although none is as detailed as Article 4.[48]

Article 4.1

Any notice or other communication that may be or is required to be given by a party under these Rules shall be in writing and shall be delivered by registered postal or courier service or transmitted by facsimile, telex, e-mail or any other means of telecommunication that provide a record of its transmission.

3.40 Article 4.1 contains specific reference to the various means of communication available to the parties, which reduces delay that could be caused by parties' queries. The inclusion of transmission by facsimile and email also brings the institution up to date with respect to modern means of communication. The only criterion established by Article 4.1 for the valid sending of notices is that the chosen method of communication provide a record of its transmission.

Article 4.2

A party's last-known residence or place of business during the arbitration shall be a valid address for the purpose of any notice or other communication in the absence of any notification of a change to such address by that party to the other parties, the Arbitral Tribunal and the Registrar.

3.41 Pursuant to Article 4.2, a party's last known residence or place of business during the arbitration constitutes a valid address of a party, in the absence of any

---

[46] *Commentary* 11.

[47] A Winstanley, 'The LCIA – history, constitution and rules' in A Berkeley and J Mimms (eds), *International Commercial Arbitration: Practical Perspectives* (Centre of Construction Law & Management, 2001) 21, 27.

[48] Art 3 ICC Rules, art 18 ICDR Rules, and art 2 UNCITRAL Rules.

notification of a change of such address. The Rules do not require any other particular formalities to be respected in making notifications in the arbitration. There is thus no requirement that notice be made to any particular person, or for the sending party to verify that the notice has been received by a duly-authorized person, provided that delivery has been made at the proper address.

However, parties should bear in mind such legal requirements that may apply to **3.42** the enforcement of awards in any given situation. Thus, while notification to a party's last known address is sufficient under the Rules, the New York Convention provides that recognition and enforcement of an award may be refused if the party against whom the award is invoked was not given proper notice of the arbitration proceedings.[49] It is therefore good practice for parties to do all that they reasonably can to ensure that notice of the arbitration proceedings is actually received from the start of the arbitration.

Article 4.3

For the purpose of determining the date of commencement of a time limit, a notice or other communication shall be treated as having been received on the day it is delivered or, in the case of telecommunications, transmitted in accordance with Articles 4.1 and 4.2.

Article 4.3 fixes the effective date of commencement of any time limit, any **3.43** notification or communication, and is self-explanatory.

Article 4.4

For the purpose of determining compliance with a time limit, a notice or other communication shall be treated as having been sent, made or transmitted if it is dispatched in accordance with Articles 4.1 and 4.2 prior to or on the date of the expiration of the time-limit.

This provision should be read in conjunction with Article 4.6 and affirms that **3.44** a notice or other communication is deemed to have been sent, made, or transmitted, if despatched in compliance with Articles 4.1 and 4.2 prior to the expiration of the time-limit.

Article 4.5

Notwithstanding the above, any notice or communication by one party may be addressed to another party in the manner agreed in writing between them or, failing such agreement, according to the practice followed in the course of their previous dealings or in whatever manner ordered by the Arbitral Tribunal.

---

[49] Art V(1)(b) New York Convention. See also art 36(1)(a)(ii) UNCITRAL Model Law.

3.45   Article 4.5 provides an exception to the default provisions set out in Articles 4.1 and 4.2 as to the means of communication available to the parties, which may be eschewed in favour of any alternate means either agreed in writing between the parties (typically specified in the contract giving rise to the dispute), according to the practice followed in the parties' course of dealing, or as ordered by the tribunal.

3.46   This provision is permissive rather than mandatory. At the start of the arbitration, the Registrar will ordinarily accept the claimant's indication as to the respondent's address, subject to inquiry if it appears peculiar to the Registrar. The claimant will bear the consequences of an erroneous indication in terms of delay in proceeding with the arbitration.

Article 4.6

For the purpose of calculating a period of time under these Rules, such period shall begin to run on the day following the day when a notice or other communication is received. If the last day of such period is an official holiday or a non-business day at the residence or place of business of the addressee, the period is extended until the first business day which follows. Official holidays or non-business days occurring during the running of the period of time are included in calculating that period.

3.47   This provision explains how the various time periods under the Rules should be calculated and, as explained earlier, is intended to avoid unnecessary debate and dispute as regards the calculation of time periods during the arbitration.

Article 4.7

The Arbitral Tribunal may at any time extend (even where the period of time has expired) or abridge any period of time prescribed under these Rules or under the Arbitration Agreement for the conduct of the arbitration, including any notice or communication to be served by one party on any other party.

3.48   This provision grants the arbitral tribunal a wide-ranging power to extend or abridge any period of time prescribed under the Rules or under the arbitration agreement for the conduct of the arbitration. The tribunal is even empowered to extend time-limits if the period of time has expired. Thus, for example, an arbitral tribunal will almost invariably accept a written pleading that is submitted a day or two late. Similarly, tribunals occasionally agree to consider applications for correction of awards, or additional awards, submitted by the parties outside the 30-day time limit specified in Article 27.[50]

---

[50]   Discussed in ch 7 below.

By ceding the power to the tribunal to extend or abridge time limits set by the **3.49** Rules, this provision thus eliminates the LCIA Court's power to do so as of the date on which the arbitral tribunal is formed. Indeed, the LCIA Court is nowhere empowered under the Rules to extend any time limits specified therein, although the Court retains the power to abridge or curtail any time limit under the Rules for the purpose of establishing an expedited tribunal pursuant to Article 9.3. This is a notable contrast with the power enjoyed by the ICC Court (and even the ICC Secretariat) to extend the various procedural time limits set forth in the ICC Rules.[51]

---

[51] eg, under arts 5(2), 18(2), and 24(2) ICC Rules.

4

THE ARBITRAL TRIBUNAL: FORMATION AND CHALLENGE (ARTICLES 5 TO 13)

A. Article 5 – Formation of the Arbitral Tribunal	4.06	Article 9.3 4.105
Article 5.1	4.07	F. Article 10 – Revocation of Arbitrator's Appointment 4.109
Article 5.2	4.08	Article 10.1 4.111
Article 5.3	4.37	Article 10.2 4.116
Article 5.4	4.42	Article 10.3 4.122
Article 5.5	4.46	Article 10.4 4.123
Article 5.6	4.49	G. Article 11 – Nomination and Replacement of Arbitrators 4.129
B. Article 6 – Nationality of Arbitrators	4.50	Article 11.1 4.130
Article 6.1	4.52	Article 11.2 4.136
Article 6.2	4.63	H. Article 12 – Majority Power to Continue Proceedings 4.137
Article 6.3	4.67	Article 12.1 4.141
C. Article 7 – Party and Other Nominations	4.69	Article 12.2 4.149
Article 7.1	4.70	Article 12.3 4.156
Article 7.2	4.74	I. Article 13 – Communications between Parties and the Arbitral Tribunal 4.158
D. Article 8 – Three or More Parties	4.75	Article 13.1 4.159
Article 8.1	4.80	Article 13.2 4.162
Article 8.2	4.85	Article 13.3 4.165
E. Article 9 – Expedited Formation	4.86	
Article 9.1	4.96	
Article 9.2	4.98	

In many ways, the formation of and challenge to the Arbitral Tribunal is the **4.01** very essence of international arbitration and, in particular, the role of an arbitral institution. That the choice of a co-arbitrator by the parties is one of the fundamental features of arbitration can be shown by the turmoil created by the judgment of the French *Cour de cassation* in the famous *Dutco* case,[1] following which

---

[1] *Cour de cassation, Sociétés BKMI et Siemens c société Dutco*, 7 January 1992, [1992] Rev arb 470. For a full description of this important jurisprudence, see *Derains & Schwartz* 177–81.

institutional rules have had to provide for multi-party arbitration with special procedures that do not give different rights to different parties when it comes to choosing a co-arbitrator.[2]

4.02 Similarly, the quality of the justice rendered by an arbitral tribunal (or, perhaps more pertinently, users' confidence in such justice and in the system of international arbitration as a reliable dispute-resolution mechanism) depends upon the impartiality of the arbitrators. This is furthermore a prerequisite for a valid award under all modern arbitration laws[3] and for the recognition of such an award under the New York Convention and local legislation. An award rendered by a partial tribunal should not be enforced as it would be contrary to international public policy to do so.

4.03 This means that the role of the institution as appointing authority is key, both in the scrutiny of initial nominations and in dealing with subsequent challenges. If the ability to nominate a co-arbitrator is a fundamental right of the parties to an arbitration agreement, as the court in *Dutco* found, the way in which the arbitral institution deals with such nominations and challenges to them is equally fundamental in ensuring that the parties' rights are respected.

4.04 It is in this context that Articles 5 to 13 of the LCIA Rules should be seen. These Articles can be divided into the formation of the tribunal (Articles 5 to 9); challenges to and the reformation of the tribunal and the power under certain circumstances for a truncated tribunal to continue with the proceedings (Articles 10 to 12); and questions of practicality in communications between the parties and the tribunal, once it has been constituted (Article 13).

4.05 In covering these topics, two matters that are peculiar to the LCIA Rules and of very great value to parties will be covered. These are, first, Article 9, which allows the LCIA Court to constitute a tribunal on an expedited basis in cases justifying such a measure and, secondly, the fact that, in deciding challenges to arbitrators under Article 10, the LCIA Court appoints a sub-committee (called a 'division') from among its members to decide the challenge, the reasoned decision of which, in contradistinction to the practice of other arbitral institutions such as the ICC, is communicated to the parties. The LCIA has recently taken the decision to publish sanitized versions of such challenge decisions, which should prove to be a very valuable resource to parties, counsel, and arbitrators alike.

---

[2] This is discussed further below in the context of art 8.
[3] eg, art 12 UNCITRAL Model Law and s 24(1) Arbitration Act 1996.

A. Article 5 – Formation of the Arbitral Tribunal

Article 5 contains the rules that govern the nomination and appointment of **4.06** arbitrators and their duties of impartiality and disclosure of matters that could justifiably be seen to jeopardize that impartiality.

Article 5.1

The expression 'the Arbitral Tribunal' in these Rules includes a sole arbitrator or all the arbitrators where more than one. All references to an arbitrator shall include the masculine and feminine. (References to the President, Vice President and members of the LCIA Court, the Registrar or deputy Registrar, expert, witness, party and legal representative shall be similarly understood.)

This provision is purely definitional. The Rules do not distinguish in terms of **4.07** duties and functions between a sole arbitrator and a three-arbitrator tribunal and there is the usual provision that the use of the masculine includes the feminine, whether the Rules are referring to an arbitrator or the LCIA's own officers.

Article 5.2

All arbitrators conducting an arbitration under these Rules shall be and remain at all times impartial and independent of the parties; and none shall act in the arbitration as advocates for any party. No arbitrator, whether before or after appointment, shall advise any party on the merits or outcome of the dispute.

Article 5.2 contains the injunction of independence and impartiality. The terms **4.08** of this requirement are fairly standard.[4] The considerable and wide-ranging debate over what the terms mean has proved that their meaning is anything but.[5] The party nominating an arbitrator therefore has to approach the choice of a party-nominated arbitrator with some care in order to ensure that his 'pick' passes the scrutiny of the institution at the appointment stage and any challenges from the other party or parties thereafter.[6]

In particular, the question of arbitrators' conflicts of interest has been examined **4.09** closely by a working party under the auspices of the International Bar Association,

---

[4] The ICDR, Swiss, SCC, UNCITRAL, CIETAC, SIAC, HKIAC, DIS, Vienna, and NAI Rules all provide that arbitrators are to be impartial and independent. The ICC Rules refer only to independence. The ICSID Rules require an arbitrator to 'judge fairly' and disclose potential conflicts.

[5] See, for example, the discussions at *Redfern & Hunter* paras 4-52 to 4-66 and, in the specific context of the ICC Rules, *Derains & Schwartz* 116–34 and the sources therein cited.

[6] On the complex issue of nominating an arbitrator in international arbitration, see generally D Bishop and L Reed 'Practical Guidelines for Interviewing, Selecting and Challenging Party-Appointed Arbitrators in International Commercial Arbitration' (1998) 14 Arb Int 395; and M Hunter, 'Ethics of the International Arbitrator' (1987) 53 Arbitration 219; as well as more general works such as *Craig, Park, Paulsson* para 12.04 and *Redfern & Hunter* paras 4-21 to 4-50.

whose work led to the promulgation of the IBA Guidelines in 2004. No international arbitral institution has gone so far as to adopt the IBA Guidelines, preferring to keep their freedom of action, as no set of guidelines can possibly cater for all of the possible permutations of relationships and interests that the real world throws up. This is certainly the position adopted by the LCIA in considering whether to confirm arbitrators' appointments and in dealing with challenges on the grounds of a lack of impartiality and/or independence. The ICC, likewise, does not consider itself bound by them.[7]

4.10 Nonetheless, even if the IBA Guidelines are not slavishly followed by the LCIA, they are important to any discussion of the independence and impartiality of arbitrators. Therefore, the extent to which they are accepted as providing useful guidance needs to be considered.[8] It has been reported that they have been 'put to use, in varying degrees' in 10 jurisdictions, most notably in western Europe and North America. Little use has been reported, however, in Asia-Pacific jurisdictions and, interestingly, Switzerland.[9] As to arbitration institutions other than the LCIA and ICC, it has been reported that the IBA Guidelines are frequently used by the SCC and WIPO and that the standard of independence of the ICDR is essentially the same. Other institutions, which profess not to use the IBA Guidelines directly, acknowledge that they may refer to them for direction.[10] At all events, the IBA Guidelines will be referred to in the discussion that follows where they are relevant.

4.11 As noted above, while the LCIA Rules require an arbitrator to be both impartial and independent, some other sets of institutional rules require only independence (see Article 7(1) of the ICC Rules[11]) and some statutes require only impartiality (see section 24(1)(a) of the English Arbitration Act 1996). The question thus arises as to whether the combination of these terms (or the absence of one of them) actually changes anything of the substance of the arbitrator's duty to disclose actual or potential conflicts or the institution's obligations when deciding whether to confirm an appointment or decide a challenge.

---

[7] AM Whitesell, 'Independence in ICC Arbitration: ICC Court Practice concerning the Appointment, Confirmation, Challenge and Replacement of Arbitrators' [2007] ICC Bull (Independence of Arbitrators Special Supplement) 7.

[8] For a general commentary on the IBA Guidelines, see J Gill, 'The IBA Conflicts Guidelines – Who's Using Them and How?' (2007) 1 Dispute Resolution International 58.

[9] Gill (n 8 above) 60. But in England the Commercial Court has referred to the IBA Guidelines with less approval. Morison J said that 'the question at issue is not whether what happened fell within the red list or not' (*ASM Shipping Ltd of India v TTMI Ltd of England* [2005] EWHC 2238 (Comm) para 39(4)). For a fuller discussion of this case, see below.

[10] *Nicholas & Partasides* 2.

[11] Although it should be noted that art 15(2) ICC Rules requires an ICC tribunal to 'act fairly and impartially'.

The better view must be that it does not. Although the ICC Rules only require an **4.12** arbitrator to be independent of the parties, there is no suggestion that this obviates the need for impartiality.[12] In the fourth edition of *Redfern and Hunter* it is said that 'there has been a distinct trend towards viewing these two elements [ie impartiality and independence] as the opposite side of the same coin'.[13] There is, however, a clear conceptual distinction to be drawn between them, even if in practice it is unusual for the precise formulation in the applicable rules or arbitration law to make a real difference to the outcome of a challenge to an arbitrator's ability to discharge his functions in an acceptable manner.[14]

Impartiality

An arbitrator is not impartial if he or she favours one of the parties to an **4.13** arbitration. The concept of impartiality is thus concerned with bias. This is a question with both an objective ('is the arbitrator actually biased?') and subjective ('are there justifiable doubts as to whether the arbitrator is or may be biased?') element, but the subjective element dominates as the arbitrator's state of mind cannot itself be ascertained. It is thus more usual to refer to the subjective test of a party's justifiable doubts rather than objective evidence of actual bias (which any half-intelligent partial arbitrator would certainly try to hide).[15]

A further refinement of the question as to whether an arbitrator is partial arises **4.14** not in relation to one of the parties to the dispute, but in relation to one of the issues to be decided. Thus, in a recent case before the courts of The Netherlands, the court held that an arbitrator could not at one and the same time act as arbitrator in one dispute and represent a party in an ICSID annulment proceeding, in which as counsel he was seeking to have an award annulled on which a party was relying in the case in which he was sitting as arbitrator.[16] This was after the arbitrator concerned had declined to resign and the Permanent Court of Arbitration, as the appointing authority under the UNCITRAL Rules in the case, had rejected the challenge.

---

[12] See *Derains & Schwartz* 117; in which it is said that 'although the word "impartiality" was not itself used in the Rules, the prevention of partiality was clearly its primary object', referring to a statement by a former Secretary-General of the ICC Court, Horacio Grigera Naón.

[13] *Redfern & Hunter* para 4-54.

[14] For a discussion in the context of investment-treaty arbitration, see C Harris, 'Arbitrator Challenges in International Investment Arbitration' (2008) 5 TDM.

[15] For a discussion of impartiality, see also G Petrochilos, *Procedural Law in International Arbitration* (Oxford University Press, 2004) para 4.55.

[16] *The Republic of Ghana v Telekom Malaysia*, District Court of The Hague, decisions of 18 October and 5 November 2004, [2005] ASA Bull 186.

4.15   That could be seen as an extreme example (and it is not without having attracted some controversy)[17] but there is obviously a delicate line to be trodden in this respect. It is not only commonplace but one of the major perceived advantages of international arbitration that the parties can each choose an arbitrator who is thought to be likely to be well-disposed to the party nominating him or her. This may be for cultural reasons, as the arbitrator shares the same nationality as the nominating party, and/or because the nominated arbitrator shares a similar outlook (commercially or legally) to the party that nominates him or her, or has expressed views on a relevant issue in the arbitration that would seem to make him or her more or less inclined to deciding that issue in that party's favour.

4.16   This has of course to be distinguished from actual or perceived bias. The fact that an arbitrator has previously decided a certain issue one way, or commented on a legal issue in an earlier publication, should not preclude him or her from sitting in a subsequent case in which a similar legal issue arises. Indeed, this forms part of the so-called 'Green List' in the IBA Guidelines, which would not lead to an obligation of disclosure in the eyes of the working party that drafted the IBA Guidelines.[18] This happens, of course, in national courts all the time, particularly those that follow the common law principle of *stare decisis*.

4.17   It may be different if the arbitrator concerned has already decided a factual question one way in a linked case, or heard a witness and formed a view about his or her credibility or truthfulness.

4.18   One striking example of a national court's view of the possibility of an arbitrator's being improperly influenced by a previous experience with a witness is the decision of the Commercial Court in England in *ASM Shipping v TTMI*.[19] ASM Shipping argued that the chairman of an arbitral tribunal (Duncan Matthews QC) should have recused himself as: (a) he had acted for other charterers against other owners in an earlier, unrelated dispute, in which the same solicitors had represented the charterers as now represented TTMI; (b) the principal witness for the owners in the earlier case was a Mr M, who was now a witness for ASM; and (c) in the earlier proceedings, Mr M's honesty had been impugned by the charterers in the context of a document production process. Thus, the essence of the complaint against Mr Matthews (who refused to stand down when challenged)

---

17   eg H Mann, 'The Emperor's Clothes Come Off: A Comment on Republic of Ghana v Telekom Malaysia' [2005] TDM. For wider issues concerning 'issue conflicts' in investment-treaty arbitration, see J Levine 'Dealing with Arbitrator "Issue Conflicts" in International Arbitration' (2006) 3 Dispute Resolution Journal 60, 61–7.

18   It is submitted that it would be otherwise were the arbitrator to have expressed a view about the case itself. This forms part of the Orange List in the IBA Guidelines, comprising a non-exhaustive list of circumstances that could give rise to justifiable doubts as to that arbitrator's impartiality and should therefore, in the view of the IBA working party, be disclosed.

19   [2005] EWHC 2238 (Comm).

was that he might have had a negative recollection of one of the parties' witnesses. Rather surprisingly, the English court ruled that Mr Matthews's participation in the arbitration amounted to a 'serious irregularity' and that he should not continue to sit.[20]

There is always a fine line to be drawn between pure 'issue conflicts' and real **4.19** conflicts of interest that would disqualify an arbitrator from sitting.[21] One interesting recent decision that has shed some further light on this distinction is the first of two challenges brought by Argentina against one of the arbitrators in the *Suez* cases, Prof Gabrielle Kaufmann-Kohler.[22] The allegation against Prof Kaufmann-Kohler was that, since she had been part of an ICSID tribunal that had rendered an award against Argentina in an earlier case, and since, according to Argentina, the earlier award had been so flawed in its findings of fact and appraisal of evidence that Prof Kaufmann-Kohler's participation in that award revealed '. . . a prima facie lack of impartiality . . . made evident through the most prominent inconsistencies of the award that result in the total lack of reliability towards [the arbitrator]'.[23] The challenge was dismissed as having been made out of time, but the substance of the allegations was also considered. These were dismissed. The two members of the tribunal deciding the challenge, as mandated by the ICSID Rules, found that the fact that an arbitrator made a determination of law or a finding of fact in one case does not mean that such arbitrator cannot decide the law and the facts impartially in another case, saying that '[a] finding of an arbitrator's or a judge's lack of impartiality requires far stronger evidence than that such arbitrator participated in a unanimous decision with two other arbitrators in a case in which a party in that case is currently a party in a case now being heard by that arbitrator or judge. To hold otherwise would have serious negative consequences for any adjudicatory system.'[24]

---

[20] To complete this saga, after Mr Matthews had stood down, ASM applied under s 24 Arbitration Act 1996 for the removal of the two co-arbitrators on the grounds that they had been tainted with the apparent bias of Mr Matthews. While finding that this was not an irrelevant issue, the court held that it did not follow as a matter of law from the finding of apparent bias against one arbitrator that each member of the original tribunal was equally tainted. As no other circumstances existed that gave rise to justifiable doubts as to the impartiality of the two other arbitrators, the application was refused (*ASM Shipping Ltd of India v Harris & Ors* [2007] EWHC 1513 (Comm)).

[21] For a general discussion, see A Sinclair and M Gearing, 'Partiality and Issue Conflicts' (2008) 5 TDM; and Levine (n 17 above).

[22] *Suez, Sociedad General de Aguas de Barcelona SA and InterAguas Servicios Integrales de Agua SA v The Argentine Republic*, ICSID Case No. ARB/03/17 and *Suez, Sociedad General de Aguas de Barcelona SA and InterAguas Servicios Integrales de Agua SA v The Argentine Republic*, ICSID Case No ARB/03/19, Decision on disqualification of a member of the arbitral tribunal, 22 October 2007. There were in fact two challenges to Prof Kaufmann-Kohler, the second being based on the fact that she had not disclosed her directorship of the Swiss bank UBS, which had shareholdings in two of the claimant companies. That challenge was also dismissed, by a decision dated 12 May 2008.

[23] Ibid, para 13.

[24] Ibid, para 36.

Independence

4.20 At least in theory, independence is a more objective test than the subjective concept of impartiality. It has been said that the former concerns the relationship the arbitrator has with the subject-matter of the dispute, while the latter concerns the relationship between the arbitrator and the parties.[25]

4.21 The IBA Guidelines spend a significant amount of time on the relations between an arbitrator, the parties, and the parties' counsel. The 'Non-Waivable Red List' and 'Waivable Red List' are entirely composed of relationships between the arbitrator and the parties and their counsel that, in the view of the working party, automatically disqualify an arbitrator from sitting. The 'Orange List' contains only one matter that would, in the view of the working party, require disclosure to the parties that could be considered to relate to impartiality rather than independence, namely if the arbitrator has advocated a specific position regarding the dispute that is being arbitrated. Even the 'Green List' is overwhelmingly concerned with relationships between arbitrator and parties rather than between the arbitrator and the subject-matter of the dispute.

4.22 It thus seems clear that the objectively assessable concept of independence is easier to reduce to writing than is impartiality. In fact, though, this does not always make the definition of what constitutes lack of independence any easier to determine in practice. For example, the question of the relationship between the arbitrator and the law firm of one of the parties has given rise to a number of borderline issues. Given that the international arbitration community is relatively small (although becoming less so as arbitration establishes itself as the preferred means of resolving international disputes), it is obvious that most specialist practitioners know each other and cross paths (and/or swords) with a greater or lesser degree of frequency. This professional frequentation also leads in many cases to social contact. This will, according to one authoritative commentary, rarely lead to a successful challenge to an arbitrator.[26] Nonetheless, as recognized by the IBA Guidelines and by other commentators,[27] such links may give rise to concern and need to be considered, at least, for possible disclosure in some cases.

4.23 Past professional links are even less likely to result in an arbitrator's disqualification than current social or professional contact, unless there is a continuing financial element; if an arbitrator was receiving a pension from a party's law firm, of which he used to be a partner, that would surely call his independence into question.[28]

---

[25] Hunter (n 6 above) 223.
[26] *Fouchard, Gaillard, Goldman* para 1031.
[27] Bishop & Reed (n 6 above) 418: 'Close personal friendships . . . probably should be disqualifying.' But how close is 'close'?
[28] The IBA Guidelines provide many examples of possibly disqualifying relationships that would at least require disclosure by potential arbitrators.

On the other hand, current professional links will almost always constitute **4.24** a conflict. In a case before the Supreme Court of Sweden, an application to set aside an arbitral award was brought on the basis of the lack of independence of an arbitrator (referred to as JL) who, at the time of the arbitration, which involved Ericsson AB, had been a consultant with the Stockholm firm of Mannheimer Swartling. Not only did Mannheimer Swartling as a firm work for companies within the Ericsson group (including Ericsson AB itself), but JL had written legal opinions for companies within the group (although it was accepted that he had had no direct contact). The Swedish Supreme Court held that JL was to be treated as any other lawyer at the firm and that all such, including therefore JL, 'were unable on grounds of professional ethics both to accept engagements for an opposite party of the Ericsson Group and to accept engagements as an arbitrator in a dispute in which one of the companies of the Group was a party'.[29]

Barrister-arbitrators

One particular issue that should be mentioned here, given the close links between **4.25** LCIA arbitration and England, is the phenomenon of barristers' chambers. In England's split legal profession, barristers (who conduct most of the advocacy before higher courts in England and who often take the same role in 'English-style' arbitrations conducted in England) are sole practitioners who practise out of 'chambers', which group a number of barristers together who, while not being in partnership (indeed barristers are forbidden from practising in partnership by their professional conduct rules), nonetheless share certain services and expenses.

It is very common for barristers from the same chambers to appear on different **4.26** sides of disputes before the English courts or to appear before judges who used to be members of the same chambers and, by the same token, it is not viewed as a problem in English legal circles to have barristers from the same chambers appear as counsel and arbitrator in the same matter.[30]

---

[29] The *Lind case*, Swedish Supreme Court case No T 2448-06, 19 November 2007, [2007] Stockholm Int Arb Rev 167, 174.

[30] See, famously, *Laker Airways v FLS Aerospace* [1999] 2 Lloyd's Rep 45, in which the English court rejected a challenge under the English Arbitration Act 1996 to an arbitrator who came from the same chambers as counsel for one of the parties. This decision (which was given in the absence of argument from the challenging party) has been much commented on (see, eg, A Merjian, 'Caveat Arbitor: *Laker Airways* and the Appointment of Barristers as Arbitrators in Cases involving Barrister-Advocates from the same Chambers' (2000) 17 J Int Arb 31; M Gearing, 'A Judge in His Own Cause? – Actual or Unconscious Bias of Arbitrators' (2000) 3 Int Arb L R 46; D Brown, 'Arbitrators, Impartiality and English Law – Did Rix J. Really Get it Wrong in *Laker Airways*?' (2001) 18 J Int Arb 123. See also the decision of the Paris Court of Appeal in *KFTCIC c Kori Estero*, 28 June 1991, which decided the same ([1992] Rev arb 568). The Swiss Federal Supreme Court indicated, in a decision dated 9 February 1998, that an arbitrator who has an office-sharing arrangement with counsel for a party can be considered to be independent: see *Poudret & Besson* para 419 n 153; and [1998] ASA Bull 634. Office-sharing arrangements are in fact becoming more common as practitioners retire

4.27 This arrangement is not always regarded by non-English parties with quite the same degree of equanimity, however, particularly if they are not used to the ways of English litigation and its split legal profession. A party unused to the particular (some might say peculiar) ways of working of the English legal profession might feel at best uneasy about the prospect of his case being decided by a tribunal containing (or even chaired by) someone who is, and may for many years have been, in almost daily professional contact with the lawyer for the opposing side and where highly sensitive, confidential, and privileged material (including draft awards and notes and records of deliberations) pass through the same clerks' room. The fact of an arbitrator's being in the same chambers as counsel for one of the parties is thus regarded as a matter for disclosure by the working party that drafted the IBA Guidelines,[31] but not as a matter for automatic disqualification.[32]

4.28 It is not the position of the LCIA Court to regard a barrister's sitting as arbitrator (co-arbitrator or chairman) in a matter in which a member of his chambers appears as counsel for one of the parties as evidence of a lack of independence or impartiality, whatever the differing cultural backgrounds and expectations of the other party or parties. This attitude could be interpreted as effectively saying to parties that they are in England and must play by English rules and accept assurances as to independence that would not be accepted in their home jurisdictions. If that were to be a widely held perception, it would not help the LCIA's professed wish to be seen and accepted as a truly international institution. In practice, however, the LCIA Court is very sensitive to such issues. The Court's membership is very international,[33] and, while it will not regard membership of the same chambers, in and of itself, as being evidence of a lack of impartiality or independence, it will take pains not to appoint arbitrators from the same chambers. It should, of course, be noted that when arbitral appointments are made by the LCIA Court, the Court will very often not know whether a party will retain an English barrister as counsel, and so cannot take this into account in appointing the arbitrators.

4.29 Whatever the theoretical position as a matter of English law and practice, barristers' chambers are these days often held out to the public at large as a single entity. Chambers' practice managers or senior clerks take initiatives or even make marketing trips on behalf of chambers as a whole, not individual barristers. Chambers' websites resemble those of law firms, which are of course partnerships. It may be hard

---

from law firms and practise as full-time arbitrators while occupying space and sharing facilities (which are paid for) in their former firms', or others', premises.

[31] On the Orange List.

[32] Derains and Schwartz record that, as at 2005, the ICC Court had not removed an arbitrator on this ground (*Derains & Schwartz* 128 n 41), although in practice the ICC Court would regard it as a disqualification for a sole or presiding arbitrator.

[33] The current membership of the LCIA Court is set out at app 5.

in such circumstances to continue to claim that there is no justifiable fear on the part of a non-English party,[34] at least, about the impartiality or independence of a barrister-arbitrator who comes from the same chambers as counsel for one of the parties.

It is therefore often the case that an arbitrator (particularly a chairman of a tribunal but also co-arbitrators; there is no logical distinction to be drawn between a presiding and co-arbitrator for the purposes of conflicts of interest) will voluntarily resign or not take up an appointment if he or she learns that counsel for one of the parties is a member of the same chambers. **4.30**

Of course, if such a position were to become generally adopted, a way would have to be found to ensure that a party could not, after the appointment of the tribunal, seek to derail the arbitration by appointing as counsel a member of the same chambers as one of the arbitrators, and particularly the presiding arbitrator, with a view to triggering a resignation and thus delaying the proceedings. **4.31**

There is nothing in the LCIA Rules that could be used to take the opposite tack, and require counsel to step down, but it should perhaps be the institution's duty to look carefully at the circumstances before accepting an arbitrator's resignation, or refusing to confirm a nomination, as a result of a conflict thus created, to ensure that there is no real risk that the party concerned has made a tactical appointment of counsel with just that end in mind. **4.32**

Indeed, while this has not, to the authors' knowledge, been the subject of any academic debate, it might be argued that arbitral tribunals should consider themselves to have the inherent power to order parties not to retain a barrister from the same chambers as one of the arbitrators in the middle of the arbitral proceedings in circumstances where the barrister-arbitrator might feel himself compelled to step down.[35] The tribunal could feel that it should have the power to regulate those who appear before it in order to ensure the interests of justice, as a state court could. **4.33**

---

[34] 'English' and 'England' are used here as a shorthand, because of the close connection between the LCIA and the English jurisdiction, but of course the same principles apply to all jurisdictions that have split legal professions, including those that are officially fused but where a separate profession of barrister has retained an existence, such as certain jurisdictions in Australia.

[35] There is at least one such published decision in which the ICSID tribunal, faced with the discovery on the eve of the final hearing that one of the parties had, unbeknownst to the other party or the tribunal, retained as counsel a barrister from the same chambers as the president of the tribunal, required the party concerned to dispense with the barrister's services. This decision was, however, grounded on a specific provision of the ICSID Convention rather than on any inherent jurisdiction of the tribunal. (*Hrvatska Elektroprivreda, d.d. v The Republic of Slovenia*, ICSID Case No ARB/05/24, Tribunal's ruling regarding the participation of David Mildon QC in further stages of the proceedings, 6 May 2008, published on <http://ita.law.uvic.ca>.) Anecdotal soundings suggest that this is not an isolated case and that other tribunals have found that they have the power to remove counsel in appropriate circumstances.

Repeat appointments

4.34 Finally, a word about the potential problem of repeat appointments and the phenomenon of the same lawyers reversing the roles of arbitrator and counsel in two proceedings that are going on at the same time. The former issue is one that has been much commented on, but it is probably impossible to state a general rule about its effect on the perception of an arbitrator's independence. The IBA Guidelines treat two prior appointments by the same party (or affiliates) or three by the same counsel within the three years preceding the present nomination, as disclosable matters under the Orange List. The issue is whether the arbitrator is, in the words of one commentator, 'making a living' from repeat appointments.[36] Where to draw that line is not something that can be answered in a work of this nature (if at all).

4.35 As to the latter, given that it is an accepted and generally beneficial part of the practice of international arbitration that practitioners act both as counsel and as arbitrator (albeit that most tend to have a preponderance of one or the other in their individual practices), it is unavoidable that one can find oneself being addressed on one day by a lawyer before whom one will be arguing the next day. In and of itself, this does not seem to present any great risk, but there are exceptions (as the Dutch Court held in the *Ghana v Telekom Malaysia* case referred to above) and in the particular context of investment arbitration, where there is very heavy reliance on precedent, there is a legitimate concern that an arbitrator could be tempted to decide a matter in a way that would be helpful to his clients in other cases where he appears as counsel.

4.36 At the end of the day, though, parties are best advised to trust an arbitrator's integrity (as in the case of personal friendships between arbitrators and counsel) since that quality is the very attribute that the arbitrator will value the most if he wishes to be appointed again.

Article 5.3

Before appointment by the LCIA Court, each arbitrator shall furnish to the Registrar a written sum of his past and present professional positions; he shall agree in writing upon fee rates conforming to the Schedule of Costs; and he shall sign a declaration to the effect that there are no circumstances known to him likely to give rise to any justified doubts as to his impartiality or independence, other than any circumstances disclosed by him in the declaration. Each arbitrator shall thereby also assume a continuing duty forthwith to disclose any such circumstances to the LCIA Court, to any other members of the Arbitral Tribunal and to all the parties if such circumstances should arise after the date of such declaration and before the arbitration is concluded.

---

[36] Hunter (n 6 above) 222, n 12 ('An arbitrator who is in effect making a living from fees generated by repeated appointments from a particular party knows very well that he will not be appointed again if he concurs with the result which an aggrieved appointing party considers to be wrong').

Article 5.3 contains three important principles. First is the need for the nominee **4.37** to provide a declaration to the Registrar that he knows of no circumstances likely to give rise to justified doubts as to his impartiality or independence. The matters that should be disclosed have been discussed above in the context of Article 5.2.

The second is the need for the prospective arbitrator to state his fee rates for acting **4.38** as arbitrator in the case at hand. The issue of costs, and in particular the LCIA's use of hourly rates rather than the *ad valorem* fee scales used by such institutions as the ICC and the SCC Arbitration Institute, and how this affects the overall costs of a given arbitration, is discussed in chapter 8 below.

The third key principle in Article 5.3 is that the duty of disclosure of circum- **4.39** stances likely to give rise to justified doubts as to the arbitrator's impartiality or independence is a continuing one. The modern landscape of international arbitration, in which many arbitrators are members of large international law firms, means that such a duty of continuing disclosure (and thus continuing vigilance) assumes very great significance. This can be both burdensome (scanning the conflicts system for a matter taken on for, or a pitch made to, an affiliate of one of the parties to an arbitration, by one's partners in Moscow or Dubai) and can also raise difficulties for arbitrators who block the acceptance of potentially profitable transactional mandates for their corporate partners.

Many arbitrators who are partners of large law firms thus ask the parties to waive **4.40** potential conflicts in advance. It is the practice of the LCIA Court not to accept such 'advance' waivers, but rather to wait until a potential conflict arises and then deal with it on a case-by-case basis. Even where this is not done, however, parties will often take a pragmatic view of an arbitrator's firm taking on a completely unrelated matter for one of the parties (or an affiliated company) if the arbitration is at an advanced stage, if only to avoid unnecessary disruption. This may also be the case where a conflict is created by the fact of an arbitrator's joining a new firm, which already acts for one of the parties. It seems clear in both these cases, how- ever, that the LCIA Court would have to allow a challenge to an arbitrator if the parties were not prepared to waive the conflict thus arising.

The extent of required disclosure is (as can be seen from the debate as to the appli- **4.41** cable standards of impartiality and independence discussed in the context of Article 5.2 above) far from being settled. The well-known English case of *AT&T Corp v Saudi Cable*[37] shows how far a seemingly trivial mistake in overlooking the disclosure of a matter that a party can seize on can lead.

---

[37] *AT&T Corp and Anor v Saudi Cable Co* [2000] 1 All ER 201 (Comm) (Court of Appeal). In this well-known case, the English Court of Appeal defined 'independence' (in that case, in the context of the ICC Rules) as 'an absence of connection with either of the parties in the sense of an

Article 5.4

The LCIA Court shall appoint the Arbitral Tribunal as soon as practicable after receipt by the Registrar of the Response or after the expiry of 30 days following service of the Request upon the Respondent if no Response is received by the Registrar (or such lesser period fixed by the LCIA Court). The LCIA Court may proceed with the formation of the Arbitral Tribunal notwithstanding that the Request is incomplete or the Response is missing, late or incomplete. A sole arbitrator shall be appointed unless the parties have agreed in writing otherwise, or unless the LCIA Court determines that in view of all the circumstances of the case a three-member tribunal is appropriate.

4.42   Article 5.4 imposes a duty on the LCIA Court to appoint the tribunal as soon as practicable after either (a) the respondent's Response (and nomination, if any, of an arbitrator) is received by the Registrar or (b), if no Response is received, after the normal time limit (or any lesser time limit filed by the LCIA Court) for its being filed has expired. The Rules therefore try, by imposing a kind of discipline on the Court itself (albeit without an enforceable deadline), to respond to the parties' wish for the procedure to be under way as quickly as possible. As noted in chapter 1 above, in the Softwood Lumber Agreement the US and Canadian governments require the LCIA Court to use its best endeavours to appoint the tribunal as soon as all of its members have been nominated and the tribunal agrees to render an award within 180 days of its appointment.

4.43   As discussed in chapter 3 above, filing a Response is not mandatory, and the Rules thus need to make provision for the possibility that a respondent may not file one (whether for tactical considerations, through inadvertence, or from a wish to seek to delay the proceedings, as respondents are sometimes wont to do). It is important to note, however, that the power of the LCIA Court to appoint the tribunal notwithstanding the failure of the respondent to file a proper timely Response is permissive only. The Court *may* constitute the tribunal despite the respondent's failure, but it does not have to. In practice, in the event that a respondent nominates an arbitrator out of time, if the Court has not by then appointed the tribunal, its nomination will be taken into account. It will not necessarily be acted upon, but it will not be ignored completely. This is also the subject of Article 7.2, as discussed below.

4.44   Again conscious of the parties' assumed wish to have a speedy and cost-effective proceeding, Article 5.4 provides that the default position of the Court in appointing a tribunal shall be for a sole arbitrator, unless either (a) the parties (as they very often do) have specified a three-member tribunal or (b) the Court considers that a three-member tribunal is appropriate. This discretion is exercised on the basis of

---

absence of interest in, or of any present or prospective business or other connection with, one of the parties, which might lead the arbitrator to favour the party concerned'.

a number of factors, among them the complexity of the case, the amounts at stake (although there is no threshold figure above which a three-member tribunal is invariably appointed), the need for particular linguistic or other skills, where these cannot all be found in one person, and where the Court feels that there are circumstances, such as cultural sensitivities, that demand a balanced tribunal. It is also worth noting that this Article, which provides only for a sole arbitrator or a three-member tribunal, while being standard to all major institutional and *ad hoc* rules, also tracks the English Arbitration Act 1996, which allows only those compositions for tribunals having their seat in England and Wales or Northern Ireland.

4.45 This provision is also notable for the first reference to the fact that it is the LCIA Court, not the parties, that 'appoints' the tribunal, as spelled out with more clarity in Article 5.5.

Article 5.5

The LCIA Court alone is empowered to appoint arbitrators. The LCIA Court will appoint arbitrators with due regard for any particular method or criteria of selection agreed in writing by the parties. In selecting arbitrators consideration will be given to the nature of the transaction, the nature and circumstances of the dispute, the nationality, location and languages of the parties and (if more than two) the number of parties.

4.46 This Article therefore confirms explicitly what was implicit in the preceding Article, namely that the LCIA Court alone is empowered to appoint arbitrators. If the parties have agreed that each shall nominate an arbitrator, therefore, such nomination is to be understood as being subject to the ultimate power of the LCIA Court to appoint.

4.47 While the LCIA has, in all cases, the role of making the final appointment of an arbitrator, it will always take party nominations into account and will usually appoint the party nominee. The reference to 'any particular method or criteria of selection' that may have been agreed by the parties is an acknowledgement that the Court will, as it does in almost all cases, appoint the parties' nominees. This is discussed more fully in the context of Article 7.1 below.

4.48 The remainder of this Article contains a non-exhaustive list of the criteria that the LCIA Court will bear in mind in appointing arbitrators. Thus, the Court may decide (at least in the absence of a party nomination) to appoint an engineer to a construction dispute, for example (or at least a lawyer who has experience of such disputes), or an arbitrator having an adequate knowledge of a relevant language, or a familiarity with the governing law of the contract out of which the dispute has arisen. The Court will also consider the location of the parties, although it is submitted that this has little to do with the suitability of the arbitrators to be appointed (whereas, on the contrary, the seat of the arbitration, and the desire to limit travelling expenses, might be of some relevance). The reference to the number of parties is intriguing in this context, since it is not immediately apparent how this would affect the qualifications or qualities of the arbitrator to be appointed. In any event, the issue of the constitution of the arbitral tribunal in cases involving multiple parties is discussed in the context of Article 8 below.

Article 5.6

In the case of a three-member Arbitral Tribunal, the chairman (who will not be a party-nominated arbitrator) shall be appointed by the LCIA Court.

4.49 This provision is very simple, which has not stopped it from being misunderstood. Since the principle that all arbitrators will be appointed by the Court has already been explicitly set out in Article 5.5, the only operative phrase in Article 5.6 is that in brackets, which does no more (and no less) than confirm that the parties cannot agree that one of them is to nominate the chairman of a three-member tribunal. It does not mean that the parties cannot agree that they will jointly nominate a chairman (who is in any event subject to appointment by the LCIA Court) or that they cannot agree that the two party-nominated arbitrators cannot nominate the chairman. Article 5.6 therefore only forbids one of the party-nominated arbitrators from being named as chairman by the Court (or the parties agreeing that the chairman should be nominated by only one of the parties). The LCIA Court, of course, retains the absolute right of appointment in all cases.

B. Article 6 – Nationality of Arbitrators

4.50 It is axiomatic that for international arbitration to be seen to be a neutral forum, the sole or presiding arbitrator should not (save by express agreement of the parties) have the nationality of either (or any) of them. There is of course no rule preventing a party from nominating an arbitrator of his own nationality, and this is (as mentioned above) very often done, to ensure that one member at least of the tribunal understands the cultural and legal traditions of the party concerned.

4.51 Article 6 sets out how the LCIA Court is to address this critical issue.

Article 6.1

Where the parties are of different nationalities, a sole arbitrator or chairman of the Arbitral Tribunal shall not have the same nationality as any party unless the parties who are not of the same nationality as the proposed appointee all agree in writing otherwise.

Article 6.1 establishes the principle set out above. Unless the parties agree **4.52** otherwise, the LCIA Court will not appoint a sole arbitrator or chairman of the nationality of one of the parties where the parties are not of the same nationality themselves.

The question of how 'nationality' is to be defined for this purpose is obviously **4.53** key in deciding whether an arbitrator falls foul of this principle. In applying Article 6.1, the LCIA Court has to consider the nationality of the parties and the arbitrator(s). In the case of the parties, they may be either legal or natural persons. The LCIA Court's reasoning in the matter of legal persons is discussed below. As to natural persons, whether parties or potential or actual arbitrators, this can be a tricky question.

A country's nationality laws may be far-reaching (for example, a citizen of a given **4.54** country may transmit citizenship to his or her offspring, who can do likewise, without subsequent generations having any real contact with the country of citizenship) or may treat all descendants in the male line as bearing a given country's nationality, whether they like it or not. Together with issues of 'dominant' or 'effective' nationality, this has been the subject of much debate in investment-treaty arbitration and other arbitrations under international law.[38]

Operation in practice

There have to date been three challenges under Article 10.4 (discussed below) to **4.55** an arbitrator based upon an alleged infringement of nationality requirements. These were not under Article 6.1, but the reasoning in them is applicable to the decision that the LCIA Court needs to take when considering the provisions of Article 6.1 in making an appointment of a sole or presiding arbitrator.

In the first such case, in 1998, an argument was raised that, while the challenged **4.56** arbitrator was not a British citizen *de jure*, his links with the United Kingdom were such that he should be regarded as a British citizen *de facto* and should thus be removed since one of the parties was British. As the arbitrator in question was in fact a party-nominated arbitrator (nominated by the claimant, which was of UK nationality), this should not in any event have been a disqualifying circumstance, but it was argued on the basis of non-disclosure of a relevant fact under Article 5.3. The division of the Court rejected the challenge. While it held that an enquiry into an arbitrator's nationality should be 'substantive and not merely formal' and said that a person's links to a given country may be such that that person's holding another nationality does not ensure neutrality, it rejected the allegation of *de facto*

---

[38] See, eg, P Turner, 'Treaties as Agreements to Arbitrate: Parties, Ownership and Control' *ICCA Congress Series No 13* (Kluwer, 2007) 444.

British nationality on the facts. The division's decision could, however, pave the way to challenges based on the meaning of 'dominant' or 'effective' nationality as in investment-treaty arbitration.

4.57   In two further decisions, in 1999 and 2005 respectively, the divisions of the Court held, in the first case, in which the LCIA acted as the appointing authority in a case proceeding under the UNCITRAL Rules, that a sole arbitrator's sharing the nationality of a party's counsel did not justify removal, while in the second it was found that, where the parties' agreement required that the sole arbitrator be neither British nor live in England, a door tenancy in barristers' chambers did not constitute residence.

4.58   As to legal persons, and subject to Article 6.2, discussed below, the practice of the LCIA Court is to regard the 'nationality' of a legal person as its place of incorporation.

Citizens of dependent territories

4.59   One question that arises (perhaps more for the LCIA than other arbitration institutions, so closely connected as it is to a former imperial power) is how to treat parties from colonies or dependent territories.

4.60   The current practice of the LCIA Court is to avoid appointing citizens of the mother country in arbitrations where there is a party from a dependent territory. The Court has not taken a definitive position as to whether citizenship of the mother country should be assimilated with that of dependent territories for the purposes of deciding nationality under Article 6.1, but (at least at present) it errs on the side of caution by avoiding appointments that could give rise to challenges on this ground. Thus, a person holding British nationality would not (without the consent of both parties) be appointed as sole arbitrator or chairman of a three-member tribunal in a case involving parties from British dependent territories. Since about 140[39] of the 701 cases that had been started under the 1998 version of the Rules up to the end of 2007 involve parties from territories that can be said to be 'dependent' on the United Kingdom,[40] the exclusion of British citizens represents a significant constraint on the available pool of arbitrators that the LCIA regularly calls upon.

---

[39] Including cases where the controlling shareholder of a party comes from such a territory: art 6.2.

[40] The territories so considered for the purposes of this book are: Bermuda; the British Virgin Islands; the Cayman Islands; Gibraltar; Guernsey; the Isle of Man; and Jersey. The last three are known as 'Crown dependencies', whereas the rest are 'British Overseas Territories'.

This is not the place for an in-depth study of British nationality law (which even **4.61** after some recent reforms has a rather confusing number of sub-categories of British nationality and accompanying anomalies) but it does not seem right that a company from the British Virgin Islands (by a long way the most popular of the British Overseas Territories as a nationality of origin for LCIA parties) should be treated as 'British' for the application of Article 6.1. Such a company is neither subject to English law nor the jurisdiction of the English Court, and the fact that its territory of incorporation is one that is still dependent on the United Kingdom (while being internally self-governing) does not, at least at first sight, appear to be a relevant consideration in a choice of sole or presiding arbitrator.

Of course, this seemingly anomalous policy may actually be an advantage, given **4.62** that to adhere to a self-denying ordinance not to appoint British nationals will in practice mean that the LCIA is forced to look further afield than its traditional English arbitrator base.[41]

Article 6.2

The nationality of parties shall be understood to include that of controlling shareholders or interests.

The LCIA Rules acknowledge in this provision that the country of incorporation **4.63** of a company need not necessarily represent the country with which it has its closest or most real connection. As with 'dominant' or 'effective' nationality for natural persons, the 'real' nationality of a company is the subject of much debate in investment-treaty law.[42] The nationality of a large quoted company is taken to be the place of incorporation: its shareholder base is both too large and too diverse to allow any other consideration. But the position will be different when a party is a shell company or a special purpose vehicle incorporated in a given jurisdiction not because of any fundamental links with that jurisdiction but for tax or other reasons.

A rule like that contained in Article 6.2 could, if not operated sensibly, impose **4.64** a considerable, indeed impossible, burden on the institution. It is for that reason that the LCIA, in regarding the nationality of a corporate party as that of its controlling shareholders, does not undertake to research such interests. It is only if it is clear from the face of the Request or Response that the controlling share-holders come from elsewhere that the LCIA Court will take this into account in applying Article 6. In cases where such nationality does not appear on the face of

---

[41] As noted in ch 1 above, British nationals (including dual nationals) were appointed by the LCIA Court (including following party or party-nominated arbitrator nominations) as sole or presiding arbitrators in just over half of the 701 fully administered cases under the 1998 Rules started up to the end of 2007.
[42] Turner (n 38 above) 448–64.

the Request or Response, it is for the parties to make representations about the nationality of the chairman or sole arbitrator on the basis of their own research.

4.65 As noted above, many parties to LCIA arbitrations come from so-called 'offshore' jurisdictions. Since the overwhelming majority of such offshore companies are controlled from somewhere else, rather than the other way around, Article 6.2 will sometimes need to be applied. Thus, for example, a Russian national could not be appointed as the sole or presiding arbitrator in a case involving a company incorporated in the Cayman Islands or the Isle of Man the majority shareholders of which were themselves Russian.

4.66 This does not, however, ameliorate the operation of the practice of the LCIA Court with regard to dependent territories. Article 6.2 does not exclude consideration of the formal nationality of a legal person: it just adds the nationality of its controlling shareholders as a further consideration for the Court to take into account. Thus, in the case referred to in the preceding paragraph of a Cayman Islands-incorporated company with Russian controlling shareholders, the LCIA Court would not, as a result of the operation of both Article 6.1 and Article 6.2, be able to appoint as chairman either a Russian or British citizen.

Article 6.3

For the purpose of this Article, a person who is a citizen of two or more states shall be treated as a national of each state; and citizens of the European Union shall be treated as nationals of its different Member States and shall not be treated as having the same nationality.

4.67 The first part of this Article covers the issue of double or multiple nationalities held by a potential arbitrator. The existence of this simple rule means that the LCIA Court does not have to decide questions of dominant or effective nationality. It leaves open, however, at least in theory, the possibility of having to decide whether a given potential arbitrator who is deemed by a state to hold its nationality under an exorbitant nationality law actually does so. So far as the authors are aware, this has not arisen in practice.

4.68 Article 6.3 also confirms that, despite the fact that all citizens of member states of the European Union are deemed to hold 'European Union' nationality as well as that of the member state in question,[43] this is not to be taken into account for the purposes of deciding the nationality of potential arbitrators in an LCIA arbitration. To do otherwise would, of course, render the selection of arbitrators in matters involving parties from the European Union quite unworkable.

---

[43] Art 17(1) EC Treaty (Rome, 25 February 1957) [1997] OJ C350/173 as amended by the Treaty on European Union (Maastricht, 17 February 1992) [1997] OJ C340/145.

C. Article 7 – Party and Other Nominations

While the LCIA Rules provide a default mechanism for the appointment of **4.69** arbitrators, they also (in common with all major institutional rules) allow the parties to make nominations for co-arbitrators in a three-member tribunal. As noted above, any such nominations are subject to confirmation by the LCIA Court, which alone has the power to make arbitral appointments, as stated expressly in Article 5.5.

Article 7.1

If the parties have agreed that any arbitrator is to be appointed by one or more of them or by any third person, that agreement shall be treated as an agreement to nominate an arbitrator for all purposes. Such nominee may only be appointed by the LCIA Court as arbitrator subject to his prior compliance with Article 5.3. The LCIA Court may refuse to appoint any such nominee if it determines that he is not suitable or independent or impartial.

The first sentence of Article 7.1 confirms the point made above, namely that an **4.70** agreement by the parties that they shall 'appoint' an arbitrator (or that a third party shall do so) is taken as a reference to 'nomination'. As to the reference to nominations by a third person, this can give rise to difficulties. First, there can be a delay while the third person is asked to make the nomination. Second, if the third person is an institution, it will usually charge a fee for making the nomination. Third, an institution can misunderstand that it is only being asked to nominate, and not appoint, an arbitrator, and that such nominations are still subject to confirmation by the Court, which makes all appointments. This can lead (and in practice has led) to confusion and yet further delay.

The rest of Article 7.1 confirms that party-nominated arbitrators, as well as those **4.71** appointed directly by the Court, must comply with all the requirements of Article 5.3 and must (as required by Article 5.2) be independent and impartial.

There is an interesting addition in Article 7.1, however, that does not appear any- **4.72** where in Article 5. That is the requirement that, in order for him to be appointed by the Court, it must determine that he is 'suitable'. This seems to mean only that he must fulfil any criteria that the parties' agreement may stipulate that an arbitrator may have (such as language ability, as to which see below), rather than that the LCIA Court can itself decide that in, say, a telecommunications-related dispute, only a person with relevant professional qualifications may be appointed to the tribunal. The parties' freedom of choice is thus not, as at first blush it may seem, restricted.

The LCIA Court has in fact only refused to appoint a party-nominated arbitrator **4.73** on the grounds of suitability on three occasions. In one, the Court was aware that the person nominated could not work in French, which was a requirement of the arbitration clause. In another, the nominee (interestingly, a joint nomination as sole arbitrator by both parties) was not a lawyer and had no prior arbitration experience. The Court decided that this would put in jeopardy the chances of his rendering an enforceable award, as required by Article 32, and thus refused to appoint the parties' nominee. In the third, the nominee of a party actually sat on the board of the nominating company and was unsurprisingly therefore held to lack independence.[44]

Article 7.2

Where the parties have howsoever agreed that the Respondent or any third person is to nominate an arbitrator and such nomination is not made within time or at all, the LCIA Court may appoint an arbitrator notwithstanding the absence of the nomination and without regard to any late nomination. Likewise, if the Request for Arbitration does not contain a nomination by the Claimant where the parties have howsoever agreed that the Claimant or a third person is to nominate an arbitrator, the LCIA Court may appoint an arbitrator notwithstanding the absence of the nomination and without regard to any late nomination.

4.74 This provision addresses the situation where a party (or a third party on whom the task of nominating an arbitrator has been conferred by the parties to the contract) fails to make a nomination in time. It gives the LCIA Court the power, but not the obligation, to make an appointment notwithstanding a late nomination. In other words, the LCIA Court is neither bound to take a late nomination into account, nor to ignore it. It may (and does) use its discretion. In practice, where a nomination is made out of time but before the LCIA Court has made an appointment in default, the parties' nominations are respected where possible.

D. Article 8 – Three or More Parties

4.75 In the absence of a provision enabling the institution to appoint all of the members of a three-member tribunal, where there are multiple claimants (or respondents) but only one respondent (or claimant), they will not all be able to nominate an arbitrator (given that the Rules only allow a sole arbitrator or a three-member tribunal and only one such can be nominated by the claimant or respondent respectively).[45]

4.76 This is the situation that pertained before the 1998 revision of the Rules. It gives rise to the situation where one party (the single claimant or respondent, as the case

---

[44] The criterion for establishing independence is discussed under art 5.2 above.
[45] See art 5.4.

may be) can nominate an arbitrator, but the multiple claimants or respondents (as the case may be) cannot. It should of course be noted that, in practice, multiple claimants who have filed one Request for Arbitration almost always act as one party; the problem described above therefore almost invariably arises in the case of multiple respondents who do not consider themselves to share the same interests.

As noted at the beginning of this chapter, the *Dutco* jurisprudence (albeit in the **4.77** context of an arbitration under the ICC Rules) determined that, theoretically only as a matter of French arbitration law, the equality of the parties in nominating arbitrators was a matter of public policy that could not be waived after the dispute had arisen.

Although, strictly speaking, this is only a matter that concerned arbitrations **4.78** (ICC or otherwise) with their seat in France, most major arbitration institutions made changes in the next version of their rules to enable the institution to appoint all members of a three-member tribunal in cases where multiple parties could not agree on joint nominations.

In the LCIA Rules, this issue is addressed by Article 8 (which had no equivalent in **4.79** the 1985 Rules, which were of course promulgated before *Dutco*, and (less understandably) did not feature in the 1996 draft revision of the rules as set out in the LCIA's Newsletter for October 1996, which appeared after *Dutco*).[46]

Article 8.1

Where the Arbitration Agreement entitles each party howsoever to nominate an arbitrator, the parties to the dispute number more than two and such parties have not all agreed in writing that the disputant parties represent two separate sides for the formation of the Arbitral Tribunal as Claimant and Respondent respectively, the LCIA Court shall appoint the Arbitral Tribunal without regard to any party's nomination.

The first point to note about Article 8 is that it only applies where the parties have **4.80** agreed that each shall have the right to nominate ('howsoever', whatever that is taken to mean[47]) an arbitrator.

The LCIA Court is thereby mandated to appoint the whole tribunal without **4.81** regard to any party's nomination if multiple claimants and/or respondents do not agree to make a single nomination as claimant or respondent respectively. They can of course so agree (and in most cases, in a well-drafted arbitration clause,

---

[46] *Commentary* 10.
[47] There is an interesting discussion of this in A Diamond, 'Procedure and Hearings' in A Berkeley and J Mimms (eds), *International Commercial Arbitration: Practical Perspectives* (Centre of Construction Law & Management, 2001) 49, 50–1.

one would certainly expect the members of, say, an oil consortium in a Production Sharing Agreement so to do). In the case of such an agreement, Article 8 finds no application.

4.82 The provision is silent as to what should happen if, despite such an agreement in writing, the parties to it in practice find themselves unable to agree. In that case, there would not be a nomination, and the LCIA Court would appoint under Article 7.2 (which applies in the case of single or multiple parties). The other party would then be free to make a nomination, since the conditions for the application of Article 8 are not present: there *is* an agreement in writing that the multiple claimants or respondents nominate an arbitrator together, but they do not apply it.

4.83 It is interesting to note that the equivalent provision in the post-*Dutco* ICC Rules, Article 10, does not contain this seeming ambiguity. Furthermore, under Article 10(2) of the ICC Rules, if the parties have not made a joint nomination and if they are otherwise unable to agree on the formation of the tribunal, the ICC Court *may* appoint all members of the tribunal, but need not, depending on its assessment of the needs of the situation.[48]

4.84 Our research has shown that, since the 1998 Rules came into effect, the Court has appointed all three members of the tribunal under Article 8.1 in 84 cases (out of 201 cases involving multiple parties). In practice, before making such appointments, the Registrar will always enquire of multiple parties whether they are prepared to nominate a single arbitrator for their respective side.

Article 8.2

In such circumstances, the Arbitration Agreement shall be treated for all purposes as a written agreement by the parties for the appointment of the Arbitral Tribunal by the LCIA Court.

4.85 As parties could argue that the application of Article 8 deprived them of the right set out in the arbitration agreement to nominate arbitrators, Article 8.2 is important in that it removes any argument that the parties might raise as to the appointment by the LCIA Court's not being in accordance with their agreement.

E. Article 9 – Expedited Formation

4.86 Article 9 is one of the most distinctive features of the LCIA Rules. One of the most-criticized aspects of international arbitration is its initial slowness. It can sometimes take literally months for a tribunal to be constituted. Urgent applications

---

[48] For a detailed discussion of the position under the ICC Rules, see *Derains & Schwartz* 183–84.

for interim measures therefore have to be made to national courts. This (while essential to support arbitration) can very often be second-best compared to an application to the arbitral tribunal that will hear the dispute. For one thing, some national courts are less well-disposed than others to order interim and conservatory measures. For another, the appropriate national court might be one in which the party wishing to bring the application feels at a disadvantage compared to the other party. Thus, any procedure that enables interim and conservatory measures to be applied for more easily to an arbitral tribunal is welcome. The Article 9 procedure has been described as 'elegant and user-friendly' by commentators.[49]

There is no strictly analogous provision in other sets of institutional rules. The **4.87** ICC has promulgated a Pre-Arbitral Referee Procedure, but the parties need to agree on its use. It takes some prescience to agree to it in the initial, pre-dispute arbitration clause and it takes little imagination to see that a party that wishes to seek urgent interim measures of protection will be unlikely to wish to discuss a submission to the Pre-Arbitral Referee Procedure with the potential respondent after the dispute has arisen. In consequence, it has only been used rarely.[50]

The NAI Rules and the ICDR Rules both allow the appointment of a sole **4.88** arbitrator (called the emergency arbitrator in the ICDR's Article 37 procedure) on application of a claimant (before the arbitration proper has been commenced) to hear an urgent application for interim measures.[51] As to the NAI Rules, the procedure can only be used if the seat of the arbitration is in The Netherlands. The ICDR procedure is more akin to the LCIA's Article 9, which applies to any arbitration, wherever the seat may be, subject, of course, to the arbitration law of the seat allowing such applications. Both the NAI and ICDR procedures differ from the LCIA's Article 9 procedure in two further ways. First, the sole or emergency arbitrator thus appointed will not hear the merits, referring the case to a full tribunal constituted in accordance with the parties' agreement once the application has been dealt with. Second, both procedures apply only to applications for the granting of interim and conservatory measures, whereas the procedure under Article 9 of the LCIA Rules can be and is used to ask for the expedited formation of a tribunal for other reasons.

WIPO adopts yet another procedure. Parties may opt for its Expedited **4.89** Arbitration Rules, which allow for the whole procedure to be completed quickly,

---

[49] V Triebel and R Hunter, 'Kommentar LCIA-Schiedsregeln' in R Schütze (ed), *Institutionelle Schiedsgerichtsbarkeit* (Carl Heymanns Verlag, 2006) 381.

[50] For a discussion of the ICC Pre-Arbitral Referee Procedure in action, see, eg, E Gaillard and P Pinsolle, 'The ICC Pre-Arbitral Referee: First Practical Experiences' (2004) 20 Arb Int 1; M Kantor, 'The ICC Pre-Arbitral Referee Procedure: Momentum for Expanded Use' (2005) 20(9) Mealey's Int Arb Rep 3; C Lécuyer-Thieffry, 'First Court Ruling on the ICC Pre-Arbitral Referee Procedure' (2003) 20 J Int Arb 599; and P Tercier, 'Le référé pré-arbitral' [2004] ASA Bull 464.

[51] Arts 42a – 42o NAI Arbitration Rules and Article 37 ICDR International Arbitration Rules.

as their name suggests. As with the ICC Pre-Arbitral Referee Procedure, the parties have to agree to the use of the WIPO Expedited Arbitration Rules, with the drawbacks referred to above. Furthermore, again as with the ICC Pre-Arbitral Referee Procedure, the WIPO Expedited Arbitration Rules only foresee the appointment of a sole arbitrator. Unlike the ICC Pre-Arbitral Referee Procedure, however, the sole arbitrator thus appointed hears the merits of the dispute.

4.90 Finally, the ICSID Rules, by Rule 39(5), allow a party to make a request for provisional measures before the constitution of the tribunal, which is then briefed according to a timetable set by the Secretary-General of ICSID, so that the tribunal can consider it immediately upon its formation.

4.91 The LCIA Rules are the only institutional rules that allow the expedited formation of the tribunal that will hear the case on the merits that can also hear an urgent application for interim measures. They thus provide the continuity that the otherwise similar procedure under Article 37 of the ICDR Rules, for example, lacks, which provides that the full tribunal (on which the emergency arbitrator may not sit) can 'reconsider, modify or vacate' any decision of the emergency arbitrator.

4.92 The power of the tribunal to order interim and conservatory measures of protection is contained in Article 25 of the Rules, discussed below. One of the major purposes of Article 9 is to enable the parties to have a tribunal formed extremely quickly so that such an application can be made with the utmost dispatch. It should be noted, however, that Article 9 is not restricted to use in cases where the claimant seeks interim measures of protection; it could be the case that an expedited decision on the merits is needed, necessitating the quick formation of the tribunal. In such cases, too, the LCIA Court has power under Article 9 to appoint the tribunal in an expedited fashion.

4.93 Since the 1998 Rules came into force, and up to the end of 2007, Article 9 has been invoked by claimants some 41 times, in slightly under half of which an application for interim measures under Article 25 was the motivating factor. Of these 41 applications under Article 9, the application for the expedited formation of the tribunal has been granted in 25 cases. In one of those cases, the tribunal was appointed only one day after the making of the application to the LCIA Court, and in many cases in less than a week. (There were some cases where the Article 9 application was indeed granted by the LCIA Court but where it nonetheless took a month or more to constitute the tribunal.)

4.94 The Article 9 procedure (as is further discussed below) does not allow for unopposed, or *ex parte*, applications.[52] The LCIA Court will give the respondent the opportunity to respond to the Article 9 application before deciding whether

---

[52] Nor do the NAI Rules, the ICDR Rules, or the ICC Pre-Arbitral Referee procedure.

to grant it, and the tribunal once constituted will then hear both parties on any application for interim measures.

This is in contrast to the draft revised rules published in 1996. Article 4 of that **4.95** proposal allowed for the LCIA Court itself to make a 'Provisional Order' for interim relief that would otherwise be within the powers of the arbitral tribunal itself to make. The application could be made *ex parte* and would be heard by a person named by the President of the Court, called the Delegate for Provisional Measures. This proposal was not taken forward.[53]

Article 9.1

In exceptional urgency, on or after the commencement of the arbitration, any party may apply to the LCIA Court for the expedited formation of the Arbitral Tribunal, including the appointment of any replacement arbitrator under Articles 10 and 11 of these Rules.

The key phrase in Article 9.1 is 'in exceptional urgency'. The LCIA Court will **4.96** need to be *prima facie* persuaded by the claimant that the case is indeed one of 'exceptional urgency' in order to accede to the application under Article 9, and the record of the Court's decisions in such applications shows that it rejects those that it does not consider to be urgent enough.

It is to be noted that the claimant does not have to make the application under **4.97** Article 9.1 when it starts the arbitration; it may be that circumstances change after the start of the proceedings and that the application is justified even if made later although, of course, before the tribunal has been constituted in the ordinary course. Thus, the LCIA Court has refused applications under Article 9 where the time for filing the Response has already passed or is imminent (in one such case, the Response was due three days after the claimant's application under Article 9). As Article 5.4 enjoins the Court to appoint the tribunal 'as soon as practicable' after the Response is filed, there would, in such circumstances, be no room for the application of Article 9.

Article 9.2

Such an application shall be made in writing to the LCIA Court, copied to all other parties to the arbitration: and it shall set out the specific grounds for exceptional urgency in the formation of the Arbitral Tribunal.

The application is to be made to the LCIA Court, which decides in the manner **4.98** discussed in chapter 2 above. The application is not, as noted above, *ex parte*, and copies have to be sent to all parties to the arbitration. The respondent thus has the

---

[53] *Commentary* 14.

opportunity to respond. The possibility of *ex parte* applications to arbitral tribunals is of course one that has generated much controversy. This issue is discussed more fully in chapter 6 below in the context of applications for interim and conservatory measures under Article 25. In any event, the fact that an Article 9 application under the LCIA Rules is on notice to the respondent might make it unattractive to claimants where the application for interim measures needs to be made without giving the respondent the chance to do the mischief that the claimant seeks to restrain.

4.99 On this note, it is interesting that the LCIA Court has granted applications under Article 9 made with the intention of asking the tribunal, once constituted, for interim relief under Article 25 to restrain a respondent from dealing with his assets on the grounds that they might be dissipated and thus defeat the enforcement of any award in favour of the claimant. It is thus clear that the Court does not consider that the fact that the respondent is on notice of the claimant's potential application, and thus has the opportunity, if he is so minded, to dissipate his assets before the application is heard by the arbitral tribunal, *ipso facto* renders any such decision moot. It is of course for this very reason, namely that a respondent liable to dissipate assets in order to defeat an award will do so on receiving notice of an application to stop him from doing so, that most claimants will be well-advised to make such applications to national courts and not to an arbitral tribunal.

4.100 The Article 9 procedure can nonetheless be extremely effective, even in this context. In one particular case in 2005 in which an asset-freezing order was to be sought by the claimant, the application under Article 9 was made on 12 January, the LCIA Court granted the application on 14 January, the tribunal was formed on 17 January, the hearing of the Article 25 application was held on 21 January and the asset-freezing order (and other interim and conservatory measures also applied for) were made the same day. Thus, within nine days of starting the arbitration, the claimant had a tribunal in place and had had its interim and conservatory measures granted. This is the kind of example that (even had there been no other cases under Article 9) would alone justify its inclusion in the Rules. It makes one wonder why other institutions have not thought along similar lines.

4.101 As to the Court's understanding of 'exceptional urgency', in one case in 2006, the claimants applied for the expedited formation of the tribunal (but not at that stage for interim measures of protection under Article 25) on the grounds that a resolution was needed quickly as the respondent was engaging in unfair competition. The Court decided that any damage to the claimants could be compensated in money terms and, thus, that the 'exceptional urgency' required by Article 9.1 had not been shown.

4.102 In another case, in 2007, however, the Court granted an application for the expedited formation of the tribunal where it believed that state court proceedings brought by the respondent (who challenged the jurisdiction of the arbitral tribunal) could render the arbitration proceedings moot.

Equally, in a case in 2005, the LCIA Court held that an application under **4.103** Article 9 based on the claimant's precarious financial position and asking for the expedited formation of the tribunal to enable it to obtain an award quickly was not the kind of matter that Article 9 was intended to address.

Reasoned decisions are given and communicated to the parties, but there is of **4.104** course no recourse against the decision (which is not an award and cannot therefore be challenged by way of an application to set aside in a state court).

Article 9.3

The LCIA Court may, in its complete discretion, abridge or curtail any time-limit under these Rules for the formation of the Arbitral Tribunal, including service of the Response and of any matters or documents adjudged to be missing from the Request. The LCIA Court shall not be entitled to abridge or curtail any other time-limit.

It makes sense that, when granting a request for the expedited formation of **4.105** the tribunal under Article 9, the LCIA Court should have the power to order the respondent to file its Response more quickly than otherwise allowed for by the Rules, so that the tribunal, once constituted, has all relevant matters before it.

Nonetheless, there have been cases in which the LCIA Court has decided to proceed with the expedited appointment of a tribunal but not abridge the time for **4.106** the Respondent's Response. It is hard to see what this achieves, but no doubt the tribunal, once formed, would be able to set a procedural timetable that reflected the urgency implicit in the Court's having granted the request under Article 9.

The LCIA Court can also ask the claimant to supplement its application under **4.107** Article 9 (and has done so). It can furthermore direct the claimant to answer matters raised by the respondent in its response to the Article 9 application before deciding on it (although if much time is taken up with such submissions it may indicate a lack of the 'exceptional urgency' that is the foundation of the Court's jurisdiction under Article 9 in the first place).

The LCIA Court cannot abridge any other time limits; that is a matter for the **4.108** arbitral tribunal under Article 4.7, as discussed above in chapter 3.

F. Article 10 – Revocation of Arbitrator's Appointment

Article 10 deals with an arbitrator's removal by the LCIA Court, whether by **4.109** acceptance of his resignation or incapacity, exercise of its discretionary power, or on the challenge of a party to the arbitration.

4.110   It sets out the circumstances that allow removal of an arbitrator; Article 11 then deals with the replacement of an arbitrator thus removed.

Article 10.1

If either (a) any arbitrator gives written notice of his desire to resign as arbitrator to the LCIA Court, to be copied to the parties and the other arbitrators (if any) or (b) any arbitrator dies, falls seriously ill, refuses, or becomes unable or unfit to act, either upon challenge by a party or at the request of the remaining arbitrators, the LCIA Court may revoke that arbitrator's appointment and appoint another arbitrator. The LCIA Court shall decide upon the amount of fees and expenses to be paid for the former arbitrator's services (if any) as it may consider appropriate in all the circumstances.

4.111   Article 10.1 provides that the LCIA Court may revoke an arbitrator's appointment in circumstances of an arbitrator's desire to resign or his death or incapacity or refusal to continue to fulfil his functions. The Court may, in the latter-named cases of unfitness or refusal to act, take action at the request of a party or the other arbitrators, if it is a three-member tribunal.

4.112   The Court's power to revoke an appointment under Article 10.1 is permissive rather than mandatory, since, among other reasons, Article 12 (discussed below) allows for truncated tribunals. One other reason why the Court is not obliged by the Rules to revoke the appointment of an arbitrator who wishes to resign is to retain flexibility in the face of what might be suspected to be a party-inspired tactical resignation by a partial arbitrator seeking to disrupt the proceedings.

4.113   The Rules do not specify on what grounds the LCIA Court may refuse to accept an arbitrator's resignation and not revoke his appointment, and the Court must thus exercise its discretion. In practice, arbitrators in LCIA arbitrations have rarely tendered their resignations, and the LCIA Court has never yet refused to accept one. More usually, an arbitrator's resignation is prompted by illness, or some other factor rendering it impossible for the arbitrator to continue, such as (certainly in the case of English arbitrators) being appointed a judge, or (as has happened in South Asian countries from time to time) being the subject of an injunction from a court to whose jurisdiction the arbitrator is subject preventing him from continuing in his functions. The arbitrator may also change law firms and be faced with an insuperable conflict in his new firm to his continuing as an arbitrator.

4.114   An arbitrator may also resign on being challenged by a party under Article 10. It is an open question, on which we do not express any view in this book, as to whether an arbitrator should resign when challenged, without waiting for the LCIA Court (in the case of an LCIA arbitration) to decide on the challenge. Arbitrators can legitimately feel (perhaps particularly in the beginning stages of the proceeding) that the interests of the arbitration are better served by resigning and not having a possibly protracted and expensive challenge procedure.[54] Equally, the LCIA Court is invested with the sole authority to decide challenges, and it can be cogently argued that the duty of the arbitrator is to wait until the challenge has been decided by the competent body before laying down his responsibilities.[55]

4.115 Any arbitrator whose appointment is revoked under this provision of the Rules is entitled to be paid for the time he served.

Article 10.2

If any arbitrator acts in deliberate violation of the Arbitration Agreement (including these Rules) or does not act fairly and impartially as between the parties or does not conduct or participate in the arbitration proceedings with reasonable diligence, avoiding unnecessary delay or expense, that arbitrator may be considered unfit in the opinion of the LCIA Court.

4.116 Article 10.2 allows the LCIA Court to revoke the appointment of an arbitrator of its own motion, as well as on a party's challenge, for serious misconduct. The power to revoke on the Court's own motion has never been exercised, but is an important power for the Court to possess.

4.117 Of note is the reference to acting 'fairly between the parties'. This can be taken to be much the same as the arbitrator's obligation to be impartial, under Article 5.2, the lack of which is also a ground for removal under Article 10.3 (as discussed immediately below), but is not always quite the same thing. The language tracks section 33(1)(a) of the English Arbitration Act 1996. It is not reflected in other institutional rules, and can thus be seen perhaps, as one of the examples of the LCIA Rules following the English Arbitration Act as the default standard for good practice.[56]

4.118 Despite its similarity to the standard of impartiality, however, this provision has been used by parties to found successful challenges to arbitrators and have them removed by the LCIA Court.

4.119 In one such, a sole arbitrator was challenged for conducting a hearing over two days with the representatives of one party where the other party was not present. The circumstances of that case were a little peculiar, in that neither side had

---

[54] Art 14(2) UNCITRAL Model Law and art 11(3) UNCITRAL Rules provide examples of the view that an arbitrator may properly decide not to await the outcome of a challenge before deciding to resign, without in any way being taken to admit the validity of that challenge.

[55] In this regard, note that there is no equivalent in the LCIA Rules of art 7(5) ICC Rules, which has been interpreted as an obligation on an arbitrator to complete the mission (as the French version of the ICC Rules has it) he has accepted, and thus not to resign without a valid reason (*Derains & Schwartz* 141).

[56] The duty to act 'fairly and impartially' between the parties is repeated in art 14.1, discussed in ch 5 below.

paid the further deposits on account of costs ordered by the Court and the claimant had said that it would not travel to London for the hearing as in its opinion the respondent (a state-owned company) was without legal existence and to attend a hearing would uselessly incur cost.

4.120   Under the circumstances, given that the further deposits had not been paid, the LCIA informed the parties that the hearing would not proceed.[57] The representatives of the respondent nonetheless turned up for the hearing and the sole arbitrator arranged to meet them in the afternoon. The Registrar informed the claimant, who protested, as the claimant could at that late stage no longer attend the hearing. The sole arbitrator nonetheless went ahead with the meeting, saying that it was not to be regarded as a 'formal hearing' but still asking the respondent's representatives questions about aspects of the case. He then decided to proceed with the hearing the following day (despite the further deposits not having been paid).

4.121   The sole arbitrator later found against the claimant, who applied for his removal under Article 10. The division of the Court did not uphold the challenge, although, despite finding that the arbitrator had done what he believed to be right, it reprimanded him on the basis that adequate notice of the hearing had not been given under Article 19.2,[58] and that the decision to meet alone with the respondent's representatives had been an 'error of judgment'. The arbitrator had thus failed to 'act fairly between the parties'. He was not paid for the costs and expenses of the hearing.

Article 10.3

An arbitrator may also be challenged by any party if circumstances exist that give rise to justifiable doubts as to his impartiality or independence. A party may challenge an arbitrator it has nominated, or in whose appointment it has participated, only for reasons of which it becomes aware after the appointment has been made.

4.122   The test for whether there may be justifiable doubts as to an arbitrator's impartiality or independence is discussed in the context of Article 5.2 above. This provision allows a party to bring a challenge to an arbitrator's appointment on that basis. A party may even challenge the arbitrator whom he has himself nominated, if circumstances justifying such a challenge come to light only after the arbitrator's appointment by the LCIA Court.

Article 10.4

A party who intends to challenge an arbitrator shall, within 15 days of the formation of the Arbitral Tribunal or (if later) after becoming aware of any circumstances

---

[57] Art 24 is discussed in ch 8 below.
[58] Discussed in ch 5 below and in *Nicholas & Partasides* 17–18.

referred to in Article 10.1, 10.2 or 10.3, send a written statement of the reasons for its challenge to the LCIA Court, the Arbitral Tribunal and all other parties. Unless the challenged arbitrator withdraws or all other parties agree to the challenge within 15 days of receipt of the written statement, the LCIA Court shall decide on the challenge.

Article 10.4 sets strict time limits to be observed by the parties in making challenges. **4.123**

As noted above, the LCIA is the only major arbitration institution that gives the parties reasoned decisions for challenges to arbitrators. This is an exception to Article 29.1, which provides that the Court is not required to give reasons for its decisions. **4.124**

In advance of the anticipated publication of challenge decisions, the best source of them is in *Nicholas & Partasides*, which contains many examples of such decisions. Parties can therefore see from these actual decisions what facts and circumstances divisions of the LCIA Court hearing challenges to arbitrators have considered could, or could not, constitute a 'justifiable doubt' as to the arbitrator's independence or impartiality. We will not repeat all of those here, but give a sample of the reasoning in decisions that have been made.[59] **4.125**

Of particular interest are challenges based on the arbitrators' conduct, whether before, during, or after a hearing. For example, unsuccessful challenges have been mounted against arbitrators on the basis of a denial of a fair hearing in circumstances where the arbitrator had defined his jurisdiction, in which the division actually examined both the substance of the jurisdictional decision by the sole arbitrator as well as procedural fairness;[60] on the basis of bias evidenced by a failure to grant the extensions of time sought by the respondent and in treating the counterclaim as withdrawn as a result of the respondent's failure to pay the deposit on account of costs.[61] **4.126**

Successful challenges have been mounted where an arbitrator reacted to a challenge (which would not, said the division, have been enough to justify his removal) in a sufficiently intemperate way as to give rise to justifiable doubts as to his impartiality;[62] and where a party-nominated arbitrator disclosed the content of the draft award and the outcome of the arbitration to the party that had nominated him. Finally, there was a challenge concerning a sole arbitrator's conduct at a hearing, involving meeting privately in his retiring room with counsel for the **4.127**

---

[59] *Nicholas & Partasides* 21–41. Summaries of decisions based on the arbitrator's nationality are dealt with under art 6.1 above.

[60] Decisions 7 and 8 in 2001, brought against the same sole arbitrator.

[61] Decisions 13, 14, and 16 in 2003 and 2004, also all against the same sole arbitrator (although not the same one as in Decisions 7 and 8).

[62] Decision 9 in 2001.

claimant, deleting parts of the transcript without both parties' consent and accusing counsel for the respondent of entering his retiring room when he was not present.[63] This challenge is also noteworthy as it was the subject of a request for reconsideration (which was refused). The division held that a challenge decision is not final, but may be subject to review if 'notwithstanding full diligence on the part of an applicant, factual elements recorded in the initial decision appear to be incorrect and knowledge of such factual elements would have led to a different legal evaluation'.

4.128 As noted in chapter 2, Article 29.2 of the Rules provides that all decisions of the Court are conclusive and binding on the parties and that they waive any right of appeal or review of such decisions to any state court (to the extent permitted under provisions of any applicable law). Challenge decisions are therefore final.

G. Article 11 – Nomination and Replacement of Arbitrators

4.129 Article 11 deals with the consequences of a rejection of an original nomination by the LCIA Court or the need to replace an appointed arbitrator after his or her removal, resignation, or death.

Article 11.1

In the event that the LCIA Court determines that any nominee is not suitable or independent or impartial or if an appointed arbitrator is to be replaced for any reason, the LCIA Court shall have a complete discretion to decide whether or not to follow the original nominating process.

4.130 The Court thus has the discretion whether or not to follow the original procedure for selecting a new nominee if the original nominee is rejected and thus not appointed, or if an arbitrator needs to be replaced.[64] It does not seem to give the LCIA Court the discretion not to replace an arbitrator it has removed. (This is discussed further in the context of truncated tribunals under Article 12.) The circumstances in which the LCIA Court should decide not to follow the original nominating process are not set out in the Rules. The LCIA Court must thus decide on a case-by-case basis. In practice, the LCIA Court follows the original procedure, unless the party concerned is being recalcitrant, for example by repeatedly nominating an arbitrator who is not 'suitable' or does not meet the criteria of independence and impartiality.

---

[63] Decision 18 in 2005.
[64] The predecessor of this provision in the 1985 Rules (art 3.5) apparently inspired the cognate provision in the ICC Rules, art 12(4) (see *Derains & Schwartz* 200).

Of course, the law of the seat of the arbitration may also have its say in this respect. **4.131**
For example, Article 15 of the UNCITRAL Model Law provides that substitute
arbitrators are to be appointed according to the rules that were applicable to the
appointment of the arbitrator being replaced. This is generally, however, agreed to
allow the parties to agree on a different procedure for appointing replacement
arbitrators, which an agreement to use the LCIA Rules would constitute.[65] In
similar vein are Article 179 of the Swiss Private International Law Act and Article
1030(1) of the Netherlands Arbitration Act 1986. In England, section 27(1) of
the Arbitration Act 1996 gives the parties full autonomy to agree on the procedure
for the replacement of an arbitrator.

Article 11 does not specify what status prior proceedings in the arbitration are to **4.132**
have if an arbitrator has to be replaced. This is in contrast to Article 12(4) of the
ICC Rules, which provides that it shall be for the tribunal to decide whether, and
to what extent, any prior proceedings are to be repeated. Article 14 of the
UNCITRAL Rules provides for previous hearings to be repeated mandatorily if
the sole or presiding arbitrator is replaced, while this is discretionary in the case of
replacement of a co-arbitrator. This reference to 'hearings' in the UNCITRAL
Rules as against 'proceedings' in the ICC Rules obviously reduces the discretion in
this respect of a tribunal sitting under the UNCITRAL Rules.[66]

The fact that the LCIA Rules do not contain a similar provision is surprising. **4.133**
Clearly, though, the tribunal must have the discretion, should it (after having
heard the parties) feel it necessary to repeat any stage of the proceedings, to do so.
This must be implicit. But it would be better were it explicit.

Equally clearly, a decision to repeat or not to repeat any part of the proceedings **4.134**
must respect the parties' right to be heard and provide them with a reasonable
opportunity to present their case. This must be balanced against the cost and delay
of repeating any stage in the proceedings. There can be no firm rules as to how
tribunals should conduct this sometimes difficult balancing act, but, if witnesses
have been heard at a hearing, a reconstituted tribunal would, it is submitted,
usually be well-advised to repeat it. Even given the existence of a transcript, the
demeanour of a witness and the atmosphere of the hearing room can be powerful
tools in the hands of the tribunal in reaching a conclusion on the outcome of the case.

---

[65] H Holtzmann and J Neuhaus, *A Guide to the UNCITRAL Model Law on International
Commercial Arbitration: Legislative History and Commentary* (Kluwer, 1989) 465–6.
[66] The UNCITRAL Rules are presently under revision. Jan Paulsson and Georgios Petrochilos
prepared a report with suggested revisions to UNCITRAL in 2006, available at <http://www.
uncitral.org/pdf/spanish/tac/events/hond07/arbrules_report.pdf>, in which it was proposed to
redraft art 14 to reflect more closely the general discretion given to a tribunal by the ICC Rules to
decide whether and to what extent any previous hearings should be repeated on the replacement of
any arbitrator.

In such circumstances, for one of the three arbitrators (and especially the chairman) not to have been present could well open up any subsequent award to challenge.

4.135 By the same token, it would usually be unnecessary to repeat purely procedural meetings or, *a fortiori*, written submissions. To do so would hardly be conducive to the efficient and cost-effective running of the proceedings that is enjoined on the tribunal by Article 10.2.

Article 11.2

If the LCIA Court should so decide, any opportunity given to a party to make a re-nomination shall be waived if not exercised within 15 days (or such lesser time as the LCIA Court may fix), after which the LCIA Court shall appoint the replacement arbitrator.

4.136 Article 11.2 deals only with the situation where the LCIA Court has exercised its discretion to follow the original nomination procedure. It sets out a very short time limit of 15 days (which can be still further reduced at the discretion of the Court) for the party concerned to make a further nomination. If it does not do so, the Court may (but need not) proceed to make the appointment itself. Late nominations and their consequences are dealt with above, in the context of Article 7.2.

H. Article 12 – Majority Power to Continue Proceedings

4.137 The phenomenon of so-called 'truncated' tribunals is well known, and it is essential that, if one member of a three-member tribunal is effectively refusing to play his or her part in the smooth running of the arbitration, the two remaining members have the discretion, should they consider it appropriate, to continue with the proceedings in the absence of the recalcitrant third member.

4.138 This is, in other words, a vital weapon in the fight against the ability of obstructionist arbitrators (no doubt acting at the behest of one of the parties) to delay or disrupt the proceedings. It would most usually be used only at the very end of the proceedings, when the delay and expense caused by the replacement of a recalcitrant arbitrator, not to mention the possible need to repeat previous hearings, would be too great to justify.

4.139 Cases in which a tribunal feels the need to continue as a truncated tribunal are rare, but often celebrated. In one of the most well known, *Himpurna California Energy Ltd v Republic of Indonesia*,[67] a case under the UNCITRAL Rules, the arbitrator appointed by the respondent, Indonesia, was prevented from taking part in a hearing convened by the tribunal in the Peace Palace in The Hague.

---

[67] (2000) 25 YCA 186.

The impeded arbitrator, Priyatna Abdurrasyid, was effectively kidnapped by Indonesian agents at Schipol Airport in Amsterdam and put on a flight to Jakarta, thus stopping him from attending the hearing. The remaining arbitrators continued with the arbitration and sat as a truncated tribunal.

Such cases are rare and extreme,[68] but, for the sake of the integrity of the arbitration process, arbitration rules need to ensure without ambiguity that the process can be protected from such tactics by unscrupulous parties and arbitrators by enabling the remaining arbitrators to see out their mission.[69]   **4.140**

Article 12.1

> If any arbitrator on a three-member Arbitral Tribunal refuses or persistently fails to participate in its deliberations, the two other arbitrators shall have the power, upon their written notice of such refusal or failure to the LCIA Court, the parties and the third arbitrator, to continue the arbitration (including the making of any decision, ruling or award), notwithstanding the absence of the third arbitrator.

Article 12.1 provides the basic power for two members of a three-member tribunal (obviously this article finds no application in the case of a sole arbitrator and the Rules do not contemplate a tribunal of more than three members) to carry on to the end of the proceedings if the third member of the tribunal 'refuses or persistently fails' to take part in deliberations.   **4.141**

Unlike Article 35 of the WIPO Rules, there is no express requirement in Article 12.1 that the refusal to take part in the tribunal's deliberations must have been 'without due cause' in order for the power to carry on regardless to come into effect. This raises the question of whether Article 12.1 applies in a case where an arbitrator cannot take part in deliberations because of illness, or some other cause that is not imputable to a wilful refusal. Given the absence of a reference to 'due cause' and the fact that a persistent failure is to be distinguished from a simple refusal, the answer is probably yes.   **4.142**

It seems as if this power does not, however, extend to cases of the death of an arbitrator (which could hardly be said to be a refusal or failure to take part in   **4.143**

---

68 See also the much-criticized decision of the Swiss Federal Supreme Court in case BGE 117 Ia 166 (*Ivan Milutinovic PIM v Deutsche Babcock AG*), in which one of the co-arbitrators in an ICC case in Zurich purported to resign after a hearing and, his resignation not having been accepted by the ICC Court, subsequently refused to take part in deliberations. The Swiss Federal Supreme Court set the resulting award aside, holding in particular that, unless the parties agreed otherwise, the award had to be made with the participation of all three arbitrators. Art 21.1 LCIA Rules would constitute such an agreement as a matter of Swiss law (see *Poudret & Besson* para 739).

69 In the *Himpurna* case, of course, the arbitrator was himself wholly blameless. For an account of his experiences, see 'They said I was going to be kidnapped' (2003) 18(6) Mealey's Int Arb Rep 29. For a different perspective on the events that led to the decision of the tribunal in that case to sit in truncated form, see L Wells and R Ahmed, *Making Foreign Investment Safe: Property Rights and National Sovereignty* (Oxford University Press, 2007).

deliberations) or the removal of an arbitrator by the LCIA Court under Article 10, for whatever reason.

4.144 The equivalent provision in the ICC Rules, Article 12(5), is very different in a number of respects from Article 12.1 of the LCIA Rules. First, it gives the power to decide to continue with the proceedings to the ICC Court, not the tribunal, as is the case with Article 12.1 of the LCIA Rules (although the ICC Court is required to take into account the views of both the remaining arbitrators and the parties).

4.145 The ICC provision also only applies after the proceedings have closed. This is a considerable restriction on the usefulness of the provision. It would not, for example, have enabled the two continuing arbitrators in the *Himpurna* case to have carried on in the face of their colleague's having been effectively kidnapped by the non-participating party. In that case, the ICC Court would have had to remove the arbitrator concerned and replace him, with all the delay and expense which that could cause (particularly if the reconstituted tribunal had decided to re-run any part of the procedure).

4.146 Furthermore, it only applies when there is a vacancy in the arbitral tribunal, caused by the death or removal of an arbitrator on any ground. This is to be contrasted with the scope of Article 12.1 of the LCIA Rules, which expressly (and indeed exclusively) finds application when all three members of the tribunal are still in office.

4.147 It might be thought preferable to have the decision as to the fitness of the third arbitrator to continue to be dealt with by the LCIA Court by way of challenge, leading to his removal, as is the case under the ICC Rules. It could be said to remove a difficult decision from the hands of the tribunal itself and perhaps lessen the chances of a successful application by the losing party to have the resulting award set aside. Nonetheless, such a process takes time and the LCIA's placing of the decision in the hands of the two participating arbitrators, without the need to go through the procedure of the removal of the offending arbitrator, seems far more suited to the object of allowing a truncated tribunal, namely to finish the proceedings with all due speed.[70]

4.148 In order to carry on in the face of the refusal or failure of the third arbitrator to take part in deliberations, the remaining members of the tribunal have to give written notice to the parties and to the LCIA Court as well as to the arbitrator in default.

---

[70] It should be noted, however, that in practice the ICC provision is more flexibly applied than its text might make it seem. There is at least one case in which, in the face of a refusal by an arbitrator to take part in deliberations, but who had not resigned or been replaced, the two other arbitrators issued the award (see *Derains & Schwartz* 207).

Article 12.2

In determining whether to continue the arbitration, the two other arbitrators shall take into account the stage of the arbitration, any explanation made by the third arbitrator for his non-participation and such other matters as they consider appropriate in the circumstances of the case. The reasons for such determination shall be stated in any award, order or other decision made by the two arbitrators without the participation of the third arbitrator.

Article 12.2 sets out the criteria that the participating arbitrators need to take into account in deciding whether to proceed as a truncated tribunal. First, they must consider the stage of the arbitration. While, unlike the ICC Rules, the power to continue as a truncated tribunal can be exercised by an LCIA tribunal at any stage in the proceedings, it is submitted that it should normally only be so exercised if the procedure has progressed to such a stage that it would be more cost-effective to carry on without having recourse to the LCIA Court to remove and replace their recalcitrant colleague. **4.149**

What that stage would be may vary from case to case, but it is likely to be relatively near the end of the arbitration. The important thing is that the Rules do not, unlike Article 12(5) of the ICC Rules, give the power to carry on as a truncated tribunal only after the proceedings have closed. The discretion of the two continuing arbitrators is thus preserved, although it is one that needs to be exercised with due care. **4.150**

The two other arbitrators must also take into account any explanation that may be given by the third arbitrator. This seems only right; on any view, if the third arbitrator is to be excluded from further participation in the proceedings, he should be heard as to why he has refused or failed to take part in deliberations to date. It is not clear how such an explanation is to be obtained: Article 12.1 requires the third arbitrator to be notified of the two other arbitrators' *decision* to carry on without him; he is not at that stage invited to comment. It must thus be implied that the two participating arbitrators must at least give the third arbitrator the opportunity to comment on their decision-in-principle before it is finally made and communicated as required by Article 12.1. **4.151**

Finally, the two other arbitrators must take into account 'such other matters as they consider appropriate in the circumstances of the case'. One of those matters should certainly be the susceptibility of the award they will render as a truncated tribunal to be set aside by the courts of the seat of the arbitration. The authority of a truncated tribunal, and awards issued by one, have been the subject of much commentary and no little controversy.[71] **4.152**

---

[71] eg, *Poudret & Besson* paras 735–9; *Redfern & Hunter* paras 4-79 to 4-81; *Lew, Mistelis, Kröll* 322–8; S Schwebel, *International Arbitration: Three Salient Problems* (Cambridge, 1987) 144

4.153   In a recent decision, the Paris Court of Appeal has added to this controversy. In a decision in 2005, the Court of Appeal refused to recognize a foreign award rendered by a truncated tribunal of two arbitrators in the United States under the International Arbitration Rules of the AAA. The grounds given were that, as the parties had submitted their dispute to a three-member tribunal, the award had been rendered in breach of the arbitrators' duties of collegiality by an irregularly constituted tribunal and was in breach of the parties' right to participate equally in the constitution of an arbitral tribunal, since the refusal of one of the co-arbitrators to take part in the proceedings had never been communicated to the parties. The remaining members of the arbitral tribunal had taken it upon themselves to carry on with the arbitration without seeking the parties' views and without explanation.[72]

4.154   All that needs to be said here is that the two other members of the tribunal would be well-advised to consider these issues before taking a decision. By contrast, there is no duty on the members of the tribunal to take likely enforceability into account. This is a matter that is of concern to the claimant only (if it is successful) and in any event (a) the tribunal cannot always know where enforcement may be sought and (b) the claimant may not need to take steps to enforce the award at all to get a benefit from it (if, for example, it has insurance that will pay out on production of a favourable award).

4.155   Finally under Article 12.2, the reasons that the two other arbitrators have for carrying on as a truncated tribunal must be stated in any subsequent award or decision made without the participation of the third arbitrator. This could of course then form the basis for scrutiny by the court of the seat on a setting-aside application, and the two signing arbitrators will therefore look to express themselves with due care in setting out the reasons for their decision.

Article 12.3

In the event that the two other arbitrators determine at any time not to continue the arbitration without the participation of the third arbitrator missing from their deliberations, the two arbitrators shall notify in writing the parties and the LCIA Court of such determination; and in that event, the two arbitrators or any party may refer the matter to the LCIA Court for the revocation of that third arbitrator's appointment and his replacement under Article 10.

(albeit more from the perspective of public international law); S Schwebel, 'The Authority of a Truncated Tribunal' in *ICCA Congress Series No 9* (Kluwer, 1999) 314; and H Holtzmann, 'Lessons of the Stockholm Congress' in *ICCA Congress Series No 5* (Kluwer, 1991) 28.

[72] *Malecki c Long*, Paris Court of Appeal, 21 April 2005, [2006] Rev arb 673; D Bensaude, '*Malecki v Long*: Truncated Tribunals and the Waiver of *Dutco* Rights' (2006) 23 J Int Arb 81.

Article 12.3 provides the two other arbitrators with the option of informing the **4.156**
LCIA Court and the parties that they will not carry on as a truncated tribunal.
They or the parties may then apply to the Court for the removal of the third
arbitrator and his replacement. (The reference is to Article 10, but this covers only
the removal of an arbitrator; Article 11 deals with an eventual replacement.) It is
to be assumed that the LCIA Court could also use its power to revoke an
arbitrator's appointment of its own motion under Article 10.2 on being notified
by the two other arbitrators of a decision under Article 12.3 not to carry on despite
the refusal or persistent failure of the third arbitrator to take part in deliberations.

There is one ambiguity in Article 12.3. The phrase 'at any time' may just be a **4.157**
confirmation that the situation can arise at any time and that there is no stage of
the proceedings by which continuation as a truncated tribunal becomes compul-
sory. It may also, however, even if this seems hard to envisage in practice, mean
that the two continuing arbitrators, having at first resolved to carry on, subsequently decide not to.

I. Article 13 – Communications between Parties and the Arbitral Tribunal

Article 13 is rather awkwardly placed in the Rules. It is a purely procedural **4.158**
provision, ensuring that the parties know how to conduct their communications
with the tribunal and the LCIA secretariat before and after the tribunal has been
formed.

Article 13.1

Until the Arbitral Tribunal is formed, all communications between parties and arbitrators shall be made through the Registrar.

This provision is straightforward enough on the surface, although one or two **4.159**
questions do arise about it in practice. The general rule set out by Article 13.1 is
that, if the tribunal has not yet been formed, the parties should not communicate
with the party-nominated arbitrators directly, but should do so instead through
the Registrar.

This is of course consistent with the general rule that the Registrar should be **4.160**
included in correspondence with the tribunal, as set out in Article 13.2, discussed
below. On a deeper level, however, it would seem that the aim of Article 13.1 is to
avoid giving the parties the impression that they can communicate freely with
their party-nominated arbitrators, which could of course give rise to a justifiable
doubt on the part of the non-communicating party as to the independence and
impartiality of those arbitrators and lead to a successful challenge. An arbitrator

who receives *ex parte* communications from the party that nominated him should refuse to deal with the party and should immediately inform the other party and the other party-nominated arbitrator of the fact and content of the communication.

4.161 On the other hand, there must be exceptions to this. The most obvious is that, where the arbitration agreement foreshadows an agreement among the party-nominated arbitrators to nominate a chairman, parties will almost invariably wish to confer with 'their' party-nominated arbitrators on the choice. This is a very well-established practice in modern international arbitration (accepted as such by its inclusion in the IBA Guidelines' Green List (at section 4.5.1), meaning that, in the opinion of the IBA working party, such contacts did not call for disclosure), while it would seem to be a breach of the strict letter of Article 13.1. Nonetheless, the LCIA accepts this practice, simply asking the party-nominated arbitrators concerned to make a formal notification that such contacts had taken place.

Article 13.2

Thereafter, unless and until the Arbitral Tribunal directs that communications shall take place directly between the Arbitral Tribunal and the parties (with simultaneous copies to the Registrar), all written communications between the parties and the Arbitral Tribunal shall continue to be made through the Registrar.

4.162 There are three aspects to Article 13.2. The first is that the same channel of communication, namely through the Registrar, is to be adopted even after the constitution of the tribunal until the tribunal directs that direct communications can take place. This is to ensure that the tribunal can direct the manner in which communications are to be made to it. It should be read in conjunction with Article 3.3, discussed in chapter 2 above, which directs all correspondence with the Court to be addressed to the Registrar.

4.163 The second aspect of Article 13.2 is that, even after the tribunal allows direct communication from the parties, the Registrar must receive simultaneous copies. This is to ensure that the LCIA has a full record of the proceedings. It is clearly vitally important that the LCIA sees what is going on in the arbitration. The Registrar may feel the need to talk to the tribunal about aspects of the procedure and if there is a doubt about any aspect of the application of the Rules, and the Court will need a full record if there is any matter that calls for its attention.

4.164 The third aspect of Article 13.2 is to ensure, as with Article 13.1, that no improper *ex parte* communication takes place between a party and one or more arbitrators. The principle of party equality demands that all parties see all communications with the arbitral tribunal. Again, as with Article 13.1, it is not hard to see that the strict application of this rule should be softened in certain circumstances, where an *ex parte* communication would not be inappropriate. It is unnecessary, and impossible, to set these out exhaustively.

Article 13.3

> Where the Registrar sends any written communication to one party on behalf of the Arbitral Tribunal, he shall send a copy to each of the other parties. Where any party sends to the Registrar any communication (including Written Statements and Documents under Article 15), it shall include a copy for each arbitrator; and it shall also send copies direct to all other parties and confirm to the Registrar in writing that it has done or is doing so.

4.165 Article 13.3 is the final part of the Rules' attempt to ensure full transparency in the proceedings. Any communication from the Registrar (on behalf of the tribunal) to one party shall be sent to all other parties at the same time. Any communication from one party to the Registrar on behalf of the tribunal shall contain copies for the arbitrators (for onward transmission by the Registrar to the tribunal) and shall also be sent to each other party, with a confirmation to this effect in writing. There is no exception to this rule: even if the Registrar asks, for example, for further clarification of an application under Article 9 for the expedited formation of the tribunal, the other parties are always notified.

5

CONDUCT OF THE ARBITRATION
(ARTICLES 14 TO 21)

A. Article 14 – Conduct of the Proceedings	5.02	
Article 14.1	5.03	
Article 14.2	5.18	
Article 14.3	5.29	
B. Article 15 – Submission of Written Statements and Documents	5.30	
Article 15.1	5.31	
Articles 15.2 to 15.7	5.43	
Article 15.8	5.56	
C. Article 16 – Seat of Arbitration and Place of Hearings	5.58	
Article 16.1	5.60	
Article 16.2	5.65	
Article 16.3	5.68	
D. Article 17 – Language of Arbitration	5.72	
Article 17.1	5.73	
Article 17.2	5.78	
Article 17.3	5.79	
Article 17.4	5.80	
E. Article 18 – Party Representation	5.81	
Article 18.1	5.82	
Article 18.2	5.85	
F. Article 19 – Hearings	5.86	
Article 19.1	5.87	
Article 19.2	5.90	
Article 19.3	5.95	
Article 19.4	5.97	
Article 19.5	5.98	
G. Article 20 – Witnesses	5.99	
Article 20.1	5.100	
Article 20.2	5.103	
Article 20.3	5.106	
Articles 20.4 and 20.5	5.108	
Article 20.6	5.112	
Article 20.7	5.113	
H. Article 21 – Experts to the Arbitral Tribunal	5.114	
Article 21.1	5.116	
Article 21.2	5.120	
Article 21.3	5.121	

5.01 This chapter deals with Articles 14 to 21 of the Rules, which address the procedure and conduct of the arbitration proceedings. Each of these eight articles addresses a particular facet of the arbitration procedure, ranging from the submission of written statements and witness evidence in Articles 15 and 19, respectively, to rules governing the determination of the seat and language of the arbitration in Articles 16 and 17, to issues of party representation, the conduct of hearings, and the appointment of experts by the tribunal, which are covered in Articles 18, 19, and 21, respectively. We follow the logical order of the Rules in this chapter and therefore start with Article 14, which unequivocally endorses the principle of party autonomy under the Rules, and thus empowers parties to determine the conduct of their arbitration by agreement.

A. Article 14 – Conduct of the Proceedings

5.02 The freedom of parties to dictate the procedure to be followed in an arbitration, encapsulated by the principle of party autonomy, is one of the most important features of international arbitration, as affirmed in modern national arbitration statutes and arbitration rules alike. The Rules are no exception. The drafters of the 1985 version of the Rules considered that the twin principles of party autonomy, on the one hand, and giving the tribunal maximum discretion and powers in the absence of party agreement, on the other hand, represented the two guiding principles underlying the Rules.[1] That remains the case today. Indeed, it may be argued that Article 14.1 of the Rules endorses the principle of party autonomy to an unprecedented degree by comparison to other institutional rules, in emphasizing the freedom of the parties to shape the procedure of their arbitration, subject only to the application of any mandatory or public policy provisions of the law governing the arbitration, also known as the *lex arbitri*, which is typically the law of the seat of the arbitration.[2]

Article 14.1

The parties may agree on the conduct of their arbitral proceedings and they are encouraged to do so, consistent with the Arbitral Tribunal's general duties at all times:

(i) to act fairly and impartially as between all parties, giving each a reasonable opportunity of putting its case and dealing with that of its opponent; and

(ii) to adopt procedures suitable to the circumstances of the arbitration, avoiding unnecessary delay or expense, so as to provide a fair and efficient means for the final resolution of the parties' dispute.

Such agreements shall be made by the parties in writing or recorded in writing by the Arbitral Tribunal at the request of and with the authority of the parties.

5.03 Article 14.1 allows the parties the greatest possible freedom in structuring the proceedings before the tribunal, subject only to the duties of the tribunal to act (i) in accordance with the principles of impartiality and natural justice and (ii) to adopt suitable procedures tailored to the circumstances of the arbitration in order to provide for a fair and expeditious resolution of the parties' dispute. As we will discuss below, these two considerations reflect the mandatory requirements imposed on arbitrators sitting in England under section 33(1) of the Arbitration Act 1996, and reflect similar public policy considerations imposed in other jurisdictions.[3]

---

[1] *Hunter & Paulsson* 168.
[2] Art 16.3.
[3] eg, under art 18 UNCITRAL Model Law.

The extent of party autonomy

Article 14.1 provides that the parties may agree on the conduct of their arbitral **5.04** proceedings and encourages them to do so, and thus fully recognizes the principle of party autonomy. Neither the parties, nor the tribunal, is bound to apply the national procedural rules and customs prevalent in civil proceedings in the courts of the country in which the arbitration is held.[4] This allows the arbitration procedure to be adapted to the requirements of the case at hand, and avoids the formalism of civil procedure rules.

Article 14.1, which adopts similar wording to that found in Article 19(1) of the **5.05** UNCITRAL Model Law, was first introduced in the 1985 version of the Rules and has been described as the 'Magna Carta' of LCIA arbitration by a leading English practitioner and one of the drafters of the Rules.[5] Article 14.1 reiterates that the parties are masters of their own procedure and grants to them complete autonomy over the conduct of the arbitration (subject to the arbitrators' duties under Article 14.1 sub-paragraphs (i) and (ii) and any considerations of international public policy at the seat of the arbitration).[6] Such freedom is missing from most other institutional rules that limit the scope of party autonomy to questions on which the rules are silent or where they expressly permit derogation. For example, the equivalent provision in ICC arbitration (Article 15(1)) provides that the proceedings are governed by the ICC Rules, and where those rules are silent, any rules which the parties or, failing them, the tribunal may settle.[7] Article 15(1) of the ICC Rules therefore establishes the following hierarchy among the governing rules: first, the ICC Rules themselves; second, any rules that the parties may agree on where the rules are silent; and third, any rules the arbitrators may settle.[8] Unlike in ICC arbitration, therefore, parties are free under the LCIA Rules to tailor the conduct of their proceedings to fit the circumstances of the case without having to contend with any obligatory procedural requirements, such as the terms of reference, the submission of a procedural timetable, or the scrutiny of draft awards by the ICC Court, which are all hallmarks of ICC arbitration. This is consistent with a further principle underlying the Rules: to grant tribunals the widest

---

[4] J Paulsson, 'Lessons of the Last Decade: The Promise and Dangers of Globalisation and Practice under the LCIA Rules' in M Hunter, A Marriott and VV Veeder (eds), *The Internationalisation of International Arbitration. The LCIA Centenary Conference* (Kluwer, 1995) 59, 66.

[5] VV Veeder, 'London Court of International Arbitration – The New 1998 LCIA Rules' (1998) 23 YCA 366, 367.

[6] Art 1.1 UNCITRAL Rules grants the parties a similar autonomy. Although see the discussion below in respect of the tribunal's authority in organizing hearings and controlling the appearance of witnesses, in accordance with arts 19 and 20.2 Rules.

[7] Art 16 ICDR Rules contains a similar provision, whereas art 19(1) SCC Rules mandates the arbitral tribunal to determine the conduct of the arbitration subject to the SCC Rules and any agreement between the parties.

[8] *Derains & Schwartz* 224.

discretion in the conduct of the arbitration, subject only to the agreement of the parties. Indeed, it is important to note that the LCIA Court is generally excluded from the procedural aspects of the arbitration as soon as the tribunal has been constituted, leaving all issues of procedure at the command of the tribunal. For this reason, it has been argued that 'the LCIA occupies an historical position halfway between full institutional arbitration and ad hoc forms of arbitration'.[9]

5.06 To be sure, Article 14.1 does not mean that the parties' autonomy remains unchecked. Apart from the tribunal's express duties set forth in Article 14.1 sub-paragraphs (i) and (ii) (and any mandatory provisions of the *lex arbitri*), discussed below, the two areas where the LCIA Court retains a continuing and close control of the arbitration concern the appointment and dismissal of arbitrators and ensuring that the LCIA is in funds sufficient to pay the fees and expenses of the tribunal and the administrative charges of the LCIA.[10] To this end, the Rules place an important economic obligation on the tribunal by restraining the arbitrators from proceeding with the arbitration without ascertaining that the LCIA holds requisite funds from the parties.[11] It is also important not to discount the important, albeit informal, supervision and follow-up of the arbitration procedure that is carried out by the Registrar (who is ordinarily copied on all communications passing between the parties and the tribunal).[12] This includes the preparation and regular updating of case summaries as part of the LCIA Court's regular review of the progress and conduct of all arbitrations conducted under the Rules.[13]

The tribunal's duties as to the conduct of the arbitration

5.07 Article 14.1 provides that, in all cases, the application of party autonomy must be consistent with the tribunal's general duties to (i) act fairly and impartially as between the parties, giving each a reasonable opportunity of putting its case and dealing with that of its opponent; and (ii) adopt procedures suitable to the circumstances of the arbitration, avoiding unnecessary delay or expense, so as to provide a fair and efficient means for resolution of the parties' dispute. Similar provisions may be found in other arbitration rules[14] and in national arbitration statutes.[15]

---

[9] Veeder (n 5 above) 366.
[10] Art 10 as regards the revocation of arbitrators' appointments and arts 24 and 28 as to the costs of the arbitration are discussed in chs 4 and 8, respectively.
[11] Art 24.2.
[12] Art 13.2.
[13] Veeder (n 5 above) 367–8.
[14] Art 15(2) ICC Rules, art 15(1) UNCITRAL Rules, and art 16(1) ICDR Rules.
[15] Art 19 UNCITRAL Model Law.

The provisions of Article 14.1 setting out the duties of the tribunal were **5.08** introduced in the current version of the Rules, and reflect the mandatory public policy provisions of section 33(1) of the English Arbitration Act 1996. Article 14.1 sub-paragraphs (i) and (ii) contain a near-verbatim reproduction of section 33(1), and represent a further example of the close coordination between the Rules and the Arbitration Act 1996.[16] This should perhaps not come as a great surprise, in light of the overwhelming proportion of cases conducted under the Rules that are seated in London, and therefore subject to the mandatory application of section 33(1) of the Arbitration Act.[17]

Article 14.1(i) requires the tribunal to comply with the rules of natural justice in **5.09** the conduct of the arbitration, referring to the two traditional limbs of natural justice, namely the requirement that the tribunal hearing the case must be unbiased and disinterested, and the requirement that each party must be given a fair opportunity to be heard.[18]

The condition that the tribunal conduct itself fairly and impartially is a basic tenet **5.10** of all systems of justice and is an essential condition of an arbitrator's appointment by the LCIA Court under the Rules.[19] Justifiable doubts as to the tribunal's impartiality will provide a ground for an arbitrator's removal under Article 10, and may also provide a ground for setting aside the award.

Each party must also be given a reasonable opportunity to present its case. This **5.11** means that each party must be given an opportunity to present its arguments to the tribunal and to adduce evidence in support of its case, and a sufficient time should be allowed for this.[20] Similarly to the requirement of impartiality, the tribunal's failure to afford a party a reasonable opportunity to present its case may render the tribunal subject to challenge under the Rules or, alternatively, provide grounds for challenging the award before the courts at the place of arbitration. A party's inability to present its case is, of course, also a possible ground for refusing enforcement of an award under Article V(1)(b) of the New York Convention.

---

[16] This was, in fact, an avowed aim of the revision process that led to the adoption of the current Rules (*Commentary* 10).

[17] In a recent decision, the English High Court affirmed the twin duties owed by arbitrators appointed under the Rules in cases with a London seat of arbitration:

> In the present case, the LCIA arbitrators have not only to comply with the statutory duty under section 33, but also a duty to the parties by virtue of article 14(1)(i) and (ii) of the LCIA Rules.

Elektrim SA v Vivendi Universal SA (No 2) [2007] 2 Lloyd's Rep 8, 19.

[18] *Russell* para 5-038.

[19] Art 5.2, discussed in ch 4 above.

[20] *Russell* para 5-042.

5.12 The Rules differ from certain other arbitration rules in providing that the parties shall have a 'reasonable' rather than a 'full' opportunity to present their case,[21] as compared to Article 15(1) of the UNCITRAL Rules, or, indeed, Article 18 of the UNCITRAL Model Law. In this respect, the Rules follow the formulation adopted in the English Arbitration Act. As explained in the DAC Report, the choice of language was deliberate in order to avoid 'any suggestion that a party is entitled to take as long as he likes, however objectively unreasonable this may be'.[22] The parties' right to present their case is not, therefore, an unfettered right to make submissions or present evidence as and when each party wishes.

5.13 The parties' right in this regard must instead be considered in light of the tribunal's duties under Article 14.1(ii) that the procedures adopted should avoid unnecessary delay or expense in order to provide a fair and efficient means of resolving the parties' dispute. This means that, in its issuance of procedural directions, the tribunal should take account of the specific circumstances of the case and tailor its conduct of the arbitration accordingly. It is therefore intended that the tribunal will have the discretion to decide when it has heard enough and whether it would be unreasonable to permit the continued exchange of further legal submissions or evidence. Indeed, in the case of arbitrations seated in England, the application of section 33(1) of the Arbitration Act means that the tribunal must actively manage the proceedings in order to comply with its mandatory duty under the *lex arbitri*.[23]

Procedural agreements to be made in writing

5.14 The final sentence of Article 14.1 requires that the agreement of the parties on the conduct of the arbitration must be in writing or recorded in writing by the arbitral tribunal at the request and with the approval of the parties. Article 14.1 appears to exact a formal requirement that any such procedural agreement must be in writing, thus reflecting the requirement that an arbitration agreement must be in writing under Article 1 of the Rules, or, indeed, the writing requirement as applied to arbitrations seated in England under section 5(1) of the Arbitration Act. Although it may be odd to consider that an agreement concluded orally or tacitly may not be binding under the Rules, the requirement that such agreements must be made in writing (or recorded in writing) is unlikely to be a significant issue in practice. This is because procedural agreements reached between the parties tend either to form part of the arbitration agreement, or to be recorded in writing, even if the initial agreement (typically between counsel) was reached orally.

---

[21] Art 15(2) ICC Rules adopts the same 'reasonable' standard.
[22] *DAC Report* para 165.
[23] *Russell* para 5-044.

Procedural clashes between the parties and the tribunal

The final issue to consider in respect of Article 14.1 is the possibility of a **5.15** disagreement between the parties and the tribunal as regards the arbitration procedure. In other words, does the principle of party autonomy authorize the parties to impose on the tribunal any procedural arrangement they wish after acceptance of their mandate by the arbitrators?

As we have already seen, the principle of party autonomy is subject to certain **5.16** limits. In addition to the application of any mandatory rules at the place of arbitration, the application of party autonomy is also fettered by the tribunal's general duties, as set forth in Article 14.1 sub-paragraphs (i) and (ii).[24] In the event, however, that these requirements present no obstacle, can an arbitral tribunal veto a procedural agreement that has been properly concluded between the parties? Although the issue remains controversial and is subject to the application of the *lex arbitri*, on the basis of the Rules alone, the answer is clear-cut: the tribunal cannot override the agreement of the parties. This is also the position under English law,[25] although it is not necessarily the case in other countries, particularly where the procedural agreement reached between the parties is considered by the arbitrators as an obstacle to the smooth conduct of the proceedings.[26] The basis for the position under English law, and the practical consequences for the arbitral tribunal, which are equally applicable under Article 14.1 of the Rules, are cogently set out in the DAC Report:

> In our view it is neither desirable nor practicable to stipulate that the tribunal can override the agreement of the parties. It is not desirable, because the type of arbitration we are discussing is a consensual process which depends on the agreement of the parties who are surely entitled (if they can agree) to have the final say on how they wish their dispute to be resolved. It is not practicable, since there is no way in which the parties can be forced to adopt a method of proceeding if they are agreed that this is not the way they wish to proceed. The latter is the case even if it could be established that their agreement was ineffective since it undermined or prevented the performance of the duty made mandatory by [section] 33.
>
> . . .
>
> In circumstances such as these, the tribunal (assuming it has failed to persuade the parties to take a different course) has the choice of adopting the course preferred by the parties or of resigning. Indeed, resignation would be the only course if the parties

---

[24] As discussed below, the parties' autonomy also appears to be limited by the tribunal's authority to organize hearings and to allow, refuse, or limit the appearance of witnesses pursuant to arts 19 and 20.2.

[25] According to s 34 Arbitration Act, 'it shall be for the tribunal to decide all procedural and evidential matters, subject to the right of the parties to agree any matter'.

[26] *Poudret & Besson* para 531.

were in agreement in rejecting the method preferred by the tribunal, and no other way of proceeding was agreed by them or considered suitable by the tribunal.[27]

5.17 It therefore follows that, if the tribunal cannot persuade the parties to adopt a different course, it must either resign or follow the parties' wishes, having satisfied itself that the course proposed by the parties can be reconciled with its general duties under Article 14.1 of the Rules.

Article 14.2

Unless otherwise agreed by the parties under Article 14.1, the Arbitral Tribunal shall have the widest discretion to discharge its duties allowed under such law(s) or rules of law as the Arbitral Tribunal may determine to be applicable; and at all times the parties shall do everything necessary for the fair, efficient and expeditious conduct of the arbitration.

5.18 Article 14.2 contains two substantive provisions. First, it provides that, in the absence of an agreement of the parties, the tribunal has the widest discretion to discharge its duties allowed under such law(s) or rules of law as the tribunal may determine to be applicable. Second, Article 14.2 mandates the parties to do everything necessary for the fair, efficient, and expeditious conduct of the arbitration. Each is considered in turn.

The tribunal's discretion to conduct the proceedings

5.19 As we discussed earlier, the Rules grant the parties the opportunity to agree on the conduct of their arbitration. In practice, however, it is rare for the parties to agree on a set of comprehensive procedural rules for the governance of the arbitration proceedings, particularly after the dispute has arisen. In most cases, therefore, and in the absence of the parties' agreement, it falls to the tribunal to determine the conduct of the proceedings, subject only to its general duties under Article 14.1 sub-paragraphs (i) and (ii) and the application of any mandatory rules under the *lex arbitri*.

The procedural framework created by the Rules

5.20 Of course, even in the absence of a specific agreement between the parties as regards the procedural conduct of the arbitration, the parties' agreement to submit the dispute for resolution under the Rules constitutes an agreement in favour of the procedural framework established by the Rules. In other words, the starting point for the tribunal in conducting the arbitration is the Rules themselves, but always subject to the parties' agreement.

---

[27] *DAC Report* paras 157 and 159.

The Rules do not provide an exhaustive procedural code designed to cover all   **5.21**
points that might arise in the course of the arbitration, and the tribunal is therefore still expected to issue one or more procedural directions during the course
of the proceedings.[28] It is noteworthy, however, that the Rules are significantly
more detailed than most other arbitration rules (institutional or ad hoc) in their
coverage of the procedural framework of the proceedings. By way of illustration,
it is instructive to compare the Rules with the ICC Rules. Articles 15, 19, 20, 21,
and 22 of the LCIA Rules, on the one hand, set out a default procedure for the
written stage of the proceedings (Article 15), address the tribunal's organization of
hearings (Article 19), include rules governing the submission of witness evidence
(Article 20), the appointment of experts by the tribunal (Article 21), as well as
providing a whole panoply of powers granted to the tribunal in its conduct of the
arbitration, including, inter alia, its appreciation of evidence and the power to
order the disclosure of documents by the parties.[29] The ICC Rules, on the other
hand, provide little more than a framework for the conduct of the proceedings,[30]
by conferring broad powers on the tribunal to establish the facts of the case 'by all
appropriate means',[31] subject to the basic guarantees generally associated with a
fair and impartial procedure, such as the right to a hearing and to a reasonable
opportunity to present one's case.[32] The prescriptive approach of the Rules
to procedural matters partly explains the relative length of the Rules, as compared
to the ICC Rules. The difference in approach between the two sets of rules is no
doubt deliberate. Certainly, the Rules were drafted and designed to contain
a more or less full agenda for the conduct of every LCIA arbitration.[33] Indeed,
it has been argued by a former President of the LCIA Court, in commenting on
the 1985 version of the Rules, that 'the content of the LCIA Rules is sufficiently
detailed and exhaustive to enable the Rules to be used as the necessary planning
instrument [at a preliminary procedural meeting] with little or no addition,
whenever they apply'.[34]

While the authors neither endorse nor reject the sentiment expressed above that   **5.22**
the Rules represent a more than adequate substitute for a checklist of procedural
issues to be debated at a preliminary meeting or procedural conference,[35]

---

[28] Art 15.7.
[29] Not forgetting the tribunal's power to order the parties to provide security for the legal or other costs of any other party by way of deposit or bank guarantee under art 25.2.
[30] *Derains & Schwartz* 224.
[31] Art 20(1) ICC Rules.
[32] Arts 15(2) and 21 ICC Rules.
[33] Sir M Kerr, 'London Court of International Arbitration' in *ICCA Congress Series No 7* (Kluwer, 1996) 213, 215.
[34] Ibid.
[35] A more exhaustive checklist of issues is set out in the Notes for Preparatory Conferences in Arbitral Proceedings adopted by UNCITRAL in 1996.

we merely note that the current version of the Rules is even more detailed than the previous version. Once again, this was deliberate on the part of the drafters of the Rules, who viewed the greater liberty granted to parties to agree their arbitral procedure under the English Arbitration Act as enfranchising the LCIA to create a 'near-exhaustive procedural code' for its users.[36] While it is unlikely that any provisions of the Rules will contravene the mandatory rules of any applicable *lex arbitri* other than English law, this is yet a further illustration that the Rules were drafted with one eye firmly on the English Arbitration Act.

Mandatory procedural rules of the lex arbitri

5.23 Article 14.2 grants the tribunal the widest discretion to discharge its duties under such law(s) or rules of law as the tribunal may determine to be applicable. The discretion of the tribunal in conducting the reference is therefore subject to the application of the mandatory rules or international public policy of the law applicable to the arbitration, also known as the *lex arbitri*. This is a fundamental tenet of international arbitration practice.[37] As we discuss below in the context of Article 16, this means that in most LCIA arbitrations the *lex arbitri* is likely to constitute English law, as the arbitration law of the seat of the arbitration.

5.24 As explained by two distinguished commentators, the *lex arbitri* encompasses all provisions governing the arbitration in a given country, particularly the formal validity of the arbitration agreement, the arbitrability of the dispute, the composition of the tribunal, fundamental procedural guarantees, assistance from the courts, and judicial review of the ensuing award(s).[38] In other words, the *lex arbitri* comprises 'a body of rules which sets a standard external to the arbitration agreement, and the wishes of the parties, for the conduct of the arbitration'.[39] Most national arbitration laws comprise fundamental procedural principles governing the conduct of the proceedings, such as the need to treat parties impartially and fairly, rather than detailed rules of procedure. The application of these fundamental procedural principles is mandatory and so they must be respected by the tribunal in its conduct of the arbitration, as affirmed in Article 14.3.

5.25 It is worth briefly addressing two possible sources of confusion as to the application of the *lex arbitri*. First, Article 14.2 does not mandate the tribunal to apply the civil procedure rules applicable at the place of arbitration, or the civil

---

[36] *Commentary* 10. Arbitration Act 1996, s 4(3) makes it clear that the parties' agreement to the application of institutional arbitration rules creates a permissible regime for all non-mandatory provisions of the Act with respect to the initiation and conduct of the arbitration.

[37] *Redfern & Hunter* paras 6-01 and 6-07; see also *Poudret & Besson* paras 545 and 555.

[38] *Poudret & Besson* para 112.

[39] *Smith Ltd v H&S International* [1991] 2 Lloyd's Rep 127, 130.

procedure rules of any other jurisdiction.[40] This is neither the intention nor the effect of modern national arbitration laws, as exemplified by the UNCITRAL Model Law. Indeed, the non-applicability of national procedural rules is one of the principal advantages of international arbitration, since this allows the arbitration procedure to be adapted to the requirements of the case at hand and avoids the formalism of national procedural rules. Second, although certain arbitration laws, the English Arbitration Act being a good example, also provide a set of optional procedural rules in addition to the fundamental procedural principles discussed above, such procedural rules only apply in the absence of a choice of specific rules by the parties or the arbitrators. Such optional rules do not therefore apply where the procedural issue is already addressed in the Rules.

The tribunal's failure to apply and ensure respect for the fundamental procedural **5.26** rights under the *lex arbitri* may render its award liable to be set aside by the courts at the seat of arbitration[41] or could see enforcement refused.[42] However, parties must be careful not to waive their right to challenge an award on this ground. Pursuant to Article 32.1 of the Rules, a party who knows that any provision of the arbitration agreement, including the Rules, has not been complied with and yet proceeds with the arbitration without promptly stating its objection to such non-compliance shall be treated as having irrevocably waived its right to object. Nor is it generally possible for parties to seek review of the tribunal's jurisdictional decisions in advance of an award.[43]

Parties' duty to comply with the tribunal's procedural orders

Article 14.2 requires that the parties shall do everything necessary for the fair, **5.27** efficient, and expeditious conduct of the arbitration. This provision is a near-verbatim reproduction of section 40(1) of the Arbitration Act 1996, which is a mandatory provision and therefore applicable to all arbitrations with seats in England, Wales, or Northern Ireland. Pursuant to this provision, the parties are duty-bound to comply without delay with the tribunal's procedural decisions and orders. The tribunal enjoys wide discretion to determine the consequences resulting from a party's failure to comply with the tribunal's directions: this will likely

---

[40] *Poudret & Besson* para 522; and Paulsson (n 4 above) 65–6.

[41] There are a few notable exceptions: eg, art 192 PILA authorizes the parties without a domicile in Switzerland to exclude any recourse against arbitral awards rendered there. Similar provisions apply in Belgium (art 1717 Belgian Judicial Code) and in Sweden (s 51 Swedish Arbitration Act 1999).

[42] Arts V(1)(b) and (d) New York Convention.

[43] The competent court's powers of review will of course depend upon the application of the *lex arbitri*. The position in respect of England is straightforward: 'the court is given no express power under the Arbitration Act to review or overrule procedural decisions in advance of an award': *Elektrim SA v Vivendi Universal SA (No 2)* [2007] 2 Lloyd's Rep 8, 20.

depend on the importance of the order or direction and the severity of the parties' non-compliance. Section 41 of the Arbitration Act sets out the tribunal's powers in cases of default, unless the parties have agreed otherwise.[44]

5.28   The most common form of procedural orders issued by tribunals concern time limits for the submission of the parties' written submissions and supporting evidence. Such time limits are often determined by agreement of the parties (and then recorded by the tribunal in the form of an order) or, if no agreement is reached, by the tribunal. They should obviously be respected by the parties to ensure an orderly and fair procedure. In international arbitration, however, there is a tendency to avoid taking severe measures to penalize a party who submits evidence and other documents out of time, especially if the tribunal considers the tardy submission to be relevant to the issues at stake, and the delay is justified on the basis of a legitimate excuse. The arbitrators' reluctance to take a firm position and simply reject late submissions can, at least partly, be explained by the power of the courts at the seat of arbitration to review the final award in order to ensure that the procedural rights of the parties have been respected during the proceedings. On the other hand, an award cannot generally be set aside or refused enforcement by the courts due to the arbitrators' having allowed the late submission of documents.[45] In order to avoid the risk of setting aside proceedings, therefore, arbitrators generally permit tardy submissions and ensure that the innocent party has sufficient time to respond, which may mean extending that party's deadline.

Article 14.3

In the case of a three-member Arbitral Tribunal the chairman may, with the prior consent of the other two arbitrators, make procedural rulings alone.

5.29   Article 14.3 delegates to the chairman of the tribunal the power to make procedural rulings alone, albeit with the prior consent of the other two arbitrators. As a matter of practice, however, it is unlikely that the chairman will make any significant procedural rulings without prior consultation of his co-arbitrators. Similar provisions are contained in most other arbitration rules, although not the ICC Rules.[46] This provision reflects common practice in international arbitration, where arbitrators are often not based in the same location, and therefore has the advantage of enabling the tribunal to make speedy decisions. It further avoids the cost and inconvenience of consulting all members of the tribunal.

---

[44] *Russell* paras 5-181 to 5-185.
[45] *Fouchard, Gaillard, Goldman* paras 1269–70.
[46] Art 31(2) UNCITRAL Arbitration Rules, art 26(2) ICDR Rules, and art 35(2) SCC Rules.

B. Article 15 – Submission of Written Statements and Documents

In the context of Article 14 above, we discussed the prescriptive approach of the **5.30** Rules to procedural matters, including the intention of the drafters of the Rules to provide a 'near-exhaustive procedural code' for users of LCIA arbitration.[47] Article 15, which sets out a full procedure for the submission of written statements and documents, represents further evidence of that prescriptive approach. The inclusion of such a procedure is intended to introduce a degree of procedural predictability in circumstances where the parties are unable to agree, either between themselves or with the procedural proposals put forward by the tribunal.[48]

Article 15.1

Unless the parties have agreed otherwise under Article 14.1 or the Arbitral Tribunal should determine differently, the written stage of the proceedings shall be as set out below.

Article 15, which applies unless the parties have agreed otherwise or the tribunal **5.31** determines differently, sets out a full procedure for the submission of written pleadings with respect to the period after the formation of the tribunal. Article 15 is one of the most distinctive features of the Rules, and is not replicated elsewhere. Other arbitration rules, most notably the ICC Rules, do not contain a similar provision and merely empower the tribunal to establish the appropriate procedure for the resolution of the parties' dispute.[49] The ICDR Rules similarly invest the tribunal with the power to establish whether the parties should present further written pleadings in addition to the request for arbitration (which must include a statement of claim) and the statement of defence, both of which are submitted prior to the tribunal's formation.[50] Even those rules that do envisage the submission of specific written pleadings following the tribunal's formation, such as the UNCITRAL Rules, empower the tribunal to determine the appropriate timing for the submission of such pleadings and to determine whether further written pleadings are required.[51]

It is important to bear in mind, however, that the procedure set out in Article 15 **5.32** is not mandatory, and will not be suitable in every case. Ideally, the arbitrators and the parties can agree – or at least attempt to agree – on a tailored set of procedural

---

[47] *Commentary* 10.
[48] *Hunter & Paulsson* 170.
[49] Art 20(1) ICC Rules (see also *Derains & Schwartz* 271–3).
[50] Art 17.1 ICDR Rules.
[51] Arts 18, 19, and 22 UNCITRAL Rules.

directions for the conduct of the arbitration, rather than rely on the procedure set out in Article 15 as a first resort. Article 15 can therefore be said to be a default procedure, applicable where the parties and the tribunal have not agreed or ordered specific procedural directions.

Arbitrators are not bound by national procedural rules

5.33 As we have seen, international arbitrators are not bound by national laws of civil procedure. This is one of the principal advantages of arbitration, where the procedure can be determined in light of the particular circumstances of the case. Determining the appropriate procedure is a task that generally requires the active management of the tribunal as well as a degree of cooperation and compromise between the parties to achieve a suitable and efficient procedure. However, such cooperation may not always be forthcoming from parties, particularly when they share different nationalities and are inexperienced in the conduct of international arbitration, and so may expect a procedure similar to their respective national rules with which they are familiar. Conversely, where counsel and the arbitrators share the same nationality and/or legal traditions, then there is a tendency for the procedures adopted to be those with which the tribunal and counsel are most familiar. This can lead to arbitrations being conducted in such a way as to mirror court proceedings. In the case of arbitrations conducted under the Rules, where a London seat is predominant and often both sets of counsel and the majority of arbitrators are English-trained and/or based in London, it is not uncommon for the procedures adopted to lean heavily on the customs and practices of the English Commercial Court and the Civil Procedure Rules 1998. Such procedures tend to share the typical characteristics of common-law civil procedure, including extensive disclosure requirements and relatively lengthy hearings, thus giving rise to a peculiarly 'English' form of procedure.

5.34 It is, of course, natural for arbitrators and counsel alike to be guided by the approach that they would follow before their national courts in devising a suitable procedure for an arbitration. This is very different, however, from adopting court-like procedures because both counsel and the arbitrators are familiar with such procedures, and without taking account of the particular circumstances of the dispute. Such conduct may well place the arbitrators in breach of their general duties to adopt procedures that are suitable, avoiding unnecessary delay or expense.[52] It also means that the arbitrators may be doing the parties – who are typically not English and should not be expected to be familiar with the practice of English civil procedure – a great injustice. The authors endorse the following

---

[52] Art 14.1(ii).

views expressed by the authors of a leading commentary on ICC arbitration, which should be equally applicable to LCIA arbitration:

> Without any sophisticated analysis, parties expect two things in practice: first, that by adopting an ICC clause in their contract, they will have escaped procedural particularities of local courts; and second, that the international arbitrators will have the power to supplement the procedures set forth in the Rules. . . . Even if the parties have chosen the place of arbitration in their contract, it is most doubtful that by such choice they intended to follow the rules of national procedure applicable to domestic arbitrations at the seat, let alone the practices followed in judicial proceedings there.[53]

Adopting a suitable arbitration procedure

In the hands of an experienced tribunal, and with the assistance and cooperation **5.35** of counsel, a sufficiently flexible arbitration procedure can be established to tailor the particular circumstances of the case. In particular, advantage can be taken of the differences between common law and civil law systems as to the conduct of the proceedings and the taking of evidence, and parties and arbitrators can pick and choose the rules which are best suited to a particular case. In practice, the liberalization of national arbitration laws, increasing contacts and interaction between international arbitration practitioners, and the issuance of transnational standards (such as the IBA Rules) have led to greater homogenization and convergence in the procedures used by international arbitrators from different legal traditions.[54] Section 34(2)(g) of the Arbitration Act, which empowers a tribunal sitting in England to take the initiative itself in ascertaining the facts and the law, is often cited as an illustration of this trend towards convergence, by permitting arbitrators to adopt an inquisitorial approach that is alien to the traditional adversarial approach adopted in common law jurisdictions. Concerns were raised during the consultation period prior to enactment of the Arbitration Act that English arbitrators were unused to such powers and might therefore abuse them. Such concerns were dismissed by the DAC on the basis that, so long as the tribunal in exercising its powers follows the duties set out in section 33(1) of the Arbitration Act (which are replicated in Article 14.1 sub-paragraphs (i) and (ii) of the Rules), then an inquisitorial approach may well be the best way of proceeding in suitable cases.[55]

In determining the arbitration procedure, arbitrators solicit the parties' views **5.36** and very often seek to obtain their agreement as to the general structure of the

---

[53] *Craig, Park, Paulsson* para 16.02.

[54] *Fouchard, Gaillard, Goldman* paras 1259–60; *Poudret & Besson* para 562; *Redfern & Hunter* paras 6-10 and 6-11; *Derains & Schwartz* 272; and A Baum 'International Arbitration: the Path towards Uniform Procedures' in *Liber Amicorum Robert Briner* (ICC Publishing, 2005) 51.

[55] *DAC Report* paras 171–2.

procedure. The exchange of views and the determination of a procedural timetable (to be set out in a subsequent procedural order) is often conducted at a preliminary meeting held between the tribunal and the parties shortly after the formation of the tribunal. There is no requirement for such a meeting, and, indeed, the default procedure of Article 15 does not specifically envisage one.[56] Nonetheless, especially where the parties and their legal representatives come from different cultural backgrounds, or from different legal systems, it is sensible for the tribunal to convene such a meeting with the parties at an early stage. This ensures that the tribunal and the parties have a common understanding of how the arbitration is to be conducted and enables a carefully designed framework for the conduct of the arbitration to be established.[57] Such meetings are also often the first time that the parties have met following the commencement of proceedings and thus provide an opportunity for valuable face-to-face contact that can sometimes act as a spur for an amicable resolution of the dispute. It is also often helpful for the parties and counsel to meet the arbitrators prior to the final hearing.

5.37 The range of matters that may be discussed at a preliminary meeting is very wide indeed and, inter alia, should include: the form and timetable for the submission of written pleadings; the form and timetable for the submission of evidence (both documentary and witness evidence); requests for further disclosure of documents; the determination of any preliminary issues, such as the applicable law or objections to the tribunal's jurisdiction, and whether such issues should be bifurcated; and date(s) for any hearings. Section 34(2) of the Arbitration Act 1996 contains a useful list of procedural and evidential matters for the tribunal and the parties to consider. A more detailed list of issues is contained in the Notes Organizing Arbitral Proceedings adopted by UNCITRAL in 1996. Although in many cases it may be difficult, at this early stage, to anticipate every step that may be required to be taken in the arbitration (for example, as regards the number of witnesses or the appointment of experts by the tribunal), the preparation of a detailed procedural order and timetable nevertheless constitutes a useful discipline that should encourage the parties and the arbitrators to decide upon the relevant procedural requirements of the case as soon as possible.[58]

---

[56] Although art 15.7 envisages the issuance of procedural directions by the tribunal following the service of the parties' written submissions, as discussed below.

[57] *Redfern & Hunter* para 6-27.

[58] *Derains & Schwartz* 265. A counter-argument to the utility of preliminary meetings holds that such meetings should be avoided, or kept to an absolute minimum, until the parties have fleshed out their respective cases and crystallized the issues at stake in their initial pleadings. Until then, it is argued that any process of planning would be largely academic and take place in a void (Kerr (n 33 above) 218).

The procedural order or directions that are issued following the preliminary   **5.38**
meeting, however, are not to be regarded as inviolate. It is quite normal for the
tribunal to modify its directions over the course of the proceedings, typically
upon the request of one or more of the parties, as the issues in the case become
crystallized. Furthermore, it may well be necessary, and in most cases advisable,
for the tribunal to issue specific directions dealing with the organization of
evidentiary hearings, but only nearer the time and once the list of all testifying
witnesses has been fixed.

The exchange of written submissions

The first step to be typically followed after the procedure has been established is   **5.39**
the exchange of written submissions between the parties. The purpose of such
submissions is to define the precise issues at stake in the arbitration by setting out
the factual assertions and legal arguments in support of the parties' positions. In
all but the smallest arbitrations, the parties will generally exchange two sets of
written submissions. The exchange of submissions permits the parties to define
more precisely the issues in dispute and to crystallize the points that need to be
determined by the tribunal. The submissions, which are typically accompanied
by documentary evidence, and, more often than not, the written statements of
factual and expert witnesses as well, constitute the principal means by which
the parties present their case to the arbitrators. In this regard, the predominant
trend in international arbitration is to adopt detailed written submissions at the
expense of a shorter oral hearing, which will principally, although not exclusively,
be devoted to the hearing of witnesses and experts.

The parties' written submissions may take a wide variety of forms and many dif-   **5.40**
ferent expressions are used to describe such submissions, often interchangeably.
At one extreme, written submissions may resemble formal pleadings served in
English civil procedure. These are generally concise submissions, the primary purpose of which is to define the issues and state the facts upon which the parties'
claims and counterclaims are founded. Such submissions typically serve as a prel-
ude to a lengthy hearing, at which the tribunal receives the oral testimony of witnesses and extensive legal submissions from counsel. The parties' detailed legal
arguments are not therefore developed at any great length in such submissions,
typically called 'pleadings', which are saved for the hearing. Although such written
submissions continue to be adopted, they do not constitute the predominant
practice in international arbitration. At the other extreme, written submissions
typically called 'memorials' are lengthy documents that set out the parties' case in
full. They contain very full arguments as to the issues of law and fact at stake and
are accompanied by supporting documents on which the parties rely, as well as

copies of relevant legal authorities.[59] Under this approach, hearings are generally kept to a minimum and are primarily reserved for the examination of witnesses, rather than extensive oral submission, in recognition that long hearings generally cause great inconvenience and cost in international arbitration, without necessarily improving the decision-making process. It is this latter approach that now represents standard practice in international arbitration.[60]

5.41 Memorials are also typically accompanied by supporting factual witness statements and expert reports. The alternative is for witness evidence to follow the exchange of written submissions, which would require the tribunal to set a series of additional dates for the different evidential stages. The simultaneous service of legal submissions together with accompanying witness evidence has a number of advantages. First, it permits each party to present its full case on the facts and the law in a coherent and organized fashion, as each submission presents a complete snapshot of that party's entire case. This is particularly useful in cases where factual or expert witness evidence plays a prominent role, as this evidence can be fully considered and taken account of in formulating the legal argument which is presented in the party's written submissions. Second, the simultaneous service of witness evidence is likely to result in a more efficient and streamlined procedure, as it avoids a separate exchange of witness evidence that would inevitably lead to a lengthier procedure.[61]

5.42 A growing tendency in international arbitration is the addition of a further round of written submissions following the evidentiary hearing. The purpose of these 'post-hearing briefs', as they are typically called, is to summarize the parties' respective cases in the light of the witness evidence presented at the hearing. Tribunals find such submissions to be especially helpful, as they collate in one document the essence of the parties' respective arguments on the facts and the law. For this reason, as well as the resulting consequence of shorter hearings, these written submissions have largely replaced the practice of oral closing statements, or at least greatly reduced these latter in length.

Articles 15.2 to 15.7

15.2 Within 30 days of receipt of written notification from the Registrar of the formation of the Arbitral Tribunal, the Claimant shall send to the Registrar a Statement of Case setting out in sufficient detail the facts and any contentions

---

[59] *Redfern & Hunter* para 6-49.
[60] *Russell* para 5-123; and *Fouchard, Gaillard, Goldman* para 1260.
[61] The simultaneous service of legal submissions and written witness statements does, however, raise greater logistical issues for the parties with respect to coordinating the submission of evidence which may be interdependent.

of law on which it relies, together with the relief claimed against all other parties, save and insofar as such matters have not been set out in its Request.

15.3 Within 30 days of receipt of the Statement of Case or written notice from the Claimant that it elects to treat the Request as its Statement of Case, the Respondent shall send to the Registrar a Statement of Defence setting out in sufficient detail which of the facts and contentions of law in the Statement of Case or Request (as the case may be) it admits or denies and on what grounds and on what other facts and contentions of law it relies. Any counterclaims shall be submitted with the Statement of Defence in the same manner as Claims are to be set out in the Statement of Case.

15.4 Within 30 days of receipt of the Statement of Defence, the Claimant shall send to the Registrar a Statement of Reply which, where there are any counterclaims, shall include a Defence of Counterclaim in the same manner as a defence is to be set out in the Statement of Defence.

15.5 If the Statement of Reply contains a Defence to Counterclaim, within 30 days of its receipt the Respondent shall send to the Registrar a Statement of Reply to Counterclaim.

15.6 All Statements referred to in this Article shall be accompanied by copies (or, if they are especially voluminous, lists) of all essential documents on which the party concerned relies and which have not previously been submitted by any party, and (where appropriate) by any relevant samples and exhibits.

15.7 As soon as practicable following receipt of the Statements specified in this Article, the Arbitral Tribunal shall proceed in such manner as has been agreed in writing by the parties or pursuant to its authority under these Rules.

Articles 15.2 to 15.6 set out the default procedure for the submission of written **5.43** statements, including supporting documents, by the parties. As discussed earlier, the default procedure under Article 15 will apply unless the parties agree otherwise or the tribunal should determine differently. The purpose for including such a procedure was to introduce a certain degree of predictability in cases where the parties are unable to agree, either between themselves or with the procedural proposals put forward by the tribunal.[62] As discussed earlier, although it is preferable for the parties and the tribunal to be able to devise a procedure that takes account of the specific circumstances of the dispute, reaching agreement on a suitable procedure is not always straightforward and can become a highly controversial exercise. In such circumstances, the tribunal and the parties may consider that following the default procedure under Article 15 represents the least contentious option. As Article 15 does not set forth a complete procedure for the conduct of the arbitration, further procedural directions (for example, as regards the submission of witness statements and expert reports) will still be required pursuant to Article 15.7.

---

[62] *Hunter & Paulsson* 170.

The procedure under Article 15

5.44   Article 15.2 provides that within 30 days of receipt of written notification of the formation of the tribunal, the claimant must submit a statement of case. This provision should be read in conjunction with Article 15.6 which requires that the statement of case (and all subsequent submissions) be accompanied by copies of all essential documents on which the parties rely.[63] In the event that the claimant elects to treat the Request as its statement of case, then the first submission following the formation of the tribunal will be the respondent's statement of defence, which must be submitted within 30 days of receipt of the claimant's notice of election.[64] If the claimant's notice of election is made prior to the constitution of the tribunal, then the time period under Article 15.3 starts to run from the tribunal's formation.

5.45   The deadline under Article 15.2 starts to run automatically as of the notification of the tribunal's formation. In fact, in his letter to the parties notifying them of the tribunal's constitution, the Registrar informs the parties that the claimant should file its statement of case within 30 days, unless otherwise agreed by the parties or directed by the tribunal. The notice of the tribunal's formation is generally the trigger for the parties to seek agreement on a suitable procedure for the written phase of the arbitration. This will typically include a discussion as regards the suitability of the default procedure under Article 15 and may also include a request (often made jointly) to the tribunal to organize a procedural meeting in order to establish a procedural timetable.

5.46   In the absence of such communication from the parties, tribunals will typically canvass the parties' views as regards the procedural conduct of the arbitration, including whether they wish to attend a procedural meeting. It is common practice for tribunals to invite the parties to agree on the procedure for the arbitration ahead of the procedural meeting in an effort to narrow down any areas of disagreement.

5.47   Any decision on the arbitration procedure, whether as a result of the parties' agreement or the tribunal's direction, should be made well before the expiration of the 30-day deadline following the tribunal's formation so that the parties at least know where they stand in respect of the default procedure set forth in Article 15.

5.48   The procedure set forth in Articles 15.2 to 15.6 envisages the exchange of two rounds of submissions, each to be served within 30 days of receipt of the

---

63   Art 15.6 permits the parties to submit lists of documents if there are voluminous accompanying documents. Although arbitrators may well elect to receive only lists of documents pending the submission of a hearing bundle in due course, it is unlikely that the parties would be content with such an arrangement.

64   Art 15.3.

prior submission: the service of statements of case and defence in the first round, to be followed, in the second round, by the claimant's statement of reply. Contrary to what is now the predominant practice in international arbitration, the respondent does not serve a second written submission under Article 15. The procedure is slightly amended in the event that the respondent pursues any counterclaims. In this case, the statement of case is served as before, but the respondent's statement of defence must also set out in detail the facts and legal arguments in support of the respondent's counterclaims. The claimant's defence to the counterclaims is then set out in the statement of reply which must also contain a defence to counterclaim. The final submission is the prerogative of the respondent, who has the right to submit a statement of reply to the claimant's defence to counterclaim.[65]

As already mentioned, Article 15.6 mandates the parties to submit their written **5.49** statements together with all essential documents on which the parties rely. It is important to add at this juncture that there is no practice of automatic disclosure of documents in international arbitration. In the absence of a separate disclosure stage in the tribunal's procedural directions, the party seeking to obtain documents must make a specific application to the tribunal. The usual practice is to limit document production as much as possible to those documents that are strictly relevant and material to the issues in dispute and are in the possession, custody, or power of the parties to the arbitration.[66] Apart from the documents served by the parties, each party will usually have the opportunity to make targeted and reasonable requests for disclosure of documents by the other parties to the arbitration, typically in the manner set forth in Article 3 of the IBA Rules, which are often explicitly adopted as part of the procedural directions of the case.

As regards the content of the parties' statements, Article 15.3 provides that the **5.50** statement of case must set out in sufficient detail the facts and any contentions of law on which the claimant relies, together with any relief claimed. The same applies to the statement of defence to be submitted by the respondent, and both submissions should be accompanied by all essential documents (including legal authorities) on which the parties rely. Article 15 therefore envisages detailed statements setting out the parties' respective cases on both the facts and the law, a process that is similar to the current prevailing international arbitration practice. It is unlikely, however, that the 30-day deadlines set out in Article 15 will prove sufficient to enable the parties to present their full case, including all factual allegations and detailed legal argument, except in the simplest cases.

---

[65] The reference in art 15.5 to the respondent's 'statement of reply to counterclaim' is a typographical error which should correctly refer to the 'statement of reply to defence to counterclaim'.

[66] The tribunal's power to order document disclosure is discussed in ch 6 below in the context of art 22.1(e).

5.51 In practice, unless the parties agree (or the tribunal so directs) to extend the deadlines set out in Article 15, it is unlikely that the parties' statements served thereunder can do much more than to identify the material facts and to clarify the principal legal arguments on which the parties' respective cases are based. In short, the statements submitted under Articles 15.2 to 15.5 are more likely to resemble English-style pleadings described above, rather than full memorials. While such submissions are suitable in English civil procedure with its emphasis on concise written pleadings and relatively lengthy hearings, they are somewhat out of step with the predominant practice in international arbitration, which envisages detailed written statements at the expense of relatively short hearings.

5.52 Nor is it envisaged that the parties submit witness statements and experts' reports together with their written statements submitted under Articles 15.2 to 15.5. The submission of witness evidence is addressed in Article 20 of the Rules and will almost certainly be the subject of a specific procedural order issued by the tribunal.

5.53 As mentioned earlier, even where the default procedure of Article 15 is followed, further procedural directions will be required to cover the remainder of the arbitration procedure. In the absence of party agreement, Article 15.7 mandates the tribunal to proceed by fixing the further conduct of the arbitration up to the making of the final award. Many of the issues considered above in relation to the organization of preliminary meetings (including the submission of witness evidence and requests for disclosure of documents) will therefore remain equally applicable in the context of the directions to be issued by the tribunal under Article 15.7.

5.54 As part of our research, we reviewed the procedural conduct of all arbitrations commenced in 2006 to determine whether the default procedure of Article 15 was followed in those cases, or whether tribunals instead issued specific procedural directions at an early stage.[67] Discounting those cases that settled prior to the formation of the tribunal, in 33 out of 78 (ie, 42 per cent of) cases, the default procedure of Article 15 was followed without amendment. In a similar number of cases (29 cases, equivalent to 37 per cent), the tribunal held a preliminary procedural meeting and issued procedural directions for the conduct of the arbitration, without having regard to Article 15. In the remaining 16 cases (equivalent to 21 per cent), the parties adopted the procedural framework of Article 15, but with modified time limits.

5.55 Taking 2006 as a representative sample, these statistics demonstrate that in well over one-third of cases conducted under the Rules, the parties were either content

---

[67] Due to the protracted nature of this research, we only focused on cases commenced in 2006 as a representative sample.

to proceed under the default procedure set out in Article 15, or were directed to do so either by the explicit stipulation of the tribunal or by default. While the Article 15 procedure for the submission of written statements may well represent a suitable procedure for the conduct of certain cases, especially if the imposed deadlines are extended to permit the service of full statements, it is unlikely that the Article 15 procedure will be suitable in all cases. Parties and tribunals are best served by engaging in an active discussion at the outset of the proceedings (in practice, upon the formation of the tribunal) in order to determine the most suitable procedural directions for the conduct of the arbitration.

Article 15.8

If the Respondent fails to submit a Statement of Defence or the Claimant a Statement of Defence to Counterclaim, or if at any point any party fails to avail itself of the opportunity to present its case in the manner determined by Article 15.2 to 15.6 or directed by the Arbitral Tribunal, the Arbitral Tribunal may nevertheless proceed with the arbitration and make an award.

This provision confirms the tribunal's authority to proceed with the arbitration **5.56** and render an award in the event of default of one of the parties. This is an important provision which prevents a defaulting party, most commonly, respondents, from being able to compromise or otherwise delay the conduct of the proceedings. Most arbitration rules contain similar provisions,[68] as do many national laws.[69] In order to satisfy the requirements of due process, and to ensure that the ensuing award is not at risk of challenge, the tribunal must ensure that the defaulting party is notified of the progress of the arbitration and given an opportunity to present its case at each stage of the proceedings.[70] If the respondent then fails to appear at any stage of the proceedings, or at all, the tribunal may proceed to render a default award based on the evidence and arguments before it.

It is important to note, however, that default does not constitute an admission of **5.57** liability, and therefore does not automatically validate the arguments of the non-defaulting party.[71] Although the tribunal is empowered (and indeed duty-bound) to proceed with the arbitration and to render an award, if the non-defaulting party so requests (and is willing to meet the costs of the arbitration),[72] the tribunal should not unquestionably accept the submissions presented by the non-defaulting party. The tribunal must instead examine the merits of the arguments presented

---

[68] Arts 6(3) and 21(2) ICC Rules, art 23 ICDR Rules, art 28 UNCITRAL Rules, and art 45 ICSID Convention.
[69] eg, art 25 UNCITRAL Model law and s 41 Arbitration Act.
[70] *Fouchard, Gaillard, Goldman* para 1224.
[71] Ibid; and *Poudret & Besson* paras 586–7.
[72] See the discussion in ch 8 below in the context of arts 24 and 28.

by the non-defaulting party, without going so far as acting as an advocate on behalf of the defaulting party.

C. Article 16 – Seat of Arbitration and Place of Hearings

5.58 One of the most critical decisions to be made during the drafting of the arbitration agreement, or at the outset of the proceedings, is the determination of the seat of the arbitration. The choice of the seat is important because the law applicable to the arbitration, or the *lex arbitri*, is the arbitration law of the seat of the arbitration.[73] In other words, by choosing the seat, the parties are choosing the 'juridical seat' of the arbitration (in the words of the English Arbitration Act),[74] which is the place to which the arbitration is legally attached. The choice of the seat, and thus the *lex arbitri*, has a number of important consequences, as discussed above in the context of Article 14.2. To summarize:[75]

- the *lex arbitri* encompasses all provisions governing the arbitration in a given country, particularly the formal validity of the arbitration agreement, the arbitrability of the dispute, and the composition of the tribunal;
- the *lex arbitri* contains fundamental procedural guarantees, which must be respected by the tribunal and the parties alike in their conduct of the arbitration;
- the *lex arbitri* determines what powers exist to enable the local courts to assist (or interfere with) the arbitration process;
- the courts at the place of arbitration enjoy the exclusive right to hear challenges to any interim or final awards rendered by the tribunal;
- the seat is also important in the context of enforcement of awards, in particular in determining whether the award rendered constitutes a New York Convention award, ie, whether the seat of the arbitration is located in a state that is party to the New York Convention, which may facilitate enforcement in other member states.[76] In addition, the grounds for resisting the recognition or enforcement of an award under the New York Convention are limited and the seat of the arbitration is specifically relevant to a number of those grounds.

---

[73] Unless and to the extent that the parties have expressly agreed in writing on the application of another law and such agreement is not prohibited by the law of the arbitral seat, in accordance with art 16.3.

[74] Arbitration Act 1996, s 3.

[75] For a more detailed discussion of the role and impact of the seat on the conduct of the arbitration, see *Redfern & Hunter* paras 2-05 to 2-30 and 6-12 to 6-26; *Poudret & Besson* paras 115–48; and *Fouchard, Gaillard, Goldman* paras 1171–208.

[76] Due to the application of the reciprocity principle under art I(3) New York Convention.

The above-mentioned factors effectively illustrate the importance attached **5.59** to the parties' choice of the seat. Quite apart from the judicial considerations cited above, however, there are also the practical considerations of neutrality and convenience at issue. Where parties in international arbitration are of different nationalities, they typically select a neutral seat, in order to ensure that neither party enjoys 'home-court advantage' in terms of familiarity with the language or court procedures in the event that court assistance (or review) is sought. The convenience of any potential seat is also an important factor, as choosing the seat will also tend to determine where meetings and hearings will typically take place. Although the tribunal enjoys an express discretion to hold hearings and meetings elsewhere for reasons of geographical convenience,[77] the parties' assumption at the start of proceedings is often that any hearings or meetings convened by the tribunal will take place at the seat of the arbitration. Accordingly, issues such as security, the ease of travel (both in terms of air links and potential visa requirements), availability of suitable hearing facilities and support services, and the cost of travel and accommodation are factors which are usually taken into account by parties in determining the seat of arbitration.

Article 16.1

The parties may agree in writing the seat (or legal place) of their arbitration. Failing such a choice, the seat of arbitration shall be London, unless and until the LCIA Court determines in view of all the circumstances, and after having given the parties an opportunity to make written comment, that another seat is more appropriate.

Article 16.1 is one of the most distinctive provisions in the Rules. It provides that **5.60** the parties may agree the seat or legal place of arbitration, although such agreement must be in writing. In the event that the parties have failed to choose the seat of arbitration, however, London becomes the default seat, unless and until the LCIA Court determines an alternative seat in view of all the circumstances of the case. The inclusion of a default seat of arbitration (absent the parties' agreement otherwise), is unique among the leading international arbitration rules.[78]

The inclusion of London as the default seat may be seen as an illustration of the **5.61** London-centric nature of LCIA arbitration, which some may regard as a possible deterrent to users in other parts of the world.[79] There are, however, a number of counter-arguments to this view. First, it is argued that the inclusion of a default

---

[77] Art 16.2.
[78] Art 14(1) ICC Rules, art 13 ICDR Rules, art 16 UNCITRAL Rules, art 20 SCC Rules, and art 16(1) Swiss Rules. However, art 16.1 DIFC-LCIA Arbitration Rules designates the Dubai International Financial Centre, which is an autonomous jurisdiction in the Emirate of Dubai (see ch 1 above), as the default seat of arbitration in the absence of a prior designation by the parties.
[79] *Commentary* 11.

seat in the absence of party choice reduces uncertainty.[80] Thus, the parties (and the competent courts) will know from the outset the location of the seat of the arbitration and can act accordingly. Second, Article 16.1 respects the principle of party autonomy and therefore parties who are deterred by London need only select a different seat. Third, the choice of London 'appears best to conform to the parties' expectation when they refer to LCIA arbitration without specifying that they desire a seat of arbitration other than London'.[81] In other words, the choice of London as the default seat of arbitration appears to form part of the overall package that arbitration users accept, and indeed expect, when choosing to resolve their disputes under the Rules.

5.62   This sentiment is borne out by our research, which revealed that some 503 out of 701 cases commenced under the Rules by the end of 2007 had their seat in London, with another six elsewhere in England and Wales, while a mere eighteen (three per cent) had their seat elsewhere. As regards these eighteen cases, eight were seated elsewhere in Europe (split across France, Switzerland, Austria, Germany, and Spain), four in the United States, three in Asia, two in Canada and one in Bermuda. Given that 173 cases had unknown or unspecified seats, and given the provision for a default seat in London, it is to be imagined that nearly all, if not all, of these 173 had (or would have had, in the case of arbitrations that settled before the seat was designated) their seat in London. The overwhelming dominance of England (and particularly London) as the seat of arbitration for cases under the LCIA Rules is therefore clear.

5.63   In light of these statistics, it should not be surprising to learn that very rarely do parties contest London as the default choice, in the absence of a prior agreement, and thus require the Court to determine the seat under Article 16.1. In the event of such a request, the Court must determine whether a different seat is appropriate in view of all the circumstances. The Court has never made such a determination in the very limited number of cases where it has considered the issue.

5.64   It is worth noting two changes in the formulation of Article 16.1 from the corresponding provision in the 1985 version of the Rules.[82] First, the former text of the Rules did not differentiate between the 'place of arbitration' and the 'seat of arbitration' and adopted the former wording. The current Rules follow the formulation of section 3 of the English Arbitration Act and refer to the 'seat of arbitration'. In so doing, the Rules clarify the distinction between the seat or juridical place of arbitration, on the one hand, and the location where certain portions of the arbitration proceedings may take place, on the other hand, and

---

[80] *Hunter & Paulsson* 168.
[81] Ibid.
[82] Art 7.1 1985 Rules.

explain that the two may not be the same.[83] Second, Article 7.1 of the 1985 Rules empowered the tribunal to determine whether a seat other than London was more appropriate, rather than the LCIA Court as is the case under Article 16.1. The current formulation of the Rules accords with the practice under the ICC Rules, which empower the ICC Court to determine the place of arbitration, and means that the seat of arbitration is fixed prior to the formation of the tribunal, a factor which will no doubt influence the selection of arbitrators either by the parties or the Court.

Article 16.2

> The Arbitral Tribunal may hold hearings, meetings and deliberations at any convenient geographical place in its discretion; and if elsewhere than the seat of the arbitration, the arbitration shall be treated as an arbitration conducted at the seat of the arbitration and any award as an award made at the seat of the arbitration for all purposes.

Article 16.2 provides the tribunal with discretion to hold hearings, meetings, and deliberations at any convenient geographical place. The tribunal's discretion to convene hearings or meetings at a convenient place of its choosing is a common feature of modern international arbitration practice and similar provisions are contained in other arbitration rules.[84] In view of the respective locations of the arbitrators, counsel, and witnesses, it may be appropriate for the tribunal to convene relevant hearings and meetings in a geographically convenient place. This is quite apart from any site visits or inspections that would naturally take place at the relevant site. **5.65**

As mentioned earlier, however, often the parties' expectation is that the arbitration will be principally conducted at the seat of the arbitration, especially if the seat was expressly chosen by the parties for reasons of neutrality and/or convenience. For this reason, it is preferable to hold hearings at the seat unless the parties agree that they may be held elsewhere,[85] even though Article 16.2 contains no such express requirement.[86] The significance of the tribunal's decision to hold hearings in a venue other than the seat of the arbitration should not be underestimated and may prove controversial, especially if the decision appears to be made for the convenience of only some of the participants involved at the hearing, **5.66**

---

[83] Art 16.2; see also A Winstanley, 'The LCIA – history, constitution and rules' in A Berkeley and J Mimms (eds), *International Commercial Arbitration: Practical Perspectives* (Centre of Construction Law & Management, 2001) 21, 28.

[84] eg, art 14(2) ICC Rules, art 13(2) ICDR Rules, and art 16(2) UNCITRAL Rules.

[85] *Redfern & Hunter* para 6-23.

[86] In contrast, art 14(2) ICC Rules requires the tribunal to consult the parties prior to conducting hearings and meetings at any location it considers appropriate (see *Derains & Schwartz* 220).

without due consideration of any inconvenience that may be caused to the other participants. In a well-known case conducted under the ICC Rules (ICC Case No 10623) between an Italian and an Ethiopian party, the European-based tribunal decided to hold the hearing in Paris, rather than Addis Ababa, which was the agreed seat of the arbitration, on the basis of its own and the Italian party's convenience, without due regard (in the eyes of the Ethiopian party) to the inconvenience that this would cause to the Ethiopian party. The tribunal's decision formed the basis of a challenge brought by the Ethiopian party which was ultimately rejected by the ICC Court, whose decision was in turn appealed to the Ethiopian courts.[87] The case provides a salutary lesson to tribunals not to underestimate the potential impact of their choice of venue for hearings, and to use caution in exercising their discretion under Article 16.2 in making such a choice.

5.67   In the event that hearings, meetings, or deliberations are held elsewhere than at the seat, Article 16.2 provides that the arbitration shall be treated as having been conducted at the seat of the arbitration and any award as an award made at the seat of the arbitration for all purposes. Article 16.2, which should be considered in conjunction with Article 26.1 in respect of the issuance of awards,[88] is a 'deeming provision' that is intended to eliminate any need for the arbitrators actually to conduct the arbitration at the seat of the arbitration, or be required to meet at the seat in order to sign the award. It was included for the first time in the current version of the Rules, partly due to queries received by the LCIA from arbitrators, seeking clarification as to whether they would need to sign the award at the seat of arbitration.[89] The confusion was partly the result of a decision of the House of Lords where the award in an otherwise entirely English arbitration was held to have been made in Paris because it was signed there.[90] So far as England is concerned, this confusion was cleared up by the introduction of the Arbitration Act.[91] A similar provision is included in many modern arbitration statutes and other arbitration rules.[92]

---

[87] Extracts from the partial award reproduced at (2003) 21 ASA Bull 82; also on this case, see E Schwartz, 'Do International Arbitrators Have a Duty to Obey the Orders of Courts at the Place of Arbitration? Reflections on the Role of the *Lex Loci Arbitri* in the Light of a Recent ICC Award' in *Liber Amicorum Robert Briner* (ICC Publishing, 2005); and R Mohtashami, 'In Defense of Injunctions Issued by the Courts at the Place of Arbitration: A Brief Reply to Professor Bachand's Commentary on *Salini Costruttori S.p.A. v. Ethiopia*' (2005) 20(5) Mealey's Int Arb Rep 44.

[88] Discussed in ch 7 below.

[89] *Commentary* 11.

[90] *Hiscox v Outhwaite* [1992] 1 AC 562, HL.

[91] Arbitration Act, ss 53 and 100(2)(b).

[92] Art 31(3) UNCITRAL Model Law, art 15(2) ICC Rules, and 27(3) ICDR Rules.

Article 16.3

The law applicable to the arbitration (if any) shall be the arbitration law of the seat of arbitration, unless and to the extent that the parties have expressly agreed in writing on the application of another arbitration law and such agreement is not prohibited by the law of the arbitral seat.

The concept that an arbitration is governed by the law of the seat of arbitration, **5.68** sometimes referred to as 'the seat theory' or 'localized arbitration', is well-established in the practice of international arbitration. This is illustrated by the adoption of the territorial link between the place of arbitration and the *lex arbitri* in the UNCITRAL Model Law and most other modern arbitration laws,[93] including the English Arbitration Act, which, as we have seen, defines the seat as the 'juridical seat' of the arbitration.[94] The New York Convention also adheres to the territorial link between the place of arbitration and the *lex arbitri*, as demonstrated by references to 'the law of the country where the award was made' and 'the law of the country where the arbitration took place' in its Article V, which sets out the limited grounds on which enforcement of an award may be refused.[95] Article 16.3 accords with this established practice by explicitly adopting the territorial link between the seat of arbitration and the *lex arbitri*.

Although the seat as a connecting factor is clearly dominant today in the practice **5.69** of international arbitration,[96] this practice is not universal. A discussion of those exceptions is strictly beyond the scope of this commentary, however, in light of the express provision of Article 16.3. A brief summary of the position in France, which represents the most prominent exception to the concept of 'localized arbitration', would therefore suffice. French arbitration law (contained in the Code de procédure civile) is based upon the conception that an international arbitration is not rooted in the legal system of the country of the seat. French arbitration law does not define its territorial scope of application and, therefore, refrains from connecting an international arbitration to a particular country's legal system.[97] Once seized in respect of an international arbitration,[98] a French court will therefore apply the French law of arbitration without taking the seat into account. French law does not entirely disregard the place of arbitration, and, in particular, the jurisdiction of the French courts to set aside an award is dependent upon the award having been rendered in France.[99] However, while accepting the value of

---

[93] eg, art 1(2) UNCITRAL Model Law, art 176(1) PILA, and art 1073 Netherlands Arbitration Act 1986.

[94] Arbitration Act, s 3.

[95] Arts V(1)(a) and V(1)(d) New York Convention, respectively.

[96] *Poudret & Besson* paras 115, 120, and 134.

[97] *Fouchard, Gaillard, Goldman* paras 94 and 1178 ff.

[98] As defined in art 1492 Code de procédure civile.

[99] Art 1504 Code de procédure civile.

a seat in France as a connecting factor, French law does not take this factor into account when the seat is outside France. Thus, a French court seized with an application for enforcement of an award rendered elsewhere, will review that award by the same enforcement rules as an award made in an international arbitration seated in France.[100] This means that French courts will not give effect to a judgment rendered by the courts at the seat of arbitration setting aside the award in question, as per Article V(1)(e) of the New York Convention.[101]

5.70   The 'delocalized' concept of arbitration, in the sense of an arbitration that is detached from a national legal system and is, thus, considered 'anational' or subject to 'transnational' principles, is based upon an extreme application of the principle of party autonomy[102] and, as mentioned earlier, has no application under the Rules. This is because, pursuant to Article 16.3, and absent an agreement of the parties, the Rules expressly endorse the territorial link between the seat and the *lex arbitri*. In light of the significant number of LCIA cases that are seated in England, it is also important to note that English law does not recognize the concept of 'delocalized' arbitral procedures.[103]

5.71   Article 16.3 does however permit the parties to choose a procedural law of the arbitration that may be different from the law at the seat of arbitration, to the extent that this is permitted by the law of the arbitral seat. It is not clear why the parties would wish to complicate further the conduct of their arbitration by seating their arbitration in one country and subjecting it to the procedural law of another. Certain national arbitration laws, including English law, permit such a possibility.[104] English law permits parties to choose a different procedural law where the seat of their arbitration is in England.[105] The choice of a foreign procedural law will not displace the application of the mandatory provisions of the Arbitration Act, however, as such provisions cannot be excluded in respect of arbitrations whose seat is in England.[106] The ensuing complications caused for both the parties and the arbitrators in having to comply with two sets of procedural laws is best avoided, wherever possible.

---

[100] Art 1502 Code de procédure civile.

[101] This practice was recently affirmed by the *Cour de Cassation, 1ère ch civ* in *Sté PT Putrabali Adyamulia*, 29 June 2007. For a commentary on this case, see P Pinsole, 'The Status of Vacated Awards in France: The Cour de Cassation decision in Putrabali' (2008) 24 Arb Int 277.

[102] P Fouchard, *L'arbitrage Commercial International* (Dalloz, 1965); and J Paulsson, 'Arbitration Unbound: Award Detached from the Law of its Country of Origin' (1981) 30 ICLQ 358.

[103] *Russell* para 2-100.

[104] *Poudret & Besson* paras 121–3.

[105] Arbitration Act, s 4(5).

[106] *Russell* para 2-103.

D. Article 17 – Language of Arbitration

Article 17 of the Rules comprises a comprehensive set of provisions dealing with **5.72** the language of the arbitration proceedings. It should be noted at the outset that Article 17 is markedly more detailed than similar provisions contained in other arbitration rules.[107] While the relative length of Article 17 is perhaps a further illustration of the LCIA's prescriptive approach towards establishing a near-exhaustive procedural code for the conduct of arbitrations under the Rules,[108] a review of Article 17 needs to be considered in light of the fact that fewer than 1 per cent of cases commenced under the Rules up to the end of 2007 were conducted in a language other than English.

Article 17.1

The initial language of the arbitration shall be the language of the Arbitration Agreement, unless the parties have agreed in writing otherwise and providing always that a non-participating or defaulting party shall have no cause for complaint if communications to and from the Registrar or the arbitration proceedings are conducted in English.

The equivalent provision to Article 17 in the 1985 Rules provided that if no agree- **5.73** ment existed between the parties, the language of the arbitration agreement would determine the language of the arbitration proceedings.[109] The 1985 Rules did not empower the LCIA or the tribunal to determine the language of the arbitration in light of any extenuating circumstances. It was argued that the inflexible nature of this rule meant that if the parties had signed a contract (containing the arbitration clause) in a little-used language, then without further agreement of the parties – which may not be forthcoming in the case of a recalcitrant or non-participating respondent – the proceedings would have to be conducted in that language with the consequences of increased costs (in terms of translators and interpreters) and delay. Article 17 introduces much-needed flexibility and should help avoid the financial repercussions mentioned above.[110]

The scheme of Article 17 is to divide the arbitration proceedings into two phases: **5.74** (i) the initial phase, which comprises the commencement of the arbitration until the formation of the tribunal; and (ii) the second phase which commences upon the formation of the tribunal and continues until the end of the proceedings. The governing principle of Article 17 in respect of both phases is that the parties may choose whatever language or languages they wish to be used in the arbitration.

---

[107] eg, art 16 ICC Rules, art 14 ICDR Rules, and art 17 UNCITRAL Rules.
[108] As discussed above in the context of art 14.2.
[109] Art 8.1 1985 Rules.
[110] *Commentary* 11–12.

5.75 As mentioned above, our review of 701 cases commenced under the Rules by the end of 2007 shows that only seven (ie, less than 1 per cent of) cases were wholly conducted in a language other than English. Of those seven cases, Russian was the language of the arbitration in six cases, with the remaining case having been conducted in Italian. Some twelve cases only were conducted in English and another language. Once again, Russian was the most popular language, representing the joint language of the arbitration in 10 cases. The remaining two cases were conducted in English and French and English and German, respectively. While the LCIA is clearly able to administer arbitrations in languages other than English, albeit with the added costs of translation, it is perhaps not surprising that the overwhelming number of cases are conducted in English.

5.76 Article 17.1 deals with the first of the two phases mentioned above. It provides that, absent the parties' agreement in writing, the initial language of the arbitration (up to the formation of the tribunal) shall be the language of the arbitration agreement. This is a sensible rule that avoids the uncertainty that would ensue in the event that the parties had not specified the language of the arbitration in their arbitration agreement, as is often the case. The parties can therefore conduct themselves accordingly in the language of their arbitration agreement during the initial phase of the arbitration, following the submission of the Request, without the need for further debate as to the proper language of the proceedings. The further benefit of this provision is to neutralize dilatory tactics by a party having signed a contract in a widely-used language but then insisting that its fundamental rights would be violated if it could not present its case in its own, less widely-used, language.[111]

5.77 Article 17.1 further provides that a defaulting party shall have no cause for complaint if communications to and from the Registrar and the arbitration proceedings are conducted in English. The purpose of this provision is to address situations where, faced with a non-participating respondent, the claimant is content to proceed in English even though the arbitration agreement is drafted in a different language. The effect of this provision is to waive the right of a defaulting party to raise any complaints as regards the language in which the proceedings are conducted.

Article 17.2

In the event that the Arbitration Agreement is written in more than one language, the LCIA Court may, unless the Arbitration Agreement provides that the arbitration proceedings shall be conducted in more than one language, decide which of those languages shall be the initial language of the arbitration.

---

[111] Ibid.

This provision addresses those situations where contracts containing the **5.78** arbitration agreement are signed in two or more languages, which is sometimes the case. Article 17.2 permits the LCIA Court to determine in which of the two languages the initial phase of the arbitration shall be conducted.[112] Under a literal application of Article 8.1 of the 1985 Rules, the arbitration would have had to be conducted in both languages.

Article 17.3

Upon the formation of the Arbitral Tribunal and unless the parties have agreed upon the language or languages of the arbitration, the Arbitral Tribunal shall decide upon the language(s) of the arbitration, after giving the parties an opportunity to make written comment and taking into account the initial language of the arbitration and any other matter it may consider appropriate in all the circumstances of the case.

Article 17.3 deals with the second phase of the arbitration proceedings described **5.79** above, and empowers the tribunal to determine the language of the proceedings, in the absence of party agreement. In determining the language of the arbitration, the tribunal is required to take account of all relevant circumstances, including the initial language of the arbitration. This is an important provision that grants the tribunal much-needed flexibility to determine the language of the proceedings in light of all appropriate circumstances, including the language proficiency of the arbitrators and counsel, as well as the language skills of potential witnesses. Such considerations might well be sufficient to persuade the tribunal to choose a language other than the language of the arbitration agreement for the conduct of the proceedings.

Article 17.4

If any document is expressed in a language other than the language(s) of the arbitration and no translation of such document is submitted by the party relying upon the document, the Arbitral Tribunal or (if the Arbitral Tribunal has not been formed) the LCIA Court may order that party to submit a translation in a form to be determined by the Arbitral Tribunal or the LCIA Court, as the case may be.

It is common practice in international arbitration for parties to provide transla- **5.80** tions of documents on which they seek to rely in the event that the documents in question are not expressed in the language of the arbitration. This is not only a question of courtesy to the tribunal and the other parties, but a pragmatic consideration to ensure that the tribunal is able to review and consider any documents on which a party seeks to rely. Article 17.4 codifies this practice by expressly empowering the tribunal (or the LCIA Court prior to the tribunal's formation)

---

[112] Winstanley (n 83 above) 29.

to request the parties to provide translations of documents on which they seek to rely in the arbitration.

E. Article 18 – Party Representation

5.81 Article 18 deals with the representation of parties in arbitration proceedings and the authority of party representatives.

Article 18.1

Any party may be represented by legal practitioners or any other representatives.

5.82 In most countries today there are no restrictions in the local law limiting the choice of party representatives in an arbitration.[113] This is in contrast to provisions contained in the internal procedural laws of most countries that restrict the representation of parties before judicial authorities. Article 18.1 therefore conforms to modern international arbitration practice and even permits the parties to be represented by non-legal practitioners.

5.83 Our research revealed many cases where the parties were not represented by external legal counsel.[114] In the bulk of those cases, however, parties were represented by in-house corporate counsel, rather than by a lay representative. The fact remains, however, that in the overwhelming majority of cases external legal counsel, typically based in England, were instructed by parties to LCIA arbitration.

5.84 It should also be noted that the effectiveness of this provision must be considered in light of the law applicable to the arbitration. If the *lex arbitri* restricts the class of party representatives, even in international arbitration, then the parties' strict adherence to Article 18.1 may subject the resulting award to challenge before the courts at the place of arbitration. This is a further consideration that parties should take into account when choosing a place of arbitration.

Article 18.2

At any time the Arbitral Tribunal may require from any party proof of authority granted to its representative(s) in such form as the Arbitral Tribunal may determine.

5.85 As discussed in chapter 3, there is no formal requirement upon the claimant to include any proof of authority granted to its representative for the purposes of the

---

[113] *Redfern & Hunter* para 6-18.
[114] Discussed in ch 1 above.

arbitration as part of its Request. If the parties have not done so prior to the formation of the tribunal, Article 18.2 empowers the tribunal to request the submission of such proof of authority.

F. Article 19 – Hearings

Article 19 groups together the provisions of the Rules that address the broad **5.86** principles regarding the organization of hearings, while leaving the detailed procedural considerations in the hands of the tribunal and the parties. It is common for tribunals to issue specific procedural directions relating to the conduct of the hearing, which will include the order of witnesses to be examined, the division of time between the parties, and other practical and logistical issues discussed below. As explained above in the context of Article 15, the prevailing trend in international arbitration is towards fuller written submissions, including written witness statements and expert reports, at the expense of shorter hearings. This does not mean, however, that hearings are disappearing from the mainstream; far from it. It is unusual for a case to be decided on the basis of written submissions and documentary evidence alone. In the overwhelming majority of international cases, the parties still insist on a hearing, in spite of the potentially considerable expense and inconvenience of gathering together arbitrators, counsel, party representatives, and witnesses, all of whom are likely to be busy professionals, in one place for a period of days or even weeks.

Article 19.1

Any party which expresses a desire to that effect has the right to be heard orally before the Arbitral Tribunal on the merits of the dispute, unless the parties have agreed in writing on documents-only arbitration.

The effect of Article 19.1 is to grant the parties the unilateral right to request a **5.87** hearing before the tribunal on the merits of the dispute, unless the parties have agreed to documents-only arbitration. A party's right to a hearing is not dependent upon agreement between the parties or the consent of the tribunal. Quite simply, if a party demands a hearing on the merits, the tribunal is duty-bound to organize such a hearing, even if it considers it unnecessary. This formulation was introduced in the current version of the Rules. The 1985 Rules provided that a hearing would take place unless the parties requested or agreed to a documents-only arbitration. This meant that if the parties remained silent on the issue, or the claimant preferred a documents-only procedure in the face of a defaulting respondent, a hearing would still have taken place.[115]

---

[115] Winstanley (n 83 above) 29.

5.88 The formulation of Article 19.1 is ambiguous as to whether, in the absence of a party's request for a hearing, the tribunal is empowered to convene such a hearing if it considers it appropriate. Article 20(2) of the ICC Rules grants tribunals an explicit right to convene hearings of their own motion. In the authors' view, a similar right may be implied in the LCIA Rules. This interpretation conforms to the current practice under the Rules where tribunals will almost invariably convene a hearing even if the parties remain silent on the issue.

5.89 The right to a hearing under Article 19.1 relates to the right to be heard orally before the tribunal on the merits. This raises the question of whether hearings organized by teleconference or video-conference satisfy the requirement of being heard orally before the tribunal, or whether Article 19.1 mandates a hearing in person. A second observation concerns the explicit reference to being heard orally on the *merits* of the parties' dispute. Do the parties have the right to a hearing in respect of the tribunal's determination of preliminary issues, such as jurisdiction? Or is the parties' right to such hearings subject to the tribunal's consent? The implication appears to be that the parties' right to a hearing is not unlimited and that it is up to the tribunal to determine what is a suitable course to follow in determining the parties' dispute, in light of the tribunal's duties under Article 14.1 sub-paragraphs (i) and (ii).[116]

Article 19.2

The Arbitral Tribunal shall fix the date, time and physical place of any meetings and hearings in the arbitration, and shall give the parties reasonable notice thereof.

5.90 Article 19.2 makes clear that it is the tribunal that fixes the date, time, and physical place of any meetings and hearings in the arbitration. It is not clear whether the parties by agreement can impose on the tribunal their own wishes as regards the date, time, and physical place of the hearing, in exercising their rights to agree on the conduct of their arbitration under Article 14.1. The mandatory formulation of Article 19.2, considered in conjunction with Articles 19.5 and 20.2, which reiterate the tribunal's control over the hearing, suggests that this provision represents one of the few limits to party autonomy under the Rules.

5.91 As a practical matter, hearing dates in international arbitrations are generally determined by the tribunal in full consultation and agreement with the parties. As it is often difficult to find convenient dates that will be suitable to all the principal participants involved (arbitrators, counsel, party representatives, and witnesses), hearing dates are often set, if only tentatively, far in advance, usually during the preliminary meeting held shortly after the tribunal's formation. The tribunal,

---

[116] The tribunal's mandatory duties under art 14.1 are discussed above in this ch 5.

however, has the last word on setting the date, if there is no agreement among the participants.

The tribunal must also determine the physical place for the hearing. The task of **5.92** organizing a hearing in a major case should not be underestimated. As discussed in the context of Article 16.2, the tribunal may hold hearings at any convenient geographical place. In doing so, however, the tribunal will wish to consult the parties and be sensitive to any potential travel or visa difficulties that the parties or their witnesses may encounter in travelling to the designated venue, and to ensure that suitable accommodation may be found near the location of the hearing. Once a convenient venue has been determined, a suitable hearing room must be found, with ancillary rooms and facilities for the parties and the arbitrators. In addition, access to standard office equipment, such as photocopying machines, telephones, and fax lines is essential. The tribunal will also need to consider the utility of whether a transcript of the hearing should be prepared, which will further add to the cost and the list of participants at the hearing. Although LCIA arbitrations can be conducted in any venue, we have seen that the overwhelming majority of cases have a London seat, and it is to be expected therefore that hearings in such cases will also likely be held in London. A popular venue for LCIA hearings is the International Dispute Resolution Centre or IDRC, where the LCIA Secretariat is based.[117] The IDRC can offer a selection of hearing rooms with all of the necessary support facilities, with the added benefit of having been designed specifically for the purpose of hosting arbitration hearings. Otherwise, hearings are commonly held in hotel meeting rooms or other conference facilities. Hearing facilities are in limited supply and therefore should be booked well in advance.

What is a reasonable length of time for a hearing will depend on the particular **5.93** circumstances of the case, including: the number of testifying witnesses to be examined; the availability of the participants for a continuous period of time; and the particular expectations of the arbitrators and the parties. As regards the latter, civil law arbitrators tend to prefer relatively shorter hearings, lasting a few days; a hearing lasting for more than a week would generally be considered lengthy. By contrast, common law arbitrators, steeped in the tradition of lengthy court trials that can last many months, would not regard a week's hearing as unduly lengthy (depending on the circumstances of the case), but would be unlikely to accept a hearing lasting more than two consecutive weeks.[118] The trend in international arbitration towards shorter hearings with greater reliance on documentary evidence and written submission means that parties should be acutely aware of such time constraints and use their allotted hearing time with care.

---

[117] Discussed in ch 1 above.
[118] *Redfern & Hunter* para 6-112.

5.94 Once the tribunal has fixed the time and place for the hearing, it must give the parties reasonable notice, which is consistent with the tribunal's duties of giving each party a reasonable opportunity of putting its case under Article 14.1(i). As explained above, since hearing dates are typically set far in advance and confirmed in the tribunal's procedural directions, the requirement of reasonable notice is likely to be fulfilled other than in the most exceptional cases.[119]

Article 19.3

The Arbitral Tribunal may in advance of any hearing submit to the parties a list of questions which it wishes them to answer with special attention.

5.95 Individual tribunals approach the determination of the procedure to be followed at the hearing in different ways, depending on the circumstances of the case, including the allotted time available and the number of testifying witnesses. Most have the common aim of keeping the duration of the hearing to a minimum so far as practicable, in order to assist the busy schedules of the arbitrators and the parties, and to reduce costs. Due to this constant time pressure, and the trend towards detailed written submissions, the principal purpose of hearings in international arbitration is to permit the cross-examination of witnesses. There is usually no, or very limited, opportunity to conduct examination-in-chief (or direct examination) of witnesses, in view of the written witness statements that are typically filed.

5.96 It is nonetheless customary to permit each side to make a brief opening statement in which the advocates have the opportunity of presenting a summary of the essential points of their case, based on the assumption that the arbitrators have studied the parties' written submissions. The parties' opening statements are also an important opportunity for the arbitrators to test the advocates and to raise any questions or clarifications that arise from their review of the written materials. Article 19.3 permits the arbitrators to raise such questions in advance of the hearing, thus ensuring that the parties arrive at the hearing prepared to respond to the tribunal's queries. By submitting its questions in advance, the tribunal takes a more active role in adjudicating the parties' dispute by influencing the scope and content of the parties' opening statements. This is typical of proceedings in the civil law inquisitorial tradition, where the arbitrators play a more active role in ascertaining the facts and the law than is the case in the common law approach. Article 19.3 reflects the growing trend in international arbitration (as reflected by section 34(2)(g) of the Arbitration Act) for a more hands-on approach by

---

[119] Such a case is discussed in ch 4 above in the context of a challenge brought against a sole arbitrator under art 10.2 on the basis that adequate notice of a hearing had not been given to one of the parties pursuant to art 19.2.

arbitrators, especially at hearings.[120] In submitting questions in advance of a hearing, tribunals should take care not to give the appearance that they have prejudged the merits.

Article 19.4

All meetings and hearings shall be in private unless the parties agree otherwise in writing or the Arbitral Tribunal directs otherwise.

Article 19.4 guarantees the privacy of the hearing unless the parties agree otherwise or the tribunal otherwise directs. This means that, in practice, no person who is not involved in the hearing and thus duly authorized as a representative of one of the parties or the tribunal (for example, an administrative secretary) can be admitted without the agreement of the parties and the tribunal.[121] It is therefore customary at the start of each hearing day for those present to identify themselves, typically by signing an attendance sheet to establish a daily attendance record. **5.97**

Article 19.5

The Arbitral Tribunal shall have the fullest authority to establish time-limits for meetings and hearings, or for any parts thereof.

Article 19.5 confers the broadest authority possible on the tribunal to establish the division of time available during the days set aside for the conduct of the hearing. As already explained, the available time at a hearing is likely to be limited and therefore the allocation of the time available by the tribunal is an important decision. Tribunals typically allocate time equally between the parties and permit the parties a degree of discretion as to how they use their allotted time. In the event that there is an imbalance between the number of witnesses presented by the respective parties, the tribunal may decide that a different allocation of time, rather than a strict 50:50 split, would be appropriate. In establishing time limits under Article 19.5, the tribunal must be aware of its duties under Article 14.1(i) to treat the parties fairly and impartially, giving each party a reasonable opportunity of putting its case and dealing with that of its opponent. In this context, fair does not always mean equal, and vice versa. **5.98**

G. Article 20 – Witnesses

Article 20 sets out the broad framework of the tribunal's powers with respect to the submission and examination of witness testimony, as well as the weight to be attached to such testimony by the tribunal. While other arbitration rules also **5.99**

---

[120] Discussed above in the context of art 15.1.
[121] *Redfern & Hunter* para 6-107; and *Derains & Schwartz* 291.

cover this issue, Article 20 is the most comprehensive set of rules on witnesses among institutional rules. It is therefore consistent with the prescriptive approach of the Rules towards the procedural conduct of the arbitration, as discussed earlier. Nonetheless, Article 20 should not be regarded as sufficiently detailed to deal with all the issues that may arise in relation to the involvement of witnesses in an arbitration. Detailed procedural rules tailored to the specific circumstances of the case will therefore need to be agreed by the parties or form part of the tribunal's procedural directions.

Article 20.1

Before any hearing, the Arbitral Tribunal may require any party to give notice of the identity of each witness that party wishes to call (including rebuttal witnesses), as well as the subject matter of that witness's testimony, its content and its relevance to the issues in the arbitration.

5.100 Article 20.1 empowers the tribunal to require any party to provide notice of the identity of each witness that party wishes to call. Such party notice should include the subject-matter of the witness's testimony, its content, and its relevance to the issues in the arbitration. The purpose of this provision is to ensure that parties (and the tribunal) have due notice of the evidence that will be served by all parties at a hearing in order to avoid the prospect of a 'trial by ambush', and to permit the parties a reasonable opportunity of dealing with the case put forward by their opponents, in accordance with Article 14.1(i).

5.101 In fact, the predominant practice in international arbitration is for parties to submit written witness statements which then stand as the witness's examination-in-chief (or direct examination) at the hearing. The submission of written statements is expressly permitted under the Rules,[122] and is consistent with the trend in international arbitration towards fuller written submissions (on points of law and facts) and shorter hearings. As a matter of practice, the tribunal's procedural directions are likely to address the submission of written witness statements. Such statements are typically served well before the hearing, which means that, in the majority of cases, the concerns addressed by Article 20.1 do not arise.

5.102 There may be situations, however, where due to circumstances or events occurring shortly before the hearing, there is no scope for the submission of witness statements prior to the hearing. In such cases, and upon request of a party, the tribunal will typically permit the appearance of a witness to testify on issues that are not covered by any previously submitted statements. In such circumstances, the tribunal should ensure that the party calling the witness gives due notice as to the

---

[122] Art 20.3.

content and relevance of the issues that the witness will address at the hearing. Furthermore, any opposing parties should normally be granted additional preparation time before exercising their right to cross-examine the witness.[123]

Article 20.2

The Arbitral Tribunal may also determine the time, manner and form in which such materials should be exchanged between the parties and presented to the Arbitral Tribunal; and it has a discretion to allow, refuse, or limit the appearance of witnesses (whether witness of fact or expert witness).

The first part of Article 20.2 refers to the materials mentioned in Article 20.1 and should be read in conjunction with that provision. As discussed above, tribunals will typically address the submission of witness statements in one or more procedural orders, often well before a hearing. **5.103**

The second part of Article 20.2 affirms the tribunal's authority to allow, refuse, or limit the appearance of witnesses. Similar provisions are contained in other arbitration rules.[124] The tribunal is not required to hear the witnesses that the parties may wish to call. It is up to the tribunal to determine, in light of the circumstances of the dispute, whether the appearance of any proposed witness is necessary.[125] Further, in the event that the tribunal agrees to hear witnesses, it has the authority to limit their appearance. The tribunal's authority over the appearance of witnesses is consistent with current international arbitration practice, as illustrated by Article 8 of the IBA Rules, which reiterates that an arbitral tribunal shall at all times have complete control over the hearing and may limit or exclude the appearance of a witness. **5.104**

The exercise of the tribunal's power to curtail the parties' presentation of witness evidence is subject to the tribunal's duties under Article 14.1(i), namely to ensure that the parties have a reasonable opportunity of putting their case and dealing with that of their opponent(s), and any mandatory provisions of the *lex arbitri*. Otherwise, the tribunal's award runs the risk of being set aside. Further, in the event that the tribunal has appointed its own expert, in accordance with the procedure set out in Article 21 (discussed below), then the parties' right to question the tribunal's expert and to present their own expert witness in response overrides the tribunal's general discretion to control the appearance of witnesses.[126] **5.105**

---

[123] Art 20.5.
[124] Art 20(3) ICC Rules and art 16(3) ICDR Rules. The UNCITRAL Rules do not contain a similar formulation, although art 25(6) provides that the tribunal shall determine the admissibility, relevance, materiality, and weight of the evidence offered.
[125] *Hunter & Paulsson* 171.
[126] Art 21.2; and *Hunter & Paulsson* 171.

Article 20.3

Subject to any order otherwise by the Arbitral Tribunal, the testimony of a witness may be presented by a party in written form, either as a signed statement or as a sworn affidavit.

5.106 Article 20.3 provides that witness testimony may be served in writing, subject to any order otherwise by the tribunal. As explained earlier, the submission of written witness statements is now standard practice in international arbitration and is usually addressed in the tribunal's procedural directions. This prevailing practice is now codified in Articles 4 and 5 of the IBA Rules in respect of witnesses of fact and party-appointed experts, respectively. Article 20.3 also provides that such statements may be either signed or sworn as an affidavit. More frequently, a statement is simply signed by the witness.

5.107 The submission of written witness statements has a number of advantages: (i) it saves time (and therefore cost) by shortening hearings; (ii) by ensuring the timely submission of evidence well before a hearing, written statements reduce the likelihood of fresh issues emerging during the giving of evidence at the hearing; and (iii) written statements force the parties to focus on the strengths and weaknesses of their case in light of the evidence submitted, which may prompt settlement before the hearing.[127]

Articles 20.4 and 20.5

20.4 Subject to Articles 14.1 and 14.2, any party may request that a witness, on whose testimony another party seeks to rely, should attend for oral questioning at a hearing before the Arbitral Tribunal. If the Arbitral Tribunal orders that other party to produce the witness and the witness fails to attend the oral hearing without good cause, the Arbitral Tribunal may place such weight on the written testimony (or exclude the same altogether) as it considers appropriate in the circumstances of the case.

20.5 Any witness who gives oral evidence at a hearing before the Arbitral Tribunal may be questioned by each of the parties under the control of the Arbitral Tribunal. The Arbitral Tribunal may put questions at any stage of his evidence.

5.108 Articles 20.4 and 20.5 should be considered together. Article 20.4 grants a party the right to call for the attendance at the hearing of any witness on whose testimony another party relies, and sets out the potential consequences should the witness not turn up. Article 20.5 affirms the parties' right to cross-examine any witness who gives oral evidence at a hearing under the control of the tribunal, and also provides that the tribunal may pose the witness questions of its own.

---

[127] *Russell* para 5-143.

As explained above, the prevailing practice in international arbitration is for parties **5.109**
to submit written witness statements that stand as the examination-in-chief
(or direct examination) of the witness. The principal purpose of evidentiary hearings
therefore is to enable the parties to test the witness testimony submitted by means
of cross-examination. An alternative method of testing witness (particularly
expert) evidence is by means of witness 'conferencing', which consists of the
simultaneous joint hearing of witnesses by the parties and the tribunal.[128] This
technique, which can be tailored to fit the particular circumstances of the case, is
enthusiastically promoted by a prominent Switzerland-based arbitrator and
is becoming increasingly popular in international arbitration (although often as
an addition to, rather than instead of, cross-examination).

If a witness who has submitted a written statement does not turn up at the notified **5.110**
hearing, his testimony cannot be tested, which in turn means that the parties are
deprived of their right to deal with the case put forward by their opponent. Articles
20.4 and 20.5 therefore enshrine the parties' due process rights to challenge the
witness evidence presented by their opponents.

In the event that a witness who has been ordered to attend the hearing fails to do **5.111**
so 'without good cause', the tribunal is authorized under Article 20.5 to place such
weight on the previously submitted written testimony as it considers appropriate.
This provision also affirms the tribunal's authority to exclude altogether any
witness statements submitted by that witness. Whether the tribunal decides to
exclude the written statement or to consider it, but give it less weight, will depend
on the circumstances of each case, especially the reasons for the witness's absence.

Article 20.6

Subject to the mandatory provisions of any applicable law, it shall not be improper
for any party or its legal representatives to interview any witness or potential witness
for the purpose of presenting his testimony in written form or producing him as an
oral witness.

An important aspect of the presentation of witnesses is the question of whether, **5.112**
and if so to what extent, it is permissible for a party or counsel to interview and
prepare the witnesses whose testimony they intend to present. This is because the
rules of certain national courts and bar associations forbid or deem it unethical for
witnesses to be contacted or interviewed by the parties or counsel before they
testify. Thus, for example, the general rule in France, Switzerland, and Belgium is
that counsel are not permitted to interview witnesses prior to trial.[129] A similar

---

[128] W Peter, 'Witness "Conferencing"' (2002) 18 Arb Int 47.
[129] H Van Houte, 'Counsel-Witness Relations and Professional Misconduct in Civil Law
Systems' (2003) 19 Arb Int 457, 458.

rule used to apply to barristers in England, but that is no longer the case.[130] Whatever limits may apply in different civil procedure rules will generally not apply in international arbitration, where it is well recognized that witnesses may be interviewed and prepared prior to giving oral testimony.[131] Article 20.6 conforms to this practice and is consistent with Article 4(3) of the IBA Rules.

Article 20.7

> Any individual intending to testify to the Arbitral Tribunal on any issue of fact or expertise shall be treated as a witness under these Rules notwithstanding that the individual is a party to the arbitration or was or is an officer, employee or shareholder of any party.

5.113 Article 20.7 deals with another cultural issue that arises in the civil procedure rules of certain civil law countries, where there are restrictions on who can be regarded as a 'witness', notably as regards party representatives or officers and employees of a party. In French procedural law, for example, a party representative is not regarded as a witness, but as a '*sachant*', and less weight is generally accorded to his evidence. As in the case of many other rules of national court procedure, this rule does not apply in international arbitration. Article 20.7 codifies this position.

H. Article 21 – Experts to the Arbitral Tribunal

5.114 Article 21 is a near-verbatim reproduction of Article 26 of the UNCITRAL Model Law and affirms the tribunal's power to appoint experts unless the parties have agreed otherwise. This provision enables the tribunal to appoint experts on matters relevant to the issues in dispute and as to which independent expertise is required. The Rules do not permit any restrictions on the kinds of experts that the tribunal may appoint and therefore permit the appointment of technical, financial, and even legal experts.

5.115 The use of tribunal-appointed experts derives from a practice common in many civil law jurisdictions, where such experts are routinely appointed by the courts in order to report on disputed factual matters.[132] The appointment of such experts is not a traditional feature of common law legal systems, however, where the role of the judge is to weigh the evidence submitted by the opposing parties rather than to undertake a primary role in the investigation of the facts. It is no doubt for this

---

[130] England & Wales Bar Standards Board, Guidance for Members of the Bar: The Preparation of Witness Statements.

[131] *Redfern & Hunter* para 6-86. For the position in civil law countries, see Van Houte (supra n 129 above) 460–1.

[132] *Derains & Schwartz* 277–8.

reason that the US and Canadian governments have excluded this rule from the dispute resolution mechanism under the Softwood Lumber Agreement.[133] The possible appointment of an expert by the tribunal has now become a standard feature of most arbitration rules,[134] and is also addressed in Article 6 of the IBA Rules, as a further demonstration that the respective traditions of the common law and civil law are often blurred in international arbitration practice.

Article 21.1

Unless otherwise agreed by the parties in writing, the Arbitral Tribunal:

(a) may appoint one or more experts to report to the Arbitral Tribunal on specific issues, who shall be and remain impartial and independent of the parties throughout the arbitration proceedings; and

(b) may require a party to give any such expert any relevant information or to provide access to any relevant documents, goods, samples, property or site for inspection by the expert.

5.116 Since it will be relatively rare for parties to agree to exclude this provision, Article 21.1 accordingly provides for the appointment of an expert by and for the tribunal without the need for any discussion or agreement of the parties after the commencement of the arbitration, and thus avoids any argument that might ensue between the parties. Although the identification of a suitable expert and their appointment is a matter for the tribunal, and there is no need for consultation of the parties, it is unlikely that a tribunal will impose an expert on the parties against their wishes. This is not only because the expert would require the cooperation of the parties in fulfilling its mandate, but also the more pragmatic reason that the expert's fees and expenses will form part of the costs of the arbitration and will therefore have to be paid by the parties.[135] Thus, the tribunal will be in a position to appoint an expert only if at least one of the parties is prepared to fund the related cost.[136]

5.117 The tribunal must ensure that the appointed expert remains impartial and independent of the parties throughout. The tribunal will also ordinarily require the parties to assist the expert in completing its mandate by providing all relevant information or access to documents, goods, samples, or sites that the expert may require. Such terms are normally included in the expert's terms of appointment, which also set out the precise issues on which the expert must opine.

5.118 The report prepared by the tribunal-appointed expert is not intended to bind the tribunal, and should be judged on the same basis as any other expert evidence

---

[133] Discussed in ch 1.
[134] Art 20(4) ICC Rules, art 22 ICDR Rules, and art 27 UNCITRAL Rules.
[135] Art 21.3.
[136] *Derains & Schwartz* 280.

proffered in the proceedings. As a matter of practice, however, such reports are generally accorded a great deal of weight by the tribunal, which is perhaps to be expected given the independence and neutrality of the expert. It is important to reiterate, though, that it falls to the arbitrators to adjudicate the parties' dispute and it is therefore inappropriate for the tribunal to delegate that task to a third party, such as a tribunal-appointed expert. Nor should the appointed expert take part in the tribunal's deliberations. In short, when appointing its own expert, the tribunal will have to be wary of the distinction between taking advice from an expert, on the one hand, and attempting to delegate its task to him, on the other.[137]

5.119 Our review of the 701 cases commenced under the Rules up to the end of 2007 revealed only six cases where experts have been appointed by the tribunal (ie in less than one per cent of cases).

Article 21.2

Unless otherwise agreed by the parties in writing, if a party so requests or if the Arbitral Tribunal considers it necessary, the expert shall, after delivery of his written or oral report to the Arbitral Tribunal and the parties, participate in one or more hearings at which the parties shall have the opportunity to question the expert on his report and to present expert witnesses in order to testify on the point at issue.

5.120 This provision encapsulates two important procedural rights of the parties. First, the parties have the right to receive the expert's report, and would typically have the opportunity to submit their observations thereon. Second, unless the parties have agreed otherwise, a party has the right to demand the organization of a hearing by the tribunal to enable: (i) the cross-examination of the tribunal-appointed expert; and (ii) the presentation of expert testimony adduced by the parties on the point at issue. The latter right overrides the discretion enjoyed by the tribunal under the Rules to allow, refuse, or limit the appearance of witnesses (whether witnesses of fact or experts).[138]

Article 21.3

The fees and expenses of any expert appointed by the Arbitral Tribunal under this Article shall be paid out of the deposits payable by the parties under Article 24 and shall form part of the costs of the arbitration.

5.121 Article 21.3 provides that the fees and expenses of an expert appointed by the tribunal shall form part of the costs of the arbitration, and shall therefore be paid out of the deposits payable by the parties under Article 24.

---

[137] *Redfern & Hunter* para 6-92.
[138] Art 20.2.

6

THE POWERS OF THE ARBITRAL
TRIBUNAL (ARTICLES 22, 23, AND 25)

A. Article 22 – Additional Powers of the Arbitral Tribunal	6.03	B. Article 23 – Jurisdiction of the Arbitral Tribunal	6.82
Article 22.1	6.06	Article 23.1	6.84
Article 22.1(a)	6.09	Article 23.2	6.98
Article 22.1(b)	6.20	Article 23.3	6.100
Article 22.1(c)	6.22	Article 23.4	6.105
Article 22.1(d)	6.24	C. Article 25 – Interim and Conservatory Measures	6.107
Article 22.1(e)	6.26	Article 25.1	6.131
Article 22.1(f)	6.37	Article 25.1(a)	6.134
Article 22.1(g)	6.39	Article 25.1(b)	6.140
Article 22.1(h)	6.44	Article 25.1(c)	6.143
Article 22.2	6.60	Article 25.2	6.152
Article 22.3	6.62	Article 25.3	6.158
Article 22.4	6.78		

This chapter covers the topics of the powers of the tribunal to conduct the proceedings (Article 22), its jurisdiction and its power to rule on its own jurisdiction (Article 23), and its power to order interim and conservatory measures (Article 25). **6.01**

Although in one sense disparate, these provisions have a common thread, namely the overall jurisdiction of the arbitral tribunal. The extent to which the powers conferred on the tribunal by these articles of the LCIA Rules can be exercised, of course, depends to a greater or lesser extent on the state of the arbitration law of the country of the seat of the arbitration. This is discussed briefly in respect of each of the articles covered in this chapter. **6.02**

A. Article 22 – Additional Powers of the Arbitral Tribunal

If the collection of articles in this chapter is eclectic, Article 22 on its own is no less so. Article 22.1 sets out a series of powers that the tribunal may exercise, subject to (a) having given the parties a reasonable opportunity to state their views and (b) **6.03**

137

the substantive law governing the dispute and the procedural law of the arbitration or *lex arbitri*.

6.04 This article has no direct counterpart in the ICC Rules. Many of the matters covered in it are dealt with in the ICC Rules, but they are not gathered together in the same way as in this article, and some of the matters contained in this article are not spelt out as powers of an ICC tribunal, although there is little doubt that the general power to 'establish the facts of the case by all appropriate means' gives ICC arbitrators the authority to do all of the things that Article 22.1, especially, gives an LCIA tribunal.

6.05 Article 22.1 is a very long sub-article, broken down into no less than eight separate additional powers given to the arbitral tribunal. We will deal with each one separately, starting with the introductory paragraph.

Article 22.1

> Unless the parties at any time agree otherwise in writing, the Arbitral Tribunal shall have the power, on the application of any party or of its own motion, but in either case only after giving the parties a reasonable opportunity to state their views:

6.06 The first thing of importance in Article 22.1 is that the list of additional powers therein set out is subject to the agreement otherwise of the parties. The parties may therefore decide to exclude or narrow some or all of the additional powers that the Rules otherwise make available to the tribunal.

6.07 Assuming that the parties' agreement does not provide otherwise, the tribunal can proceed to exercise the powers given in Article 22.1 on its own motion or on the application of any party. The question of the extent to which a tribunal can act *sua sponte* is heavily debated, but the issue is rendered moot in Article 22.1 by the qualification that, whether of its own motion or on application by a party, the tribunal cannot exercise any of the additional powers without having given the parties a 'reasonable opportunity to state their views'.

6.08 This tracks the phrasing of the obligation imposed on the tribunal by Article 14.1(i) to give each party a 'reasonable opportunity of putting its case and dealing with that of its opponent'.[1] It cannot mean that the tribunal must hear the parties to whatever extent the parties wish, but it does impose a duty on the tribunal not to use any of the powers set out in the rest of Article 22.1 without at least giving the parties the opportunity to make representations before the power is actually exercised. This will, in normal circumstances, be limited to short submissions on the appropriateness of the actual exercise of the power; the provision does not restrict the parties' right to make full submissions on the manner in which the power is to be exercised.

---

[1] Discussed in ch 5 above.

Article 22.1(a)

to allow any party, upon such terms (as to costs and otherwise) as it shall determine, to amend any claim, counterclaim, defence and reply;

This provision is the nearest equivalent in the LCIA Rules of Article 19 of the ICC **6.09** Rules relating to the introduction of new claims. As the LCIA Rules do not have a corresponding procedural step to the ICC's Terms of Reference, the way in which the respective sets of Rules deal with the question of amendments and new claims differs procedurally, and could give rise to significant differences in practice.

There is one important distinction, however. The ICC provision refers only **6.10** to 'claims', while the LCIA refers to 'amendments', which is both a wider and a narrower concept. On the one hand, the ability of a party to make amendments can allow greater flexibility to the tribunal to allow, for example, the introduction of new facts or arguments that do not amount to 'claims' but are simply alternative or better ways of making the same 'claim'. On the other hand, amendments to existing claims are not new claims. Indeed, there does not seem to be a mechanism whereby a party can introduce new claims into an existing arbitration.

Thus, the debates that can bedevil ICC arbitrations as to when a new claim is not **6.11** a claim, and whether or not it falls outside the 'limits of the Terms of Reference', as Article 19 of the ICC Rules puts it, are avoided in LCIA cases.[2] The arbitrators do not thus have to consider whether claims based on the same facts as already pleaded, but on different legal grounds, or ones that seek the same relief based on new or different facts, or increases in the amounts claimed, are or are not 'new claims' and are or are not within the 'limits' of the Terms of Reference. Equally, the arbitrators in an LCIA arbitration are not able to admit new claims (however they are defined) and a party wishing to raise a new claim must start a new proceeding (and run the risk of possible issue estoppel).

The equivalent provision in the UNCITRAL Rules, Article 20, is phrased, like **6.12** the LCIA provision, in terms of amendments, but refers only to amendments to a party's claim or defence, generic terms that should not necessarily be taken to refer to the statement of claim or statement of defence, the only actual written submissions referred to in the UNCITRAL Rules.[3] Indeed, the US-Iran Claims Tribunal has allowed amendments to counterclaims.[4]

In any event, the wording of this provision owes a great deal to English litigation **6.13** practice, where pleadings can, with the leave of the Court, be amended as the case

---

[2] For a discussion of the practice of ICC tribunals in this regard, see generally *Derains & Schwartz* 266–70.
[3] At arts 18 and 19 respectively.
[4] See D Caron, L Caplan and M Pellonpää, *The UNCITRAL Arbitration Rules: A Commentary* (Oxford University Press, 2006) 466–7.

progresses, and indeed have to be as (as a general rule) the parties are bound by their written pleadings. The similarities between the LCIA default procedure contained in Article 15 and the usual procedure of a piece of English High Court litigation has been discussed in chapter 5 above, and it is interesting to see another manifestation of the Rules' essential 'Englishness' in this provision also.

6.14 In international arbitration practice, parties very rarely actually revisit their written submissions. It is in fact very common in practice for a party's case to evolve substantially between the first and second round of memorials without there being any question of amending the first round to take account of the changes in the second. This can, of course, sometimes create the need for the tribunal to rule on whether the altered presentation in the second round memorial is allowable under the rules governing the arbitration in question, but this is dealt with after the filing and not before.

6.15 That having been said, the power to allow the parties to amend is an important one. It could be that facts come to light after the filing of the claimant's first round submission that necessitate a change of tack or even the addition of new claims based on facts that have recently come to light.[5] In such a case, it can be to the advantage of both parties (and the efficiency of the proceedings) for the claimant to ask for leave to amend the original memorial so that the respondent's defence can take account of the new matters and thus reply on all points. To have such new material emerge only in the claimant's second memorial would lead to probable complaint by the respondent, certain delay and additional cost, and the possibility that the tribunal would refuse to allow the new material, to the detriment of the claimant.

6.16 As to the circumstances in which the tribunal should allow an amendment, it is submitted that this should be governed by practical considerations. The tribunal is enjoined by Article 14.1(ii) to avoid unnecessary delay and expense, and by Article 14.1(i) to allow each party a reasonable opportunity of putting its case. It would thus seem appropriate for leave to amend to be given by the tribunal where it considers that the amendment is necessary to enable the party concerned to put its case and where it will not cause unnecessary delay and expense in the prosecution of the proceedings.

6.17 As to the former, the tribunal will be on its guard not to let a review of the usefulness or coherence of the proposed amendments become a summary determination of any part of the merits of the claim or defence, as the case may be, while still assessing whether the amendment is necessary in order to allow the party concerned a reasonable opportunity to put its case.[6] As to the latter, the stage of

---

[5] As one of the authors has recently done in a case under the SCC Rules.
[6] A consideration equally valid in the tribunal's decision on a request for interim measures under art 25, as discussed below.

the proceedings will inevitably be an important factor. If the proposed amendment comes at an early stage of the proceedings, and can be accommodated without significant change to the procedural timetable, it should almost always be allowed.

6.18 If, however, it is made at a late stage, the tribunal will need to ensure that any necessary adjustment to the procedural timetable, including a possible change of hearing dates, to give the other party a reasonable opportunity to deal with the new case put forward by its opponent, is not disproportionate to the benefit to the amending party. While the tribunal can allow the amendment 'upon such terms (as to costs and otherwise) as it shall determine', thus ensuring that the amending party bears the costs of the disruption thereby caused, that might not be enough if the delay is too great. The decision on any proposed amendment will therefore be a balancing act for the tribunal to perform on a case-by-case basis.

6.19 There is one quirk in the wording of the provision. It refers to the submissions that can be amended as the 'claim, counterclaim, defence and reply' but does not refer to a rejoinder. In so doing, the wording tracks the default procedure of Article 15. It is hardly to be thought that the tribunal does not have the inherent power to allow an amendment even to the second-round submission of the respondent, late in the life of the arbitration though that may be, but the words of the provision are there. It is interesting to note in this context that the equivalent provision of the UNCITRAL Rules, Article 20, also refers to a party's 'claim or defence', without even a reference to counterclaims, although it has been the practice of UNCITRAL Rules tribunals, especially the Iran-US Claims Tribunal, to allow amendments to counterclaims under that provision.[7]

Article 22.1(b)

to extend or abbreviate any time-limit provided by the Arbitration Agreement or these Rules for the conduct of the arbitration or by the Arbitral Tribunal's own orders;

6.20 This is an essential power for any arbitral tribunal or court to have. It would need to be implied in the Rules were it not express. Just as the LCIA Court can abbreviate the time for filing the respondent's Response in an application by the claimant under Article 9,[8] and the tribunal can extend or abridge the time limits set by the Rules themselves under Article 4.7,[9] the tribunal must have the power both to abridge and extend any time limit set by its own orders, as the interests and circumstances of the case dictate. In fact, Article 22.1(b) partially duplicates Article 4.7,

---

[7] Caron, Caplan and Pellonpää (n 4 above) 475–95.
[8] Discussed in ch 4 above.
[9] Discussed in ch 3 above.

in that it, too, refers to time limits prescribed both by the Rules and the arbitration agreement, but it goes further in adding to the list the tribunal's own orders.

6.21 It is interesting that this power to abridge time limits has been expressly referred to. While it may be less common for a given deadline to be brought forward than to be put back, circumstances can easily be envisaged that necessitate such amendments to the procedural timetable. Extensions to deadlines are, of course, sought by parties with what arbitrators consider monotonous regularity. They should be granted where there is a good reason (a category that cannot be defined here, or indeed at all, and must be determined on a case-by-case basis) and where the prejudice caused to the other party or parties, and the damage to the overall procedural timetable and the tribunal's duty to avoid unnecessary delay, is not disproportionate.

Article 22.1(c)

to conduct such enquiries as may appear to the Arbitral Tribunal to be necessary or expedient, including whether and to what extent the Arbitral Tribunal should itself take the initiative in identifying the issues and ascertaining the relevant facts and the law(s) or rules of law applicable to the arbitration, the merits of the parties' dispute and the Arbitration Agreement;

6.22 This provision closely follows section 34(2)(g) of the Arbitration Act, which empowers a tribunal sitting in England to take the initiative itself in ascertaining the facts and the law, as part of the tribunal's discretion to decide all procedural and evidential matters, subject to the parties' agreement. As discussed in chapter 5, by permitting arbitrators to adopt an inquisitorial approach that is a feature of civil law procedure, this provision is often cited as an illustration of the trend towards procedural convergence in international arbitration.

6.23 This provision caters for the possibility that the parties' submissions are not up to the task of allowing the tribunal to decide between opposing arguments. In that case, in order to be able to fulfil its obligations in a proper manner, the tribunal may have to carry out its own enquiries. This cannot be done without having given the parties a reasonable opportunity to state their views, and it is of course possible that, given the opportunity to comment on the tribunal's proposal to conduct its own enquiries, the parties would rise to the challenge and provide the sensible submissions that were hitherto lacking.

Article 22.1(d)

to order any party to make any property, site or thing under its control and relating to the subject matter of the arbitration available for inspection by the Arbitral Tribunal, any other party, its expert or any expert to the Arbitral Tribunal;

This provision is to be distinguished from a possible order to preserve evidence, **6.24** which could be granted by the tribunal as an interim measure of protection under Article 25.1(c), discussed below.

It is thus a simple power enabling the tribunal, should it consider it necessary or **6.25** helpful, to order a party to ensure that a site visit or inspection can be made. It is interesting that the provision refers specifically to the possibility that only the inspection itself could be limited to experts (including any tribunal-appointed expert). This could be a useful power of the tribunal if it considered that the experts on their own might be able to narrow the issues in dispute. In such circumstances, to exclude the parties' representatives from an inspection could help in this laudable aim, given the propensity of party representatives to recoil from any suggestion that any of their claims or defences could be dispensed with.

Article 22.1(e)

to order any party to produce to the Arbitral Tribunal, and to the other parties for inspection, and to supply copies of, any documents or classes of documents in their possession, custody or power which the Arbitral Tribunal determines to be relevant;

In any international arbitration, LCIA or not, there is no right to automatic **6.26** disclosure of documents as there is in common law litigation. Therefore, a party seeking to obtain documents must (in the absence of a separate 'disclosure' stage in the proceedings) make a specific application to the arbitral tribunal.

Article 22.1(e) is the general power of the tribunal to order disclosure of **6.27** documents. Such a procedure is of course an integral part of any common law-inspired procedure and it is not surprising to see it in such detailed terms in the LCIA Rules, complete with the reference to the standard English formulation of documents in a party's 'possession, custody or power'.[10] This is to be contrasted with the ICC Rules, which, in Article 20(5), refer rather coyly to the power of the tribunal to 'summon any party to provide additional evidence'.

In substance, rather than form, though, the two provisions are identical. Whether **6.28** and to what extent documentary evidence is sought and production granted depends on the parties, their counsel, and the arbitrators. In a more-or-less English-style procedure, in which the parties (wherever they come from) are represented by English lawyers before a tribunal composed of English lawyers (a rather common outcome in LCIA arbitration), one can expect more rather than less disclosure. If the parties are represented by lawyers from continental Europe

---

[10] Although it should be admitted that this phrase (or rather its predecessor in the English discovery lexicon, referring to 'control' rather than 'power') appears in art 3(3) IBA Rules, discussed below.

(or those, from whatever legal background, who regularly practise before international tribunals composed of non-English arbitrators) and have nominated arbitrators from a similar legal tradition, there is likely to be more limited disclosure.

6.29 In that context, it needs to be recalled that the Rules provide that, as is now generally accepted as standard procedure in international arbitration, the parties' written submissions are to be accompanied by copies (or lists) of all documents on which the party making the submission relies.[11] By definition, therefore, the documents it is envisaged will be sought by an application under this article will be supplemental to those already disclosed by the parties. This reinforces the expectation that document production ordered under Article 22.1(e) will be limited.

6.30 There is no other guidance in the Rules as to how the tribunal should exercise its discretion to order disclosure of documents. Indeed, it is to be expected that (unless the parties have, by their appointment of counsel and nomination of arbitrators, subscribed to an English procedure) the tribunal will take into account the differing expectations of the parties in deciding the extent of documentary disclosure that will be allowed and issues such as whether documents that are regarded as confidential should be disclosed, and to what extent, and how the concept of legal professional or attorney-client privilege is to be applied.

6.31 The question of document disclosure is therefore again to be dealt with on a case-by-case basis, unless the parties have agreed otherwise. It is in this context that the IBA Rules have a role to play.[12]

6.32 The IBA Rules were drawn up by a working party comprising practitioners from different legal traditions, both common law and civil law, and are designed to be acceptable to both. They are widely used and, while it is more common to see them used as a guideline to the scope of document production that will be ordered by the tribunal, rather than incorporated wholesale into the procedural rules governing the arbitration (and thus binding the hands of the tribunal in what should be the exercise of a power best applied on a case-by-case basis), they have had considerable influence.

---

[11] Art 15.6; see ch 5 above.

[12] For commentary on the IBA Rules and document disclosure generally in international arbitration, see, eg, *Poudret & Besson* paras 649–655; *Redfern & Hunter* paras 6-69 to 6-81; G Kaufmann-Kohler and A Bärtsch, 'Discovery in international arbitration: How much is too much?' (2004) 1 SchiedsVZ 13; K Sachs, 'Use of documents and document discovery: Fishing expeditions versus transparency and burden of proof' (2003) 5 SchiedsVZ 193; H Raeschke-Kessler, 'The Production of Documents in International Arbitration – A Commentary on Art 3 of the New IBA Rules of Evidence' (2002) 18 Arb Int 411; L Reed and J Sutcliffe, 'The Americanization of International Arbitration' (2001) 16 Mealey's Int Arb Rep 37; T Webster, 'Obtaining Documents from Third Parties in International Arbitration' (2001) 17 Arb Int 41; and many more.

The basic approach of the IBA Rules, and of most international arbitral tribunals, **6.33** whether or not they follow the IBA Rules, is to discourage wide-ranging requests for document production and limit orders for production to documents, or classes of document, that are both relevant and able to be identified with reasonable specificity.[13]

The IBA Rules further set out, in Article 9(2), reasons why production of docu- **6.34** ments can be refused by the tribunal. These reasons include the grounds of privilege and confidentiality, both of which will bear different meanings in different jurisdictions. It is for the tribunal to ensure that its orders to produce or not to produce take full account of the legal background of the parties and their counsel in making orders of this sort. While an English party will know that all relevant documents could be disclosed as a matter of English practice and will take great care to ensure that all sensitive documents passed through the hands of his in-house counsel, thus (under English law) attracting privilege from disclosure, a French party will not consider that internal, confidential documents would be disclosable and will not therefore take care to ensure that such documents are protected by privilege (which, as a matter of French law, would not in any event be attracted by being sent through in-house counsel).

Just as it would be unthinkable for the English party to have to disclose docu- **6.35** ments that he considered protected by privilege by contact with in-house counsel, in order to put him and his French opponent on the same level, the French party would be horrified to think that he would have to hand over internal documents that he regarded as confidential because they would be regarded as disclosable by the English party. These different expectations need somehow to be reconciled by an arbitral tribunal in considering issues of document production.

Finally, what are the consequences of a failure to comply with an order for **6.36** production? As arbitrators notoriously have no *imperium*, they are unable to impose direct sanctions for non-compliance. The tribunal, however, draws adverse inferences from a party's failure or refusal to comply with an order under this provision (and indeed any other order). This is expressly foreshadowed in the IBA

---

[13] Art 3(3) IBA Rules provides that a request for documents shall contain:

   (a) (i) a description of a requested document sufficient to indentify it, or (ii) a description in sufficient detail (including subject-matter) of a narrow and specific category of documents that are reasonably believed to exist;

   (b) a description of how the documents requested are relevant and material to the outcome of the case; and

   (c) a statement that the documents requested are not in the possession, custody or control of the requesting Party, and the reason why that Party assumes the documents requested to be in the possession, custody or control of the other Party.

Rules themselves,[14] and is seen as the expected and natural consequence of such non-compliance.[15]

Article 22.1(f)

to decide whether or not to apply any strict rules of evidence (or any other rules) as to the admissibility, relevance or weight of any material tendered by a party on any matter of fact or expert opinion; and to determine the time, manner and form in which such material should be exchanged between the parties and presented to the Arbitral Tribunal;

6.37   The 'strict rules of evidence' referred to here will be taken to refer to the rules of evidence applicable in the procedural law of the seat of the arbitration. As the overwhelming majority of LCIA arbitrations have their seat in England and Wales, this phrase will usually be taken to refer to the rules applicable in an English court. Indeed, the wording of this provision closely tracks that of section 34(2)(f) of the Arbitration Act. It would perhaps be natural for parties, counsel and arbitrators in an English-style arbitration in London (a not uncommon occurrence in LCIA arbitration) to consider that the rules of evidence in English court proceedings should apply. This provision makes it clear that (subject to the parties having a reasonable opportunity to state their views) the tribunal is not bound so to do.

6.38   Thus, the tribunal has full control over the admissibility of evidence, the manner of proof that it will accept, and the weight that it will accord to any given piece of evidence.

Article 22.1(g)

to order the correction of any contract between the parties or the Arbitration Agreement, but only to the extent required to rectify any mistake which the Arbitral Tribunal determines to be common to the parties and then only if and to the extent to which the law(s) or rules of law applicable to the contract or Arbitration Agreement permit such correction;

6.39   Whether an arbitral tribunal has, or should have, the power to fill gaps in contracts, or revise them, is the subject of much academic debate.[16] The so-called 'transnational' approach would argue that arbitrators should be able to rewrite contracts to reflect and preserve the economic equilibrium between the parties, whereas others would argue that the arbitrator's job, unless acting as *ex aequo et bono* or as *amiable compositeur*,[17] is to construe the contract and decide whether a party has breached the terms of the contract and assess damages for the breach.

---

[14] Art 9(4).

[15] *Poudret & Besson* para 650.

[16] For a full discussion, see, eg, KP Berger, 'Power of Arbitrators to Fill Gaps and Revise Contracts to Make Sense' (2001) 17 Arb Int 1.

[17] As to which, see the discussion of art 22.4 below.

Of course, there are some principles of substantive law, which the arbitrator may **6.40** be called upon to apply, that do involve rewriting the contract. The principle of *clausula rebus sic stantibus* in, for example, Swiss law, allows a contract to be amended by a court or arbitral tribunal applying the law where there has been a fundamental change of circumstances in order to maintain the initial economic balance of the contract.[18] Other laws give the court (or arbitral tribunal) the power to amend contracts. Certain other laws allow contracts to be amended by a state court or arbitral tribunal on grounds of 'unfairness' or 'unconscionability'.[19] As to English law, it allows a contract to be rectified, for example.

The LCIA Rules seem to say that an arbitral tribunal applying the law cannot do **6.41** this, since Article 22.1(g) restricts the ability of a tribunal to rewrite the main contract or the arbitration agreement (which may of course be governed by different laws) to cases of mistake 'common to the parties'. It is submitted that this cannot be the right interpretation of this provision (or that, if it is, it should be removed as soon as possible). If the parties' contract or the arbitration agreement is governed by Swiss law, the tribunal must be able to apply all aspects of Swiss law, including *clausula rebus sic stantibus*. Similarly, if the contract is governed by Finnish or Chinese law, the tribunal must be able to amend it on grounds of unfairness. If (as is rather more common in LCIA arbitration) the contract is governed by English law, the tribunal should be able to rectify it without the need for this oddly drafted provision, particularly since rectification does not strictly need a mistake 'common to the parties' but can be ordered when one party knew of and took advantage of the other's mistake.

It has been suggested by one commentator[20] that the origins of this provision lie **6.42** in the position taken by English law before 1988 which prevented an arbitrator from rectifying the contract containing the arbitral clause.[21] Whatever the reason, it is potentially problematic.

The clause is furthermore potentially ambiguous in that it gives the power to the **6.43** tribunal to correct both the main contract and the arbitration agreement but does not clearly say that in either case it must be by reference to the right governing law; as a matter of principle, the law governing the arbitration agreement cannot

---

[18] Often seen nowadays as a part of the general duty of good faith contained in art 2 of the Swiss Civil Code: P Tercier, 'La clausula rebus sic stantibus en droit suisse des obligations' [1979] JT I 201.

[19] For example, s 36 Finnish (and other Nordic) Contract Act and art 54 Contract Law of the People's Republic of China.

[20] A Samuel, 'Jurisdiction, interim relief and awards under the LCIA Rules' in A Berkeley and J Mimms (eds), *International Commercial Arbitration: Practical Perspectives* (Centre of Construction Law & Management, 2001) 35, 42.

[21] The position was changed by *Ashville Investments Ltd v Elmer Contractors Ltd* [1989] QB 488, CA.

(if different) be used to justify a correction of the main contract and vice versa, but the drafting of this provision does not make the point clear.

Article 22.1(h)

to allow, only upon the application of a party, one or more third persons to be joined in the arbitration as a party provided any such third person and the applicant party have consented thereto in writing, and thereafter to make a single final award, or separate awards, in respect of all parties so implicated in the arbitration;

6.44 This is a potentially far-reaching power. The applicant party may, without the consent of the other original party or parties to the arbitration, apply to join a third party 'as a party' to the arbitration. Provided the third party also agrees, the tribunal can join the third party 'as a party' over the opposition of the other party or parties.

6.45 The roots of the power clearly lie in English litigation procedure, where a defendant can join third parties, who can themselves join fourth and subsequent parties, to ensure, in the interests of the efficient administration of justice, that the whole dispute is dealt with in one proceeding, thus avoiding delay and the risk of inconsistent decisions arising from the same facts. Much as English law has made use of the power to join third parties to smooth the path of court proceedings, it has set its face against it in respect of arbitration in the absence of consent of all of the parties to the original arbitration (as well as the third party).[22]

6.46 In considering the scope of this provision, a distinction should be drawn between two differing sets of circumstances. In the case of a multi-party contract, it may be that an arbitration is started without all parties to the contract being parties to the arbitration. Can one of the original parties join one of the non-parties, or can one of the non-parties apply to join the existing arbitration? In principle, the answer should be yes, if the arbitration clause by which all parties are bound provides that all disputes arising out of the contract are to be settled by arbitration. This may, of course, depend on the terms of the arbitration rules governing the arbitration and indeed the law of the seat, but it is not strange to think of a further party to the arbitration agreement becoming a party to an existing arbitration, whether on his application or the application of an original party to the arbitration.

6.47 This is to be contrasted with the situation where the third party is not a party to the same contract at all, but perhaps a linked contract (where, for example, Party A had contracted with Party B to build a house and Party B had sub-contracted parts of that work to Parties C, D, E, etc). Thus, ICC tribunals have rejected the power to join third parties (as opposed to extending the scope of the arbitration clause).

---

[22] *The Bay Hotel and Resort Ltd v Cavalier Construction Co Ltd* [2001] UKPC 34.

In ICC Case No 12171, the tribunal rejected an attempt to join a third party in the following terms:

> the question whether the arbitration clause can be extended to additional parties is subject to the interpretation of the arbitration agreement and its scope . . . the issue, however, whether a request for third person notice is to be admitted in arbitration proceedings is of a procedural nature and is subject to the rules governing the proceedings.[23]

It is this difficulty that the provision in Article 22.1(h) seeks to overcome, by **6.48** providing an express power to join third parties who may not necessarily be parties to the arbitration agreement.[24] This remains, however, a controversial area. Arbitration is consent-based, and, while there is much debate on the ways in which a party's consent to submit to arbitration can be found, and much controversy surrounding such constructs as the 'group of companies' theory, tribunals always look to find that consent, express or implied, exists before accepting jurisdiction over a party.[25] Similarly, enforcement courts will have regard to the same issues under the New York Convention.

Thus, the idea that a third party can be joined without the consent of all parties to **6.49** the arbitration could be seen as a departure from normal practice. Of course, the non-consenting party can be taken to have consented in theory by having agreed to arbitration under the LCIA Rules, which give the tribunal the power under discussion.[26] This will therefore satisfy the requirements of Article II of the New York Convention and section 6 of the Arbitration Act 1996 that the arbitration agreement be in writing.

It has been suggested that Article 22.1(h) is wide enough to encompass claims **6.50** between the applicant party and the third party itself, but should not extend to situations where the applicant party and the third party wish an issue between the third party and the non-applicant party to be decided in the same arbitration.[27] There is, however, nothing in the drafting of Article 22.1(h) to support such a restrictive construction and, given that all parties will have consented to its use in agreeing to LCIA arbitration, there is no reason to apply a restrictive interpretation at all.

---

[23] ICC Case No 12171 [2005] ASA Bull 2770.
[24] *Hunter & Paulsson* 169.
[25] For an excellent in-depth study of such matters, see B Hanotiau, *Complex Arbitrations: Multiparty, Multicontract, Multi-issue and Class Actions* (Kluwer, 2005).
[26] *Commentary* 12.
[27] A Diamond, 'Procedure and Hearings' in A Berkeley and J Mimms (eds), *International Commercial Arbitration: Practical Perspectives* (Centre of Construction Law & Management, 2001) 49, 55.

6.51 The nearest equivalent provision in other sets of institutional rules is probably that contained in Article 4(2) of the Swiss Rules, which provides: 'Where a third party requests to participate in arbitral proceedings already pending under these Rules or where a party to arbitral proceedings under these Rules intends to cause a third party to participate in the arbitration, the arbitral tribunal shall decide on such request, after consulting with all the parties, taking into account all circumstances it deems relevant and applicable'.[28] It is not clear whether this provision purports to give a Swiss Rules tribunal the power to join a third party without his consent (which is not specifically referred to) but the better answer must be that it could only do so if the third party was already a party to the arbitration agreement, without which the element of consent would be totally missing. Equally, it is not clear whether a consenting third party could be joined without the consent of all parties to the original arbitration; again, the better view must be that it could, as there would otherwise be little point in having the provision in the first place. It is thus fairly similar in scope to the LCIA provision.

6.52 In any event, the matter of the joinder of a third party 'as a party' raises a number of questions. Clearly, such third party would not have all of the rights of a party: he would not be able to nominate an arbitrator, for instance, if the original arbitration clause had foreseen party nominations. For this reason, it may be that some potential third parties (whose consent is needed for them to be joined) may decline to give their consent. Given the importance attached to the ability to choose one of the members of the tribunal, a potential third party can be expected to look long and hard at the composition of the tribunal to which it would be subject and to decline to join if it thought that that particular combination of arbitrators would not look favourably on the position it would take in the proceedings.

6.53 But in other respects he should presumably be treated as a full party to the proceedings, going so far as having the same right to join a fourth party under Article 22.1(h) as the original applicant party who caused him to be joined. Thus, in theory, the cycle of joinder of further parties (say, a long chain of sub-contractors in a large construction dispute) could continue *ad infinitum*, or at least until the tribunal decided that to join further such parties came into conflict with its duty under Article 14.1(ii) to conduct the arbitration efficiently and avoid unnecessary delay and expense.

6.54 Our research shows this provision to have been used by a tribunal in 21 cases up to the end of 2007. From the authors' research, it seems as if there has not yet been a case in which the third party has been joined against the wishes of one of the

---

[28] The UNCITRAL Working Group on the revision of the UNCITRAL Rules is also considering a similar provision: see paras 121ff of the Report of the 46th Session in New York, February 2007 at <http://www.uncitral.org.>

original parties. To the authors' knowledge, Article 22.1(h) has not been the subject of a decision of a supervisory court.

Consolidation

There is no provision in the LCIA Rules that deals with the question of the consolidation of two or more otherwise distinct arbitrations, which is another issue related to questions of jurisdiction and consent that has generated much discussion.[29] This is to be contrasted with the ICC Rules and the SCC Rules, which both allow consolidation of a case with a pending case under the same rules but only, to take the example of the ICC Rules, 'in connection with a legal relationship in respect of which arbitration proceedings between the same parties' are already pending and before the Terms of Reference have been signed.[30] Under both the ICC and SCC provisions, the power is exercised by the institution, not the tribunal. **6.55**

In England, the position is governed by section 35 of the Arbitration Act 1996, which forbids the consolidation of two or more cases, or even their being heard together, without the consent of all of the parties to each arbitration. Put another way, with the consent of each party in each arbitration, there is no absolute bar to consolidation as a matter of English arbitration law. Had the Rules included a provision allowing consolidation of two pending LCIA arbitrations, the parties' agreement by reference to such a provision would, one imagines, have been taken to represent consent under the Arbitration Act. Since there is no such provision in the Rules as they stand, however, the question is moot. **6.56**

Despite the absence of an express provision in the Rules governing consolidation and the requirement of consent in the English Arbitration Act, our research shows that consolidation has been asked for some 48 times. In all, 16 orders for consolidation of a total of some 36 different proceedings have been made, in each case following the agreement of the parties. In no such case was the seat outside London. **6.57**

Interestingly, in several cases there was no formal consolidation but the LCIA Court appointed the same tribunal, on some occasions, but not all, at the request of the parties, who wished the proceedings to be heard together but not (for whatever reason) have them formally consolidated. Indeed, the LCIA Court has a practice of appointing the same tribunal (or sole arbitrator) in cases arising out of the same facts and/or agreement, in one such instance appointing the same sole arbitrator in no less than seven related cases between the same parties but arising out of technically separate contracts, started by a claimant who was awaiting consent to consolidation from the other side's counsel. **6.58**

---

[29] For a full discussion, see generally Hanotiau (n 25 above) 179–90.
[30] Art 4(6) ICC Rules; and *Derains & Schwartz* 58–62.

6.59 In one interesting case, a claimant creatively argued that the wide discretion given to the tribunal under Article 14.2[31] extended to ordering consolidation where that appeared to be helpful to the 'fair, efficient and expeditious conduct of the arbitration' under that provision. The tribunal, unsurprisingly, disagreed. Since the seat of the arbitration was London, and, as noted above, section 35 of the Arbitration Act forbids consolidation without consent, that was surely the right decision.

Article 22.2

By agreeing to arbitration under these Rules, the parties shall be treated as having agreed not to apply to any state court or other judicial authority for any order available from the Arbitral Tribunal under Article 22.1, except with the agreement in writing of all parties.

6.60 In reviewing Article 22.2, one of the advantages of having set out *in extenso* all of the additional powers of the tribunal in Article 22.1 becomes clear. The fact that they are specified enables the Rules to provide in Article 22.2 that, in respect of these named additional powers, there is to be no recourse to a state court without the written consent of all parties to the arbitration. This keeps such matters in the hands of the arbitral tribunal and avoids time-consuming and costly excursions to the courts in respect of matters that are better dealt with by the tribunal that will hear the merits of the case.

6.61 It is to be contrasted with the parties' ability to apply to a state court for interim and conservatory measures, even after the formation of the tribunal.[32]

Article 22.3

The Arbitral Tribunal shall decide the parties' dispute in accordance with the law(s) or rules of law chosen by the parties as applicable to the merits of their dispute. If and to the extent that the Arbitral Tribunal determines that the parties have made no such choice, the Arbitral Tribunal shall apply the law(s) or rules of law which it considers appropriate.

6.62 The first sentence of Article 22.3 provides that the default position of an LCIA arbitration is that the tribunal shall decide it according to law. There is no mention, unlike in Article 17(2) of the ICC Rules, of allowing or requiring the tribunal to take account of 'relevant trade usages', unless, of course, these also form part of the applicable law.

6.63 The tribunal's first obligation is therefore to ascertain whether the parties have agreed that the dispute should be subject to a particular law or laws, or rules of law, and to decide it in accordance with the parties' agreement. This will be clear in the

---

[31] Discussed in ch 5 above.
[32] Art 25.3.

overwhelming majority of contractual arbitrations, since it is nowadays very rare for parties not to specify the law to which they have subjected their contract.

'Rules of Law'

6.64 Should there be no express agreement, the tribunal is enjoined to apply such law(s) or rules of law that it 'considers appropriate'. There is no requirement to apply particular rules of conflicts of laws.[33] The tribunal may simply apply the law, laws or rules of law that it considers 'appropriate'.[34]

6.65 In common with Article 17(1) of the ICC Rules, as well as the AAA, SCC, WIPO, and other arbitration rules, Article 22.3 refers both to law and 'rules of law'. The former has a plural alternative, which recognizes that the same dispute may be subject to more than one substantive law. Having distinct issues governed by different laws (referred to as *dépeçage*) is specifically recognized by the Rome Convention, Article 3(1) of which provides that 'the parties can select the law applicable to the whole or a part only of the contract'.[35] The expression 'rules of law' seems to have gained wide currency with its inclusion in Article 28 of the UNCITRAL Model Law.

6.66 Similarly, there is nothing that stops the parties from agreeing that their contract or relationship should be governed by common principles of more than one national law, rather than dividing issues up among them. This is the so-called *tronc commun* method and may be based on the inability of the parties to decide which of their respective national laws should govern the contract and a decision therefore to adopt both insofar as they contain principles in common.[36]

6.67 As to the meaning of 'rules of law', it would certainly cover anational or transnational rules, such as the much-discussed *lex mercatoria* or the UNIDROIT principles.[37] The *lex mercatoria* (the law merchant) has received much attention by commentators on international arbitration, although, as Jan Paulsson has rightly said, 'despite its intellectual fascination, the debate on the *lex mercatoria*

---

[33] A position reflected in s 46(2) Arbitration Act 1996 in respect of arbitrations with their seat in England, Wales, and Northern Ireland (although (unless the parties have agreed otherwise) s 46(3) mandates the application of some conflicts rules, albeit those that the tribunal 'considers appropriate'.)

[34] The substantive law applicable to international arbitration has been the subject of much learned discussion. See, eg, *Poudret & Besson* paras 676–720; *Redfern & Hunter* paras 2-31 to 2-85; and *Lew, Mistelis, Kröll* 411–72.

[35] Art 3(1) of the Convention on the Law Applicable to Contractual Obligations (Rome, 19 April 1980, as amended) [1980] OJ L266/1, [1998] OJ C27/34 (consolidated version).

[36] As was the case for the contract for the construction of the Channel Tunnel between England and France.

[37] *UNIDROIT Principles of International Commercial Contracts 2004*, International Institute for the Unification of Private Law (UNIDROIT) (Rome, 2004).

does not seem to have had more than marginal influence on international commercial practice'.[38] In addition, one might add, the choice of a national law has the advantages of both foreseeability and accessability, in that the materials are more easily available than for the extremely diffuse *lex mercatoria*, whose sources could be argued to be almost infinite, including international trade usages and precedents created by previous arbitral awards, both of which are of an almost infinite variety (or alternatively express such general principles that they are too vague to be applied), although certain sources, such as the UNIDROIT principles, are incontestably definite.[39]

6.68 It is now almost universally accepted that the parties can choose such anational or transnational rules of law to govern their dispute and that awards based upon such rules will be enforceable. It is sometimes less clear whether the arbitrators have the same power in all cases, although this is also now generally accepted.[40] Whether they should so do is of course another matter, and arbitrators will need to be persuaded that the application of anational rules of law is really the most appropriate way of resolving a dispute.

6.69 Whether a good idea or not, our research has shown that in only three of the 701 cases under the 1998 Rules that the authors have studied did the parties choose a non-national law (in one case public international law and in the two others the Vienna Convention on the International Sale of Goods).[41] It is not known how many tribunals determined that the most applicable rules of law were anational in the 40-odd cases where no governing law was specified in the parties' contract. We hazard a guess that the answer is nil.

The freedom of the parties to choose the applicable substantive law

6.70 The issue of the meaning of 'rules of law' aside, the freedom of the parties to choose the law governing their dispute is not in doubt.[42] Where there is an agreement, the tribunal has no discretion but to apply it under the wording of Article 22.3.

---

[38] J Paulsson, 'La lex mercatoria dans l'arbitrage CCI' [1990] Rev arb 55, 58, quoted in *Poudret & Besson* para 676.

[39] *Poudret & Besson* para 681; and *Redfern & Hunter* para 2-40.

[40] This is the case now even in England. Arbitration Act, s 46(1)(b) provides that the parties may agree that their dispute may be decided according to the law they have chosen or 'such other considerations' as they agree or as are determined by the tribunal (see *Russell* 2-091).

[41] United Nations Convention on Contracts for the International Sale of Goods (Vienna, 11 April 1980) (1988) 1489 UNTS 3.

[42] In England, since the House of Lords decided that the choice of England as the seat of the arbitration did not necessarily imply a choice of English law under the maxim *qui eligit judicem eligit jus* (*Compagnie d'Armement Maritime v Compagnie Tunisienne de Navigation* [1971] AC 572).

The UNIDROIT principles, though, state that they can be used even where the **6.71** parties have designated a national law or laws. The Preamble to the 2004 edition states that they may be applied not only where the parties have agreed that their contract is to be governed by 'general principles of law, the *lex mercatoria* or the like' or 'when the parties have not chosen the law governing their contract' but also 'to interpret or supplement' international uniform law instruments or domestic law. It is not known how often this is done by tribunals in practice, and there would be an obvious risk, in basing a decision on the UNIDROIT principles where the parties had expressly chosen a national law or laws, that the resulting award would be set aside by the courts of the seat of the arbitration or would be otherwise unenforceable.

Restrictions on the parties' freedom

The parties' freedom is not, however, unlimited. They cannot avoid the manda- **6.72** tory application of public policy by choosing a law that would otherwise enable them so to do. The Rome Convention does not allow a choice of foreign law to override the mandatory rules of a country to which all the factual elements of the contract point.[43] Redfern and Hunter point, in this respect, to the issue of tax evasion.[44] Furthermore, enforcement courts are able to apply international public policy in deciding whether to enforce an award, as the English case of *Soleimany v Soleimany* showed.[45] The contract in question, for the smuggling of carpets out of Iran in breach of Iranian law, was governed by Jewish law (which took no account of the illegality under Iranian law), and the dispute arising under it had been decided by the London Beth Din (the customary court of the Chief Rabbi). The English Court of Appeal refused to enforce the award, stating:

> The Court is in our view concerned to preserve the integrity of its process, and to see that it is not abused. The parties cannot override that concern by private agreement. They cannot by procuring an arbitration conceal that they, or rather one of them, is seeking to enforce an illegal contract. Public policy will not allow it.[46]

The same issue arises with regard to antitrust or competition law. Such matters **6.73** have been recognized as arbitrable.[47] In the European Union, the European Court of Justice has established the principle that the courts of the Member States must set aside arbitral awards that themselves breach Articles 81 and 82 of the EC Treaty

---

[43] Rome Convention, art 3(3).
[44] *Redfern & Hunter* para 2-37.
[45] [1999] QB 785, CA.
[46] [1999] QB 785, CA, 800.
[47] For a full discussion, see B Hanotiau, *L'arbitrabilité, Recueil des Cours, Académie de Droit International de la Haye 2002* (Martinus Nijhoff, 2003) 29.

where the applicable national arbitration laws require awards to be set aside for breach of international public policy.[48]

6.74 The French courts have recently upheld this principle in two cases. In the *Thalès* case, the Paris Court of Appeal rejected an application to set aside an arbitral award on the basis of an alleged breach of European competition law, saying that the breach would have to be 'blatant, actual and concrete' (*'violation flagrante, effective et concrète'*). The Paris Court of Appeal followed the ECJ's decision in *Eco Swiss* that, although EC competition law might be considered part of the principles of international public policy of Member States, a review of awards on this ground should be limited in scope and in conformity with national arbitration law (in this case, the timing of the challenge).[49] The reasoning in the *Thalès* decision was confirmed by the *Cour de cassation* in a different case in 2008.[50]

Determination by the tribunal

6.75 As noted above, the tribunals in determining the applicable law(s) or rules of law are not bound to apply any rules of conflicts of laws, but nor are they precluded from so doing. They can approach the matter, in other words, in the manner that they consider best gets to the most 'appropriate' law or rules of law.

6.76 Different methods can include the use of the conflicts rules of the country of the seat of the arbitration, some other conflicts rules or a combination of more than one set of rules or the so-called *voie directe* method. This enables the arbitrators to go directly to the substantive law they consider appropriate, without taking a detour via any conflicts of laws rules. In effect, it gives the arbitrators freedom to choose the substantive law rather than the rules of conflicts of laws. Of course, in practice, in adopting such a method, the arbitrators must have taken some factors into consideration, probably including conflicts of laws rules of one sort or another. Thus, the *voie directe* method in practice just enables the arbitrators to hide their reasoning and escape scrutiny for it. It is hardly the most satisfactory way to determine the rules that will decide the outcome of the parties' dispute.

---

[48] *Eco Swiss China Time Ltd v Benetton International*, Case No C-126/97, [1999] ECR I-3055.

[49] Court of Appeal of Paris, *Thalès Air Defence BV c GIE Euromissile, EADS France and EADS Deutschland GmbH*, 18 November 2004, [2005] Rev arb 529, note L G Radiati di Brozolo; A Mourre [2005] JDI 357; D Bensaude, '*Thalès Air Defence B.V. v. GIE Euromissile*: Defining the Limits of Scrutiny of Awards Based on Alleged Violations of European Competition Law' (2005) 22 J Int Arb 239; G Blanke, 'Defining the Limits of Scrutiny of Awards Based on Alleged Violations of European Competition Law: A Réplique to Denis Bensaude's "*Thalès Air Defence B.V. v. GIE Euromissile*"' (2006) 23 J Int Arb 249.

[50] *Cour de cassation, 1ère ch civ, Société SNF SAS c Société Cytec Industries BV*, 4 June 2008, Bull civ I No 06-15.320.

Poudret and Besson rightly say that 'the choice must not be arbitrary, in particular dictated solely by the solution which the arbitrators intend to reach on the merits, but must be based on objective criteria, with the result that a conflict-of-laws approach is indispensable'.[51]

As a matter of practice, it is obviously highly advisable for a decision as to the applicable law to be made in a partial award on a preliminary issue. This is to ensure that the parties know under which law they should be arguing and under which law the arbitrators will decide on the scope of their respective rights and obligations. **6.77**

Article 22.4

> The Arbitral Tribunal shall only apply to the merits of the dispute principles deriving from 'ex aequo et bono', 'amiable composition' or 'honourable engagement' where the parties have so agreed expressly in writing.

The three phrases used in Article 22.4 equate to the English concept of equity and good conscience. In effect, to confer such a power on the arbitrators enables them to decide a dispute on the basis of what they, as individuals, consider to be 'fair and reasonable'. While this does not give the arbitrators licence to decide whatever they wish (they must, if charged with deciding in equity, be equitable), it does not limit them to the application of any particular, or indeed arguably any, rules of law.[52] **6.78**

In practice, it is generally accepted that arbitrators mandated with the duty to decide *ex aequo et bono* must have regard to the relevant law (as to which, see above) but to feel free to derogate from any strict rule of law that would, according to their conception of the case, lead to an unfair result. They might also seek to imply a higher duty to act in good faith than might always be present in a given national law and/or to decide on the basis of what they perceive to have been the initial and intended economic equilibrium of the contract.[53] **6.79**

It is an interesting question whether, in the light of the provisions of Article 22.1(g), an arbitral tribunal deciding in equity or as *amiable compositeur* could modify provisions of the contract. There is the philosophical question of whether the parties could be taken to have agreed their contract and at the same time, in agreeing to submit disputes to an *amiable compositeur*, given a third party the **6.80**

---

[51] *Poudret & Besson* para 687.
[52] The better view is that the arbitrators cannot depart from the law entirely. They certainly cannot in England: *Home and Overseas Insurance v Mentor Insurance* [1989] 1 Lloyd's Rep 473, CA 487. The reference to 'other considerations' in s 46(1)(b) Arbitration Act 1996 is a statutory recognition of the ability of arbitrators to decide *ex aequo et bono*.
[53] For a general discussion, see *Poudret & Besson* paras 709–20.

power to change it. It is perhaps one thing to argue that the tribunal in such circumstances can decide whether to apply the full rigour of the contract to past situations giving rise to the dispute; it is another to allow the tribunal to change the parties' rights and obligations for the future. Are the parties to be taken to have agreed to oust not only the law but the contract as well?[54] It is submitted not.

6.81 In any event, the duty imposed by Article 26.1 to produce a reasoned award is not lifted by the tribunal's being designated to decide in equity.

B. Article 23 – Jurisdiction of the Arbitral Tribunal

6.82 Article 23 raises two issues at the heart of international arbitration, namely the separability of the arbitration clause and the jurisdiction of the tribunal to decide on its own jurisdiction.

6.83 The two are interlinked to the extent that the former resolves the logical difficulty of an arbitral tribunal deciding that it did not have jurisdiction on the basis, for example, of the non-existence or lack of validity of the contract, which could imply that the tribunal should not have assumed jurisdiction in the first place. The doctrine of the separability of the arbitration clause gives the arbitration clause an independent existence of its own, rather than only as part of the contract in which it may be embedded.

Article 23.1

The Arbitral Tribunal shall have the power to rule on its own jurisdiction, including any objection to the initial or continuing existence, validity or effectiveness of the Arbitration Agreement. For that purpose, an arbitration clause which forms or was intended to form part of another agreement shall be treated as an arbitration agreement independent of that other agreement. A decision by the Arbitral Tribunal that such other agreement is non-existent, invalid or ineffective shall not entail ipso jure the non-existence, invalidity or ineffectiveness of the arbitration clause.

Compétence-compétence

6.84 It is now generally accepted that an arbitral tribunal has the jurisdiction to decide on its own jurisdiction.[55] This is often known as competence-competence or,

---

[54] The French courts consider that there is, in this respect, no difference between acting *ex aequo et bono* and as an *amiable compositeur* (see *Derains & Schwartz* 246 and the references therein cited).

[55] Redfern and Hunter describe this as an 'inherent power' of an arbitral tribunal: see *Redfern & Hunter* para 5-39.

because the word 'competence' is rarely used in English to mean 'jurisdiction' in this context, by its French equivalent, *compétence-compétence*.[56]

Although it has been said that the principle of *compétence-compétence* is itself a **6.85** 'customary international rule',[57] it is submitted that the better view is that the power of the arbitral tribunal to decide on its own jurisdiction is not absolute, but is subject to the control of the courts of the seat of the arbitration. It is hard to imagine that a decision by an arbitral tribunal to rule on its own jurisdiction would long survive a setting-aside application if the law of the seat of the arbitration did not allow the arbitrators that power.

Thus, the existence of the *compétence-compétence* principle in a given case is **6.86** dependent on both the law of the seat of the arbitration and the relevant procedural rules (in our case the LCIA Rules) conferring the power on the tribunal. The conferral by the national arbitration law (in the UNCITRAL Model Law by Article 16, in England by section 30 of the Arbitration Act 1996 and in similar terms in the arbitration statutes of all major commercial centres) is permissive: it allows the parties to agree to confer the power on their tribunal. The applicable procedural rules then confer the power directly: in agreeing to arbitration under those rules the parties have agreed to the principle of *compétence-compétence*.

Unlike under the ICC Rules, there is no formal two-stage process for deciding **6.87** jurisdiction. In an ICC arbitration, if the respondent raises a plea of lack of jurisdiction, the ICC Secretariat first conducts a prima facie review of the existence of an arbitration agreement between the parties to the arbitration. Only if it is satisfied that an agreement exists will the debate progress to the second stage, which is the determination by the arbitral tribunal itself of its own jurisdiction.[58]

In practice, though, something rather similar happens, albeit informally. Under **6.88** the LCIA Rules, the Request for Arbitration should be accompanied by a copy of the arbitration clause.[59] If, on review of the documents submitted, the Registrar considers that there is doubt as to the existence of an arbitration agreement, or if it covers the parties to or the subject-matter of the dispute, the Registrar will enter into discussions with the claimant to seek to resolve the apparent anomaly (at the same time, of course, inviting the comments of the respondent).

---

[56] In German, *Kompetenzprüfung durch das Schiedsgericht*, not *Kompetenz-Kompetenz*, which would mean that the arbitral tribunal would have the power to make a *final* ruling on its own jurisdiction, without any supervision by a state court, which is not the case in international arbitration. See *Poudret & Besson* para 457, n 3, citing P Fouchard, E Gaillard, B Goldman *Traité de l'arbitrage international* (1st ed, Litec, 1996) para 651.

[57] M de Boisséson, *Le droit français de l'arbitrage interne et international* (Joly, 1990) 715.

[58] Art 6(2) ICC Rules; and *Derains & Schwartz* 76–110.

[59] Art 1.1(b).

If, following such discussions, however, there is no glaring or obvious inconsistency, the matter will be referred to the arbitral tribunal for decision under Article 23.1.[60]

6.89 There are two aspects to the *compétence-compétence* principle, the negative and the positive effect of the principle.[61] The positive effect is the ability of the tribunal to determine its own jurisdiction. The negative effect, equally important, indeed essential for the positive effect to have any real substance, is the principle that the state courts will decline jurisdiction to decide on the existence or validity of an arbitration agreement or the jurisdiction of the arbitral tribunal, referring such matters to the arbitral tribunal.[62]

6.90 As noted in chapter 1 above, the LCIA submitted an *amicus curiae* brief in the Canadian Supreme Court case of *Dell Computer Corporation v Union des Consommateurs* in 2007.[63] This case concerned the enforceability of an arbitration clause in the conditions of sale of a company selling over the internet in circumstances where the buyers wanted to institute a class action. The Supreme Court of Canada supported the LCIA's stance on the major issues, holding that:

(i) the challenge to the jurisdiction of the arbitrator should be determined by the arbitrator, not the court, thus upholding the principle of *compétence-compétence*;

(ii) a challenge to the principle of *compétence-compétence* should only be entertained if the challenge is based solely on a question of law and then only if the court is satisfied that the challenge is not brought merely as a delaying tactic and will not unduly impede the conduct of the arbitration;

(iii) an arbitration agreement in a click-through agreement on the internet is enforceable; and

(iv) a commitment to arbitrate should prevail over the procedural right to commence a class action.[64]

Separability

6.91 As noted above, this is the essential corollary to the *compétence-compétence* principle. The issue is simple. Given that the tribunal's jurisdiction derives from the

---

60 The Registrar's review of the Request for Arbitration is discussed in more detail in ch 3 above.

61 As first described in *Fouchard, Gaillard, Goldman* paras 660 and 671–82.

62 In France, art 1458 Code de procédure civile.

63 *Dell Computer Corporation v Union des Consommateurs and Olivier Demoulin* 2007 SCC 34.

64 Although on this last point it is interesting to note that two Canadian provinces legislated to bar the enforceability of arbitration clauses in consumer agreements.

arbitration agreement, if it decides that one or both of the parties never agreed to be bound in whatever way (lack of legal capacity, illegality, *non est factum*, fraud, forgery, termination by effluxion of time, invalidity *ab initio*, etc), this creates the logical impossibility of the parties' ever having conferred jurisdiction on the tribunal for any purpose whatsoever.

The solution to this logical conundrum is the doctrine of separability, that is to say, the arbitration agreement having an independent legal existence as a separate and self-standing contract, divorced from the overall contract in which it is embedded. Thus, even in cases where the whole contract was found to have been a forgery, the jurisdiction of the arbitral tribunal to decide that point (which, if decided in the sense of the contract's never having existed, would remove the existence both of the contract and the arbitration agreement) is unaffected. Article 23.1 makes this clear in saying that '[a] decision by the Arbitral Tribunal that such other agreement is non-existent, invalid or ineffective shall not entail ipso jure the non-existence, invalidity or ineffectiveness of the arbitration clause'. **6.92**

This doctrine has recently seen important developments in two major arbitral jurisdictions, France and England. In France, the *Cour de cassation* decided in 2005 that the autonomy of the arbitration clause was not affected by the invalidity or non-existence of the main contract.[65] **6.93**

As to English law, the House of Lords confirmed the application of this important principle, and that of *compétence-compétence*, in the *Fiona Trust* case in 2007.[66] The appeal before the House of Lords concerned the scope and effect of arbitration clauses in eight charterparties. It was alleged that the charterparties had been procured by bribery. The arbitration clause provided that disputes 'arising under this charter' would be referred to arbitration in London. The owners purported to rescind the contracts and then sought a declaration that the rescissions were valid; the charterers subsequently applied for a stay of proceedings under section 9 of the Arbitration Act. **6.94**

---

[65] *Cour de cassation, 1ère ch civ, Société Omenex c M Hugon*, 25 October 2005, [2006] Rev arb 106, note J-B Racine.

[66] *Premium Nafta Products Ltd v Fili Shipping Company Ltd* [2007] UKHL 40, on appeal from *Fiona Trust and Holding Corporation and others v Privalov and Others* [2007] EWCA Civ 20. This case has already been the subject of much commentary: S Gee, 'Jurisdiction – the Validity and Width of Arbitration Agreements, and the House of Lords Decision in *Premium Nafta Products Ltd v Fili Shipping Co Ltd*' (2008) 24 Arb Int 467; M McNeill and B Juratowitch, 'The Doctrine of Separability and Consent to Arbitrate' (2008) 24 Arb Int 475; A Samuel, 'Separability and Construing Arbitration Clauses' (2008) 24 Arb Int 489; C Style and M Knowles, '*Fiona Trust*: 10 Years On, the Fresh Start Entrenched' (2008) 24 Arb Int 499; and E Snodgrass, '*Fiona Trust v Privalov*: The Arbitration Act 1996 Comes of Age' (2007) 10 Int ALR 27.

6.95 The owners argued that the arbitration clause contained in the charterparties did not apply for two reasons:

(a) as a matter of construction, the dispute as to the validity of the arbitration clause was not a matter 'arising under' the contract, and therefore fell outside the scope of the arbitration clause; and

(b) as the contract was liable to be rescinded for bribery, the arbitration clause was therefore not binding.

6.96 On the issue of construction, the House of Lords dismissed the distinction between disputes 'arising under' and 'arising out of' a contract. The House of Lords held that the words 'arising out of' should indeed cover a dispute about the validity of the contract, although a distinction was drawn as to 'a dispute as to whether there was ever a contract at all'.[67]

6.97 On the issue of bribery, the owners argued that they were entitled to rescind the whole of the contract, including the arbitration agreement, and that the arbitral tribunal had as a consequence no jurisdiction. The House of Lords, however, upheld the doctrine of separability. Thus, the invalidity of the main contract did not necessarily entail the invalidity or rescission of the arbitration agreement. The House of Lords confirmed that the arbitration agreement is a distinct agreement that is void or voidable only on grounds that relate directly to it (as distinct from the main contract). On the facts, this meant that even though the main charter-party may have been void or voidable on the grounds of bribery, the arbitration agreement contained therein survived, vesting the arbitral tribunal with the jurisdiction to determine the issue of bribery.

Article 23.2

A plea by a Respondent that the Arbitral Tribunal does not have jurisdiction shall be treated as having been irrevocably waived unless it is raised not later than the Statement of Defence; and a like plea by a Respondent to Counterclaim shall be similarly treated unless it is raised no later than the Statement of Defence to Counterclaim. A plea that the Arbitral Tribunal is exceeding the scope of its authority shall be raised promptly after the Arbitral Tribunal has indicated its intention to decide on the matter alleged by any party to be beyond the scope of its authority, failing which such plea shall also be treated as having been waived irrevocably. In any case, the Arbitral Tribunal may nevertheless admit an untimely plea if it considers the delay justified in the particular circumstances.

6.98 It is axiomatic that a respondent should not be able to raise an objection to jurisdiction at a late stage of the arbitration, at a point when time and costs will have been expended, possibly uselessly. To allow this would be to open the possibility of serious abuse of the arbitral process. The primary rule laid down by Article 23.2

---

67 *Premium Nafta Products Ltd v Fili Shipping Company Ltd* [2007] UKHL 40 at para 34.

is that any such objection has to be made in the first full memorial of the party raising the objection, namely the Statement of Defence for the respondent and, if there is an objection from the claimant that matters raised in a counterclaim are beyond the jurisdiction of the arbitral tribunal, in the Statement of Defence to Counterclaim.

Article 23.2 further provides that an objection that the tribunal intends 'to decide on the matter alleged by any party to be beyond the scope of its authority' must be made 'promptly', failing which it, too, is taken to have been irrevocably waived. There is no definition of how prompt is prompt for the purposes of this provision, and in any event the tribunal has a general discretion in Article 23.2 to allow a late objection if it is considered justified.[68] This is obviously a vital provision to preserve the tribunal's discretion, to be exercised on a case-by-case basis, depending on the facts of the particular case. The whole of Article 23.2 closely tracks the wording of Article 16(2) of the UNCITRAL Model Law.

6.99

Article 23.3

The Arbitral Tribunal may determine the plea to its jurisdiction or authority in an award as to jurisdiction or later in an award on the merits, as it considers appropriate in the circumstances.

Faced with a challenge to their jurisdiction, the arbitrators have a number of options. They can decide to hear the objection to jurisdiction as a preliminary issue, and then either render an award declaring that they have no jurisdiction, putting an end to the proceedings completely, or upholding (in whole or in part) their jurisdiction, so that the case goes forward, either in its original or a modified form. In either case, their decision should be rendered in the form of a partial award. This will almost certainly be after having received the parties' written submissions on jurisdiction and, usually, an oral hearing (with or, more usually without, witnesses of fact, but often with expert witnesses in the relevant law or laws).[69]

6.100

Alternatively, they could decide that, because the facts on which a decision on the issue of jurisdiction would be based are inextricably intertwined with those of the merits, they should hear the issues of jurisdiction and the merits at the same time.

6.101

Article 23.3 provides authority to the tribunal to take either of these routes.

6.102

---

[68] This is in addition to the general power in art 22.1(b).

[69] Given that the LCIA Secretariat will have checked as to the existence of a document at least purporting to be the arbitration agreement, it is very unlikely that the question of jurisdiction can be dealt with by the tribunal without full written submissions and a hearing.

6.103 In many cases, the former course of action is the more sensible. If the tribunal does not have jurisdiction, it is better for the parties to know that before committing themselves to the time and cost of fighting the dispute on the merits. Another factor for the tribunal to consider, however, is that a partial award on the subject of jurisdiction is open to challenge at the seat of the arbitration in setting-aside proceedings. Thus, the tribunal can be faced with the prospect of having to decide whether to stay the proceedings pending the outcome of the setting-aside application, with the concomitant delay, or carrying on, with the possibility that it will be found to have had no jurisdiction from the start and that the proceedings on the merits were a waste of time and money. It is to be noted that section 31(4) of the Arbitration Act provides that, if the parties agree that the tribunal should decide the jurisdictional objection in a partial award, or to combine it with the merits and deal with both in a final award, the tribunal must do so.

6.104 The English Arbitration Act 1996 provides in section 67(2) that there is no automatic stay of proceedings. The Model Law adopts the same approach. Article 16(3) provides that, while the supervisory court is seized with an application to set aside an award on jurisdiction, the arbitral tribunal may continue with the reference and make a final award.

Article 23.4

By agreeing to arbitration under these Rules, the parties shall be treated as having agreed not to apply to any state court or other judicial authority for any relief regarding the Arbitral Tribunal's jurisdiction or authority, except with the agreement in writing of all parties to the arbitration or the prior authorization of the Arbitral Tribunal or following the latter's award ruling on the objection to its jurisdiction or authority.

6.105 Article 23.4 confirms the principle of *compétence-compétence* in the sense that the parties themselves agree not to make an application to the court in respect of jurisdiction. The only exceptions are:

   (i) with the consent of all parties; or
  (ii) with the authorization of the arbitral tribunal; or
 (iii) in proceedings for the setting-aside of an award on jurisdiction.

6.106 This provision is really only belt-and-braces, as it follows from everything else in Article 23.

C. Article 25 – Interim and Conservatory Measures

6.107 The power contained in Article 25 to order interim and conservatory measures should be seen together with the power to order the expedited formation of the arbitral tribunal in Article 9, for the two often go together.[70] The explicit preservation of the parties' right to apply for such measures before 'any state court or other judicial authority' both before and, in exceptional cases, after the formation of the tribunal is also necessary, in that it prevents such an application to a state court from being taken to constitute a waiver of the applicant party's right to have recourse to arbitration under the arbitration agreement.

6.108 It is the case for the grant of interim and conservatory measures under Article 25, as with other powers granted to the tribunal under the Rules, that its exercise is dependent upon the arbitration law of the seat of the arbitration making this power available to the arbitrators, or at least not forbidding it. In practice, it is recognized in all major arbitral jurisdictions that the tribunal has the power to grant interim and conservatory measures, although only since 1989 in the case of one of the most important such jurisdictions, Switzerland.[71]

6.109 The availability of interim and conservatory measures is clearly an essential part of the workability of the Rules. Interim and conservatory measures can be themselves a prerequisite to the successful working of the arbitral process in some cases, where a freezing order is needed to ensure the practical enforceability of the award, or the preservation of an asset that is the subject-matter of the proceedings. Indeed, of the 701 cases under the 1998 Rules that we have studied in our research, no fewer than 126 have been the subject of applications under Article 25, of which, however, only 45 were granted by the arbitral tribunal.

6.110 The Rules do not set out any test for the granting of an application for interim and conservatory measures. This is left to the discretion of the tribunal. Some guidelines can, however, be inferred from various sources. Of these, the most useful are the 2006 amendments to the UNCITRAL Model Law, in that the Model Law can be taken to represent, while not exactly a consensus among international arbitration commentators and practitioners, at least a view that commands wide support.[72]

6.111 The tests for granting interim relief under the UNCITRAL Model Law come in two parts. Article 17(2) sets out the circumstances in which, and the purposes for which, interim and conservatory measures can be sought. These are:

(i) to maintain or restore the *status quo* pending determination of the dispute;
(ii) to take action that would prevent, or refrain from taking action that is likely to cause, current or imminent harm to the arbitral process itself;

---

[70] Art 9 is discussed in ch 4 above.
[71] Art 183 PILA.
[72] For a further discussion of interim and conservatory measures in international arbitration, see A Redfern, 'Interim Measures' in L Newman and R Hill (eds), *The Leading Arbitrators' Guide to International Arbitration* (Juris Publishing, 2008) 203.

(iii) to provide a means of preserving assets out of which a subsequent award may be satisfied; or

(iv) to preserve evidence that may be relevant and material to the resolution of the dispute.

6.112 The following provision, Article 17.A, provides three qualifications to the right of the requesting party to obtain the interim and conservatory measures sought. The requesting party must satisfy the tribunal that:

(i) the applicant party will suffer harm not adequately reparable in damages if the interim and conservatory measures are not granted;

(ii) such harm to the applicant party substantially outweighs the harm to the other party if the interim and conservatory measures are granted; and

(iii) there is (while not affecting the discretion of the tribunal to decide otherwise in a final award) a 'reasonable possibility that the requesting party will succeed on the merits of the claim'.

6.113 Article 17.A(2) makes clear that these two last requirements are not applicable if the interim and conservatory measures sought are just to preserve evidence.

6.114 If these are accepted to be the main principles guiding a tribunal's decision as to the granting of interim and conservatory measures, how are they to be applied? Again, there is nothing to be gleaned from the Rules themselves, but some idea of the relevant principles that should be applied by international arbitral tribunals can be obtained from several sources.

6.115 Thus, international arbitral practice shows that a claimant will generally be expected to show that, to some degree, he has a *prima facie* case on the merits of one or more of his claims without forcing a tribunal to pre-hear the merits:

> In dealing with a request for an interim measure, an arbitral tribunal must refrain from pre-judging the merits of the case . . . A tribunal will always wish to leave the parties the opportunity for their full cases to be heard. Although a tribunal should not pre-judge the merits of a case, the applicant should nevertheless demonstrate the prima-facie establishment of its case.[73]

6.116 The language used in the Model Law only requires the applicant party to prove to the tribunal that he has a 'reasonable possibility' of success on the merits, a significantly lower threshold than the initial formulation posed by the working group in the 2003 draft of the Model Law, which called for a 'substantial possibility'.[74] On the assumption, discussed above, that the test as finally set out in the Model Law reflects international arbitral practice, and so long as it does not conflict with any

---

[73] J Lew, 'Commentary on Interim and Conservatory Measures in ICC Arbitration Cases' (2000) 11 ICC Bull 23, 27.
[74] Working Group draft CN.9/WGII/WP.123, para 16 (3 April 2003).

mandatory rules of the seat of the arbitration, it should be followed by arbitral tribunals applying the LCIA Rules, as well as other rules that invest the tribunal with the power to grant interim and conservatory measures.

In the ICSID annulment proceedings in *CDC Group PLC v Republic of the* **6.117** *Seychelles*,[75] the *ad hoc* committee briefly considered the meaning and applicability of Article 17(3)(b) of the draft UNCITRAL Model Law prepared by the working group, which later became Article 17.A. The committee noted that the application of a merits-based test to determine whether an interim measure should be granted was relatively unheard of in international practice at the time. However, the committee did state that:

> Leaving to one side the fact that the Working Group has not yet completed its work, however, it is clear that a 'reasonable possibility' of success is markedly less than a 'probability'. In addition, an important motivation for inserting any such requirement in the Model Law would seem to be to enhance the chances that a municipal court will be persuaded to enforce an award of interim measures.[76]

A leading commentator has remarked that: **6.118**

> this latest formulation [of the Model Law], by narrowly limiting the inquiry, will undoubtedly reduce the plaintiff's burden to an even greater degree — and at the same time minimize the likelihood that the arbitrators may be led to 'prejudge' the merits at an early stage of the proceedings.[77]

In fact, it has been suggested that the merits of the claimant's case rarely play a role **6.119** in determining whether or not interim and conservatory measures are granted:

> the requirement of a good arguable case on the merits, which is considered in some laws to be a prerequisite for interim relief in support of court proceedings, has received mixed reactions. This is due to the fact that unlike court proceedings, where the judge granting interim relief will frequently be different from the judge dealing with the merits of the case, in arbitration the same tribunal will deal with both issues. To avoid any appearance of pre-judgment arbitrators are invariably reluctant to express their views on the merits before they have considered at least a significant amount of the evidence presented by the parties. For this reason the merits of the case rarely play any direct role in determining whether or not interim relief is granted.[78]

The rationale behind this practice is both easy to understand and compelling. An **6.120** arbitral tribunal must be mindful of the fact that it is the sole trier of fact in the case and that to be seen to pre-judge the final outcome on the events at such an

---

[75] *CDC Group PLC v Republic of the Seychelles*, ICSID Case No ARB/02/14, decision of *ad hoc* committee (Judge Brower, presiding, M Hwang SC, D Williams QC) on the Respondent's application for a stay of execution of the award, 14 July 2004.

[76] See *CDC Group PLC v Republic of the Seychelles*, above, para 13.

[77] A Rau, *Provisional Relief in Arbitration: How Things Stand in the United States* (2005) 22 J Int Arb 1, n 156.

[78] *Lew, Mistelis, Kröll* 604.

early stage of the proceedings could lead to grave doubt being expressed as to the fairness of the procedure, which in turn could imperil the final award. At the same time, it is sometimes imperative that interim and conservatory measures be granted. The test set out in the new Article 17.A of the Model Law, namely that the claimant should show a 'reasonable possibility' of ultimate success, is therefore the appropriate one.

6.121   As to the meaning of the notion of 'harm not adequately reparable by an award of damages',[79] it has been suggested that it should be understood in the economic sense:

> In this respect 'irreparable' must be understood in an economic, not a literal, sense. It must take account of the fact that it may not always be possible to compensate for actual losses suffered or sullied business reputation through damages.[80]

6.122   Schwartz, however, states the definition construed by arbitral bodies is even broader, in that although 'Anglo-American lawyers often understand "irreparable" harm as meaning harm that cannot readily be compensated by an award of monetary damages', ICC arbitral tribunals have sometimes also construed risk of financial loss to be included within this definition.[81]

6.123   The remaining principle in Article 17.A of the Model Law that should be applied is that of proportionality, or 'the balance of convenience' as it is known to common lawyers, namely the need for the tribunal to weigh the advantage to the claimant of granting the interim and conservatory measures sought against the harm to the respondent. Even if the requesting party can show that he would suffer harm through not being granted the interim and conservatory measures sought, the tribunal must ensure that the harm to be done to the other party in granting such interim and conservatory measures is not disproportionate to the benefit.

6.124   It is also this consideration that leads to the need for an arbitral tribunal granting interim and conservatory measures to consider whether, and if so to what extent, countervailing security is needed from the applicant if the interim and conservatory measures are subsequently found to have been wrongly granted. This principle is referred to specifically in two provisions of the LCIA Rules, namely Article 25.1(a) and Article 25.2, and is considered further in the discussion of those provisions.

6.125   A final consideration in reflecting on the circumstances in which a tribunal should entertain a request for interim and conservatory measures is the overriding duty

---

[79]   UNCITRAL Model Law, art 17.A(1)(a).
[80]   *Lew, Mistelis, Kröll* 604.
[81]   E Schwartz, 'The Practices and Experiences of the ICC Court' in *Conservatory and Provisional Measures in International Arbitration* (ICC Publishing, 1993) 45.

in arbitral practice to conduct the proceedings in good faith. It has indeed become a principle of international arbitral practice that the parties should refrain from any act or omission that would result in an aggravation of their dispute. This can be seen, for example, in the partial award in ICC Case No 3896, in which the tribunal, composed of Professors Lalive, Robert, and Goldman, stated that:

> [i]n conclusion, the Arbitral Tribunal considers that there exists, undeniably, the risk of the dispute before it becoming aggravated or magnified, and that the parties should, in the same spirit of goodwill that they have already demonstrated in signing the Terms of Reference, refrain from any action likely to widen or aggravate the dispute, or to complicate the task of the Tribunal or even make more difficult, one way or another, the observance of the final arbitral award.[82]

6.126 This principle is reflected in the provisions of Article 17 of the Model Law discussed above. It combines the need to preserve the *status quo*[83] with the ability of the tribunal to order interim and conservatory measures to prevent 'current or imminent harm or prejudice to the arbitral process itself'.[84] The obligation on the parties to conduct the proceedings in good faith could therefore be used by an arbitral tribunal in combination with generally accepted powers to grant interim and conservatory measures in order both to preserve the *status quo* pending the final resolution of the dispute and also to prevent a party from taking steps that would, in the opinion of the tribunal, aggravate the dispute.

6.127 Indeed, in the experience of one of the authors, an arbitral tribunal (sitting under the SCC Rules, which are less detailed than the LCIA Rules in setting out the powers of a tribunal to grant interim and conservatory measures) ordered the preservation of the *status quo* even pending final determination of the substance of a heavy application for interim and conservatory measures. It could therefore be seen as a further ground upon which a grant of interim and conservatory measures could be ordered.

6.128 It is interesting to note that this principle appears explicitly in the rules of only one major international arbitration institution, namely CIETAC. The CIETAC Rules provide, in Article 7, that '[t]he parties shall proceed with the arbitration in bona fide cooperation'.[85] While this principle does not appear in the LCIA Rules,

---

[82] Partial Award in ICC Case No 3896, 23 December 1982 (1974–1985) Collection of ICC Arbitral Awards 161.

[83] UNCITRAL Model Law, art 17(2)(a).

[84] UNCITRAL Model Law, art 17(2)(b).

[85] It should be noted, however, that the CIETAC Rules by arts 17 and 18 only allow for very restrictive interim and conservatory measures (essentially for the preservation of evidence) and further provide that such requests have to be referred to and granted only by state courts. See generally N Darwazeh and M Moser, 'Arbitration Inside China' in M Moser (ed), *Managing Business Disputes in Today's China: Duelling with Dragons* (Kluwer, 2007) 45, 79–81.

it is submitted that it infuses all international arbitration, including that conducted according to the LCIA Rules.

6.129 One particular issue that arises in the context of grants of interim and conservatory measures is enforceability. While there is always doubt over the enforceability of orders for interim and conservatory measures that are made in the form of orders and not awards, a defaulting party can be pretty sure that his delinquency will not go unpunished by the tribunal in the final award, even if this is limited to the drawing of adverse inferences. Parties are thus generally reluctant to flout orders made by the tribunal. Furthermore, in most jurisdictions, state courts will assist parties seeking to have orders for interim and conservatory measures made by arbitral tribunals enforced. In England, section 42 of the Arbitration Act allows a court to enforce 'peremptory' orders of an arbitral tribunal, namely those requiring that a particular act be done within a given time.[86] Equivalent provisions exist in both Switzerland and Germany, for example.[87]

6.130 An arbitral tribunal might be faced with this question in particularly acute form when having to decide an application for an asset-freezing order under Article 25.1(b) and/or Article 25.1(c), discussed below.

Article 25.1

The Arbitral Tribunal shall have the power, unless otherwise agreed by the parties in writing, on the application of any party:

6.131 The LCIA Rules adopt an interesting descriptive method for setting out the powers that they grant to the tribunal to order interim and conservatory measures. Rather than simply say, as do the ICC Rules in Article 23(1) and the SCC Rules in Article 32(1), that the tribunal may grant such interim and conservatory measures as 'it deems appropriate', the LCIA Rules set out specific powers of the tribunal to grant interim and conservatory measures.[88] It has been suggested[89] that this was needed as a result of section 39 of the English Arbitration Act. While section 39 does indeed set out examples of the interim and conservatory measures that parties may agree to allow the tribunal to grant, it is not in any way restrictive (nor a mandatory provision), so this explanation seems unlikely.

---

[86] Although *Russell* at para 6-130 states that there are doubts as to the applicability of s 42 to orders for interim and conservatory measures.

[87] Art 183(2) PILA and s 1041(2) ZPO, respectively.

[88] For a general review of the differences in institutional rules with respect to the grant of interim and conservatory measures, see G Marchac, 'Interim Measures in International Commercial Arbitration under the ICC, AAA, LCIA and UNCITRAL Rules' (2000) 10 Am Rev Int Arb 123.

[89] V Triebel and R Hunter, 'Kommentar LCIA-Schiedsregeln' in R Schütze (ed), *Institutionelle Schiedsgerichtsbarkeit* (Carl Heymanns Verlag, 2006) 413.

The structure of Article 25 is that it first sets out that the tribunal may make orders **6.132** securing the amounts in dispute (Article 25.1(a)) and the preservation or other dealing with property (Article 25.1(b)) before giving the tribunal a more general power to order on a provisional basis any relief that it could grant in a final award in Article 25.1(c) (which does, indeed, correspond to section 39(1) of the Arbitration Act). Article 25.2 then deals specifically with security for costs, which could give the impression that the LCIA Rules consider this to be of particular importance, which, if true, would have an unfortunate resonance in the English context given the controversy that the exercise of the power to award security for costs has had in the past.

In an English context, the general authorization to grant interim and conserva- **6.133** tory measures is contained in section 39 of the Arbitration Act. This is headed 'Power to make provisional awards', which might lead to the conclusion that only those matters that could be the subject of a partial final award could be the subject of applications for interim and conservatory measures in an arbitration with its seat in England. Confusingly, sub-section 39(1) refers to the power of the tribunal to make provisional orders. In practice, it seems as if this presents no difficulty in enabling the tribunal to order interim and conservatory measures in the form of an order and not an award.[90] Indeed, it may be that the real power to order provisional relief can be found in sub-section 38(1), which allows the parties to agree on powers exercisable by the tribunal. Since section 38 covers both security for costs and orders for the preservation and inspection of property, this is wholly plausible. In any event, as seen below, orders under Article 25.1(b) have been made by tribunals sitting in England without being overturned as an excess of jurisdiction.

Article 25.1(a)

to order any respondent party to a claim or counterclaim to provide security for all or part of the amount in dispute, by way of deposit or bank guarantee or in any other manner and upon such terms as the Arbitral Tribunal considers appropriate. Such terms may include the provision by the claiming or counterclaiming party of a cross-indemnity, itself secured in such manner as the Arbitral Tribunal considers appropriate, for any costs or losses incurred by such respondent in providing security. The amount of any costs and losses payable under such cross-indemnity may be determined by the Arbitral Tribunal in one or more awards;

Article 25.1(a) enables a tribunal to order security for the amount of a claim or **6.134** counterclaim. It will cater for situations where the respondent or respondent to

---

[90] Another solution was adopted in *Ronly Holdings Ltd v JSC Zestafoni G Nikoladze Ferralloy Plant* [2004] EWHC 1354, where Gross J held that relief granted under s 39 Arbitration Act was an exception to the general principle that an award must be final as to the issues it decides (*Russell* para 6-020).

counterclaim is shown by the applicant to be impecunious and is thus exercisable in similar circumstances to grants of security for costs under Article 25.2, discussed below. It appears to be the case that the relief envisaged by this provision to order 'security' for the amounts in dispute is not the same as an asset-freezing order, applications for which have been made under Article 25.1(b).

6.135 Applications have been made under Article 25.1(a) on 15 occasions in the 701 cases that were the subject of our research, four of which were applications by counterclaimants.

6.136 Article 25.1(a) allows the tribunal to order a cross-indemnity in such form as shall be considered appropriate. This is in itself relatively uncontroversial, and is widely accepted as proper in international arbitration. For example, Article 17.E(1) of the Model Law provides that '[t]he arbitral tribunal may require the party requesting an interim measure to provide appropriate security in connection with the measure'.

6.137 In similar vein, the Swedish Arbitration Act provides that:

> Unless the parties have agreed otherwise, the arbitrators may, at the request of a party, decide that, during the proceedings, the opposing party must undertake a certain interim measure to secure the claim which is to be adjudicated by the arbitrators. The arbitrators may prescribe that the party requesting the interim measure must provide reasonable security for the damage which may be incurred by the opposing party as a result of the interim measure.[91]

6.138 Interestingly, there is no express power in the English Arbitration Act to enable a tribunal to order the provision of a cross-indemnity, despite its being generally required in English litigation practice for the applicant for interim relief to provide a cross-undertaking in damages, but it seems clearly to be catered for by section 38(1).

6.139 What is somewhat strange, however, is that the power to order security by the claimant to cover potential losses by the respondent if the interim or conservatory measures are later found to have been wrongly granted is specifically referred to in the Rules only here, in Article 25.1(a) and in respect of the grant of an order of security for costs under Article 25.2 (dealt with below). It surely cannot be the case that a tribunal granting other relief, for example under Article 25.1(b), which seems to cover, among other things, asset-freezing orders, which could cause very significant harm to those bound by them, does not have this power.

Article 25.1(b)

to order the preservation, storage, sale or other disposal of any property or thing under the control of any party and relating to the subject matter of the arbitration;

---

91 Swedish Arbitration Act, s 25.

This provision covers the same ground as section 38(4) of the English Arbitration Act 1996. It is to be distinguished from Article 22.1(d), relating to inspection by the tribunal (although the two may sometimes be connected). **6.140**

This provision, in conjunction with Article 25.1(c), discussed below, has also been relied upon to enable the tribunal to order injunctions freezing the assets of a respondent who might otherwise put them beyond the reach of the claimant, even if he ultimately prevails and obtains a favourable award on the merits. **6.141**

Apart from its ancillary use in asset-freezing cases (which are very rare), Article 25.1(b) can be used to preserve monies in bank accounts as well as physical assets and in one case to justify an order (which was granted) to require shares in a third party company in the claimant's hands to stay there pending the outcome of the proceedings and to prevent the respondent from recovering them. **6.142**

Article 25.1(c)

to order on a provisional basis, subject to final determination in an award, any relief which the Arbitral Tribunal would have power to grant in an award, including a provisional order for the payment of money or the disposition of property as between any parties.

Article 25.1(c) uses the same phrasing as section 39 of the Arbitration Act, in that it empowers the tribunal to order on a provisional basis relief that it could order in a final award. As a commentator has noted, this could be dangerous territory for a tribunal that could rightly be concerned not to give the impression that it had already made up its mind on the merits of the case. Nonetheless, this power could be used, for example, to order payment of sums unquestionably due.[92] **6.143**

In practice, as shown by our research, this provision has been used to justify many sorts of interim and conservatory measures. For example, in a very recent case, the tribunal used Article 25.1(c) to order the respondent to procure that its subsidiary have court proceedings that the subsidiary had started against the claimant stayed pending the outcome of the arbitration. The tribunal made it clear that this was not an anti-suit injunction to enforce the arbitration agreement (the subsidiary was not a party to the arbitration agreement and no application had been made to join it to the proceedings). The tribunal further made it clear that the state court proceedings could be resumed should the claimant not succeed in the arbitration. **6.144**

Article 25.1(c) has also been used as a basis for seeking an injunction to restrain threatened dissipation of assets (in such cases, which are, as noted above, rare, often in combination with Article 25.1(b)), orders for disclosure of related awards, orders prohibiting dealing in shares, etc. Its scope of application is very wide, and probably **6.145**

---

[92] Samuel (n 20 above) 45.

corresponds most closely to the general powers to grant interim and conservatory measures found in the ICC Rules and other more broadly worded provisions.

6.146 As to asset-freezing orders, the ability to freeze all or part of the assets of a party in order to prevent that party dissipating or otherwise dealing with his assets in order to render any award subsequently rendered against him futile is an essential weapon in the armoury of interim and conservatory measures. It is to be distinguished from the power to order security contained in Article 25.1(a), which seems to envisage less urgent applications and not necessarily a fear that assets that would otherwise have been available to the claimant (or counterclaimant) would be deliberately put beyond reach in order to defeat any award.

6.147 By its very nature, however, as discussed in relation to Article 9 above, it is more likely that such applications will be made to a state court rather than to an arbitral tribunal. This is for two straightforward reasons. The first is that the apprehension of a risk of dissipation of assets to render a respondent (or respondent to counterclaim) judgment-proof is one that almost in and of itself needs the application to freeze assets to be made *ex parte*. As noted above, if the respondent to the application for an asset-freezing order is the type of person who is likely to dissipate his assets, the last thing an applicant for such an order would normally want is to give him notice beforehand, thus giving him the opportunity to do the very thing that the application is designed to prevent.

6.148 This raises the question of whether an LCIA tribunal can hear *ex parte* applications. In England, the Arbitration Act does not give a specific power so to do, but nor does it expressly forbid it (despite a provision enabling *ex parte* applications being contained in clause 34 of the July 1995 draft of the Arbitration Bill). The Rules themselves are silent. This is certainly a delicate area.

6.149 The 2006 amendment to the UNCITRAL Model Law allows applications for interim and conservatory measures without notice to the other party. It was a controversial issue when the Model Law was being revised.[93] There are certainly practical difficulties: how, for example, should a tribunal deal with an unsuccessful application? Should it tell the other party that the application has been made? What if it did so when the applicant was making a successful application to a state court, only to find that the tribunal's notification to the respondent had caused the latter to put his assets beyond reach? This possibility alone might deter an applicant and send him instead running to the state court, where at least he can be assured that an unsuccessful *ex parte* application for interim and conservatory measures will remain secret.

---

[93] H van Houtte, 'Ten Reasons against a Proposal for *ex parte* Interim Measures of Protection in Arbitration' (2004) 20 Arb Int 85. See also Redfern (n 72 above) 221.

Second, as noted above, an arbitral tribunal has no power to ensure compliance **6.150** with its orders (although for arbitrations with their seat in England section 42 of the Arbitration Act allows the court to enforce peremptory orders of the tribunal, as noted above). It is therefore to be expected that a party would wish to have the order made by a court that could exercise jurisdiction over the respondent and sanction any breach of the order, rather than rely on the power of the tribunal to draw adverse inferences from a breach (by which time the mischief sought to be guarded against, namely that the claimant is left with a paper award to be enforced against a respondent with no assets, is the only possible result).

Despite apprehensions about the effectiveness of freezing orders made by arbitral **6.151** tribunals, these have in very rare cases been ordered, as shown by the example of such an order combined with an application under Article 9 for the expedited formation of the tribunal, discussed above.[94] In that case, the claimant applied under Article 25.1(b) for the preservation of monies in an escrow account and asked for an order to prevent the respondent from dealing with or diminishing the value of its shares in a third party company under Article 25.1(c). The orders were granted by the tribunal.

Article 25.2

The Arbitral Tribunal shall have the power, upon the application of a party, to order any claiming or counterclaiming party to provide security for the legal or other costs of any other party by way of deposit or bank guarantee or in any other manner and upon such terms as the Arbitral Tribunal considers appropriate. Such terms may include the provision by that other party of a cross-indemnity, itself secured in such manner as the Arbitral Tribunal considers appropriate, for any costs and losses incurred by such claimant or counterclaimant in providing security. The amount of any costs and losses payable under such cross-indemnity may be determined by the Arbitral Tribunal in one or more awards. In the event that a claiming or counter-claiming party does not comply with any order to provide security, the Arbitral Tribunal may stay that party's claims or counterclaims or dismiss them in an award.

Despite the alarm that could grow in seeing the reference in the arbitration rules **6.152** of an English-based institution to the express power of an arbitral tribunal to grant security for costs, after all of the controversy generated by the *Ken-Ren* case,[95] this provision is in fact part of the solution, not part of the problem.[96]

---

[94] Discussed in ch 4 above.

[95] *Coppée-Lavalin SA/NV v Ken-Ren Chemicals and Fertilizers Ltd (In Liquidation)* [1994] 2 All ER 449, HL.

[96] Although Derains and Schwartz say that the 1998 ICC Rules did not wish to state the power to grant security for costs explicitly, despite the *Ken-Ren* experience, because those drafting them were unwilling to encourage the making of such applications (*Derains & Schwartz* 297).

6.153   The *Ken-Ren* case was conducted under the ICC Rules of 1975, which by their Article 8(5) gave the power to the tribunal to order interim and conservatory measures by implication only, referring to 'the relevant powers reserved to the arbitrator'. The failure of the 1975 ICC Rules to say expressly that all applications for interim and conservatory measures should, wherever possible and in the absence of a legal impediment, be made to the tribunal led to the widely criticized decision of the House of Lords in *Ken-Ren* to order security for costs after the respondent applied to the courts of England, as the seat of the arbitration, rather than to the tribunal. One of the factors that led the House of Lords to take this decision was the uncertainty of the extent of the power of the tribunal to order security for costs under Article 8(5) of the 1975 ICC Rules.[97]

6.154   The criticism that this gave rise to led directly to the adoption of section 38(3) of the English Arbitration Act 1996, which makes it clear that the tribunal has the authority to order security for costs. It is this same controversy, therefore, that led to this power being explicitly spelled out in Article 25 of the 1998 LCIA Rules. Applications under Article 25.2 have only been made in seven cases of the 701 we have studied in our research, and granted in only three.

6.155   Neither the Arbitration Act (for arbitrations with their seat in England) nor the Rules specify the circumstances in which the tribunal is to exercise this power, which is therefore left to the tribunal to be used on a case-by-case basis. Article 25.2 provides that the tribunal may order security against a respondent or a respondent to counterclaim and that the security may be in such form as the tribunal thinks appropriate. This will usually be in the form of a bank guarantee. The tribunal may also require the applicant to put up a form of cross-security, any amounts due under which being determined by the tribunal in an award or awards. This provision echoes the terms of Article 25.1(a) discussed above. The seeming oddity that this power is not expressly made available in respect of other interim and conservatory measures ordered by the tribunal under Article 25 has been discussed above.

6.156   Article 25.2 empowers the tribunal to stay or dismiss the claim (or counterclaim, as the case may be) for failure to comply with an order for security for costs. This is interesting. While it conforms to English court practice, it is not a power that the LCIA Rules confer on the tribunal in relation to breaches of any other order for interim and conservatory measures. This is a power that is expressly enshrined in section 41(6) of the Arbitration Act 1996, and so would be available to a tribunal sitting in England and Wales even if the power had not been conferred upon the tribunal by the parties as part of the LCIA Rules. It would certainly be seen as a draconian power by many non-English supervisory courts were they to be seized

---

[97]   *Derains & Schwartz* 296.

with a complaint by a respondent that it had been deprived of the right to put his case (a right enshrined in Article 14.1(i)) by his inability to put up security for the other party's costs. A tribunal would be wise to think twice before using this power in an arbitration with its seat outside England and Wales.

Given the injunction to make every effort to render an enforceable award con- **6.157** tained in Article 32.2,[98] a tribunal, even one sitting in England, would also do well to think how an enforcement court would view a default award being made in furtherance of this power.

Article 25.3

The power of the Arbitral Tribunal under Article 25.1 shall not prejudice howsoever any party's right to apply to any state court or other judicial authority for interim or conservatory measures before the formation of the Arbitral Tribunal and, in exceptional cases, thereafter. Any application and any order for such measures after the formation of the Arbitral Tribunal shall be promptly communicated by the applicant to the Arbitral Tribunal and all other parties. However, by agreeing to arbitration under these Rules, the parties shall be taken to have agreed not to apply to any state court or other judicial authority for any order for security for its legal or other costs available from the Arbitral Tribunal under Article 25.2.

Article 25.3 has three basic premises. First, the fact that the tribunal has the power **6.158** to order interim and conservatory measures does not 'howsoever' remove a party's right to apply for any such interim and conservatory measures from a state court. Second, this right is only to be used after the formation of the tribunal in 'exceptional cases'. Third, in respect of applications for security for costs, these can only be made to the tribunal, thus putting the final nail in the coffin of *Ken-Ren*. Article 25.2 is therefore an exclusive remedy.

The purpose of the first principle established by Article 25.3, the ability to apply **6.159** to state courts for interim and conservatory measures, is needed to ensure that there is no room for the other party to argue that the application constitutes a waiver of the right to rely on the arbitration agreement. It is universally accepted in major arbitral jurisdictions. Indeed, applying for urgent interim and conservatory measures will very often be the natural thing for a party to do. As discussed above in the context of asset-freezing orders under Article 25.1(b), these are probably best sought from a state court with jurisdiction over the respondent, and such orders will certainly be better enforced than if granted by an arbitral tribunal. The same will be true of other measures.

As to the parties' right to make such applications after the formation of the arbitral **6.160** tribunal, this is preserved by Article 25.3 but with the important qualifier that

---

[98] Discussed in ch 9 below.

such an application may only be made in 'exceptional cases'. All turns, therefore, on the meaning of the word 'exceptional'.[99] It is submitted that this should mean no more and no less than that there is a presumption that the application for interim and conservatory measures should be made to the arbitral tribunal. It will of course be for the applicant to justify a derogation in a particular case from this presumption.

6.161 It would seem that an application for an asset-freezing order would qualify, if the applicant can show the state court concerned that the application needs to be made *ex parte* to avoid tipping off the respondent: that would surely justify recourse to a state court despite the ability of the tribunal to make such an order. The meaning of 'exceptional' will be determined by state courts on a case-by-case basis.

---

[99] It is interesting to note that the ICC Rules did away with this qualification in their 1998 version (*Derains & Schwartz* 295–6).

7

AWARDS
(ARTICLES 26 AND 27)

A. Article 26 – The Award	7.02
Article 26.1	7.03
Article 26.2	7.12
Article 26.3	7.14
Article 26.4	7.16
Article 26.5	7.19
Article 26.6	7.23
Article 26.7	7.25
Article 26.8	7.30
Article 26.9	7.32
B. Article 27 – Correction of Award and Additional Awards	7.38
Article 27.1	7.39
Article 27.2	7.50
Article 27.3	7.52

The issuance of an award represents the culmination of the arbitration process, **7.01** at least with respect to a particular issue or head of claim in the case of partial awards. Articles 26 and 27 of the Rules bring together all of the relevant provisions dealing with awards (Article 26) and the post-award remedies available to the parties (Article 27).

A. Article 26 – The Award

Article 26 is split into nine sub-articles, each dealing with a distinct issue relating to **7.02** the form, content, issuance, and effect of awards. It has been suggested that the heading of Article 26 should more correctly be 'awards' in the plural, since Article 26.7 allows a tribunal to make as many awards as it likes, as and when it considers appropriate.[1]

---

[1] A Samuel, 'Jurisdiction, interim relief and awards under the LCIA Rules' in A Berkeley and J Mimms (eds), *International Commercial Arbitration: Practical Perspectives* (Centre of Construction Law & Management, 2001) 35, 45.

Article 26.1

The Arbitral Tribunal shall make its award in writing and, unless all parties agree in writing otherwise, shall state the reasons upon which its award is based. The award shall also state the date when the award is made and the seat of the arbitration; and it shall be signed by the Arbitral Tribunal or those of its members assenting to it.

The requirement to provide a reasoned award

7.03 Article 26.1 mandates the tribunal to make its award in writing, and unless all parties agree in writing otherwise, to render a reasoned award. Whereas the parties are able to agree that the tribunal should dispense with the requirement to render a reasoned award, the Rules do not permit the parties to request that the tribunal dispense with a written award altogether. In this respect, the Rules reflect the requirements of most arbitration laws, including Article 31(1) of the UNCITRAL Model Law. The Rules are more restrictive than section 52(1) of the English Arbitration Act, which gives the parties complete freedom to agree on the form of an award. In other respects, however, Article 26.1 closely follows the default provisions of section 52(2) of the Arbitration Act as regards the form of an award.

7.04 The requirement to provide reasons (absent the parties' written agreement otherwise) reflects modern arbitration practice and is, in fact, a requirement in many jurisdictions. The reasons contained in an award demonstrate, moreover, the basis on which the tribunal has reached its decision in light of the parties' submissions and, it is argued, enhances the likelihood that the parties will voluntarily abide by the arbitrators' decision.[2]

7.05 The requirement to provide a reasoned award applies to all types of awards rendered by tribunals and is specifically reiterated in Article 28.4 in connection with the tribunal's order on costs in the award containing such order.

7.06 While the Rules do not address the extent or sufficiency of reasons, it should be borne in mind that the very purpose of rendering a reasoned award is to enable the parties (and the relevant courts at the seat of arbitration or in the enforcing jurisdiction) to understand the basis for the tribunal's decision. In this respect, the authors endorse the following statement of the English high court stated in the context of an application for setting aside of an LCIA award under section 68 of the Arbitration Act:

> Whilst the court will never dictate to arbitrators how their conclusions should be expressed, it must be obvious that the giving of clearly expressed reasons responsive to the issues as they were debated before the arbitrators will reduce the scope for the making of unmeritorious challenges as this ultimately has proved to be. . . . Reasons which were a little less compressed at the essential points might have been

---

[2] *Derains & Schwartz* 309.

more transparent as to their meaning and might even have dissuaded the unsuccessful party from challenging the award, or at any rate, from mounting so wide ranging a challenge.[3]

The award shall state the date of the award and the seat of the arbitration

7.07 The requirements that awards shall state the date of the award and the seat of the arbitration closely track the default provisions of section 52(2) of the Arbitration Act, which apply in the absence of the parties' agreement otherwise and are equally applicable under most other arbitration laws, including Article 31(3) of the UNCITRAL Model Law.

7.08 The requirement that the award state the date when it is made facilitates the subsequent performance of the award by the parties to the extent that the award contains time limits running as of the issuance of the award, for example, as regards the calculation of interest. It also avoids unnecessary debate or confusion as regards the date of the award where (as is very often the case) the arbitrators do not sign the award simultaneously but on three different dates. Article 26.1 therefore permits the tribunal to specify an appropriate date.

7.09 The award should also state the seat of the arbitration, as determined by application of Article 16 of the Rules. This is intended to eliminate any need for the arbitrators actually to meet at the seat in order to sign the award and should be read in conjunction with Article 16.2, which provides that any award rendered shall be treated as an award made at the seat of the arbitration for all purposes.[4] A similar provision is found in most other arbitration rules, for example, Article 25(3) of the ICC Rules. Without such a provision, the award might be at risk of challenge in jurisdictions which require the award to be made (ie, physically signed by the arbitrators) at the seat of the arbitration, although this should no longer be a concern under modern arbitration statutes.[5]

Signature of the award

7.10 Article 26.1 also provides that the award should be signed by the arbitral tribunal or those members assenting to it. In this regard, the Rules adopt the formulation of section 52(3) of the Arbitration Act in a further example of the close

---

[3] *ABB AG v Hochtief Airport GmbH* [2006] EWHC 388.

[4] Art 16.2 is discussed in ch 5 above.

[5] *Redfern & Hunter* para 6-24. The position under English law was confused following the judgment of the House of Lords in *Hiscox v Outhwaite* [1991] 2 Lloyd's Rep 435, HL, where the award in an otherwise entirely English arbitration was held to have been made in Paris because it was signed there. This confusion was cleared up by s 53 Arbitration Act.

cooperation between the Rules and the English Act. The effect of Article 26.1, as reinforced by Article 26.4, is that it is sufficient that the award contains only the signature of those arbitrators who approve of the award, ie the majority (or in the absence of a majority, solely the chairman's signature). In other words, dissenting arbitrators need not sign the award.[6] This is a clear departure from Article 31(1) of the Model Law and practice elsewhere where signing the award is an arbitrator's duty and does not imply the ratification of its contents, but merely participation in the deliberations and the very existence of the award, be it rendered unanimously or by majority.[7]

No time limit for issuance of awards

7.11   The Rules do not impose a time limit on the arbitrators to render their award. This is the case with respect to most other international arbitration rules, although the ICC Rules impose upon the tribunal a time limit of six months that starts to run from the date of the last signature of the Terms of Reference.[8] However, as discussed in chapter 5 above, arbitrators are under a duty to adopt procedures suitable to the circumstances of the case, avoiding unnecessary delay or expense, pursuant to Article 14.1(ii).[9]

Article 26.2

If any arbitrator fails to comply with the mandatory provisions of any applicable law relating to the making of the award, having been given a reasonable opportunity to do so, the remaining arbitrators may proceed in his absence and state in their award the circumstances of the other arbitrator's failure to participate in the making of the award.

7.12   This article provides that where an arbitrator fails to comply with a mandatory provision of any applicable law relating to the making of an award, the other arbitrators may nonetheless proceed with the award. This provision is intended to serve as a further 'belt-and-braces' measure to protect the enforceability of the award (pursuant to Article 32.2), by ensuring that a majority of the arbitrators can proceed with the issuance of an award in circumstances where a non-cooperating arbitrator might otherwise be able to delay or derail the issuance of the award.

7.13   It has been suggested, however, that the reference to a failure by the defaulting arbitrator to 'comply with the mandatory provisions of any applicable law' serves

---

[6] *Russell* para 6-049.

[7] *Poudret & Besson* para 756.

[8] Art 24(1) ICC Rules.

[9] In the case of arbitrations seated in England, arbitrators are also subject to the statutory duties set forth in s 33(1) Arbitration Act (discussed in ch 5 above).

no useful purpose, except possibly to allow a court to set aside an award that is unsigned by an arbitrator where the defaulting member has not done anything that can be identified as a breach of a mandatory applicable law provision.[10] It is instead suggested that a better formulation would be as follows: 'If an arbitrator fails to cooperate in the rendering of the award, the remaining arbitrators may proceed in his absence.'[11] While the authors do not share the unduly pessimistic view of the current formulation cited above, they agree that the proposed alternative language has the benefit of brevity and would be likely to cause less confusion.

Article 26.3

Where there are three arbitrators and the Arbitral Tribunal fails to agree on any issue, the arbitrators shall decide that issue by a majority. Failing a majority decision on any issue, the chairman of the Arbitral Tribunal shall decide that issue.

Article 26.3 follows the modern pattern of first requiring a majority vote on any **7.14** issue and then, if no majority can be found, the vote of the chairman of the tribunal will prevail. Similar provisions are found in most other arbitral rules, but not in the UNCITRAL Rules, where Article 30(1) requires a majority in all circumstances. The latter approach has the disadvantage of forcing the chairman to obtain the agreement of at least one of the co-arbitrators, which can force compromises that may be neither legitimate nor reasonable. The shortcomings of the UNCITRAL Rules in this regard are vividly illustrated in the context of certain awards rendered by the Iran-US Claims Tribunal.[12] Article 26.3, in contrast, permits the chairman to maintain an independent position and discourages partisan conduct on the part of the co-arbitrators, who know that the chairman is not required to agree with either of them in order to issue an award. In fact, we understand that no chairman of an LCIA arbitration has ever been required to decide alone any issue dealt with in an award.

Irrespective of whether the award is made unanimously, by majority, or by deci- **7.15** sion of the chairman alone, arbitrators are under a duty to deliberate among all members of the tribunal prior to rendering their decision. Although the Rules do not deal with the issue expressly, the duty to deliberate is clearly implied in Article 12.1 of the Rules dealing with the authority of truncated tribunals.[13] Certain commentators consider that the existence of proper deliberations is in itself

---

[10] Samuel (n 1 above), 45.
[11] Ibid.
[12] KH Böckstiegel, 'Experience as an Arbitrator Using the UNCITRAL Arbitration Rules' in *Etudes de Droit International en l'Honneur de Pierre Lalive* (Helbing & Lichtenhahn, 1993) 423.
[13] Discussed in ch 4 above. Art 16.2 also refers to the tribunal's deliberations, which may occur at any convenient place.

a requirement of international procedural public policy, a breach of which will also constitute a ground for setting aside of the award.[14]

Article 26.4

If any arbitrator refuses or fails to sign the award, the signatures of the majority or (failing a majority) of the chairman shall be sufficient, provided that the reason for the omitted signature is stated in the award by the majority or chairman.

7.16 Article 26.4 is a logical consequence of Articles 26.1 and 26.3 and provides that the signature of the majority (or the chairman alone failing a majority) is sufficient, if any arbitrator fails to sign the award; provided that the reason for the omitted signature(s) is stated in the award.

7.17 A statement of reasons to explain an omitted signature is particularly important where the tribunal decides to render an award in truncated form in the face of the refusal or failure of the third arbitrator to take part in deliberations and to sign the award. The authority of a truncated tribunal and the status of awards issued by one have been the subject of much commentary and no little controversy, as discussed in chapter 4 above in the context of Article 12.

7.18 The authors understand that, as a matter of practice, dissenting arbitrators sign the award in the majority of cases conducted under the Rules. Although the Rules are silent on the practice of dissenting opinions, dissenting arbitrators may set out their separate views in a dissenting opinion which are given for the parties' information only and do not form part of the award under English law.[15] Dissenting opinions may take one of three possible forms: (a) the dissenting views with respect to a particular issue or finding may be incorporated in the award; (b) the dissenting opinion may be set out in a separate memorandum that is adjoined to the award and acknowledged therein; or (c) the dissenting opinion may be expressed in a separate document to the award. There is no prevailing practice in LCIA arbitration. According to a leading arbitrator and experienced practitioner, dissenting opinions are best avoided whenever possible, or should at least be 'kept short, polite and restrained', because a detailed dissenting opinion risks bringing the arbitral process into disrepute and may encourage a challenge to the award.[16] In practice, this sound advice is not always followed by dissenting arbitrators.

---

[14] *Poudret & Besson* paras 732–43; and *Fouchard, Gaillard, Goldman* para 1369.

[15] *Russell* paras 6-029 and 6-058.

[16] A Redfern, 'Dissenting Opinions in International Commercial Arbitration – The Good, the Bad and the Ugly' in J Lew and L Mistelis (eds), *Arbitration Insights, Twenty Years of the Annual Lecture of the School of International Arbitration* (Kluwer, 2007) 367, 389.

Article 26.5

The sole arbitrator or chairman shall be responsible for delivering the award to the LCIA Court, which shall transmit certified copies to the parties provided that the costs of arbitration have been paid to the LCIA in accordance with Article 28.

Article 26.5 tasks the sole arbitrator or the chairman of the tribunal with the responsibility of delivering a signed award to the LCIA Court. It is then up to the LCIA, rather than the arbitrators, to transmit certified copies of the award to the parties. In fact, pursuant to Articles D.2 and G(i) of the Court's Constitution, the Court's function in receiving and transmitting awards to the parties is deemed to be an administrative function and is therefore delegated to the Registrar.[17] **7.19**

Review of awards by the LCIA

The Rules do not provide for the review and scrutiny of awards (whether in final or draft form) by the LCIA Court or the Registrar prior to their transmission to the parties. Indeed, LCIA awards are not seen by the LCIA Court.[18] In this respect, the Rules are consistent with the practice of the overwhelming majority of arbitral institutions. The most prominent exception concerns ICC arbitration, where the ICC Court is empowered to scrutinize draft awards and may lay down modifications as to the form of the award and suggest points of substance to the arbitrators.[19] This is a key feature of ICC arbitration, whereas, in LCIA arbitration, once the arbitral tribunal has been constituted, the Court's role in the proceedings is essentially limited to decisions on financial matters and, exceptionally, revocation of appointment of arbitrators.[20] The constitution of the arbitral tribunal effectively marks the transfer of all other procedural responsibilities from the Court to the tribunal.[21] **7.20**

In the absence of any formal scrutiny of awards by the LCIA, the Registrar is often requested by tribunals to undertake an informal review of awards, in particular to ensure that the relevant dates, procedural history, and the correct names of the parties have been accurately transcribed in the award. It is important to note, **7.21**

---

[17] The Court's directive delegating this task to the Registrar is reproduced at app 6.

[18] VV Veeder, 'London Court of International Arbitration – The New 1998 LCIA Rules' (1998) 23 YCA 366, 368.

[19] Art 27 ICC Rules. For a general discussion of the ICC Court's powers of review, see *Derains & Schwartz* 312–16.

[20] As discussed in chs 4 and 8; see also WL Craig 'The LCIA and ICC Rules: the 1998 Revisions Compared' in A Berkeley and J Mimms (eds), *International Commercial Arbitration: Practical Perspectives* (Centre of Construction Law & Management, 2001) 79, 87.

[21] An example of the Court's limited role in procedural matters is illustrated by the fact that, with the exception of the constitution of an expedited tribunal pursuant to art 9, the Court lacks the power to extend or abridge any period of time prescribed under the Rules. This power is instead reserved for the tribunal pursuant to art 4.7, as discussed in ch 3 above.

however, that any such review is informal and is carried out solely at the instigation of the tribunal. Nor is the Registrar, once seized by the tribunal, empowered to direct the tribunal to take account of any suggested modifications or additions. In practice, however, arbitrators are likely to pay close attention to the comments made by the Registrar, particularly as to the form of the award and with respect to any suggested clerical, typographical, or similar such modifications.

Transmission of the award is conditioned on the parties' payment of the costs of the arbitration

7.22 Pursuant to Article 28.1, the parties are jointly and severally liable to the tribunal and the LCIA in respect of the costs of the arbitration, which comprise the fees and expenses of the arbitrators and the administrative charges and disbursements of the LCIA. The costs of the arbitration are determined by the LCIA Court. The LCIA Court directs the parties to make one or more payments on account of such costs, which deposits are held by the LCIA and released from time to time to meet the fees and expenses of the arbitrators and the LCIA, in accordance with Article 24.[22] The LCIA does not release the award until it has received an amount equivalent to the costs of the arbitration. In this respect, the LCIA's practice is similar to that of other arbitral institutions.[23] As discussed in further detail in chapter 8, as part of our research, we came across several instances where a shortfall of funds delayed the transmission of the award to the parties until the additional deposits directed by the LCIA Court were met by either one or both parties.

Article 26.6

An award may be expressed in any currency. The Arbitral Tribunal may order that simple or compound interest shall be paid by any party on any sum awarded at such rates as the Arbitral Tribunal determines to be appropriate, without being bound by legal rates of interest imposed by any state court, in respect of any period which the Arbitral Tribunal determines to be appropriate ending not later than the date upon which the award is complied with.

7.23 Article 26.6 deals with the tribunal's award of damages and provides that an award may be expressed in any currency. As to interest, this rule (introduced in the 1985 version of the Rules) signals a move away from the traditional English law view that an arbitrator is not allowed to award compound interest. It accords with section 40 of the Arbitration Act 1996, which itself reflected a change from

---

[22] A detailed discussion of arts 24 and 28 is set out in ch 8 below.

[23] Pursuant to art 28(1) ICC Rules, the notification of the signed award by the ICC Secretariat to the parties is conditioned on the full payment to the ICC of the costs of the arbitration by the parties.

its predecessor that referred only to simple interest.[24] By explicitly empowering arbitrators to award compound interest at such rates as they deem appropriate, without being bound by legal rates of interest, the drafters of the Rules intended to create a disincentive for parties who might otherwise drag their feet in complying with awards.[25] Furthermore, this provision enables LCIA arbitrators to conform to commercial realities and to ensure that delays in making payment are compensated for in amounts that accurately reflect the loss caused to the prevailing party.

The provision on interest mirrors a further change brought about by the **7.24** Arbitration Act (sections 49(3) and 49(4)) in permitting awards of interest to run to the date of payment. This was not the position under English law previously, where the judgment rate was applied for the period after the date of the award.[26] By empowering arbitrators to award interest on 'any sum awarded', Article 26.6 is, however, potentially more restrictive than the Arbitration Act by not explicitly empowering arbitrators to award interest on a sum due at the commencement of the arbitration (and so claimed in the arbitration) but which is paid before the date of the award, as section 49(3)(b) of the Arbitration Act does.[27] It remains to be seen whether this provision will be applied in such a restrictive manner by tribunals.

Article 26.7

> The Arbitral Tribunal may make separate awards on different issues at different times. Such awards shall have the same status and effect as any other award made by the Arbitral Tribunal.

7.25

As mentioned at the start of this chapter, Article 26.7 empowers the tribunal to issue more than one award dealing with different issues at different times, as and when it considers appropriate. In so doing, the Rules maintain their perfect harmony with the Arbitration Act.[28] The issuance of more than a single award in an arbitration proceeding is common practice in international arbitration generally and, based on our review of awards rendered under the Rules, LCIA arbitration is no exception. Indeed, the DAC Report emphasizes the importance of the arbitrators' discretion to render multiple awards and encourages arbitrators to do so 'in any case where it appears that time and money will be saved by doing so, and where such an approach would not be at the expense of any of the other requirements of justice'.[29]

---

[24] Arbitration Act 1950, s 19A.
[25] *Hunter & Paulsson* 171–2.
[26] Arbitration Act 1950, s 20.
[27] *Russell* para 6-118.
[28] Arbitration Act, s 47(1).
[29] *DAC Report* para 230.

7.26   The Rules do not contain a definition of what constitutes an award, despite the important consequences that flow from an award being made. As mentioned at the start of this chapter, an award is a final determination of a particular issue or claim in the arbitration, and may be contrasted with orders and directions which address the procedural mechanisms to be adopted in the arbitration. Awards, which finally determine an issue or claim, should further be contrasted with provisional awards, which by definition are provisional and are subject to the tribunal's final adjudication. The distinction between awards, on the one hand, and orders, directions, or provisional awards, on the other, is important because only the former are final and binding and can be the subject of a challenge, whereas an order or direction in itself cannot be challenged. The legal effect of awards is discussed in more detail below in the context of Article 26.9.

7.27   The limited scope of review of a tribunal's procedural directions was affirmed recently by the English court in the context of a request for the issuance of an anti-suit injunction to restrain a pending LCIA arbitration seated in London, following the tribunal's refusal to stay the proceedings:

> [T]he court is given no express power under the 1996 Act to review or overrule those procedural decisions in advance of an award by the LCIA arbitrators. Fifthly, to attempt to invoke section 37 [of the Supreme Court Act 1981] as a means of reviewing or overruling the tribunal's decisions would undermine the principles of the 1996 Act and would grant the court a general supervisory power which it has never had.[30]

7.28   The Rules do not provide any guidance as to the nomenclature of awards, which may explain the variety of awards that have been rendered under the Rules, variously labelled as, inter alia, 'Final', 'Partial', 'Partial Final', 'Partial on One Preliminary Issue', 'Interim', 'Jurisdiction', 'Costs', 'Final save as to Costs' and 'Award on Respondent's Application for Interim and Conservatory Measures'. In short, the arbitrators have broad discretion in this respect. Under Article 26.7, moreover, all such awards have the same status and effect as any other award rendered by the tribunal.

7.29   It is the substance of the tribunal's decision rather than its title that determines the qualification of a decision as an award rather than a procedural order, direction, or provisional award. Thus, for example, in the well-known *Brasoil* case, the Paris Court of Appeal held that a reasoned decision, designated as an order, that was rendered by an ICC tribunal dealing with Brasoil's application for revision of the tribunal's partial award based on documents that had been allegedly fraudulently withheld, should be regarded not as a procedural order but as an arbitral award.[31]

---

[30] *Elektrim SA v Vivendi Universal SA (No 2)* [2007] 2 Lloyd's Rep 8, 20.
[31] Paris Court of Appeal, *Société Braspetro Oil Services (Brasoil) c GMRA*, 1 July 1999, [1999] Rev arb 834.

The court reached its decision, inter alia, on the basis that the tribunal had discussed the points at issue at length and (after a five-month deliberation) had decided them in a definitive way, terminating the dispute as to Brasoil's request for revision, thereby clearly exercising its jurisdictional power.

Article 26.8

In the event of a settlement of the parties' dispute, the Arbitral Tribunal may render an award recording the settlement if the parties so request in writing ('a Consent Award'), provided always that such award contains an express statement that it is an award made by the parties' consent. A Consent Award need not contain reasons. If the parties do not require a Consent Award, then on written conformation by the parties to the LCIA Court that a settlement has been reached, the Arbitral Tribunal shall be discharged and the arbitration proceedings concluded, subject to payment by the parties of any outstanding costs of the arbitration under Article 28.

7.30 Article 26.8 is the sole provision in the Rules that explicitly addresses the possible settlement of the arbitration (although Article 28.5 deals with the costs implications of an arbitration that is abandoned, suspended, or concluded by agreement, or otherwise, and therefore also contemplates settlement of the arbitration). Article 26.8 provides that the tribunal may render an award by consent, if the parties so request in writing. Parties are under no obligation to record their amicable settlement in the form of a consent award, and in most cases, they do not. A potential ambiguity concerns whether the tribunal must also agree to the issuance of a consent award, or whether the tribunal is obliged to issue such an award upon the parties' request. The ambiguity arises because Article 26.8 states that the tribunal 'may' render an award, if the parties so request, rather than 'shall' render an award.[32] The better construction in the authors' view is that the tribunal has discretion in deciding whether to accede to the parties' request for the issuance of a consent award. This construction has the added advantage of consistency with section 51(2) of the Arbitration Act, which also deals with the issuance of a consent award, following settlement of the parties' dispute. As a matter of practice, it is unlikely that a tribunal would not accede to the parties' request for issuance of a consent award.

7.31 The parties may, alternatively, withdraw or abandon their respective claims and counterclaims without requesting the issuance of a consent award. Pursuant to the second sentence of Article 26.8, upon written notification of a settlement having been reached, the tribunal shall be discharged and the arbitration proceedings concluded, subject to the payment of any outstanding costs of the arbitration pursuant to Article 28. To the extent that the costs of the arbitration

---

[32] By way of comparison, art 26 ICC Rules expressly conditions the issuance of a consent award upon the tribunal's consent.

remain outstanding, however, the parties remain jointly and severally liable to the tribunal and the LCIA for such arbitration costs, as per Article 28.1.[33] It must follow that the tribunal is not discharged and thus does not become *functus officio* until such time as all outstanding payments on account of the costs of the arbitration have been made, or until the LCIA Court deems the parties' respective claims and counterclaims as withdrawn pursuant to Article 24.4.[34]

Article 26.9

All awards shall be final and binding on the parties. By agreeing to arbitration under these Rules, the parties undertake to carry out any award immediately and without any delay (subject only to Article 27); and the parties also waive irrevocably their right to any form of appeal, review or recourse to any state court or other judicial authority, insofar as such waiver may be validly made.

7.32 As mentioned earlier in the context of Article 26.7, tribunals may render more than one award in any arbitration proceeding, and all such awards shall have the same status and effect. Pursuant to Article 26.9, all awards shall be final and binding.

Final and binding nature of awards

7.33 Final in this context means that, as between the parties to the arbitration, the award is conclusive as to the issues with which it deals, unless and until there is a successful challenge to the award. In other words, an award can be enforced, even if there are other issues outstanding in the arbitration. The qualification of an award as 'final' can also mean, however, that (a) the award determines all the issues in the arbitration, or determines all the issues which remain outstanding following earlier awards dealing with only some of the issues in the arbitration; or (b) the award is final in the sense of being a complete decision on the particular issues considered without leaving aspects of those issues to be dealt with subsequently or by third parties. It was this scope for confusion that prompted the drafters of the ICC Rules to replace the word 'final' with 'binding' in the current version of those rules. Article 26.9 refers to both 'final' and 'binding' and in so doing should be understood as referring to the conclusive and enforceable nature of an award, subject to any available challenges.

---

[33] Art 28.5 affirms that the debt owed by the parties to the tribunal and the LCIA on account of the costs of the arbitration remains pending in the event that the arbitration is abandoned, suspended, or concluded.

[34] Discussed in ch 8 below.

Waiver of any right of appeal, review, or recourse

The second sentence of Article 26.9 sets forth the general obligation of the parties **7.34** to comply with awards promptly and voluntarily, and contains a waiver of any form of appeal, review, or recourse, in so far as such waiver can validly be made. The waiver of appeal (or exclusion agreement) was introduced in the 1985 version of the Rules in light of court decisions, particularly in England, upholding the validity of the waiver of appeal on the merits of the arbitrators' decision (which was possible under the previous arbitration regime in England) contained in similarly worded clauses in other arbitration rules. The extent to which the parties' deemed waiver is recognized and given effect varies between different jurisdictions, however, and is a matter to be determined in accordance with the applicable law.

Article 26(9) should have the general effect of preventing appeals of the tribunal's **7.35** findings of fact or law in jurisdictions where such appeals are permitted.[35] In England, appeals on points of law are allowed under section 69 of the Arbitration Act 1996, but this provision of the Arbitration Act is not mandatory and therefore can be waived. Article 28.6 of the ICC Rules, which contains similar waiver language to Article 26.9 of the LCIA Rules, was recently held by the House of Lords to exclude an appeal under section 69 of the Arbitration Act (confirming earlier decisions under the predecessor to the Arbitration Act).[36]

However, most jurisdictions will not give effect to a waiver of all recourse, particu- **7.36** larly in respect of violations of due process, competence of the arbitral tribunal, or considerations of international public policy which constitute grounds for setting aside of an award. This is the case in England, for example, where the rights of recourse pursuant to sections 67 and 68 of the Arbitration Act (relating to the tribunal's substantive jurisdiction and serious irregularity) are mandatory and cannot be waived. This is also the position in most other jurisdictions,[37] with the notable exceptions of Switzerland and Belgium.[38] However, even in those jurisdictions, there are strict conditions for an effective waiver of all recourse before national courts, including the fact that the parties (none of whom must be domiciled in Switzerland or Belgium, as the case may be) must expressly state that they waive any challenge against the award. In other words, a tacit agreement,

---

[35] *Poudret & Besson* para 838.

[36] *Lesotho Highlands Development Authority v Impregilo SpA* [2006] 1 AC 221, HL.

[37] In France, for example, pursuant to art 1504 Code de procédure civile, the recourse available against awards is considered to be a matter of public policy (*Fouchard, Gaillard, Goldman* para 1596).

[38] Pursuant to art 192 PILA and art 1717(4) Belgian Judicial Code, respectively.

an agreement implied by conduct of the parties, or even an indirect agreement by submission to rules of arbitration which provide for a waiver of any possible appeal or challenge is insufficient.[39] Article 26.9 of the Rules would not, therefore, operate as a complete waiver in either Switzerland or Belgium.

7.37 It is worth mentioning, moreover, that the waiver provision of Article 26.9 might have unintended consequences. A similar provision contained in Article 28(6) of the ICC Rules was held by the French *Cour de cassation* to constitute a waiver of sovereign immunity from execution in France.[40]

B. Article 27 – Correction of Award and Additional Awards

7.38 This Article was introduced in the 1985 version of the Rules and was inspired by Article 33 of the UNCITRAL Model Law. It represents a limited exception to the finality of awards and allows the tribunal, although otherwise *functus officio*, to correct accidental errors contained in the award or to make additional awards if the initial award failed to dispose of all claims. The drafters of the 1985 Rules were concerned that, if such an authority did not exist, there might be a problem if arbitrators having rendered an award were considered *functus officio* and therefore without jurisdiction to correct the clerical mistakes or omissions which occasionally may be made.[41] This would lead to the reconstitution of the tribunal, which would be both costly and cumbersome.

Article 27.1

Within 30 days of receipt of any award, or such lesser period as may be agreed in writing by the parties, a party may by written notice to the Registrar (copied to all other parties) request the Arbitral Tribunal to correct in the award any errors in computation, clerical or typographical errors or any errors of a similar nature. If the Arbitral Tribunal considers the request to be justified, it shall make the corrections within 30 days of receipt of the request. Any correction shall take the form of separate memorandum dated and signed by the Arbitral Tribunal or (if three arbitrators) those of its members assenting to it; and such memorandum shall become part of the award for all purposes.

---

[39] *Poudret & Besson* para 839; and D Baizeau, 'Waiving the Right to Challenge an Arbitral Award Rendered in Switzerland: Caveats and Drafting Considerations for Foreign Parties' [2005] Int ALR 1.

[40] *Cour de cassation, 1ère ch civ, Gouvernement de l'Etat du Qatar c Creighton Ltd*, 6 July 2000, [2001] Rev arb 114, note Leboulanger.

[41] *Hunter & Paulsson* 172.

Procedure and timing of an application for correction

This provision deals with possible requests by a party (or joint requests by two or **7.39** more parties) for the correction of an award. It establishes a 30-day time-limit for the application to be made. The time period in this regard shall start to run from the date of receipt by the party making the application, rather than from the date of the award, as determined by the tribunal pursuant to Article 26.1. The 30-day time-limit is not irrevocable, however, and may be extended by the tribunal pursuant to its general authority under Article 4.7 to extend any time-limit under the Rules, even where the period of time has expired. This is an important provision which provides a welcome degree of flexibility to alleviate the otherwise potentially harsh effects of such a tight deadline. Our review of the practice of LCIA tribunals under Article 27 shows that tribunals have occasionally exercised have their discretionary power to consider applications under Article 27.1, even after expiry of the 30-day time-limit.

Although the application for correction of the award is made to the arbitral **7.40** tribunal, it should not be sent directly to the tribunal, but to the Registrar, who will then forward the application to the tribunal. The Registrar makes no assessment as regards the validity or merits of the application for correction. This diversion is made for practical reasons, as following the issuance of a final award, the Secretariat is typically occupied with making the final arrangements relating to the closure of the proceedings and can therefore determine whether, for example, the LCIA is in possession of sufficient funds to cover the costs of the application or whether the tribunal is *functus officio*.

The tribunal must make any corrections that it considers to be justified within **7.41** 30 days of receipt of the application. However, as explained above, it is open to the tribunal to extend any time limit specified in the Rules, if it believes this to be appropriate, including the deadline for the issuance of its decision with respect to an application for correction.

Grounds for an application

Article 27.1 empowers the parties to seek correction of computational, clerical, or **7.42** typographical errors, or any errors of a similar nature. Not surprisingly, the bulk of memoranda issued by tribunals pursuant to Article 27.1 deals with issues such as amending dates, the names of parties, or arithmetical errors in the tribunal's calculations. It is up to the tribunal to determine whether such requested corrections are justified in the circumstances of the case. In several cases, the parties' proposed amendments were dismissed by tribunals for 'bordering on stylistic preferences'.

7.43 On its face, the grounds on which an application under Article 27.1 may be based are limited and do not include the possibility of seeking either interpretation or revision of the award, as is the case with a number of other arbitral rules.[42] The omission of such remedies is deliberate on the part of the drafters of the Rules, particularly as regards the remedy of interpretation:

> On balance the LCIA felt that such a provision would lead to more mischief than good, in that it would tempt the parties seeking to delay matters to formulate never-ending and complicated requests for interpretation. The 1985 Rules therefore internationally omit the possibility of requests to the arbitrators for interpretation of awards.[43]

7.44 The concerns expressed by the drafters of the 1985 Rules certainly seem prescient in light of the experience of the Iran-US Claims Tribunal, where the Tribunal faced the repeated invocation of Article 35 of the UNCITRAL Rules, as a thinly disguised attempt by the unsuccessful party to re-argue the case or disagree with the tribunal's conclusions stated in the award.[44] The repeated invocation of the interpretation remedy before the Iran-US Claims Tribunal may be due, however, to the very particular circumstances surrounding the Tribunal and its mandate, which are not readily transferable to the general practice of international commercial arbitration. It is worth noting that there have been only two requests for interpretation submitted to date in ICSID arbitration, in spite of the absence of any time limit for making such an application pursuant to Article 50 of the ICSID Convention.[45]

7.45 As we have seen throughout our discussion of the Rules, many provisions of the Rules concord with the default provisions set forth in the English Arbitration Act. This is not the case, however, in respect of post-award remedies, where the default provisions of the Arbitration Act provide a broader range of such remedies, including the power to 'clarify or remove any ambiguity in the award'.[46] The tribunal is thus empowered under the Arbitration Act to clarify or interpret an award which

---

[42] eg, article 29(2) ICC Rules permits an application for correction or interpretation of an award; whereas art 35 UNCITRAL Rules also permits the parties to seek an interpretation of the award, in addition to the post-award remedies of correction (art 36) and issuance of an additional award (art 37). Similarly, the post-award remedies of interpretation and revision (in addition to correction) are available to parties in ICSID arbitration, in accordance with arts 50 and 51 ICSID Convention, respectively.

[43] *Hunter & Paulsson* 172.

[44] D Caron, L Caplan & M Pellonpää, *The UNCITRAL Arbitration Rules: A Commentary* (Oxford University Press, 2006) 881–91.

[45] *Wena Hotels Limited v Arab Republic of Egypt* (ICSID Case No ARB/98/4), Decision on Application by Wena Hotels Ltd for Interpretation of the Arbitral Award dated 8 December 2000, rendered on 31 October 2005 is the sole such decision rendered to date. A second interpretation application was registered by ICSID in July 2008 in *Tanzania Electric Supply Company Limited v Independent Power Tanzania Limited* (ICSID Case No ARB/98/8).

[46] Arbitration Act, s 57(3)(a).

contains inadequate rationale or incomplete reasons. In other words, section 57(3)(a) may provide a means to request further reasons from the tribunal or to request reasons where none has previously been given in relation to a particular issue, but only where there is genuine ambiguity.[47] While the authors share the apprehensions of the drafters of the Rules as regards the risks of expanding the range of post-award remedies, the limited expansion represented by the default mechanism of section 57(3) of the Arbitration Act could be a welcome addition to an LCIA tribunal's armoury, and would further maintain the harmony between the Rules and the Arbitration Act. Our research covering memoranda issued by tribunals pursuant to Article 27 suggests that, on occasion, tribunals are, in fact, prepared to expand the restrictive grounds of Article 27.1, where they consider this to be necessary. Thus, we found two instances where, upon the request of one or more of the parties, tribunals issued memoranda in order to clarify their award or provide additional reasoning. In the first such case, the tribunal clarified the relief ordered in the dispositive part of the award further to a request by a party concerned that the relief awarded was ambiguous. In the second case, the tribunal issued a memorandum providing further reasoning, in response to a request from a party whose request invoked the tribunal's obligation to render a reasoned award pursuant to Article 26.1.

A debatable point with a long lineage is whether an international arbitral tribunal has an inherent power to reconsider its award in the face of alleged due process or public policy violations, typically fraud, based on evidence that comes to light after an award has been issued. The Rules, like most other arbitration rules, provide no explicit authority to the tribunal to reconsider its award. A number of tribunals, relying on the principle of *fraus omnia corrumpit* (fraud negates everything), which represents a narrow exception to the principle of finality, have held that they enjoy such an inherent power[48] to revise their decisions upon discovery of fraudulent conduct by the parties.[49] Although inherent powers may be denied or limited by the parties' arbitration agreement, the more such powers are necessary to the judicial nature of the tribunal, then the more strictly the limitation or denial is likely to be construed.[50] Whether an arbitral tribunal constituted under the Rules enjoys such an inherent power remains to be seen.

7.46

---

[47] *Russell* para 6-170.

[48] ie, those powers that are not explicitly granted to the tribunal but must be seen as a necessary consequence of the parties' fundamental intent to create an institution with a judicial nature.

[49] Two relatively recent cases where the tribunal's inherent power was discussed were: *Ram International Industries, Inc and Others v The Air Force of the Islamic Republic of Iran*, Decision No DEC 118-148-1, 28 December 1993, reprinted in 29 Iran-US Cl Trib Rep 383; and *Antoine Biloune et al v Ghana Investments et al*, Award on Damages and Costs dated 30 June 1990, (1994) 19 YCA 11, 22.

[50] *Poudret & Besson* paras 843–7; and Caron, Caplan & Pellonpää (n 44 above) 914–918.

The answer may depend on the specific circumstances of the case before the tribunal, and whether an alternative remedy exists before the courts.

7.47 The principle of *fraus omnia corrumpit*, as applied in the context of international arbitration, is also found in many municipal arbitration statutes, either expressly, as in the case of The Netherlands,[51] or as a consequence of the inherent power of the court, as is the case in Switzerland and in France.[52] The position in England is more restrictive. The previous legislation contained a power to remit an award in cases where new evidence had subsequently come to light after the award. The Arbitration Act, however, gives the court no such power; and the English courts will now adopt a restrictive attitude in respect of fresh evidence that comes to light after an award has been made.[53]

Corrections take the form of signed and dated memoranda that become part of the award

7.48 If the tribunal considers that an application for correction is justified, it shall make any corrections in the form of a memorandum, which shall become part of the award for all purposes.[54] It logically follows that any such memorandum should be subject to all of the provisions of the Rules (pursuant to Article 26) applicable to the original award, including that it be dated and signed by the tribunal or, in the event of a dissent, those arbitrators assenting to the memorandum.

7.49 The Rules do not specifically address decisions of tribunals that dismiss applications for correction as unjustified. Such decisions do not form part of the award. They would not therefore need to comply with the provisions of Article 26 relating to the issuance of awards.

Article 27.2

The Arbitral Tribunal may likewise correct any error of the nature described in Article 27.1 on its own initiative within 30 days of the date of the award, to the same effect.

7.50 Article 27.2 permits a tribunal, on its own initiative, to correct any error of the nature covered by Article 27.1, ie errors in computation, clerical errors, or any

---

[51] Netherlands Arbitration Act 1986, art 1068 specifically addresses the revocation of awards in the case of fraud, forgery, or new documents.

[52] As regards the position in Switzerland, see the judgment of the Swiss Federal Supreme Court in *Société P c Société S Ltd*, 11 March 1992, note P Tschanz [1993] Rev arb 115; and *Cour de cassation, 1ère ch civ, Fougerolle SA c Procofrance SA*, 25 May 1992, note B Oppetit [1992] RCDIP 700, for the position in France.

[53] *Russell* para 8-100.

[54] It is therefore not necessary for the tribunal to render an additional award, unless a party's application concerns a request for determination of claims and counterclaims presented in the arbitration, but not determined by the tribunal, under art 27.3.

errors of a similar nature contained in the award. Any such corrections should be issued as a memorandum that will form part of the award, as per Article 27.1, within 30 days of the date of the award.[55] The same considerations discussed above in connection with Article 27.1 as regards the grounds and the form of issuing such memoranda are equally applicable here. In practice, the issuance of memoranda by tribunals *sua sponte* is likely to be a rare occurrence, as confirmed by the fact that we found only two such memoranda issued to date under the Rules.

An interesting issue that arises is whether a tribunal is empowered to render an **7.51** additional award (as per Article 27.3) without the request of the parties, if it were to discover that it had failed to deal with a particular claim or counterclaim presented in the arbitration. On the face of the Rules, tribunals appear not to enjoy such a power. Such a scenario is, admittedly, unlikely in practice, as the parties are bound to discover such omissions and make an appropriate application for an additional award pursuant to Article 27.3. A similar issue arose, however, in a case where, in the absence of any claim for costs by the parties, the tribunal failed to issue an award of costs, as it is bound to do pursuant to Article 28.2. Having realized its omission, the tribunal awarded costs by issuing a memorandum, even though such an order clearly exceeds the scope of the tribunal's powers under Article 27.2, and is tantamount to an additional award.

Article 27.3

> Within 30 days of receipt of the final award, a party may by written notice to the Registrar (copied to all other parties), request the Arbitral Tribunal to make an additional award as to claims or counterclaims presented in the arbitration but not determined in any award. If the Arbitral Tribunal considers the request to be justified, it shall make the additional award within 60 days of receipt of the request. The provisions of Article 26 shall apply to any additional award.

Pursuant to Article 27.3, the tribunal also has the power to make an additional **7.52** award in respect of any claim or counterclaim, including a claim for interest or costs. However, the tribunal's power under this provision is limited to claims which were presented in the arbitration but were omitted from the award. Article 27.3 does not therefore enable parties to raise new claims after the award has been made. Although, in one case, the tribunal issued an additional award dealing with the apportionment of the costs of the arbitration, at the request of the successful party, even though neither of the parties had raised a claim for costs in the arbitration. The applicant party had based its application for an additional

---

[55] Pursuant to art 4.7, the tribunal is empowered to extend any time limit specified in the Rules.

award on the tribunal's duty to specify in the award the total amount of the costs of the arbitration, and to apportion such costs among the parties, in accordance with Article 28.2.

7.53 The same procedure for making an application under Article 27.1 should be followed here as well. If the tribunal considers such an application to be justified, it must issue an additional award rather than issuing a separate memorandum that forms a part of the original award under Article 27.1. The provisions of Article 26 relating to awards logically apply to any additional awards rendered pursuant to Article 27.3.

8

COSTS
(ARTICLES 24 AND 28)

A. **Article 28 – Arbitration and Legal Costs**   8.02
  Article 28.1   8.04
  Article 28.2   8.19
  Article 28.3   8.23
  Article 28.4   8.26
  Article 28.5   8.33
B. **Article 24 – Deposits**   8.35
  Article 24.1   8.36
  Article 24.2   8.44
  Article 24.3   8.46
  Article 24.4   8.51

With regard to costs, the LCIA Rules continue their slightly disconcerting pattern **8.01** of separating provisions dealing with related issues throughout the body of the Rules. In this case, Articles 24 and 28 contain the relevant provisions relating to the costs of the arbitration and the deposits to be made by the parties to the LCIA on account thereof. Articles 24 and 28 are separated, however, by provisions dealing with interim and conservatory measures (Article 25) and those relating to the form, content, and issuance of awards and their correction (Articles 26 and 27, respectively). Given that Article 28 contains the principal provisions in connection with the costs of the arbitration, we will address Article 28 first, before turning to consider the provisions of Article 24 as to the payment of deposits by the parties.

A. Article 28 – Arbitration and Legal Costs

It is perhaps helpful at the outset to distinguish between what the LCIA Rules **8.02** regard as 'the costs of the arbitration' (ie the fees and expenses of the arbitrators and the LCIA's own administrative charges) and the parties' 'legal costs' or 'costs of representation' (ie the legal and other costs incurred by the parties in connection with the arbitration). In distinguishing between these two categories, the Rules adopt a different approach from the ICC Rules (and the UNCITRAL Rules[1]) which define the 'costs of the arbitration' as comprising not only the fees and expenses of the tribunal and the ICC's administrative fees, but also the 'reasonable legal and other costs incurred by the parties for the arbitration'.[2]

8.03 Article 28 is split among six sub-articles and contains a comprehensive set of rules dealing with the determination of the costs of the arbitration by the LCIA Court, and the subsequent allocation of those costs (as well as the parties' legal costs) by the tribunal.

Article 28.1

The costs of the arbitration (other than the legal or other costs incurred by the parties themselves) shall be determined by the LCIA Court in accordance with the Schedule of Costs. The parties shall be jointly and severally liable to the Arbitral Tribunal and the LCIA for such arbitration costs.

8.04 Article 28.1 establishes the principle – common to most forms of institutional arbitration – that the costs of the arbitration are determined by the LCIA Court, rather than by the arbitrators.[3] This means that any dispute regarding the administrative charges or the fees and expenses of the tribunal are determined by the Court, rather than by the arbitrators.

8.05 The costs of the arbitration are determined by the Court on the basis of the Schedule of Costs. As set out in the preamble to the Rules, the Schedule of Costs forms a part of the Rules and may be separately amended by the Court from time to time. It is therefore possible that an arbitration may be subject to more than one Schedule of Costs, if a new Schedule is established by the Court during the course of the arbitration.

The costs of the arbitration are based on time spent by the LCIA and the arbitrators

8.06 The first point to note is that the LCIA's charges, and the fees charged by the arbitrators it appoints, are not based on the amounts in dispute (*ad valorem*), but are based on the time actually spent by the LCIA (both the Court and the Secretariat)

---

[1] Art 38 UNCITRAL Rules.

[2] Art 31(1) ICC Rules.

[3] Under the 1985 version of the Rules (art 18.2), this was the task of the arbitral tribunal, subject to 'confirmation' by the LCIA Court that the tribunal's determination was in conformity with the Schedule of Costs (*Commentary* 10); see also W L Craig, 'The LCIA and the ICC Rules: the 1998 revisions compared' in A Berkeley and J Mimms (eds), *International Commercial Arbitration: Practical Perspectives* (Centre of Construction Law & Management, 2001) 79, 99.

and by the arbitrators. This method of calculating the costs of the arbitration has a number of consequences for the parties. The most obvious is that parties will be unable, at the outset of commencing an LCIA arbitration, to estimate the likely costs of the arbitration which they would otherwise be able to do if the arbitrators' fees and administrative costs were based on an *ad valorem* scale.[4] As a further consequence, the costs of the arbitration do not relate to the amounts at stake, which is the case when an *ad valorem* fee scale is applied. Proponents of the ICC fee scale argue that such a scale provides a financial framework for the arbitration that is broadly compatible with the amount at stake. In other words, it is to be expected that the costs of the arbitration will be greater when there is a significant sum at stake and vice versa. The LCIA is of the view, however, that a very substantial monetary claim does not necessarily mean a technically or legally complex claim, and that arbitration costs should be based on time actually spent by the administrator and arbitrators alike, which, according to the LCIA, is the fairest means for establishing the arbitrators' fees.[5]

While the authors do not endorse one methodology over another, based on their **8.07** own experience and anecdotal evidence, parties could confidently expect that certain types of dispute will likely cost less under an *ad valorem* scale, than on a time-cost basis, and vice versa. For example, the costs of a technically and legally complex case heard by a panel of three arbitrators where the sums in dispute are not substantial are likely to be markedly less when calculated on the basis of an *ad valorem* scale, rather than on a time-cost basis. Conversely, when there are substantial sums in dispute, then the application of an *ad valorem* scale will invariably lead to inflated costs of the arbitration. Two examples from our research illustrate the point. At one extreme: in a case heard by a sole arbitrator appointed under the Rules where the amount in dispute was $1 million, the total costs of the arbitration amounted to approximately $80,000. The costs of the arbitration of a hypothetical similar case heard under the ICC Rules would be approximately $60,000, according to the costs calculator available on the ICC's website.[6] At the other extreme: the costs of the arbitration of a case heard by a three-member tribunal under the LCIA Rules where the amount in dispute was $50 million was approximately $190,000. However, a similar case conducted under the ICC Rules would likely generate approximately $570,000 as costs of the arbitration, based on the ICC's costs calculator. The difference can thus be quite substantial.

---

[4] eg, the ICC's Scales of Administrative Expenses and Arbitrator's Fees. Although, prior to the commencement of proceedings, claimant parties frequently ask the LCIA Secretariat for an estimate of the likely costs of the arbitration.

[5] *Hunter & Paulsson* 167.

[6] <http://iccwbo.org/court/arbitration/id4097/index.html>.

8.08 Whether the basis on which an arbitral institution determines the costs of the arbitration should play an important part in the parties' choice of arbitration rules is a matter for debate, particularly in circumstances where the costs of the arbitration are likely to represent only a small proportion of the parties' overall legal costs. That being said, the authors certainly agree with the sentiment expressed by Derains and Schwartz in their commentary on the ICC Rules that, apart from the ultimate outcome and the time that may be required for the conduct of the arbitration, there is usually no aspect of the arbitration process that is of greater concern to the parties than its cost.[7]

8.09 It has also been argued that an *ad valorem* fee scale has a disciplinary effect both on the parties and the arbitrators alike. As to the former, it is said that the ICC system discourages the submission of frivolous claims and counterclaims, which will have a direct impact on the costs of the arbitration.[8] Anecdotal evidence based on the authors' experience suggests, however, that arbitration costs (as distinct from a party's legal costs) tend not to constitute a significant (or certainly, an overriding) consideration in formulating the litigation strategy of an arbitrating party, perhaps because of the relatively small proportion of the overall costs represented by the arbitrators' fees and administration costs. As for creating an incentive for efficiency on the part of arbitrators, while it is true that the ICC system does not encourage arbitrators to prolong the case, it does not follow that the LCIA's method of determining arbitrators' fees does. Indeed, as discussed in more detail below, arbitrators appointed by the LCIA are encouraged to adopt methodical record-keeping procedures in support of their fees, which are closely reviewed by the Secretariat prior to their approval by the Court, once it is satisfied that the claimed fees are reasonable.

The Schedule of Costs

8.10 The current Schedule of Costs, which came into effect in May 2007, determines the rate and method of calculation of the LCIA's administrative charges, as well as the arbitrators' fees.

8.11 Apart from an initial registration fee (of £1,500) that is payable with the Request for Arbitration, the administrative fees of the LCIA, covering the work conducted in connection with the arbitration by the Registrar and the Court, are based on time spent on the arbitration. At present, the work of the Registrar, his deputy, and counsel are charged at £200 per hour, whereas the time of other Secretariat personnel is charged at half that amount. The time spent by members of the LCIA

---

[7] *Derains & Schwartz* 329.
[8] *Derains & Schwartz* 331; and *Craig, Park, Paulsson* 390.

Court in carrying out their functions (such as appointment of arbitrators or deciding arbitrator challenges) is based on the hourly rates advised by members of the LCIA Court. Such rates are normally subject to the hourly fee range applicable to arbitrators, as discussed below. In addition, the LCIA charges the parties a sum equivalent to 5 per cent of the tribunal's fees in respect of the LCIA's general overhead.

Similarly, the tribunal's fees are calculated by reference to work done by its **8.12** members in connection with the arbitration and will be charged at rates appropriate to the particular circumstances of the case, including its complexity and the special qualifications of the arbitrators. At present, arbitrators' fees must be within the range of £150 to £350 per hour and arbitrators must agree their rates in writing prior to their appointment. This is an important condition of an arbitrator's appointment by the Court. Upon the tribunal's appointment, the Registrar will inform the parties of the respective hourly rates of the arbitrators, which may well be different among the panel members, albeit within the specified range.[9] It is possible, however, in exceptional circumstances, for the arbitrators' fees to exceed the stipulated range, provided that the fees are fixed by the Court on the recommendation of the Registrar, and the parties expressly agree to such higher rates.

Although the arbitrators are remunerated on the basis of time spent on the arbitra- **8.13** tion, the Schedule of Costs explicitly provides that the tribunal's fees may also include a charge for time reserved but not used as a result of late postponement or cancellation, provided that such charge is approved by the Court. Depending on the particular circumstances of the case, such fees are commonplace and are intended to compensate arbitrators who may have blocked extensive time, particularly in respect of hearings which are ultimately cancelled following a settlement or postponement. One such formula approved by the Court that is often used advises the parties that, in the event of cancellation or postponement less than four weeks before the start of a hearing, the tribunal would charge 50 per cent of a notional daily sitting rate based on an 8-hour day, multiplied by the number of days reserved; and in the event of a cancellation or postponement more than four weeks, but less than twelve weeks, before the start of a hearing, 30 per cent of the daily sitting rate multiplied by the number of days reserved.

Procedure for determining the costs of the arbitration

Article 28.1 tasks the LCIA Court with the responsibility of determining the **8.14** costs of the arbitration. In so doing, the Court relies on a financial dossier prepared by the Secretariat for each arbitration. The procedure in this regard is set out in a directive issued by the Court in relation to the performance of its

---

[9] Since arbitrators may have significantly different overheads, a same-rate policy may be illusory.

duties under Articles 28.1, 28.2, and 28.5.[10] For the purposes of Article 28.1, the Secretariat provides the Court with a financial dossier, which includes a complete financial summary of sums lodged by the parties, sums paid to the arbitrators, outstanding fees and expenses, and interest accrued. The dossier also includes a copy of the original confirmation to the parties of the arbitrators' fee rate, copies of the arbitrators' accounts, a copy of the LCIA's own time and disbursements ledger, copies of directions for deposits, and copies of all notices given to the parties of payments made from deposits. The Court reviews the dossier and, if necessary, calls for any further information, or initiates any investigation, it may require to satisfy itself that the costs are reasonable and are in accordance with the Schedule of Costs, before notifying the Secretariat of the amount it has determined as the costs of the arbitration.

8.15 As part of its duties, the Court will therefore review the fee claims submitted by the arbitrators and must satisfy itself that they are reasonable (both as to amount and consistency across the three members of the tribunal), in light of its knowledge of the arbitration procedure. The review and settling of the costs of the arbitration by the Court requires arbitrators to maintain a diligent record of the time they have spent in connection with the arbitration, as well as with respect to any related disbursements, in order to satisfy the Court. It is therefore unsurprising to learn that requests made of arbitrators by the Registrar (on behalf of the Court) for more detailed time records and explanations of tasks undertaken to justify their fees are not uncommon, and, from the users' standpoint, the LCIA's vigilance in this respect is to be applauded.

The parties are jointly liable as regards the costs of the arbitration

8.16 The parties are jointly and severally liable to the tribunal and the LCIA as regards the costs of the arbitration. This is a consequence of calculating the costs of the arbitration on the basis of time spent by the administrator and the arbitrators alike. There is no scope under such an arrangement for the possibility of establishing discrete deposits in respect of the parties' respective claims and counterclaims, as is the case in ICC arbitration.[11] This does not mean, however, that the Court must apportion the costs of the arbitration equally between the parties, although this is the Court's general practice. As discussed below in the context of Article 24.1, the Court enjoys wide discretion in directing the parties to meet one or more payments on account of the costs of the arbitration 'in such proportions as it thinks appropriate'.

8.17 The sanction available against a party that does not contribute its share of ordered deposits is the deemed withdrawal of any claims or counterclaims

---

[10] The Court's directive is reproduced at app 6.
[11] *Derains & Schwartz* 341.

pursued by that party, in accordance with Article 24.4. However, such a sanction will have little impact upon a respondent who is only defending a claim.[12] Thus, when faced with a respondent who refuses to contribute its share of the directed deposits, the claimant has little choice but to meet the entire costs of the arbitration until the issuance of a final award disposing of its claims, including an award of costs pursuant to Article 24.3 (discussed below).

In practice, the interest of the claimant in pursuing the arbitration to the end, **8.18** coupled with the arbitrators' inability (and understandable reluctance) to proceed with the arbitration without ascertaining that the LCIA is in requisite funds under Article 24.2, means that the LCIA is unlikely to find itself out of funds for long.

Article 28.2

The Arbitral Tribunal shall specify in the award the total amount of the costs of the arbitration as determined by the LCIA Court. Unless the parties agree otherwise in writing, the Arbitral Tribunal shall determine the proportions in which the parties shall bear all or part of such arbitration costs. If the Arbitral Tribunal has determined that all or any part of the arbitration costs shall be borne by a party other than a party which has already paid them to the LCIA, the latter party shall have the right to recover the appropriate amount from the former party.

Once the LCIA Court has determined the costs of the arbitration, the tribunal **8.19** must put the set amount in the award and then, unless the parties have agreed otherwise, determine who bears the costs as between the parties. In so doing, the tribunal has no discretion to amend or otherwise determine an alternative amount as to the costs of the arbitration, although the tribunal is empowered to determine the apportionment of such costs between the parties, subject to the general principle set forth in Article 28.4, discussed below. It follows that the tribunal must determine the issue of the costs of the arbitration in its award even in the absence of any claims for such costs raised by the parties.

Our research revealed more than one instance where tribunals had initially failed **8.20** to carry out their duty under Article 28.2, by determining the costs of the arbitration in the final award. On one occasion, the tribunal's omission was remedied of its own motion in the form of a post-award memorandum, in accordance with Article 27.2.[13] On a second occasion, the tribunal's omission formed the basis for a party's request for an additional award dealing with costs under Article 27.3.

---

[12] Similarly, a respondent to a claim brought by an insolvent claimant could be placed in real difficulties if it is unable to obtain an order from the tribunal securing the costs of the arbitration. The power under the Rules to order security for costs is contained in art 25.2, discussed in ch 6 above.

[13] Although, as discussed in ch 7 above, it is not clear whether art 27.2 empowers the tribunal to issue a memorandum (which forms an integral part of the award) in respect of a new issue, as opposed to addressing any corrections in an existing award as to any computational or clerical errors.

8.21 As we have seen, the costs of the arbitration must be included in the tribunal's award, which, in cases where more than one award is rendered by the tribunal (as expressly foreseen in Article 26.7), typically means the final award. Indeed, as discussed in chapter 7, the despatch of the final award by the LCIA to the parties is conditioned on the costs of the arbitration having been paid to the LCIA in full.

8.22 It remains open to tribunals to reserve the issue of the parties' legal costs to be dealt with in a separate and dedicated costs award. This practice has the merit of permitting the parties the opportunity to brief the issue of costs after having received the tribunal's final decision on the merits of their dispute.

Article 28.3

The Arbitral Tribunal shall also have the power to order in its award that all or part of the legal or other costs incurred by a party be paid by another party, unless the parties agree otherwise in writing. The Arbitral Tribunal shall determine and fix the amount of each item comprising such costs on such reasonable basis as it thinks fit.

8.23 In addition to determining which party should bear the costs of the arbitration, the tribunal is empowered to order costs of representation, ie the party's legal or other costs incurred in connection with the arbitration, subject to a contrary agreement of the parties. Whereas the tribunal is mandated to address the costs of the arbitration in its award under Article 28.2, it is not required to do so in respect of the parties' legal costs. The tribunal's power to order costs of representation under Article 28.3 is discretionary. Parties should therefore expressly raise a claim for legal costs if they wish to ensure that the tribunal deals with this issue in its award. Our research revealed a number of cases where tribunals declined to address the issue of the parties' costs of representation (contrary to the costs of the arbitration) on the basis that the parties had failed to make any submissions on this issue. Tribunals enjoy wide discretion to determine both the scope of what constitutes legal and other costs borne by the parties, as well as to determine whether such costs are reasonable in light of the particular circumstances of the arbitration. The tribunal's discretion in this regard means that it can decide that only part of a party's legal costs should be borne by the other party, if appropriate under the circumstances.

8.24 One issue that regularly confronts arbitrators is where there is a great disparity between the parties' respective legal costs. In such circumstances, tribunals must determine the parties' costs on the basis of what is reasonable in the circumstances of the case. In one recent case, the tribunal was confronted with a situation where the prevailing party's legal costs were approximately three times greater than the legal costs of the losing party. The disparity was explained by the fact that the prevailing party had instructed a large international law firm, whereas the other party had instructed a small national law firm. In its award on costs, the tribunal found that: (a) a party in arbitration is entitled to an unfettered choice of counsel; and (b) the fees of the prevailing party's law firm were consistent with fees charged by large firms in complex disputes and were therefore not unreasonable; but (c) what is reasonable is not determined by prevailing market rates, but rather by looking at the circumstances of a particular case. Accordingly, the tribunal held that, in light of the great disparity in the respective legal costs of the parties, it was indeed unreasonable for the losing party to bear more than half of the prevailing party's legal costs (but the entirety of the costs of the arbitration), in accordance with Article 28.4.

The extent of tribunals' discretion in determining and fixing the parties' legal **8.25** costs is illustrated by two awards covered by our research where the tribunal awarded the costs of representation in favour of the successful party, subject to their assessment by the Supreme Court Costs Office of the English High Court, which deals with contested hearings on costs in English civil litigation. These examples represent somewhat extreme, but nonetheless valid, illustrations of the tribunal's discretion in fixing the costs of representation to be awarded.

Article 28.4

Unless the parties otherwise agree in writing, the Arbitral Tribunal shall make its orders on both arbitration and legal costs on the general principle that costs should reflect the parties' relative success and failure in the award or arbitration, except where it appears to the Arbitral Tribunal that in the particular circumstances this general approach is inappropriate. Any order for costs shall be made with reasons in the award containing such order.

Article 28.4 provides that, in determining the apportionment of the costs of **8.26** the arbitration and the parties' legal costs, tribunals should follow the general principle that costs should reflect the parties' relative success and failure in the arbitration, except in exceptional circumstances as determined by the tribunal. This provision was introduced in the current version of the Rules. It represents a less rigid application of the English civil procedure rule that costs should follow the event, as also adopted in section 61 of the Arbitration Act 1996. The default rule under Article 28.4 is less rigid because it encourages tribunals to apportion costs based on the *relative* success or failure of the parties, rather than to follow the traditional English civil procedure approach of awarding costs to the ultimately successful party (subject to the application of the principle of reasonableness). Tribunals are not bound to follow the default rule of Article 28.4, and have the power to determine the costs of the arbitration and the parties' legal costs in any way that they see fit.

Application of the default rule

8.27   In spite of the inherent flexibility of the default rule, based on our research, it appears that in the vast majority of cases tribunals tend to follow the general (English) principle that costs should follow the event. Indeed, our research covering over 300 awards rendered under the Rules up to the end of 2007 demonstrates that in the majority of cases where the tribunal determined the issue of costs, it did so by ordering the losing party to bear the costs of the arbitration in their entirety, without any further analysis of the relative success or failure of the parties across different issues or heads of claim. Whereas this practice is perhaps to be expected in instances of a complete victory for one party, such as where a tribunal declines jurisdiction (and thus orders costs against the claimant), the authors would have expected to see a more nuanced application by tribunals of the default rule of Article 28.4, in particular, as is often the case, when neither party is wholly successful in pursuing its respective claims and counterclaims. The practice of tribunals to date is therefore more rigid than need be under the default rule of Article 28.4 and more closely reflects the principle that costs should follow the event, as enunciated in section 61 of the Arbitration Act.[14]

8.28   Only in a minority of cases, therefore, have tribunals rendered a more nuanced costs award by reviewing the respective success and failure of the parties at different stages of the arbitration or with respect to different substantive issues. In those instances, tribunals arrived at many different combinations of apportioning the costs of the arbitration by reference to the particular circumstances of the case, such as to make it difficult to discern an overriding or universally applicable practice. To the extent that it is possible to discern a broad pattern, the considerations most often cited by tribunals in support of their apportionment of costs included: (i) the relative success and failure of the parties on the merits; (ii) the respective conduct of the parties in the arbitration; and (iii) the parties' relative success at different stages of the arbitration procedure, for example, in challenging an arbitrator under Article 11, or requesting correction of an award under Article 27.

8.29   Nor, in most cases, do tribunals appear to treat the parties' legal costs as being distinct from the costs of the arbitration in awarding costs against the losing party. Our research shows that in very few instances did tribunals appear to apportion the costs of the arbitration and the parties' legal costs on different grounds. Where this was the case, however, tribunals tended to order the losing party to bear a greater portion of the costs of the arbitration as compared to the winning party's legal costs. Thus, in one case, although the claimant had succeeded in full on the merits, the tribunal ordered the respondent to bear 75 per cent of the costs of

---

[14]   Indeed, in more than one instance, tribunals justified their awards of costs by reference to s 61 Arbitration Act, rather than art 28.4.

the arbitration, but only 50 per cent of the claimant's legal costs on the basis that the respondent had raised a number of legitimate defences.[15] This decision is a good illustration of the wide discretion enjoyed by tribunals under Article 28.4.

Agreement in writing of the parties

The default rule may be displaced by an agreement in writing of the parties, **8.30** although such agreements are not common. In light of the overwhelming number of cases that are seated in London and therefore subject to the mandatory provisions of the Arbitration Act 1996, it is important to note that an agreement which has the effect that a party is to pay the costs of the arbitration in any event is only valid if made after the dispute in question has arisen.[16]

In our research, we only came across two examples of costs agreements, both **8.31** concerning sealed offers made by respondents to settle claims, in accordance with Part 36 of the English Civil Procedure Rules 1998. In both cases, the tribunals determined their award of costs in the context of the sealed offers to settle, which they treated akin to an agreement of the parties for the purposes of Article 28.4. In the first case, where the claimant was ultimately successful, but failed to better the sealed offer from the respondent, the tribunal awarded the claimant recovery of its share of the costs of the arbitration incurred up to the allotted time for the acceptance of the respondent's offer. With respect to costs incurred thereafter, however, the claimant was ordered to bear half of the respondent's share of the costs. In the second such case, where the respondent also made a sealed offer, the claimant was not successful in establishing its claim for damages. The tribunal therefore held that each party should bear half of the costs of the arbitration and their own legal costs until the allotted time for the acceptance of the respondent's offer, and further ordered the claimant to bear the entirety of the respondent's arbitration and legal costs incurred from the date of the claimant's rejection of the sealed offer.

An order on costs must be reasoned

The requirement that a tribunal's decision on costs must be reasoned is consistent **8.32** with the broader requirement under Article 26.1 of the Rules that a tribunal shall state the reasons upon which its award is based.[17] The reasons requirement is not particularly burdensome in the context of a costs award, and is typically satisfied by a reference to the default rule of Article 28.4 as the basis for the tribunal's decision.

---

[15] See also the example discussed above in the context of art 28.3.
[16] Arbitration Act, s 60.
[17] Discussed in ch 7 above.

Article 28.5

If the arbitration is abandoned, suspended or concluded, by agreement or otherwise, before the final award is made, the parties shall remain jointly and severally liable to pay to the LCIA and the Arbitral Tribunal the costs of the arbitration as determined by the LCIA Court in accordance with the Schedule of Costs. In the event that such arbitration costs are less than the deposits made by the parties, there shall be a refund by the LCIA in such proportions as the parties may agree in writing, or failing such agreement, in the same proportions as the deposits were made by the parties to the LCIA.

8.33 Article 28.5 affirms the parties' joint and several liability to pay the costs of the arbitration in the event that the arbitration is abandoned or otherwise concluded prior to the issuance of the final award. The most common application of this provision arises following the parties' notification of settlement of their dispute to the LCIA and the tribunal, in accordance with Article 26.8. Upon receipt of such notification, the Secretariat will request the arbitrators to provide a final accounting of their fees and expenses, which the Secretariat needs in order to prepare the financial dossier for review by the Court, in accordance with Article 28.1, as discussed earlier. Shortly thereafter, the Secretariat will provide the parties with a financial summary showing the costs of the arbitration, as approved by the Court, in accordance with the Schedule of Costs.

8.34 In the event that the costs of the arbitration, as determined by the Court, are less than the deposits made by the parties, which should ideally be the case pursuant to Article 24.2, the LCIA will refund the remaining funds in accordance with the tribunal's directions or the terms of the parties' settlement agreement, as the case may be. Although not expressly foreseen in the Rules, it is possible (albeit unlikely in practice), that the costs of the arbitration exceed the amounts already deposited by the parties. In such a case, the LCIA will have to seek a further payment from the parties to make up the shortfall.

B. Article 24 – Deposits

8.35 Article 24 deals with the payment of deposits by parties on account of the costs of the arbitration. Such deposits are made at the request of the LCIA Court to cover the arbitrators' and the LCIA's on-going fees and expenses, and are therefore subject to such awards on costs as tribunals deem appropriate pursuant to Article 28.2. It is important to bear in mind that the LCIA does not seek to make profits from fees paid by the parties; nor do its administrative charges fund any activities extraneous to its functions. The purpose of deposits is to ensure that arbitrators will encounter no difficulty in being remunerated for services rendered, and that expenses are covered.

Article 24.1

The LCIA Court may direct the parties, in such proportions as it thinks appropriate, to make one or several interim or final payments on account of the costs of the arbitration. Such deposits shall be made to and held by the LCIA and from time to time may be released by the LCIA Court to the arbitrator(s), any expert appointed by the Arbitral Tribunal and the LCIA itself as the arbitration progresses.

8.36

Article 24.1 empowers the LCIA Court to direct parties to make one or more payments on account of the costs of the arbitration. As mentioned above, such deposits supplement the amount required to be paid by the claimant upon the submission of the Request for Arbitration, and ensure that the LCIA and the arbitrators are in funds throughout the arbitration proceedings. The deposits submitted by the parties are held on trust in interest-bearing client bank accounts which are controlled by reference to each individual case until the funds are disbursed.[18] Any interest accrued on the sums deposited shall be credited to the account of each party depositing them.[19] The practice of the LCIA in this respect is not universally followed by other arbitral institutions. In ICC arbitration, for example, any interest earned on the advance on costs paid by the parties accrues to the benefit of the ICC rather than the parties, a practice that has been criticized.[20]

The LCIA Court's delegated authority

8.37

Although the Rules vest the Court with the power to direct the parties to make deposits on account of the costs of the arbitration, the Court has, in fact, delegated to the Registrar its authority to make such directions under Article 24.1, and to approve the payments contemplated thereunder, subject to the Court's supervision.[21] The decision to delegate such authority to the Registrar (in practice, the Secretariat) is sensible given the practicalities involved in the application of Article 24.1, which requires a constant monitoring of ongoing arbitrations, and the maintenance of regular dialogue with tribunals. Under the authority delegated by the Court, the Registrar is empowered to issue individual directions for interim or final payments in an aggregate sum up to £120,000 (or $240,000) per direction, without seeking prior approval of the Court. However, the written authority of the Court is required before the Registrar is able to issue a direction exceeding £120,000 (or $240,000). Furthermore, the Registrar must, in all cases, advise the Court when the cumulative total of directions issued in any one case

---

[18] Art 5(e) Schedule of Costs.

[19] Art 6 Schedule of Costs.

[20] *Derains & Schwartz* 352; and C Salans, 'The 1985 Rules of the London Court of International Arbitration' (1986) 2 Arb Int 40, 41.

[21] The Court's directive is reproduced at app 6. The LCIA Court is permitted to delegate its authority in administrative matters pursuant to art G(i) of its Constitution.

exceeds £250,000 (or $500,000), and must advise the Court of all further deposits thereafter.

Timing and frequency of deposit payments

8.38 Although the Rules and the Schedule of Costs are silent as to the timing and frequency of such directions, the LCIA typically calls for the payment of deposits: (i) shortly following the tribunal's constitution;[22] and (ii) in anticipation of a hearing, although this will depend on the circumstances of each case. As to the frequency of calls for payment, this entirely depends on the circumstances of the case. Article 24.1 expressly provides that the Court may direct the payment of one or several interim or final payments. In practice, the LCIA directs deposits to be paid in stages (following consultations with the arbitrators) and will limit such directions for payment to a sum sufficient to cover the fees, expenses, and costs for the next stage of the arbitration, as per Article 5(a) of the Schedule of Costs. This is a sensible policy, not only because it spreads out the parties' financial burden, but also because it is difficult to predict the likely total costs of the arbitration at the start of the proceedings.

8.39 The LCIA's sensible practice of collecting deposits as the case progresses is also likely to impose less financial demands on the parties than the practice under the ICC Rules, which requires the payment of the costs of the arbitration (as determined on the basis of the ICC's Scales of Administrative Expenses and Arbitrator's Fees) in full at an early stage of the proceedings, in the form of the 'advance on costs'.[23] The latter may well require a substantial, interest-free, deposit to be made.

Special considerations in respect of multi-party arbitrations

8.40 Article 24.1 empowers the Court to direct the parties to pay deposits on account of the costs of the arbitration in such proportions as it thinks fit. In other words, the Court – and subject to the Court's delegated authority, the Registrar – has considerable discretion to apportion the directed payments among the parties, as it thinks appropriate. The discretion enjoyed by the LCIA can be contrasted with Article 30(3) of the ICC Rules, which refers to the payment of the advance on

---

[22] The payment of such a deposit is not a formal requirement, unlike the practice under art 13 ICC Rules, which makes the transmission of the file to the arbitral tribunal upon its constitution conditional on the advance on costs having been paid. For a discussion of the ICC Secretariat's practice, see *Derains & Schwartz* 209–11.

[23] Art 30(2) ICC Rules. For a discussion of the ICC Secretariat's practice, see *Derains & Schwartz* 335–41.

costs in equal shares by the claimant and the respondent (although the ICC Court is empowered to fix separate advances on costs in respect of claims and counterclaims).[24] In fact, the practice of the LCIA is also to apportion costs equally between the parties.

The equal apportionment of deposit payments is a practice that the Court departs **8.41** from whenever appropriate. One such circumstance relates to recalcitrant claimants who insist on proceeding with an LCIA arbitration notwithstanding an obvious or glaring inconsistency as to the existence of the arbitration agreement or as to whether it covers the parties to or the subject-matter of the dispute. As discussed in chapter 3 above, unless the Court considers the matter to be clear-cut, for example, if the arbitration agreement unequivocally provides for arbitration under the ICC Rules, the LCIA Court is likely to decide to proceed with the arbitration, but may direct the claimant alone to bear the costs of the arbitration until the tribunal has determined the issue of its jurisdiction. Another example of the Court's flexible practice in apportioning the costs of the arbitration is demonstrated by a case involving a non-participating respondent who nonetheless introduced a counterclaim in the proceedings. In response, the Court directed the respondent alone to bear the cost of an interim deposit payment, as the costs of the arbitration until then had been met solely by the claimant.

The position also becomes more complicated where there are multiple parties. **8.42** Generally, notwithstanding the multiplicity of parties, where there can be said to be two sides in the arbitration, the LCIA will apportion the costs of the arbitration equally between the two sides. It will then be up to the parties on each side to make arrangements among themselves for the payment of that side's share of deposits. Where there are three or more distinct sides in the arbitration, however, the Court will determine the appropriate apportionment of the payments to be made based on the circumstances of the case. It may be appropriate in such instances, for example, for the LCIA to divide the costs of the arbitration in three or more equal shares.

The release of payments

Article 24.1 empowers the LCIA Court to release from time to time the deposits **8.43** it holds to arbitrators, any experts appointed by the arbitral tribunal pursuant to Article 21, and the LCIA itself as the arbitration progresses.[25] In this respect, the Registrar is empowered to submit interim invoices in respect of all current arbitrations on a quarterly basis for payment direct by the parties or from funds

---

[24] Ibid.
[25] Art 7(a) Schedule of Costs.

held on deposit.[26] As explained earlier, the Court has delegated its powers under Article 24.1, including its power to release payments, to the Registrar.[27] Prior to approving the release of any such payments, the Registrar must notify the parties of the fact and the amount of such payments. As discussed earlier in the context of Article 28, any request by arbitrators for payment on account of their fees must be supported by a fee note, which includes detail of the time spent at the rates that have been advised to the parties by the LCIA.[28] Following any such payments, the Registrar will provide the tribunal and the parties with a financial summary, accounting for such payments and recording the balance of the funds held on deposit.

Article 24.2

The Arbitral Tribunal shall not proceed with the arbitration without ascertaining at all times from the Registrar or any deputy Registrar that the LCIA is in requisite funds.

8.44 As mentioned earlier in the context of Article 28, upon appointment by the LCIA Court, arbitrators are instructed by the Registrar not to proceed with an arbitration without ascertaining from the Registrar that the LCIA is in requisite funds. This provision calls for the establishment and maintenance of a consistent dialogue between tribunals and the Registrar as regards the financial state of the arbitration. In practice, it is up to the arbitrators to keep a methodical record of the time spent on their arbitrations and diligently to submit that record to the Registrar on a regular basis. The Registrar, for his part, is responsible for monitoring the progress of all LCIA arbitrations, which includes keeping abreast of the financial state of every arbitration.

8.45 There will inevitably be occasions where arbitrations will progress in circumstances where the LCIA is not in requisite funds. In such cases, and upon discovery of the shortage of funds, the Registrar will call for the payment of further deposits and direct the arbitrators not to proceed any further until such payment has been made. The authors' research revealed numerous instances where arbitrations were brought to a halt due to the lack of funds, most often just before the commencement of a hearing or at the very end of the arbitration when the award is ready for despatch to the parties. Unless the outstanding deposits are forthcoming (whether by the directed parties or in the form of substitute payments under Article 24.3), the arbitration will remain, in effect, suspended before an eventual withdrawal of claims or counterclaims pursuant to Article 24.4. The authors' research also revealed several instances where the lack of funds delayed the

---

[26] Art 7(b) Schedule of Costs.
[27] Art 8(b) Schedule of Costs.
[28] Art 8(c) Schedule of Costs.

issuance of the award in accordance with Article 26.5, which conditions the Registrar's despatch of the arbitrators' award to the parties on the costs of the arbitration having been paid. A similar provision is found in Article 9(b) of the Schedule of Costs.

Article 24.3

In the event that a party fails or refuses to provide any deposit as directed by the LCIA Court, the LCIA Court may direct the other party or parties to effect a substitute payment to allow the arbitration to proceed (subject to any award on costs). In such circumstances, the party paying the substitute payment shall be entitled to recover that amount as a debt immediately due from the defaulting party.

The first point to note in respect to Article 24.3 is that the Court's powers there- **8.46** under have been delegated to the Registrar, in the same manner as the Court's delegated authority in respect of Article 24.1. In the event that a party fails to pay its share of deposits and the other party nevertheless wishes to proceed with the arbitration, the non-defaulting party has no alternative other than to effect a substitute payment, irrespective of whether the Court directs the non-defaulting party to effect such payment.[29]

Although the Rules were not intended to facilitate a practice where one party **8.47** refuses to pay its share of the deposits and thus leaves it to the other party to pay the entirety of the costs of the arbitration, the Rules contain no sanction precluding the continued participation of the defaulting (usually the respondent) party, at least for the purposes of defending itself. Indeed, in our research, we came across scores of cases where parties (overwhelmingly, but not exclusively, respondents) refused to pay their share of the deposits and thus forced the other party to effect one or more substitute payments pursuant to Article 24.3. The sanction available against a defaulting party is contained in Article 24.4 (discussed below), which prevents a party from pursuing any claims or counterclaims if any directed deposits have not been paid.

Further, it is not possible under the Rules for the Court to fix separate deposits on **8.48** account of the parties' respective claims and counterclaims, as is the case pursuant to Article 30(3) of the ICC Rules. This is a consequence of the fact that, as discussed earlier, the costs of the arbitration under the Rules are not calculated *ad valorem*, but on the basis of time spent on the case by arbitrators and the LCIA alike.

It has to be acknowledged, however, that respondents in a significant majority **8.49** of cases fully contribute their share of the deposits directed by the Registrar. In the absence of any meaningful sanctions, particularly against respondents not

---

[29] Art 24.3 empowers, but does not mandate, the Court to direct one or more parties to effect substitute payments when confronted with a party's refusal to make a directed payment.

pursuing counterclaims, this conduct is probably explained by most parties' desire to be viewed in the eyes of the arbitral tribunal as responsible and helpful participants in the arbitration process.

8.50 The sole immediate relief available under the Rules to parties who make substitute payments directed by the Registrar, acting under his delegated authority, is an entitlement to recover the amounts paid on behalf of the defaulting party as a debt immediately due by the defaulting party. The entitlement to recovery of substitute payments is independent of the ultimate outcome of the case (subject to any final award on costs) and forms an immediate debt owed by the defaulting party to the party or parties who effected the substitute payments. In order to facilitate the recovery of such a debt, and upon request of the non-defaulting party, arbitral tribunals have agreed, on several occasions, to issue partial awards ordering defaulting parties to pay their outstanding shares of the directed deposits. The issuance of such partial awards enables the recipient of such an award to seek enforcement of the award in order to recover the substitute payments made during the progress of the arbitration.

Article 24.4

Failure by a claimant or counterclaiming party to provide promptly and in full the required deposit may be treated by the LCIA Court and the Arbitral Tribunal as a withdrawal of the claim or counter-claim respectively.

8.51 Pursuant to Article 24.4, the claims and counterclaims of either party may be deemed to be withdrawn if the directed deposit is not made promptly and in full. This provision represents the sole sanction available under the Rules against a party that fails to pay its share of the costs of the arbitration. As mentioned above, however, such a sanction has no practical effect with respect to a respondent who is merely defending a claim, rather than pursuing separate counterclaims. Indeed, in our research, we came across several instances where respondents, in affirming their refusal to pay the requested funds, explicitly acknowledged the absence of any adverse effect pursuant to Article 24.4 on their ability to defend themselves.

8.52 Article 24.4 enables the tribunal and the LCIA Court to end the arbitration in respect of either or both parties' claims, if the corresponding deposit has not been paid. This provision also applies in respect of substitute payments that may be directed by the Court. In one case, for example, the claimant was directed to effect a substitute payment on behalf of a non-participating respondent. The claimant's failure to effect such a payment on a timely basis eventually led to its claim being deemed as withdrawn by the Court.

8.53 In circumstances where a tribunal has been constituted and the LCIA is in sufficient funds to enable the tribunal to act under Article 24.2, it falls to the tribunal to determine whether a party's claim or counterclaim should be treated as withdrawn. The LCIA Court will invariably follow the tribunal's lead and confirm the deemed withdrawal. In circumstances where either no tribunal is in place or the tribunal is constrained from taking action by a lack of funds, then it falls to the LCIA Court to determine the withdrawal of the respective claims and/or counterclaims.

Once withdrawn, it remains possible (at least in principle) for the respective claim **8.54** or counterclaim to be re-introduced in the arbitration at the discretion of the tribunal, provided of course that the directed payment is subsequently made. Although this is unlikely to occur very often in practice, we understand that such a scenario has occurred in at least one case where the tribunal accepted the re-introduction of the respondent's counterclaims in the arbitration after their initial withdrawal, following the subsequent payment by the respondent of the directed deposit payments. It is interesting to note that the re-introduction of withdrawn claims or counterclaims in the same arbitration is not possible under Article 30(4) of the ICC Rules.[30]

Article 24.4 does not specify a time limit within which the parties must ensure the **8.55** payment of their share of the deposits, although any such payment must be made 'promptly', in order to avoid the prospect of sanctions. The absence of such a deadline provides the tribunal and the Court with a welcome degree of flexibility in their application of this provision, in accordance with the particular circumstances of the case. In practice, before treating any claims as withdrawn, they will notify defaulting parties of the consequences of their failure to pay the directed deposits pursuant to Article 24.4, and will grant such parties a reasonable opportunity to make any outstanding payments. It is not the practice of LCIA tribunals or the Court to treat the withdrawal of claims lightly and therefore they will, in most cases, be amenable to reasonable (and reasoned) extensions of time sought by parties in which to effect payments. Indeed, the practice of the LCIA also extends to accepting requests from parties to pay directed deposits in several tranches over time. However, their patience should not be treated as infinitely elastic. Our research reveals that a party's persistent failure to pay its share of the costs of the arbitration in full will inevitably cause that party's respective claims or counterclaims to be treated as withdrawn, albeit there is no consistent practice as to how long defaulting parties are granted to pay outstanding deposits.

Claimant's failure to pay

Occasionally, it is the claimant that is unable or refuses to pay its share of **8.56** the directed deposits. In such instances, and unless the respondent effects a

---

[30] Unless the parties agree otherwise: see *Derains & Schwartz* 354.

substitute payment – which is unlikely unless it is pursuing counterclaims – the tribunal (if already constituted) and the Court will treat the claimant's claims as withdrawn pursuant to Article 24.4 and terminate the arbitration. This may follow the tribunal's issuance of an award on costs, at the respondent's request, if there are sufficient funds available. This occurred in one recent case, where the respondent had paid its share of the directed deposits, whereas the claimant had not and had subsequently failed to participate in the arbitration. In the circumstances, in addition to the withdrawal of the claimant's claims pursuant to Article 24.4, the tribunal also rendered an award of costs in favour of the respondent.

8.57 Article 24.4 also enables the Court to bring the proceedings to an end in the absence of an arbitral tribunal. In one case, where the claimant had failed to participate in the arbitration shortly after submitting the Request for Arbitration, and no tribunal had been constituted, the LCIA was faced by a request from the respondent to terminate the proceedings. The Court responded by directing the parties to pay initial deposits, and upon the parties' failure to do so, the Court was able to treat the claimant's claims as withdrawn pursuant to Article 24.4 and to bring the arbitration to an end.

9

MISCELLANEOUS PROVISIONS
(ARTICLES 30, 31, AND 32)

A.	Article 30 – Confidentiality	9.03
	Article 30.1	9.21
	Article 30.2	9.26
	Article 30.3	9.27
B.	Article 31 – Exclusion of Liability	9.30
	Article 31.1	9.31
	Article 31.2	9.35
C.	Article 32 – General Rules	9.36
	Article 32.1	9.37
	Article 32.2	9.46

9.01 Like all sets of institutional rules, the LCIA Rules have gathered together rules governing some aspects of an LCIA arbitration at the end. Their relative position by reference to the rest of the Rules, and their lack of interrelationship among themselves, does not, however, make them any less important.

9.02 These provisions, gathered together in this chapter under the heading of 'miscellaneous provisions', in fact cover some very significant issues. The first is confidentiality (Article 30).

A. Article 30 – Confidentiality

Background

9.03 One of the most oft-cited supposed benefits of arbitration is its confidentiality. Parties are assumed to wish that their private disputes be resolved in private and that one of the principal reasons for their having chosen arbitration was to avoid the public nature of the litigation process in state courts. This may be to overstate the importance to sophisticated users of international arbitration (for whom finality, a fair result and, perhaps most of all, neutrality can perhaps be expected to weigh more heavily than confidentiality).

9.04   The LCIA Rules recognize this perceived benefit and by Article 30 explicitly provide that the proceedings are to be confidential. Article 30 imposes an overall duty of confidentiality on the parties, although the parties may agree not to be bound by it. This duty of confidentiality should be distinguished from two related issues, the privacy of hearings and the power of the arbitral tribunal to make special arrangements to protect confidential information (contained in documents or otherwise) even from the other party or parties to the arbitration, especially where issues of commercial confidence and trade secrets are in play. Among major institutional rules, only the LCIA Rules and the Swiss Rules[1] impose a similar duty (although the terms of the Swiss Rules are even wider than the LCIA Rules).[2] The ICDR Rules (Article 34) and the current SCC Rules (Article 46) enjoin the arbitrators and institutions to respect the confidentiality of information disclosed during the proceedings, but not the parties.

9.05   The relative rarity of a confidentiality obligation in institutional rules thus further distinguishes the LCIA Rules from most competing sets of rules (as does Article 9 on the expedited formation of the tribunal, discussed in chapter 4 above). It is a reason for parties to choose, or to avoid, the LCIA Rules, depending on their concern or dislike for confidentiality in arbitration.

The existence of an implied duty of confidentiality

9.06   Before turning to the specifics of the Article 30 obligations, it is helpful to rehearse briefly the state of the implied duty of confidentiality in international commercial arbitration.[3] It was historically assumed that this implied duty was the logical corollary of the privacy of hearings. But these are very different concepts. The 'privacy' of hearings refers to the *in camera* nature of arbitral hearings. It ensures that only the parties, their representatives and witnesses (expert and factual) are allowed to attend the hearings.[4] The concept of 'confidentiality' is far wider, extending to documents created for or submitted in the proceedings (including pleadings and witness statements and the like) and indeed to the very existence of the arbitration.

9.07   While there is a strong consensus as to the privacy of hearings, recognized by all major institutional rules, the same is no longer true (if it ever was) in relation to

---

[1]   By art 43(1).

[2]   A Jolles and M Canals de Cediel, 'Confidentiality' in G Kaufmann-Kohler and B Tucki (eds) *International Arbitration in Switzerland* (Kluwer, 2004) 89, 107.

[3]   The adjective 'commercial' is important in this context to distinguish commercial cases from investment-treaty arbitration, in which it is becoming accepted not only that there is no obligation of confidentiality on the parties, but also that third parties may even intervene in the proceedings as *amici curiae*. This is, however, outside the scope of this book, which confines itself to a review of the position in international *commercial* arbitration.

[4]   See the discussion of art 19.3 in ch 5 above.

the notion of 'confidentiality' in its broader sense. As a general principle, it is undeniable that in the modern law of arbitration there is a strong trend away from an assumption that arbitration is confidential. At the same time, English law is perhaps one of the last bastions of such an implied duty and, given the close connection between LCIA arbitration and England, the general trend needs to be seen through English spectacles in order to understand Article 30.

The position in England

The traditional formulation of the duty of confidentiality in English law was **9.08** expressed by Potter LJ in the Court of Appeal in *Ali Shipping v Shipyard Trogir* as:

> [a term] which arises as the nature of the contract itself implicitly requires [and] which the law will necessarily imply as a necessary incident of a definable category of contractual relationship.[5]

Potter LJ went on to say that: **9.09**

> the boundaries of the obligations of confidence which thereby arise have yet to be delineated.[6]

This categorization of the duty of confidentiality as an implied term in English **9.10** law has been challenged by two more recent decisions, however. In the first, *Associated Electric & Gas Insurance Services Ltd v European Reinsurance Co of Zurich*,[7] the Privy Council had to consider the specific case of a party's seeking to use the award rendered by a different arbitral tribunal in a previous arbitration between the same parties arising out of the same reinsurance agreement. The Privy Council held that, despite the existence of an express confidentiality agreement between the parties, it was allowable to use the award in subsequent proceedings on which it was sought to rely on it as an issue estoppel. This was justified as part of the general exception to the obligation of confidentiality which is necessary to allow a party to enforce its legal rights.

Because the case at hand involved the construction of an express confidentiality **9.11** agreement, the Privy Council declined to comment directly on *Ali Shipping* or define more precisely the scope of the duty of confidentiality. Indeed, the Privy Council expressed reservations about the categorization of the duty as an implied term with exceptions.[8]

---

[5] [1996] 1 Lloyd's Rep 643, CA, 651.
[6] Ibid.
[7] [2003] UKPC 11.
[8] N Rawding and K Seeger, '*Aegis v European Re* and the Confidentiality of Arbitration Awards' (2003) 19 Arb Int 483.

9.12 This theme was taken up again by the Court of Appeal in *Emmott v Michael Wilson & Partners Ltd*.[9] In that case, Lawrence Collins LJ held that 'the implied agreement is really a rule of substantive law masquerading as an implied term'.[10]

The position elsewhere

9.13 Elsewhere than in England, the consensus in favour of the existence of an obligation of confidentiality in international commercial arbitration is in full retreat.[11]

9.14 This can be for various reasons. First, there is the fact that parties may have legal duties of disclosure, but this cannot be said to be the driving force because the existence of such legal duties is recognized by English law as an exception that would allow the court to lift the general duty of confidentiality. More pertinently, national courts have recognized that there is little by way of sensible sanction that can be applied for a breach of an obligation of confidentiality, as graphically shown by the decision of the Stockholm City Court in the *Bulbank* case, later reversed by the Swedish Supreme Court.[12]

9.15 In that case, one of the parties had arranged for the tribunal's partial award on jurisdiction to be published in an arbitration journal, before the final award on the merits was rendered. The respondent argued before the Stockholm City Court that this was a fundamental breach of an implied term of the arbitration agreement requiring confidentiality. While the arbitral tribunal rejected this argument, it was accepted by the court, which discharged the arbitration agreement and annulled the by now rendered final award.

9.16 In a complete about-turn in response to this swingeing sanction, the Supreme Court not only reversed the decision of the Stockholm City Court, but held that

---

[9] [2008] EWCA Civ 184.

[10] [2008] EWCA Civ 184 at para 84.

[11] The one (now rather dated) seeming exception to this is the decision of the Paris Court of Appeal in *Aita c Ojjeh*, 18 February 1986, [1986] Rev arb 583. The Court of Appeal ruled in that case that the mere bringing of court proceedings in France to annul an arbitration award rendered in England violated the principle of confidentiality by causing a 'public debate of facts that should remain confidential'. In so finding, the court held that it was in 'the very nature of arbitral proceedings that they ensure the highest degree of discretion in the resolution of private disputes, as the two parties had agreed'. This seems highly unsatisfactory in that it gives no explanation as to what the limits of such a duty may be, or where it comes from. Two commentators have surmised that this decision can perhaps best be understood in the context of the Court of Appeal's determination to censure what it considered to be an entirely hopeless attempt to set aside an English award in France with the apparent aim of embarrassing the winning party by publicity (the contract concerned the sale of military material): see J Paulsson and N Rawding, 'The Trouble with Confidentiality' (1995) 11 Arb Int 303.

[12] *AI Trade Finance Inc v Bulgarian Foreign Trade Bank Ltd* (1999) YCA 321.

there was no implied duty of confidentiality at all. In so doing, the Supreme Court carefully distinguished between the wider duty of 'confidentiality' and the narrower concept of 'privacy', such that the parties would be allowed to disclose information to third parties while their proceedings remained closed to the public.

9.17 Similarly, in the United States, there is no implied duty of confidentiality,[13] although the parties can agree that they should be bound by an obligation to keep documents and information disclosed in the arbitration confidential.

9.18 The most influential development against the existence of a general, implied duty of confidentiality is the decision of the High Court of Australia in the *Esso v Plowman* case.[14] The High Court in that case held that there was a distinction between the privacy of oral hearings and the secrecy of proceedings in general. Thus, an obligation to hold hearings *in camera* does not imply a requirement not to disclose documents and information provided in and for the purposes of the arbitration. The High Court held that, even though a certain degree of confidentiality might arise in certain circumstances, it was not absolute and that a public interest exception applied.

9.19 On this last point Mason CJ held:

> The courts have consistently viewed governmental secrets differently from personal and commercial secrets. As I stated in *The Commonwealth of Australia v John Fairfax and Sons Ltd*, the judiciary must view the disclosure of governmental information 'through different spectacles'. This involves a reversal of the onus of proof: the government must prove that the public interest demands non-disclosure.[15]

9.20 It is in the light of this debate that the decision of the drafters of the LCIA Rules to provide as the default position (from which the parties can opt out) that the proceedings should be confidential should be viewed.

Article 30.1

> Unless the parties expressly agree in writing to the contrary, the parties undertake as a general principle to keep confidential all awards in their arbitration, together with all materials in the proceedings created for the purpose of the arbitration and all other documents produced by another party in the proceedings not otherwise in the public domain – save and to the extent that disclosure may be required of a party by legal duty, to protect or pursue a legal right or to enforce or challenge an award in bona fide legal proceedings before a state court or other judicial authority.

---

[13] *United States v Panhandle Eastern Corp et al* 118 FRD 346 (D Del 1988).

[14] *Esso Australia Resources Ltd & Ors v The Honourable Sidney James Plowman & Ors* (1995) 128 ALR 391.

[15] (1995) 128 ALR 391 at para 39. See, by way of example of the commentary on this momentous decision, Paulsson and Rawding (n 11 above).

9.21 Article 30.1 establishes the basic principle of the parties' agreement that the proceedings will be confidential. Thus, even if the seat of the arbitration is in a jurisdiction where there is no implied duty of confidentiality (which is most of them except England and Wales), the parties will have expressly undertaken to keep the arbitration confidential by agreeing to conduct their arbitration under the LCIA Rules.

9.22 This is the default position: as the first phrase of Article 30.1 makes clear, it is not mandatory and the parties can opt out. By implication, the United States and Canada have so opted out in the Softwood Lumber Agreement. Although there is no express exclusion of this article (as there is for Article 21 (tribunal-appointed experts)), it is excluded by necessary implication as the agreement provides for all documents to be made public subject to arrangements being asked for and ordered by the tribunal on the specific application of a party in respect of specific documents or information. As noted above in chapter 1, even the hearings are public.

9.23 Article 30.1 refers specifically to awards and 'all materials in the proceedings created for the purpose of the arbitration and all other documents produced by another party in the proceedings not otherwise in the public domain'. As to awards, it was the use of an award that was the subject of the decisions in *Aegis v European Re* and *Bulbank* discussed above and awards have also been the subject of several other decisions of state courts on the subject of the existence and extent of a duty of confidentiality (express or implied). These decisions mainly concern the right of a party to use an award to enforce its rights, and this is specifically provided for in the exception to Article 30.1, which allows all documents to be used by a party under a legal duty or to protect or enforce a legal right, including to enforce or challenge the award in question.

9.24 As to the reference to 'all materials … and all other documents', this must include submissions, witness statements, expert reports, and all documents (other than those in the public domain) that were produced by the other parties to the proceedings (unless, of course, they are also within the possession of the disclosing party).

9.25 It has been suggested that there is a tension between the obligation of confidentiality imposed by Article 30 and the power of the tribunal to join a third party under Article 22.1(h).[16] This is on the basis that a third party cannot be joined without giving the parties an opportunity to be heard and then only with the consent of the third party, who would presumably want to know about the issues in the case before agreeing. Given that the power conferred on the tribunal by Article 22.1(h)

---

[16] A Diamond, 'Procedure and Hearings' in A Berkeley and J Mimms (eds), *International Commercial Arbitration: Practical Perspectives* (Centre of Construction Law & Management, 2001) 49, 54.

can be exercised over the opposition of the non-applicant party or parties, there can indeed be seen to be some tension. This tension, however, is surely resolved by seeing Article 22.1(h) as a derogation from the obligations in Article 30, to which, by agreeing to submit their disputes to arbitration under the LCIA Rules, all parties to the arbitration have consented.

Article 30.2

The deliberations of the Arbitral Tribunal are likewise confidential to its members, save and to the extent that disclosure of an arbitrator's refusal to participate in the arbitration is required of the other members of the Arbitral Tribunal under Articles 10, 12 and 26.

The confidentiality of the tribunal's deliberations is universally accepted. As has already been discussed,[17] the violation of the secrecy of deliberations is a prima facie ground for challenge for an arbitrator. There is an express exception to allow arbitrators to make public (to the LCIA and the parties) an arbitrator's refusal to take part in deliberations where such disclosure is required by Articles 10 (challenge), 12 (truncated tribunals), and 26 (awards). **9.26**

Article 30.3

The LCIA Court does not publish any award or any part of an award without the prior written consent of all parties and the Arbitral Tribunal.

The refusal to publish awards (even in anonymous form) is to be contrasted with the laudable decision to publish sanitized versions of decisions of the Court on arbitrator challenges. It is also to be contrasted to the practice of the ICC. Previous arbitral awards can be of considerable value to practitioners, arbitrators, and counsel alike. While there is no system of precedent in arbitration, and while decisions of commercial tribunals are more likely to turn on their own facts than decisions of investment-treaty tribunals, awards are a rich source of arbitral practice and have a real influence on the development of such practice. **9.27**

The LCIA is not only depriving itself of the opportunity to present its awards and help itself as well as the international arbitral community: it can be seen actually to be doing a disservice, since some favoured arbitrators and counsel will have access to many confidential awards that are not available to less-experienced parties and their representatives. This can go so far as to unbalance the playing field in arbitrations between those parties who are represented by counsel 'in the know' and those who are not. It can also mean that experienced arbitrators take decisions based upon their own, and other tribunals', past practice of which they are aware but which is not known to the parties. The LCIA's concern with confidentiality **9.28**

---

[17] In ch 4 above.

(which the ICC overcomes by publishing awards in such a form as to protect the parties' right to privacy) could be said to have caused it, in adopting this principle, to throw the baby out with the bathwater.

9.29 It is understood that the LCIA's retention of a strict requirement of confidentiality, even extending to the refusal to publish arbitral awards in sanitized form, comes from its perception of its users' concern to safeguard the strict confidentiality of the proceedings. Nonetheless, it must be possible to ensure that the legitimate concerns of users to preserve the confidentiality of their proceedings be respected while at the same time serving the interests of the wider international arbitration community by publishing sanitized awards.

B. Article 31 – Exclusion of Liability

9.30 Article 31 sets out the principle of the immunity from suit of the LCIA and its officers from parties dissatisfied with its decisions. Given the administrative nature of the LCIA Court (established in Article 29, discussed in chapter 2 above) and the obviously administrative nature of the LCIA's other functions in an LCIA arbitration, to the extent that there is no immunity for the acts of an administrative body (as there would be for those exercising a quasi-judicial function, such as arbitrators),[18] the principle needs to be agreed by the parties in the form of a grant of immunity.[19] This provision seeks therefore both to protect the members of the Court and other officers of the LCIA and also (as with Article 29) to minimize any satellite litigation based on a Court decision (even if it is impossible to avoid it entirely).

Article 31.1

None of the LCIA, the LCIA Court (including its President, Vice Presidents and individual members), the Registrar, any deputy Registrar, any arbitrator and any expert to the Arbitral Tribunal shall be liable to any party howsoever for any act or omission in connection with any arbitration conducted by reference to these Rules, save where the act or omission is shown by that party to constitute conscious and deliberate wrongdoing committed by the body or person alleged to be liable to that party.

9.31 If arbitrators have been the beneficiaries of an increasing tendency to resolve disputes by way of arbitration rather than litigation in state courts, they (and the institutions that administer the arbitrations in which they serve) could also be its victims.[20] Disgruntled (that is to say, losing) parties might, faced with the difficulties of challenging an award, seek to take their frustration out on

---

[18] Arbitration Act 1996, s 29.
[19] As noted below, in England immunity is extended to arbitral institutions by s 74 Arbitration Act.
[20] A Redfern, 'The Immunity of Arbitrators' in *The Status of the Arbitrator* (ICC Publishing, 1995).

the members of the tribunal. While in many countries this is dealt with by conferring immunity on arbitrators for acts committed in the furtherance of their quasi-judicial functions,[21] arbitral institutions make sure that this is also a part of their respective rules.[22] As noted above, the English Arbitration Act also extends the statutory immunity for arbitrators to arbitral institutions.[23] If an action cannot be brought against the arbitrators, or perhaps even if it can, there may be action against the LCIA or its individual officers. To the extent that this is not covered by Article 29.2, discussed in chapter 2 above, Article 31.1 is designed to ensure that no such claims can be maintained.

How effective this provision would be is a matter of some considerable debate. **9.32** The provision will obviously depend upon the willingness of local jurisdictions to give it effect. As a matter of English law (still the most relevant jurisdiction for any consideration of the effectiveness of this provision given the number of LCIA arbitrations with their seat in England, although the DIFC Court will become highly relevant as cases begin to emerge under the DIFC-LCIA Arbitration Centre Rules referred to in chapter 1 above), the position is wholly covered by statute.

For arbitrations with their seat in England and Wales (as is the case for 97 per cent **9.33** of LCIA arbitrations), section 74 of the English Arbitration Act 1996 provides for immunity for all acts of arbitral institutions and their employees and agents for all acts otherwise in connection with their functions unless such acts were committed in bad faith (including an exclusion of liability for acts done by an arbitrator appointed by the institution, which goes further than Article 31). Similarly, as mentioned above, section 29 of the Arbitration Act provides the same immunity for an arbitrator (or an agent or employee of an arbitrator). The exclusion of acts committed in bad faith in both of those statutory provisions is mirrored by the reference in Article 31.1 to the exclusion of 'conscious and deliberate wrongdoing'. (By contrast, Article 34 of the ICC Rules contains no such exclusion, which has given rise to considerable criticism and doubts in both France, where the ICC's headquarters is situated, and Switzerland.)[24]

As noted above, no decision of the LCIA Court has been challenged in court pro- **9.34** ceedings (unlike the ICC, as evidenced by the *Cubic* case referred to in note 24 below

---

[21] *Fouchard, Gaillard, Goldman* paras 1142–56; *Redfern & Hunter* paras 5-14 to 5-22; *Poudret & Besson* paras 395–98; and *Lew, Mistelis, Kröll* 288–99.

[22] Apart from art 31 LCIA Rules, see, for example, art 34 ICC Rules, art 35 ICDR Rules, and art 77 WIPO Arbitration Rules.

[23] Arbitration Act 1996, s 74.

[24] See, eg, P Lalive, 'Sur l'irresponsabilité arbitrale' in *Etudes de procédure et d'arbitrage en l'honneur de Jean-François Poudret* (1999) and the decision of the French *Cour de cassation* in *Société Cubic Defense Systems Inc c Chambre de commerce internationale, Cour de cassation, 1ère ch civ* (20 February 2001), note Clay [2001] Rev arb 511; and Paris Court of Appeal (15 September 1998), note Lalive [1999] Rev arb 103. See also *Fouchard, Gaillard, Goldman* para 1110 n 217 and paras 1153–55.

and by proceedings brought against the ICC in Cairo in relation to the *Westland* case[25] and, most recently, in Argentina arising out of a challenge to an arbitrator in one of the many investment-treaty cases against that country).[26] The effectiveness and scope of Article 31.1, as with Article 29.2, thus remains untested.

Article 31.2

After the award has been made and the possibilities of correction and additional awards referred to in Article 27 have lapsed or been exhausted, neither the LCIA, the LCIA Court (including its President, Vice Presidents and individual members), the Registrar, any deputy Registrar, any arbitrator or expert to the Arbitral Tribunal shall be under any legal obligation to make any statement to any person about any matter concerning the arbitration, nor shall any party seek to make any of these persons a witness in any legal or other proceedings arising out of the arbitration.

9.35 Article 31.2 is of less theoretical but perhaps more practical importance. It draws a line, in effect, under the arbitration. Once an award has been rendered and all possibility of correction and additional awards has been exhausted or has lapsed, the LCIA, its officers, and the arbitrators (and experts to the tribunal) shall have no liability to appear as witnesses or make any other comment on the case.[27] Again, the effectiveness of this provision will depend upon local law, but the intention to bring proceedings to a clean end and to avoid them dragging on for ever in ancillary or satellite litigation is sound.

C. Article 32 – General Rules

9.36 As its title of 'General Rules' suggests, the two paragraphs of Article 32 are not related to one another. Article 32.1 regulates the question of when a party can be said to have waived its rights under the Rules, while Article 32.2 sets out a general exhortation to all players in an LCIA arbitration to act in the spirit of the Rules.

---

[25] A celebrated case arising out of a contract between Westland Helicopters Ltd and the Arab Organization for Industrialization, giving rise to an arbitration in Switzerland, a court case before the courts of the Canton of Geneva and a subsequent appeal, a setting-aside application before the Swiss Federal Supreme Court and much commentary. See the judgment of the Geneva court [1989] Rev arb 514; first decision of the Swiss Federal Supreme Court BGE 120 II 155; and the final decision of the Swiss Federal Supreme Court [1996] ASA Bull 496.

[26] Causa 2.660/2006 *Procuración del Tesoro v International Chamber of Commerce* (Deci 15-XII-05).

[27] This is perhaps not an entirely fanciful possibility. In the famous case of *CME v Czech Republic*, an arbitration brought under the Bilateral Investment Treaty between The Netherlands and the Czech Republic, the losing respondent sought to set the award aside in the Svea Court of Appeal (the seat of the arbitration having been Stockholm). All three arbitrators were called to, and did, give evidence about the deliberations of the arbitral tribunal (see *Czech Republic v CME Czech Republic BV*, Judgment of the Svea Court of Appeal, 15 June 2003, in case T 8735-01 (2003) 42 ILM 915).

Article 32.1

A party who knows that any provision of the Arbitration Agreement (including these Rules) has not been complied with and yet proceeds with the arbitration without promptly stating its objection to such non-compliance, shall be treated as having irrevocably waived its right to object.

Waiver

Article 32.1 is the expression of the widely accepted principle that a party should **9.37** not be allowed to complain about something that it could and should have objected to at some earlier time. It is reflected in substantive law in the doctrines of waiver, estoppel, etc. It is also reflected as a principle of some arbitration laws and is contained, for example, in Article 4 of the UNCITRAL Model Law and section 73 of the English Arbitration Act.

This is a fairly standard provision, comparable to Article 33 of the ICC Rules, **9.38** Article 30 of the UNCITRAL Rules, and Article 31 of the SCC Rules, for example. There are some differences, however. The LCIA and SCC provisions talk about objections to both the arbitration agreement and the Rules (the LCIA provision rightly regarding the latter as part of the former). The ICC provision refers to the 'Rules, or . . . any other rules applicable to the proceedings, any direction given by the Arbitral Tribunal, or any requirement under the arbitration agreement *relating to the constitution of the Arbitral Tribunal*, or to the conduct of the proceedings'. (Emphasis added.) This is (for once) a wordier provision than its LCIA cognate but possibly less wide insofar as objections to the arbitration agreement are concerned, as these are restricted to objections relating to the constitution of the tribunal. The UNCITRAL Rules refer only to provisions or requirements of the rules.

In all cases, the principle of waiver extends to any action taken under the **9.39** respective rules, whether by the tribunal, the institution, or any of the parties themselves. Thus, in an LCIA arbitration, it would cover acts of the Court and the Secretariat as well as the arbitrators and the parties.

Because it covers the arbitration agreement, any objection as to the jurisdiction of **9.40** the tribunal, its formation, and the independence or impartiality of its members must be raised at the appropriate time or be deemed waived. It would therefore logically also cover the fairness of the proceedings, the right of the parties to be heard, and other fundamental aspects of the procedure. It should, therefore, help to defeat any application to set an award aside, or to resist its enforcement, based upon any such ground, unless the objection was made at the right time and refused by the tribunal. A word of caution, however. In all cases, a waiver is effective only if it can validly be made under the applicable law. Mandatory rules cannot, by definition, be waived. Under the English Arbitration Act, section 73 confirms the effectiveness of a waiver of a right to object to the tribunal's jurisdiction, the conduct of the proceedings, failure to comply with the arbitration agreement, or any irregularity affecting the tribunal or the proceedings.

9.41 The waiver principle operates both before the arbitral tribunal and before a state court. In other words, whether a party first raises an objection in the arbitration itself, or in proceedings, such as setting-aside proceedings, before a state court, he will be taken to have waived the objection if it could have been raised earlier.

9.42 Two areas of controversy could be expected in relation to Article 32.1. The first is the question of knowledge. In order to waive a right, one must know that that right exists. The issue that arises is when such knowledge should be deemed, if actual knowledge cannot be shown. The second is the meaning of the requirement that objections, if they are not to be deemed waived, are to be raised 'promptly'.

9.43 As to knowledge, the concept of imputed knowledge is a widespread one, and arbitrators should have little difficulty in conducting an enquiry to determine whether a party had actual knowledge of an event about which complaint could have been made earlier, and, if not, to set the test for establishing whether such knowledge should be imputed. It may be, in that regard, that there will be circumstances that will lead to a presumption of knowledge, to be rebutted by the party concerned. The knowledge test for effective waiver in the English Arbitration Act is contained in section 73(1)(d), which says that a party will have waived his right to object if he could have raised the objection at an earlier stage of the proceedings unless 'he shows that, at the time he took part or continued to take part in the proceedings, he did not know or could not with reasonable diligence have discovered the grounds for the objection'.

9.44 As to the meaning of the requirement to raise an objection 'promptly', it can only mean that a party must raise any objection within a reasonable time of having knowledge of it (or when such knowledge could with reasonable diligence have been obtained). When exactly that will be in any given procedure is left for the tribunal or the court to determine on a case-by-case basis.

9.45 Should an objection be raised promptly, of course, the party concerned is able to continue with the proceedings subject to the objection. Nor does a party whose objection has been turned down by the tribunal need to make an immediate application to the court in order to preserve his right to raise it later.[28]

---

[28] *Société Nihon Plast Co Ltd c Société Takata-Petri Aktiengesellschaft*, Paris Court of Appeal, 4 March 2004 [2004] Rev arb 452.

Article 32.2

In all matters not expressly provided for in these Rules, the LCIA Court, the Arbitral Tribunal and the parties shall act in the spirit of these Rules and shall make every reasonable effort to ensure that an award is legally enforceable.

The spirit of the Rules

Since the Rules do not and cannot cater for every eventuality, the first part of **9.46** Article 32.2 provides the parties, the tribunal, and the LCIA Court with the injunction to act in the spirit of the Rules when they come across a point that is not 'expressly provided for' (that is to say, to consider what the Rules would have said had they dealt with the point to hand).

It is worth noting that, although this provision is effectively the same as its equiva- **9.47** lents in, for example, the ICC and SCC Rules, the LCIA Rules are far more detailed than the ICC Rules and there are therefore likely to be far fewer gaps to be filled.

One intriguing question is what the drafters of the Rules meant by the spirit of the **9.48** Rules. One clue may be in the statement by one of their drafters, VV Veeder QC, made shortly after the 1998 Rules came into force, that the 1998 Rules put the LCIA 'halfway between full institutional arbitration and *ad hoc* forms of arbitration'.[29] By this, this most knowledgeable 'insider' seems to have meant the provision in Article 14.1 that '[t]he parties may agree on the conduct of their arbitration and they are encouraged to do so'.[30] If that is so, then arbitrators (and the LCIA Court and Registrar, to the extent that the Rules allow them to do so) will, in filling any *lacunae* in the Rules, wish to ensure that they are filled first and foremost by the parties' wishes, to respect the fundamental principle of party autonomy that is the guiding light of the Rules.

Despite the significant differences between the LCIA and ICC Rules, many of **9.49** which have been highlighted in this book, some guidance can, perhaps, be drawn in this respect from a court decision in an arbitration that had been conducted under the ICC Rules. In the one such case referred to by Derains and Schwartz, the US federal Court of Appeals for the Sixth Circuit invoked the analogous provision of the ICC Rules, Article 35, to justify remanding an award to the tribunal under section 68(3)(a) of the English Arbitration Act 1996 (England being the seat of the arbitration) to deal with ambiguities impeding the enforcement of the award.[31]

---

[29] VV Veeder, 'London Court of International Arbitration – The New 1998 LCIA Rules' (1998) 23 YCA 366.
[30] Discussed in more depth in ch 5 above.
[31] *Derains & Schwartz* 384–5.

Enforceability of awards

9.50 The second part of Article 32.2 requires all of 'the LCIA Court, the Arbitral Tribunal and the parties' to make 'every reasonable effort' to ensure the enforceability of awards. This is more than a platitude (especially when seen in conjunction with Article 26.2, discussed in chapter 7 above, which requires conformity with the mandatory rules of the seat), but nor can it be taken to mean that the Court, tribunal, and parties should always bear in mind the possible difficulties of enforcement of an award in any given country in deciding how to proceed or determine issues.

9.51 Arbitrators cannot be expected to be aware of all formal requirements to ensure the enforceability of an award in any given country, or even to know where the award may be enforced (it is up to the parties to make submissions if needed on such points). Moreover, if there is a doubt as to the enforcement of an award because one of the parties has said that it will not abide by it and if it is thought that the courts of the jurisdiction from which that party comes would not uphold the award, the tribunal should nonetheless proceed as it thinks fit if its decisions are in conformity with its interpretation of the substantive or procedural merits of the case.

9.52 Furthermore, it is hard to see what the parties and, especially, the LCIA Court, can do to ensure the enforceability of the award before it is rendered (although the LCIA will provide parties with help in the enforcement of awards, such as letting them have statements as to the establishment of the tribunal, certified copies of notices to parties, certified copies of awards and such like). As to the parties, one of them may very well have every incentive to ensure that the award is never enforced, and the provisions of Article 32.2 are unlikely to stop him. As to the Court, in the absence of a formal scrutiny of awards such as that undertaken by the ICC Court, it is by no means clear what the Court could do to help the enforceability of awards.

9.53 In any event, it is in general for the claimant to take the risk of enforcement. The claimant may himself be well aware that any award rendered in his favour will not be enforceable in the place most propitious for enforcement to be sought. But there may be other places where the respondent has assets, and in any event the claimant may only need an award in order to claim some other right, such as under an insurance policy. Thus, in the *Himpurna* case referred to above in the context of truncated tribunals,[32] it was clear to the tribunal that the Indonesian courts would not allow the award to be enforced, having already purported to

---

[32] In ch 4.

enjoin the continuation of the arbitration. As the claimant still wished to proceed, however, the tribunal acquiesced and rendered an award in the full knowledge that it would not be enforced in Indonesia. While that decision was rendered under the UNCITRAL Rules, the result should be the same under the LCIA Rules, and indeed under any set of arbitration rules.

It is thus to be supposed that this provision is limited in its application to be a **9.54** reminder to arbitrators not to do anything in the conduct of the arbitration that they know will render their award unenforceable. It is for that reason that tribunals will often err on the side of caution when confronted with requests for extensions of time and suchlike; they do not wish to be faced with a setting-aside application or a refusal of enforcement on the grounds that they did not give the parties a fair hearing. Tribunals will furthermore be keen to ensure that notice of procedural steps is duly served on all parties.

APPENDICES

1. Recommended LCIA Arbitration Clauses   237
2. LCIA Arbitration Rules   239
3. Schedule of the LCIA's Arbitration Fees and Costs   255
4. Constitution of the LCIA Arbitration Court   259
5. Membership of the LCIA Arbitration Court   261
6. Directives of the LCIA Arbitration Court under Articles 24, 26, and 28   263
7. Constitution of the LCIA Users' Councils   267
8. The English Arbitration Act 1996   271
9. UNCITRAL Model Law on International Commercial Arbitration   323
10. LCIA Mediation Procedure   355
11. DIFC-LCIA Arbitration Rules   359

APPENDIX 1

Recommended LCIA Arbitration Clauses*

Future Disputes

For contracting parties who wish to have future disputes referred to arbitration and/or mediation under the auspices of the LCIA, the following clauses are recommended. Words/blanks in square brackets should be deleted/completed as appropriate.

A. Arbitration only

"Any dispute arising out of or in connection with this contract, including any question regarding its existence, validity or termination, shall be referred to and finally resolved by arbitration under the Rules of the LCIA, which Rules are deemed to be incorporated by reference into this clause.

The number of arbitrators shall be [one/three].

The seat, or legal place, of arbitration shall be [City and/or Country].

The language to be used in the arbitration shall be [   ].

The governing law of the contract shall be the substantive law of [   ]."

B. Mediation only

"In the event of a dispute arising out of or relating to this contract, including any question regarding its existence, validity or termination, the parties shall seek settlement of that dispute by mediation in accordance with the LCIA Mediation Procedure, which Procedure is deemed to be incorporated by reference into this clause."

C. Mediation and Arbitration

"In the event of a dispute arising out of or relating to this contract, including any question regarding its existence, validity or termination, the parties shall first seek settlement of that dispute by mediation in accordance with the LCIA Mediation Procedure, which Procedure is deemed to be incorporated by reference into this clause.

If the dispute is not settled by mediation within [   ] days of the commencement of the mediation, or such further period as the parties shall agree in writing, the dispute shall be referred to and finally resolved by arbitration under the LCIA Rules, which Rules are deemed to be incorporated by reference into this clause.

The language to be used in the mediation and in the arbitration shall be [   ].

The governing law of the contract shall be the substantive law of [   ].

In any arbitration commenced pursuant to this clause,

  (i) the number of arbitrators shall be [one/three]; and
 (ii) the seat, or legal place, of the arbitration shall be [City and/or Country]."

---

* Reproduced with the permission of the LCIA.

D. Arbitration under the UNCITRAL Rules

"Any dispute arising out of or in connection with this contract, including any question regarding its existence, validity or termination, shall be referred to and finally resolved by arbitration under the UNCITRAL Arbitration Rules, which Rules are deemed to be incorporated by reference into this clause.

Any arbitration commenced pursuant to this clause shall be administered by the LCIA.

The appointing authority shall be the LCIA.

The LCIA schedule of fees and costs shall apply,

The number of arbitrators shall be [one/three].

The seat, or legal place of arbitration shall be [City and/or Country].

The language to be used in the arbitral proceedings shall be [   ].

The governing law of the contract shall be the substantive law of [   ]."

Modification to Recommended Clauses

The LCIA Secretariat will be pleased to discuss any modifications to these standard clauses. For example, to provide for party nomination of arbitrators or for expedited procedures.

Existing Disputes

If a dispute has already arisen, but there is no agreement between the parties to mediate and/or to arbitrate, the parties may enter into an agreement for those purposes. In such cases, please contact the LCIA Secretariat if recommended wording is required.

APPENDIX 2

LCIA Arbitration Rules[*]

Effective 1 January 1998

Where any agreement, submission or reference provides in writing and in whatsoever manner for arbitration under the rules of the LCIA or by the Court of the LCIA ("the LCIA Court"), the parties shall be taken to have agreed in writing that the arbitration shall be conducted in accordance with the following rules ("the Rules") or such amended rules as the LCIA may have adopted hereafter to take effect before the commencement of the arbitration. The Rules include the Schedule of Costs in effect at the commencement of the arbitration, as separately amended from time to time by the LCIA Court.

CONTENTS

Article 1	The Request for Arbitration
Article 2	The Response
Article 3	The LCIA Court and Registrar
Article 4	Notices and Periods of Time
Article 5	Formation of the Arbitral Tribunal
Article 6	Nationality of Arbitrators
Article 7	Party and Other Nominations
Article 8	Three or More Parties
Article 9	Expedited Formation
Article 10	Revocation of Arbitrator's Appointment
Article 11	Nomination and Replacement Arbitrators
Article 12	Majority Power to Continue Proceedings
Article 13	Communications
Article 14	Conduct of the Proceedings
Article 15	Submission of Written Statements and Documents
Article 16	Seat of Arbitration and Place of Hearings
Article 17	Language of Arbitration
Article 18	Party Representation
Article 19	Hearings
Article 20	Witnesses
Article 21	Experts to the Arbitral Tribunal
Article 22	Additional Powers of the Arbitral Tribunal
Article 23	Jurisdiction of the Arbitral Tribunal
Article 24	Deposits
Article 25	Interim and Conservatory Measures
Article 26	The Award
Article 27	Correction of Awards and Additional Awards
Article 28	Arbitration and Legal Costs
Article 29	Decisions by the LCIA Court

---

[*] Reproduced with the permission of the LCIA.

Article 30   Confidentiality
Article 31   Exclusion of Liability
Article 32   General Rules

Article 1
The Request for Arbitration

1.1 Any party wishing to commence an arbitration under these Rules ("the Claimant") shall send to the Registrar of the LCIA Court ("the Registrar") a written request for arbitration ("the Request"), containing or accompanied by:

(a) the names, addresses, telephone, facsimile, telex and e-mail numbers (if known) of the parties to the arbitration and of their legal representatives;

(b) a copy of the written arbitration clause or separate written arbitration agreement invoked by the Claimant ("the Arbitration Agreement"), together with a copy of the contractual documentation in which the arbitration clause is contained or in respect of which the arbitration arises;

(c) a brief statement describing the nature and circumstances of the dispute, and specifying the claims advanced by the Claimant against another party to the arbitration ("the Respondent");

(d) a statement of any matters (such as the seat or language(s) of the arbitration, or the number of arbitrators, or their qualifications or identities) on which the parties have already agreed in writing for the arbitration or in respect of which the Claimant wishes to make a proposal;

(e) if the Arbitration Agreement calls for party nomination of arbitrators, the name, address, telephone, facsimile, telex and e-mail numbers (if known) of the Claimant's nominee;

(f) the fee prescribed in the Schedule of Costs (without which the Request shall be treated as not having been received by the Registrar and the arbitration as not having been commenced);

(g) confirmation to the Registrar that copies of the Request (including all accompanying documents) have been or are being served simultaneously on all other parties to the arbitration by one or more means of service to be identified in such confirmation.

1.2 The date of receipt by the Registrar of the Request shall be treated as the date on which the arbitration has commenced for all purposes. The Request (including all accompanying documents) should be submitted to the Registrar in two copies where a sole arbitrator should be appointed, or, if the parties have agreed or the Claimant considers that three arbitrators should be appointed, in four copies.

Article 2
The Response

2.1 Within 30 days of service of the Request on the Respondent, (or such lesser period fixed by the LCIA Court), the Respondent shall send to the Registrar a written response to the Request ("the Response"), containing or accompanied by:

(a) confirmation or denial of all or part of the claims advanced by the Claimant in the Request;

(b) a brief statement describing the nature and circumstances of any counterclaims advanced by the Respondent against the Claimant;

(c) comment in response to any statements contained in the Request, as called for under Article 1.1(d), on matters relating to the conduct of the arbitration;

(d) if the Arbitration Agreement calls for party nomination of arbitrators, the name, address, telephone, facsimile, telex and e-mail numbers (if known) of the Respondent's nominee; and

(e) confirmation to the Registrar that copies of the Response (including all accompanying documents) have been or are being served simultaneously on all other parties to the arbitration by one or more means of service to be identified in such confirmation.

2.2 The Response (including all accompanying documents) should be submitted to the Registrar in two copies, or if the parties have agreed or the Respondent considers that three arbitrators should be appointed, in four copies.

2.3 Failure to send a Response shall not preclude the Respondent from denying any claim or from advancing a counterclaim in the arbitration. However, if the Arbitration Agreement calls for party nomination of arbitrators, failure to send a Response or to nominate an arbitrator within time or at all shall constitute an irrevocable waiver of that party's opportunity to nominate an arbitrator.

Article 3
The LCIA Court and Registrar

3.1 The functions of the LCIA Court under these Rules shall be performed in its name by the President or a Vice-President of the LCIA Court or by a division of three or five members of the LCIA Court appointed by the President or a Vice-President of the LCIA Court, as determined by the President.

3.2 The functions of the Registrar under these Rules shall be performed by the Registrar or any deputy Registrar of the LCIA Court under the supervision of the LCIA Court.

3.3 All communications from any party or arbitrator to the LCIA Court shall be addressed to the Registrar.

Article 4
Notices and Periods of Time

4.1 Any notice or other communication that may be or is required to be given by a party under these Rules shall be in writing and shall be delivered by registered postal or courier service or transmitted by facsimile, telex, e-mail or any other means of telecommunication that provide a record of its transmission.

4.2 A party's last-known residence or place of business during the arbitration shall be a valid address for the purpose of any notice or other communication in the absence of any notification of a change to such address by that party to the other parties, the Arbitral Tribunal and the Registrar.

4.3 For the purpose of determining the date of commencement of a time limit, a notice or other communication shall be treated as having been received on the day it is delivered or, in the case of telecommunications, transmitted in accordance with Articles 4.1 and 4.2.

4.4 For the purpose of determining compliance with a time limit, a notice or other communication shall be treated as having been sent, made or transmitted if it is dispatched in accordance with Articles 4.1 and 4.2 prior to or on the date of the expiration of the time-limit.

4.5 Notwithstanding the above, any notice or communication by one party may be addressed to another party in the manner agreed in writing between them or, failing such agreement, according to the practice followed in the course of their previous dealings or in whatever manner ordered by the Arbitral Tribunal.

4.6 For the purpose of calculating a period of time under these Rules, such period shall begin to run on the day following the day when a notice or other communication is received. If the last day of such period is an official holiday or a non-business day at the residence or place of business of the addressee, the period is extended until the first business day which follows. Official holidays or non-business days occurring during the running of the period of time are included in calculating that period.

4.7 The Arbitral Tribunal may at any time extend (even where the period of time has expired) or abridge any period of time prescribed under these Rules or under the Arbitration Agreement for the conduct of the arbitration, including any notice or communication to be served by one party on any other party.

Article 5
Formation of the Arbitral Tribunal

5.1 The expression "the Arbitral Tribunal" in these Rules includes a sole arbitrator or all the arbitrators where more than one. All references to an arbitrator shall include the masculine and feminine. (References to the President, Vice-President and members of the LCIA Court, the Registrar or deputy Registrar, expert, witness, party and legal representative shall be similarly understood).

5.2 All arbitrators conducting an arbitration under these Rules shall be and remain at all times impartial and independent of the parties; and none shall act in the arbitration as advocates for any party. No arbitrator, whether before or after appointment, shall advise any party on the merits or outcome of the dispute.

5.3 Before appointment by the LCIA Court, each arbitrator shall furnish to the Registrar a written resume of his past and present professional positions; he shall agree in writing upon fee rates conforming to the Schedule of Costs; and he shall sign a declaration to the effect that there are no circumstances known to him likely to give rise to any justified doubts as to his impartiality or independence, other than any circumstances disclosed by him in the declaration. Each arbitrator shall thereby also assume a continuing duty forthwith to disclose any such circumstances to the LCIA Court, to any other members of the Arbitral Tribunal and to all the parties if such circumstances should arise after the date of such declaration and before the arbitration is concluded.

5.4 The LCIA Court shall appoint the Arbitral Tribunal as soon as practicable after receipt by the Registrar of the Response or after the expiry of 30 days following service of the Request upon the Respondent if no Response is received by the Registrar (or such lesser period fixed by the LCIA Court). The LCIA Court may proceed with the formation of the Arbitral Tribunal notwithstanding that the Request is incomplete or the Response is missing, late or incomplete. A sole arbitrator shall be appointed unless the parties have agreed in writing otherwise, or unless the LCIA Court determines that in view of all the circumstances of the case a three-member tribunal is appropriate.

5.5 The LCIA Court alone is empowered to appoint arbitrators. The LCIA Court will appoint arbitrators with due regard for any particular method or criteria of selection agreed in writing by the parties. In selecting arbitrators consideration will be given to the nature of the transaction, the nature and circumstances of the dispute, the nationality, location and languages of the parties and (if more than two) the number of parties.

5.6 In the case of a three-member Arbitral Tribunal, the chairman (who will not be a party-nominated arbitrator) shall be appointed by the LCIA Court.

Article 6
Nationality of Arbitrators

6.1 Where the parties are of different nationalities, a sole arbitrator or chairman of the Arbitral Tribunal shall not have the same nationality as any party unless the parties who are not of the same nationality as the proposed appointee all agree in writing otherwise.

6.2 The nationality of parties shall be understood to include that of controlling shareholders or interests.

6.3 For the purpose of this Article, a person who is a citizen of two or more states shall be treated as a national of each state; and citizens of the European Union shall be treated as nationals of its different Member States and shall not be treated as having the same nationality.

Article 7
Party and Other Nominations

7.1 If the parties have agreed that any arbitrator is to be appointed by one or more of them or by any third person, that agreement shall be treated as an agreement to nominate an arbitrator for

242

all purposes. Such nominee may only be appointed by the LCIA Court as arbitrator subject to his prior compliance with Article 5.3. The LCIA Court may refuse to appoint any such nominee if it determines that he is not suitable or independent or impartial.

7.2 Where the parties have howsoever agreed that the Respondent or any third person is to nominate an arbitrator and such nomination is not made within time or at all, the LCIA Court may appoint an arbitrator notwithstanding the absence of the nomination and without regard to any late nomination. Likewise, if the Request for Arbitration does not contain a nomination by the Claimant where the parties have howsoever agreed that the Claimant or a third person is to nominate an arbitrator, the LCIA Court may appoint an arbitrator notwithstanding the absence of the nomination and without regard to any late nomination.

Article 8
Three or More Parties

8.1 Where the Arbitration Agreement entitles each party howsoever to nominate an arbitrator, the parties to the dispute number more than two and such parties have not all agreed in writing that the disputant parties represent two separate sides for the formation of the Arbitral Tribunal as Claimant and Respondent respectively, the LCIA Court shall appoint the Arbitral Tribunal without regard to any party's nomination.

8.2 In such circumstances, the Arbitration Agreement shall be treated for all purposes as a written agreement by the parties for the appointment of the Arbitral Tribunal by the LCIA Court.

Article 9
Expedited Formation

9.1 In exceptional urgency, on or after the commencement of the arbitration, any party may apply to the LCIA Court for the expedited formation of the Arbitral Tribunal, including the appointment of any replacement arbitrator under Articles 10 and 11 of these Rules.

9.2 Such an application shall be made in writing to the LCIA Court, copied to all other parties to the arbitration; and it shall set out the specific grounds for exceptional urgency in the formation of the Arbitral Tribunal.

9.3 The LCIA Court may, in its complete discretion, abridge or curtail any time-limit under these Rules for the formation of the Arbitral Tribunal, including service of the Response and of any matters or documents adjudged to be missing from the Request. The LCIA Court shall not be entitled to abridge or curtail any other time-limit.

Article 10
Revocation of Arbitrator's Appointment

10.1 If either (a) any arbitrator gives written notice of his desire to resign as arbitrator to the LCIA Court, to be copied to the parties and the other arbitrators (if any) or (b) any arbitrator dies, falls seriously ill, refuses, or becomes unable or unfit to act, either upon challenge by a party or at the request of the remaining arbitrators, the LCIA Court may revoke that arbitrator's appointment and appoint another arbitrator. The LCIA Court shall decide upon the amount of fees and expenses to be paid for the former arbitrator's services (if any) as it may consider appropriate in all the circumstances.

10.2 If any arbitrator acts in deliberate violation of the Arbitration Agreement (including these Rules) or does not act fairly and impartially as between the parties or does not conduct or participate in the arbitration proceedings with reasonable diligence, avoiding unnecessary delay or expense, that arbitrator may be considered unfit in the opinion of the LCIA Court.

10.3 An arbitrator may also be challenged by any party if circumstances exist that give rise to justifiable doubts as to his impartiality or independence. A party may challenge an arbitrator it has nominated, or in whose appointment it has participated, only for reasons of which it becomes aware after the appointment has been made.

10.4 A party who intends to challenge an arbitrator shall, within 15 days of the formation of the Arbitral Tribunal or (if later) after becoming aware of any circumstances referred to in Article 10.1, 10.2 or 10.3, send a written statement of the reasons for its challenge to the LCIA Court, the Arbitral Tribunal and all other parties. Unless the challenged arbitrator withdraws or all other parties agree to the challenge within 15 days of receipt of the written statement, the LCIA Court shall decide on the challenge.

Article 11
Nomination and Replacement of Arbitrators

11.1 In the event that the LCIA Court determines that any nominee is not suitable or independent or impartial or if an appointed arbitrator is to be replaced for any reason, the LCIA Court shall have a complete discretion to decide whether or not to follow the original nominating process.

11.2 If the LCIA Court should so decide, any opportunity given to a party to make a renomination shall be waived if not exercised within 15 days (or such lesser time as the LCIA Court may fix), after which the LCIA Court shall appoint the replacement arbitrator.

Article 12
Majority Power to Continue Proceedings

12.1 If any arbitrator on a three-member Arbitral Tribunal refuses or persistently fails to participate in its deliberations, the two other arbitrators shall have the power, upon their written notice of such refusal or failure to the LCIA Court, the parties and the third arbitrator, to continue the arbitration (including the making of any decision, ruling or award), notwithstanding the absence of the third arbitrator.

12.2 In determining whether to continue the arbitration, the two other arbitrators shall take into account the stage of the arbitration, any explanation made by the third arbitrator for his non-participation and such other matters as they consider appropriate in the circumstances of the case. The reasons for such determination shall be stated in any award, order or other decision made by the two arbitrators without the participation of the third arbitrator.

12.3 In the event that the two other arbitrators determine at any time not to continue the arbitration without the participation of the third arbitrator missing from their deliberations, the two arbitrators shall notify in writing the parties and the LCIA Court of such determination; and in that event, the two arbitrators or any party may refer the matter to the LCIA Court for the revocation of that third arbitrator's appointment and his replacement under Article 10.

Article 13
Communications between Parties and the Arbitral Tribunal

13.1 Until the Arbitral Tribunal is formed, all communications between parties and arbitrators shall be made through the Registrar.

13.2 Thereafter, unless and until the Arbitral Tribunal directs that communications shall take place directly between the Arbitral Tribunal and the parties (with simultaneous copies to the Registrar), all written communications between the parties and the Arbitral Tribunal shall continue to be made through the Registrar.

13.3 Where the Registrar sends any written communication to one party on behalf of the Arbitral Tribunal, he shall send a copy to each of the other parties. Where any party sends to the Registrar any communication (including Written Statements and Documents under Article 15), it shall include a copy for each arbitrator; and it shall also send copies direct to all other parties and confirm to the Registrar in writing that it has done or is doing so.

Article 14
Conduct of the Proceedings

14.1 The parties may agree on the conduct of their arbitral proceedings and they are encouraged to do so, consistent with the Arbitral Tribunal's general duties at all times:
- (i) to act fairly and impartially as between all parties, giving each a reasonable opportunity of putting its case and dealing with that of its opponent; and
- (ii) to adopt procedures suitable to the circumstances of the arbitration, avoiding unnecessary delay or expense, so as to provide a fair and efficient means for the final resolution of the parties' dispute.

Such agreements shall be made by the parties in writing or recorded in writing by the Arbitral Tribunal at the request of and with the authority of the parties.

14.2 Unless otherwise agreed by the parties under Article 14.1, the Arbitral Tribunal shall have the widest discretion to discharge its duties allowed under such law(s) or rules of law as the Arbitral Tribunal may determine to be applicable; and at all times the parties shall do everything necessary for the fair, efficient and expeditious conduct of the arbitration.

14.3 In the case of a three-member Arbitral Tribunal the chairman may, with the prior consent of the other two arbitrators, make procedural rulings alone.

Article 15
Submission of Written Statements and Documents

15.1 Unless the parties have agreed otherwise under Article 14.1 or the Arbitral Tribunal should determine differently, the written stage of the proceedings shall be as set out below.

15.2 Within 30 days of receipt of written notification from the Registrar of the formation of the Arbitral Tribunal, the Claimant shall send to the Registrar a Statement of Case setting out in sufficient detail the facts and any contentions of law on which it relies, together with the relief claimed against all other parties, save and insofar as such matters have not been set out in its Request.

15.3 Within 30 days of receipt of the Statement of Case or written notice from the Claimant that it elects to treat the Request as its Statement of Case, the Respondent shall send to the Registrar a Statement of Defence setting out in sufficient detail which of the facts and contentions of law in the Statement of Case or Request (as the case may be) it admits or denies, on what grounds and on what other facts and contentions of law it relies. Any counterclaims shall be submitted with the Statement of Defence in the same manner as claims are to be set out in the Statement of Case.

15.4 Within 30 days of receipt of the Statement of Defence, the Claimant shall send to the Registrar a Statement of Reply which, where there are any counterclaims, shall include a Defence to Counterclaim in the same manner as a defence is to be set out in the Statement of Defence.

15.5 If the Statement of Reply contains a Defence to Counterclaim, within 30 days of its receipt the Respondent shall send to the Registrar a Statement of Reply to Counterclaim.

15.6 All Statements referred to in this Article shall be accompanied by copies (or, if they are especially voluminous, lists) of all essential documents on which the party concerned relies and which have not previously been submitted by any party, and (where appropriate) by any relevant samples and exhibits.

15.7 As soon as practicable following receipt of the Statements specified in this Article, the Arbitral Tribunal shall proceed in such manner as has been agreed in writing by the parties or pursuant to its authority under these Rules.

15.8 If the Respondent fails to submit a Statement of Defence or the Claimant a Statement of Defence to Counterclaim, or if at any point any party fails to avail itself of the opportunity to present its case in the manner determined by Article 15.2 to 15.6 or directed by the Arbitral Tribunal, the Arbitral Tribunal may nevertheless proceed with the arbitration and make an award.

Article 16
Seat of Arbitration and Place of Hearings

16.1 The parties may agree in writing the seat (or legal place) of their arbitration. Failing such a choice, the seat of arbitration shall be London, unless and until the LCIA Court determines in view of all the circumstances, and after having given the parties an opportunity to make written comment, that another seat is more appropriate.

16.2 The Arbitral Tribunal may hold hearings, meetings and deliberations at any convenient geographical place in its discretion; and if elsewhere than the seat of the arbitration, the arbitration shall be treated as an arbitration conducted at the seat of the arbitration and any award as an award made at the seat of the arbitration for all purposes.

16.3 The law applicable to the arbitration (if any) shall be the arbitration law of the seat of arbitration, unless and to the extent that the parties have expressly agreed in writing on the application of another arbitration law and such agreement is not prohibited by the law of the arbitral seat.

Article 17
Language of Arbitration

17.1 The initial language of the arbitration shall be the language of the Arbitration Agreement, unless the parties have agreed in writing otherwise and providing always that a non-participating or defaulting party shall have no cause for complaint if communications to and from the Registrar and the arbitration proceedings are conducted in English.

17.2 In the event that the Arbitration Agreement is written in more than one language, the LCIA Court may, unless the Arbitration Agreement provides that the arbitration proceedings shall be conducted in more than one language, decide which of those languages shall be the initial language of the arbitration.

17.3 Upon the formation of the Arbitral Tribunal and unless the parties have agreed upon the language or languages of the arbitration, the Arbitration Tribunal shall decide upon the language(s) of the arbitration, after giving the parties an opportunity to make written comment and taking into account the initial language of the arbitration and any other matter it may consider appropriate in all the circumstances of the case.

17.4 If any document is expressed in a language other than the language(s) of the arbitration and no translation of such document is submitted by the party relying upon the document, the Arbitral Tribunal or (if the Arbitral Tribunal has not been formed) the LCIA Court may order that party to submit a translation in a form to be determined by the Arbitral Tribunal or the LCIA Court, as the case may be.

Article 18
Party Representation

18.1 Any party may be represented by legal practitioners or any other representatives.

18.2 At any time the Arbitral Tribunal may require from any party proof of authority granted to its representative(s) in such form as the Arbitral Tribunal may determine.

Article 19
Hearings

19.1 Any party which expresses a desire to that effect has the right to be heard orally before the Arbitral Tribunal on the merits of the dispute, unless the parties have agreed in writing on documents-only arbitration.

19.2 The Arbitral Tribunal shall fix the date, time and physical place of any meetings and hearings in the arbitration, and shall give the parties reasonable notice thereof.

19.3 The Arbitral Tribunal may in advance of any hearing submit to the parties a list of questions which it wishes them to answer with special attention.

19.4 All meetings and hearings shall be in private unless the parties agree otherwise in writing or the Arbitral Tribunal directs otherwise.

19.5 The Arbitral Tribunal shall have the fullest authority to establish time-limits for meetings and hearings, or for any parts thereof.

Article 20
Witnesses

20.1 Before any hearing, the Arbitral Tribunal may require any party to give notice of the identity of each witness that party wishes to call (including rebuttal witnesses), as well as the subject matter of that witness's testimony, its content and its relevance to the issues in the arbitration.

20.2 The Arbitral Tribunal may also determine the time, manner and form in which such materials should be exchanged between the parties and presented to the Arbitral Tribunal; and it has a discretion to allow, refuse, or limit the appearance of witnesses (whether witness of fact or expert witness).

20.3 Subject to any order otherwise by the Arbitral Tribunal, the testimony of a witness may be presented by a party in written form, either as a signed statement or as a sworn affidavit.

20.4 Subject to Article 14.1 and 14.2, any party may request that a witness, on whose testimony another party seeks to rely, should attend for oral questioning at a hearing before the Arbitral Tribunal. If the Arbitral Tribunal orders that other party to produce the witness and the witness fails to attend the oral hearing without good cause, the Arbitral Tribunal may place such weight on the written testimony (or exclude the same altogether) as it considers appropriate in the circumstances of the case.

20.5 Any witness who gives oral evidence at a hearing before the Arbitral Tribunal may be questioned by each of the parties under the control of the Arbitral Tribunal. The Arbitral Tribunal may put questions at any stage of his evidence.

20.6 Subject to the mandatory provisions of any applicable law, it shall not be improper for any party or its legal representatives to interview any witness or potential witness for the purpose of presenting his testimony in written form or producing him as an oral witness.

20.7 Any individual intending to testify to the Arbitral Tribunal on any issue of fact or expertise shall be treated as a witness under these Rules notwithstanding that the individual is a party to the arbitration or was or is an officer, employee or shareholder of any party.

Article 21
Experts to the Arbitral Tribunal

21.1 Unless otherwise agreed by the parties in writing, the Arbitral Tribunal:

(a) may appoint one or more experts to report to the Arbitral Tribunal on specific issues, who shall be and remain impartial and independent of the parties throughout the arbitration proceedings; and

(b) may require a party to give any such expert any relevant information or to provide access to any relevant documents, goods, samples, property or site for inspection by the expert.

21.2 Unless otherwise agreed by the parties in writing, if a party so requests or if the Arbitral Tribunal considers it necessary, the expert shall, after delivery of his written or oral report to the Arbitral Tribunal and the parties, participate in one or more hearings at which the parties shall have the opportunity to question the expert on his report and to present expert witnesses in order to testify on the points at issue.

21.3 The fees and expenses of any expert appointed by the Arbitral Tribunal under this Article shall be paid out of the deposits payable by the parties under Article 24 and shall form part of the costs of the arbitration.

Article 22
Additional Powers of the Arbitral Tribunal

22.1 Unless the parties at any time agree otherwise in writing, the Arbitral Tribunal shall have the power, on the application of any party or of its own motion, but in either case only after giving the parties a reasonable opportunity to state their views:

(a) to allow any party, upon such terms (as to costs and otherwise) as it shall determine, to amend any claim, counterclaim, defence and reply;

(b) to extend or abbreviate any time-limit provided by the Arbitration Agreement or these Rules for the conduct of the arbitration or by the Arbitral Tribunal's own orders;

(c) to conduct such enquiries as may appear to the Arbitral Tribunal to be necessary or expedient, including whether and to what extent the Arbitral Tribunal should itself take the initiative in identifying the issues and ascertaining the relevant facts and the law(s) or rules of law applicable to the arbitration, the merits of the parties' dispute and the Arbitration Agreement;

(d) to order any party to make any property, site or thing under its control and relating to the subject matter of the arbitration available for inspection by the Arbitral Tribunal, any other party, its expert or any expert to the Arbitral Tribunal;

(e) to order any party to produce to the Arbitral Tribunal, and to the other parties for inspection, and to supply copies of, any documents or classes of documents in their possession, custody or power which the Arbitral Tribunal determines to be relevant;

(f) to decide whether or not to apply any strict rules of evidence (or any other rules) as to the admissibility, relevance or weight of any material tendered by a party on any matter of fact or expert opinion; and to determine the time, manner and form in which such material should be exchanged between the parties and presented to the Arbitral Tribunal;

(g) to order the correction of any contract between the parties or the Arbitration Agreement, but only to the extent required to rectify any mistake which the Arbitral Tribunal determines to be common to the parties and then only if and to the extent to which the law(s) or rules of law applicable to the contract or Arbitration Agreement permit such correction; and

(h) to allow, only upon the application of a party, one or more third persons to be joined in the arbitration as a party provided any such third person and the applicant party have consented thereto in writing, and thereafter to make a single final award, or separate awards, in respect of all parties so implicated in the arbitration;

22.2 By agreeing to arbitration under these Rules, the parties shall be treated as having agreed not to apply to any state court or other judicial authority for any order available from the Arbitral Tribunal under Article 22.1, except with the agreement in writing of all parties.

22.3 The Arbitral Tribunal shall decide the parties' dispute in accordance with the law(s) or rules of law chosen by the parties as applicable to the merits of their dispute. If and to the extent that the Arbitral Tribunal determines that the parties have made no such choice, the Arbitral Tribunal shall apply the law(s) or rules of law which it considers appropriate.

22.4 The Arbitral Tribunal shall only apply to the merits of the dispute principles deriving from "ex aequo et bono", "amiable composition" or "honourable engagement" where the parties have so agreed expressly in writing.

Article 23
Jurisdiction of the Arbitral Tribunal

23.1 The Arbitral Tribunal shall have the power to rule on its own jurisdiction, including any objection to the initial or continuing existence, validity or effectiveness of the Arbitration Agreement. For that purpose, an arbitration clause which forms or was intended to form part of another agreement shall be treated as an arbitration agreement independent of that other agreement. A decision by the Arbitral Tribunal that such other agreement is non-existent, invalid or ineffective shall not entail ipso jure the non-existence, invalidity or ineffectiveness of the arbitration clause.

23.2 A plea by a Respondent that the Arbitral Tribunal does not have jurisdiction shall be treated as having been irrevocably waived unless it is raised not later than the Statement of Defence; and a like plea by a Respondent to Counterclaim shall be similarly treated unless it is raised no later than the Statement of Defence to Counterclaim. A plea that the Arbitral Tribunal is exceeding the scope of its authority shall be raised promptly after the Arbitral Tribunal has indicated its intention to decide on the matter alleged by any party to be beyond the scope of its authority, failing which such plea shall also be treated as having been waived irrevocably. In any case, the Arbitral Tribunal may nevertheless admit an untimely plea if it considers the delay justified in the particular circumstances.

23.3 The Arbitral Tribunal may determine the plea to its jurisdiction or authority in an award as to jurisdiction or later in an award on the merits, as it considers appropriate in the circumstances.

23.4 By agreeing to arbitration under these Rules, the parties shall be treated as having agreed not to apply to any state court or other judicial authority for any relief regarding the Arbitral Tribunal's jurisdiction or authority, except with the agreement in writing of all parties to the arbitration or the prior authorisation of the Arbitral Tribunal or following the latter's award ruling on the objection to its jurisdiction or authority.

Article 24
Deposits

24.1 The LCIA Court may direct the parties, in such proportions as it thinks appropriate, to make one or several interim or final payments on account of the costs of the arbitration. Such deposits shall be made to and held by the LCIA and from time to time may be released by the LCIA Court to the arbitrator(s), any expert appointed by the Arbitral Tribunal and the LCIA itself as the arbitration progresses.

24.2 The Arbitral Tribunal shall not proceed with the arbitration without ascertaining at all times from the Registrar or any deputy Registrar that the LCIA is in requisite funds.

24.3 In the event that a party fails or refuses to provide any deposit as directed by the LCIA Court, the LCIA Court may direct the other party or parties to effect a substitute payment to allow the arbitration to proceed (subject to any award on costs). In such circumstances, the party paying the substitute payment shall be entitled to recover that amount as a debt immediately due from the defaulting party.

24.4 Failure by a claimant or counterclaiming party to provide promptly and in full the required deposit may be treated by the LCIA Court and the Arbitral Tribunal as a withdrawal of the claim or counterclaim respectively.

Article 25
Interim and Conservatory Measures

25.1 The Arbitral Tribunal shall have the power, unless otherwise agreed by the parties in writing, on the application of any party:

(a) to order any respondent party to a claim or counterclaim to provide security for all or part of the amount in dispute, by way of deposit or bank guarantee or in any other manner and upon such terms as the Arbitral Tribunal considers appropriate. Such terms may include the provision by the claiming or counterclaiming party of a cross-indemnity, itself secured in such manner as the Arbitral Tribunal considers appropriate, for any costs or losses incurred by such respondent in providing security. The amount of any costs and losses payable under such cross-indemnity may be determined by the Arbitral Tribunal in one or more awards;

(b) to order the preservation, storage, sale or other disposal of any property or thing under the control of any party and relating to the subject matter of the arbitration; and

(c) to order on a provisional basis, subject to final determination in an award, any relief which the Arbitral Tribunal would have power to grant in an award, including a provisional order for the payment of money or the disposition of property as between any parties.

25.2 The Arbitral Tribunal shall have the power, upon the application of a party, to order any claiming or counterclaiming party to provide security for the legal or other costs of any other party by way of deposit or bank guarantee or in any other manner and upon such terms as the Arbitral Tribunal considers appropriate. Such terms may include the provision by that other party of a cross-indemnity, itself secured in such manner as the Arbitral Tribunal considers appropriate, for any costs and losses incurred by such claimant or counterclaimant in providing security. The amount of any costs and losses payable under such cross-indemnity may be determined by the Arbitral Tribunal in one or more awards. In the event that a claiming or counterclaiming party does not comply with any order to provide security, the Arbitral Tribunal may stay that party's claims or counterclaims or dismiss them in an award.

25.3 The power of the Arbitral Tribunal under Article 25.1 shall not prejudice howsoever any party's right to apply to any state court or other judicial authority for interim or conservatory measures before the formation of the Arbitral Tribunal and, in exceptional cases, thereafter. Any application and any order for such measures after the formation of the Arbitral Tribunal shall be promptly communicated by the applicant to the Arbitral Tribunal and all other parties. However, by agreeing to arbitration under these Rules, the parties shall be taken to have agreed not to apply to any state court or other judicial authority for any order for security for its legal or other costs available from the Arbitral Tribunal under Article 25.2.

Article 26
The Award

26.1 The Arbitral Tribunal shall make its award in writing and, unless all parties agree in writing otherwise, shall state the reasons upon which its award is based. The award shall also state the date when the award is made and the seat of the arbitration; and it shall be signed by the Arbitral Tribunal or those of its members assenting to it.

26.2 If any arbitrator fails to comply with the mandatory provisions of any applicable law relating to the making of the award, having been given a reasonable opportunity to do so, the remaining arbitrators may proceed in his absence and state in their award the circumstances of the other arbitrator's failure to participate in the making of the award.

26.3 Where there are three arbitrators and the Arbitral Tribunal fails to agree on any issue, the arbitrators shall decide that issue by a majority. Failing a majority decision on any issue, the chairman of the Arbitral Tribunal shall decide that issue.

26.4 If any arbitrator refuses or fails to sign the award, the signatures of the majority or (failing a majority) of the chairman shall be sufficient, provided that the reason for the omitted signature is stated in the award by the majority or chairman.

26.5 The sole arbitrator or chairman shall be responsible for delivering the award to the LCIA Court, which shall transmit certified copies to the parties provided that the costs of arbitration have been paid to the LCIA in accordance with Article 28.

26.6 An award may be expressed in any currency. The Arbitral Tribunal may order that simple or compound interest shall be paid by any party on any sum awarded at such rates as the Arbitral Tribunal determines to be appropriate, without being bound by legal rates of interest imposed by any state court, in respect of any period which the Arbitral Tribunal determines to be appropriate ending not later than the date upon which the award is complied with.

26.7 The Arbitral Tribunal may make separate awards on different issues at different times. Such awards shall have the same status and effect as any other award made by the Arbitral Tribunal.

26.8 In the event of a settlement of the parties' dispute, the Arbitral Tribunal may render an award recording the settlement if the parties so request in writing (a "Consent Award"), provided always that such award contains an express statement that it is an award made by the parties' consent. A Consent Award need not contain reasons. If the parties do not require a consent award, then on written confirmation by the parties to the LCIA Court that a settlement has been reached, the Arbitral Tribunal shall be discharged and the arbitration proceedings concluded, subject to payment by the parties of any outstanding costs of the arbitration under Article 28.

26.9 All awards shall be final and binding on the parties. By agreeing to arbitration under these Rules, the parties undertake to carry out any award immediately and without any delay (subject only to Article 27); and the parties also waive irrevocably their right to any form of appeal, review or recourse to any state court or other judicial authority, insofar as such waiver may be validly made.

Article 27
Correction of Awards and Additional Awards

27.1 Within 30 days of receipt of any award, or such lesser period as may be agreed in writing by the parties, a party may by written notice to the Registrar (copied to all other parties) request the Arbitral Tribunal to correct in the award any errors in computation, clerical or typographical errors or any errors of a similar nature. If the Arbitral Tribunal considers the request to be justified, it shall make the corrections within 30 days of receipt of the request. Any correction shall take the form of separate memorandum dated and signed by the Arbitral Tribunal or (if three arbitrators) those of its members assenting to it; and such memorandum shall become part of the award for all purposes.

27.2 The Arbitral Tribunal may likewise correct any error of the nature described in Article 27.1 on its own initiative within 30 days of the date of the award, to the same effect.

27.3 Within 30 days of receipt of the final award, a party may by written notice to the Registrar (copied to all other parties), request the Arbitral Tribunal to make an additional award as to claims or counterclaims presented in the arbitration but not determined in any award. If the Arbitral Tribunal considers the request to be justified, it shall make the additional award within 60 days of receipt of the request. The provisions of Article 26 shall apply to any additional award.

Article 28
Arbitration and Legal Costs

28.1 The costs of the arbitration (other than the legal or other costs incurred by the parties themselves) shall be determined by the LCIA Court in accordance with the Schedule of Costs. The parties shall be jointly and severally liable to the Arbitral Tribunal and the LCIA for such arbitration costs.

28.2 The Arbitral Tribunal shall specify in the award the total amount of the costs of the arbitration as determined by the LCIA Court. Unless the parties agree otherwise in writing, the Arbitral Tribunal shall determine the proportions in which the parties shall bear all or part of such arbitration costs. If the Arbitral Tribunal has determined that all or any part of the arbitration costs shall be borne by a party other than a party which has already paid them to the LCIA, the latter party shall have the right to recover the appropriate amount from the former party.

28.3 The Arbitral Tribunal shall also have the power to order in its award that all or part of the legal or other costs incurred by a party be paid by another party, unless the parties agree otherwise in writing. The Arbitral Tribunal shall determine and fix the amount of each item comprising such costs on such reasonable basis as it thinks fit.

28.4 Unless the parties otherwise agree in writing, the Arbitral Tribunal shall make its orders on both arbitration and legal costs on the general principle that costs should reflect the parties' relative success and failure in the award or arbitration, except where it appears to the Arbitral

Tribunal that in the particular circumstances this general approach is inappropriate. Any order for costs shall be made with reasons in the award containing such order.

28.5 If the arbitration is abandoned, suspended or concluded, by agreement or otherwise, before the final award is made, the parties shall remain jointly and severally liable to pay to the LCIA and the Arbitral Tribunal the costs of the arbitration as determined by the LCIA Court in accordance with the Schedule of Costs. In the event that such arbitration costs are less than the deposits made by the parties, there shall be a refund by the LCIA in such proportion as the parties may agree in writing, or failing such agreement, in the same proportions as the deposits were made by the parties to the LCIA.

Article 29
Decisions by the LCIA Court

29.1 The decisions of the LCIA Court with respect to all matters relating to the arbitration shall be conclusive and binding upon the parties and the Arbitral Tribunal. Such decisions are to be treated as administrative in nature and the LCIA Court shall not be required to give any reasons.

29.2 To the extent permitted by the law of the seat of the arbitration, the parties shall be taken to have waived any right of appeal or review in respect of any such decisions of the LCIA Court to any state court or other judicial authority. If such appeals or review remain possible due to mandatory provisions of any applicable law, the LCIA Court shall, subject to the provisions of that applicable law, decide whether the arbitral proceedings are to continue, notwithstanding an appeal or review.

Article 30
Confidentiality

30.1 Unless the parties expressly agree in writing to the contrary, the parties undertake as a general principle to keep confidential all awards in their arbitration, together with all materials in the proceedings created for the purpose of the arbitration and all other documents produced by another party in the proceedings not otherwise in the public domain - save and to the extent that disclosure may be required of a party by legal duty, to protect or pursue a legal right or to enforce or challenge an award in bona fide legal proceedings before a state court or other judicial authority.

30.2 The deliberations of the Arbitral Tribunal are likewise confidential to its members, save and to the extent that disclosure of an arbitrator's refusal to participate in the arbitration is required of the other members of the Arbitral Tribunal under Articles 10, 12 and 26.

30.3 The LCIA Court does not publish any award or any part of an award without the prior written consent of all parties and the Arbitral Tribunal.

Article 31
Exclusion of Liability

31.1 None of the LCIA, the LCIA Court (including its President, Vice-Presidents and individual members), the Registrar, any deputy Registrar, any arbitrator and any expert to the Arbitral Tribunal shall be liable to any party howsoever for any act or omission in connection with any arbitration conducted by reference to these Rules, save where the act or omission is shown by that party to constitute conscious and deliberate wrongdoing committed by the body or person alleged to be liable to that party.

31.2 After the award has been made and the possibilities of correction and additional awards referred to in Article 27 have lapsed or been exhausted, neither the LCIA, the LCIA Court (including its President, Vice-Presidents and individual members), the Registrar, any deputy Registrar, any arbitrator or expert to the Arbitral Tribunal shall be under any legal obligation to make any statement to any person about any matter concerning the arbitration, nor shall any party seek to make any of these persons a witness in any legal or other proceedings arising out of the arbitration.

Article 32
General Rules

32.1 A party who knows that any provision of the Arbitration Agreement (including these Rules) has not been complied with and yet proceeds with the arbitration without promptly stating its objection to such non-compliance, shall be treated as having irrevocably waived its right to object.

32.2 In all matters not expressly provided for in these Rules, the LCIA Court, the Arbitral Tribunal and the parties shall act in the spirit of these Rules and shall make every reasonable effort to ensure that an award is legally enforceable.

APPENDIX 3

Schedule of the LCIA's Arbitration‡
Fees and Costs

(EFFECTIVE 11 MAY 2007)

For all arbitrations in which the LCIA provides services, whether as administrator, or as appointing authority only, and whether under the LCIA Rules, UNCITRAL Rules or other, *ad hoc,* rules or procedures agreed by the parties to the arbitration.

1. Administrative charges under LCIA Rules, UNCITRAL Rules, or other, *ad hoc,* rules or procedures*

1(a) Registration Fee (payable in advance with Request for Arbitration non-refundable).

£1,500

1(b) Time spent** by the Secretariat of the LCIA in the administration of the arbitration.***

Registrar / Deputy Registrar / Counsel   **£200 per hour**
Other Secretariat personnel   **£100 per hour**

1(c) Time spent by members of the LCIA Court in carrying out their functions in deciding any challenge brought under the applicable rules.***

at hourly rates advised by members of the LCIA Court

1(d) A sum equivalent to 5% of the fees of the Tribunal (excluding expenses) in respect of the LCIA's general overhead.***

1(e) Expenses incurred by the Secretariat and by members of the LCIA Court, in connection with the arbitration (such as postage, telephone, facsimile, travel etc.), and additional arbitration support services, whether provided by the Secretariat or the members of the LCIA Court from their own resources or otherwise.***

at applicable hourly rates or at cost

1(f) The LCIA's fees and expenses will be invoiced in sterling, but may be paid in other convertible currencies, at rates prevailing at the time of payment, provided that any transfer and/or currency exchange charges shall be borne by the payer.

2. Request to act as Appointing Authority only*

2(a) Appointment Fee (payable in advance with request – non-refundable).   **£1,000**
2(b) As for 1(b) and 1(e), above.

3. Request to act in deciding challenges to arbitrators in non-LCIA arbitrations*

3(a) As for 2(a) and 2(b), above; plus

---

‡ Reproduced with the permission of the LCIA.
* Charges may be subject to Value Added Tax at the prevailing rate.
** Minimum unit of time in all cases: 15 minutes.
*** Items 1(b), 1(c), 1(d) and 1(e) above, are payable on interim invoice; with the award, or as directed by the LCIA Court under Article 24.1 of the Rules.

3(b) Time spent by members of the LCIA Court in carrying out their functions in deciding the challenge.

at hourly rates advised by members of the LCIA Court

4. Fees and expenses of the Tribunal*

4(a) The Tribunal's fees will be calculated by reference to work done by its members in connection with the arbitration and will be charged at rates appropriate to the particular circumstances of the case, including its complexity and the special qualifications of the arbitrators. The Tribunal shall agree in writing upon fee rates conforming to this Schedule of Arbitration Costs prior to its appointment by the LCIA Court. The rates will be advised by the Registrar to the parties at the time of the appointment of the Tribunal, but may be reviewed annually if the duration of the arbitration requires.

The fee rates shall be within the following range: **£150 to £350 per hour**

However, in exceptional cases, the rate may be higher or lower, provided that, in such cases, (a) the fees of the Tribunal shall be fixed by the LCIA Court on the recommendation of the Registrar, following consultation with the arbitrator(s), and (b) the fees shall be agreed expressly by all parties.

4(b) The Tribunal's fees may include a charge for time spent travelling.

4(c) The Tribunal's fees may also include a charge for time reserved but not used as a result of late postponement or cancellation, provided that the basis for such charge shall be advised in writing to, and approved by, the LCIA Court.

4(d) The Tribunal may also recover such expenses as are reasonably incurred in connection with the arbitration, and as are in a reasonable amount, provided that claims for expenses should be supported by invoices or receipts.

4(e) The Tribunal's fees may be invoiced either in the currency of account between the Tribunal and the parties, or in sterling. The Tribunal's expenses may be invoiced in the currency in which they were incurred, or in sterling.

4(f) In the event of the revocation of the appointment of any arbitrator, pursuant to the provisions of Article 10 of the LCIA Rules, the LCIA Court shall decide upon the amount of fees and expenses to be paid for the former arbitrator's services (if any) as it may consider appropriate in all the circumstances.

5. Deposits

5(a) The LCIA Court may direct the parties, in such proportions as it thinks appropriate, to make one or several interim or final payments on account of the costs of the arbitration. The LCIA Court may limit such payments to a sum sufficient to cover fees, expenses and costs for the next stage of the arbitration.

5(b) The Tribunal shall not proceed with the arbitration without ascertaining at all times from the Registrar or any deputy Registrar that the LCIA is in requisite funds.

5(c) In the event that a party fails or refuses to provide any deposit as directed by the LCIA Court, the LCIA Court may direct the other party or parties to effect a substitute payment to allow the arbitration to proceed (subject to any award on costs). In such circumstances, the party paying the substitute payment shall be entitled to recover that amount as a debt immediately due from the defaulting party.

5(d) Failure by a claimant or counterclaiming party to provide promptly and in full the required deposit may be treated by the LCIA Court and the Arbitral Tribunal as a withdrawal of the claim or counterclaim, respectively.

5(e) Funds lodged by the parties on account of the fees and expenses of the Tribunal and of the LCIA are held on trust in client bank accounts which are controlled by reference to each individual case and are disbursed by the LCIA, in accordance with the LCIA Rules and with this Schedule of Arbitration Costs. In the event that funds lodged by the parties exceed the costs of the arbitration at the conclusion of the arbitration, surplus monies will be returned to the parties as the ultimate default beneficiaries under the trust.

6. Interest on deposits

Interest on sums deposited shall be credited to the account of each party depositing them, at the rate applicable to an amount equal to the amount so credited.

7. Interim payments

7(a) When interim payments are required to cover the LCIA's administrative costs or the fees or expenses of the members of the LCIA Court, or the Tribunal's fees or expenses, including the fees or expenses of any expert appointed by the Tribunal, such payments may be made out of deposits held, upon the approval of the LCIA Court.

7(b) The LCIA may, in any event, submit interim invoices in respect of all current arbitrations, in March, June, September and December of each year, for payment direct by the parties or from funds held on deposit.

8. Registrar's authority

8(a) For the purposes of sections 5(a) and 5(c) above, and of Articles 24.1 and 24.3 of the LCIA Rules, the Registrar has the authority of the LCIA Court to make the directions referred to, under the supervision of the Court.

8(b) For the purposes of section 7(a) above, and of Article 24.1 of the LCIA Rules, the Registrar has the authority of the LCIA Court to approve the payments referred to.

8(c) Any request by an arbitrator for payment on account of his fees shall be supported by a fee note, which shall include, or be accompanied by, details of the time spent at the rates that have been advised to the parties by the LCIA.

8(d) Any dispute regarding administration costs or the fees and expenses of the Tribunal shall be determined by the LCIA Court.

9. Arbitration costs

9(a) The parties shall be jointly and severally liable to the Arbitral Tribunal and the LCIA for the arbitration costs (other than the legal or other costs incurred by the parties themselves).

9(b) The Tribunal's Award(s) shall be transmitted to the parties by the LCIA Court provided that the costs of the arbitration have been paid in accordance with Article 28 of the LCIA Rules.

APPENDIX 4

Constitution of the LCIA Arbitration Court[*]

(ADOPTED 1990, AMENDED 1998, 2002 AND 2008)

A. Composition

1. The Arbitration Court ("the Court") shall consist of up to thirty five members appointed by the Board of Directors of the LCIA ("the Board") on the recommendation of the Court, of whom up to six shall be from the United Kingdom and the remainder from other countries.
2. The members of the Court shall serve for a five-year term. Save in exceptional circumstances, they shall not be re-appointed to consecutive terms.
3. The Court shall make recommendations to the Board to fill appointments arising from retirements or casual vacancies and on other issues relating to the composition of the Court from time to time as appropriate.

B. Officers of the Court

1. The Officers of the Court shall consist of:
   (a) a President appointed by the Board on the recommendation of the Court, to serve for a period of up to three years, and to be eligible for reappointment; and
   (b) up to seven Vice-Presidents appointed by the Court, to serve until expiry of their terms as members of the Court. Due regard shall be given to a balanced international representation.
2. At the request of the President or, if not available, of the Registrar or a Deputy Registrar, any Vice-President shall be entitled to exercise any of the functions and powers of the President.
3. Former Presidents will be invited by the Court to attend and to vote at Court meetings as Honorary Presidents or Honorary Vice Presidents, for as long as they wish, and are not deemed to be ordinary members for the purposes of the number of members prescribed by Article A.1.

C. Registrars and Deputy Registrars

1. There shall be a Registrar and may be a Deputy Registrar or Deputy Registrars appointed by the Board.
2. There may be additional Registrars and/or Deputy Registrars appointed by the Board, to fulfil such roles pursuant to such rules and/or procedures as the Court or Board may publish in connection with any branch of the LCIA, whether independently of, or in a joint venture with, a third party or parties.

D. Functions of the Court

1. The Court shall have power to do anything which it may consider appropriate for the proper performance of its functions and shall in particular:
   (a) act as appointing authority under the LCIA Rules, the UNCITRAL Rules and in any other case where an agreement provides for appointments by the LCIA;
   (b) perform the functions conferred on it by any applicable rules of arbitration, mediation or conciliation, whether the LCIA Rules, the UNCITRAL Rules or any other arbitration, mediation or conciliation rules;

---

[*] Reproduced with the permission of the LCIA.

(c) keep the LCIA Rules under review;

(d) make recommendations to the Board as appropriate concerning the introduction of new general or specialist rules; and

(e) promote the objectives of the LCIA and of international commercial arbitration generally.

2. The functions of the Court under 1(a) and (b) above shall be performed in the name of the Court by the President or a Vice-President, or by divisions of 3 or 5 members of the Court appointed by the President and chaired by the President or a Vice-President, or in the case of administrative functions by a Registrar or Deputy Registrar pursuant to G.(i) below.

3. For the purpose of performing specific tasks in relation to the functions of the Court under 1.(c) to (e) above, the President may set up ad hoc sub-committees of the Court chaired by any members appointed by the President which shall report back to the Court.

4. In the performance of its functions under this Constitution, the Court, its Officers and members shall at all times act independently of the Board.

5. No member of the Court who has a connection with an arbitration in relation to which the LCIA exercises any functions of any kind may participate in or influence any decision of the Court relating to such arbitration.

E. Meetings of the Court

1. The Court shall meet as often as required and at least once a year.

2. Meetings shall be chaired by the President or a Vice-President. A quorum shall be seven. The Chairman of the meeting shall have a casting vote.

F. Appointment of arbitrators and mediators

1. All appointments of arbitrators and mediators in the name of the Court pursuant to D.1(a) and D.1(b) shall be made by the President or by a Vice-President on the President's behalf pursuant to B.2 above.

2. All members of the Court shall be eligible for appointment as arbitrators. However:

(a) the President shall only be eligible if the parties agree to nominate him as sole arbitrator or as Chairman; and

(b) the Vice-Presidents shall only be eligible to serve as arbitrators if nominated by a party or the parties.

The President or Vice Presidents so nominated shall take no part in the appointment of an arbitral tribunal to which they have been nominated or in any other function of the Court relating to such an arbitration.

G. Functions of the Registrars and Deputy Registrars

The Registrars and the Deputy Registrars shall:

(i) carry out in the name of the Court such day to day operations of the Court and administrative functions under any applicable arbitration, mediation or conciliation rules as may be authorised by the President from time to time; and

(ii) service the Court and any division or sub-committee set up under D.2 or D.3 above.

H. Amendments

The provisions of this Constitution may only be amended with the mutual consent of the Court and the Board.

APPENDIX 5

Membership of the LCIA Arbitration Court[*]

Members as at October 2008

President

Jan Paulsson	France

Vice Presidents

José Astigarraga	US
Teresa Giovannini	Switzerland
Paul Hannon	Ireland (UK)
Dr Laurent Lévy	Switzerland/Brazil (Switzerland)
Professor William W Park	US
Dr Klaus Sachs	Germany
V V Veeder QC	UK

Honorary Vice Presidents

Professor Dr Karl-Heinz Böckstiegel	Germany
L Yves Fortier CC OQ QC	Canada
Professor Dr Gerold Herrmann	Germany (Austria)

Other Members

Makhdoom Ali Khan SA	Pakistan
Hassan Ali Radhi	Bahrain
Henri C Alvarez QC	Canada
C Mark Baker	US
James Castello	US (France)
Andrew Clarke	UK
Professor Dr Filip De Ly	Belgium (Netherlands)
Paul D Friedland	US
Hamid Gharavi	Iran (France)
Gilberto Giusti	Brazil
Karim Hafez	Egypt
Kaj Hobér	Sweden
Michael Hwang SC	Singapore
Boris Karabelnikov	Russia
Kap-You (Kevin) Kim	Korea
Peter Leaver QC	UK
Zia Mody	India
Michael J Moser	US (Hong Kong)
Professor Dr Fidelis Oditah QC SAN	Nigeria (UK)

[*] Reproduced with the permission of the LCIA.

Dr Wolfgang Peter	Switzerland
J William F Rowley QC	Canada/UK (Canada)
Jernej Sekolec	Slovenia (Austria)
Dr Guido Tawil	Argentina
Professor Wang Sheng Chang	China
Adrian Winstanley **Director General**	UK

Registrar
James Clanchy

APPENDIX 6

Directives of the LCIA Arbitration Court under Articles 24, 26, and 28[†]

ARTICLE 24 PROCEDURE

Procedure for the Registrar in the application of Articles 24.1 and 24.3 of the LCIA Rules (the Rules)

Introduction

Article 24.1 of the Rules provides that the LCIA Court (the Court) may direct the parties to make one or several interim or final payments, on account of the costs of the arbitration. It provides, further, that the Court may, from time to time, release such deposits to the arbitrators, any expert appointed by the Tribunal, and the LCIA itself, as the arbitration progresses.

Article 24.3 of the Rules provides that the Court may direct a party to effect a substitute payment in the event another party defaults in the payment of a deposit directed by the Court.

Given the practicalities of the application [of] Articles 24.1 and 24.3, it has been agreed that the LCIA Registrar be given the general delegated authority of the Court to make the directions, and to approve the payments, contemplated by those Articles.

Procedure

For the purposes of Articles 24.1 and 24.3 of the Rules, the following procedure will apply.

1. The Registrar may, without the prior approval of the Court, issue individual directions for interim or final payments, on account of the costs of the arbitration, in an aggregate sum up to US$100,000[*] per direction.
2. The Registrar will obtain the written authority of the Court prior to issuing any single direction, exceeding, in the aggregate, US$100,000.[*]
3. The Registrar will, in all cases, advise the Court as and when the cumulative total of directions issued in any one arbitration exceeds US$250,000,[‡] and will advise the Court of all directions for deposits thereafter.
4. Prior to approving the payments referred to in [in] Article 24.1 of the Rules, the Registrar will ensure that the parties have been notified of the fact, and of the amount, of such payments.
5. When payments have been made from deposits, pursuant to Article 24.1, the Registrar will ensure that the parties and the Tribunal are provided with a financial summary, accounting for such payments, and recording the balance of the funds held on deposit.
6. The Registrar will ensure that a file of all correspondence generated pursuant to Articles 24.1 and 24.3, and to the operation of these procedures, is maintained and is available for inspection by the Court on request and will, in any event, make such material available to the Court in accordance with the established procedures for the operation of Articles 28.1 and [28.2] of the Rules.

[†] Reproduced with the permission of the LCIA.
[*] Subsequently amended to US$240,000 or £120,000.
[‡] Subsequently amended to US$500,000 or £240,000.

Signed: L Yves Fortier CC QC
                    President
                    LCIA Court

Date: 19 October 2000

Article 26 Procedure

**Procedure for the LCIA Court (the Court) in the application of Article 26.5 of the
LCIA Rules (the Rules)**

Introduction

Article 26.5 of the Rules provides that a sole arbitrator or Chairman shall be responsible for
delivering Awards to the LCIA Court, which shall transmit certified copies to the parties, provided
that the costs of arbitration have been paid to [the] LCIA in accordance with Article 28.

Procedure

Pursuant to Articles D.2 and G(i) of the Constitution of the Court, the Court's function in receiving
and transmitting Awards to the parties, in accordance with Article 26.5 of the Rules, shall be deemed
an administrative function, which may be performed by the Registrar or Deputy Registrar.

Signed: Jan Paulsson
                    Vice President
                    LCIA Court

Date: 10 May 2002

Article 28 Procedure

**Procedure for the LCIA Court (the Court) in the application of Articles 28.1, 28.2
and 28.5 of the LCIA Rules (the Rules)**

Introduction

Article 28.1 of the Rules requires the Court to determine the costs of an arbitration in accordance
with the schedule of costs.

Article 28.2 requires that the total amount of the costs of the arbitration specified in an Award shall
be the sum determined by the Court.

Article 28.5 requires that, if an arbitration is abandoned, suspended or concluded, by agreement or
otherwise, before the final Award is made, the parties shall remain jointly and severally liable to pay
the LCIA and the Tribunal, the costs of the arbitration as determined by the Court.

Procedure

For the purposes of Articles 28.1, 28.2 and 28.5 of the Rules, the following procedure will apply:

1. The Registrar will furnish the Court with

    (a) a financial summary, which will show
        (i) the registration fee filed with the Request;
        (ii) all amounts deposited by the parties to the arbitration, pursuant to section 5 of the
            schedule of costs, and to Articles 24.1 and 24.3 of the Rules;

    (iii) all amounts paid to the arbitrator(s) on account of the arbitrator(s)' fees and expenses, pursuant to section 7 of the schedule of costs;

    (iv) all amounts claimed by the arbitrator(s), but unpaid;

    (v) all amounts paid to the LCIA on account of its own administrative charges and expenses, pursuant to section 7 of the schedule of costs;

    (vi) all amounts due to the LCIA, but unpaid; and

    (vii) the amount of interest accruing to the sums deposited by the parties;

(b) a copy of the LCIA's notice to the parties of the fee rates agreed by the arbitrator(s) at the time of the appointment of the Tribunal;

(c) copies of the arbitrator(s)' accounts for fees and expenses, in relation to (a) (iii) and (a) (iv) above, together with any supporting receipts;

(d) a copy of the LCIA Secretariat's computerised time and disbursements ledger;

(e) copies of all directions given to the parties, pursuant to section 5 of the schedule of costs and Article 24 of the Rules; and

(f) copies of all notices given to the parties of payments made from deposits pursuant to section 7 of the schedule of costs.

2. As soon as practicable following its receipt of the above, the Court will

(a) review the financial summary and all supporting materials;

(b) in the event it considers the records to be incomplete or otherwise deficient, instruct the Registrar to supply such further information as it requires;

(c) satisfy itself that the costs of the arbitration are reasonable and in accordance with the schedule of costs; and

(d) notify the Registrar, in writing, of the total amount of the costs of the arbitration, for the purposes of Article 28.2 or 28.5 of the Rules.

Signed: Jan Paulsson
               Vice President
               LCIA Court

Date: 10 May 2002

APPENDIX 7

Constitution of the LCIA Users' Councils[*]

(APPROVED BY THE LCIA BOARD AND ADOPTED BY THE LCIA COURT
ON 5 MAY 2006)

A. Aims and Objectives

1. To establish, foster and maintain links between the LCIA and users, and prospective users, of its services, to enable the LCIA to ensure that the arbitration and ADR services it provides to its users worldwide are relevant, cost effective, efficient and consistent with current best practice.
2. Through conferences, meetings, publications and personal contacts, to instil in members of the Users' Councils, and others, confidence in the LCIA's arbitration and ADR services, such that, whenever appropriate, they adopt, or recommend the adoption of, LCIA dispute resolution clauses.

B. The Users' Councils

1. The LCIA Court has established the following Users' Councils and may, from time to time, establish others.

   (a) The European Users' Council.
   (b) The Arab Users' Council.
   (c) The North American Users' Council.
   (d) The Latin American and Caribbean Users' Council.
   (e) The Asia-Pacific Users' Council.
   (f) The African Users' Council.

C. Membership

1. Membership of the Users' Councils is open to any person or body of good standing with a *bona fide* interest in international commercial arbitration or ADR, including lawyers, arbitrators, mediators, experts, academics, businessmen, law firms and commercial and trading organisations.
2. Members may elect to which Users' Council or Councils they wish to be affiliated, whether on the basis of origin, domicile, nationality or language.
3. Members shall pay an annual membership subscription, at the rate advised from time to time by the LCIA.
4. The membership of members who do not pay their annual subscription within the period stipulated in the relevant invoice shall be cancelled, though this will not preclude reapplication for membership at a later date.
5. Membership is available at three levels:

   (a) individual membership for arbitration and ADR practitioners;
   (b) individual membership for full-time academics; and

---

[*] Reproduced with the permission of the LCIA.

(c) corporate membership, for firms and businesses, for whom the annual subscription covers up to four individuals from the corporate member's office or offices, and who may, for an additional subscription, enrol additional members.

6. Application for membership shall be made to the membership department of the LCIA and shall be supported (in the case of an individual applicant) by a personal résumé or (in the case of a corporate applicant) by information sufficient to confirm its *bona fides*.

7. Membership may be refused if, in its discretion, the LCIA Court considers that an applicant does not meet the criteria for membership.

8. Membership may be cancelled if, in its discretion, the LCIA Court considers that a current member no longer meets the criteria for membership, for reasons that have become known to the LCIA since membership was granted.

D. Services to Members

1. Members will receive, free of charge, the quarterly journal *"Arbitration International"*, which is recognised as one of the leading scholarly journals on the development and application of international commercial arbitration.

2. Members will receive, free of charge, the LCIA's occasional Newsletter, to which members are invited to submit contributions.

3. Members' names, contact details, nationality, areas of specialisation and languages spoken will be published in the LCIA's annual Directory of Members, which is distributed to all members and to arbitral institutions worldwide.

4. Members will enjoy discounted registration fees for selected LCIA symposia.

5. The LCIA intends, whenever practically possible, to hold at least one symposium or conference each year in the region of each of the Users' Councils.

6. The LCIA will, in its discretion, on the timely request of a member and where reasonably practical, provide, or recommend, a speaker at a seminar, symposium or conference organised by that member for the promotion of arbitration and ADR.

E. Officers

1. The business of the Users' Councils will be administered by the membership department of the LCIA, in consultation with the LCIA Court and the Officers of each of the Users' Council, of which there shall be:

   (a) a President;
   (b) up to 4 Vice Presidents;
   (c) up to 4 Councillors; and
   (d) a Secretary.

2. Sitting members of the LCIA Court shall be eligible for appointment as Officers of the Users' Councils.

3. Officers shall serve for a period of up to 3 years and shall be eligible for reappointment, provided that no Officer shall be appointed for more than two consecutive terms.

4. The first Officers of each Users' Council have been, or will be, selected and appointed by the LCIA Court.

5. Vacancies arising after the initial appointments will be filled by candidates appointed by the LCIA Court following consultation with the then-current Officers.

6. In selecting Officers, the Court will endeavour to achieve a balance of representation across the jurisdictions of the Users' Council to which the appointment is being made.

7. The Officers shall be responsible for recommending to the LCIA Court and the membership department of the LCIA such initiatives and activities as will best meet the aims and objectives set out at Article A of this Constitution.

8. The Officers will, whenever reasonably practical, make themselves available to participate in the LCIA conferences organised under the auspices of the Users' Council to which they are appointed and to represent the LCIA at such other meetings and presentations as may be organised from time to time in accordance with Article A of this Constitution.

9. The Officers shall meet as often as required and at least once a year, working to an agenda that should routinely include

    (a) a report on significant developments in arbitration and ADR practice and procedure within the jurisdiction of the Users' Council;

    (b) a report on any known Court proceedings relating to LCIA arbitrations and/or Awards;

    (c) recommendations to be made to the LCIA Court pursuant to Article E.7 of this Constitution; and

    (d) a report on any symposium held, or to be held, in that year, within the region of their Users' Council.

10. A quorum for meetings of Officers shall be 3, one of whom shall be the President or a Vice President, who shall also chair the meeting.

11. The decisions of the Officers shall be taken by a simple majority, provided that, in the event of deadlock, the Chairman of the meeting shall have a casting vote.

12. The Officers may, in consultation with the LCIA Court, establish such committees or working groups, whose members shall be appointed from the membership of their Users' Council, as may be required to assist with the fulfilment of their obligations under this Constitution and with the achievement of its aims and objectives.

F. Amendments

The provisions of this Constitution may only be amended with the mutual consent of the LCIA Court and LCIA Board.

APPENDIX 8

The English Arbitration Act 1996[*]

1996 CHAPTER 23

ARRANGEMENT OF SECTIONS

Part I

Arbitration pursuant to an arbitration agreement

Introductory

1. General principles.

2. Scope of application of provisions.

3. The seat of the arbitration.

4. Mandatory and non-mandatory provisions.

5. Agreements to be in writing.

The arbitration agreement

6. Definition of arbitration agreement.

7. Separability of arbitration agreement.

8. Whether agreement discharged by death of a party.

Stay of legal proceedings

9. Stay of legal proceedings.

10. Reference of interpleader issue to arbitration.

11. Retention of security where Admiralty proceedings stayed.

Commencement of arbitral proceedings

12. Power of court to extend time for beginning arbitral proceedings, &c.

13. Application of Limitation Acts.

14. Commencement of arbitral proceedings.

The arbitral tribunal

15. The arbitral tribunal.

16. Procedure for appointment of arbitrators.

17. Power in case of default to appoint sole arbitrator.

18. Failure of appointment procedure.

19. Court to have regard to agreed qualifications.

---

[*] Crown copyright material is reproduced under Class Licence Number C01P0000148 with the permission of OPSI and the Queen's Printer for Scotland

20. Chairman.

21. Umpire.

22. Decision-making where no chairman or umpire.

23. Revocation of arbitrator's authority.

24. Power of court to remove arbitrator.

25. Resignation of arbitrator.

26. Death of arbitrator or person appointing him.

27. Filling of vacancy, &c.

28. Joint and several liability of parties to arbitrators for fees and expenses.

29. Immunity of arbitrator.

Jurisdiction of the arbitral tribunal

30. Competence of tribunal to rule on its own jurisdiction.

31. Objection to substantive jurisdiction of tribunal.

32. Determination of preliminary point of jurisdiction.

The arbitral proceedings

33. General duty of the tribunal.

34. Procedural and evidential matters.

35. Consolidation of proceedings and concurrent hearings.

36. Legal or other representation.

37. Power to appoint experts, legal advisers or assessors.

38. General powers exercisable by the tribunal.

39. Power to make provisional awards.

40. General duty of parties.

41. Powers of tribunal in case of party's default.

Powers of court in relation to arbitral proceedings

42. Enforcement of peremptory orders of tribunal.

43. Securing the attendance of witnesses.

44. Court powers exercisable in support of arbitral proceedings.

45. Determination of preliminary point of law.

The award

46. Rules applicable to substance of dispute.

47. Awards on different issues, &c.

48. Remedies.

49. Interest.

50. Extension of time for making award.

51. Settlement.

52. Form of award.

53. Place where award treated as made.

54. Date of award.

55. Notification of award.

56. Power to withhold award in case of non-payment.

57. Correction of award or additional award.

58. Effect of award.

Costs of the arbitration

59. Costs of the arbitration.

60. Agreement to pay costs in any event.

61. Award of costs.

62. Effect of agreement or award about costs.

63. The recoverable costs of the arbitration.

64. Recoverable fees and expenses of arbitrators.

65. Power to limit recoverable costs.

Powers of the court in relation to award

66. Enforcement of the award.

67. Challenging the award: substantive jurisdiction.

68. Challenging the award: serious irregularity.

69. Appeal on point of law.

70. Challenge or appeal: supplementary provisions.

71. Challenge or appeal: effect of order of court.

Miscellaneous

72. Saving for rights of person who takes no part in proceedings.

73. Loss of right to object.

74. Immunity of arbitral institutions, &c.

75. Charge to secure payment of solicitors' costs.

Supplementary

76. Service of notices, &c.

77. Powers of court in relation to service of documents.

78. Reckoning periods of time.

79. Power of court to extend time limits relating to arbitral proceedings.

80. Notice and other requirements in connection with legal proceedings.

81. Saving for certain matters governed by common law.

82. Minor definitions.

83. Index of defined expressions: Part I.

84. Transitional provisions.

Part II

Other provisions relating to arbitration

Domestic arbitration agreements

85. Modification of Part I in relation to domestic arbitration agreement.

86. Staying of legal proceedings.

87. Effectiveness of agreement to exclude court's jurisdiction.

88. Power to repeal or amend sections 85 to 87.

Consumer arbitration agreements

89. Application of unfair terms regulations to consumer arbitration agreements.

90. Regulations apply where consumer is a legal person.

91. Arbitration agreement unfair where modest amount sought.

Small claims arbitration in the county court

92. Exclusion of Part I in relation to small claims arbitration in the county court.

Appointment of judges as arbitrators

93. Appointment of judges as arbitrators.

Statutory arbitrations

94. Application of Part I to statutory arbitrations.

95. General adaptation of provisions in relation to statutory arbitrations.

96. Specific adaptations of provisions in relation to statutory arbitrations.

97. Provisions excluded from applying to statutory arbitrations.

98. Power to make further provision by regulations.

Part III

Recognition and enforcement of certain foreign awards

Enforcement of Geneva Convention awards

99. Continuation of Part II of the Arbitration Act 19501950.

Recognition and enforcement of New York Convention awards

100. New York Convention awards.

101. Recognition and enforcement of awards.

102. Evidence to be produced by party seeking recognition or enforcement.

103. Refusal of recognition or enforcement.

104. Saving for other bases of recognition or enforcement.

Part IV

General provisions

105. Meaning of "the court": jurisdiction of High Court and county court.

106. Crown application.

107. Consequential amendments and repeals.

108. Extent.

109. Commencement.

110. Short title.

Schedules:

Schedule 1

Mandatory provisions of Part I.

Schedule 2

Modifications of Part I in relation to judge-arbitrators.

Schedule 3

Consequential amendments.

Schedule 4

Repeals.

An Act to restate and improve the law relating to arbitration pursuant to an arbitration agreement; to make other provision relating to arbitration and arbitration awards; and for connected purposes.

[17th June 1996]

Be it enacted by the Queen's most Excellent Majesty, by and with the advice and consent of the Lords Spiritual and Temporal, and Commons, in this present Parliament assembled, and by the authority of the same, as follows:—

PART I
ARBITRATION PURSUANT TO AN ARBITRATION AGREEMENT

Introductory

1 General principles

The provisions of this Part are founded on the following principles, and shall be construed accordingly—

(a) the object of arbitration is to obtain the fair resolution of disputes by an impartial tribunal without unnecessary delay or expense;

(b) the parties should be free to agree how their disputes are resolved, subject only to such safeguards as are necessary in the public interest;

(c) in matters governed by this Part the court should not intervene except as provided by this Part.

2 Scope of application of provisions

(1) The provisions of this Part apply where the seat of the arbitration is in England and Wales or Northern Ireland.

(2) The following sections apply even if the seat of the arbitration is outside England and Wales or Northern Ireland or no seat has been designated or determined—

(a) sections 9 to 11 (stay of legal proceedings, &c.), and

(b) section 66 (enforcement of arbitral awards).

(3) The powers conferred by the following sections apply even if the seat of the arbitration is outside England and Wales or Northern Ireland or no seat has been designated or determined—

(a) section 43 (securing the attendance of witnesses), and

(b) section 44 (court powers exercisable in support of arbitral proceedings);

but the court may refuse to exercise any such power if, in the opinion of the court, the fact that the seat of the arbitration is outside England and Wales or Northern Ireland, or that when designated or determined the seat is likely to be outside England and Wales or Northern Ireland, makes it inappropriate to do so.

(4) The court may exercise a power conferred by any provision of this Part not mentioned in subsection (2) or (3) for the purpose of supporting the arbitral process where—

(a) no seat of the arbitration has been designated or determined, and

(b) by reason of a connection with England and Wales or Northern Ireland the court is satisfied that it is appropriate to do so.

(5) Section 7 (separability of arbitration agreement) and section 8 (death of a party) apply where the law applicable to the arbitration agreement is the law of England and Wales or Northern Ireland even if the seat of the arbitration is outside England and Wales or Northern Ireland or has not been designated or determined.

3 The seat of the arbitration

In this Part "the seat of the arbitration" means the juridical seat of the arbitration designated—

(a) by the parties to the arbitration agreement, or

(b) by any arbitral or other institution or person vested by the parties with powers in that regard, or

(c) by the arbitral tribunal if so authorised by the parties,

or determined, in the absence of any such designation, having regard to the parties' agreement and all the relevant circumstances.

4 Mandatory and non-mandatory provisions

(1) The mandatory provisions of this Part are listed in Schedule 1 and have effect notwithstanding any agreement to the contrary.

(2) The other provisions of this Part (the "non-mandatory provisions") allow the parties to make their own arrangements by agreement but provide rules which apply in the absence of such agreement.

(3) The parties may make such arrangements by agreeing to the application of institutional rules or providing any other means by which a matter may be decided.

(4) It is immaterial whether or not the law applicable to the parties' agreement is the law of England and Wales or, as the case may be, Northern Ireland.

(5) The choice of a law other than the law of England and Wales or Northern Ireland as the applicable law in respect of a matter provided for by a non-mandatory provision of this Part is equivalent to an agreement making provision about that matter.

For this purpose an applicable law determined in accordance with the parties' agreement, or which is objectively determined in the absence of any express or implied choice, shall be treated as chosen by the parties.

5 Agreements to be in writing

(1) The provisions of this Part apply only where the arbitration agreement is in writing, and any other agreement between the parties as to any matter is effective for the purposes of this Part only if in writing.

The expressions "agreement", "agree" and "agreed" shall be construed accordingly.

(2) There is an agreement in writing—

(a) if the agreement is made in writing (whether or not it is signed by the parties),

(b) if the agreement is made by exchange of communications in writing, or

(c) if the agreement is evidenced in writing.

(3) Where parties agree otherwise than in writing by reference to terms which are in writing, they make an agreement in writing.

(4) An agreement is evidenced in writing if an agreement made otherwise than in writing is recorded by one of the parties, or by a third party, with the authority of the parties to the agreement.

(5) An exchange of written submissions in arbitral or legal proceedings in which the existence of an agreement otherwise than in writing is alleged by one party against another party and not denied by the other party in his response constitutes as between those parties an agreement in writing to the effect alleged.

(6) References in this Part to anything being written or in writing include its being recorded by any means.

The arbitration agreement

6 Definition of arbitration agreement

(1) In this Part an "arbitration agreement" means an agreement to submit to arbitration present or future disputes (whether they are contractual or not).

(2) The reference in an agreement to a written form of arbitration clause or to a document containing an arbitration clause constitutes an arbitration agreement if the reference is such as to make that clause part of the agreement.

7 Separability of arbitration agreement

Unless otherwise agreed by the parties, an arbitration agreement which forms or was intended to form part of another agreement (whether or not in writing) shall not be regarded as invalid, non-existent or ineffective because that other agreement is invalid, or did not come into existence or has become ineffective, and it shall for that purpose be treated as a distinct agreement.

8 Whether agreement discharged by death of a party

(1) Unless otherwise agreed by the parties, an arbitration agreement is not discharged by the death of a party and may be enforced by or against the personal representatives of that party.

(2) Subsection (1) does not affect the operation of any enactment or rule of law by virtue of which a substantive right or obligation is extinguished by death.

Stay of legal proceedings

9 Stay of legal proceedings

(1) A party to an arbitration agreement against whom legal proceedings are brought (whether by way of claim or counterclaim) in respect of a matter which under the agreement is to be referred to arbitration may (upon notice to the other parties to the proceedings) apply to the court in which the proceedings have been brought to stay the proceedings so far as they concern that matter.

(2) An application may be made notwithstanding that the matter is to be referred to arbitration only after the exhaustion of other dispute resolution procedures.

(3) An application may not be made by a person before taking the appropriate procedural step (if any) to acknowledge the legal proceedings against him or after he has taken any step in those proceedings to answer the substantive claim.

(4) On an application under this section the court shall grant a stay unless satisfied that the arbitration agreement is null and void, inoperative, or incapable of being performed.

(5) If the court refuses to stay the legal proceedings, any provision that an award is a condition precedent to the bringing of legal proceedings in respect of any matter is of no effect in relation to those proceedings.

10 Reference of interpleader issue to arbitration

(1) Where in legal proceedings relief by way of interpleader is granted and any issue between the claimants is one in respect of which there is an arbitration agreement between them, the court granting the relief shall direct that the issue be determined in accordance with the agreement unless the circumstances are such that proceedings brought by a claimant in respect of the matter would not be stayed.

(2) Where subsection (1) applies but the court does not direct that the issue be determined in accordance with the arbitration agreement, any provision that an award is a condition precedent to the bringing of legal proceedings in respect of any matter shall not affect the determination of that issue by the court.

11 Retention of security where Admiralty proceedings stayed

(1) Where Admiralty proceedings are stayed on the ground that the dispute in question should be submitted to arbitration, the court granting the stay may, if in those proceedings property has been arrested or bail or other security has been given to prevent or obtain release from arrest—

(a) order that the property arrested be retained as security for the satisfaction of any award given in the arbitration in respect of that dispute, or

(b) order that the stay of those proceedings be conditional on the provision of equivalent security for the satisfaction of any such award.

(2) Subject to any provision made by rules of court and to any necessary modifications, the same law and practice shall apply in relation to property retained in pursuance of an order as would apply if it were held for the purposes of proceedings in the court making the order.

Commencement of arbitral proceedings

12 Power of court to extend time for beginning arbitral proceedings, & c

(1) Where an arbitration agreement to refer future disputes to arbitration provides that a claim shall be barred, or the claimant's right extinguished, unless the claimant takes within a time fixed by the agreement some step—

(a) to begin arbitral proceedings, or

(b) to begin other dispute resolution procedures which must be exhausted before arbitral proceedings can be begun,

the court may by order extend the time for taking that step.

(2) Any party to the arbitration agreement may apply for such an order (upon notice to the other parties), but only after a claim has arisen and after exhausting any available arbitral process for obtaining an extension of time.

(3) The court shall make an order only if satisfied—

(a) that the circumstances are such as were outside the reasonable contemplation of the parties when they agreed the provision in question, and that it would be just to extend the time, or

(b) that the conduct of one party makes it unjust to hold the other party to the strict terms of the provision in question.

(4) The court may extend the time for such period and on such terms as it thinks fit, and may do so whether or not the time previously fixed (by agreement or by a previous order) has expired.

(5) An order under this section does not affect the operation of the Limitation Acts (see section 13).

(6) The leave of the court is required for any appeal from a decision of the court under this section.

13 Application of Limitation Acts

(1) The Limitation Acts apply to arbitral proceedings as they apply to legal proceedings.

(2) The court may order that in computing the time prescribed by the Limitation Acts for the commencement of proceedings (including arbitral proceedings) in respect of a dispute which was the subject matter—

(a) of an award which the court orders to be set aside or declares to be of no effect, or

(b) of the affected part of an award which the court orders to be set aside in part, or declares to be in part of no effect,

the period between the commencement of the arbitration and the date of the order referred to in paragraph (a) or (b) shall be excluded.

(3) In determining for the purposes of the Limitation Acts when a cause of action accrued, any provision that an award is a condition precedent to the bringing of legal proceedings in respect of a matter to which an arbitration agreement applies shall be disregarded.

(4) In this Part "the Limitation Acts" means—

    (a) in England and Wales, the [1980 c. 58.] Limitation Act 1980, the [1984 c. 16.] Foreign Limitation Periods Act 1984 and any other enactment (whenever passed) relating to the limitation of actions;

    (b) in Northern Ireland, the [S.I. 1989/1339 (N.I. 11).] Limitation (Northern Ireland) Order 1989, the [S.I. 1985/754 (N.I. 5).] Foreign Limitation Periods (Northern Ireland) Order 1985 and any other enactment (whenever passed) relating to the limitation of actions.

14 Commencement of arbitral proceedings

(1) The parties are free to agree when arbitral proceedings are to be regarded as commenced for the purposes of this Part and for the purposes of the Limitation Acts.

(2) If there is no such agreement the following provisions apply.

(3) Where the arbitrator is named or designated in the arbitration agreement, arbitral proceedings are commenced in respect of a matter when one party serves on the other party or parties a notice in writing requiring him or them to submit that matter to the person so named or designated.

(4) Where the arbitrator or arbitrators are to be appointed by the parties, arbitral proceedings are commenced in respect of a matter when one party serves on the other party or parties notice in writing requiring him or them to appoint an arbitrator or to agree to the appointment of an arbitrator in respect of that matter.

(5) Where the arbitrator or arbitrators are to be appointed by a person other than a party to the proceedings, arbitral proceedings are commenced in respect of a matter when one party gives notice in writing to that person requesting him to make the appointment in respect of that matter.

The arbitral tribunal

15 The arbitral tribunal

(1) The parties are free to agree on the number of arbitrators to form the tribunal and whether there is to be a chairman or umpire.

(2) Unless otherwise agreed by the parties, an agreement that the number of arbitrators shall be two or any other even number shall be understood as requiring the appointment of an additional arbitrator as chairman of the tribunal.

(3) If there is no agreement as to the number of arbitrators, the tribunal shall consist of a sole arbitrator.

16 Procedure for appointment of arbitrators

(1) The parties are free to agree on the procedure for appointing the arbitrator or arbitrators, including the procedure for appointing any chairman or umpire.

(2) If or to the extent that there is no such agreement, the following provisions apply.

(3) If the tribunal is to consist of a sole arbitrator, the parties shall jointly appoint the arbitrator not later than 28 days after service of a request in writing by either party to do so.

(4) If the tribunal is to consist of two arbitrators, each party shall appoint one arbitrator not later than 14 days after service of a request in writing by either party to do so.

(5) If the tribunal is to consist of three arbitrators—

    (a) each party shall appoint one arbitrator not later than 14 days after service of a request in writing by either party to do so, and

    (b) the two so appointed shall forthwith appoint a third arbitrator as the chairman of the tribunal.

(6) If the tribunal is to consist of two arbitrators and an umpire—

    (a) each party shall appoint one arbitrator not later than 14 days after service of a request in writing by either party to do so, and

(b) the two so appointed may appoint an umpire at any time after they themselves are appointed and shall do so before any substantive hearing or forthwith if they cannot agree on a matter relating to the arbitration.

(7) In any other case (in particular, if there are more than two parties) section 18 applies as in the case of a failure of the agreed appointment procedure.

17 Power in case of default to appoint sole arbitrator

(1) Unless the parties otherwise agree, where each of two parties to an arbitration agreement is to appoint an arbitrator and one party ("the party in default") refuses to do so, or fails to do so within the time specified, the other party, having duly appointed his arbitrator, may give notice in writing to the party in default that he proposes to appoint his arbitrator to act as sole arbitrator.

(2) If the party in default does not within 7 clear days of that notice being given—

(a) make the required appointment, and
(b) notify the other party that he has done so,

the other party may appoint his arbitrator as sole arbitrator whose award shall be binding on both parties as if he had been so appointed by agreement.

(3) Where a sole arbitrator has been appointed under subsection (2), the party in default may (upon notice to the appointing party) apply to the court which may set aside the appointment.

(4) The leave of the court is required for any appeal from a decision of the court under this section.

18 Failure of appointment procedure

(1) The parties are free to agree what is to happen in the event of a failure of the procedure for the appointment of the arbitral tribunal.
There is no failure if an appointment is duly made under section 17 (power in case of default to appoint sole arbitrator), unless that appointment is set aside.

(2) If or to the extent that there is no such agreement any party to the arbitration agreement may (upon notice to the other parties) apply to the court to exercise its powers under this section.

(3) Those powers are—

(a) to give directions as to the making of any necessary appointments;
(b) to direct that the tribunal shall be constituted by such appointments (or any one or more of them) as have been made;
(c) to revoke any appointments already made;
(d) to make any necessary appointments itself.

(4) An appointment made by the court under this section has effect as if made with the agreement of the parties.

(5) The leave of the court is required for any appeal from a decision of the court under this section.

19 Court to have regard to agreed qualifications

In deciding whether to exercise, and in considering how to exercise, any of its powers under section 16 (procedure for appointment of arbitrators) or section 18 (failure of appointment procedure), the court shall have due regard to any agreement of the parties as to the qualifications required of the arbitrators.

20 Chairman

(1) Where the parties have agreed that there is to be a chairman, they are free to agree what the functions of the chairman are to be in relation to the making of decisions, orders and awards.

(2) If or to the extent that there is no such agreement, the following provisions apply.

(3) Decisions, orders and awards shall be made by all or a majority of the arbitrators (including the chairman).

(4) The view of the chairman shall prevail in relation to a decision, order or award in respect of which there is neither unanimity nor a majority under subsection (3).

21 Umpire

(1) Where the parties have agreed that there is to be an umpire, they are free to agree what the functions of the umpire are to be, and in particular—

(a) whether he is to attend the proceedings, and
(b) when he is to replace the other arbitrators as the tribunal with power to make decisions, orders and awards.

(2) If or to the extent that there is no such agreement, the following provisions apply.

(3) The umpire shall attend the proceedings and be supplied with the same documents and other materials as are supplied to the other arbitrators.

(4) Decisions, orders and awards shall be made by the other arbitrators unless and until they cannot agree on a matter relating to the arbitration.
In that event they shall forthwith give notice in writing to the parties and the umpire, whereupon the umpire shall replace them as the tribunal with power to make decisions, orders and awards as if he were sole arbitrator.

(5) If the arbitrators cannot agree but fail to give notice of that fact, or if any of them fails to join in the giving of notice, any party to the arbitral proceedings may (upon notice to the other parties and to the tribunal) apply to the court which may order that the umpire shall replace the other arbitrators as the tribunal with power to make decisions, orders and awards as if he were sole arbitrator.

(6) The leave of the court is required for any appeal from a decision of the court under this section.

22 Decision-making where no chairman or umpire

(1) Where the parties agree that there shall be two or more arbitrators with no chairman or umpire, the parties are free to agree how the tribunal is to make decisions, orders and awards.

(2) If there is no such agreement, decisions, orders and awards shall be made by all or a majority of the arbitrators.

23 Revocation of arbitrator's authority

(1) The parties are free to agree in what circumstances the authority of an arbitrator may be revoked.

(2) If or to the extent that there is no such agreement the following provisions apply.

(3) The authority of an arbitrator may not be revoked except—

(a) by the parties acting jointly, or
(b) by an arbitral or other institution or person vested by the parties with powers in that regard.

(4) Revocation of the authority of an arbitrator by the parties acting jointly must be agreed in writing unless the parties also agree (whether or not in writing) to terminate the arbitration agreement.

(5) Nothing in this section affects the power of the court—

(a) to revoke an appointment under section 18 (powers exercisable in case of failure of appointment procedure), or
(b) to remove an arbitrator on the grounds specified in section 24.

24 Power of court to remove arbitrator

(1) A party to arbitral proceedings may (upon notice to the other parties, to the arbitrator concerned and to any other arbitrator) apply to the court to remove an arbitrator on any of the following grounds—

(a) that circumstances exist that give rise to justifiable doubts as to his impartiality;
(b) that he does not possess the qualifications required by the arbitration agreement;
(c) that he is physically or mentally incapable of conducting the proceedings or there are justifiable doubts as to his capacity to do so;

(d) that he has refused or failed—

    (i) properly to conduct the proceedings, or

    (ii) to use all reasonable despatch in conducting the proceedings or making an award,

and that substantial injustice has been or will be caused to the applicant.

(2) If there is an arbitral or other institution or person vested by the parties with power to remove an arbitrator, the court shall not exercise its power of removal unless satisfied that the applicant has first exhausted any available recourse to that institution or person.

(3) The arbitral tribunal may continue the arbitral proceedings and make an award while an application to the court under this section is pending.

(4) Where the court removes an arbitrator, it may make such order as it thinks fit with respect to his entitlement (if any) to fees or expenses, or the repayment of any fees or expenses already paid.

(5) The arbitrator concerned is entitled to appear and be heard by the court before it makes any order under this section.

(6) The leave of the court is required for any appeal from a decision of the court under this section.

25 Resignation of arbitrator

(1) The parties are free to agree with an arbitrator as to the consequences of his resignation as regards—

    (a) his entitlement (if any) to fees or expenses, and

    (b) any liability thereby incurred by him.

(2) If or to the extent that there is no such agreement the following provisions apply.

(3) An arbitrator who resigns his appointment may (upon notice to the parties) apply to the court—

    (a) to grant him relief from any liability thereby incurred by him, and

    (b) to make such order as it thinks fit with respect to his entitlement (if any) to fees or expenses or the repayment of any fees or expenses already paid.

(4) If the court is satisfied that in all the circumstances it was reasonable for the arbitrator to resign, it may grant such relief as is mentioned in subsection (3)(a) on such terms as it thinks fit.

(5) The leave of the court is required for any appeal from a decision of the court under this section.

26 Death of arbitrator or person appointing him

(1) The authority of an arbitrator is personal and ceases on his death.

(2) Unless otherwise agreed by the parties, the death of the person by whom an arbitrator was appointed does not revoke the arbitrator's authority.

27 Filling of vacancy, & c

(1) Where an arbitrator ceases to hold office, the parties are free to agree—

    (a) whether and if so how the vacancy is to be filled,

    (b) whether and if so to what extent the previous proceedings should stand, and

    (c) what effect (if any) his ceasing to hold office has on any appointment made by him (alone or jointly).

(2) If or to the extent that there is no such agreement, the following provisions apply.

(3) The provisions of sections 16 (procedure for appointment of arbitrators) and 18 (failure of appointment procedure) apply in relation to the filling of the vacancy as in relation to an original appointment.

(4) The tribunal (when reconstituted) shall determine whether and if so to what extent the previous proceedings should stand.

This does not affect any right of a party to challenge those proceedings on any ground which had arisen before the arbitrator ceased to hold office.

(5) His ceasing to hold office does not affect any appointment by him (alone or jointly) of another arbitrator, in particular any appointment of a chairman or umpire.

28 Joint and several liability of parties to arbitrators for fees and expenses

(1) The parties are jointly and severally liable to pay to the arbitrators such reasonable fees and expenses (if any) as are appropriate in the circumstances.

(2) Any party may apply to the court (upon notice to the other parties and to the arbitrators) which may order that the amount of the arbitrators' fees and expenses shall be considered and adjusted by such means and upon such terms as it may direct.

(3) If the application is made after any amount has been paid to the arbitrators by way of fees or expenses, the court may order the repayment of such amount (if any) as is shown to be excessive, but shall not do so unless it is shown that it is reasonable in the circumstances to order repayment.

(4) The above provisions have effect subject to any order of the court under section 24(4) or 25(3)(b) (order as to entitlement to fees or expenses in case of removal or resignation of arbitrator).

(5) Nothing in this section affects any liability of a party to any other party to pay all or any of the costs of the arbitration (see sections 59 to 65) or any contractual right of an arbitrator to payment of his fees and expenses.

(6) In this section references to arbitrators include an arbitrator who has ceased to act and an umpire who has not replaced the other arbitrators.

29 Immunity of arbitrator

(1) An arbitrator is not liable for anything done or omitted in the discharge or purported discharge of his functions as arbitrator unless the act or omission is shown to have been in bad faith.

(2) Subsection (1) applies to an employee or agent of an arbitrator as it applies to the arbitrator himself.

(3) This section does not affect any liability incurred by an arbitrator by reason of his resigning (but see section 25).

Jurisdiction of the arbitral tribunal

30 Competence of tribunal to rule on its own jurisdiction

(1) Unless otherwise agreed by the parties, the arbitral tribunal may rule on its own substantive jurisdiction, that is, as to—

    (a) whether there is a valid arbitration agreement,
    (b) whether the tribunal is properly constituted, and
    (c) what matters have been submitted to arbitration in accordance with the arbitration agreement.

(2) Any such ruling may be challenged by any available arbitral process of appeal or review or in accordance with the provisions of this Part.

31 Objection to substantive jurisdiction of tribunal

(1) An objection that the arbitral tribunal lacks substantive jurisdiction at the outset of the proceedings must be raised by a party not later than the time he takes the first step in the proceedings to contest the merits of any matter in relation to which he challenges the tribunal's jurisdiction.
A party is not precluded from raising such an objection by the fact that he has appointed or participated in the appointment of an arbitrator.

(2) Any objection during the course of the arbitral proceedings that the arbitral tribunal is exceeding its substantive jurisdiction must be made as soon as possible after the matter alleged to be beyond its jurisdiction is raised.

(3) The arbitral tribunal may admit an objection later than the time specified in subsection (1) or (2) if it considers the delay justified.

(4) Where an objection is duly taken to the tribunal's substantive jurisdiction and the tribunal has power to rule on its own jurisdiction, it may—

    (a) rule on the matter in an award as to jurisdiction, or

    (b) deal with the objection in its award on the merits.

If the parties agree which of these courses the tribunal should take, the tribunal shall proceed accordingly.

(5) The tribunal may in any case, and shall if the parties so agree, stay proceedings whilst an application is made to the court under section 32 (determination of preliminary point of jurisdiction).

32 Determination of preliminary point of jurisdiction

(1) The court may, on the application of a party to arbitral proceedings (upon notice to the other parties), determine any question as to the substantive jurisdiction of the tribunal.

A party may lose the right to object (see section 73).

(2) An application under this section shall not be considered unless—

    (a) it is made with the agreement in writing of all the other parties to the proceedings, or

    (b) it is made with the permission of the tribunal and the court is satisfied—

        (i) that the determination of the question is likely to produce substantial savings in costs,

        (ii) that the application was made without delay, and

        (iii) that there is good reason why the matter should be decided by the court.

(3) An application under this section, unless made with the agreement of all the other parties to the proceedings, shall state the grounds on which it is said that the matter should be decided by the court.

(4) Unless otherwise agreed by the parties, the arbitral tribunal may continue the arbitral proceedings and make an award while an application to the court under this section is pending.

(5) Unless the court gives leave, no appeal lies from a decision of the court whether the conditions specified in subsection (2) are met.

(6) The decision of the court on the question of jurisdiction shall be treated as a judgment of the court for the purposes of an appeal.

But no appeal lies without the leave of the court which shall not be given unless the court considers that the question involves a point of law which is one of general importance or is one which for some other special reason should be considered by the Court of Appeal.

The arbitral proceedings

33 General duty of the tribunal

(1) The tribunal shall—

    (a) act fairly and impartially as between the parties, giving each party a reasonable opportunity of putting his case and dealing with that of his opponent, and

    (b) adopt procedures suitable to the circumstances of the particular case, avoiding unnecessary delay or expense, so as to provide a fair means for the resolution of the matters falling to be determined.

(2) The tribunal shall comply with that general duty in conducting the arbitral proceedings, in its decisions on matters of procedure and evidence and in the exercise of all other powers conferred on it.

34 Procedural and evidential matters

(1) It shall be for the tribunal to decide all procedural and evidential matters, subject to the right of the parties to agree any matter.

(2) Procedural and evidential matters include—

(a) when and where any part of the proceedings is to be held;

(b) the language or languages to be used in the proceedings and whether translations of any relevant documents are to be supplied;

(c) whether any and if so what form of written statements of claim and defence are to be used, when these should be supplied and the extent to which such statements can be later amended;

(d) whether any and if so which documents or classes of documents should be disclosed between and produced by the parties and at what stage;

(e) whether any and if so what questions should be put to and answered by the respective parties and when and in what form this should be done;

(f) whether to apply strict rules of evidence (or any other rules) as to the admissibility, relevance or weight of any material (oral, written or other) sought to be tendered on any matters of fact or opinion, and the time, manner and form in which such material should be exchanged and presented;

(g) whether and to what extent the tribunal should itself take the initiative in ascertaining the facts and the law;

(h) whether and to what extent there should be oral or written evidence or submissions.

(3) The tribunal may fix the time within which any directions given by it are to be complied with, and may if it thinks fit extend the time so fixed (whether or not it has expired).

35 Consolidation of proceedings and concurrent hearings

(1) The parties are free to agree—

(a) that the arbitral proceedings shall be consolidated with other arbitral proceedings, or

(b) that concurrent hearings shall be held,

on such terms as may be agreed.

(2) Unless the parties agree to confer such power on the tribunal, the tribunal has no power to order consolidation of proceedings or concurrent hearings.

36 Legal or other representation

Unless otherwise agreed by the parties, a party to arbitral proceedings may be represented in the proceedings by a lawyer or other person chosen by him.

37 Power to appoint experts, legal advisers or assessors

(1) Unless otherwise agreed by the parties—

(a) the tribunal may—

(i) appoint experts or legal advisers to report to it and the parties, or

(ii) appoint assessors to assist it on technical matters,

and may allow any such expert, legal adviser or assessor to attend the proceedings; and

(b) the parties shall be given a reasonable opportunity to comment on any information, opinion or advice offered by any such person.

(2) The fees and expenses of an expert, legal adviser or assessor appointed by the tribunal for which the arbitrators are liable are expenses of the arbitrators for the purposes of this Part.

38 General powers exercisable by the tribunal

(1) The parties are free to agree on the powers exercisable by the arbitral tribunal for the purposes of and in relation to the proceedings.

(2) Unless otherwise agreed by the parties the tribunal has the following powers.

(3) The tribunal may order a claimant to provide security for the costs of the arbitration.

This power shall not be exercised on the ground that the claimant is—

    (a) an individual ordinarily resident outside the United Kingdom, or

    (b) a corporation or association incorporated or formed under the law of a country outside the United Kingdom, or whose central management and control is exercised outside the United Kingdom.

(4) The tribunal may give directions in relation to any property which is the subject of the proceedings or as to which any question arises in the proceedings, and which is owned by or is in the possession of a party to the proceedings—

    (a) for the inspection, photographing, preservation, custody or detention of the property by the tribunal, an expert or a party, or

    (b) ordering that samples be taken from, or any observation be made of or experiment conducted upon, the property.

(5) The tribunal may direct that a party or witness shall be examined on oath or affirmation, and may for that purpose administer any necessary oath or take any necessary affirmation.

(6) The tribunal may give directions to a party for the preservation for the purposes of the proceedings of any evidence in his custody or control.

39 Power to make provisional awards

(1) The parties are free to agree that the tribunal shall have power to order on a provisional basis any relief which it would have power to grant in a final award.

(2) This includes, for instance, making—

    (a) a provisional order for the payment of money or the disposition of property as between the parties, or

    (b) an order to make an interim payment on account of the costs of the arbitration.

(3) Any such order shall be subject to the tribunal's final adjudication; and the tribunal's final award, on the merits or as to costs, shall take account of any such order.

(4) Unless the parties agree to confer such power on the tribunal, the tribunal has no such power.

This does not affect its powers under section 47 (awards on different issues, &c.).

40 General duty of parties

(1) The parties shall do all things necessary for the proper and expeditious conduct of the arbitral proceedings.

(2) This includes—

    (a) complying without delay with any determination of the tribunal as to procedural or eviden-tial matters, or with any order or directions of the tribunal, and

    (b) where appropriate, taking without delay any necessary steps to obtain a decision of the court on a preliminary question of jurisdiction or law (see sections 32 and 45).

41 Powers of tribunal in case of party's default

(1) The parties are free to agree on the powers of the tribunal in case of a party's failure to do something necessary for the proper and expeditious conduct of the arbitration.

(2) Unless otherwise agreed by the parties, the following provisions apply.

(3) If the tribunal is satisfied that there has been inordinate and inexcusable delay on the part of the claimant in pursuing his claim and that the delay—

    (a) gives rise, or is likely to give rise, to a substantial risk that it is not possible to have a fair resolution of the issues in that claim, or

    (b) has caused, or is likely to cause, serious prejudice to the respondent,

the tribunal may make an award dismissing the claim.

(4) If without showing sufficient cause a party—

    (a) fails to attend or be represented at an oral hearing of which due notice was given, or

    (b) where matters are to be dealt with in writing, fails after due notice to submit written evidence or make written submissions,

the tribunal may continue the proceedings in the absence of that party or, as the case may be, without any written evidence or submissions on his behalf, and may make an award on the basis of the evidence before it.

(5) If without showing sufficient cause a party fails to comply with any order or directions of the tribunal, the tribunal may make a peremptory order to the same effect, prescribing such time for compliance with it as the tribunal considers appropriate.

(6) If a claimant fails to comply with a peremptory order of the tribunal to provide security for costs, the tribunal may make an award dismissing his claim.

(7) If a party fails to comply with any other kind of peremptory order, then, without prejudice to section 42 (enforcement by court of tribunal's peremptory orders), the tribunal may do any of the following—

    (a) direct that the party in default shall not be entitled to rely upon any allegation or material which was the subject matter of the order;

    (b) draw such adverse inferences from the act of non-compliance as the circumstances justify;

    (c) proceed to an award on the basis of such materials as have been properly provided to it;

    (d) make such order as it thinks fit as to the payment of costs of the arbitration incurred in consequence of the non-compliance.

Powers of court in relation to arbitral proceedings

42 Enforcement of peremptory orders of tribunal

(1) Unless otherwise agreed by the parties, the court may make an order requiring a party to comply with a peremptory order made by the tribunal.

(2) An application for an order under this section may be made—

    (a) by the tribunal (upon notice to the parties),

    (b) by a party to the arbitral proceedings with the permission of the tribunal (and upon notice to the other parties), or

    (c) where the parties have agreed that the powers of the court under this section shall be available.

(3) The court shall not act unless it is satisfied that the applicant has exhausted any available arbitral process in respect of failure to comply with the tribunal's order.

(4) No order shall be made under this section unless the court is satisfied that the person to whom the tribunal's order was directed has failed to comply with it within the time prescribed in the order or, if no time was prescribed, within a reasonable time.

(5) The leave of the court is required for any appeal from a decision of the court under this section.

43 Securing the attendance of witnesses

(1) A party to arbitral proceedings may use the same court procedures as are available in relation to legal proceedings to secure the attendance before the tribunal of a witness in order to give oral testimony or to produce documents or other material evidence.

(2) This may only be done with the permission of the tribunal or the agreement of the other parties.

(3) The court procedures may only be used if—

    (a) the witness is in the United Kingdom, and

    (b) the arbitral proceedings are being conducted in England and Wales or, as the case may be, Northern Ireland.

(4) A person shall not be compelled by virtue of this section to produce any document or other material evidence which he could not be compelled to produce in legal proceedings.

44 Court powers exercisable in support of arbitral proceedings

(1) Unless otherwise agreed by the parties, the court has for the purposes of and in relation to arbitral proceedings the same power of making orders about the matters listed below as it has for the purposes of and in relation to legal proceedings.

(2) Those matters are—

    (a) the taking of the evidence of witnesses;

    (b) the preservation of evidence;

    (c) making orders relating to property which is the subject of the proceedings or as to which any question arises in the proceedings—

        (i) for the inspection, photographing, preservation, custody or detention of the property, or

        (ii) ordering that samples be taken from, or any observation be made of or experiment conducted upon, the property;

    and for that purpose authorising any person to enter any premises in the possession or control of a party to the arbitration;

    (d) the sale of any goods the subject of the proceedings;

    (e) the granting of an interim injunction or the appointment of a receiver.

(3) If the case is one of urgency, the court may, on the application of a party or proposed party to the arbitral proceedings, make such orders as it thinks necessary for the purpose of preserving evidence or assets.

(4) If the case is not one of urgency, the court shall act only on the application of a party to the arbitral proceedings (upon notice to the other parties and to the tribunal) made with the permission of the tribunal or the agreement in writing of the other parties.

(5) In any case the court shall act only if or to the extent that the arbitral tribunal, and any arbitral or other institution or person vested by the parties with power in that regard, has no power or is unable for the time being to act effectively.

(6) If the court so orders, an order made by it under this section shall cease to have effect in whole or in part on the order of the tribunal or of any such arbitral or other institution or person having power to act in relation to the subject-matter of the order.

(7) The leave of the court is required for any appeal from a decision of the court under this section.

45 Determination of preliminary point of law

(1) Unless otherwise agreed by the parties, the court may on the application of a party to arbitral proceedings (upon notice to the other parties) determine any question of law arising in the course of the proceedings which the court is satisfied substantially affects the rights of one or more of the parties.

An agreement to dispense with reasons for the tribunal's award shall be considered an agreement to exclude the court's jurisdiction under this section.

(2) An application under this section shall not be considered unless—

    (a) it is made with the agreement of all the other parties to the proceedings, or

    (b) it is made with the permission of the tribunal and the court is satisfied—

        (i) that the determination of the question is likely to produce substantial savings in costs, and

        (ii) that the application was made without delay.

(3) The application shall identify the question of law to be determined and, unless made with the agreement of all the other parties to the proceedings, shall state the grounds on which it is said that the question should be decided by the court.

(4) Unless otherwise agreed by the parties, the arbitral tribunal may continue the arbitral proceedings and make an award while an application to the court under this section is pending.

(5) Unless the court gives leave, no appeal lies from a decision of the court whether the conditions specified in subsection (2) are met.

(6) The decision of the court on the question of law shall be treated as a judgment of the court for the purposes of an appeal.

But no appeal lies without the leave of the court which shall not be given unless the court considers that the question is one of general importance, or is one which for some other special reason should be considered by the Court of Appeal.

The award

46 Rules applicable to substance of dispute

(1) The arbitral tribunal shall decide the dispute—

    (a) in accordance with the law chosen by the parties as applicable to the substance of the dispute, or

    (b) if the parties so agree, in accordance with such other considerations as are agreed by them or determined by the tribunal.

(2) For this purpose the choice of the laws of a country shall be understood to refer to the substantive laws of that country and not its conflict of laws rules.

(3) If or to the extent that there is no such choice or agreement, the tribunal shall apply the law determined by the conflict of laws rules which it considers applicable.

47 Awards on different issues, & c

(1) Unless otherwise agreed by the parties, the tribunal may make more than one award at different times on different aspects of the matters to be determined.

(2) The tribunal may, in particular, make an award relating—

    (a) to an issue affecting the whole claim, or

    (b) to a part only of the claims or cross-claims submitted to it for decision.

(3) If the tribunal does so, it shall specify in its award the issue, or the claim or part of a claim, which is the subject matter of the award.

48 Remedies

(1) The parties are free to agree on the powers exercisable by the arbitral tribunal as regards remedies.

(2) Unless otherwise agreed by the parties, the tribunal has the following powers.

(3) The tribunal may make a declaration as to any matter to be determined in the proceedings.

(4) The tribunal may order the payment of a sum of money, in any currency.

(5) The tribunal has the same powers as the court—

    (a) to order a party to do or refrain from doing anything;

    (b) to order specific performance of a contract (other than a contract relating to land);

    (c) to order the rectification, setting aside or cancellation of a deed or other document.

49 Interest

(1) The parties are free to agree on the powers of the tribunal as regards the award of interest.

(2) Unless otherwise agreed by the parties the following provisions apply.

(3) The tribunal may award simple or compound interest from such dates, at such rates and with such rests as it considers meets the justice of the case—

    (a) on the whole or part of any amount awarded by the tribunal, in respect of any period up to the date of the award;

    (b) on the whole or part of any amount claimed in the arbitration and outstanding at the commencement of the arbitral proceedings but paid before the award was made, in respect of any period up to the date of payment.

(4) The tribunal may award simple or compound interest from the date of the award (or any later date) until payment, at such rates and with such rests as it considers meets the justice of the case, on

the outstanding amount of any award (including any award of interest under subsection (3) and any award as to costs).

(5) References in this section to an amount awarded by the tribunal include an amount payable in consequence of a declaratory award by the tribunal.

(6) The above provisions do not affect any other power of the tribunal to award interest.

50 Extension of time for making award

(1) Where the time for making an award is limited by or in pursuance of the arbitration agreement, then, unless otherwise agreed by the parties, the court may in accordance with the following provisions by order extend that time.

(2) An application for an order under this section may be made—

    (a) by the tribunal (upon notice to the parties), or

    (b) by any party to the proceedings (upon notice to the tribunal and the other parties),

but only after exhausting any available arbitral process for obtaining an extension of time.

(3) The court shall only make an order if satisfied that a substantial injustice would otherwise be done.

(4) The court may extend the time for such period and on such terms as it thinks fit, and may do so whether or not the time previously fixed (by or under the agreement or by a previous order) has expired.

(5) The leave of the court is required for any appeal from a decision of the court under this section.

51 Settlement

(1) If during arbitral proceedings the parties settle the dispute, the following provisions apply unless otherwise agreed by the parties.

(2) The tribunal shall terminate the substantive proceedings and, if so requested by the parties and not objected to by the tribunal, shall record the settlement in the form of an agreed award.

(3) An agreed award shall state that it is an award of the tribunal and shall have the same status and effect as any other award on the merits of the case.

(4) The following provisions of this Part relating to awards (sections 52 to 58) apply to an agreed award.

(5) Unless the parties have also settled the matter of the payment of the costs of the arbitration, the provisions of this Part relating to costs (sections 59 to 65) continue to apply.

52 Form of award

(1) The parties are free to agree on the form of an award.

(2) If or to the extent that there is no such agreement, the following provisions apply.

(3) The award shall be in writing signed by all the arbitrators or all those assenting to the award.

(4) The award shall contain the reasons for the award unless it is an agreed award or the parties have agreed to dispense with reasons.

(5) The award shall state the seat of the arbitration and the date when the award is made.

53 Place where award treated as made

Unless otherwise agreed by the parties, where the seat of the arbitration is in England and Wales or Northern Ireland, any award in the proceedings shall be treated as made there, regardless of where it was signed, despatched or delivered to any of the parties.

54 Date of award

(1) Unless otherwise agreed by the parties, the tribunal may decide what is to be taken to be the date on which the award was made.

(2) In the absence of any such decision, the date of the award shall be taken to be the date on which it is signed by the arbitrator or, where more than one arbitrator signs the award, by the last of them.

55 Notification of award

(1) The parties are free to agree on the requirements as to notification of the award to the parties.

(2) If there is no such agreement, the award shall be notified to the parties by service on them of copies of the award, which shall be done without delay after the award is made.

(3) Nothing in this section affects section 56 (power to withhold award in case of non-payment).

56 Power to withhold award in case of non-payment

(1) The tribunal may refuse to deliver an award to the parties except upon full payment of the fees and expenses of the arbitrators.

(2) If the tribunal refuses on that ground to deliver an award, a party to the arbitral proceedings may (upon notice to the other parties and the tribunal) apply to the court, which may order that—

> (a) the tribunal shall deliver the award on the payment into court by the applicant of the fees and expenses demanded, or such lesser amount as the court may specify,
>
> (b) the amount of the fees and expenses properly payable shall be determined by such means and upon such terms as the court may direct, and
>
> (c) out of the money paid into court there shall be paid out such fees and expenses as may be found to be properly payable and the balance of the money (if any) shall be paid out to the applicant.

(3) For this purpose the amount of fees and expenses properly payable is the amount the applicant is liable to pay under section 28 or any agreement relating to the payment of the arbitrators.

(4) No application to the court may be made where there is any available arbitral process for appeal or review of the amount of the fees or expenses demanded.

(5) References in this section to arbitrators include an arbitrator who has ceased to act and an umpire who has not replaced the other arbitrators.

(6) The above provisions of this section also apply in relation to any arbitral or other institution or person vested by the parties with powers in relation to the delivery of the tribunal's award.

As they so apply, the references to the fees and expenses of the arbitrators shall be construed as including the fees and expenses of that institution or person.

(7) The leave of the court is required for any appeal from a decision of the court under this section.

(8) Nothing in this section shall be construed as excluding an application under section 28 where payment has been made to the arbitrators in order to obtain the award.

57 Correction of award or additional award

(1) The parties are free to agree on the powers of the tribunal to correct an award or make an additional award.

(2) If or to the extent there is no such agreement, the following provisions apply.

(3) The tribunal may on its own initiative or on the application of a party—

> (a) correct an award so as to remove any clerical mistake or error arising from an accidental slip or omission or clarify or remove any ambiguity in the award, or
>
> (b) make an additional award in respect of any claim (including a claim for interest or costs) which was presented to the tribunal but was not dealt with in the award.

These powers shall not be exercised without first affording the other parties a reasonable opportunity to make representations to the tribunal.

(4) Any application for the exercise of those powers must be made within 28 days of the date of the award or such longer period as the parties may agree.

(5) Any correction of an award shall be made within 28 days of the date the application was received by the tribunal or, where the correction is made by the tribunal on its own initiative, within 28 days of the date of the award or, in either case, such longer period as the parties may agree.

(6) Any additional award shall be made within 56 days of the date of the original award or such longer period as the parties may agree.

(7) Any correction of an award shall form part of the award.

58 Effect of award

(1) Unless otherwise agreed by the parties, an award made by the tribunal pursuant to an arbitration agreement is final and binding both on the parties and on any persons claiming through or under them.

(2) This does not affect the right of a person to challenge the award by any available arbitral process of appeal or review or in accordance with the provisions of this Part.

Costs of the arbitration

59 Costs of the arbitration

(1) References in this Part to the costs of the arbitration are to—

(a) the arbitrators' fees and expenses,

(b) the fees and expenses of any arbitral institution concerned, and

(c) the legal or other costs of the parties.

(2) Any such reference includes the costs of or incidental to any proceedings to determine the amount of the recoverable costs of the arbitration (see section 63).

60 Agreement to pay costs in any event

An agreement which has the effect that a party is to pay the whole or part of the costs of the arbitration in any event is only valid if made after the dispute in question has arisen.

61 Award of costs

(1) The tribunal may make an award allocating the costs of the arbitration as between the parties, subject to any agreement of the parties.

(2) Unless the parties otherwise agree, the tribunal shall award costs on the general principle that costs should follow the event except where it appears to the tribunal that in the circumstances this is not appropriate in relation to the whole or part of the costs.

62 Effect of agreement or award about costs

Unless the parties otherwise agree, any obligation under an agreement between them as to how the costs of the arbitration are to be borne, or under an award allocating the costs of the arbitration, extends only to such costs as are recoverable.

63 The recoverable costs of the arbitration

(1) The parties are free to agree what costs of the arbitration are recoverable.

(2) If or to the extent there is no such agreement, the following provisions apply.

(3) The tribunal may determine by award the recoverable costs of the arbitration on such basis as it thinks fit.

If it does so, it shall specify—

(a) the basis on which it has acted, and

(b) the items of recoverable costs and the amount referable to each.

(4) If the tribunal does not determine the recoverable costs of the arbitration, any party to the arbitral proceedings may apply to the court (upon notice to the other parties) which may—

(a) determine the recoverable costs of the arbitration on such basis as it thinks fit, or

(b) order that they shall be determined by such means and upon such terms as it may specify.

(5) Unless the tribunal or the court determines otherwise—

(a) the recoverable costs of the arbitration shall be determined on the basis that there shall be allowed a reasonable amount in respect of all costs reasonably incurred, and

(b) any doubt as to whether costs were reasonably incurred or were reasonable in amount shall be resolved in favour of the paying party.

(6) The above provisions have effect subject to section 64 (recoverable fees and expenses of arbitrators).

(7) Nothing in this section affects any right of the arbitrators, any expert, legal adviser or assessor appointed by the tribunal, or any arbitral institution, to payment of their fees and expenses.

64 Recoverable fees and expenses of arbitrators

(1) Unless otherwise agreed by the parties, the recoverable costs of the arbitration shall include in respect of the fees and expenses of the arbitrators only such reasonable fees and expenses as are appropriate in the circumstances.

(2) If there is any question as to what reasonable fees and expenses are appropriate in the circumstances, and the matter is not already before the court on an application under section 63(4), the court may on the application of any party (upon notice to the other parties)—

  (a) determine the matter, or
  (b) order that it be determined by such means and upon such terms as the court may specify.

(3) Subsection (1) has effect subject to any order of the court under section 24(4) or 25(3)(b) (order as to entitlement to fees or expenses in case of removal or resignation of arbitrator).

(4) Nothing in this section affects any right of the arbitrator to payment of his fees and expenses.

65 Power to limit recoverable costs

(1) Unless otherwise agreed by the parties, the tribunal may direct that the recoverable costs of the arbitration, or of any part of the arbitral proceedings, shall be limited to a specified amount.

(2) Any direction may be made or varied at any stage, but this must be done sufficiently in advance of the incurring of costs to which it relates, or the taking of any steps in the proceedings which may be affected by it, for the limit to be taken into account.

Powers of the court in relation to award

66 Enforcement of the award

(1) An award made by the tribunal pursuant to an arbitration agreement may, by leave of the court, be enforced in the same manner as a judgment or order of the court to the same effect.

(2) Where leave is so given, judgment may be entered in terms of the award.

(3) Leave to enforce an award shall not be given where, or to the extent that, the person against whom it is sought to be enforced shows that the tribunal lacked substantive jurisdiction to make the award.

The right to raise such an objection may have been lost (see section 73).

(4) Nothing in this section affects the recognition or enforcement of an award under any other enactment or rule of law, in particular under Part II of the [1950 c. 27.] Arbitration Act 1950 (enforcement of awards under Geneva Convention) or the provisions of Part III of this Act relating to the recognition and enforcement of awards under the New York Convention or by an action on the award.

67 Challenging the award: substantive jurisdiction

(1) A party to arbitral proceedings may (upon notice to the other parties and to the tribunal) apply to the court—

  (a) challenging any award of the arbitral tribunal as to its substantive jurisdiction; or
  (b) for an order declaring an award made by the tribunal on the merits to be of no effect, in whole or in part, because the tribunal did not have substantive jurisdiction.

A party may lose the right to object (see section 73) and the right to apply is subject to the restrictions in section 70(2) and (3).

(2) The arbitral tribunal may continue the arbitral proceedings and make a further award while an application to the court under this section is pending in relation to an award as to jurisdiction.

(3) On an application under this section challenging an award of the arbitral tribunal as to its substantive jurisdiction, the court may by order—

  (a) confirm the award,
  (b) vary the award, or

(c) set aside the award in whole or in part.

(4) The leave of the court is required for any appeal from a decision of the court under this section.

68 Challenging the award: serious irregularity

(1) A party to arbitral proceedings may (upon notice to the other parties and to the tribunal) apply to the court challenging an award in the proceedings on the ground of serious irregularity affecting the tribunal, the proceedings or the award.

A party may lose the right to object (see section 73) and the right to apply is subject to the restrictions in section 70(2) and (3).

(2) Serious irregularity means an irregularity of one or more of the following kinds which the court considers has caused or will cause substantial injustice to the applicant—

    (a) failure by the tribunal to comply with section 33 (general duty of tribunal);

    (b) the tribunal exceeding its powers (otherwise than by exceeding its substantive jurisdiction: see section 67);

    (c) failure by the tribunal to conduct the proceedings in accordance with the procedure agreed by the parties;

    (d) failure by the tribunal to deal with all the issues that were put to it;

    (e) any arbitral or other institution or person vested by the parties with powers in relation to the proceedings or the award exceeding its powers;

    (f) uncertainty or ambiguity as to the effect of the award;

    (g) the award being obtained by fraud or the award or the way in which it was procured being contrary to public policy;

    (h) failure to comply with the requirements as to the form of the award; or

    (i) any irregularity in the conduct of the proceedings or in the award which is admitted by the tribunal or by any arbitral or other institution or person vested by the parties with powers in relation to the proceedings or the award.

(3) If there is shown to be serious irregularity affecting the tribunal, the proceedings or the award, the court may—

    (a) remit the award to the tribunal, in whole or in part, for reconsideration,

    (b) set the award aside in whole or in part, or

    (c) declare the award to be of no effect, in whole or in part.

The court shall not exercise its power to set aside or to declare an award to be of no effect, in whole or in part, unless it is satisfied that it would be inappropriate to remit the matters in question to the tribunal for reconsideration.

(4) The leave of the court is required for any appeal from a decision of the court under this section.

69 Appeal on point of law

(1) Unless otherwise agreed by the parties, a party to arbitral proceedings may (upon notice to the other parties and to the tribunal) appeal to the court on a question of law arising out of an award made in the proceedings.

An agreement to dispense with reasons for the tribunal's award shall be considered an agreement to exclude the court's jurisdiction under this section.

(2) An appeal shall not be brought under this section except—

    (a) with the agreement of all the other parties to the proceedings, or

    (b) with the leave of the court.

The right to appeal is also subject to the restrictions in section 70(2) and (3).

(3) Leave to appeal shall be given only if the court is satisfied—

    (a) that the determination of the question will substantially affect the rights of one or more of the parties,

    (b) that the question is one which the tribunal was asked to determine,

(c) that, on the basis of the findings of fact in the award—

    (i) the decision of the tribunal on the question is obviously wrong, or

    (ii) the question is one of general public importance and the decision of the tribunal is at least open to serious doubt, and

(d) that, despite the agreement of the parties to resolve the matter by arbitration, it is just and proper in all the circumstances for the court to determine the question.

(4) An application for leave to appeal under this section shall identify the question of law to be determined and state the grounds on which it is alleged that leave to appeal should be granted.

(5) The court shall determine an application for leave to appeal under this section without a hearing unless it appears to the court that a hearing is required.

(6) The leave of the court is required for any appeal from a decision of the court under this section to grant or refuse leave to appeal.

(7) On an appeal under this section the court may by order—

(a) confirm the award,

(b) vary the award,

(c) remit the award to the tribunal, in whole or in part, for reconsideration in the light of the court's determination, or

(d) set aside the award in whole or in part.

The court shall not exercise its power to set aside an award, in whole or in part, unless it is satisfied that it would be inappropriate to remit the matters in question to the tribunal for reconsideration.

(8) The decision of the court on an appeal under this section shall be treated as a judgment of the court for the purposes of a further appeal.

But no such appeal lies without the leave of the court which shall not be given unless the court considers that the question is one of general importance or is one which for some other special reason should be considered by the Court of Appeal.

70 Challenge or appeal: supplementary provisions

(1) The following provisions apply to an application or appeal under section 67, 68 or 69.

(2) An application or appeal may not be brought if the applicant or appellant has not first exhausted—

(a) any available arbitral process of appeal or review, and

(b) any available recourse under section 57 (correction of award or additional award).

(3) Any application or appeal must be brought within 28 days of the date of the award or, if there has been any arbitral process of appeal or review, of the date when the applicant or appellant was notified of the result of that process.

(4) If on an application or appeal it appears to the court that the award—

(a) does not contain the tribunal's reasons, or

(b) does not set out the tribunal's reasons in sufficient detail to enable the court properly to consider the application or appeal,

the court may order the tribunal to state the reasons for its award in sufficient detail for that purpose.

(5) Where the court makes an order under subsection (4), it may make such further order as it thinks fit with respect to any additional costs of the arbitration resulting from its order.

(6) The court may order the applicant or appellant to provide security for the costs of the application or appeal, and may direct that the application or appeal be dismissed if the order is not complied with.

The power to order security for costs shall not be exercised on the ground that the applicant or appellant is—

(a) an individual ordinarily resident outside the United Kingdom, or

(b) a corporation or association incorporated or formed under the law of a country outside the United Kingdom, or whose central management and control is exercised outside the United Kingdom.

(7) The court may order that any money payable under the award shall be brought into court or otherwise secured pending the determination of the application or appeal, and may direct that the application or appeal be dismissed if the order is not complied with.

(8) The court may grant leave to appeal subject to conditions to the same or similar effect as an order under subsection (6) or (7).

This does not affect the general discretion of the court to grant leave subject to conditions.

71 Challenge or appeal: effect of order of court

(1) The following provisions have effect where the court makes an order under section 67, 68 or 69 with respect to an award.

(2) Where the award is varied, the variation has effect as part of the tribunal's award.

(3) Where the award is remitted to the tribunal, in whole or in part, for reconsideration, the tribunal shall make a fresh award in respect of the matters remitted within three months of the date of the order for remission or such longer or shorter period as the court may direct.

(4) Where the award is set aside or declared to be of no effect, in whole or in part, the court may also order that any provision that an award is a condition precedent to the bringing of legal proceedings in respect of a matter to which the arbitration agreement applies, is of no effect as regards the subject matter of the award or, as the case may be, the relevant part of the award.

Miscellaneous

72 Saving for rights of person who takes no part in proceedings

(1) A person alleged to be a party to arbitral proceedings but who takes no part in the proceedings may question—

(a) whether there is a valid arbitration agreement,

(b) whether the tribunal is properly constituted, or

(c) what matters have been submitted to arbitration in accordance with the arbitration agreement,

by proceedings in the court for a declaration or injunction or other appropriate relief.

(2) He also has the same right as a party to the arbitral proceedings to challenge an award—

(a) by an application under section 67 on the ground of lack of substantive jurisdiction in relation to him, or

(b) by an application under section 68 on the ground of serious irregularity (within the meaning of that section) affecting him;

and section 70(2) (duty to exhaust arbitral procedures) does not apply in his case.

73 Loss of right to object

(1) If a party to arbitral proceedings takes part, or continues to take part, in the proceedings without making, either forthwith or within such time as is allowed by the arbitration agreement or the tribunal or by any provision of this Part, any objection—

(a) that the tribunal lacks substantive jurisdiction,

(b) that the proceedings have been improperly conducted,

(c) that there has been a failure to comply with the arbitration agreement or with any provision of this Part, or

(d) that there has been any other irregularity affecting the tribunal or the proceedings,

he may not raise that objection later, before the tribunal or the court, unless he shows that, at the time he took part or continued to take part in the proceedings, he did not know and could not with reasonable diligence have discovered the grounds for the objection.

(2) Where the arbitral tribunal rules that it has substantive jurisdiction and a party to arbitral proceedings who could have questioned that ruling—

    (a) by any available arbitral process of appeal or review, or

    (b) by challenging the award,

does not do so, or does not do so within the time allowed by the arbitration agreement or any provision of this Part, he may not object later to the tribunal's substantive jurisdiction on any ground which was the subject of that ruling.

74 Immunity of arbitral institutions, &c

(1) An arbitral or other institution or person designated or requested by the parties to appoint or nominate an arbitrator is not liable for anything done or omitted in the discharge or purported discharge of that function unless the act or omission is shown to have been in bad faith.

(2) An arbitral or other institution or person by whom an arbitrator is appointed or nominated is not liable, by reason of having appointed or nominated him, for anything done or omitted by the arbitrator (or his employees or agents) in the discharge or purported discharge of his functions as arbitrator.

(3) The above provisions apply to an employee or agent of an arbitral or other institution or person as they apply to the institution or person himself.

75 Charge to secure payment of solicitors' costs

The powers of the court to make declarations and orders under section 73 of the [1974 c. 47.] Solicitors Act 1974 or Article 71H of the [S.I. 1976/582 (N.I. 12).] Solicitors (Northern Ireland) Order 1976 (power to charge property recovered in the proceedings with the payment of solicitors' costs) may be exercised in relation to arbitral proceedings as if those proceedings were proceedings in the court.

Supplementary

76 Service of notices, &c

(1) The parties are free to agree on the manner of service of any notice or other document required or authorised to be given or served in pursuance of the arbitration agreement or for the purposes of the arbitral proceedings.

(2) If or to the extent that there is no such agreement the following provisions apply.

(3) A notice or other document may be served on a person by any effective means.

(4) If a notice or other document is addressed, pre-paid and delivered by post—

    (a) to the addressee's last known principal residence or, if he is or has been carrying on a trade, profession or business, his last known principal business address, or

    (b) where the addressee is a body corporate, to the body's registered or principal office,

it shall be treated as effectively served.

(5) This section does not apply to the service of documents for the purposes of legal proceedings, for which provision is made by rules of court.

(6) References in this Part to a notice or other document include any form of communication in writing and references to giving or serving a notice or other document shall be construed accordingly.

77 Powers of court in relation to service of documents

(1) This section applies where service of a document on a person in the manner agreed by the parties, or in accordance with provisions of section 76 having effect in default of agreement, is not reasonably practicable.

(2) Unless otherwise agreed by the parties, the court may make such order as it thinks fit—

    (a) for service in such manner as the court may direct, or

(b) dispensing with service of the document.

(3) Any party to the arbitration agreement may apply for an order, but only after exhausting any available arbitral process for resolving the matter.

(4) The leave of the court is required for any appeal from a decision of the court under this section.

78 Reckoning periods of time

(1) The parties are free to agree on the method of reckoning periods of time for the purposes of any provision agreed by them or any provision of this Part having effect in default of such agreement.

(2) If or to the extent there is no such agreement, periods of time shall be reckoned in accordance with the following provisions.

(3) Where the act is required to be done within a specified period after or from a specified date, the period begins immediately after that date.

(4) Where the act is required to be done a specified number of clear days after a specified date, at least that number of days must intervene between the day on which the act is done and that date.

(5) Where the period is a period of seven days or less which would include a Saturday, Sunday or a public holiday in the place where anything which has to be done within the period falls to be done, that day shall be excluded.

In relation to England and Wales or Northern Ireland, a "public holiday" means Christmas Day, Good Friday or a day which under the [1971 c. 80.] Banking and Financial Dealings Act 1971 is a bank holiday.

79 Power of court to extend time limits relating to arbitral proceedings

(1) Unless the parties otherwise agree, the court may by order extend any time limit agreed by them in relation to any matter relating to the arbitral proceedings or specified in any provision of this Part having effect in default of such agreement.

This section does not apply to a time limit to which section 12 applies (power of court to extend time for beginning arbitral proceedings, &c.).

(2) An application for an order may be made—

(a) by any party to the arbitral proceedings (upon notice to the other parties and to the tribunal), or

(b) by the arbitral tribunal (upon notice to the parties).

(3) The court shall not exercise its power to extend a time limit unless it is satisfied—

(a) that any available recourse to the tribunal, or to any arbitral or other institution or person vested by the parties with power in that regard, has first been exhausted, and

(b) that a substantial injustice would otherwise be done.

(4) The court's power under this section may be exercised whether or not the time has already expired.

(5) An order under this section may be made on such terms as the court thinks fit.

(6) The leave of the court is required for any appeal from a decision of the court under this section.

80 Notice and other requirements in connection with legal proceedings

(1) References in this Part to an application, appeal or other step in relation to legal proceedings being taken "upon notice" to the other parties to the arbitral proceedings, or to the tribunal, are to such notice of the originating process as is required by rules of court and do not impose any separate requirement.

(2) Rules of court shall be made—

(a) requiring such notice to be given as indicated by any provision of this Part, and

(b) as to the manner, form and content of any such notice.

(3) Subject to any provision made by rules of court, a requirement to give notice to the tribunal of legal proceedings shall be construed—

(a) if there is more than one arbitrator, as a requirement to give notice to each of them; and

(b) if the tribunal is not fully constituted, as a requirement to give notice to any arbitrator who has been appointed.

(4) References in this Part to making an application or appeal to the court within a specified period are to the issue within that period of the appropriate originating process in accordance with rules of court.

(5) Where any provision of this Part requires an application or appeal to be made to the court within a specified time, the rules of court relating to the reckoning of periods, the extending or abridging of periods, and the consequences of not taking a step within the period prescribed by the rules, apply in relation to that requirement.

(6) Provision may be made by rules of court amending the provisions of this Part—

(a) with respect to the time within which any application or appeal to the court must be made,

(b) so as to keep any provision made by this Part in relation to arbitral proceedings in step with the corresponding provision of rules of court applying in relation to proceedings in the court, or

(c) so as to keep any provision made by this Part in relation to legal proceedings in step with the corresponding provision of rules of court applying generally in relation to proceedings in the court.

(7) Nothing in this section affects the generality of the power to make rules of court.

81 Saving for certain matters governed by common law

(1) Nothing in this Part shall be construed as excluding the operation of any rule of law consistent with the provisions of this Part, in particular, any rule of law as to—

(a) matters which are not capable of settlement by arbitration;

(b) the effect of an oral arbitration agreement; or

(c) the refusal of recognition or enforcement of an arbitral award on grounds of public policy.

(2) Nothing in this Act shall be construed as reviving any jurisdiction of the court to set aside or remit an award on the ground of errors of fact or law on the face of the award.

82 Minor definitions

(1) In this Part—

"arbitrator", unless the context otherwise requires, includes an umpire;

"available arbitral process", in relation to any matter, includes any process of appeal to or review by an arbitral or other institution or person vested by the parties with powers in relation to that matter;

"claimant", unless the context otherwise requires, includes a counterclaimant, and related expressions shall be construed accordingly;

"dispute" includes any difference;

"enactment" includes an enactment contained in Northern Ireland legislation;

"legal proceedings" means civil proceedings in the High Court or a county court;

"peremptory order" means an order made under section 41(5) or made in exercise of any corresponding power conferred by the parties;

"premises" includes land, buildings, moveable structures, vehicles, vessels, aircraft and hovercraft;

"question of law" means—

> (a) for a court in England and Wales, a question of the law of England and Wales, and
>
> (b) for a court in Northern Ireland, a question of the law of Northern Ireland;

"substantive jurisdiction", in relation to an arbitral tribunal, refers to the matters specified in section 30(1)(a) to (c), and references to the tribunal exceeding its substantive jurisdiction shall be construed accordingly.

(2) References in this Part to a party to an arbitration agreement include any person claiming under or through a party to the agreement.

83 Index of defined expressions: Part I

In this Part the expressions listed below are defined or otherwise explained by the provisions indicated—

agreement, agree and agreed	section 5(1)
agreement in writing	section 5(2) to (5)
arbitration agreement	sections 6 and 5(1)
arbitrator	section 82(1)
available arbitral process	section 82(1)
claimant	section 82(1)
commencement (in relation to arbitral proceedings)	section 14
costs of the arbitration	section 59
the court	section 105
dispute	section 82(1)
enactment	section 82(1)
legal proceedings	section 82(1)
Limitation Acts	section 13(4)
notice (or other document)	section 76(6)
party—	
—in relation to an arbitration agreement	section 82(2)
—where section 106(2) or (3) applies	section 106(4)
peremptory order	section 82(1) (and see section 41(5))
premises	section 82(1)
question of law	section 82(1)
recoverable costs	sections 63 and 64
seat of the arbitration	section 3
serve and service (of notice or other document)	section 76(6)
substantive jurisdiction (in relation to an arbitral tribunal)	section 82(1) (and see section 30(1)(a) to (c))
upon notice (to the parties or the tribunal)	section 80
written and in writing	section 5(6)

84 Transitional provisions

(1) The provisions of this Part do not apply to arbitral proceedings commenced before the date on which this Part comes into force.

(2) They apply to arbitral proceedings commenced on or after that date under an arbitration agreement whenever made.

(3) The above provisions have effect subject to any transitional provision made by an order under section 109(2) (power to include transitional provisions in commencement order).

PART II
OTHER PROVISIONS RELATING TO ARBITRATION

Domestic arbitration agreements

85 Modification of Part I in relation to domestic arbitration agreement

(1) In the case of a domestic arbitration agreement the provisions of Part I are modified in accordance with the following sections.

(2) For this purpose a "domestic arbitration agreement" means an arbitration agreement to which none of the parties is—

(a) an individual who is a national of, or habitually resident in, a state other than the United Kingdom, or

(b) a body corporate which is incorporated in, or whose central control and management is exercised in, a state other than the United Kingdom,

and under which the seat of the arbitration (if the seat has been designated or determined) is in the United Kingdom.

(3) In subsection (2) "arbitration agreement" and "seat of the arbitration" have the same meaning as in Part I (see sections 3, 5(1) and 6).

86 Staying of legal proceedings

(1) In section 9 (stay of legal proceedings), subsection (4) (stay unless the arbitration agreement is null and void, inoperative, or incapable of being performed) does not apply to a domestic arbitration agreement.

(2) On an application under that section in relation to a domestic arbitration agreement the court shall grant a stay unless satisfied—

(a) that the arbitration agreement is null and void, inoperative, or incapable of being performed, or

(b) that there are other sufficient grounds for not requiring the parties to abide by the arbitration agreement.

(3) The court may treat as a sufficient ground under subsection (2)(b) the fact that the applicant is or was at any material time not ready and willing to do all things necessary for the proper conduct of the arbitration or of any other dispute resolution procedures required to be exhausted before resorting to arbitration.

(4) For the purposes of this section the question whether an arbitration agreement is a domestic arbitration agreement shall be determined by reference to the facts at the time the legal proceedings are commenced.

87 Effectiveness of agreement to exclude court's jurisdiction

(1) In the case of a domestic arbitration agreement any agreement to exclude the jurisdiction of the court under—

(a) section 45 (determination of preliminary point of law), or

(b) section 69 (challenging the award: appeal on point of law),

is not effective unless entered into after the commencement of the arbitral proceedings in which the question arises or the award is made.

(2) For this purpose the commencement of the arbitral proceedings has the same meaning as in Part I (see section 14).

(3) For the purposes of this section the question whether an arbitration agreement is a domestic arbitration agreement shall be determined by reference to the facts at the time the agreement is entered into.

88 Power to repeal or amend sections 85 to 87

(1) The Secretary of State may by order repeal or amend the provisions of sections 85 to 87.

(2) An order under this section may contain such supplementary, incidental and transitional provisions as appear to the Secretary of State to be appropriate.

(3) An order under this section shall be made by statutory instrument and no such order shall be made unless a draft of it has been laid before and approved by a resolution of each House of Parliament.

Consumer arbitration agreements

89 Application of unfair terms regulations to consumer arbitration agreements

(1) The following sections extend the application of the [S.I. 1994/3159] Unfair Terms in Consumer Contracts Regulations 1994 in relation to a term which constitutes an arbitration agreement.

For this purpose "arbitration agreement" means an agreement to submit to arbitration present or future disputes or differences (whether or not contractual).

(2) In those sections "the Regulations" means those regulations and includes any regulations amending or replacing those regulations.

(3) Those sections apply whatever the law applicable to the arbitration agreement.

90 Regulations apply where consumer is a legal person

The Regulations apply where the consumer is a legal person as they apply where the consumer is a natural person.

91 Arbitration agreement unfair where modest amount sought

(1) A term which constitutes an arbitration agreement is unfair for the purposes of the Regulations so far as it relates to a claim for a pecuniary remedy which does not exceed the amount specified by order for the purposes of this section.

(2) Orders under this section may make different provision for different cases and for different purposes.

(3) The power to make orders under this section is exercisable—

    (a) for England and Wales, by the Secretary of State with the concurrence of the Lord Chancellor,

    (b) for Scotland, by the Secretary of State with the concurrence of the Lord Advocate, and

    (c) for Northern Ireland, by the Department of Economic Development for Northern Ireland with the concurrence of the Lord Chancellor.

(4) Any such order for England and Wales or Scotland shall be made by statutory instrument which shall be subject to annulment in pursuance of a resolution of either House of Parliament.

(5) Any such order for Northern Ireland shall be a statutory rule for the purposes of the [S.I. 1979/1573 (N.I. 12).] Statutory Rules (Northern Ireland) Order 1979 and shall be subject to negative resolution, within the meaning of section 41(6) of the [1954 c. 33 (N.I.).] Interpretation Act (Northern Ireland) 1954.

Small claims arbitration in the county court

92 Exclusion of Part I in relation to small claims arbitration in the county court

Nothing in Part I of this Act applies to arbitration under section 64 of the [1984 c. 28.] County Courts Act 1984.

Appointment of judges as arbitrators

93 Appointment of judges as arbitrators

(1) A judge of the Commercial Court or an official referee may, if in all the circumstances he thinks fit, accept appointment as a sole arbitrator or as umpire by or by virtue of an arbitration agreement.

(2) A judge of the Commercial Court shall not do so unless the Lord Chief Justice has informed him that, having regard to the state of business in the High Court and the Crown Court, he can be made available.

(3) An official referee shall not do so unless the Lord Chief Justice has informed him that, having regard to the state of official referees' business, he can be made available.

(4) The fees payable for the services of a judge of the Commercial Court or official referee as arbitrator or umpire shall be taken in the High Court.

(5) In this section—

"arbitration agreement" has the same meaning as in Part I; and

"official referee" means a person nominated under section 68(1)(a) of the [1981 c. 54.] Supreme Court Act 1981 to deal with official referees' business.

(6) The provisions of Part I of this Act apply to arbitration before a person appointed under this section with the modifications specified in Schedule 2.

Statutory arbitrations

94 Application of Part I to statutory arbitrations

(1) The provisions of Part I apply to every arbitration under an enactment (a "statutory arbitration"), whether the enactment was passed or made before or after the commencement of this Act, subject to the adaptations and exclusions specified in sections 95 to 98.

(2) The provisions of Part I do not apply to a statutory arbitration if or to the extent that their application—

(a) is inconsistent with the provisions of the enactment concerned, with any rules or procedure authorised or recognised by it, or

(b) is excluded by any other enactment.

(3) In this section and the following provisions of this Part "enactment"—

(a) in England and Wales, includes an enactment contained in subordinate legislation within the meaning of the [1978 c. 30.] Interpretation Act 1978;

(b) in Northern Ireland, means a statutory provision within the meaning of section 1(f) of the [1954 c. 33 (N.I.).] Interpretation Act (Northern Ireland) 1954.

95 General adaptation of provisions in relation to statutory arbitrations

(1) The provisions of Part I apply to a statutory arbitration—

(a) as if the arbitration were pursuant to an arbitration agreement and as if the enactment were that agreement, and

(b) as if the persons by and against whom a claim subject to arbitration in pursuance of the enactment may be or has been made were parties to that agreement.

(2) Every statutory arbitration shall be taken to have its seat in England and Wales or, as the case may be, in Northern Ireland.

96 Specific adaptations of provisions in relation to statutory arbitrations

(1) The following provisions of Part I apply to a statutory arbitration with the following adaptations.

(2) In section 30(1) (competence of tribunal to rule on its own jurisdiction), the reference in paragraph (a) to whether there is a valid arbitration agreement shall be construed as a reference to whether the enactment applies to the dispute or difference in question.

(3) Section 35 (consolidation of proceedings and concurrent hearings) applies only so as to authorise the consolidation of proceedings, or concurrent hearings in proceedings, under the same enactment.

(4) Section 46 (rules applicable to substance of dispute) applies with the omission of subsection (1)(b) (determination in accordance with considerations agreed by parties).

97 Provisions excluded from applying to statutory arbitrations

The following provisions of Part I do not apply in relation to a statutory arbitration—

    (a) section 8 (whether agreement discharged by death of a party);

    (b) section 12 (power of court to extend agreed time limits);

    (c) sections 9(5), 10(2) and 71(4) (restrictions on effect of provision that award condition precedent to right to bring legal proceedings).

98 Power to make further provision by regulations

(1) The Secretary of State may make provision by regulations for adapting or excluding any provision of Part I in relation to statutory arbitrations in general or statutory arbitrations of any particular description.

(2) The power is exercisable whether the enactment concerned is passed or made before or after the commencement of this Act.

(3) Regulations under this section shall be made by statutory instrument which shall be subject to annulment in pursuance of a resolution of either House of Parliament.

PART III

RECOGNITION AND ENFORCEMENT OF CERTAIN FOREIGN AWARDS

Enforcement of Geneva Convention awards

99 Continuation of Part II of the Arbitration Act 1950

Part II of the [1950 c. 27.] Arbitration Act 1950 (enforcement of certain foreign awards) continues to apply in relation to foreign awards within the meaning of that Part which are not also New York Convention awards.

Recognition and enforcement of New York Convention awards

100 New York Convention awards

(1) In this Part a "New York Convention award" means an award made, in pursuance of an arbitration agreement, in the territory of a state (other than the United Kingdom) which is a party to the New York Convention.

(2) For the purposes of subsection (1) and of the provisions of this Part relating to such awards—

    (a) "arbitration agreement" means an arbitration agreement in writing, and

    (b) an award shall be treated as made at the seat of the arbitration, regardless of where it was signed, despatched or delivered to any of the parties.

In this subsection "agreement in writing" and "seat of the arbitration" have the same meaning as in Part I.

(3) If Her Majesty by Order in Council declares that a state specified in the Order is a party to the New York Convention, or is a party in respect of any territory so specified, the Order shall, while in force, be conclusive evidence of that fact.

(4) In this section "the New York Convention" means the Convention on the Recognition and Enforcement of Foreign Arbitral Awards adopted by the United Nations Conference on International Commercial Arbitration on 10th June 1958.

101 Recognition and enforcement of awards

(1) A New York Convention award shall be recognised as binding on the persons as between whom it was made, and may accordingly be relied on by those persons by way of defence, set-off or otherwise in any legal proceedings in England and Wales or Northern Ireland.

(2) A New York Convention award may, by leave of the court, be enforced in the same manner as a judgment or order of the court to the same effect.

As to the meaning of "the court" see section 105.

(3) Where leave is so given, judgment may be entered in terms of the award.

102 Evidence to be produced by party seeking recognition or enforcement

(1) A party seeking the recognition or enforcement of a New York Convention award must produce—

    (a) the duly authenticated original award or a duly certified copy of it, and

    (b) the original arbitration agreement or a duly certified copy of it.

(2) If the award or agreement is in a foreign language, the party must also produce a translation of it certified by an official or sworn translator or by a diplomatic or consular agent.

103 Refusal of recognition or enforcement

(1) Recognition or enforcement of a New York Convention award shall not be refused except in the following cases.

(2) Recognition or enforcement of the award may be refused if the person against whom it is invoked proves—

    (a) that a party to the arbitration agreement was (under the law applicable to him) under some incapacity;

    (b) that the arbitration agreement was not valid under the law to which the parties subjected it or, failing any indication thereon, under the law of the country where the award was made;

    (c) that he was not given proper notice of the appointment of the arbitrator or of the arbitration proceedings or was otherwise unable to present his case;

    (d) that the award deals with a difference not contemplated by or not falling within the terms of the submission to arbitration or contains decisions on matters beyond the scope of the submission to arbitration (but see subsection (4));

    (e) that the composition of the arbitral tribunal or the arbitral procedure was not in accordance with the agreement of the parties or, failing such agreement, with the law of the country in which the arbitration took place;

    (f) that the award has not yet become binding on the parties, or has been set aside or suspended by a competent authority of the country in which, or under the law of which, it was made.

(3) Recognition or enforcement of the award may also be refused if the award is in respect of a matter which is not capable of settlement by arbitration, or if it would be contrary to public policy to recognise or enforce the award.

(4) An award which contains decisions on matters not submitted to arbitration may be recognised or enforced to the extent that it contains decisions on matters submitted to arbitration which can be separated from those on matters not so submitted.

(5) Where an application for the setting aside or suspension of the award has been made to such a competent authority as is mentioned in subsection (2)(f), the court before which the award is sought to be relied upon may, if it considers it proper, adjourn the decision on the recognition or enforcement of the award.

It may also on the application of the party claiming recognition or enforcement of the award order the other party to give suitable security.

104 Saving for other bases of recognition or enforcement

Nothing in the preceding provisions of this Part affects any right to rely upon or enforce a New York Convention award at common law or under section 66.

Part IV
General Provisions

105 Meaning of "the court": jurisdiction of High Court and county court

(1) In this Act "the court" means the High Court or a county court, subject to the following provisions.

(2) The Lord Chancellor may by order make provision—

(a) allocating proceedings under this Act to the High Court or to county courts; or

(b) specifying proceedings under this Act which may be commenced or taken only in the High Court or in a county court.

(3) The Lord Chancellor may by order make provision requiring proceedings of any specified description under this Act in relation to which a county court has jurisdiction to be commenced or taken in one or more specified county courts.

Any jurisdiction so exercisable by a specified county court is exercisable throughout England and Wales or, as the case may be, Northern Ireland.

(4) An order under this section—

(a) may differentiate between categories of proceedings by reference to such criteria as the Lord Chancellor sees fit to specify, and

(b) may make such incidental or transitional provision as the Lord Chancellor considers necessary or expedient.

(5) An order under this section for England and Wales shall be made by statutory instrument which shall be subject to annulment in pursuance of a resolution of either House of Parliament.

(6) An order under this section for Northern Ireland shall be a statutory rule for the purposes of the [S.I. 1979/1573 (N.I. 12).] Statutory Rules (Northern Ireland) Order 1979 which shall be subject to annulment in pursuance of a resolution of either House of Parliament in like manner as a statutory instrument and section 5 of the [1946 c. 36.] Statutory Instruments Act 1946 shall apply accordingly.

106 Crown application

(1) Part I of this Act applies to any arbitration agreement to which Her Majesty, either in right of the Crown or of the Duchy of Lancaster or otherwise, or the Duke of Cornwall, is a party.

(2) Where Her Majesty is party to an arbitration agreement otherwise than in right of the Crown, Her Majesty shall be represented for the purposes of any arbitral proceedings—

(a) where the agreement was entered into by Her Majesty in right of the Duchy of Lancaster, by the Chancellor of the Duchy or such person as he may appoint, and

(b) in any other case, by such person as Her Majesty may appoint in writing under the Royal Sign Manual.

(3) Where the Duke of Cornwall is party to an arbitration agreement, he shall be represented for the purposes of any arbitral proceedings by such person as he may appoint.

(4) References in Part I to a party or the parties to the arbitration agreement or to arbitral proceedings shall be construed, where subsection (2) or (3) applies, as references to the person representing Her Majesty or the Duke of Cornwall.

107 Consequential amendments and repeals

(1) The enactments specified in Schedule 3 are amended in accordance with that Schedule, the amendments being consequential on the provisions of this Act.

(2) The enactments specified in Schedule 4 are repealed to the extent specified.

108 Extent

(1) The provisions of this Act extend to England and Wales and, except as mentioned below, to Northern Ireland.

(2) The following provisions of Part II do not extend to Northern Ireland—
section 92 (exclusion of Part I in relation to small claims arbitration in the county court), and
section 93 and Schedule 2 (appointment of judges as arbitrators).

(3) Sections 89, 90 and 91 (consumer arbitration agreements) extend to Scotland and the provisions of Schedules 3 and 4 (consequential amendments and repeals) extend to Scotland so far as they relate to enactments which so extend, subject as follows.

(4) The repeal of the [1975 c. 3.] Arbitration Act 1975 extends only to England and Wales and Northern Ireland.

109 Commencement

(1) The provisions of this Act come into force on such day as the Secretary of State may appoint by order made by statutory instrument, and different days may be appointed for different purposes.

(2) An order under subsection (1) may contain such transitional provisions as appear to the Secretary of State to be appropriate.

110 Short title

This Act may be cited as the Arbitration Act 1996.

SCHEDULES

Section 4(1).

SCHEDULE 1 Mandatory provisions of Part I

sections 9 to 11 (stay of legal proceedings);

section 12 (power of court to extend agreed time limits);

section 13 (application of Limitation Acts);

section 24 (power of court to remove arbitrator);

section 26(1) (effect of death of arbitrator);

section 28 (liability of parties for fees and expenses of arbitrators);

section 29 (immunity of arbitrator);

section 31 (objection to substantive jurisdiction of tribunal);

section 32 (determination of preliminary point of jurisdiction);

section 33 (general duty of tribunal);

section 37(2) (items to be treated as expenses of arbitrators);

section 40 (general duty of parties);

section 43 (securing the attendance of witnesses);

section 56 (power to withhold award in case of non-payment);

section 60 (effectiveness of agreement for payment of costs in any event);

section 66 (enforcement of award);

sections 67 and 68 (challenging the award: substantive jurisdiction and serious irregularity), and sections 70 and 71 (supplementary provisions; effect of order of court) so far as relating to those sections;

section 72 (saving for rights of person who takes no part in proceedings);

section 73 (loss of right to object);

section 74 (immunity of arbitral institutions, &c.);

section 75 (charge to secure payment of solicitors' costs).

Section 93(6).

SCHEDULE 2 Modifications of Part I in relation to judge-arbitrators

Introductory

1 In this Schedule "judge-arbitrator" means a judge of the Commercial Court or official referee appointed as arbitrator or umpire under section 93.

General

2—(1) Subject to the following provisions of this Schedule, references in Part I to the court shall be construed in relation to a judge-arbitrator, or in relation to the appointment of a judge-arbitrator, as references to the Court of Appeal.

(2) The references in sections 32(6), 45(6) and 69(8) to the Court of Appeal shall in such a case be construed as references to the House of Lords.

Arbitrator's fees

3—(1) The power of the court in section 28(2) to order consideration and adjustment of the liability of a party for the fees of an arbitrator may be exercised by a judge-arbitrator.

(2) Any such exercise of the power is subject to the powers of the Court of Appeal under sections 24(4) and 25(3)(b) (directions as to entitlement to fees or expenses in case of removal or resignation).

Exercise of court powers in support of arbitration

4—(1) Where the arbitral tribunal consists of or includes a judge-arbitrator the powers of the court under sections 42 to 44 (enforcement of peremptory orders, summoning witnesses, and other court powers) are exercisable by the High Court and also by the judge-arbitrator himself.

(2) Anything done by a judge-arbitrator in the exercise of those powers shall be regarded as done by him in his capacity as judge of the High Court and have effect as if done by that court.
Nothing in this sub-paragraph prejudices any power vested in him as arbitrator or umpire.

Extension of time for making award

5—(1) The power conferred by section 50 (extension of time for making award) is exercisable by the judge-arbitrator himself.

(2) Any appeal from a decision of a judge-arbitrator under that section lies to the Court of Appeal with the leave of that court.

Withholding award in case of non-payment

6—(1) The provisions of paragraph 7 apply in place of the provisions of section 56 (power to withhold award in the case of non-payment) in relation to the withholding of an award for non-payment of the fees and expenses of a judge-arbitrator.

(2) This does not affect the application of section 56 in relation to the delivery of such an award by an arbitral or other institution or person vested by the parties with powers in relation to the delivery of the award.

7—(1) A judge-arbitrator may refuse to deliver an award except upon payment of the fees and expenses mentioned in section 56(1).

(2) The judge-arbitrator may, on an application by a party to the arbitral proceedings, order that if he pays into the High Court the fees and expenses demanded, or such lesser amount as the judge-arbitrator may specify—

(a) the award shall be delivered,

(b) the amount of the fees and expenses properly payable shall be determined by such means and upon such terms as he may direct, and

(c) out of the money paid into court there shall be paid out such fees and expenses as may be found to be properly payable and the balance of the money (if any) shall be paid out to the applicant.

(3) For this purpose the amount of fees and expenses properly payable is the amount the applicant is liable to pay under section 28 or any agreement relating to the payment of the arbitrator.

(4) No application to the judge-arbitrator under this paragraph may be made where there is any available arbitral process for appeal or review of the amount of the fees or expenses demanded.

(5) Any appeal from a decision of a judge-arbitrator under this paragraph lies to the Court of Appeal with the leave of that court.

(6) Where a party to arbitral proceedings appeals under sub-paragraph (5), an arbitrator is entitled to appear and be heard.

Correction of award or additional award

8 Subsections (4) to (6) of section 57 (correction of award or additional award: time limit for application or exercise of power) do not apply to a judge-arbitrator.

Costs

9 Where the arbitral tribunal consists of or includes a judge-arbitrator the powers of the court under section 63(4) (determination of recoverable costs) shall be exercised by the High Court.

10—(1) The power of the court under section 64 to determine an arbitrator's reasonable fees and expenses may be exercised by a judge-arbitrator.

(2) Any such exercise of the power is subject to the powers of the Court of Appeal under sections 24(4) and 25(3)(b) (directions as to entitlement to fees or expenses in case of removal or resignation).

Enforcement of award

11 The leave of the court required by section 66 (enforcement of award) may in the case of an award of a judge-arbitrator be given by the judge-arbitrator himself.

Solicitors' costs

12 The powers of the court to make declarations and orders under the provisions applied by section 75 (power to charge property recovered in arbitral proceedings with the payment of solicitors' costs) may be exercised by the judge-arbitrator.

Powers of court in relation to service of documents

13—(1) The power of the court under section 77(2) (powers of court in relation to service of documents) is exercisable by the judge-arbitrator.

(2) Any appeal from a decision of a judge-arbitrator under that section lies to the Court of Appeal with the leave of that court.

Powers of court to extend time limits relating to arbitral proceedings

14—(1) The power conferred by section 79 (power of court to extend time limits relating to arbitral proceedings) is exercisable by the judge-arbitrator himself.

(2) Any appeal from a decision of a judge-arbitrator under that section lies to the Court of Appeal with the leave of that court.

Section 107(1).

SCHEDULE 3 *Consequential amendments*

Merchant Shipping Act 1894 (c. 60)

1 In section 496 of the Merchant Shipping Act 1894 (provisions as to deposits by owners of goods), after subsection (4) insert—

"(5) In subsection (3) the expression "legal proceedings" includes arbitral proceedings and as respects England and Wales and Northern Ireland the provisions of section 14 of the Arbitration Act 1996 apply to determine when such proceedings are commenced."

Stannaries Court (Abolition) Act 1896 (c. 45)

2 In section 4(1) of the Stannaries Court (Abolition) Act 1896 (references of certain disputes to arbitration), for the words from "tried before" to "any such reference" substitute "referred to arbitration before himself or before an arbitrator agreed on by the parties or an officer of the court".

Tithe Act 1936 (c. 43)

3 In section 39(1) of the Tithe Act 1936 (proceedings of Tithe Redemption Commission)—

    (a) for "the Arbitration Acts 1889 to 1934" substitute "Part I of the Arbitration Act 1996";
    (b) for paragraph (e) substitute—
       "(e) the making of an application to the court to determine a preliminary point of law and the bringing of an appeal to the court on a point of law;";
    (c) for "the said Acts" substitute "Part I of the Arbitration Act 1996".

Education Act 1944 (c. 31)

4 In section 75(2) of the Education Act 1944 (proceedings of Independent School Tribunals) for "the Arbitration Acts 1889 to 1934" substitute "Part I of the Arbitration Act 1996".

Commonwealth Telegraphs Act 1949 (c. 39)

5 In section 8(2) of the Commonwealth Telegraphs Act 1949 (proceedings of referees under the Act) for "the Arbitration Acts 1889 to 1934, or the Arbitration Act (Northern Ireland) 1937," substitute "Part I of the Arbitration Act 1996".

Lands Tribunal Act 1949 (c. 42)

6 In section 3 of the Lands Tribunal Act 1949 (proceedings before the Lands Tribunal)—

    (a) in subsection (6)(c) (procedural rules: power to apply Arbitration Acts), and
    (b) in subsection (8) (exclusion of Arbitration Acts except as applied by rules),
      for "the Arbitration Acts 1889 to 1934" substitute "Part I of the Arbitration Act 1996".

Wireless Telegraphy Act 1949 (c. 54)

7 In the Wireless Telegraphy Act 1949, Schedule 2 (procedure of appeals tribunal), in paragraph 3(1)—

    (a) for the words "the Arbitration Acts 1889 to 1934" substitute "Part I of the Arbitration Act 1996";
    (b) after the word "Wales" insert "or Northern Ireland"; and
    (c) for "the said Acts" substitute "Part I of that Act".

Patents Act 1949 (c. 87)

8 In section 67 of the Patents Act 1949 (proceedings as to infringement of pre-1978 patents referred to comptroller), for "The Arbitration Acts 1889 to 1934" substitute "Part I of the Arbitration Act 1996".

National Health Service (Amendment) Act 1949 (c. 93)

9 In section 7(8) of the [1946 c. 81.] National Health Service (Amendment) Act 1949 (arbitration in relation to hardship arising from the National Health Service Act 1946 or the Act), for "the Arbitration Acts 1889 to 1934" substitute "Part I of the Arbitration Act 1996" and for "the said Acts" substitute "Part I of that Act".

Arbitration Act 1950 (c. 27)

10 In section 36(1) of the Arbitration Act 1950 (effect of foreign awards enforceable under Part II of that Act) for "section 26 of this Act" substitute "section 66 of the Arbitration Act 1996".

Interpretation Act (Northern Ireland) 1954 (c. 33 (N.I.))

11 In section 46(2) of the Interpretation Act (Northern Ireland) 1954 (miscellaneous definitions), for the definition of "arbitrator" substitute—
""arbitrator" has the same meaning as in Part I of the Arbitration Act 1996;".

Agricultural Marketing Act 1958 (c. 47)

12 In section 12(1) of the Agricultural Marketing Act 1958 (application of provisions of Arbitration Act 1950)—

 (a) for the words from the beginning to "shall apply" substitute "Sections 45 and 69 of the Arbitration Act 1996 (which relate to the determination by the court of questions of law) and section 66 of that Act (enforcement of awards) apply"; and

 (b) for "an arbitration" substitute "arbitral proceedings".

Carriage by Air Act 1961 (c. 27)

13—(1) The Carriage by Air Act 1961 is amended as follows.

(2) In section 5(3) (time for bringing proceedings)—

 (a) for "an arbitration" in the first place where it occurs substitute "arbitral proceedings"; and

 (b) for the words from "and subsections (3) and (4)" to the end substitute "and the provisions of section 14 of the Arbitration Act 1996 apply to determine when such proceedings are commenced.".

(3) In section 11(c) (application of section 5 to Scotland)—

 (a) for "subsections (3) and (4)" substitute "the provisions of section 14 of the Arbitration Act 1996"; and

 (b) for "an arbitration" substitute "arbitral proceedings".

Factories Act 1961 (c. 34)

14 In the Factories Act 1961, for section 171 (application of Arbitration Act 1950), substitute—
"171 Application of the Arbitration Act 1996
Part I of the Arbitration Act 1996 does not apply to proceedings under this Act except in so far as it may be applied by regulations made under this Act.".

Clergy Pensions Measure 1961 (No. 3)

15 In the Clergy Pensions Measure 1961, section 38(4) (determination of questions), for the words "The Arbitration Act 1950" substitute "Part I of the Arbitration Act 1996".

Transport Act 1962 (c. 46)

16—(1) The Transport Act 1962 is amended as follows.

(2) In section 74(6)(f) (proceedings before referees in pension disputes), for the words "the Arbitration Act 1950" substitute "Part I of the Arbitration Act 1996".

(3) In section 81(7) (proceedings before referees in compensation disputes), for the words "the Arbitration Act 1950" substitute "Part I of the Arbitration Act 1996".

(4) In Schedule 7, Part IV (pensions), in paragraph 17(5) for the words "the Arbitration Act 1950" substitute "Part I of the Arbitration Act 1996".

Corn Rents Act 1963 (c. 14)

17 In the Corn Rents Act 1963, section 1(5) (schemes for apportioning corn rents, &c.), for the words "the Arbitration Act 1950" substitute "Part I of the Arbitration Act 1996".

Plant Varieties and Seeds Act 1964 (c. 14)

18 In section 10(6) of the Plant Varieties and Seeds Act 1964 (meaning of "arbitration agreement"), for "the meaning given by section 32 of the Arbitration Act 1950" substitute "the same meaning as in Part I of the Arbitration Act 1996".

Lands Tribunal and Compensation Act (Northern Ireland) 1964 (c. 29 (N.I.))

19 In section 9 of the Lands Tribunal and Compensation Act (Northern Ireland) 1964 (proceedings of Lands Tribunal), in subsection (3) (where Tribunal acts as arbitrator) for "the Arbitration Act (Northern Ireland) 1937" substitute "Part I of the Arbitration Act 1996".

Industrial and Provident Societies Act 1965 (c. 12)

20—(1) Section 60 of the Industrial and Provident Societies Act 1965 is amended as follows.

(2) In subsection (8) (procedure for hearing disputes between society and member, &c.)—

    (a) in paragraph (a) for "the Arbitration Act 1950" substitute "Part I of the Arbitration Act 1996"; and

    (b) in paragraph (b) omit "by virtue of section 12 of the said Act of 1950".

(3) For subsection (9) substitute—

"(9) The court or registrar to whom any dispute is referred under subsections (2) to (7) may at the request of either party state a case on any question of law arising in the dispute for the opinion of the High Court or, as the case may be, the Court of Session.".

Carriage of Goods by Road Act 1965 (c. 37)

21 In section 7(2) of the Carriage of Goods by Road Act 1965 (arbitrations: time at which deemed to commence), for paragraphs (a) and (b) substitute—

"(a) as respects England and Wales and Northern Ireland, the provisions of section 14(3) to (5) of the Arbitration Act 1996 (which determine the time at which an arbitration is commenced) apply;".

Factories Act (Northern Ireland) 1965 (c. 20 (N.I.))

22 In section 171 of the Factories Act (Northern Ireland) 1965 (application of Arbitration Act), for "The Arbitration Act (Northern Ireland) 1937" substitute "Part I of the Arbitration Act 1996".

Commonwealth Secretariat Act 1966 (c. 10)

23 In section 1(3) of the Commonwealth Secretariat Act 1966 (contracts with Commonwealth Secretariat to be deemed to contain provision for arbitration), for "the Arbitration Act 1950 and the Arbitration Act (Northern Ireland) 1937" substitute "Part I of the Arbitration Act 1996".

Arbitration (International Investment Disputes) Act 1966 (c. 41)

24 In the Arbitration (International Investment Disputes) Act 1966, for section 3 (application of Arbitration Act 1950 and other enactments) substitute—

"3 Application of provisions of Arbitration Act 1996

(1) The Lord Chancellor may by order direct that any of the provisions contained in sections 36 and 38 to 44 of the Arbitration Act 1996 (provisions concerning the conduct of arbitral proceedings, &c.) shall apply to such proceedings pursuant to the Convention as are specified in the order with or without any modifications or exceptions specified in the order.

(2) Subject to subsection (1), the Arbitration Act 1996 shall not apply to proceedings pursuant to the Convention, but this subsection shall not be taken as affecting section 9 of that Act (stay of legal proceedings in respect of matter subject to arbitration).

(3) An order made under this section—

    (a) may be varied or revoked by a subsequent order so made, and

    (b) shall be contained in a statutory instrument.".

Poultry Improvement Act (Northern Ireland) 1968 (c. 12 (N.I.))

25 In paragraph 10(4) of the Schedule to the Poultry Improvement Act (Northern Ireland) 1968 (reference of disputes), for "The Arbitration Act (Northern Ireland) 1937" substitute "Part I of the Arbitration Act 1996".

Industrial and Provident Societies Act (Northern Ireland) 1969 (c. 24 (N.I.))

26—(1) Section 69 of the Industrial and Provident Societies Act (Northern Ireland) 1969 (decision of disputes) is amended as follows.

(2) In subsection (7) (decision of disputes)—

(a) in the opening words, omit the words from "and without prejudice" to "1937";

(b) at the beginning of paragraph (a) insert "without prejudice to any powers exercisable by virtue of Part I of the Arbitration Act 1996,"; and

(c) in paragraph (b) omit "the registrar or" and "registrar or" and for the words from "as might have been granted by the High Court" to the end substitute "as might be granted by the registrar".

(3) For subsection (8) substitute—

"(8) The court or registrar to whom any dispute is referred under subsections (2) to (6) may at the request of either party state a case on any question of law arising in the dispute for the opinion of the High Court.".

Health and Personal Social Services (Northern Ireland) Order 1972 (N.I.14)

27 In Article 105(6) of the Health and Personal Social Services (Northern Ireland) Order 1972 (arbitrations under the Order), for "the Arbitration Act (Northern Ireland) 1937" substitute "Part I of the Arbitration Act 1996".

Consumer Credit Act 1974 (c. 39)

28—(1) Section 146 of the Consumer Credit Act 1974 is amended as follows.

(2) In subsection (2) (solicitor engaged in contentious business), for "section 86(1) of the Solicitors Act 1957" substitute "section 87(1) of the Solicitors Act 1974".

(3) In subsection (4) (solicitor in Northern Ireland engaged in contentious business), for the words from "business done" to "Administration of Estates (Northern Ireland) Order 1979" substitute "contentious business (as defined in Article 3(2) of the Solicitors (Northern Ireland) Order 1976.".

Friendly Societies Act 1974 (c. 46)

29—(1) The Friendly Societies Act 1974 is amended as follows.

(2) For section 78(1) (statement of case) substitute—

"(1) Any arbitrator, arbiter or umpire to whom a dispute falling within section 76 above is referred under the rules of a registered society or branch may at the request of either party state a case on any question of law arising in the dispute for the opinion of the High Court or, as the case may be, the Court of Session.".

(3) In section 83(3) (procedure on objections to amalgamations &c. of friendly societies), for "the Arbitration Act 1950 or, in Northern Ireland, the Arbitration Act (Northern Ireland) 1937" substitute "Part I of the Arbitration Act 1996".

Industry Act 1975 (c. 68)

30 In Schedule 3 to the Industry Act (arbitration of disputes relating to vesting and compensation orders), in paragraph 14 (application of certain provisions of Arbitration Acts)—

(a) for "the Arbitration Act 1950 or, in Northern Ireland, the Arbitration Act (Northern Ireland) 1937" substitute "Part I of the Arbitration Act 1996", and

(b) for "that Act" substitute "that Part".

Industrial Relations (Northern Ireland) Order 1976 (N.I.16)

31 In Article 59(9) of the Industrial Relations (Northern Ireland) Order 1976 (proceedings of industrial tribunal), for "The Arbitration Act (Northern Ireland) 1937" substitute "Part I of the Arbitration Act 1996".

Aircraft and Shipbuilding Industries Act 1977 (c. 3)

32 In Schedule 7 to the Aircraft and Shipbuilding Industries Act 1977 (procedure of Arbitration Tribunal), in paragraph 2—

(a) for "the Arbitration Act 1950 or, in Northern Ireland, the Arbitration Act (Northern Ireland) 1937" substitute "Part I of the Arbitration Act 1996", and

(b) for "that Act" substitute "that Part".

Patents Act 1977 (c. 37)

33 In section 130 of the Patents Act 1977 (interpretation), in subsection (8) (exclusion of Arbitration Act) for "The Arbitration Act 1950" substitute "Part I of the Arbitration Act 1996".

Judicature (Northern Ireland) Act 1978 (c. 23)

34—(1) The Judicature (Northern Ireland) Act 1978 is amended as follows.

(2) In section 35(2) (restrictions on appeals to the Court of Appeal), after paragraph (f) insert—
"(fa) except as provided by Part I of the Arbitration Act 1996, from any decision of the High Court under that Part;".

(3) In section 55(2) (rules of court) after paragraph (c) insert—
"(cc) providing for any prescribed part of the jurisdiction of the High Court in relation to the trial of any action involving matters of account to be exercised in the prescribed manner by a person agreed by the parties and for the remuneration of any such person;".

Health and Safety at Work (Northern Ireland) Order 1978 (N.I.9)

35 In Schedule 4 to the Health and Safety at Work (Northern Ireland) Order 1978 (licensing provisions), in paragraph 3, for "The Arbitration Act (Northern Ireland) 1937" substitute "Part I of the Arbitration Act 1996".

County Courts (Northern Ireland) Order 1980 (N.I.3)

36—(1) The County Courts (Northern Ireland) Order 1980 is amended as follows.

(2) In Article 30 (civil jurisdiction exercisable by district judge)—

(a) for paragraph (2) substitute—
"(2) Any order, decision or determination made by a district judge under this Article (other than one made in dealing with a claim by way of arbitration under paragraph (3)) shall be embodied in a decree which for all purposes (including the right of appeal under Part VI) shall have the like effect as a decree pronounced by a county court judge.";

(b) for paragraphs (4) and (5) substitute—

"(4) Where in any action to which paragraph (1) applies the claim is dealt with by way of arbitration under paragraph (3)—

(a) any award made by the district judge in dealing with the claim shall be embodied in a decree which for all purposes (except the right of appeal under Part VI) shall have the like effect as a decree pronounced by a county court judge;

(b) the district judge may, and shall if so required by the High Court, state for the determination of the High Court any question of law arising out of an award so made;

(c) except as provided by sub-paragraph (b), any award so made shall be final; and

(d) except as otherwise provided by county court rules, no costs shall be awarded in connection with the action.

(5) Subject to paragraph (4), county court rules may—

(a) apply any of the provisions of Part I of the Arbitration Act 1996 to arbitrations under paragraph (3) with such modifications as may be prescribed;

(b) prescribe the rules of evidence to be followed on any arbitration under paragraph (3) and, in particular, make provision with respect to the manner of taking and questioning evidence.

(5A) Except as provided by virtue of paragraph (5)(a), Part I of the Arbitration Act 1996 shall not apply to an arbitration under paragraph (3).".

(3) After Article 61 insert—

"Appeals from decisions under Part I of Arbitration Act 1996

61A—(1) Article 61 does not apply to a decision of a county court judge made in the exercise of the jurisdiction conferred by Part I of the Arbitration Act 1996.

(2) Any party dissatisfied with a decision of the county court made in the exercise of the jurisdiction conferred by any of the following provisions of Part I of the Arbitration Act 1996, namely—

(a) section 32 (question as to substantive jurisdiction of arbitral tribunal);

(b) section 45 (question of law arising in course of arbitral proceedings);

(c) section 67 (challenging award of arbitral tribunal: substantive jurisdiction);

(d) section 68 (challenging award of arbitral tribunal: serious irregularity);

(e) section 69 (appeal on point of law),

may, subject to the provisions of that Part, appeal from that decision to the Court of Appeal.

(3) Any party dissatisfied with any decision of a county court made in the exercise of the jurisdiction conferred by any other provision of Part I of the Arbitration Act 1996 may, subject to the provisions of that Part, appeal from that decision to the High Court.

(4) The decision of the Court of Appeal on an appeal under paragraph (2) shall be final.".

Supreme Court Act 1981 (c. 54)

37—(1) The Supreme Court Act 1981 is amended as follows.

(2) In section 18(1) (restrictions on appeals to the Court of Appeal), for paragraph (g) substitute—

"(g) except as provided by Part I of the Arbitration Act 1996, from any decision of the High Court under that Part;".

(3) In section 151 (interpretation, &c.), in the definition of "arbitration agreement", for "the Arbitration Act 1950 by virtue of section 32 of that Act;" substitute "Part I of the Arbitration Act 1996;".

Merchant Shipping (Liner Conferences) Act 1982 (c. 37)

38 In section 7(5) of the Merchant Shipping (Liner Conferences) Act 1982 (stay of legal proceedings), for the words from "section 4(1)" to the end substitute "section 9 of the Arbitration Act 1996 (which also provides for the staying of legal proceedings).".

Agricultural Marketing (Northern Ireland) Order 1982 (N.I.12)

39 In Article 14 of the Agricultural Marketing (Northern Ireland) Order 1982 (application of provisions of Arbitration Act (Northern Ireland) 1937)—

(a) for the words from the beginning to "shall apply" substitute "Section 45 and 69 of the Arbitration Act 1996 (which relate to the determination by the court of questions of law) and section 66 of that Act (enforcement of awards)" apply; and

(b) for "an arbitration" substitute "arbitral proceedings".

Mental Health Act 1983 (c. 20)

40 In section 78 of the Mental Health Act 1983 (procedure of Mental Health Review Tribunals), in subsection (9) for "The Arbitration Act 1950" substitute "Part I of the Arbitration Act 1996".

Registered Homes Act 1984 (c. 23)

41 In section 43 of the Registered Homes Act 1984 (procedure of Registered Homes Tribunals), in subsection (3) for "The Arbitration Act 1950" substitute "Part I of the Arbitration Act 1996".

Housing Act 1985 (c. 68)

42 In section 47(3) of the Housing Act 1985 (agreement as to determination of matters relating to service charges) for "section 32 of the Arbitration Act 1950" substitute "Part I of the Arbitration Act 1996".

Landlord and Tenant Act 1985 (c. 70)

43 In section 19(3) of the Landlord and Tenant Act 1985 (agreement as to determination of matters relating to service charges), for "section 32 of the Arbitration Act 1950" substitute "Part I of the Arbitration Act 1996".

Credit Unions (Northern Ireland) Order 1985 (N.I.12)

44—(1) Article 72 of the Credit Unions (Northern Ireland) Order 1985 (decision of disputes) is amended as follows.

(2) In paragraph (7)—

   (a) in the opening words, omit the words from "and without prejudice" to "1937";
   (b) at the beginning of sub-paragraph (a) insert "without prejudice to any powers exercisable by virtue of Part I of the Arbitration Act 1996,"; and
   (c) in sub-paragraph (b) omit "the registrar or" and "registrar or" and for the words from "as might have been granted by the High Court" to the end substitute "as might be granted by the registrar".

(3) For paragraph (8) substitute—

   "(8) **The court or registrar to whom any dispute is referred under paragraphs (2) to (6) may at the request of either party state a case on any question of law arising in the dispute for the opinion of the High Court.".**

Agricultural Holdings Act 1986 (c. 5)

45 In section 84(1) of the Agricultural Holdings Act 1986 (provisions relating to arbitration), for "the Arbitration Act 1950" substitute "Part I of the Arbitration Act 1996".

Insolvency Act 1986 (c. 45)

46 In the Insolvency Act 1986, after section 349 insert—

"349A Arbitration agreements to which bankrupt is party

   (1) This section applies where a bankrupt had become party to a contract containing an arbitration agreement before the commencement of his bankruptcy.

   (2) If the trustee in bankruptcy adopts the contract, the arbitration agreement is enforceable by or against the trustee in relation to matters arising from or connected with the contract.

   (3) If the trustee in bankruptcy does not adopt the contract and a matter to which the arbitration agreement applies requires to be determined in connection with or for the purposes of the bankruptcy proceedings—

   (a) the trustee with the consent of the creditors' committee, or
   (b) any other party to the agreement,

   may apply to the court which may, if it thinks fit in all the circumstances of the case, order that the matter be referred to arbitration in accordance with the arbitration agreement.

   (4) In this section—

   "arbitration agreement" has the same meaning as in Part I of the Arbitration Act 1996; and "the court" means the court which has jurisdiction in the bankruptcy proceedings.".

Building Societies Act 1986 (c. 53)

47 In Part II of Schedule 14 to the Building Societies Act 1986 (settlement of disputes: arbitration), in paragraph 5(6) for "the Arbitration Act 1950 and the Arbitration Act 1979 or, in Northern

Ireland, the Arbitration Act (Northern Ireland) 1937" substitute "Part I of the Arbitration Act 1996".

Mental Health (Northern Ireland) Order 1986 (N.I.4)

48 In Article 83 of the Mental Health (Northern Ireland) Order 1986 (procedure of Mental Health Review Tribunal), in paragraph (8) for "The Arbitration Act (Northern Ireland) 1937" substitute "Part I of the Arbitration Act 1996".

Multilateral Investment Guarantee Agency Act 1988 (c. 8)

49 For section 6 of the Multilateral Investment Guarantee Agency Act 1988 (application of Arbitration Act) substitute—
"6 Application of Arbitration Act
(1) The Lord Chancellor may by order made by statutory instrument direct that any of the provisions of sections 36 and 38 to 44 of the Arbitration Act 1996 (provisions in relation to the conduct of the arbitral proceedings, &c.) apply, with such modifications or exceptions as are specified in the order, to such arbitration proceedings pursuant to Annex II to the Convention as are specified in the order.
(2) Except as provided by an order under subsection (1) above, no provision of Part I of the Arbitration Act 1996 other than section 9 (stay of legal proceedings) applies to any such proceedings.".

Copyright, Designs and Patents Act 1988 (c. 48)

50 In section 150 of the Copyright, Designs and Patents Act 1988 (Lord Chancellor's power to make rules for Copyright Tribunal), for subsection (2) substitute—
"(2) The rules may apply in relation to the Tribunal, as respects proceedings in England and Wales or Northern Ireland, any of the provisions of Part I of the Arbitration Act 1996.".

Fair Employment (Northern Ireland) Act 1989 (c. 32)

51 In the Fair Employment (Northern Ireland) Act 1989, section 5(7) (procedure of Fair Employment Tribunal), for "The Arbitration Act (Northern Ireland) 1937" substitute "Part I of the Arbitration Act 1996".

Limitation (Northern Ireland) Order 1989 (N.I.11)

52 In Article 2(2) of the Limitation (Northern Ireland) Order 1989 (interpretation), in the definition of "arbitration agreement", for "the Arbitration Act (Northern Ireland) 1937" substitute "Part I of the Arbitration Act 1996".

Insolvency (Northern Ireland) Order 1989 (N.I.19)

53 In the Insolvency (Northern Ireland) Order 1989, after Article 320 insert—
"Arbitration agreements to which bankrupt is party.
320A—(1) This Article applies where a bankrupt had become party to a contract containing an arbitration agreement before the commencement of his bankruptcy.
(2) If the trustee in bankruptcy adopts the contract, the arbitration agreement is enforceable by or against the trustee in relation to matters arising from or connected with the contract.
(3) If the trustee in bankruptcy does not adopt the contract and a matter to which the arbitration agreement applies requires to be determined in connection with or for the purposes of the bankruptcy proceedings—
(a) the trustee with the consent of the creditors' committee, or
(b) any other party to the agreement,
may apply to the court which may, if it thinks fit in all the circumstances of the case, order that the matter be referred to arbitration in accordance with the arbitration agreement.

(4) In this Article—
"arbitration agreement" has the same meaning as in Part I of the Arbitration Act 1996; and
"the court" means the court which has jurisdiction in the bankruptcy proceedings.".

Social Security Administration Act 1992 (c. 5)

54 In section 59 of the Social Security Administration Act 1992 (procedure for inquiries, &c.), in subsection (7), for "The Arbitration Act 1950" substitute "Part I of the Arbitration Act 1996".

Social Security Administration (Northern Ireland) Act 1992 (c. 8)

55 In section 57 of the Social Security Administration (Northern Ireland) Act 1992 (procedure for inquiries, &c.), in subsection (6) for "the Arbitration Act (Northern Ireland) 1937" substitute "Part I of the Arbitration Act 1996".

Trade Union and Labour Relations (Consolidation) Act 1992 (c. 52)

56 In sections 212(5) and 263(6) of the Trade Union and Labour Relations (Consolidation) Act 1992 (application of Arbitration Act) for "the Arbitration Act 1950" substitute "Part I of the Arbitration Act 1996".

Industrial Relations (Northern Ireland) Order 1992 (N.I.5)

57 In Articles 84(9) and 92(5) of the Industrial Relations (Northern Ireland) Order 1992 (application of Arbitration Act) for "The Arbitration Act (Northern Ireland) 1937" substitute "Part I of the Arbitration Act 1996".

Registered Homes (Northern Ireland) Order 1992 (N.I.20)

58 In Article 33(3) of the Registered Homes (Northern Ireland) Order 1992 (procedure of Registered Homes Tribunal) for "The Arbitration Act (Northern Ireland) 1937" substitute "Part I of the Arbitration Act 1996".

Education Act 1993 (c. 35)

59 In section 180(4) of the Education Act 1993 (procedure of Special Educational Needs Tribunal), for "The Arbitration Act 1950" substitute "Part I of the Arbitration Act 1996".

Roads (Northern Ireland) Order 1993 (N.I.15)

60—(1) The Roads (Northern Ireland) Order 1993 is amended as follows.
(2) In Article 131 (application of Arbitration Act) for "the Arbitration Act (Northern Ireland) 1937" substitute "Part I of the Arbitration Act 1996".
(3) In Schedule 4 (disputes), in paragraph 3(2) for "the Arbitration Act (Northern Ireland) 1937" substitute "Part I of the Arbitration Act 1996".

Merchant Shipping Act 1995 (c. 21)

61 In Part II of Schedule 6 to the Merchant Shipping Act 1995 (provisions having effect in connection with Convention Relating to the Carriage of Passengers and Their Luggage by Sea), for paragraph 7 substitute—
"7 Article 16 shall apply to arbitral proceedings as it applies to an action; and, as respects England and Wales and Northern Ireland, the provisions of section 14 of the Arbitration Act 1996 apply to determine for the purposes of that Article when an arbitration is commenced.".

Industrial Tribunals Act 1996 (c. 17)

62 In section 6(2) of the Industrial Tribunals Act 1996 (procedure of industrial tribunals), for "The Arbitration Act 1950" substitute "Part I of the Arbitration Act 1996".

Section 107(2).

SCHEDULE 4 REPEALS

Chapter	Short title	Extent of repeal
1892 c. 43.	Military Lands Act 1892.	In section 21(b), the words "under the Arbitration Act 1889".
1922 c. 51.	Allotments Act 1922.	In section 21(3), the words "under the Arbitration Act 1889".
1937 c. 8 (N.I.).	Arbitration Act (Northern Ireland) 1937.	The whole Act.
1949 c. 54.	Wireless Telegraphy Act 1949.	In Schedule 2, paragraph 3(3).
1949 c. 97.	National Parks and Access to the Countryside Act 1949.	In section 18(4), the words from "Without prejudice" to "England or Wales".
1950 c. 27.	Arbitration Act 1950.	Part I. Section 42(3).
1958 c. 47.	Agricultural Marketing Act 1958.	Section 53(8).
1962 c. 46.	Transport Act 1962.	In Schedule 11, Part II, paragraph 7.
1964 c. 14.	Plant Varieties and Seeds Act 1964.	In section 10(4) the words from "or in section 9" to "three arbitrators)". Section 39(3)(b)(i).
1964 c. 29 (N.I.).	Lands Tribunal and Compensation Act (Northern Ireland) 1964.	In section 9(3) the words from "so, however, that" to the end.
1965 c. 12.	Industrial and Provident Societies Act 1965.	In section 60(8)(b), the words "by virtue of section 12 of the said Act of 1950".
1965 c. 37.	Carriage of Goods by Road Act 1965.	Section 7(2)(b).
1965 c. 13 (N.I.).	New Towns Act (Northern Ireland) 1965.	In section 27(2), the words from "under and in accordance with" to the end.
1969 c. 24 (N.I.).	Industrial and Provident Societies Act (Northern Ireland) 1969.	In section 69(7)— (a) in the opening words, the words from "and without prejudice" to "1937"; (b) in paragraph (b), the words "the registrar or" and "registrar or".
1970 c. 31.	Administration of Justice Act 1970.	Section 4. Schedule 3.
1973 c. 41.	Fair Trading Act 1973.	Section 33(2)(d).
1973 N.I. 1.	Drainage (Northern Ireland) Order 1973.	In Article 15(4), the words from "under and in accordance" to the end. Article 40(4). In Schedule 7, in paragraph 9(2), the words from "under and in accordance" to the end.
1974 c. 47.	Solicitors Act 1974.	In section 87(1), in the definition of "contentious business", the words "appointed under the Arbitration Act 1950".

319

Chapter	Short title	Extent of repeal
1975 c. 3.	Arbitration Act 1975.	The whole Act.
1975 c. 74.	Petroleum and Submarine Pipe-Lines Act 1975.	In Part II of Schedule 2—
		(a) in model clause 40(2), the words "in accordance with the Arbitration Act 1950";
		(b) in model clause 40(2B), the words "in accordance with the Arbitration Act (Northern Ireland) 1937".
		In Part II of Schedule 3, in model clause 38(2), the words "in accordance with the Arbitration Act 1950".
1976 N.I. 12.	Solicitors (Northern Ireland) Order 1976.	In Article 3(2), in the entry "contentious business", the words "appointed under the Arbitration Act (Northern Ireland) 1937".
		Article 71H(3).
1977 c. 37.	Patents Act 1977.	In section 52(4) the words "section 21 of the Arbitration Act 1950 or, as the case may be, section 22 of the Arbitration Act (Northern Ireland) 1937 (statement of cases by arbitrators); but".
		Section 131(e).
1977 c. 38.	Administration of Justice Act 1977.	Section 17(2).
1978 c. 23.	Judicature (Northern Ireland) Act 1978.	In section 35(2), paragraph (g)(v).
		In Schedule 5, the amendment to the Arbitration Act 1950.
1979 c. 42.	Arbitration Act 1979.	The whole Act.
1980 c. 58.	Limitation Act 1980.	Section 34.
1980 N.I. 3.	County Courts (Northern Ireland) Order 1980.	Article 31(3).
1981 c. 54.	Supreme Court Act 1981.	Section 148.
1982 c. 27.	Civil Jurisdiction and Judgments Act 1982.	Section 25(3)(c) and (5).
		In section 26—
		(a) in subsection (1), the words "to arbitration or";
		(b) in subsection (1)(a)(i), the words "arbitration or";
		(c) in subsection (2), the words "arbitration or".
1982 c. 53.	Administration of Justice Act 1982.	Section 15(6).
		In Schedule 1, Part IV.
1984 c. 5.	Merchant Shipping Act 1984.	Section 4(8).

Chapter	Short title	Extent of repeal
1984 c. 12.	Telecommunications Act 1984.	Schedule 2, paragraph 13(8).
1984 c. 16.	Foreign Limitation Periods Act 1984.	Section 5.
1984 c. 28.	County Courts Act 1984.	In Schedule 2, paragraph 70.
1985 c. 61.	Administration of Justice Act 1985.	Section 58.
		In Schedule 9, paragraph 15.
1985 c. 68.	Housing Act 1985.	In Schedule 18, in paragraph 6(2) the words from "and the Arbitration Act 1950" to the end.
1985 N.I. 12.	Credit Unions (Northern Ireland) Order 1985.	In Article 72(7)— (a) in the opening words, the words from "and without prejudice" to "1937"; (b) in sub-paragraph (b), the words "the registrar or" and "registrar or".
1986 c. 45.	Insolvency Act 1986.	In Schedule 14, the entry relating to the Arbitration Act 1950.
1988 c. 8.	Multilateral Investment Guarantee Agency Act 1988.	Section 8(3).
1988 c. 21.	Consumer Arbitration Agreements Act 1988.	The whole Act.
1989 N.I. 11.	Limitation (Northern Ireland) Order 1989.	Article 72.
		In Schedule 3, paragraph 1.
1989 N.I. 19.	Insolvency (Northern Ireland) Order 1989.	In Part II of Schedule 9, paragraph 66.
1990 c. 41.	Courts and Legal Services Act 1990.	Sections 99 and 101 to 103.
1991 N.I. 7.	Food Safety (Northern Ireland) Order 1991.	In Articles 8(8) and 11(10), the words from "and the provisions" to the end.
1992 c. 40.	Friendly Societies Act 1992.	In Schedule 16, paragraph 30(1).
1995 c. 8.	Agricultural Tenancies Act 1995.	Section 28(4).
1995 c. 21.	Merchant Shipping Act 1995.	Section 96(10).
		Section 264(9).
1995 c. 42.	Private International Law (Miscellaneous Provisions) Act 1995.	Section 3.

APPENDIX 9

UNCITRAL Model Law on International Commercial Arbitration*

1985

WITH AMENDMENTS AS ADOPTED IN 2006

CONTENTS

Resolutions adopted by the General Assembly

General Assembly Resolution 40/72 (11 December 1985)

General Assembly Resolution 61/33 (4 December 2006)

PART ONE

UNCITRAL MODEL LAW ON INTERNATIONAL COMMERCIAL ARBITRATION

Chapter I. General provisions

Article 1.	Scope of application
Article 2.	Definitions and rules of interpretation
Article 2A.	International origin and general principles
Article 3.	Receipt of written communications
Article 4.	Waiver of right to object
Article 5.	Extent of court intervention
Article 6.	Court or other authority for certain functions of arbitration assistance and supervision

Chapter II. Arbitration agreement

Article 7.	Option I Definition and form of arbitration agreement
	Option II Definition of arbitration agreement
Article 8.	Arbitration agreement and substantive claim before court
Article 9.	Arbitration agreement and interim measures by court

Chapter III. Composition of arbitral tribunal

Article 10.	Number of arbitrators
Article 11.	Appointment of arbitrators
Article 12.	Grounds for challenge
Article 13.	Challenge procedure
Article 14.	Failure or impossibility to act
Article 15.	Appointment of substitute arbitrator

Chapter IV. Jurisdiction of arbitral tribunal

Article 16.	Competence of arbitral tribunal to rule on its jurisdiction

---

* Reproduced with the permission of the LCIA.

Chapter IV A. Interim measures and preliminary orders

Section 1.   Interim measures
  Article 17.   Power of arbitral tribunal to order interim measures
  Article 17 A.   Conditions for granting interim measures
Section 2.   Preliminary orders
  Article 17 B.   Applications for preliminary orders and conditions for granting
                  preliminary orders
  Article 17 C.   Specific regime for preliminary orders
Section 3.   Provisions applicable to interim measures and preliminary orders
  Article 17 D.   Modification, suspension, termination
  Article 17 E.   Provision of security
  Article 17 F.   Disclosure
  Article 17 G.   Costs and damages
Section 4.   Recognition and enforcement of interim measures
  Article 17 H.   Recognition and enforcement
  Article 17 I.   Grounds for refusing recognition or enforcement
Section 5.   Court-ordered interim measures
  Article 17 J.   Court-ordered interim measures

Chapter V. Conduct of arbitral proceedings

Article 18.   Equal treatment of parties
Article 19.   Determination of rules of procedure
Article 20.   Place of arbitration
Article 21.   Commencement of arbitral proceedings
Article 22.   Language
Article 23.   Statements of claim and defence
Article 24.   Hearings and written proceedings
Article 25.   Default of a party
Article 26.   Expert appointed by arbitral tribunal
Article 27.   Court assistance in taking evidence

Chapter VI. Making of award and termination of proceedings

Article 28.   Rules applicable to substance of dispute
Article 29.   Decision-making by panel of arbitrators
Article 30.   Settlement
Article 31.   Form and contents of award
Article 32.   Termination of proceedings
Article 33.   Correction and interpretation of award; additional award

Chapter VII. Recourse against award

Article 34.   Application for setting aside as exclusive recourse against arbitral award

Chapter VIII. Recognition and enforcement of awards

Article 35.   Recognition and enforcement
Article 36.   Grounds for refusing recognition or enforcement

PART TWO

EXPLANATORY NOTE BY THE UNICITRAL SECRETARIAT ON THE MODEL LAW ON
INTERNATIONAL COMMERCIAL ARBITRATION

A. Background to the Model Law
   1. Inadequacy of domestic laws
   2. Disparity between national laws

B. Salient features of the Model Law
1. Special procedural regime for international commercial arbitration
2. Arbitration agreement
3. Composition of arbitral tribunal
4. Jurisdiction of arbitral tribunal
5. Conduct of arbitral proceedings
6. Making of award and termination of proceedings
7. Recourse against award
8. Recognition and enforcement of awards

PART THREE

"Recommendation regarding the interpretation of article II, paragraph 2, and article VII, paragraph 1, of the Convention on the Recognition and Enforcement of Foreign Arbitral Awards, done in New York, 10 June 1958", adopted by the United Nations Commission on International Trade Law on 7 July 2006 at its thirty-ninth session

Resolutions Adopted by the General Assembly

*40/72. Model Law on International Commercial Arbitration
of the United Nations Commission on International Trade Law*

The General Assembly,

Recognizing the value of arbitration as a method of settling disputes arising in international commercial relations,

Convinced that the establishment of a model law on arbitration that is acceptable to States with different legal, social and economic systems contributes to the development of harmonious international economic relations,

Noting that the Model Law on International Commercial Arbitration[**] was adopted by the United Nations Commission on International Trade Law at its eighteenth session, after due deliberation and extensive consultation with arbitral institutions and individual experts on international commercial arbitration,

Convinced that the Model Law, together with the Convention on the Recognition and Enforcement of Foreign Arbitral Awards[***] and the Arbitration Rules of the United Nations Commission on International Trade Law[****] recommended by the General Assembly in its resolution 31/98 of 15 December 1976, significantly contributes to the establishment of a unified legal framework for the fair and efficient settlement of disputes arising in international commercial relations,

1. *Requests* the Secretary-General to transmit the text of the Model Law on International Commercial Arbitration of the United Nations Commission on International Trade Law, together with the *travaux préparatoires* from the eighteenth session of the Commission, to Governments and to arbitral institutions and other interested bodies, such as chambers of commerce;

2. *Recommends* that all States give due consideration to the Model Law on International Commercial Arbitration, in view of the desirability of uniformity of the law of arbitral procedures and the specific needs of international commercial arbitration practice.

*112th plenary meeting
11 December 1985*

[on the report of the Sixth Committee (A/61/453)]

*61/33. Revised articles of the Model Law on International Commercial
Arbitration of the United Nations Commission on International Trade Law,
and the recommendation regarding the interpretation of article II, paragraph 2,
and article VII, paragraph 1, of the Convention on the Recognition and
Enforcement of Foreign Arbitral Awards, done at New York, 10 June 1958*

The General Assembly,

Recognizing the value of arbitration as a method of settling disputes arising in the context of international commercial relations,

Recalling its resolution 40/72 of 11 December 1985 regarding the Model Law on International Commercial Arbitration,[*****]

Recognizing the need for provisions in the Model Law to conform to current practices in international trade and modern means of contracting with regard to the form of the arbitration agreement and the granting of interim measures,

---

[**]   *Official Records of the General Assembly, Fortieth Session, Supplement No. 17* (A/40/17), annex I.
[***]   United Nations, *Treaty Series*, vol. 330, No. 4739, p. 38.
[****]   United Nations publication, Sales No. E.77.V.6.
[*****]   *Official Records of the General Assembly, Fortieth Session, Supplement No. 17* (A/40/17), annex I.

Believing that revised articles of the Model Law on the form of the arbitration agreement and interim measures reflecting those current practices will significantly enhance the operation of the Model Law,

Noting that the preparation of the revised articles of the Model Law on the form of the arbitration agreement and interim measures was the subject of due deliberation and extensive consultations with Governments and interested circles and would contribute significantly to the establishment of a harmonized legal framework for a fair and efficient settlement of international commercial disputes,

Believing that, in connection with the modernization of articles of the Model Law, the promotion of a uniform interpretation and application of the Convention on the Recognition and Enforcement of Foreign Arbitral Awards, done at New York, 10 June 1958,****** is particularly timely,

1. *Expresses its appreciation* to the United Nations Commission on International Trade Law for formulating and adopting the revised articles of its Model Law on International Commercial Arbitration on the form of the arbitration agreement and interim measures, the text of which is contained in annex I to the report of the United Nations Commission on International Trade Law on the work of its thirty-ninth session,******* and recommends that all States give favourable consideration to the enactment of the revised articles of the Model Law, or the revised Model Law on International Commercial Arbitration of the United Nations Commission on International Trade Law, when they enact or revise their laws, in view of the desirability of uniformity of the law of arbitral procedures and the specific needs of international commercial arbitration practice;

2. *Also expresses its appreciation* to the United Nations Commission on International Trade Law for formulating and adopting the recommendation regarding the interpretation of article II, paragraph 2, and article VII, paragraph 1, of the Convention on the Recognition and Enforcement of Foreign Arbitral Awards, done at New York, 10 June 1958,[5] the text of which is contained in annex II to the report of the United Nations Commission on International Trade Law on the work of its thirty-ninth session;[6]

3. *Requests* the Secretary-General to make all efforts to ensure that the revised articles of the Model Law and the recommendation become generally known and available.

64th plenary meeting
4 December 2006

****** United Nations, *Treaty Series*, vol. 330, No. 4739.
******* *Official Records of the General Assembly, Sixty-first Session, Supplement No. 17* (A/61/17).

Part One
UNCITRAL Model Law on International Commercial Arbitration

(United Nations documents A/40/17, annex I and A/61/17, annex I)

(As adopted by the United Nations Commission on International Trade Law on 21 June 1985, and as amended by the United Nations Commission on International Trade Law on 7 July 2006)

Chapter I
General Provisions

Article 1
Scope of Application********

(1) This Law applies to international commercial******** arbitration, subject to any agreement in force between this State and any other State or States.

(2) The provisions of this Law, except articles 8, 9, 17 H, 17 I, 17 J, 35 and 36, apply only if the place of arbitration is in the territory of this State.

(Article 1(2) has been amended by the Commission at its thirty-ninth session, in 2006)

(3) An arbitration is international if:

  (a) the parties to an arbitration agreement have, at the time of the conclusion of that agreement, their places of business in different States; or

  (b) one of the following places is situated outside the State in which the parties have their places of business:

   (i) the place of arbitration if determined in, or pursuant to, the arbitration agreement;

   (ii) any place where a substantial part of the obligations of the commercial relationship is to be performed or the place with which the subject-matter of the dispute is most closely connected; or

  (c) the parties have expressly agreed that the subject matter of the arbitration agreement relates to more than one country.

(4) For the purposes of paragraph (3) of this article:

  (a) if a party has more than one place of business, the place of business is that which has the closest relationship to the arbitration agreement;

  (b) if a party does not have a place of business, reference is to be made to his habitual residence.

(5) This Law shall not affect any other law of this State by virtue of which certain disputes may not be submitted to arbitration or may be submitted to arbitration only according to provisions other than those of this Law.

Article 2
Definitions and Rules of Interpretation

For the purposes of this Law:

  (a) "arbitration" means any arbitration whether or not administered by a permanent arbitral institution;

  (b) "arbitral tribunal" means a sole arbitrator or a panel of arbitrators;

******** Article headings are for reference purposes only and are not to be used for purposes of interpretation.

******** The term "commercial" should be given a wide interpretation so as to cover matters arising from all relationships of a commercial nature, whether contractual or not. Relationships of a commercial nature include, but are not limited to, the following transactions: any trade transaction for the supply or exchange of goods or services; distribution agreement; commercial representation or agency; factoring; leasing; construction of works; consulting; engineering; licensing; investment; financing; banking; insurance; exploitation agreement or concession; joint venture and other forms of industrial or business cooperation; carriage of goods or passengers by air, sea, rail or road.

(c) "court" means a body or organ of the judicial system of a State;

(d) where a provision of this Law, except article 28, leaves the parties free to determine a certain issue, such freedom includes the right of the parties to authorize a third party, including an institution, to make that determination;

(e) where a provision of this Law refers to the fact that the parties have agreed or that they may agree or in any other way refers to an agreement of the parties, such agreement includes any arbitration rules referred to in that agreement;

(f) where a provision of this Law, other than in articles 25*(a)* and 32(2) *(a)*, refers to a claim, it also applies to a counter-claim, and where it refers to a defence, it also applies to a defence to such counter-claim.

Article 2 A
International Origin and General Principles
(As adopted by the Commission at its thirty-ninth session, in 2006)

(1) In the interpretation of this Law, regard is to be had to its international origin and to the need to promote uniformity in its application and the observance of good faith.

(2) Questions concerning matters governed by this Law which are not expressly settled in it are to be settled in conformity with the general principles on which this Law is based.

Article 3
Receipt of Written Communications

(1) Unless otherwise agreed by the parties:

(a) any written communication is deemed to have been received if it is delivered to the addressee personally or if it is delivered at his place of business, habitual residence or mailing address; if none of these can be found after making a reasonable inquiry, a written communication is deemed to have been received if it is sent to the addressee's last-known place of business, habitual residence or mailing address by registered letter or any other means which provides a record of the attempt to deliver it;

(b) the communication is deemed to have been received on the day it is so delivered.

(2) The provisions of this article do not apply to communications in court proceedings.

Article 4
Waiver of Right to Object

A party who knows that any provision of this Law from which the parties may derogate or any requirement under the arbitration agreement has not been complied with and yet proceeds with the arbitration without stating his objection to such non-compliance without undue delay or, if a time-limit is provided therefor, within such period of time, shall be deemed to have waived his right to object.

Article 5
Extent of Court Intervention

In matters governed by this Law, no court shall intervene except where so provided in this Law.

Article 6
Court or Other Authority for Certain Functions of Arbitration
Assistance and Supervision

The functions referred to in articles 11(3), 11(4), 13(3), 14, 16(3) and 34(2) shall be performed by . . . [Each State enacting this model law specifies the court, courts or, where referred to therein, other authority competent to perform these functions.]

CHAPTER II
ARBITRATION AGREEMENT

Option I

Article 7

Definition and Form of Arbitration Agreement

(As adopted by the Commission at its thirty-ninth session, in 2006)

(1) "Arbitration agreement" is an agreement by the parties to submit to arbitration all or certain disputes which have arisen or which may arise between them in respect of a defined legal relationship, whether contractual or not. An arbitration agreement may be in the form of an arbitration clause in a contract or in the form of a separate agreement.

(2) The arbitration agreement shall be in writing.

(3) An arbitration agreement is in writing if its content is recorded in any form, whether or not the arbitration agreement or contract has been concluded orally, by conduct, or by other means.

(4) The requirement that an arbitration agreement be in writing is met by an electronic communication if the information contained therein is accessible so as to be useable for subsequent reference; "electronic communication" means any communication that the parties make by means of data messages; "data message" means information generated, sent, received or stored by electronic, magnetic, optical or similar means, including, but not limited to, electronic data interchange (EDI), electronic mail, telegram, telex or telecopy.

(5) Furthermore, an arbitration agreement is in writing if it is contained in an exchange of statements of claim and defence in which the existence of an agreement is alleged by one party and not denied by the other.

(6) The reference in a contract to any document containing an arbitration clause constitutes an arbitration agreement in writing, provided that the reference is such as to make that clause part of the contract.

Option II

Article 7

Definition of Arbitration Agreement

*(*As adopted by the Commission at its thirty-ninth session, in 2006)

"Arbitration agreement" is an agreement by the parties to submit to arbitration all or certain disputes which have arisen or which may arise between them in respect of a defined legal relationship, whether contractual or not.

Article 8

Arbitration Agreement and Substantive Claim Before Court

(1) A court before which an action is brought in a matter which is the subject of an arbitration agreement shall, if a party so requests not later than when submitting his first statement on the substance of the dispute, refer the parties to arbitration unless it finds that the agreement is null and void, inoperative or incapable of being performed.

(2) Where an action referred to in paragraph (1) of this article has been brought, arbitral proceedings may nevertheless be commenced or continued, and an award may be made, while the issue is pending before the court.

Article 9

Arbitration Agreement and Interim Measures by Court

It is not incompatible with an arbitration agreement for a party to request, before or during arbitral proceedings, from a court an interim measure of protection and for a court to grant such measure.

CHAPTER III.
COMPOSITION OF ARBITRAL TRIBUNAL

Article 10
Number of Arbitrators

(1) The parties are free to determine the number of arbitrators.

(2) Failing such determination, the number of arbitrators shall be three.

Article 11
Appointment of Arbitrators

(1) No person shall be precluded by reason of his nationality from acting as an arbitrator, unless otherwise agreed by the parties.

(2) The parties are free to agree on a procedure of appointing the arbitrator or arbitrators, subject to the provisions of paragraphs (4) and (5) of this article.

(3) Failing such agreement,

    (a) in an arbitration with three arbitrators, each party shall appoint one arbitrator, and the two arbitrators thus appointed shall appoint the third arbitrator; if a party fails to appoint the arbitrator within thirty days of receipt of a request to do so from the other party, or if the two arbitrators fail to agree on the third arbitrator within thirty days of their appointment, the appointment shall be made, upon request of a party, by the court or other authority specified in article 6;

    (b) in an arbitration with a sole arbitrator, if the parties are unable to agree on the arbitrator, he shall be appointed, upon request of a party, by the court or other authority specified in article 6.

(4) Where, under an appointment procedure agreed upon by the parties,

    (a) a party fails to act as required under such procedure, or

    (b) the parties, or two arbitrators, are unable to reach an agreement expected of them under such procedure, or

    (c) a third party, including an institution, fails to perform any function entrusted to it under such procedure,

any party may request the court or other authority specified in article 6 to take the necessary measure, unless the agreement on the appointment procedure provides other means for securing the appointment.

(5) A decision on a matter entrusted by paragraph (3) or (4) of this article to the court or other authority specified in article 6 shall be subject to no appeal. The court or other authority, in appointing an arbitrator, shall have due regard to any qualifications required of the arbitrator by the agreement of the parties and to such considerations as are likely to secure the appointment of an independent and impartial arbitrator and, in the case of a sole or third arbitrator, shall take into account as well the advisability of appointing an arbitrator of a nationality other than those of the parties.

Article 12
Grounds for Challenge

(1) When a person is approached in connection with his possible appointment as an arbitrator, he shall disclose any circumstances likely to give rise to justifiable doubts as to his impartiality or independence. An arbitrator, from the time of his appointment and throughout the arbitral proceedings, shall without delay disclose any such circumstances to the parties unless they have already been informed of them by him.

(2) An arbitrator may be challenged only if circumstances exist that give rise to justifiable doubts as to his impartiality or independence, or if he does not possess qualifications agreed to by the parties. A party may challenge an arbitrator appointed by him, or in whose appointment he has participated, only for reasons of which he becomes aware after the appointment has been made.

Article 13
Challenge Procedure

(1) The parties are free to agree on a procedure for challenging an arbitrator, subject to the provisions of paragraph (3) of this article.

(2) Failing such agreement, a party who intends to challenge an arbitrator shall, within fifteen days after becoming aware of the constitution of the arbitral tribunal or after becoming aware of any circumstance referred to in article 12(2), send a written statement of the reasons for the challenge to the arbitral tribunal. Unless the challenged arbitrator withdraws from his office or the other party agrees to the challenge, the arbitral tribunal shall decide on the challenge.

(3) If a challenge under any procedure agreed upon by the parties or under the procedure of paragraph (2) of this article is not successful, the challenging party may request, within thirty days after having received notice of the decision rejecting the challenge, the court or other authority specified in article 6 to decide on the challenge, which decision shall be subject to no appeal; while such a request is pending, the arbitral tribunal, including the challenged arbitrator, may continue the arbitral proceedings and make an award.

Article 14
Failure or Impossibility to Act

(1) If an arbitrator becomes *de jure* or *de facto* unable to perform his functions or for other reasons fails to act without undue delay, his mandate terminates if he withdraws from his office or if the parties agree on the termination. Otherwise, if a controversy remains concerning any of these grounds, any party may request the court or other authority specified in article 6 to decide on the termination of the mandate, which decision shall be subject to no appeal.

(2) If, under this article or article 13(2), an arbitrator withdraws from his office or a party agrees to the termination of the mandate of an arbitrator, this does not imply acceptance of the validity of any ground referred to in this article or article 12(2).

Article 15
Appointment of Substitute Arbitrator

Where the mandate of an arbitrator terminates under article 13 or 14 or because of his withdrawal from office for any other reason or because of the revocation of his mandate by agreement of the parties or in any other case of termination of his mandate, a substitute arbitrator shall be appointed according to the rules that were applicable to the appointment of the arbitrator being replaced.

CHAPTER IV
JURISDICTION OF ARBITRAL TRIBUNAL

Article 16
Competence of Arbitral Tibunal to Rule on its Jurisdiction

(1) The arbitral tribunal may rule on its own jurisdiction, including any objections with respect to the existence or validity of the arbitration agreement. For that purpose, an arbitration clause which forms part of a contract shall be treated as an agreement independent of the other terms of the contract. A decision by the arbitral tribunal that the contract is null and void shall not entail *ipso jure* the invalidity of the arbitration clause.

(2) A plea that the arbitral tribunal does not have jurisdiction shall be raised not later than the submission of the statement of defence. A party is not precluded from raising such a plea by the fact that he has appointed, or participated in the appointment of, an arbitrator. A plea that the arbitral

tribunal is exceeding the scope of its authority shall be raised as soon as the matter alleged to be beyond the scope of its authority is raised during the arbitral proceedings. The arbitral tribunal may, in either case, admit a later plea if it considers the delay justified.

(3) The arbitral tribunal may rule on a plea referred to in paragraph (2) of this article either as a preliminary question or in an award on the merits. If the arbitral tribunal rules as a preliminary question that it has jurisdiction, any party may request, within thirty days after having received notice of that ruling, the court specified in article 6 to decide the matter, which decision shall be subject to no appeal; while such a request is pending, the arbitral tribunal may continue the arbitral proceedings and make an award.

Chapter IV A
Interim Measures and Preliminary Orders

(As adopted by the Commission at its thirty-ninth session, in 2006)

Section 1 Interim Measures

Article 17
Power of Arbitral Tribunal to Order Interim Measures

(1) Unless otherwise agreed by the parties, the arbitral tribunal may, at the request of a party, grant interim measures.

(2) An interim measure is any temporary measure, whether in the form of an award or in another form, by which, at any time prior to the issuance of the award by which the dispute is finally decided, the arbitral tribunal orders a party to:

> *(a)* Maintain or restore the status quo pending determination of the dispute;
> *(b)* Take action that would prevent, or refrain from taking action that is likely to cause, current or imminent harm or prejudice to the arbitral process itself;
> *(c)* Provide a means of preserving assets out of which a subsequent award may be satisfied; or
> *(d)* Preserve evidence that may be relevant and material to the resolution of the dispute.

Article 17 A
Conditions for Granting Interim Measures

(1) The party requesting an interim measure under article 17(2)*(a)*, *(b)* and *(c)* shall satisfy the arbitral tribunal that:

> *(a)* Harm not adequately reparable by an award of damages is likely to result if the measure is not ordered, and such harm substantially outweighs the harm that is likely to result to the party against whom the measure is directed if the measure is granted; and
> *(b)* There is a reasonable possibility that the requesting party will succeed on the merits of the claim. The determination on this possibility shall not affect the discretion of the arbitral tribunal in making any subsequent determination.

(2) With regard to a request for an interim measure under article 17(2)*(d)*, the requirements in paragraphs (1)*(a)* and *(b)* of this article shall apply only to the extent the arbitral tribunal considers appropriate.

Section 2 Preliminary Orders

Article 17 B
Applications for Preliminary Orders and Conditions for Granting Preliminary Orders

(1) Unless otherwise agreed by the parties, a party may, without notice to any other party, make a request for an interim measure together with an application for a preliminary order directing a party not to frustrate the purpose of the interim measure requested.

(2) The arbitral tribunal may grant a preliminary order provided it considers that prior disclosure of the request for the interim measure to the party against whom it is directed risks frustrating the purpose of the measure.

(3) The conditions defined under article 17A apply to any preliminary order, provided that the harm to be assessed under article 17A(1)*(a)*, is the harm likely to result from the order being granted or not.

Article 17 C
Specific Regime for Preliminary Orders

(1) Immediately after the arbitral tribunal has made a determination in respect of an application for a preliminary order, the arbitral tribunal shall give notice to all parties of the request for the interim measure, the application for the preliminary order, the preliminary order, if any, and all other communications, including by indicating the content of any oral communication, between any party and the arbitral tribunal in relation thereto.

(2) At the same time, the arbitral tribunal shall give an opportunity to any party against whom a preliminary order is directed to present its case at the earliest practicable time.

(3) The arbitral tribunal shall decide promptly on any objection to the preliminary order.

(4) A preliminary order shall expire after twenty days from the date on which it was issued by the arbitral tribunal. However, the arbitral tribunal may issue an interim measure adopting or modifying the preliminary order, after the party against whom the preliminary order is directed has been given notice and an opportunity to present its case.

(5) A preliminary order shall be binding on the parties but shall not be subject to enforcement by a court. Such a preliminary order does not constitute an award.

Section 3 Provisions Applicable to Interim Measures and Preliminary Orders
Article 17 D
Modification, Suspension, Termination

The arbitral tribunal may modify, suspend or terminate an interim measure or a preliminary order it has granted, upon application of any party or, in exceptional circumstances and upon prior notice to the parties, on the arbitral tribunal's own initiative.

Article 17 E
Provision of Security

(1) The arbitral tribunal may require the party requesting an interim measure to provide appropriate security in connection with the measure.

(2) The arbitral tribunal shall require the party applying for a preliminary order to provide security in connection with the order unless the arbitral tribunal considers it inappropriate or unnecessary to do so.

Article 17 F
Disclosure

(1) The arbitral tribunal may require any party promptly to disclose any material change in the circumstances on the basis of which the measure was requested or granted.

(2) The party applying for a preliminary order shall disclose to the arbitral tribunal all circumstances that are likely to be relevant to the arbitral tribunal's determination whether to grant or maintain the order, and such obligation shall continue until the party against whom the order has been requested has had an opportunity to present its case. Thereafter, paragraph (1) of this article shall apply.

Article 17 G
Costs and Damages

The party requesting an interim measure or applying for a preliminary order shall be liable for any costs and damages caused by the measure or the order to any party if the arbitral tribunal later determines that, in the circumstances, the measure or the order should not have been granted. The arbitral tribunal may award such costs and damages at any point during the proceedings.

Section 4 Recognition and Enforcement of Interim Measures

Article 17 H
Recognition and Enforcement

(1) An interim measure issued by an arbitral tribunal shall be recognized as binding and, unless otherwise provided by the arbitral tribunal, enforced upon application to the competent court, irrespective of the country in which it was issued, subject to the provisions of article 17 I.

(2) The party who is seeking or has obtained recognition or enforcement of an interim measure shall promptly inform the court of any termination, suspension or modification of that interim measure.

(3) The court of the State where recognition or enforcement is sought may, if it considers it proper, order the requesting party to provide appropriate security if the arbitral tribunal has not already made a determination with respect to security or where such a decision is necessary to protect the rights of third parties.

Article 17 I
Grounds for Refusing Recognition or Enforcement********

(1) Recognition or enforcement of an interim measure may be refused only:

    (a) At the request of the party against whom it is invoked if the court is satisfied that:
        (i) Such refusal is warranted on the grounds set forth in article 36(1)*(a)*(i), (ii), (iii) or (iv); or
        (ii) The arbitral tribunal's decision with respect to the provision of security in connection with the interim measure issued by the arbitral tribunal has not been complied with; or
        (iii) The interim measure has been terminated or suspended by the arbitral tribunal or, where so empowered, by the court of the State in which the arbitration takes place or under the law of which that interim measure was granted; or
    (b) If the court finds that:
        (i) The interim measure is incompatible with the powers conferred upon the court unless the court decides to reformulate the interim measure to the extent necessary to adapt it to its own powers and procedures for the purposes of enforcing that interim measure and without modifying its substance; or
        (ii) Any of the grounds set forth in article 36(1)*(b)*(i) or (ii), apply to the recognition and enforcement of the interim measure.

(2) Any determination made by the court on any ground in paragraph (1) of this article shall be effective only for the purposes of the application to recognize and enforce the interim measure. The court where recognition or enforcement is sought shall not, in making that determination, undertake a review of the substance of the interim measure.

Section 5 Court-ordered Interim Measures

Article 17 J
Court-ordered Interim Measures

A court shall have the same power of issuing an interim measure in relation to arbitration proceedings, irrespective of whether their place is in the territory of this State, as it has in relation to proceedings in courts. The court shall exercise such power in accordance with its own procedures in consideration of the specific features of international arbitration.

******** The conditions set forth in article 17 I are intended to limit the number of circumstances in which the court may refuse to enforce an interim measure. It would not be contrary to the level of harmonization sought to be achieved by these model provisions if a State were to adopt fewer circumstances in which enforcement may be refused.

CHAPTER V
CONDUCT OF ARBITRAL PROCEEDINGS

Article 18
Equal Treatment of Parties

The parties shall be treated with equality and each party shall be given a full opportunity of presenting his case.

Article 19
Determination of Rules of Procedure

(1) Subject to the provisions of this Law, the parties are free to agree on the procedure to be followed by the arbitral tribunal in conducting the proceedings.

(2) Failing such agreement, the arbitral tribunal may, subject to the provisions of this Law, conduct the arbitration in such manner as it considers appropriate. The power conferred upon the arbitral tribunal includes the power to determine the admissibility, relevance, materiality and weight of any evidence.

Article 20
Place of Arbitration

(1) The parties are free to agree on the place of arbitration. Failing such agreement, the place of arbitration shall be determined by the arbitral tribunal having regard to the circumstances of the case, including the convenience of the parties.

(2) Notwithstanding the provisions of paragraph (1) of this article, the arbitral tribunal may, unless otherwise agreed by the parties, meet at any place it considers appropriate for consultation among its members, for hearing witnesses, experts or the parties, or for inspection of goods, other property or documents.

Article 21
Commencement of Arbitral proceedings

Unless otherwise agreed by the parties, the arbitral proceedings in respect of a particular dispute commence on the date on which a request for that dispute to be referred to arbitration is received by the respondent.

Article 22
Language

(1) The parties are free to agree on the language or languages to be used in the arbitral proceedings. Failing such agreement, the arbitral tribunal shall determine the language or languages to be used in the proceedings. This agreement or determination, unless otherwise specified therein, shall apply to any written statement by a party, any hearing and any award, decision or other communication by the arbitral tribunal.

(2) The arbitral tribunal may order that any documentary evidence shall be accompanied by a translation into the language or languages agreed upon by the parties or determined by the arbitral tribunal.

Article 23
Statements of Claim and Defence

(1) Within the period of time agreed by the parties or determined by the arbitral tribunal, the claimant shall state the facts supporting his claim, the points at issue and the relief or remedy sought, and the respondent shall state his defence in respect of these particulars, unless the parties have otherwise agreed as to the required elements of such statements. The parties may submit with their

statements all documents they consider to be relevant or may add a reference to the documents or other evidence they will submit.

(2) Unless otherwise agreed by the parties, either party may amend or supplement his claim or defence during the course of the arbitral proceedings, unless the arbitral tribunal considers it inappropriate to allow such amendment having regard to the delay in making it.

Article 24
Hearings and Written Proceedings

(1) Subject to any contrary agreement by the parties, the arbitral tribunal shall decide whether to hold oral hearings for the presentation of evidence or for oral argument, or whether the proceedings shall be conducted on the basis of documents and other materials. However, unless the parties have agreed that no hearings shall be held, the arbitral tribunal shall hold such hearings at an appropriate stage of the proceedings, if so requested by a party.

(2) The parties shall be given sufficient advance notice of any hearing and of any meeting of the arbitral tribunal for the purposes of inspection of goods, other property or documents.

(3) All statements, documents or other information supplied to the arbitral tribunal by one party shall be communicated to the other party. Also any expert report or evidentiary document on which the arbitral tribunal may rely in making its decision shall be communicated to the parties.

Article 25
Default of a Party

Unless otherwise agreed by the parties, if, without showing sufficient cause,

(a) the claimant fails to communicate his statement of claim in accordance with article 23(1), the arbitral tribunal shall terminate the proceedings;

(b) the respondent fails to communicate his statement of defence in accordance with article 23(1), the arbitral tribunal shall continue the proceedings without treating such failure in itself as an admission of the claimant's allegations;

(c) any party fails to appear at a hearing or to produce documentary evidence, the arbitral tribunal may continue the proceedings and make the award on the evidence before it.

Article 26
Expert Appointed by Arbitral Tribunal

(1) Unless otherwise agreed by the parties, the arbitral tribunal

(a) may appoint one or more experts to report to it on specific issues to be determined by the arbitral tribunal;

(b) may require a party to give the expert any relevant information or to produce, or to provide access to, any relevant documents, goods or other property for his inspection.

(2) Unless otherwise agreed by the parties, if a party so requests or if the arbitral tribunal considers it necessary, the expert shall, after delivery of his written or oral report, participate in a hearing where the parties have the opportunity to put questions to him and to present expert witnesses in order to testify on the points at issue.

Article 27
Court Assistance in Taking Evidence

The arbitral tribunal or a party with the approval of the arbitral tribunal may request from a competent court of this State assistance in taking evidence.

The court may execute the request within its competence and according to its rules on taking evidence.

Chapter VI
Making of Award and Termination of Proceedings

Article 28
Rules Applicable to Substance of Dispute

(1) The arbitral tribunal shall decide the dispute in accordance with such rules of law as are chosen by the parties as applicable to the substance of the dispute. Any designation of the law or legal system of a given State shall be construed, unless otherwise expressed, as directly referring to the substantive law of that State and not to its conflict of laws rules.

(2) Failing any designation by the parties, the arbitral tribunal shall apply the law determined by the conflict of laws rules which it considers applicable.

(3) The arbitral tribunal shall decide *ex aequo et bono* or as *amiable compositeur* only if the parties have expressly authorized it to do so.

(4) In all cases, the arbitral tribunal shall decide in accordance with the terms of the contract and shall take into account the usages of the trade applicable to the transaction.

Article 29
Decision-making by Panel of Arbitrators

In arbitral proceedings with more than one arbitrator, any decision of the arbitral tribunal shall be made, unless otherwise agreed by the parties, by a majority of all its members. However, questions of procedure may be decided by a presiding arbitrator, if so authorized by the parties or all members of the arbitral tribunal.

Article 30
Settlement

(1) If, during arbitral proceedings, the parties settle the dispute, the arbitral tribunal shall terminate the proceedings and, if requested by the parties and not objected to by the arbitral tribunal, record the settlement in the form of an arbitral award on agreed terms.

(2) An award on agreed terms shall be made in accordance with the provisions of article 31 and shall state that it is an award. Such an award has the same status and effect as any other award on the merits of the case.

Article 31
Form and Contents of Award

(1) The award shall be made in writing and shall be signed by the arbitrator or arbitrators. In arbitral proceedings with more than one arbitrator, the signatures of the majority of all members of the arbitral tribunal shall suffice, provided that the reason for any omitted signature is stated.

(2) The award shall state the reasons upon which it is based, unless the parties have agreed that no reasons are to be given or the award is an award on agreed terms under article 30.

(3) The award shall state its date and the place of arbitration as determined in accordance with article 20(1). The award shall be deemed to have been made at that place.

(4) After the award is made, a copy signed by the arbitrators in accordance with paragraph (1) of this article shall be delivered to each party.

Article 32
Termination of Proceedings

(1) The arbitral proceedings are terminated by the final award or by an order of the arbitral tribunal in accordance with paragraph (2) of this article.

(2) The arbitral tribunal shall issue an order for the termination of the arbitral proceedings when:

    (a) the claimant withdraws his claim, unless the respondent objects thereto and the arbitral tribunal recognizes a legitimate interest on his part in obtaining a final settlement of the dispute;

(b) the parties agree on the termination of the proceedings;

(c) the arbitral tribunal finds that the continuation of the proceedings has for any other reason become unnecessary or impossible.

(3) The mandate of the arbitral tribunal terminates with the termination of the arbitral proceedings, subject to the provisions of articles 33 and 34(4).

Article 33
Correction and Interpretation of Award; Additional Award

(1) Within thirty days of receipt of the award, unless another period of time has been agreed upon by the parties:

(a) *a party, with notice to the other party, may request the arbitral* tribunal to correct in the award any errors in computation, any clerical or typographical errors or any errors of similar nature;

(b) if so agreed by the parties, a party, with notice to the other party, may request the arbitral tribunal to give an interpretation of a specific point or part of the award. If the arbitral tribunal considers the request to be justified, it shall make the correction or give the interpretation within thirty days of receipt of the request. The interpretation shall form part of the award.

(2) The arbitral tribunal may correct any error of the type referred to in paragraph (1)*(a)* of this article on its own initiative within thirty days of the date of the award.

(3) Unless otherwise agreed by the parties, a party, with notice to the other party, may request, within thirty days of receipt of the award, the arbitral tribunal to make an additional award as to claims presented in the arbitral proceedings but omitted from the award. If the arbitral tribunal considers the request to be justified, it shall make the additional award within sixty days.

(4) The arbitral tribunal may extend, if necessary, the period of time within which it shall make a correction, interpretation or an additional award under paragraph (1) or (3) of this article.

(5) The provisions of article 31 shall apply to a correction or interpretation of the award or to an additional award.

CHAPTER VII
RECOURSE AGAINST AWARD

Article 34
Application for Setting Aside as Exclusive Recourse Against Arbitral Award

(1) Recourse to a court against an arbitral award may be made only by an application for setting aside in accordance with paragraphs (2) and (3) of this article.

(2) An arbitral award may be set aside by the court specified in article 6 only if:

(a) the party making the application furnishes proof that:

(i) a party to the arbitration agreement referred to in article 7 was under some incapacity; or the said agreement is not valid under the law to which the parties have subjected it or, failing any indication thereon, under the law of this State; or

(ii) the party making the application was not given proper notice of the appointment of an arbitrator or of the arbitral proceedings or was otherwise unable to present his case; or

(iii) the award deals with a dispute not contemplated by or not falling within the terms of the submission to arbitration, or contains decisions on matters beyond the scope of the submission to arbitration, provided that, if the decisions on matters submitted to arbitration can be separated from those not so submitted, only that part of the award which contains decisions on matters not submitted to arbitration may be set aside; or

(iv) the composition of the arbitral tribunal or the arbitral procedure was not in accordance with the agreement of the parties, unless such agreement was in conflict with a provision of this Law from which the parties cannot derogate, or, failing such agreement, was not in accordance with this Law; or (*b*) the court finds that:

    (i) the subject-matter of the dispute is not capable of settlement by arbitration under the law of this State; or

    (ii) the award is in conflict with the public policy of this State.

(3) An application for setting aside may not be made after three months have elapsed from the date on which the party making that application had received the award or, if a request had been made under article 33, from the date on which that request had been disposed of by the arbitral tribunal.

(4) The court, when asked to set aside an award, may, where appropriate and so requested by a party, suspend the setting aside proceedings for a period of time determined by it in order to give the arbitral tribunal an opportunity to resume the arbitral proceedings or to take such other action as in the arbitral tribunal's opinion will eliminate the grounds for setting aside.

CHAPTER VIII
RECOGNITION AND ENFORCEMENT OF AWARDS

Article 35
Recognition and Enforcement

(1) An arbitral award, irrespective of the country in which it was made, shall be recognized as binding and, upon application in writing to the competent court, shall be enforced subject to the provisions of this article and of article 36.

(2) The party relying on an award or applying for its enforcement shall supply the original award or a copy thereof. If the award is not made in an official language of this State, the court may request the party to supply a translation thereof into such language.********

(Article 35(2) has been amended by the Commission at its thirty-ninth session, in 2006)

Article 36
Grounds for Refusing Recognition or Enforcement

(1) Recognition or enforcement of an arbitral award, irrespective of the country in which it was made, may be refused only:

    (*a*) at the request of the party against whom it is invoked, if that party furnishes to the competent court where recognition or enforcement is sought proof that:

        (i) a party to the arbitration agreement referred to in article 7 was under some incapacity; or the said agreement is not valid under the law to which the parties have subjected it or, failing any indication thereon, under the law of the country where the award was made; or

        (ii) the party against whom the award is invoked was not given proper notice of the appointment of an arbitrator or of the arbitral proceedings or was otherwise unable to present his case; or

        (iii) the award deals with a dispute not contemplated by or not falling within the terms of the submission to arbitration, or it contains decisions on matters beyond the scope of the submission to arbitration, provided that, if the decisions on matters submitted to arbitration can be separated from those not so submitted, that part of the award which contains decisions on matters submitted to arbitration may be recognized and enforced; or

        (iv) the composition of the arbitral tribunal or the arbitral procedure was not in accordance with the agreement of the parties or, failing such agreement, was not in accordance with the law of the country where the arbitration took place; or

---

******** The conditions set forth in this paragraph are intended to set maximum standards. It would, thus, not be contrary to the harmonization to be achieved by the model law if a State retained even less onerous conditions.

    (v) the award has not yet become binding on the parties or has been set aside or suspended by a court of the country in which, or under the law of which, that award was made; or

  (b) if the court finds that:

    (i) the subject-matter of the dispute is not capable of settlement by arbitration under the law of this State; or

    (ii) the recognition or enforcement of the award would be contrary to the public policy of this State.

(2) If an application for setting aside or suspension of an award has been made to a court referred to in paragraph (1)*(a)*(v) of this article, the court where recognition or enforcement is sought may, if it considers it proper, adjourn its decision and may also, on the application of the party claiming recognition or enforcement of the award, order the other party to provide appropriate security.

PART TWO

EXPLANATORY NOTE BY THE UNCITRAL SECRETARIAT ON THE 1985 MODEL LAW ON
INTERNATIONAL COMMERCIAL ARBITRATION AS AMENDED IN 2006********

1. The UNCITRAL Model Law on International Commercial Arbitration ("the Model Law") was adopted by the United Nations Commission on International Trade Law (UNCITRAL) on 21 June 1985, at the end of the eighteenth session of the Commission. The General Assembly, in its resolution 40/72 of 11 December 1985, recommended "that all States give due consideration to the Model Law on International Commercial Arbitration, in view of the desirability of uniformity of the law of arbitral procedures and the specific needs of international commercial arbitration practice". The Model Law was amended by UNCITRAL on 7 July 2006, at the thirty-ninth session of the Commission (see below, paragraphs 4, 19, 20, 27, 29 and 53). The General Assembly, in its resolution 61/33 of 4 December 2006, recommended "that all States give favourable consideration to the enactment of the revised articles of the UNCITRAL Model Law on International Commercial Arbitration, or the revised UNCITRAL Model Law on International Commercial Arbitration, when they enact or revise their laws (. . .)".

2. The Model Law constitutes a sound basis for the desired harmonization and improvement of national laws. It covers all stages of the arbitral process from the arbitration agreement to the recognition and enforcement of the arbitral award and reflects a worldwide consensus on the principles and important issues of international arbitration practice. It is acceptable to States of all regions and the different legal or economic systems of the world. Since its adoption by UNCITRAL, the Model Law has come to represent the accepted international legislative standard for a modern arbitration law and a significant number of jurisdictions have enacted arbitration legislation based on the Model Law.

3. The form of a model law was chosen as the vehicle for harmonization and modernization in view of the flexibility it gives to States in preparing new arbitration laws. Notwithstanding that flexibility, and in order to increase the likelihood of achieving a satisfactory degree of harmonization, States are encouraged to make as few changes as possible when incorporating the Model Law into their legal systems. Efforts to minimize variation from the text adopted by UNCITRAL are also expected to increase the visibility of harmonization, thus enhancing the confidence of foreign parties, as the primary users of international arbitration, in the reliability of arbitration law in the enacting State.

4. The revision of the Model Law adopted in 2006 includes article 2 A, which is designed to facilitate interpretation by reference to internationally accepted principles and is aimed at promoting a uniform understanding of the Model Law. Other substantive amendments to the Model Law relate to the form of the arbitration agreement and to interim measures. The original 1985 version of the provision on the form of the arbitration agreement (article 7) was modelled on the language used in article II (2) of the Convention on the Recognition and Enforcement of Foreign Arbitral Awards (New York, 1958) ("the New York Convention"). The revision of article 7 is intended to address evolving practice in international trade and technological developments. The extensive revision of article 17 on interim measures was considered necessary in light of the fact that such measures are increasingly relied upon in the practice of international commercial arbitration. The revision also includes an enforcement regime for such measures in recognition of the fact that the effectiveness of arbitration frequently depends upon the possibility of enforcing interim measures. The new provisions are contained in a new chapter of the Model Law on interim measures and preliminary orders (chapter IV A).

******** This note was prepared by the secretariat of the United Nations Commission on International Trade Law (UNCITRAL) for informational purposes only; it is not an official commentary on the Model Law. A commentary prepared by the Secretariat on an early draft of the Model Law appears in document A/CN.9/264 (reproduced in UNCITRAL Yearbook, vol. XVI — 1985, United Nations publication, Sales No. E.87.V.4).

A. Background to the Model Law

5. The Model Law was developed to address considerable disparities in national laws on arbitration. The need for improvement and harmonization was based on findings that national laws were often particularly inappropriate for international cases.

1. Inadequacy of domestic laws

6. Recurrent inadequacies to be found in outdated national laws include provisions that equate the arbitral process with court litigation and fragmentary provisions that fail to address all relevant substantive law issues. Even most of those laws that appear to be up-to-date and comprehensive were drafted with domestic arbitration primarily, if not exclusively, in mind. While this approach is understandable in view of the fact that even today the bulk of cases governed by arbitration law would be of a purely domestic nature, the unfortunate consequence is that traditional local concepts are imposed on international cases and the needs of modern practice are often not met.

7. The expectations of the parties as expressed in a chosen set of arbitration rules or a "one-off" arbitration agreement may be frustrated, especially by mandatory provisions of applicable law. Unexpected and undesired restrictions found in national laws may prevent the parties, for example, from submitting future disputes to arbitration, from selecting the arbitrator freely, or from having the arbitral proceedings conducted according to agreed rules of procedure and with no more court involvement than appropriate. Frustration may also ensue from non-mandatory provisions that may impose undesired requirements on unwary parties who may not think about the need to provide otherwise when drafting the arbitration agreement. Even the absence of any legislative provision may cause difficulties simply by leaving unanswered some of the many procedural issues relevant in arbitration and not always settled in the arbitration agreement. The Model Law is intended to reduce the risk of such possible frustration, difficulties or surprise.

2. Disparity between national laws

8. Problems stemming from inadequate arbitration laws or from the absence of specific legislation governing arbitration are aggravated by the fact that national laws differ widely. Such differences are a frequent source of concern in international arbitration, where at least one of the parties is, and often both parties are, confronted with foreign and unfamiliar provisions and procedures. Obtaining a full and precise account of the law applicable to the arbitration is, in such circumstances often expensive, impractical or impossible.

9. Uncertainty about the local law with the inherent risk of frustration may adversely affect the functioning of the arbitral process and also impact on the selection of the place of arbitration. Due to such uncertainty, a party may hesitate or refuse to agree to a place, which for practical reasons would otherwise be appropriate. The range of places of arbitration acceptable to parties is thus widened and the smooth functioning of the arbitral proceedings is enhanced where States adopt the Model Law, which is easily recognizable, meets the specific needs of international commercial arbitration and provides an international standard based on solutions acceptable to parties from different legal systems.

B. Salient features of the Model Law

1. Special procedural regime for international commercial arbitration

10. The principles and solutions adopted in the Model Law aim at reducing or eliminating the above-mentioned concerns and difficulties. As a response to the inadequacies and disparities of national laws, the Model Law presents a special legal regime tailored to international commercial arbitration, without affecting any relevant treaty in force in the State adopting the Model Law. While the Model Law was designed with international commercial arbitration in mind, it offers a set of basic rules that are not, in and of themselves, unsuitable to any other type of arbitration. States may thus consider extending their enactment of the Model Law to cover also domestic disputes, as a number of enacting States already have.

(a) Substantive and territorial scope of application

11. Article 1 defines the scope of application of the Model Law by reference to the notion of "international commercial arbitration". The Model Law defines an arbitration as international if "the parties to an arbitration agreement have, at the time of the conclusion of that agreement, their places of business in different States" (article 1 (3)). The vast majority of situations commonly regarded as international will meet this criterion. In addition, article 1 (3) broadens the notion of internationality so that the Model Law also covers cases where the place of arbitration, the place of contract performance, or the place of the subject-matter of the dispute is situated outside the State where the parties have their place of business, or cases where the parties have expressly agreed that the subject-matter of the arbitration agreement relates to more than one country. Article 1 thus recognizes extensively the freedom of the parties to submit a dispute to the legal regime established pursuant to the Model Law.

12. In respect of the term "commercial", the Model Law provides no strict definition. The footnote to article 1 (1) calls for "a wide interpretation" and offers an illustrative and open-ended list of relationships that might be described as commercial in nature, "whether contractual or not". The purpose of the footnote is to circumvent any technical difficulty that may arise, for example, in determining which transactions should be governed by a specific body of "commercial law" that may exist in some legal systems.

13. Another aspect of applicability is the territorial scope of application. The principle embodied in article 1 (2) is that the Model Law as enacted in a given State applies only if the place of arbitration is in the territory of that State. However, article 1 (2) also contains important exceptions to that principle, to the effect that certain articles apply, irrespective of whether the place of arbitration is in the enacting State or elsewhere (or, as the case may be, even before the place of arbitration is determined). These articles are the following: articles 8 (1) and 9, which deal with the recognition of arbitration agreements, including their compatibility with interim measures ordered by a court, article 17 J on court-ordered interim measures, articles 17 H and 17 I on the recognition and enforcement of interim measures ordered by an arbitral tribunal, and articles 35 and 36 on the recognition and enforcement of arbitral awards.

14. The territorial criterion governing most of the provisions of the Model Law was adopted for the sake of certainty and in view of the following facts. In most legal systems, the place of arbitration is the exclusive criterion for determining the applicability of national law and, where the national law allows parties to choose the procedural law of a State other than that where the arbitration takes place, experience shows that parties rarely make use of that possibility. Incidentally, enactment of the Model Law reduces any need for the parties to choose a "foreign" law, since the Model Law grants the parties wide freedom in shaping the rules of the arbitral proceedings. In addition to designating the law governing the arbitral procedure, the territorial criterion is of considerable practical importance in respect of articles 11, 13, 14, 16, 27 and 34, which entrust State courts at the place of arbitration with functions of supervision and assistance to arbitration. It should be noted that the territorial criterion legally triggered by the parties' choice regarding the place of arbitration does not limit the arbitral tribunal's ability to meet at any place it considers appropriate for the conduct of the proceedings, as provided by article 20 (2).

(b) Delimitation of court assistance and supervision

15. Recent amendments to arbitration laws reveal a trend in favour of limiting and clearly defining court involvement in international commercial arbitration. This is justified in view of the fact that the parties to an arbitration agreement make a conscious decision to exclude court jurisdiction and prefer the finality and expediency of the arbitral process.

16. In this spirit, the Model Law envisages court involvement in the following instances. A first group comprises issues of appointment, challenge and termination of the mandate of an arbitrator (articles 11, 13 and 14), jurisdiction of the arbitral tribunal (article 16) and setting aside of the arbitral award (article 34). These instances are listed in article 6 as functions that should be

entrusted, for the sake of centralization, specialization and efficiency, to a specially designated court or, with respect to articles 11, 13 and 14, possibly to another authority (for example, an arbitral institution or a chamber of commerce). A second group comprises issues of court assistance in taking evidence (article 27), recognition of the arbitration agreement, including its compatibility with court-ordered interim measures (articles 8 and 9), court-ordered interim measures (article 17 J), and recognition and enforcement of interim measures (articles 17 H and 17 I) and of arbitral awards (articles 35 and 36).

17. Beyond the instances in these two groups, "no court shall intervene, in matters governed by this Law". Article 5 thus guarantees that all instances of possible court intervention are found in the piece of legislation enacting the Model Law, except for matters not regulated by it (for example, consolidation of arbitral proceedings, contractual relationship between arbitrators and parties or arbitral institutions, or fixing of costs and fees, including deposits). Protecting the arbitral process from unpredictable or disruptive court interference is essential to parties who choose arbitration (in particular foreign parties).

2. Arbitration agreement

18. Chapter II of the Model Law deals with the arbitration agreement, including its recognition by courts.

(a) Definition and form of arbitration agreement

19. The original 1985 version of the provision on the definition and form of arbitration agreement (article 7) closely followed article II (2) of the New York Convention, which requires that an arbitration agreement be in writing. If the parties have agreed to arbitrate, but they entered into the arbitration agreement in a manner that does not meet the form requirement, any party may have grounds to object to the jurisdiction of the arbitral tribunal. It was pointed out by practitioners that, in a number of situations, the drafting of a written document was impossible or impractical. In such cases, where the willingness of the parties to arbitrate was not in question, the validity of the arbitration agreement should be recognized. For that reason, article 7 was amended in 2006 to better conform to international contract practices. In amending article 7, the Commission adopted two options, which reflect two different approaches on the question of definition and form of arbitration agreement. The first approach follows the detailed structure of the original 1985 text. It confirms the validity and effect of a commitment by the parties to submit to arbitration an existing dispute ("*compromis*") or a future dispute ("*clause compromissoire*"). It follows the New York Convention in requiring the written form of the arbitration agreement but recognizes a record of the "contents" of the agreement "in any form" as equivalent to traditional "writing". The agreement to arbitrate may be entered into in any form (e.g. including orally) as long as the content of the agreement is recorded. This new rule is significant in that it no longer requires signatures of the parties or an exchange of messages between the parties. It modernizes the language referring to the use of electronic commerce by adopting wording inspired from the 1996 UNCITRAL Model Law on Electronic Commerce and the 2005 United Nations Convention on the Use of Electronic Communications in International Contracts. It covers the situation of "an exchange of statements of claim and defence in which the existence of an agreement is alleged by one party and not denied by another". It also states that "the reference in a contract to any document" (for example, general conditions) "containing an arbitration clause constitutes an arbitration agreement in writing provided that the reference is such as to make that clause part of the contract". It thus clarifies that applicable contract law remains available to determine the level of consent necessary for a party to become bound by an arbitration agreement allegedly made "by reference". The second approach defines the arbitration agreement in a manner that omits any form requirement. No preference was expressed by the Commission in favour of either option I or II, both of which are offered for enacting States to consider, depending on their particular needs, and by reference to the legal context in which the Model Law is enacted, including the general contract law of the enacting State.

Both options are intended to preserve the enforceability of arbitration agreements under the New York Convention.

20. In that respect, the Commission also adopted, at its thirty-ninth session in 2006, a "Recommendation regarding the interpretation of article II, paragraph 2, and article VII, paragraph 1, of the Convention on the Recognition and Enforcement of Foreign Arbitral Awards, done in New York, 10 June 1958" (A/61/17, Annex 2).******** The General Assembly, in its resolution 61/33 of 4 December 2006 noted that "in connection with the modernization of articles of the Model Law, the promotion of a uniform interpretation and application of the Convention on the Recognition and Enforcement of Foreign Arbitral Awards, done in New York, 10 June 1958, is particularly timely". The Recommendation was drafted in recognition of the widening use of electronic commerce and enactments of domestic legislation as well as case law, which are more favourable than the New York Convention in respect of the form requirement governing arbitration agreements, arbitration proceedings, and the enforcement of arbitral awards. The Recommendation encourages States to apply article II (2) of the New York Convention "recognizing that the circumstances described therein are not exhaustive". In addition, the Recommendation encourages States to adopt the revised article 7 of the Model Law. Both options of the revised article 7 establish a more favourable regime for the recognition and enforcement of arbitral awards than that provided under the New York Convention. By virtue of the "more favourable law provision" contained in article VII (1) of the New York Convention, the Recommendation clarifies that "any interested party" should be allowed "to avail itself of rights it may have, under the law or treaties of the country where an arbitration agreement is sought to be relied upon, to seek recognition of the validity of such an arbitration agreement".

(b) Arbitration agreement and the courts

21. Articles 8 and 9 deal with two important aspects of the complex relationship between the arbitration agreement and the resort to courts. Modelled on article II (3) of the New York Convention, article 8 (1) of the Model Law places any court under an obligation to refer the parties to arbitration if the court is seized with a claim on the same subject-matter unless it finds that the arbitration agreement is null and void, inoperative or incapable of being performed. The referral is dependent on a request, which a party may make not later than when submitting its first statement on the substance of the dispute. This provision, where adopted by a State enacting the Model Law, is by its nature binding only on the courts of that State. However, since article 8 is not limited in scope to agreements providing for arbitration to take place in the enacting State, it promotes the universal recognition and effect of international commercial arbitration agreements.

22. Article 9 expresses the principle that any interim measures of protection that may be obtained from courts under their procedural law (for example, pre-award attachments) are compatible with an arbitration agreement. That provision is ultimately addressed to the courts of any State, insofar as it establishes the compatibility between interim measures possibly issued by any court and an arbitration agreement, irrespective of the place of arbitration. Wherever a request for interim measures may be made to a court, it may not be relied upon, under the Model Law, as a waiver or an objection against the existence or effect of the arbitration agreement.

3. Composition of arbitral tribunal

23. Chapter III contains a number of detailed provisions on appointment, challenge, termination of mandate and replacement of an arbitrator. The chapter illustrates the general approach taken by the Model Law in eliminating difficulties that arise from inappropriate or fragmentary laws or rules. First, the approach recognizes the freedom of the parties to determine, by reference to an existing set of arbitration rules or by an ad hoc agreement, the procedure to be followed, subject to the fundamental requirements of fairness and justice. Secondly, where the parties have not exercised

******** Reproduced in Part Three hereafter.

their freedom to lay down the rules of procedure or they have failed to cover a particular issue, the Model Law ensures, by providing a set of suppletive rules, that the arbitration may commence and proceed effectively until the dispute is resolved.

24. Where under any procedure, agreed upon by the parties or based upon the suppletive rules of the Model Law, difficulties arise in the process of appointment, challenge or termination of the mandate of an arbitrator, articles 11, 13 and 14 provide for assistance by courts or other competent authorities designated by the enacting State. In view of the urgency of matters relating to the composition of the arbitral tribunal or its ability to function, and in order to reduce the risk and effect of any dilatory tactics, short time-periods are set and decisions rendered by courts or other authorities on such matters are not appealable.

4. Jurisdiction of arbitral tribunal

(a) Competence to rule on own jurisdiction

25. Article 16 (1) adopts the two important (not yet generally recognized) principles of "*Kompetenz-Kompetenz*" and of separability or autonomy of the arbitration clause. "*Kompetenz-Kompetenz*" means that the arbitral tribunal may independently rule on the question of whether it has jurisdiction, including any objections with respect to the existence or validity of the arbitration agreement, without having to resort to a court. Separability means that an arbitration clause shall be treated as an agreement independent of the other terms of the contract. As a consequence, a decision by the arbitral tribunal that the contract is null and void shall not entail *ipso jure* the invalidity of the arbitration clause. Detailed provisions in paragraph (2) require that any objections relating to the arbitrators' jurisdiction be made at the earliest possible time.

26. The competence of the arbitral tribunal to rule on its own jurisdiction (i.e. on the foundation, content and extent of its mandate and power) is, of course, subject to court control. Where the arbitral tribunal rules as a preliminary question that it has jurisdiction, article 16 (3) allows for immediate court control in order to avoid waste of time and money. However, three procedural safeguards are added to reduce the risk and effect of dilatory tactics: short time-period for resort to court (30 days), court decision not appealable, and discretion of the arbitral tribunal to continue the proceedings and make an award while the matter is pending before the court. In those cases where the arbitral tribunal decides to combine its decision on jurisdiction with an award on the merits, judicial review on the question of jurisdiction is available in setting aside proceedings under article 34 or in enforcement proceedings under article 36.

(b) Power to order interim measures and preliminary orders

27. Chapter IV A on interim measures and preliminary orders was adopted by the Commission in 2006. It replaces article 17 of the original 1985 version of the Model Law. Section 1 provides a generic definition of interim measures and sets out the conditions for granting such measures. An important innovation of the revision lies in the establishment (in section 4) of a regime for the recognition and enforcement of interim measures, which was modelled, as appropriate, on the regime for the recognition and enforcement of arbitral awards under articles 35 and 36 of the Model Law.

28. Section 2 of chapter IV A deals with the application for, and conditions for the granting of, preliminary orders. Preliminary orders provide a means for preserving the status quo until the arbitral tribunal issues an interim measure adopting or modifying the preliminary order. Article 17 B (1) provides that "a party may, without notice to any other party, make a request for an interim measure together with an application for a preliminary order directing a party not to frustrate the purpose of the interim measure requested". Article 17 B (2) permits an arbitral tribunal to grant a preliminary order if "it considers that prior disclosure of the request for the interim measure to the party against whom it is directed risks frustrating the purpose of the measure". Article 17 C contains carefully drafted safeguards for the party against whom the preliminary order is directed, such as

prompt notification of the application for the preliminary order and of the preliminary order itself (if any), and an opportunity for that party to present its case "at the earliest practicable time". In any event, a preliminary order has a maximum duration of twenty days and, while binding on the parties, is not subject to court enforcement and does not constitute an award. The term "preliminary order" is used to emphasize its limited nature.

29. Section 3 sets out rules applicable to both preliminary orders and interim measures.

30. Section 5 includes article 17 J on interim measures ordered by courts in support of arbitration, and provides that "a court shall have the same power of issuing an interim measure in relation to arbitration proceedings irrespective of whether their place is in the territory of the enacting State, as it has in relation to proceedings in courts". That article has been added in 2006 to put it beyond any doubt that the existence of an arbitration agreement does not infringe on the powers of the competent court to issue interim measures and that the party to such an arbitration agreement is free to approach the court with a request to order interim measures.

5. Conduct of arbitral proceedings

31. Chapter V provides the legal framework for a fair and effective conduct of the arbitral proceedings. Article 18, which sets out fundamental requirements of procedural justice, and article 19 on the rights and powers to determine the rules of procedure, express principles that are central to the Model Law.

(a) Fundamental procedural rights of a party

32. Article 18 embodies the principles that the parties shall be treated with equality and given a full opportunity of presenting their case. A number of provisions illustrate those principles. For example, article 24 (1) provides that, unless the parties have agreed that no oral hearings be held for the presentation of evidence or for oral argument, the arbitral tribunal shall hold such hearings at an appropriate stage of the proceedings, if so requested by a party. It should be noted that article 24 (1) deals only with the general entitlement of a party to oral hearings (as an alternative to proceedings conducted on the basis of documents and other materials) and not with the procedural aspects, such as the length, number or timing of hearings.

33. Another illustration of those principles relates to evidence by an expert appointed by the arbitral tribunal. Article 26 (2) requires the expert, after delivering his or her written or oral report, to participate in a hearing where the parties may put questions to the expert and present expert witnesses to testify on the points at issue, if such a hearing is requested by a party or deemed necessary by the arbitral tribunal. As another provision aimed at ensuring fairness, objectivity and impartiality, article 24 (3) provides that all statements, documents and other information supplied to the arbitral tribunal by one party shall be communicated to the other party, and that any expert report or evidentiary document on which the arbitral tribunal may rely in making its decision shall be communicated to the parties. In order to enable the parties to be present at any hearing and at any meeting of the arbitral tribunal for inspection purposes, they shall be given sufficient notice in advance (article 24 (2)).

(b) Determination of rules of procedure

34. Article 19 guarantees the parties' freedom to agree on the procedure to be followed by the arbitral tribunal in conducting the proceedings, subject to a few mandatory provisions on procedure, and empowers the arbitral tribunal, failing agreement by the parties, to conduct the arbitration in such a manner as it considers appropriate. The power conferred upon the arbitral tribunal includes the power to determine the admissibility, relevance, materiality and weight of any evidence.

35. Autonomy of the parties in determining the rules of procedure is of special importance in international cases since it allows the parties to select or tailor the rules according to their specific wishes and needs, unimpeded by traditional and possibly conflicting domestic concepts, thus obviating the earlier mentioned risk of frustration or surprise (see above, paras. 7 and 9). The supplementary

discretion of the arbitral tribunal is equally important in that it allows the tribunal to tailor the conduct of the proceedings to the specific features of the case without being hindered by any restraint that may stem from traditional local law, including any domestic rule on evidence. Moreover, it provides grounds for displaying initiative in solving any procedural question not regulated in the arbitration agreement or the Model Law.

36. In addition to the general provisions of article 19, other provisions in the Model Law recognize party autonomy and, failing agreement, empower the arbitral tribunal to decide on certain matters. Examples of particular practical importance in international cases are article 20 on the place of arbitration and article 22 on the language to be used in the proceedings.

(c) Default of a party

37. The arbitral proceedings may be continued in the absence of a party, provided that due notice has been given. This applies, in particular, to the failure of the respondent to communicate its statement of defence (article 25 *(b)*). The arbitral tribunal may also continue the proceedings where a party fails to appear at a hearing or to produce documentary evidence without showing sufficient cause for the failure (article 25 *(c)*). However, if the claimant fails to submit its statement of claim, the arbitral tribunal is obliged to terminate the proceedings (article 25 *(a)*).

38. Provisions that empower the arbitral tribunal to carry out its task even if one of the parties does not participate are of considerable practical importance. As experience shows, it is not uncommon for one of the parties to have little interest in cooperating or expediting matters. Such provisions therefore provide international commercial arbitration its necessary effectiveness, within the limits of fundamental requirements of procedural justice.

6. Making of award and termination of proceedings

(a) Rules applicable to substance of dispute

39. Article 28 deals with the determination of the rules of law governing the substance of the dispute. Under paragraph (1), the arbitral tribunal decides the dispute in accordance with the rules of law chosen by the parties. This provision is significant in two respects. It grants the parties the freedom to choose the applicable substantive law, which is important where the national law does not clearly or fully recognize that right. In addition, by referring to the choice of "rules of law" instead of "law", the Model Law broadens the range of options available to the parties as regards the designation of the law applicable to the substance of the dispute. For example, parties may agree on rules of law that have been elaborated by an international forum but have not yet been incorporated into any national legal system. Parties could also choose directly an instrument such as the United Nations Convention on Contracts for the International Sale of Goods as the body of substantive law governing the arbitration, without having to refer to the national law of any State party to that Convention. The power of the arbitral tribunal, on the other hand, follows more traditional lines. When the parties have not chosen the applicable law, the arbitral tribunal shall apply the law (i.e., the national law) determined by the conflict-of-laws rules that it considers applicable.

40. Article 28 (3) recognizes that the parties may authorize the arbitral tribunal to decide the dispute *ex aequo et bono* or as *amiables compositeur*. This type of arbitration (where the arbitral tribunal may decide the dispute on the basis of principles it believes to be just, without having to refer to any particular body of law) is currently not known or used in all legal systems. The Model Law does not intend to regulate this area. It simply calls the attention of the parties on the need to provide clarification in the arbitration agreement and specifically to empower the arbitral tribunal. However, paragraph (4) makes it clear that in all cases where the dispute relates to a contract (including arbitration *ex aequo et bono*) the arbitral tribunal must decide in accordance with the terms of the contract and shall take into account the usages of the trade applicable to the transaction.

(b) Making of award and other decisions

41. In its rules on the making of the award (articles 29–31), the Model Law focuses on the situation where the arbitral tribunal consists of more than one arbitrator. In such a situation, any award and other decision shall be made by a majority of the arbitrators, except on questions of procedure, which may be left to a presiding arbitrator. The majority principle applies also to the signing of the award, provided that the reason for any omitted signature is stated.

42. Article 31 (3) provides that the award shall state the place of arbitration and shall be deemed to have been made at that place. The effect of the deeming provision is to emphasize that the final making of the award constitutes a legal act, which in practice does not necessarily coincide with one factual event. For the same reason that the arbitral proceedings need not be carried out at the place designated as the legal "place of arbitration", the making of the award may be completed through deliberations held at various places, by telephone or correspondence. In addition, the award does not have to be signed by the arbitrators physically gathering at the same place.

43. The arbitral award must be in writing and state its date. It must also state the reasons on which it is based, unless the parties have agreed otherwise or the award is "on agreed terms" (i.e., an award that records the terms of an amicable settlement by the parties). It may be added that the Model Law neither requires nor prohibits "dissenting opinions".

7. Recourse against award

44. The disparity found in national laws as regards the types of recourse against an arbitral award available to the parties presents a major difficulty in harmonizing international arbitration legislation. Some outdated laws on arbitration, by establishing parallel regimes for recourse against arbitral awards or against court decisions, provide various types of recourse, various (and often long) time periods for exercising the recourse, and extensive lists of grounds on which recourse may be based. That situation (of considerable concern to those involved in international commercial arbitration) is greatly improved by the Model Law, which provides uniform grounds upon which (and clear time periods within which) recourse against an arbitral award may be made.

(a) Application for setting aside as exclusive recourse

45. The first measure of improvement is to allow only one type of recourse, to the exclusion of any other recourse regulated in any procedural law of the State in question. Article 34 (1) provides that the sole recourse against an arbitral award is by application for setting aside, which must be made within three months of receipt of the award (article 34 (3)). In regulating "recourse" (i.e., the means through which a party may actively "attack" the award), article 34 does not preclude a party from seeking court control by way of defence in enforcement proceedings (articles 35 and 36). Article 34 is limited to action before a court (i.e., an organ of the judicial system of a State). However, a party is not precluded from appealing to an arbitral tribunal of second instance if the parties have agreed on such a possibility (as is common in certain commodity trades).

(b) Grounds for setting aside

46. As a further measure of improvement, the Model Law lists exhaustively the grounds on which an award may be set aside. This list essentially mirrors that contained in article 36 (1), which is taken from article V of the New York Convention. The grounds provided in article 34 (2) are set out in two categories. Grounds which are to be proven by one party are as follows: lack of capacity of the parties to conclude an arbitration agreement; lack of a valid arbitration agreement; lack of notice of appointment of an arbitrator or of the arbitral proceedings or inability of a party to present its case; the award deals with matters not covered by the submission to arbitration; the composition of the arbitral tribunal or the conduct of arbitral proceedings are contrary to the effective agreement of the parties or, failing such agreement, to the Model Law. Grounds that a court may consider of its own

initiative are as follows: non-arbitrability of the subject-matter of the dispute or violation of public policy (which is to be understood as serious departures from fundamental notions of procedural justice).

47. The approach under which the grounds for setting aside an award under the Model Law parallel the grounds for refusing recognition and enforcement of the award under article V of the New York Convention is reminiscent of the approach taken in the European Convention on International Commercial Arbitration (Geneva, 1961). Under article IX of the latter Convention, the decision of a foreign court to set aside an award for a reason other than the ones listed in article V of the New York Convention does not constitute a ground for refusing enforcement. The Model Law takes this philosophy one step further by directly limiting the reasons for setting aside.

48. Although the grounds for setting aside as set out in article 34 (2) are almost identical to those for refusing recognition or enforcement as set out in article 36 (1), a practical difference should be noted. An application for setting aside under article 34 (2) may only be made to a court in the State where the award was rendered whereas an application for enforcement might be made in a court in any State. For that reason, the grounds relating to public policy and non-arbitrability may vary in substance with the law applied by the court (in the State of setting aside or in the State of enforcement).

8. Recognition and enforcement of awards

49. The eighth and last chapter of the Model Law deals with the recognition and enforcement of awards. Its provisions reflect the significant policy decision that the same rules should apply to arbitral awards whether made in the country of enforcement or abroad, and that those rules should follow closely the New York Convention.

(a) Towards uniform treatment of all awards irrespective of country of origin

50. By treating awards rendered in international commercial arbitration in a uniform manner irrespective of where they were made, the Model Law distinguishes between "international" and "non-international" awards instead of relying on the traditional distinction between "foreign" and "domestic" awards. This new line is based on substantive grounds rather than territorial borders, which are inappropriate in view of the limited importance of the place of arbitration in international cases. The place of arbitration is often chosen for reasons of convenience of the parties and the dispute may have little or no connection with the State where the arbitration legally takes place. Consequently, the recognition and enforcement of "international" awards, whether "foreign" or "domestic", should be governed by the same provisions.

51. By modelling the recognition and enforcement rules on the relevant provisions of the New York Convention, the Model Law supplements, without conflicting with, the regime of recognition and enforcement created by that successful Convention.

(b) Procedural conditions of recognition and enforcement

52. Under article 35 (1) any arbitral award, irrespective of the country in which it was made, shall be recognized as binding and enforceable, subject to the provisions of article 35 (2) and of article 36 (the latter of which sets forth the grounds on which recognition or enforcement may be refused). Based on the above consideration of the limited importance of the place of arbitration in international cases and the desire of overcoming territorial restrictions, reciprocity is not included as a condition for recognition and enforcement.

53. The Model Law does not lay down procedural details of recognition and enforcement, which are left to national procedural laws and practices. The Model Law merely sets certain conditions for obtaining enforcement under article 35 (2). It was amended in 2006 to liberalize formal requirements and reflect the amendment made to article 7 on the form of the arbitration agreement. Presentation of a copy of the arbitration agreement is no longer required under article 35 (2).

(c) Grounds for refusing recognition or enforcement

54. Although the grounds on which recognition or enforcement may be refused under the Model Law are identical to those listed in article V of the New York Convention, the grounds listed in the Model Law are relevant not only to foreign awards but to all awards rendered in the sphere of application of the piece of legislation enacting the Model Law. Generally, it was deemed desirable to adopt, for the sake of harmony, the same approach and wording as this important Convention. However, the first ground on the list as contained in the New York Convention (which provides that recognition and enforcement may be refused if "the parties to the arbitration agreement were, under the law applicable to them, under some incapacity") was modified since it was viewed as containing an incomplete and potentially misleading conflict-of-laws rule.

Further information on the Model Law may be obtained from:

UNCITRAL secretariat
Vienna International Centre
P.O. Box 500
1400 Vienna
Austria

Telephone: (+43-1) 26060-4060
Telefax: (+43-1) 26060-5813
Internet: www.uncitral.org
E-mail: uncitral@uncitral.org

PART THREE

RECOMMENDATION REGARDING THE INTERPRETATION OF ARTICLE II,
PARAGRAPH 2, AND ARTICLE VII, PARAGRAPH 1, OF THE CONVENTION ON THE
RECOGNITION AND ENFORCEMENT OF FOREIGN ARBITRAL AWARDS, DONE IN
NEW YORK, 10 JUNE 1958, ADOPTED BY THE UNITED NATIONS COMMISSION ON
INTERNATIONAL TRADE LAW ON 7 JULY 2006 AT ITS THIRTY-NINTH SESSION

The United Nations Commission on International Trade Law,

Recalling General Assembly resolution 2205 (XXI) of 17 December 1966, which established the United Nations Commission on International Trade Law with the object of promoting the progressive harmonization and unification of the law of international trade by, inter alia, promoting ways and means of ensuring a uniform interpretation and application of international conventions and uniform laws in the field of the law of international trade,

Conscious of the fact that the different legal, social and economic systems of the world, together with different levels of development, are represented in the Commission,

Recalling successive resolutions of the General Assembly reaffirming the mandate of the Commission as the core legal body within the United Nations system in the field of international trade law to coordinate legal activities in this field,

Convinced that the wide adoption of the Convention on the Recognition and Enforcement of Foreign Arbitral Awards, done in New York on 10 June 1958,******** has been a significant achievement in the promotion of the rule of law, particularly in the field of international trade,

Recalling that the Conference of Plenipotentiaries which prepared and opened the Convention for signature adopted a resolution, which states, inter alia, that the Conference "considers that greater uniformity of national laws on arbitration would further the effectiveness of arbitration in the settlement of private law disputes",

Bearing in mind differing interpretations of the form requirements under the Convention that result in part from differences of expression as between the five equally authentic texts of the Convention,

Taking into account article VII, paragraph 1, of the Convention, a purpose of which is to enable the enforcement of foreign arbitral awards to the greatest extent, in particular by recognizing the right of any interested party to avail itself of law or treaties of the country where the award is sought to be relied upon, including where such law or treaties offer a regime more favourable than the Convention,

Considering the wide use of electronic commerce,

Taking into account international legal instruments, such as the 1985 UNCITRAL Model Law on International Commercial Arbitration,******** as subsequently revised, particularly with respect to article 7,******** the UNCITRAL Model Law on Electronic Commerce,******** the UNCITRAL Model Law on Electronic Signatures******** and the United Nations Convention on the Use of Electronic Communications in International Contracts,********

******** United Nations, *Treaty Series*, vol. 330, No. 4739.

******** *Official Records of the General Assembly, Fortieth Session, Supplement No. 17* (A/40/17), annex I, and United Nations publication, Sales No. E.95.V.18.

******** Ibid., *Sixty-first Session, Supplement No. 17* (A/61/17), annex I.

******** Ibid., *Fifty-first Session, Supplement No. 17* (A/51/17), annex I, and United Nations publication, Sales No. E.99.V.4, which contains also an additional article 5 bis, adopted in 1998, and the accompanying Guide to Enactment.

******** Ibid., *Fifty-sixth Session, Supplement No. 17* and corrigendum (A/56/17 and Corr.3), annex II, and United Nations publication, Sales No. E.02.V.8, which contains also the accompanying Guide to Enactment.

******** General Assembly resolution 60/21, annex.

Taking into account also enactments of domestic legislation, as well as case law, more favourable than the Convention in respect of form requirement governing arbitration agreements, arbitration proceedings and the enforcement of arbitral awards,

Considering that, in interpreting the Convention, regard is to be had to the need to promote recognition and enforcement of arbitral awards,

1. *Recommends* that article II, paragraph 2, of the Convention on the Recognition and Enforcement of Foreign Arbitral Awards, done in New York, 10 June 1958, be applied recognizing that the circumstances described therein are not exhaustive;

2. *Recommends also* that article VII, paragraph 1, of the Convention on the Recognition and Enforcement of Foreign Arbitral Awards, done in New York, 10 June 1958, should be applied to allow any interested party to avail itself of rights it may have, under the law or treaties of the country where an arbitration agreement is sought to be relied upon, to seek recognition of the validity of such an arbitration agreement.

APPENDIX 10

LCIA Mediation Procedure[*]

EFFECTIVE 1 OCTOBER 1999

Where any agreement provides for mediation of existing or future disputes under the procedure or rules of the LCIA, the parties shall be taken to have agreed that the mediation shall be conducted in accordance with the following procedure (the "Procedure") or such amended procedure as the LCIA may have adopted hereafter to take effect before the commencement of the mediation. The Procedure includes the Schedule of Mediation Fees and Expenses (the "Schedule") in effect at the commencement of the mediation, as separately amended from time to time by the LCIA Court.

CONTENTS

Article

1. Commencing Mediation – Prior Existing Agreements to Mediate

2. Commencing Mediation – no Prior Agreement

3. Appointment of Mediator

4. Statements by the Parties

5. Conduct of the Mediation

6. Conclusion of the Mediation

7. Settlement Agreement

8. Costs

9. Judicial or Arbitral Proceedings

10. Confidentiality and Privacy

11. Exclusion of Liability

Article 1
Commencing Mediation – Prior Existing Agreements to Mediate

1.1 Where there is a prior existing agreement to mediate under the Procedure (a "Prior Agreement"), any party or parties wishing to commence a mediation shall send to the Registrar of the LCIA Court ("the Registrar") a written request for mediation (the "Request for Mediation"), which shall briefly state the nature of the dispute and the value of the claim, and should include, or be accompanied by a copy of the Prior Agreement, the names, addresses, telephone, facsimile, telex and e-mail numbers (if known) of the parties to the mediation, and of their legal representatives (if known) and of the mediator proposed (if any) by the party or parties requesting mediation.

1.2 If the Request for Mediation is not made jointly by all parties to the Prior Agreement, the party commencing the mediation shall, at the same time, send a copy of the Request for Mediation to the other party or parties.

---

[*] Reproduced with the permission of the LCIA.

1.3 The Request for Mediation shall be accompanied by the registration fee prescribed in the Schedule.

1.4 The LCIA Court shall appoint a mediator as soon as practicable after receipt by the Registrar of the Request for Mediation, with due regard for any nomination, or method or criteria of selection agreed in writing by the parties, and subject always to Article 8 of the Procedure.

1.5 Where there is a Prior Agreement, the date of commencement of the mediation shall be the date of receipt by the Registrar of the Request for Mediation.

Article 2
Commencing Mediation – no Prior Agreement

2.1 Where there is no Prior Agreement, any party or parties wishing to commence a mediation under the Procedure shall send to the Registrar a Request for Mediation, which shall briefly state the nature of the dispute and the value of the claim, and should include, or be accompanied by, the names, addresses, telephone, facsimile, telex and e-mail numbers (if known) of the parties to the mediation, and of their legal representatives (if known) and of the mediator proposed (if any) by the party or parties requesting mediation.

2.2 The Request for Mediation shall be accompanied by the registration fee prescribed in the Schedule.

2.3 If the Request for Mediation is not made jointly by all parties to the dispute,

   a) the party wishing to commence the mediation shall, at the same time, send a copy of the Request for Mediation to the other party or parties; and

   b) the other party or parties shall, within 14 days of receiving the Request for Mediation, advise the Registrar in writing whether or not they agree to the mediation of the dispute.

2.4 In the event that the other party or parties either declines mediation, or fails to agree to mediation within the 14 days referred to at Article 2.3 b), there shall be no mediation under the Procedure and the Registrar shall so advise the parties, in writing.

2.5 The LCIA Court shall appoint a mediator as soon as practicable after agreement to mediate has been reached between the parties, with due regard for any nomination, or method or criteria of selection agreed in writing by the parties, and subject always to Article 8 of the Procedure.

2.6 Where there is no Prior Agreement, the date of commencement of the mediation shall be the date that agreement to mediate is reached in accordance with Article 2.3(b).

Article 3
Appointment of Mediator

3.1 Before appointment by the LCIA Court, pursuant to Article 1.4 or Article 2.5, the mediator shall furnish the Registrar with a written résumé of his or her past and present professional positions; and he or she shall sign a declaration to the effect that there are no circumstances known to him or her likely to give rise to any justified doubts as to his or her impartiality or independence, other than any circumstances disclosed by him or her in the declaration. A copy of the mediator's résumé and declaration shall be provided to the parties.

3.2 Where the mediator has made a disclosure, pursuant to Article 3.1, or where a party independently knows of circumstances likely to give rise to justified doubts as to his or her impartiality or independence, a party shall be at liberty to object to his or her appointment; in which case the LCIA Court shall appoint another mediator.

Article 4
Statements by the Parties

4.1 The parties are free to agree how, and in what form, they will inform the mediator of their respective cases, provided that, unless they have agreed otherwise, each party shall submit to the mediator, no later than 7 days before the date agreed between the mediator and the parties for the first scheduled mediation session, a brief written statement summarising his case; the background to the dispute; and the issues to be resolved.

4.2 Each written statement should be accompanied by copies of any documents to which it refers.

4.3 Each party shall, at the same time, submit a copy of his written statement and supporting documents to the other party or parties.

Article 5
Conduct of the Mediation

5.1 The mediator may conduct the mediation in such manner as he or she sees fit, having in mind at all times the circumstances of the case and the wishes of the parties.

5.2 The mediator may communicate with the parties orally or in writing, together, or individually, and may convene a meeting or meetings at a venue to be determined by the mediator after consultations with the parties.

5.3 Nothing which is communicated to the mediator in private during the course of the mediation shall be repeated to the other party or parties, without the express consent of the party making the communication.

5.4 Each party shall notify the other party and the mediator of the number and identity of those persons who will attend any meeting convened by the mediator.

5.5 Each party shall identify a representative of that party who is authorised to settle the dispute on behalf of that party, and shall confirm that authority in writing.

5.6 Unless otherwise agreed by the parties, the mediator will decide the language(s) in which the mediation will be conducted.

Article 6
Conclusion of the Mediation

The mediation will be at an end when, either

(a) a settlement agreement is signed by the parties; or

(b) the parties advise the mediator that it is their view that a settlement cannot be reached and that it is their wish to terminate the mediation; or

(c) the mediator advises the parties that, in his or her judgement, the mediation process will not resolve the issues in dispute; or

(d) the time limit for mediation provided in a Prior Agreement has expired and the parties have not agreed to extend that time limit.

Article 7
Settlement Agreement

7.1 If terms are agreed in settlement of the dispute, the parties, with the assistance of the mediator if the parties so request, shall draw up and sign a settlement agreement, setting out such terms.

7.2 By signing the settlement agreement, the parties agree to be bound by its terms.

Article 8
Costs

8.1 The costs of the mediation (the "Costs") shall include the fees and expenses of the mediator and the administrative charges of the LCIA, as set out in the Schedule.

8.2 The Costs shall be borne equally by the parties (or in such other proportions as they have agreed in writing).

8.3 As soon as practicable after receipt of the Request for Mediation, pursuant to Article 1 of the Procedure, or after the parties have agreed to mediate, pursuant to Article 2 of the Procedure, the LCIA will request the parties to file a deposit to be held on account of the Costs ("the Deposit"). The Deposit shall be paid by the parties in equal shares (or in such other proportions as they have agreed) prior to the appointment of the mediator.

8.4 A mediator shall not be appointed and the mediation shall not proceed until and unless the Deposit has been paid in full.

8.5 At the conclusion of the mediation, the LCIA, in consultation with the mediator, will fix the Costs of the mediation.

8.6 If the Deposit exceeds the Costs, the excess will be reimbursed to the parties in the proportions in which they paid the deposit. If the Costs exceed the Deposit, the shortfall will be invoiced to the parties for immediate payment in equal shares (or in such other proportions as they have agreed).

8.7 Any other costs incurred by the parties, whether in regard to legal fees, experts' fees or expenses of any other nature will not be part of the Costs for the purposes of the Procedure.

Article 9
Judicial or Arbitral Proceedings

Unless they have agreed otherwise, and notwithstanding the mediation, the parties may initiate or continue any arbitration or judicial proceedings in respect of the dispute which is the subject of the mediation.

Article 10
Confidentiality and Privacy

10.1 All mediation sessions shall be private, and shall be attended only by the mediator, the parties and those individuals identified pursuant to Article 5.4.

10.2 The mediation process and all negotiations, and statements and documents prepared for the purposes of the mediation, shall be confidential and covered by "without prejudice" or negotiation privilege.

10.3 The mediation shall be confidential. Unless agreed among the parties, or required by law, neither the mediator nor the parties may disclose to any person any information regarding the mediation or any settlement terms, or the outcome of the mediation.

10.4 All documents or other information produced for or arising in relation to the mediation will be privileged and will not be admissible in evidence or otherwise discoverable in any litigation or arbitration in connection with the dispute referred to mediation, except for any documents or other information which would in any event be admissible or discoverable in any such litigation or arbitration.

10.5 There shall be no formal record or transcript of the mediation.

10.6 The parties shall not rely upon, or introduce as evidence in any arbitral or judicial proceedings, any admissions, proposals or views expressed by the parties or by the mediator during the course of the mediation.

Article 11
Exclusion of Liability

11.1 None of the LCIA, the LCIA Court (including its President, Vice-Presidents and individual members), the Registrar, any Deputy Registrar and any mediator shall be liable to any party howsoever for any act or omission in connection with any mediation conducted by reference to the Procedure, save where the act or omission is shown by that party to constitute conscious and deliberate wrongdoing committed by the body or person alleged to be liable to that party.

11.2 None of the LCIA, the LCIA Court (including its President, Vice-Presidents and individual members), the Registrar, any Deputy Registrar, or the Mediator shall be under any legal obligation to make any statement to any person about any matter concerning the mediation, nor shall any party seek to make any of these persons a witness in any legal or other proceedings arising out of the mediation.

APPENDIX 11

DIFC-LCIA Arbitration Rules*

EFFECTIVE 17 FEBRUARY 2008

Where any agreement, submission or reference provides in writing and in whatsoever manner for arbitration under the rules of the DIFC-LCIA Arbitration Centre, the parties shall be taken to have agreed in writing that the arbitration shall be conducted in accordance with the following rules (the Rules) or such amended rules as the DIFC-LCIA Arbitration Centre and the Court of the LCIA (the LCIA Court) may have adopted hereafter to take effect before the commencement of the arbitration. The Rules include the Schedule of Costs in effect at the commencement of the arbitration, as separately amended from time to time by the DIFC-LCIA Arbitration Centre and the LCIA Court.

CONTENTS

Article 1   The Request for Arbitration
Article 2   The Response
Article 3   The LCIA Court, the Registrar and the DIFC-LCIA Registrar
Article 4   Notices and Periods of Time
Article 5   Formation of the Arbitral Tribunal
Article 6   Nationality of Arbitrators
Article 7   Party and Other Nominations
Article 8   Three or More Parties
Article 9   Expedited Formation
Article 10 Revocation of Arbitrator's Appointment
Article 11 Nomination and Replacement Arbitrators
Article 12 Majority Power to Continue Proceedings
Article 13 Communications
Article 14 Conduct of the Proceedings
Article 15 Submission of Written Statements and Documents
Article 16 Seat of Arbitration and Place of Hearings
Article 17 Language of Arbitration
Article 18 Party Representation
Article 19 Hearings
Article 20 Witnesses
Article 21 Experts to the Arbitral Tribunal
Article 22 Additional Powers of the Arbitral Tribunal
Article 23 Jurisdiction of the Arbitral Tribunal
Article 24 Deposits
Article 25 Interim and Conservatory Measures
Article 26 The Award
Article 27 Correction of Awards and Additional Awards
Article 28 Arbitration and Legal Costs
Article 29 Decisions by the LCIA Court

---

* Reproduced with the permission of the DIFC-LCIA Arbitration Centre.

Article 30   Confidentiality
Article 31   Exclusion of Liability
Article 32   General Rules

Article 1
The Request for Arbitration

1.1 Any party wishing to commence an arbitration under these Rules (the Claimant) shall send to the Registrar of the DIFC-LCIA Arbitration Centre (the DIFC-LCIA Registrar) a written request for arbitration (the Request), containing or accompanied by:

(a) the names, addresses, telephone, facsimile, telex and e-mail numbers (if known) of the parties to the arbitration and of their legal representatives;

(b) a copy of the written arbitration clause or separate written arbitration agreement invoked by the Claimant (the Arbitration Agreement), together with a copy of the contractual documentation in which the arbitration clause is contained or in respect of which the arbitration arises;

(c) a brief statement describing the nature and circumstances of the dispute, and specifying the claims advanced by the Claimant against another party to the arbitration (the Respondent);

(d) a statement of any matters (such as the seat or language(s) of the arbitration, or the number of arbitrators, or their qualifications or identities) on which the parties have already agreed in writing for the arbitration or in respect of which the Claimant wishes to make a proposal;

(e) if the Arbitration Agreement calls for party nomination of arbitrators, the name, address, telephone, facsimile, telex and e-mail numbers (if known) of the Claimant's nominee;

(f) the fee prescribed in the Schedule of Costs (without which the Request shall be treated as not having been received by the DIFC-LCIA Registrar and the arbitration as not having been commenced);

(g) confirmation to the DIFC-LCIA Registrar that copies of the Request (including all accompanying documents) have been or are being served simultaneously on all other parties to the arbitration by one or more means of service to be identified in such confirmation.

1.2 The date of receipt by the DIFC-LCIA Registrar of the Request shall be treated as the date on which the arbitration has commenced for all purposes. The Request (including all accompanying documents) should be submitted to the DIFC-LCIA Registrar in two copies where a sole arbitrator should be appointed, or, if the parties have agreed or the Claimant considers that three arbitrators should be appointed, in four copies.

Article 2
The Response

2.1 Within 30 days of service of the Request on the Respondent, (or such lesser period fixed by the LCIA Court), the Respondent shall send to the DIFC-LCIA Registrar a written response to the Request (the Response), containing or accompanied by:

(a) confirmation or denial of all or part of the claims advanced by the Claimant in the Request;

(b) a brief statement describing the nature and circumstances of any counterclaims advanced by the Respondent against the Claimant;

(c) comment in response to any statements contained in the Request, as called for under Article 1.1(d), on matters relating to the conduct of the arbitration;

(d) if the Arbitration Agreement calls for party nomination of arbitrators, the name, address, telephone, facsimile, telex and e-mail numbers (if known) of the Respondent's nominee; and

(e) confirmation to the DIFC-LCIA Registrar that copies of the Response (including all accompanying documents) have been or are being served simultaneously on all other parties to the arbitration by one or more means of service to be identified in such confirmation.

2.2 The Response (including all accompanying documents) should be submitted to the DIFC-LCIA Registrar in two copies, or if the parties have agreed or the Respondent considers that three arbitrators should be appointed, in four copies.

2.3 Failure to send a Response shall not preclude the Respondent from denying any claim or from advancing a counterclaim in the arbitration. However, if the Arbitration Agreement calls for party nomination of arbitrators, failure to send a Response or to nominate an arbitrator within time or at all shall constitute an irrevocable waiver of that party's opportunity to nominate an arbitrator.

Article 3
The LCIA Court, the Registrar and the DIFC-LCIA Registrar

3.1 The functions of the LCIA Court under these Rules shall be performed in its name by the President or a Vice-President of the LCIA Court or by a division of three or five members of the LCIA Court appointed by the President or a Vice-President of the LCIA Court, as determined by the President.

3.2 The functions of the DIFC-LCIA Registrar under these Rules shall be performed by the DIFC-LCIA Registrar under the supervision of the Registrar of the LCIA Court and of the LCIA Court.

3.3 All communications from any party or arbitrator to the LCIA Court shall be addressed to the DIFC-LCIA Registrar.

Article 4
Notices and Periods of Time

4.1 Any notice or other communication that may be or is required to be given by a party under these Rules shall be in writing and shall be delivered by registered postal or courier service or transmitted by facsimile, telex, e-mail or any other means of telecommunication that provide a record of its transmission.

4.2 A party's last-known residence or place of business during the arbitration shall be a valid address for the purpose of any notice or other communication in the absence of any notification of a change to such address by that party to the other parties, the Arbitral Tribunal and the DIFC-LCIA Registrar.

4.3 For the purpose of determining the date of commencement of a time limit, a notice or other communication shall be treated as having been received on the day it is delivered or, in the case of telecommunications, transmitted in accordance with Articles 4.1 and 4.2.

4.4 For the purpose of determining compliance with a time limit, a notice or other communication shall be treated as having been sent, made or transmitted if it is dispatched in accordance with Articles 4.1 and 4.2 prior to or on the date of the expiration of the time-limit.

4.5 Notwithstanding the above, any notice or communication by one party may be addressed to another party in the manner agreed in writing between them or, failing such agreement, according to the practice followed in the course of their previous dealings or in whatever manner ordered by the Arbitral Tribunal.

4.6 For the purpose of calculating a period of time under these Rules, such period shall begin to run on the day following the day when a notice or other communication is received. If the last day of such period is an official holiday or a non-business day at the residence or place of business of the addressee, the period is extended until the first business day which follows. Official holidays or non-business days occurring during the running of the period of time are included in calculating that period.

4.7 The Arbitral Tribunal may at any time extend (even where the period of time has expired) or abridge any period of time prescribed under these Rules or under the Arbitration Agreement for the conduct of the arbitration, including any notice or communication to be served by one party on any other party.

Article 5
Formation of the Arbitral Tribunal

5.1 The expression "the Arbitral Tribunal" in these Rules includes a sole arbitrator or all the arbitrators where more than one. All references to an arbitrator shall include the masculine and feminine. (References to the President, Vice-President and members of the LCIA Court, the Registrar or deputy Registrar, the DIFC-LCIA Registrar, expert, witness, party and legal representative shall be similarly understood).

5.2 All arbitrators conducting an arbitration under these Rules shall be and remain at all times impartial and independent of the parties; and none shall act in the arbitration as advocates for any party. No arbitrator, whether before or after appointment, shall advise any party on the merits or outcome of the dispute.

5.3 Before appointment by the LCIA Court, each arbitrator shall furnish to the DIFC-LCIA Registrar a written resume of his past and present professional positions; he shall agree in writing upon fee rates conforming to the Schedule of Costs; and he shall sign a declaration to the effect that there are no circumstances known to him likely to give rise to any justified doubts as to his impartiality or independence, other than any circumstances disclosed by him in the declaration. Each arbitrator shall thereby also assume a continuing duty forthwith to disclose any such circumstances to the LCIA Court, to any other members of the Arbitral Tribunal and to all the parties if such circumstances should arise after the date of such declaration and before the arbitration is concluded.

5.4 The LCIA Court shall appoint the Arbitral Tribunal as soon as practicable after receipt by the DIFC-LCIA Registrar of the Response or after the expiry of 30 days following service of the Request upon the Respondent if no Response is received by the DIFC-LCIA Registrar (or such lesser period fixed by the LCIA Court). The LCIA Court may proceed with the formation of the Arbitral Tribunal notwithstanding that the Request is incomplete or the Response is missing, late or incomplete. A sole arbitrator shall be appointed unless the parties have agreed in writing otherwise, or unless the LCIA Court determines that in view of all the circumstances of the case a three-member tribunal is appropriate.

5.5 The LCIA Court alone is empowered to appoint arbitrators. The LCIA Court will appoint arbitrators with due regard for any particular method or criteria of selection agreed in writing by the parties. In selecting arbitrators consideration will be given to the nature of the transaction, the nature and circumstances of the dispute, the nationality, location and languages of the parties and (if more than two) the number of parties.

5.6 In the case of a three-member Arbitral Tribunal, the chairman (who will not be a party-nominated arbitrator) shall be appointed by the LCIA Court.

Article 6
Nationality of Arbitrators

6.1 Where the parties are of different nationalities, a sole arbitrator or chairman of the Arbitral Tribunal shall not have the same nationality as any party unless the parties who are not of the same nationality as the proposed appointee all agree in writing otherwise.

6.2 The nationality of parties shall be understood to include that of controlling shareholders or interests.

6.3 For the purpose of this Article, a person who is a citizen of two or more states shall be treated as a national of each state; and citizens of the European Union shall be treated as nationals of its different Member States and shall not be treated as having the same nationality.

Article 7
Party and Other Nominations

7.1 If the parties have agreed that any arbitrator is to be appointed by one or more of them or by any third person, that agreement shall be treated as an agreement to nominate an arbitrator for all purposes. Such nominee may only be appointed by the LCIA Court as arbitrator subject to his prior compliance with Article 5.3. The LCIA Court may refuse to appoint any such nominee if it determines that he is not suitable or independent or impartial.

7.2 Where the parties have howsoever agreed that the Respondent or any third person is to nominate an arbitrator and such nomination is not made within time or at all, the LCIA Court may appoint an arbitrator notwithstanding the absence of the nomination and without regard to any late nomination. Likewise, if the Request for Arbitration does not contain a nomination by the Claimant where the parties have howsoever agreed that the Claimant or a third person is to nominate an arbitrator, the LCIA Court may appoint an arbitrator notwithstanding the absence of the nomination and without regard to any late nomination.

Article 8
Three or More Parties

8.1 Where the Arbitration Agreement entitles each party howsoever to nominate an arbitrator, the parties to the dispute number more than two and such parties have not all agreed in writing that the disputant parties represent two separate sides for the formation of the Arbitral Tribunal as Claimant and Respondent respectively, the LCIA Court shall appoint the Arbitral Tribunal without regard to any party's nomination.

8.2 In such circumstances, the Arbitration Agreement shall be treated for all purposes as a written agreement by the parties for the appointment of the Arbitral Tribunal by the LCIA Court.

Article 9
Expedited Formation

9.1 In exceptional urgency, on or after the commencement of the arbitration, any party may apply to the LCIA Court for the expedited formation of the Arbitral Tribunal, including the appointment of any replacement arbitrator under Articles 10 and 11 of these Rules.

9.2 Such an application shall be made in writing to the LCIA Court, copied to all other parties to the arbitration; and it shall set out the specific grounds for exceptional urgency in the formation of the Arbitral Tribunal.

9.3 The LCIA Court may, in its complete discretion, abridge or curtail any time-limit under these Rules for the formation of the Arbitral Tribunal, including service of the Response and of any matters or documents adjudged to be missing from the Request. The LCIA Court shall not be entitled to abridge or curtail any other time-limit.

Article 10
Revocation of Arbitrator's Appointment

10.1 If either (a) any arbitrator gives written notice of his desire to resign as arbitrator to the LCIA Court, to be copied to the parties and the other arbitrators (if any) or (b) any arbitrator dies, falls seriously ill, refuses, or becomes unable or unfit to act, either upon challenge by a party or at the request of the remaining arbitrators, the LCIA Court may revoke that arbitrator's appointment and appoint another arbitrator. The LCIA Court shall decide upon the amount of fees and expenses to be paid for the former arbitrator's services (if any) as it may consider appropriate in all the circumstances.

10.2 If any arbitrator acts in deliberate violation of the Arbitration Agreement (including these Rules) or does not act fairly and impartially as between the parties or does not conduct or participate in the arbitration proceedings with reasonable diligence, avoiding unnecessary delay or expense, that arbitrator may be considered unfit in the opinion of the LCIA Court.

10.3 An arbitrator may also be challenged by any party if circumstances exist that give rise to justifiable doubts as to his impartiality or independence. A party may challenge an arbitrator it has nominated, or in whose appointment it has participated, only for reasons of which it becomes aware after the appointment has been made.

10.4 A party who intends to challenge an arbitrator shall, within 15 days of the formation of the Arbitral Tribunal or (if later) after becoming aware of any circumstances referred to in Article 10.1, 10.2 or 10.3, send a written statement of the reasons for its challenge to the LCIA Court, the Arbitral Tribunal and all other parties. Unless the challenged arbitrator withdraws or all other parties agree to the challenge within 15 days of receipt of the written statement, the LCIA Court shall decide on the challenge.

Article 11
Nomination and Replacement of Arbitrators

11.1 In the event that the LCIA Court determines that any nominee is not suitable or independent or impartial or if an appointed arbitrator is to be replaced for any reason, the LCIA Court shall have a complete discretion to decide whether or not to follow the original nominating process.

11.2 If the LCIA Court should so decide, any opportunity given to a party to make a re-nomination shall be waived if not exercised within 15 days (or such lesser time as the LCIA Court may fix), after which the LCIA Court shall appoint the replacement arbitrator.

Article 12
Majority Power to Continue Proceedings

12.1 If any arbitrator on a three-member Arbitral Tribunal refuses or persistently fails to participate in its deliberations, the two other arbitrators shall have the power, upon their written notice of such refusal or failure to the LCIA Court, the parties and the third arbitrator, to continue the arbitration (including the making of any decision, ruling or award), notwithstanding the absence of the third arbitrator.

12.2 In determining whether to continue the arbitration, the two other arbitrators shall take into account the stage of the arbitration, any explanation made by the third arbitrator for his non-participation and such other matters as they consider appropriate in the circumstances of the case. The reasons for such determination shall be stated in any award, order or other decision made by the two arbitrators without the participation of the third arbitrator.

12.3 In the event that the two other arbitrators determine at any time not to continue the arbitration without the participation of the third arbitrator missing from their deliberations, the two arbitrators shall notify in writing the parties and the LCIA Court of such determination; and in that event, the two arbitrators or any party may refer the matter to the LCIA Court for the revocation of that third arbitrator's appointment and his replacement under Article 10.

Article 13
Communications between Parties and the Arbitral Tribunal

13.1 Until the Arbitral Tribunal is formed, all communications between parties and arbitrators shall be made through the DIFC-LCIA Registrar.

13.2 Thereafter, unless and until the Arbitral Tribunal directs that communications shall take place directly between the Arbitral Tribunal and the parties (with simultaneous copies to the DIFC-LCIA Registrar), all written communications between the parties and the Arbitral Tribunal shall continue to be made through the DIFC-LCIA Registrar.

13.3 Where the DIFC-LCIA Registrar sends any written communication to one party on behalf of the Arbitral Tribunal, he shall send a copy to each of the other parties. Where any party sends to the DIFC-LCIA Registrar any communication (including Written Statements and Documents under Article 15), it shall include a copy for each arbitrator; and it shall also send copies direct to all other parties and confirm to the DIFC-LCIA Registrar in writing that it has done or is doing so.

Article 14
Conduct of the Proceedings

14.1 The parties may agree on the conduct of their arbitral proceedings and they are encouraged to do so, consistent with the Arbitral Tribunal's general duties at all times:

(i) to act fairly and impartially as between all parties, giving each a reasonable opportunity of putting its case and dealing with that of its opponent; and

(ii) to adopt procedures suitable to the circumstances of the arbitration, avoiding unnecessary delay or expense, so as to provide a fair and efficient means for the final resolution of the parties' dispute.

Such agreements shall be made by the parties in writing or recorded in writing by the Arbitral Tribunal at the request of and with the authority of the parties.

14.2 Unless otherwise agreed by the parties under Article 14.1, the Arbitral Tribunal shall have the widest discretion to discharge its duties allowed under such law(s) or rules of law as the Arbitral Tribunal may determine to be applicable; and at all times the parties shall do everything necessary for the fair, efficient and expeditious conduct of the arbitration.

14.3 In the case of a three-member Arbitral Tribunal the chairman may, with the prior consent of the other two arbitrators, make procedural rulings alone.

Article 15
Submission of Written Statements and Documents

15.1 Unless the parties have agreed otherwise under Article 14.1 or the Arbitral Tribunal should determine differently, the written stage of the proceedings shall be as set out below.

15.2 Within 30 days of receipt of written notification from the DIFC-LCIA Registrar of the formation of the Arbitral Tribunal, the Claimant shall send to the DIFC-LCIA Registrar a Statement of Case setting out in sufficient detail the facts and any contentions of law on which it relies, together with the relief claimed against all other parties, save and insofar as such matters have not been set out in its Request.

15.3 Within 30 days of receipt of the Statement of Case or written notice from the Claimant that it elects to treat the Request as its Statement of Case, the Respondent shall send to the DIFC-LCIA Registrar a Statement of Defence setting out in sufficient detail which of the facts and contentions of law in the Statement of Case or Request (as the case may be) it admits or denies, on what grounds and on what other facts and contentions of law it relies. Any counterclaims shall be submitted with the Statement of Defence in the same manner as claims are to be set out in the Statement of Case.

15.4 Within 30 days of receipt of the Statement of Defence, the Claimant shall send to the DIFC-LCIA Registrar a Statement of Reply which, where there are any counterclaims, shall include a Defence to Counterclaim in the same manner as a defence is to be set out in the Statement of Defence.

15.5 If the Statement of Reply contains a Defence to Counterclaim, within 30 days of its receipt the Respondent shall send to the DIFC-LCIA Registrar a Statement of Reply to Counterclaim.

15.6 All Statements referred to in this Article shall be accompanied by copies (or, if they are especially voluminous, lists) of all essential documents on which the party concerned relies and which have not previously been submitted by any party, and (where appropriate) by any relevant samples and exhibits.

15.7 As soon as practicable following receipt of the Statements specified in this Article, the Arbitral Tribunal shall proceed in such manner as has been agreed in writing by the parties or pursuant to its authority under these Rules.

15.8 If the Respondent fails to submit a Statement of Defence or the Claimant a Statement of Defence to Counterclaim, or if at any point any party fails to avail itself of the opportunity to present its case in the manner determined by Article 15.2 to 15.6 or directed by the Arbitral Tribunal, the Arbitral Tribunal may nevertheless proceed with the arbitration and make an award.

Article 16
Seat of Arbitration and Place of Hearings

16.1 The parties may agree in writing the seat (or legal place) of their arbitration. Failing such a choice, the seat of arbitration shall be the Dubai International Financial Centre, Dubai, unless and until the LCIA Court determines in view of all the circumstances, and after having given the parties an opportunity to make written comment, that another seat is more appropriate.

16.2 The Arbitral Tribunal may hold hearings, meetings and deliberations at any convenient geographical place in its discretion; and if elsewhere than the seat of the arbitration, the arbitration shall be treated as an arbitration conducted at the seat of the arbitration and any award as an award made at the seat of the arbitration for all purposes.

16.3 The law applicable to the arbitration (if any) shall be the arbitration law of the seat of arbitration, unless and to the extent that the parties have expressly agreed in writing on the application of another arbitration law and such agreement is not prohibited by the law of the arbitral seat.

Article 17
Language of Arbitration

17.1 The initial language of the arbitration shall be the language of the Arbitration Agreement, unless the parties have agreed in writing otherwise and providing always that a non-participating or defaulting party shall have no cause for complaint if communications to and from the DIFC-LCIA Registrar and the arbitration proceedings are conducted in English.

17.2 In the event that the Arbitration Agreement is written in more than one language, the LCIA Court may, unless the Arbitration Agreement provides that the arbitration proceedings shall be conducted in more than one language, decide which of those languages shall be the initial language of the arbitration.

17.3 Upon the formation of the Arbitral Tribunal and unless the parties have agreed upon the language or languages of the arbitration, the Arbitration Tribunal shall decide upon the language(s) of the arbitration, after giving the parties an opportunity to make written comment and taking into account the initial language of the arbitration and any other matter it may consider appropriate in all the circumstances of the case.

17.4 If any document is expressed in a language other than the language(s) of the arbitration and no translation of such document is submitted by the party relying upon the document, the Arbitral Tribunal or (if the Arbitral Tribunal has not been formed) the LCIA Court may order that party to submit a translation in a form to be determined by the Arbitral Tribunal or the LCIA Court, as the case may be.

Article 18
Party Representation

18.1 Any party may be represented by legal practitioners or any other representatives.

18.2 At any time the Arbitral Tribunal may require from any party proof of authority granted to its representative(s) in such form as the Arbitral Tribunal may determine.

Article 19
Hearings

19.1 Any party which expresses a desire to that effect has the right to be heard orally before the Arbitral Tribunal on the merits of the dispute, unless the parties have agreed in writing on documents-only arbitration.

19.2 The Arbitral Tribunal shall fix the date, time and physical place of any meetings and hearings in the arbitration, and shall give the parties reasonable notice thereof.

19.3 The Arbitral Tribunal may in advance of any hearing submit to the parties a list of questions which it wishes them to answer with special attention.

19.4 All meetings and hearings shall be in private unless the parties agree otherwise in writing or the Arbitral Tribunal directs otherwise.

19.5 The Arbitral Tribunal shall have the fullest authority to establish time-limits for meetings and hearings, or for any parts thereof.

Article 20
Witnesses

20.1 Before any hearing, the Arbitral Tribunal may require any party to give notice of the identity of each witness that party wishes to call (including rebuttal witnesses), as well as the subject matter of that witness's testimony, its content and its relevance to the issues in the arbitration.

20.2 The Arbitral Tribunal may also determine the time, manner and form in which such materials should be exchanged between the parties and presented to the Arbitral Tribunal; and it has a discretion to allow, refuse, or limit the appearance of witnesses (whether witness of fact or expert witness).

20.3 Subject to any order otherwise by the Arbitral Tribunal, the testimony of a witness may be presented by a party in written form, either as a signed statement or as a sworn affidavit.

20.4 Subject to Article 14.1 and 14.2, any party may request that a witness, on whose testimony another party seeks to rely, should attend for oral questioning at a hearing before the Arbitral Tribunal. If the Arbitral Tribunal orders that other party to produce the witness and the witness fails to attend the oral hearing without good cause, the Arbitral Tribunal may place such weight on the written testimony (or exclude the same altogether) as it considers appropriate in the circumstances of the case.

20.5 Any witness who gives oral evidence at a hearing before the Arbitral Tribunal may be questioned by each of the parties under the control of the Arbitral Tribunal. The Arbitral Tribunal may put questions at any stage of his evidence.

20.6 Subject to the mandatory provisions of any applicable law, it shall not be improper for any party or its legal representatives to interview any witness or potential witness for the purpose of presenting his testimony in written form or producing him as an oral witness.

20.7 Any individual intending to testify to the Arbitral Tribunal on any issue of fact or expertise shall be treated as a witness under these Rules notwithstanding that the individual is a party to the arbitration or was or is an officer, employee or shareholder of any party.

Article 21
Experts to the Arbitral Tribunal

21.1 Unless otherwise agreed by the parties in writing, the Arbitral Tribunal:

(a) may appoint one or more experts to report to the Arbitral Tribunal on specific issues, who shall be and remain impartial and independent of the parties throughout the arbitration proceedings; and

(b) may require a party to give any such expert any relevant information or to provide access to any relevant documents, goods, samples, property or site for inspection by the expert.

21.2 Unless otherwise agreed by the parties in writing, if a party so requests or if the Arbitral Tribunal considers it necessary, the expert shall, after delivery of his written or oral report to the Arbitral Tribunal and the parties, participate in one or more hearings at which the parties shall have the opportunity to question the expert on his report and to present expert witnesses in order to testify on the points at issue.

21.3 The fees and expenses of any expert appointed by the Arbitral Tribunal under this Article shall be paid out of the deposits payable by the parties under Article 24 and shall form part of the costs of the arbitration.

Article 22
Additional Powers of the Arbitral Tribunal

22.1 Unless the parties at any time agree otherwise in writing, the Arbitral Tribunal shall have the power, on the application of any party or of its own motion, but in either case only after giving the parties a reasonable opportunity to state their views:

(a) to allow any party, upon such terms (as to costs and otherwise) as it shall determine, to amend any claim, counterclaim, defence and reply;

(b) to extend or abbreviate any time-limit provided by the Arbitration Agreement or these Rules for the conduct of the arbitration or by the Arbitral Tribunal's own orders;

(c) to conduct such enquiries as may appear to the Arbitral Tribunal to be necessary or expedient, including whether and to what extent the Arbitral Tribunal should itself take the initiative in identifying the issues and ascertaining the relevant facts and the law(s) or rules of law applicable to the arbitration, the merits of the parties' dispute and the Arbitration Agreement;

(d) to order any party to make any property, site or thing under its control and relating to the subject matter of the arbitration available for inspection by the Arbitral Tribunal, any other party, its expert or any expert to the Arbitral Tribunal;

(e) to order any party to produce to the Arbitral Tribunal, and to the other parties for inspection, and to supply copies of, any documents or classes of documents in their possession, custody or power which the Arbitral Tribunal determines to be relevant;

(f) to decide whether or not to apply any strict rules of evidence (or any other rules) as to the admissibility, relevance or weight of any material tendered by a party on any matter of fact or expert opinion; and to determine the time, manner and form in which such material should be exchanged between the parties and presented to the Arbitral Tribunal;

(g) to order the correction of any contract between the parties or the Arbitration Agreement, but only to the extent required to rectify any mistake which the Arbitral Tribunal determines to be common to the parties and then only if and to the extent to which the law(s) or rules of law applicable to the contract or Arbitration Agreement permit such correction; and

(h) to allow, only upon the application of a party, one or more third persons to be joined in the arbitration as a party provided any such third person and the applicant party have consented thereto in writing, and thereafter to make a single final award, or separate awards, in respect of all parties so implicated in the arbitration;

22.2 By agreeing to arbitration under these Rules, the parties shall be treated as having agreed not to apply to any state court or other judicial authority for any order available from the Arbitral Tribunal under Article 22.1, except with the agreement in writing of all parties.

22.3 The Arbitral Tribunal shall decide the parties' dispute in accordance with the law(s) or rules of law chosen by the parties as applicable to the merits of their dispute. If and to the extent that the Arbitral Tribunal determines that the parties have made no such choice, the Arbitral Tribunal shall apply the law(s) or rules of law which it considers appropriate.

22.4 The Arbitral Tribunal shall only apply to the merits of the dispute principles deriving from "ex aequo et bono", "amiable composition" or "honourable engagement" where the parties have so agreed expressly in writing.

Article 23
Jurisdiction of the Arbitral Tribunal

23.1 The Arbitral Tribunal shall have the power to rule on its own jurisdiction, including any objection to the initial or continuing existence, validity or effectiveness of the Arbitration Agreement. For that purpose, an arbitration clause which forms or was intended to form part of another agreement shall be treated as an arbitration agreement independent of that other agreement. A decision by the Arbitral Tribunal that such other agreement is non-existent, invalid or ineffective shall not entail ipso jure the non-existence, invalidity or ineffectiveness of the arbitration clause.

23.2 A plea by a Respondent that the Arbitral Tribunal does not have jurisdiction shall be treated as having been irrevocably waived unless it is raised not later than the Statement of Defence; and a like plea by a Respondent to Counterclaim shall be similarly treated unless it is raised no later than the Statement of Defence to Counterclaim. A plea that the Arbitral Tribunal is exceeding the scope of its authority shall be raised promptly after the Arbitral Tribunal has indicated its intention to decide on the matter alleged by any party to be beyond the scope of its authority, failing which such plea shall also be treated as having been waived irrevocably. In any case, the Arbitral Tribunal may nevertheless admit an untimely plea if it considers the delay justified in the particular circumstances.

23.3 The Arbitral Tribunal may determine the plea to its jurisdiction or authority in an award as to jurisdiction or later in an award on the merits, as it considers appropriate in the circumstances.

23.4 By agreeing to arbitration under these Rules, the parties shall be treated as having agreed not to apply to any state court or other judicial authority for any relief regarding the Arbitral Tribunal's jurisdiction or authority, except with the agreement in writing of all parties to the arbitration or the prior authorisation of the Arbitral Tribunal or following the latter's award ruling on the objection to its jurisdiction or authority.

Article 24
Deposits

24.1 The LCIA Court may, through the DIFC-LCIA Registrar, direct the parties, in such proportions as it thinks appropriate, to make one or several interim or final payments on account of the costs of the arbitration. Such deposits shall be made to and held by the DIFC-LCIA Arbitration Centre and from time to time may be released by the LCIA Court, through the DIFC-LCIA Arbitration Centre, to the arbitrator(s), any expert appointed by the Arbitral Tribunal, any division of the LCIA Court appointed pursuant to these Rules, and the DIFCLCIA Arbitration Centre itself as the arbitration progresses.

24.2 The Arbitral Tribunal shall not proceed with the arbitration without ascertaining at all times from the DIFC-LCIA Registrar that the DIFC-LCIA Arbitration Centre is in requisite funds.

24.3 In the event that a party fails or refuses to provide any deposit as directed by the LCIA Court, through the DIFC-LCIA Registrar, the LCIA Court may, through the DIFC-LCIA Registrar, direct the other party or parties to effect a substitute payment to allow the arbitration to proceed (subject to any award on costs). In such circumstances, the party paying the substitute payment shall be entitled to recover that amount as a debt immediately due from the defaulting party.

24.4 Failure by a claimant or counterclaiming party to provide promptly and in full the required deposit may be treated by the LCIA Court and the Arbitral Tribunal as a withdrawal of the claim or counterclaim respectively.

Article 25
Interim and Conservatory Measures

25.1 The Arbitral Tribunal shall have the power, unless otherwise agreed by the parties in writing, on the application of any party:

(a) to order any respondent party to a claim or counterclaim to provide security for all or part of the amount in dispute, by way of deposit or bank guarantee or in any other manner and upon such terms as the Arbitral Tribunal considers appropriate. Such terms may include the provision by the claiming or counterclaiming party of a cross-indemnity, itself secured in such manner as the Arbitral Tribunal considers appropriate, for any costs or losses incurred by such respondent in providing security. The amount of any costs and losses payable under such cross-indemnity may be determined by the Arbitral Tribunal in one or more awards;

(b) to order the preservation, storage, sale or other disposal of any property or thing under the control of any party and relating to the subject matter of the arbitration; and

(c) to order on a provisional basis, subject to final determination in an award, any relief which the Arbitral Tribunal would have power to grant in an award, including a provisional order for the payment of money or the disposition of property as between any parties.

25.2 The Arbitral Tribunal shall have the power, upon the application of a party, to order any claiming or counterclaiming party to provide security for the legal or other costs of any other party by way of deposit or bank guarantee or in any other manner and upon such terms as the Arbitral Tribunal considers appropriate. Such terms may include the provision by that other party of a cross-indemnity, itself secured in such manner as the Arbitral Tribunal considers appropriate, for any costs and losses incurred by such claimant or counterclaimant in providing security. The amount of any costs and losses payable under such cross-indemnity may be determined by the Arbitral Tribunal in one or more awards. In the event that a claiming or counterclaiming party does not comply with any order to provide security, the Arbitral Tribunal may stay that party's claims or counterclaims or dismiss them in an award.

25.3 The power of the Arbitral Tribunal under Article 25.1 shall not prejudice howsoever any party's right to apply to any state court or other judicial authority for interim or conservatory measures before the formation of the Arbitral Tribunal and, in exceptional cases, thereafter. Any application and any order for such measures after the formation of the Arbitral Tribunal shall be promptly communicated by the applicant to the Arbitral Tribunal and all other parties. However, by agreeing to arbitration under these Rules, the parties shall be taken to have agreed not to apply to any state court or other judicial authority for any order for security for its legal or other costs available from the Arbitral Tribunal under Article 25.2.

Article 26
The Award

26.1 The Arbitral Tribunal shall make its award in writing and, unless all parties agree in writing otherwise, shall state the reasons upon which its award is based. The award shall also state the date when the award is made and the seat of the arbitration; and it shall be signed by the Arbitral Tribunal or those of its members assenting to it.

26.2 If any arbitrator fails to comply with the mandatory provisions of any applicable law relating to the making of the award, having been given a reasonable opportunity to do so, the remaining arbitrators may proceed in his absence and state in their award the circumstances of the other arbitrator's failure to participate in the making of the award.

26.3 Where there are three arbitrators and the Arbitral Tribunal fails to agree on any issue, the arbitrators shall decide that issue by a majority. Failing a majority decision on any issue, the chairman of the Arbitral Tribunal shall decide that issue.

26.4 If any arbitrator refuses or fails to sign the award, the signatures of the majority or (failing a majority) of the chairman shall be sufficient, provided that the reason for the omitted signature is stated in the award by the majority or chairman.

26.5 The sole arbitrator or chairman shall be responsible for delivering the award to the LCIA Court, through the DIFC-LCIA Registrar, who shall transmit certified copies to the parties provided that the costs of arbitration have been paid to the DIFC-LCIA Arbitration Centre in accordance with Article 28.

26.6 An award may be expressed in any currency. The Arbitral Tribunal may order that simple or compound interest shall be paid by any party on any sum awarded at such rates as the Arbitral

Tribunal determines to be appropriate, without being bound by legal rates of interest imposed by any state court, in respect of any period which the Arbitral Tribunal determines to be appropriate ending not later than the date upon which the award is complied with.

26.7 The Arbitral Tribunal may make separate awards on different issues at different times. Such awards shall have the same status and effect as any other award made by the Arbitral Tribunal.

26.8 In the event of a settlement of the parties' dispute, the Arbitral Tribunal may render an award recording the settlement if the parties so request in writing (a Consent Award), provided always that such award contains an express statement that it is an award made by the parties' consent. A Consent Award need not contain reasons. If the parties do not require a consent award, then on written confirmation by the parties to the LCIA Court that a settlement has been reached, the Arbitral Tribunal shall be discharged and the arbitration proceedings concluded, subject to payment by the parties of any outstanding costs of the arbitration under Article 28.

26.9 All awards shall be final and binding on the parties. By agreeing to arbitration under these Rules, the parties undertake to carry out any award immediately and without any delay (subject only to Article 27); and the parties also waive irrevocably their right to any form of appeal, review or recourse to any state court or other judicial authority, insofar as such waiver may be validly made.

Article 27
Correction of Awards and Additional Awards

27.1 Within 30 days of receipt of any award, or such lesser period as may be agreed in writing by the parties, a party may by written notice to the DIFC-LCIA Registrar (copied to all other parties) request the Arbitral Tribunal to correct in the award any errors in computation, clerical or typographical errors or any errors of a similar nature. If the Arbitral Tribunal considers the request to be justified, it shall make the corrections within 30 days of receipt of the request. Any correction shall take the form of separate memorandum dated and signed by the Arbitral Tribunal or (if three arbitrators) those of its members assenting to it; and such memorandum shall become part of the award for all purposes.

27.2 The Arbitral Tribunal may likewise correct any error of the nature described in Article 27.1 on its own initiative within 30 days of the date of the award, to the same effect.

27.3 Within 30 days of receipt of the final award, a party may by written notice to the DIFC-LCIA Registrar (copied to all other parties), request the Arbitral Tribunal to make an additional award as to claims or counterclaims presented in the arbitration but not determined in any award. If the Arbitral Tribunal considers the request to be justified, it shall make the additional award within 60 days of receipt of the request. The provisions of Article 26 shall apply to any additional award.

Article 28
Arbitration and Legal Costs

28.1 The costs of the arbitration (other than the legal or other costs incurred by the parties themselves) shall be determined by the LCIA Court in accordance with the Schedule of Costs. The parties shall be jointly and severally liable to the Arbitral Tribunal and the DIFC-LCIA Arbitration Centre for such arbitration costs.

28.2 The Arbitral Tribunal shall specify in the award the total amount of the costs of the arbitration as determined by the LCIA Court. Unless the parties agree otherwise in writing, the Arbitral Tribunal shall determine the proportions in which the parties shall bear all or part of such arbitration costs. If the Arbitral Tribunal has determined that all or any part of the arbitration costs shall be borne by a party other than a party which has already paid them to the DIFC-LCIA Arbitration Centre, the latter party shall have the right to recover the appropriate amount from the former party.

28.3 The Arbitral Tribunal shall also have the power to order in its award that all or part of the legal or other costs incurred by a party be paid by another party, unless the parties agree otherwise in writing. The Arbitral Tribunal shall determine and fix the amount of each item comprising such costs on such reasonable basis as it thinks fit.

28.4 Unless the parties otherwise agree in writing, the Arbitral Tribunal shall make its orders on both arbitration and legal costs on the general principle that costs should reflect the parties' relative success and failure in the award or arbitration, except where it appears to the Arbitral Tribunal that in the particular circumstances this general approach is inappropriate. Any order for costs shall be made with reasons in the award containing such order.

28.5 If the arbitration is abandoned, suspended or concluded, by agreement or otherwise, before the final award is made, the parties shall remain jointly and severally liable to pay to the DIFC-LCIA Arbitration Centre and the Arbitral Tribunal the costs of the arbitration as determined by the LCIA Court in accordance with the Schedule of Costs. In the event that such arbitration costs are less than the deposits made by the parties, there shall be a refund by the DIFC-LCIA Arbitration Centre in such proportion as the parties may agree in writing, or failing such agreement, in the same proportions as the deposits were made by the parties to the LCIA.

Article 29
Decisions by the LCIA Court

29.1 The decisions of the LCIA Court with respect to all matters relating to the arbitration shall be conclusive and binding upon the parties and the Arbitral Tribunal. Such decisions are to be treated as administrative in nature and the LCIA Court shall not be required to give any reasons.

29.2 To the extent permitted by the law of the seat of the arbitration, the parties shall be taken to have waived any right of appeal or review in respect of any such decisions of the LCIA Court to any state court or other judicial authority. If such appeals or review remain possible due to mandatory provisions of any applicable law, the LCIA Court shall, subject to the provisions of that applicable law, decide whether the arbitral proceedings are to continue, notwithstanding an appeal or review.

Article 30
Confidentiality

30.1 Unless the parties expressly agree in writing to the contrary, the parties undertake as a general principle to keep confidential all awards in their arbitration, together with all materials in the proceedings created for the purpose of the arbitration and all other documents produced by another party in the proceedings not otherwise in the public domain - save and to the extent that disclosure may be required of a party by legal duty, to protect or pursue a legal right or to enforce or challenge an award in bona fide legal proceedings before a state court or other judicial authority.

30.2 The deliberations of the Arbitral Tribunal are likewise confidential to its members, save and to the extent that disclosure of an arbitrator's refusal to participate in the arbitration is required of the other members of the Arbitral Tribunal under Articles 10, 12 and 26.

30.3 The LCIA Court does not publish any award or any part of an award without the prior written consent of all parties and the Arbitral Tribunal.

Article 31
Exclusion of Liability

31.1 None of the LCIA, the DIFC-LCIA Arbitration Centre, the LCIA Court (including its President, Vice-Presidents and individual members), the DIFCLCIA Registrar, the Registrar, any deputy Registrar, any arbitrator and any expert to the Arbitral Tribunal shall be liable to any party howsoever for any act or omission in connection with any arbitration conducted by reference to these Rules, save where the act or omission is shown by that party to constitute conscious and deliberate wrongdoing committed by the body or person alleged to be liable to that party.

31.2 After the award has been made and the possibilities of correction and additional awards referred to in Article 27 have lapsed or been exhausted, neither the LCIA, the DIFC-LCIA Arbitration Centre, the LCIA Court (including its President, Vice-Presidents and individual members), the DIFC-LCIA Registrar, the Registrar, any deputy Registrar, any arbitrator or expert to the Arbitral Tribunal shall be under any legal obligation to make any statement to any person about any matter concerning the arbitration, nor shall any party seek to make any of these persons a witness in any legal or other proceedings arising out of the arbitration.

Article 32
General Rules

32.1 A party who knows that any provision of the Arbitration Agreement (including these Rules) has not been complied with and yet proceeds with the arbitration without promptly stating its objection to such non-compliance, shall be treated as having irrevocably waived its right to object.

32.2 In all matters not expressly provided for in these Rules, the DIFC-LCIA Arbitration Centre, the LCIA Court, the Arbitral Tribunal and the parties shall act in the spirit of these Rules and shall make every reasonable effort to ensure that an award is legally enforceable.

BIBLIOGRAPHY

Abdurrasyid, P, 'They said I was going to be kidnapped' (2003) 18(6) Mealey's Int Arb Rep 29

Baizeau, D, 'Waiving the Right to Challenge an Arbitral Award Rendered in Switzerland: Caveats and Drafting Considerations for Foreign Parties' [2005] Int ALR 1

Baum, A, 'International Arbitration: the Path toward Uniform Procedures' in *Liber Amicorum Robert Briner* (ICC Publishing, 2005) 51

Bensaude, D, '*Thalès Air Defence B.V. v. GIE Euromissile*: Defining the Limits of Scrutiny of Awards Based on Alleged Violations of European Competition Law' (2005) 22 J Int Arb 239

—— '*Malecki v Long*: Truncated Tribunals and the Waiver of *Dutco* Rights' (2006) 23 J Int Arb 81

Berger, KP, 'Power of Arbitrators to Fill Gaps and Revise Contracts to Make Sense' (2001) 17 Arb Int 1

Berkeley, A, and J Mimms (eds), *International Commercial Arbitration: Practical Perspectives* (Centre of Construction Law & Management, 2001)

Bishop, D, and L Reed 'Practical Guidelines for Interviewing, Selecting and Challenging Party-Appointed Arbitrators in International Commercial Arbitration' (1998) 14 Arb Int 395

Blanke, G, 'Defining the Limits of Scrutiny of Awards Based on Alleged Violations of European Competition Law: A Réplique to Denis Bensaude's "*Thalès Air Defence B.V. v. GIE Euromissile*"' (2006) 23 J Int Arb 249

Böckstiegel, KH, 'Experience as an Arbitrator Using the UNCITRAL Arbitration Rules' in *Etudes de Droit International en l'Honneur de Pierre Lalive* (Helbing & Lichtenhahn, 1993) 423

de Boisséson, M, *Le droit français de l'arbitrage interne et international* (Joly, 1990)

Bourke, P, and D Hennessy 'Brighter times – developments in arbitration in the United Arab Emirates' (2008) 13(2) IBA Arb News 24

Brown, D, 'Arbitrators, Impartiality and English Law – Did Rix J. Really Get it Wrong in *Laker Airways*?' (2001) 18 J Int Arb 123

Caron, D, L Caplan and M Pellonpää, *The UNCITRAL Arbitration Rules: A Commentary* (Oxford University Press, 2006)

Craig, WL, W Park and J Paulsson, *International Chamber of Commerce Arbitration* (3rd edn, Oceana/ICC, 2000)

Craig, WL, 'The LCIA and the ICC Rules: the 1998 Revisions Compared' in A Berkeley and J Mimms (eds), *International Commercial Arbitration: Practical Perspectives* (Centre of Construction Law & Management, 2001) 79

Darwazeh, N, and M Moser 'Arbitration Inside China' in M Moser (ed), *Managing Business Disputes in Today's China: Duelling with Dragons* (Kluwer, 2007)

Delvolvé, JL, 'Le centenaire de la LCIA (London Court of International Arbitration)' [1993] Rev arb 599

Derains, Y, and E Schwartz, *A Guide to the ICC Rules of Arbitration* (2nd edn, Kluwer, 2005)

Diamond, A, 'Procedure and Hearings' in A Berkeley and J Mimms (eds), *International Commercial Arbitration: Practical Perspectives* (Centre of Construction Law & Management, 2001) 49

England & Wales Bar Standards Board, Guidance for Members of the Bar: The Preparation of Witness Statements

Fouchard, P, *L'arbitrage Commercial International* (Dalloz, 1965)

Fouchard, P, E Gaillard, and B Goldman, *Traité de l'arbitrage international* (1st edn, Litec, 1996)

Gaillard, E, and J Savage (eds), *Fouchard, Gaillard, Goldman on International Commercial Arbitration* (Kluwer, 2000)

Gaillard, E, and P Pinsolle, 'The ICC Pre-Arbitral Referee: First Practical Experiences' (2004) 20 Arb Int 1

Gearing, M, 'A Judge in His Own Cause? – Actual or Unconscious Bias of Arbitrators' (2000) 3 Int ALR 46

Gee, S, 'Jurisdiction – the Validity and Width of Arbitration Agreements, and the House of Lords Decision in *Premium Nafta Products Ltd v Fili Shipping Co Ltd*' (2008) 24 Arb Int 467

Gill, J, 'The IBA Conflicts Guidelines – Who's Using Them and How?' (2007) 1 Dispute Resolution International 58

Hanotiau, B, *L'arbitrabilité, Recueil des Cours, Académie de Droit International de la Haye 2002* (Martinus Nijhoff, 2003)

—— *Complex Arbitrations: Multiparty, Multicontract, Multi-issue and Class Actions* (Kluwer, 2005)

Harris, C, 'Arbitrator Challenges in International Investment Arbitration' (2008) 5 TDM

Holtzmann, H, and J Neuhaus, *A Guide to the UNCITRAL Model Law on International Commercial Arbitration: Legislative History and Commentary* (Kluwer, 1989)

Holtzmann, H, 'Lessons of the Stockholm Congress' in *ICCA Congress Series No 5* (Kluwer, 1991) 28

Hunter, M, and J Paulsson, 'A Commentary on the Rules of the London Court of International Arbitration' (1985) 10 YCA 167

Hunter, M, 'Ethics of the International Arbitrator' (1987) 53 Arbitration 219

Jolles, A, and M Canals de Cediel, 'Confidentiality' in G Kaufmann-Kohler and B Stucki (eds) *International Arbitration in Switzerland* (Kluwer, 2004) 89

Kantor, M, 'The ICC Pre-Arbitral Referee Procedure: Momentum for Expanded Use' (2005) 20(9) Mealey's Int Arb Rep 3

Kaufmann-Kohler, G, and A Bärtsch, 'Discovery in international arbitration: How much is too much?' (2004) 1 SchiedsVZ 13

Kerr, M, 'The London Court of International Arbitration 1892-1992' (1992) 8 Arb Int 317

—— 'London Court of International Arbitration' in *ICCA Congress Series No 7* (Kluwer, 1996) 213

Lalive, P, 'Sur l'irresponsabilité arbitrale' in *Etudes de procédure et d'arbitrage en l'honneur de Jean-François Poudret* (1999)

Lebedev, S, 'The LCIA Rules for International Commercial Arbitration' (1992) 8 Arb Int 321

Lécuyer-Thieffry, C, 'First Court Ruling on the ICC Pre-Arbitral Referee Procedure' (2003) 20 J Int Arb 599

Levine, J, 'Dealing with Arbitrator "Issue Conflicts" in International Arbitration' (2006) 3 Dispute Resolution Journal 60

Lew, J, 'Commentary on Interim and Conservatory Measures in ICC Arbitration Cases' (2000) 11 ICC Bull 23

Lew, J, L Mistelis and S Kröll, *Comparative International Commercial Arbitration* (Kluwer, 2003)

Mann, H, 'The Emperor's Clothes Come Off: A Comment on Republic of Ghana v Telekom Malaysia' [2005] TDM

Marchac, G, 'Interim Measures in International Commercial Arbitration under the ICC, AAA, LCIA and UNCITRAL Rules' (2000) 10 Am Rev Int Arb 123

McNeill, M, and B Juratowitch, 'The Doctrine of Separability and Consent to Arbitrate' (2008) 24 Arb Int 475

Merjian, A, 'Caveat Arbitor: *Laker Airways* and the Appointment of Barristers as Arbitrators in Cases involving Barrister-Advocates from the same Chambers' (2000) 17 J Int Arb 31

Mohtashami, R, 'In Defense of Injunctions Issued by the Courts at the Place of Arbitration: A Brief Reply to Professor Bachand's Commentary on *Salini Costruttori S.p.A. v. Ethiopia*' (2005) 20(5) Mealey's Int Arb Rep 44

—— 'Recent Arbitration-Related Developments in the UAE' (2008) 25 J Int Arb 631

Paulsson, J, 'Arbitration Unbound: Award Detached from the Law of its Country of Origin' (1981) 30 ICLQ 358

—— '*La lex mercatoria dans l'arbitrage CCI*' [1990] Rev arb 55

—— 'Lessons of the Last Decade: The Promise and Dangers of Globalisation and Practice under the LCIA Rules' in M Hunter, A Marriott and VV Veeder (eds), *The Internationalisation of International Arbitration: The LCIA Centenary Conference* (Kluwer, 1995) 59

—— and N Rawding, 'The Trouble with Confidentiality' (1995) 11 Arb Int 303

—— and G Petrochilos, *Revision of the UNCITRAL Arbitration Rules,* 2006

Peter, W, 'Witness "Conferencing"' (2002) 18 Arb Int 47

Petrochilos, G, *Procedural Law in International Arbitration* (Oxford University Press, 2004)

Pinsole, P, 'The Status of Vacated Awards in France: The Cour de Cassation decision in Putrabali' (2008) 24 Arb Int 277

Poudret, JF, and Besson, S, *Comparative Law of International Arbitration* (2nd edn, Sweet & Maxwell, 2007)

Raeschke-Kessler, H, 'The Production of Documents in International Arbitration – A Commentary on Art 3 of the New IBA Rules of Evidence' (2002) 18 Arb Int 411

Rau, A, *Provisional Relief in Arbitration: How Things Stand in the United States* (2005) 22 J Int Arb 1

Rawding, N, and K Seeger, '*Aegis v European Re* and the Confidentiality of Arbitration Awards' (2003) 19 Arb Int 483

Redfern, A, 'The Immunity of Arbitrators' in *The Status of the Arbitrator* (ICC Publishing, 1995)

—— 'Dissenting Opinions in International Commercial Arbitration – The Good, the Bad and the Ugly' in J Lew and L Mistelis (eds), *Arbitration Insights, Twenty Years of the Annual Lecture of the School of International Arbitration* (Kluwer, 2007) 367

—— 'Interim Measures' in L Newman and R Hill (eds), *The Leading Arbitrators' Guide to International Arbitration* (Juris Publishing, 2008)

—— and M Hunter with N Blackaby and C Partasides, *Law and Practice of International Commercial Arbitration* (4th edn, Sweet & Maxwell, 2004)

Reed, L, and J Sutcliffe, 'The Americanization of International Arbitration' (2001) 16 Mealey's Int Arb Rep 37

Rivkin, D, '1997: A Year of Rule Changes' Int ALR 1998 1(2) 91

Sachs, K, 'Use of documents and document discovery: Fishing expeditions versus transparency and burden of proof' (2003) 5 SchiedsVZ 193

Salans, C, 'The 1985 Rules of the London Court of International Arbitration' (1986) 2 Arb Int 40

Samuel, A, 'Jurisdiction, interim relief and awards under the LCIA Rules' in A Berkeley and J Mimms (eds), *International Commercial Arbitration: Practical Perspectives* (Centre of Construction Law & Management, 2001) 35

—— 'Separability and Construing Arbitration Clauses' (2008) 24 Arb Int 489

Schwartz, E, 'The Practices and Experiences of the ICC Court' in *Conservatory and Provisional Measures in International Arbitration* (ICC Publishing, 1993) 45

—— 'Do International Arbitrators Have a Duty to Obey the Orders of Courts at the Place of Arbitration? Reflections on the Role of the *Lex Loci Arbitri* in the Light of a Recent ICC Award' in *Liber Amicorum Robert Briner* (ICC Publishing, 2005)

Schwebel, S, *International Arbitration: Three Salient Problems* (Cambridge, 1987) 144

—— 'The Authority of a Truncated Tribunal' in *ICCA Congress Series No 9* (Kluwer, 1999) 314

Sinclair, A, and M Gearing, 'Partiality and Issue Conflicts' (2008) 5 TDM

Snodgrass, E, '*Fiona Trust v Privalov*: The Arbitration Act 1996 Comes of Age' (2007) 10 Int ALR 27

St John Sutton, D, J Gill, and M Gearing, *Russell on Arbitration* (23rd edn, Sweet & Maxwell, 2007)

Style, C, and M Knowles '*Fiona Trust*: 10 Years On, the Fresh Start Entrenched' (2008) 24 Arb Int 499

Tercier, P, 'La clausula rebus sic stantibus en droit suisse des obligations' [1979] JT I 201

—— 'Le référé pré-arbitral' [2004] ASA Bull 464

Triebel, V, and R Hunter, 'Kommentar LCIA-Schiedsregeln' in R Schütze (ed), *Institutionelle Schiedsgerichtsbarkeit* (Carl Heymanns Verlag, 2006)

Turner, P, 'Treaties as Agreements to Arbitrate: Parties, Ownership and Control' *ICCA Congress Series No 13* (Kluwer, 2007) 444

van Houtte, H, 'Counsel-Witness Relations and Professional Misconduct in Civil Law Systems' (2003) 19 Arb Int 457, 458

—— 'Ten Reasons against a Proposal for *ex parte* Interim Measures of Protection in Arbitration' (2004) 20 Arb Int 85

Veeder, VV, 'London Court of International Arbitration – The New 1998 LCIA Rules' (1998) 23 YCA 366

Webster, T, 'Obtaining Documents from Third Parties in International Arbitration' (2001) 17 Arb Int 41

Wells, L, and R Ahmed, *Making Foreign Investment Safe: Property Rights and National Sovereignty* (Oxford University Press, 2007)

Whitesell, AM, 'Independence in ICC Arbitration: ICC Court Practice concerning the Appointment, Confirmation, Challenge and Replacement of Arbitrators' [2007] ICC Bull (Independence of Arbitrators Special Supplement) 7

Winstanley, A, 'The New Rules of the London Court of International Arbitration', (1997) 8 Am Rev Int Arb 59

—— 'The LCIA – History, Constitution and Rules' in A Berkeley and J Mimms (eds), *International Commercial Arbitration: Practical Perspectives* (Centre of Construction Law & Management, 2001) 21

INDEX

additional awards *see* awards
amendments
    powers of arbitral tribunal 6.09–6.19
amiable composition
    powers of arbitral tribunal 6.78–6.81
applicable law
    determination by tribunal 6.75–6.77
    freedom of parties to choose applicable
        substantive law 6.70, 6.71
    lex mercatoria 6.67, 6.71
    procedure *see lex arbitri*
    seat of arbitration 5.68–5.71
Arbitral Tribunal
    appointment
        barrister-arbitrators 4.25–4.33
        challenging appointment 4.122–4.128
        criteria 4.46–4.48
        disclosure 4.37–4.41
        impartiality 4.08–4.19
        importance 4.01–4.05
        independence 4.08–4.12, 4.20–4.41
        nationality of arbitrators 4.50–4.68
        nominations 4.69–4.74
        power to appoint 4.46–4.48
        repeat appointments 4.34–4.36
        revocation 4.109–4.128
        timescale 4.42–4.45
    barrister-arbitrators 4.25–4.33
    chairman
        three-member tribunal 4.49
    challenges 4.122–4.128
    communications between parties 4.158–4.165
    confidentiality of deliberations 9.26
    criteria for appointment 4.46–4.48
    disclosure 4.37–4.41
    expedited formation 4.86–4.108
    formation of arbitral tribunal
        criteria for appointment 4.46–4.48
        disclosure 4.37–4.41
        expedition 4.86–4.108
        impartiality 4.08–4.19
        importance 4.01–4.05
        independence 4.08–4.12, 4.20–4.41
        nationality of arbitrators 4.50–4.68
        nominations 4.69–4.74
        power to appoint 4.46–4.48

        repeat appointments 4.34–4.36
        timescale 4.42–4.45
    impartiality 4.08–4.19
    independence 4.08–4.12, 4.20–4.41
    jurisdiction
        applications to court 6.105, 6.106
        challenging 6.100–6.104
        compétence-compétence 6.82, 6.84–6.90
        deciding own jurisdiction 6.82, 6.84–6.90
        generally 1.11
        objections 6.98, 6.99
        powers of arbitral tribunal 6.82–6.106
        separability of arbitration clause 6.82, 6.83,
          6.91–6.97
        stay of proceedings 6.104
    language 5.78
    majority power to continue
        proceedings 4.137–4.157
    meaning 4.07
    nationality of arbitrators 4.50–4.68
    nominations 4.69–4.74
    obstructionist arbitrators 4.138
    powers *see* powers of arbitral tribunal
    repeat appointments 4.34–4.36
    replacement of arbitrators 4.129–4.136
    revocation of arbitrator's
        appointment 4.109–4.128
    three-member
        appointment of chairman 4.49
        nominations 4.75–4.85
    truncated tribunals 4.137–4.157
arbitration agreement/clause
    acting in violation of 4.115
    additional parties 6.47, 6.48, 6.49, 6.51
    admissibility of evidence 6.38
    ambiguities 3.35
    co-arbitrator, nomination of 4.03, 4.79
    correction of mistakes 6.41–6.43
    conduct of arbitration 3.13, 3.32
    confidentiality 9.15
    construction 3.38
    determining existence 3.08, 3.09, 6.87, 6.88,
        6.89, 8.41
    discharge 9.15
    domestic agreement 1.11
    drafting 5.58

arbitration agreement/clause (*cont.*)
internet agreements 6.90
jurisdiction of tribunal 6.83
language 5.78
nomination of arbitrator 3.14, 3.15, 3.16, 3.33,
3.35, 4.161
non-compliance 5.26, 9.36
objections 9.38–9.40
oral 3.06
reconsideration of award 10.46
Request for Arbitration 3.06, 3.07
Response to Request 3.31
seat of arbitration 5.58
seperability 6.91–6.97
time periods 3.47, 3.48, 6.19, 6.20, 6.21
validity 5.24
writing requirement 5.14
arbitration clause *see* arbitration agreement/clause
arbitrators
see also Arbitral Tribunal
appointment 2.12–2.14, 4.06–4.50
barrister-arbitrators 4.25–4.33
challenges to 2.26
conflicts of interest 4.09, 4.10
controlling shareholders/interests 4.63–4.66
court members serving as 2.12–2.14
criteria for appointment 4.46–4.48
death 4.111
dependent territory citizens 4.59–4.62
IBA Guidelines 4.09, 4.10
impartiality 4.08–4.19
incapacity 4.111
independence 4.08–4.12, 4.20–4.41
language 4.48
majority power to continue
proceedings 4.137–4.157
multiple nationalities 4.67, 4.68
nationality 4.50–4.68
citizenship 4.54
controlling shareholders/interests 4.63–4.66
definition of nationality 4.53
dependent territory citizens 4.59–4.62
double nationalities 4.67, 4.68
importance 4.50
multiple nationalities 4.67, 4.68
parties' nationality 4.52
practical operation of rules 4.55–4.58
nomination
absence 3.37
claimant, by 3.14–3.16
disputed 3.38
late 3.37
waiver of right 3.35–3.38

obstructionist 4.138
refusal to act 4.111
repeat appointments 4.34–4.36
replacement 4.129–4.136
resignation 4.111–4.114
revocation of arbitrator's
appointment 4.109–4.128
serious misconduct 4.116–4.121
asset freezing order
interim and conservatory
measures 6.130, 6.161
awards
additional awards 7.52, 7.53
consent award 7.30, 7.31
correction of award
application for correction 7.39–7.41
generally 7.38
grounds 7.42–7.47
initiative of tribunal, on 7.50, 7.51
procedure 7.39–7.41
purpose of award 7.38
currency 7.23, 7.24
date 7.07–7.09
definition 7.26
deliberations on 7.15
delivery 7.19
dissenting arbitrators 7.16–7.18
enforceability 7.12, 9.50–9.54
failure to sign 7.16–7.18
final and binding nature 7.32–7.37
generally 7.01
majority voting 7.14, 7.15
multiple awards 7.02, 7.23, 7.24
nomenclature 7.28
non-compliance with provisions 7.12, 7.13
number of 7.02, 7.25–7.29
payment of costs 7.22
publication 9.27–9.29
reasoned award required 7.03–7.06
refusal to sign 7.16–7.18
review 7.20, 7.21
scrutiny 7.20, 7.21
seat of arbitration 7.07–7.09
settlement of dispute 7.30, 7.31
signature 7.10
structure of rules 7.02
sufficiency of reasons 7.06
time limit 7.11
transmission 7.22
truncated tribunals 7.15
voting 7.14, 7.15
waiver of right to appeal 7.34–7.37
writing 7.03

Board of Directors of the LCIA
appointment of LCIA Court members 2.06
responsibility 1.05
role 1.05

commencement of arbitration
see also Request for Arbitration; Response
expedited formation of arbitral
tribunal 4.97
notices 3.39–3.49
time periods 3.43–3.49
communications between parties
arbitral tribunal 4.158–4.165
communications to LCIA Court
language 2.17
Registrar 2.17, 2.18
compétence-compétence
jurisdiction of arbitral tribunal 6.84–6.90
competition law
powers of arbitral tribunal 6.73, 6.74
conduct of arbitration
see also experts; hearings; language of arbitration;
party representation; seat of arbitration;
submission of written statements/
documents; witnesses
compliance with procedural orders 5.27, 5.28
delegation of power to make decisions to
chairman 5.29
discretion of tribunal 5.19–5.26
duties of tribunal 5.07–5.13
generally 5.01
lex arbitri 5.23–5.26
mandatory procedural rules of *lex
arbitri* 5.23–5.26
natural justice 5.03, 5.09
party autonomy 5.02, 5.03–5.06
powers of arbitral tribunal 6.03–6.81
procedural agreements to be in writing 5.14
procedural clashes between parties and
tribunal 5.15–5.17
procedural framework 5.20–5.22
Request for Arbitration 3.13
confidentiality
agreement 9.21–9.25
background 9.03–9.05
benefit of arbitration 9.03, 9.04
deliberations of arbitral tribunal 9.26
duty 9.04, 9.06, 9.07
implied duty 9.06, 9.07
importance 9.03
international position 9.13–9.19
privacy of hearings 9.04, 9.07
publication of award 9.27–9.29

special arrangements to protect confidential
information 9.04
conflicts of interest
arbitrators 4.09, 4.10
conservatory measures *see* interim and
conservatory measures
consolidation
powers of arbitral tribunal 6.55–6.59
contact details
Request for Arbitration 3.05
contractual documentation
Request for Arbitration 3.06, 3.07
controlling shareholders/interests
arbitrators 4.63–4.66
nationality 4.63–4.66
copies
expedited formation of arbitral tribunal 4.98
Request for Arbitration 3.23
Response 3.33
correction of award
form of corrections 7.48, 7.49
generally 7.38
grounds 7.42–7.47
initiative of tribunal, on 7.50, 7.51
procedure 7.39–7.41
purpose of rules 7.38
timing of application 7.39–7.41
correction of contracts
powers of arbitral tribunal 6.39–6.43
costs
agreement in writing of the parties 8.30, 8.31
allocation of costs 8.03
apportionment 8.26
arbitration costs 8.02–8.34
calculation 8.06–8.09
costs of the arbitration 8.02
costs of representation 8.02, 8.23–8.25
default rule 8.27–8.29
determination of costs 8.03–8.05
determining who bears costs 8.19–8.22
general rule 8.01
joint liability 8.16–8.18, 8.33, 8.34
legal costs 8.02–8.34
less than deposit 8.34
procedure for determination 8.14, 8.15
reasoned order 8.32
Schedule of Costs 8.05, 8.10–8.13
time spent by LCIA and arbitrators 8.06–8.09
counsel
nationality 1.22, 1.23
counterclaims
statement of case 5.48
Court *see* LCIA Arbitration Court

cross-examination
experts 5.120
currency
awards 7.23, 7.24

death
arbitrators 4.111
delegated authority, exercise of
LCIA Arbitration Court 2.08–2.11
deliberations
at place other than seat of arbitration 5.65–5.67
awards 7.15
confidentiality 9.26
delivery
awards 7.19
dépeçage
meaning 6.65
dependent territory citizens
arbitrators 4.59–4.62
nationality 4.59–4.62
deposits
claimant's failure to pay 8.56, 8.57
collection 8.38, 8.39
costs less than 8.34
delegated authority of LCIA Arbitration
Court 8.37
direction to pay 8.36–8.43
failure to pay 8.46–8.50, 8.56, 8.57
frequency of payment 8.38, 8.39
generally 8.35
multi-party arbitrations 8.40–8.42
proceeding with arbitration 8.44, 8.45
purpose 8.35
refusal to pay 8.46–8.50
release of payments 8.43
timing of payment 8.38, 8.39
withdrawal of claim 8.51–8.55
deposits on account of costs
Registrar 2.18
description of dispute
Request for Arbitration 3.10–3.12
description of the parties
Request for Arbitration 3.04, 3.05
disclosure
independence 4.37–4.41
powers of arbitral tribunal 6.26–6.36
Dubai International Finance
Centre 1.31, 1.32

enforcement of awards
defaulting arbitrator 7.12, 7.13
New York Convention 3.42, 4.02, 5.11
non-compliance with provisions as to
making of award 7.12, 7.13

notices 3.42
rules 9.50–9.54
ex aequo et bono
powers of arbitral tribunal 6.78–6.81
exclusion agreement 7.34
exclusion of liability
immunity from suit 9.30–9.35
expedited formation of arbitral
tribunal 4.86–4.108
advantages 4.91
challenging decisions 4.104
commencement of arbitration 4.97
conservatory measures 4.92
copies 4.98
decisions 4.104
effectiveness 4.100
ex parte applications 4.94, 4.98
exceptional urgency 4.96, 4.101
interim measures 4.92, 4.99
other Rules, in 4.87–4.90
precarious financial position of claimant 4.103
provisional orders 4.95
rationale 4.86
requirements of application 4.98–4.104
Response 4.105–4.108
state court proceedings 4.102
supplementary information
required 4.107
time limits 4.108
unopposed applications 4.94
use of procedure 4.93
experts
cross-examination 5.120
expenses 5.121
fees 5.121
impartiality 5.117
independence 5.117
power to appoint 5.114–5.119
presentation of testimony 5.120
procedural rights of parties 5.120
receipt of report 5.120
report 5.118
role 5.118
statistics on appointment 5.119
tribunal-appointed 5.114–5.119
types of expert 5.114

fees
experts 5.121
registration
Request for Arbitration 3.17, 3.18
Schedule of Costs 3.17
finality of decisions
LCIA Arbitration Court 2.21

formation of arbitral tribunal
see also Arbitral Tribunal; arbitrators
challenging appointment 4.122–4.128
disclosure 4.37–4.41
impartiality 4.08–4.19
importance 4.01–4.05
independence 4.08–4.12, 4.20–4.41

hearings
absence of request for 5.88
attendance sheet 5.97
date 5.90, 5.91
generally 5.86
nature of right 5.89
notice 5.94
opening statement 5.96
oral hearing on the merits 5.89
physical place 5.90, 5.92
private 5.97
purpose 5.95
questions submitted in advance 5.95, 5.96
requesting 5.87–5.89
right to 5.87–5.89
teleconference 5.89
time for 5.90, 5.93
time limits 5.98
use 5.86
video-conference 5.89

hearings, meetings and deliberations at place other than
seat of arbitration 5.65–5.67

IBA Guidelines on Conflicts
adoption 4.09
bias 4.16
conflicts of interest 4.09
disclosure 4.16, 4.27
importance 4.10
independence of arbitrator 4.21, 4.22
party-nominated arbitrators 4.161
repeat appointments 4.34

IBA Rules of Evidence
disclosure 1.13
experts 5.115
witnesses 5.104, 5.112

immunity from suit
arbitrators 9.30–9.35
exclusion of liability 9.30–9.35
LCIA Court 2.24, 9.30–9.35

impartiality
arbitral tribunal 4.08–4.19
arbitrators 4.08–4.19
experts 5.117
revocation of arbitrator's appointment 4.122

incapacity
arbitrators 4.111

independence
arbitral tribunal 4.08–4.12, 4.20–4.41
arbitrators 4.08–4.12, 4.20–4.41
barrister-arbitrators 4.25–4.33
current professional links 4.24
declaration 4.37–4.41
disclosure 4.37–4.41
experts 5.117
IBA Guidelines 4.21, 4.22
meaning 4.20
objective standard 4.20, 4.22
past professional links 4.23
professional links
current 4.24
past 4.23
repeat appointments 4.34–4.36
revocation of arbitrator's appointment 4.122

inspections
powers of arbitral tribunal 6.24, 6.25

interim and conservatory measures
appropriate measures 6.131
asset freezing order 6.130, 6.161
balance of convenience 6.123
bona fide cooperation of parties 6.128
countervailing security 6.124
enforceability 6.129
exercise of power 6.108
expedited formation of arbitral tribunal 4.92, 4.99
final award, orders granted in 6.132, 6.143–6.151
generally 6.107
guidelines 6.110
harm irreparable by damages 6.121, 6.122
merits of case 6.119, 6.120
overriding duty of good faith 6.125, 6.126
parties' right to apply 6.107
powers 6.131–6.151
preservation of property 6.132, 6.140–6.142
proportionality 6.123
seat of arbitration 6.108
securing disputed amounts 6.132, 6.134–6.142
security for costs 6.152–6.157
state courts, application to 6.158–6.161
status quo, preservation of 6.126, 6.127
test 6.110, 6.111
UNCITRAL Model Law 6.111–6.116
workability of Rules 6.109

International Dispute Resolution Centre 1.36

joinder
powers of arbitral tribunal 6.44–6.54

jurisdiction of arbitral tribunal
applications to court 6.105, 6.106
challenging 6.100–6.104
compétence-compétence 6.82, 6.84–6.90
deciding own jurisdiction 6.82, 6.84–6.90
generally 1.11
objections 6.98, 6.99
powers of arbitral tribunal 6.82–6.106
separability of arbitration clause 6.82, 6.83,
    6.91–6.97
stay of proceedings 6.104

language
arbitral tribunal decision on 5.79
arbitration 5.72–5.80
arbitration agreement 5.78
arbitrators 4.48
both languages, conduct of arbitration in 5.78
communications to LCIA Court 2.17
determination 5.79
seat of arbitration 5.59
translations of documents 5.80
LCIA Arbitration Court
administrative body 2.03
appointment of members 2.06
challenging decisions 2.23–2.28
composition 2.03–2.07
court members serving as arbitrator 2.12–2.14
decisions 2.21–2.28
delegated authority, exercise of 2.08–2.11
exercise of court's functions 2.08–2.11
finality of decisions 2.21
functions 1.08, 2.03
importance 1.06
membership 1.07, 2.06, 2.07
organization of LCIA 1.06–1.08
performance of functions 2.02, 2.03
President 2.03, 2.04
reasons for decisions 2.22
role 1.06
role of LCIA's organs 2.02–2.20
scrutiny of awards, no 1.08
selection of tribunals 1.08
sub-divisions 2.02
Vice President 2.03, 2.04, 2.05
lex arbitri
conduct of arbitration 5.23–5.26
party representation 5.84
powers of arbitral tribunal 6.03
seat of arbitration 5.58, 5.70
lex mercatoria
applicable law 6.67, 6.71
London Chamber of Arbitration 1.02

mediators
appointment 2.12–2.14
memorials
written submissions 5.40, 5.41
multi-party arbitrations
deposits 8.40–8.42

natural justice
conduct of proceedings 5.03, 5.09
party autonomy 1.42
notices
address for service 3.41
commencement of arbitration 3.39–3.49
enforcement of awards 3.42
formalities 3.41
requirements 3.40
residence 3.41

objections
jurisdiction of arbitral tribunal 6.98, 6.99
oral arbitration agreements 3.06
organization of LCIA
company 1.05
general structure 1.04
incorporation 1.05
LCIA Arbitration Court 1.06–1.08
Secretariat 1.09, 1.10

party autonomy 5.02, 5.03–5.06
party representation
external legal counsel 5.82–5.84
general rule 5.81–5.84
lex arbitri 5.84
proof of authority 5.85
payment of costs
awards 7.22
periods of time *see* time periods
place of arbitration *see* seat of arbitration
power of attorney
Request for Arbitration 3.05
powers of arbitral tribunal
see also jurisdiction of arbitral tribunal; interim
    and conservatory measures
agreement of parties 6.06–6.08
amendments 6.09–6.19
amiable composition 6.78–6.81
carrying out own enquiries 6.22, 6.23
competition law 6.73, 6.74
conduct of proceedings 6.03–6.81
consolidation 6.55–6.59
correction of contracts 6.39–6.43
deciding dispute in accordance with law
    determination by the tribunal 6.75–6.77

freedom of parties to choose applicable
    substantive law 6.70, 6.71
generally 6.62, 6.63
restrictions on parties' freedom 6.72–6.74
rules of law 6.64–6.69
determination of applicable law by the
    tribunal 6.75–6.77
disclosure 6.26–6.36
establishing facts of case by all appropriate
    means 6.04
evidential rules, application of 6.38
ex aequo et bono 6.78–6.81
freedom of parties to choose applicable
    substantive law 6.70, 6.71
generally 6.01, 6.02, 6.03
giving parties reasonable opportunity to state
    views 6.06–6.08
initiative, taking 6.22, 6.23
inspections 6.24, 6.25
interim and conservatory measures 6.107–6.161
joinder 6.44–6.54
jurisdiction 6.82–6.106
lex arbitri 6.03
reasonable opportunity of putting its case and
    dealing with that of its opponent 6.08
recourse to state court 6.60, 6.61
restrictions on parties' freedom 6.72–6.74
Rome Convention 6.72
rules of law 6.64–6.69
security for costs 6.152–6.157
site visits 6.24, 6.25
strict rules of evidence, application of 6.37, 6.38
sua sponte, acting 6.07
third parties 6.44–6.54
time limits 6.20–6.21
trade usages 6.62
publication of award
confidentiality 9.27–9.29

Registrar
communications to LCIA Court 2.17, 2.18
delegated functions 2.19, 2.20
deposits on account of costs 2.18
deputy Registrars 2.15
exercise of functions 2.15
functions 2.20
operation 2.02
Request for Arbitration 2.16, 3.22
responsibility 2.16
role 2.15–2.20
supervision of court 2.02
registration fee
Request for Arbitration 3.17, 3.18

replacement
arbitrators 4.129–4.136
Request for Arbitration
appointment of arbitral tribunal 3.13
arbitration agreement 3.06, 3.07
claims 3.10–3.12
commencement of arbitration 3.03
conduct of arbitration 3.13
confirmation of service 3.19–3.23
contact details 3.05
contents 3.02
contractual documentation 3.06, 3.07
copies 3.23
date of receipt 3.21
description of dispute 3.10–3.12
description of the parties 3.04, 3.05
dispute, description of 3.10–3.12
generally 3.01
incomplete 3.12
initial review 3.06, 3.08, 3.09
late 3.12
missing 3.12
nomination of arbitrator 3.14–3.16
oral arbitration agreements 3.06
particulars of claim 3.02
parties 3.04, 3.05
power of attorney 3.05
proof of authority 3.05
purpose 3.02
Registrar 2.16, 3.22
registration fee 3.17, 3.18
review of documents 3.09
review upon receipt 3.22
service 3.19–3.23
statement of case 5.44
sufficiency of contents disputed 3.12
summary of case 3.11
written requirement 3.06
resignation *see* revocation of arbitrator's
    appointment
Response
consequences of non-submission 3.24
content 3.31, 3.32
copies 3.33
expedited formation of arbitral
    tribunal 4.105–4.108
form 3.31, 3.32
importance 3.24
non-submission 3.24, 3.34
not required 3.24
optional 3.14, 3.34
purpose 3.24
submission 3.24

Response (*cont.*)
  time period 3.25–3.30
  uses 3.24
  waiver of right to nominate arbitrator 3.35–3.38
revocation of arbitrator's
  appointment 4.109–4.128
  challenging appointment 4.122–4.128
  circumstances of 4.110–4.115
  death 4.111
  impartiality 4.122
  incapacity to act 4.111
  independence 4.122
  payment for time served 4.115
  permissive nature of power 4.112
  replacement of arbitrators 4.129–4.136
  resignation 4.111–4.114
  serious misconduct 4.116–4.121

Schedule of Costs 8.05, 8.10–8.13
seat of arbitration
  agreement in writing 5.60–5.64
  applicable law 5.68–5.71
  awards 7.07–7.09
  consequences of choice 5.58
  convenience 5.59
  default seat 5.61, 5.63
  delocalized concept of arbitration 5.70
  enforcement of awards 5.58
  generally 1.20
  geographical convenience 5.59
  hearing facilities 5.59
  hearings, meetings and deliberations at
    place other than 5.65–5.67
  home-court advantage 5.59
  importance of decision 5.58, 5.59
  interim and conservatory measures 6.108
  juridical seat 5.58
  language 5.59
  lex arbitri 5.58, 5.70
  localized arbitration 5.68
  meaning 5.64
  national arbitration laws 5.71
  neutral seat 5.59
  New York Convention 5.58, 5.68, 5.69
  place of arbitration 5.64
  seat theory 5.68
  security 5.59
  selection of arbitrators 5.64
  statistics 5.62
  support services 5.59
  travel arrangements 5.59
Secretariat
  membership 1.10
  organization of LCIA 1.09, 1.10

  responsibility 1.09
  interim and conservatory measures 6.152–6.157
serious misconduct
  arbitrators 4.116–4.121
  revocation of arbitrator's
    appointment 4.116–4.121
service
  Request for Arbitration 3.19–3.23
signature
  awards 7.10
site visits
  powers of arbitral tribunal 6.24, 6.25
Softwood Lumber Arbitration 1.50–1.53
spirit of rules, acting in 9.36, 9.46–9.49
submission of written statements/documents
  see also written submissions
  adoption of suitable procedure 5.35–5.38
  agreement of parties 5.32
  default by one of parties 5.56, 5.57
  default procedure 5.32, 5.43–5.57
  exchange of written submissions 5.39–5.42
  exchanging views on 5.36
  form of submissions 5.40
  full procedure 5.31, 5.32
  further submissions after evidentiary hearing 5.42
  generally 5.30
  initiative taken by tribunal 5.35
  memorials 5.40, 5.41
  national procedural rules 5.33, 5.34
  order following preliminary meeting 5.38
  other Rules, in 5.31
  post-hearing briefs 5.42
  preliminary meeting 5.36, 5.37
  prescriptive approach 5.30
  soliciting parties' views on 5.36
  statement of case 5.44–5.55
  statistics 5.55
  witness evidence 5.41, 5.52
summary of case
  Request for Arbitration 3.11
support services
  seat of arbitration 5.59

third parties
  powers of arbitral tribunal 6.44–6.54
time periods
  calculation 3.47
  commencement of arbitration 3.43–3.49
  compliance 3.44
  date of commencement 3.43
  exception to default provisions 3.45, 3.46
  expedited formation of arbitral tribunal 4.108
  expiry 3.48
  extension 3.48

power of arbitral tribunal to extend 6.20
trade usages
powers of arbitral tribunal 6.62
translation
documents 5.80
transmission
awards 7.22
truncated tribunals
arbitral tribunal 4.137–4.157
awards 7.15

waiver of rights
appeal 7.34–7.37
determination 9.36–9.45
nomination of arbitrator 3.35–3.38
WIPO
expedited arbitration rules 4.89
witnesses
cultural issues 5.113
exchange of material 5.103–5.105
failure to attend 5.110, 5.111
generally 5.99
limiting appearance 5.104, 5.105
non-attendance 5.110, 5.111
notice of identity 5.100–5.102

preparation of witness 5.112
presentation of testimony 5.106, 5.107
refusal to appear 5.104
right to call 5.108–5.111
subject-matter of testimony 5.100
submission of written statements/
documents 5.41, 5.52, 5.107
testimony 5.106, 5.107
treatment as 5.113
written witness statements 5.102, 5.103
written procedure 1.44
written submissions
approach to 5.40
documentary evidence 5.39
exchange 5.39–5.42
form 5.40
memorials 5.40, 5.41
number of sets 5.39
purpose 5.39
statement of case *see* statement of case
submission *see* submission of written
statements/documents
use 5.40

young arbitrators groups 1.35